LAW AND MORALITY:
READINGS IN LEGAL PHILOSOPHY

This anthology fills a longstanding need for a contemporary Canadian textbook in the philosophy of law. It includes articles, readings, and cases in legal philosophy that give students the conceptual tools necessary to consider the general problems of jurisprudence.

The collection begins with general questions about morality and law, drawing on both traditional literature on legal positivism and contemporary debates about the role of law in the pursuit of equality. It explores the tensions between law as a protector of individual liberty and as a tool of democratic self-rule. The second part deals with these philosophical questions as they apply to contemporary issues. Included is an extensive sampling of the feminist writings that have been influential in legal theory and Canadian law. Transcripts of judicial decisions are presented throughout to give students an appropriate sense of the complexity of legal reasoning.

This book strikes a balance between practical problems and the more analytic, philosophical frameworks. Its treatment of the philosophy of law as a branch of political philosophy enables students to understand law in its function as a social institution. This important resource book will be a valuable text in both departments of philosophy and faculties of law for years to come.

DAVID DYZENHAUS and ARTHUR RIPSTEIN are professors of philosophy and law at the University of Toronto.

EDITED BY DAVID DYZENHAUS
AND ARTHUR RIPSTEIN

Law and Morality:
Readings in Legal Philosophy

UNIVERSITY OF TORONTO PRESS
Toronto Buffalo London

© University of Toronto Press Incorporated 1996
Toronto Buffalo London
Printed in Canada

Reprinted 1998

ISBN 0-8020-0896-8 (cloth)
ISBN 0-8020-7878-8 (paper)

Printed on acid-free paper

Toronto Studies in Philosophy
Editors: James R. Brown and Calvin Normore

Canadian Cataloguing in Publication Data

Main entry under title:

Law and morality : readings in a legal philosophy

(Toronto studies in philosophy)
ISBN 0-8020-0896-8 (bound)
ISBN 0-8020-7878-8 (pbk.)

1. Law – Philosophy.   2. Law and ethics.
I. Dyzenhaus, David.   II. Ripstein, Arthur.
III. Series

K235.L39 1996   340'.112   C96-931037-4

University of Toronto Press acknowledges the financial assistance to its
publishing program of the Canada Council and the Ontario Arts Council.

Contents

PART TWO: SOME CONTEMPORARY ISSUES

Preface

For most students, a course in legal philosophy marks their first encounter with a rigorous examination of the conceptual apparatus of the law. Yet it is hardly their first encounter with many of the law's central questions. Law has long shaped ordinary life. From regulations concerning auto emissions to common-law rules governing warranties and product liability, the law affects our everyday existence. Indeed, these rules and regulations are so pervasive that most people seldom notice them, let alone reflect on them. By providing conceptual tools with which to consider the general problems of jurisprudence, this book aims to be an aid to students both in their intellectual pursuits and in their role as informed citizens.

Courses in the philosophy of law often break up into two sharply divided sections, one exploring conceptual questions about the nature of law, the other looking at a series of questions concerning the proper limits of the criminal law. These two sections sometimes sit together uneasily. In our view, the philosophy of law is far too important a subject to be treated in such a disjointed way. Part of the difficulty is that most discussion of the nature of law focuses on administrative rules or grand questions of constitutional theory. As a result, questions about the reach of the criminal law too often seem unrelated to those about its nature. A deeper reason for avoiding the usual approach is that it probably rests on a particular resolution to one of the problems considered in the first part of such courses in the philosophy of law. Standard versions of legal positivism suppose that the law can take on any content whatsoever. One consequence of such a view is that questions about the appropriate reach of the criminal law are in principle open to any sort of argumentation, because the concept of law by itself provides no constraints on its content. Yet legal reasoning often employs reasoning from other areas of the law, and these often seem to constrain the law's content. An adequate understanding of these challenges to positivism, or a version of positivism adequate to meet them, allows for a more sophisticated approach to contemporary issues. While we do not offer this anthology for use only by anti-positivists, we regard it as a virtue of our approach that it is neutral on those questions. Our central organizing assumption in compiling this anthology is that questions about morality and the law are at root questions of political theory.

The traditional questions of jurisprudence concern the distinguishing features of a legal order. What makes a legal order different from other types of social order? Answers to those questions, in turn, make a difference to the ways in which law can be used. For example, different views of legal order have profound implications for any account of the relation between democracy and the rule of law, and so for questions about the limits to criminalization. Again, views about the nature of law have implications for the ways in which the law might appropriately address those who object to it on moral grounds. Of course, there is no direct relationship – one might be a positivist or anti-positivist and still suppose the criminal law should be limited. But views about the general relation between law, morality, and democracy give shape to the types of arguments that are available, and assumptions about the nature of law will sometimes dictate which of those arguments seem most compelling. At the same time, views about the appropriate limits of state action may well lend credence to views about what is or is not an acceptable account of the nature of law. Again, questions about the nature of adjudication seem to straddle both sets of issues. In the end, all of the issues revolve around whether, or under what conditions, law is an appropriate place to pin our hopes for justice.

Since the introduction of the *Charter of Rights and Freedoms* in 1982, Canada's legal and political culture has changed dramatically. The political vocabulary of Canadians has become increasingly legalized. Perhaps the most noticeable feature is the way in which claims about fundamental justice and individual rights are traded in debates about most issues of public concern. But there have been subtler and deeper changes also. Although this collection contains brief excerpts from and discussions of American cases, its main focus will be Canadian. While some critics have described the introduction of the *Charter* as the "American-ization" of Canadian law, such a characterization is at best misleading. Judicial review has assumed an increased importance since the *Charter* was introduced, but the content of Canadian and American legal thought is very different. The differences are perhaps most obvious on issues of freedom of expression, where Canadian and American courts have come to such different conclusions. Those conclusions reveal yet deeper differences in their views of equality and the rule of law more generally. The central debates of legal theory and public policy that face Canadians in the 1990s are not the same as those that divided the United States in the 1960s. While those American struggles, especially the struggle for racial equality, are worthy of serious study, America's specific political and constitutional history has given these issues a shape that does not transfer readily to the rest of the world. Canada's legal culture is distinctive and important, and must be taken seriously in its own right. For similar reasons, we include a sample of the feminist writings which have been so influential in both legal theory and Canadian law.

The collection is divided into two sections. The first deals with general questions about morality and law, drawing both on the traditional literature discussing legal positivism and on contemporary debates about the role of law as a tool in pursuit of equality. Then it looks at a series of questions revolving around the tensions between the role of law as a protector of individual liberty and as a tool of democratic self-rule. Law has been defended as each of these, yet they are in apparent tension. The second section considers a series of contemporary issues in which the questions considered in the first section present themselves especially forcefully. The collection contains somewhat more material than would ordinarily be included in a one-semester course, so as to allow instructors some flexibility in designing a course using it, and in varying the course from year to year. For example, different contemporary problems might be covered, and the conceptual and practical materials integrated in a number of ways. At the same time, it does not contain so much material as to make prohibitive the cost of using additional material, either because this is better suited to the particular instructor's aims or because the instructor wishes to use the collection as the basis for a full-year course.

We have included reading questions for each of the selections. We have not suggested additional readings, leaving that instead to the discretion of instructors using the book.

THE EDITORS

David Dyzenhaus is Associate Professor of Law and Philosophy at the University of Toronto. He holds a BA and LLB from the University of the Witwatersrand, and a DPhil from Oxford. He is the author of *Hard Cases in Wicked Legal Systems* (Oxford, 1991) and numerous articles and reviews. In 1992–3 he was the holder of a Humboldt Fellowship at the University of Heidelberg.

Arthur Ripstein is Professor of Philosophy and Law at the University of Toronto. He holds a BA from the University of Manitoba, a PhD from the University of Pittsburgh, and an MSL from Yale Law School. He has published numerous articles and reviews in philosophy journals and law reviews. For 1995–6 he holds a Rockefeller Fellowship at Princeton University.

PART ONE

MORALITY AND THE RULE OF LAW

1

Positivism, Legal Ordering, and Morality

Careful reflection about the law's relationship to morality requires inquiry into a variety of questions about its other features. Lawyers regularly make claims about what the law requires in a particular case. What other facts fix the truth of such claims? Does moral argument enter into them? If so, what sorts of moral argument? What determines whether a moral argument is admissible? Must every legal system incorporate moral arguments?

Philosophical thought about the nature of law has fallen into two broad camps. Legal positivism is the view that law is best understood as a sociological phenomenon, a particular way of structuring social life. For the positivist, it is essential to the nature of law that it can be identified without appeal to controversial moral arguments. Law is thus identified with positive law, that is law that has been promulgated or enacted in appropriate ways. Different positivists have different views of the necessary and sufficient conditions for appropriate enactment. Some make the command of a sovereign essential; others the existence of structures for changing laws, and others the availability of non-controversial ways of applying the law to particular cases. Whatever their other differences, positivists share the view that it is essential to a legal system that what the law *is* can be established without considering what the law morally *ought to be*.

Opposed to positivists are defenders of natural law, according to whom a system of official power only qualifies as a legal system if it meets certain moral demands. Natural lawyers differ on what those demands might be, but share an insistence that the difference between the rule of law and other ways of organizing power can only be drawn in terms of the fundamental moral conceptions at the heart of a legal system.

So described, the traditional questions of jurisprudence sometimes seem narrowly conceptual and lacking in political implications. At one level, this is plainly true; answers to them do not, by themselves, dictate answers to pressing political disputes. Yet jurisprudence was born of political ferment, and many people continue to see it as profoundly related to questions of justice and legitimacy. The connection can be found in the issue of adjudication. Any account of the nature of law is thereby also an account of the distinction between a judge or other official *applying* established law and *making* new law. One of the core ideals of the rule of law is that the task of judges is to apply the law rather than to make it. Depending on how this distinction is drawn, the role of courts can be seen as anything from a usurpation of majority rule (or a bulwark against tyranny), to a direct instrument of state control. Positivists will regard most intrusions of morality into official decisions as making law rather than applying it; natural lawyers will suppose that correctly applying the law requires moral argument. The distinction between making and applying law also has important implications for understanding the demands placed on judges as legal actors. Does the law allow a judge to reach morally desirable results contrary to the wishes of the state? Does it ever require such results?

Both positivists and their opponents sometimes accuse each other of authoritarianism. Positivists claim that seeing law as essentially moral is likely to lead to either of two pathologies. It may lead to authoritarianism, because people will suppose that whatever law is on the books is therefore just, and thus blindly obey it. Alternatively, it may lead to anarchy, as people suppose themselves to be the appropriate judges of whether or not to obey. For their part, anti-positivists sometimes charge that positivism leads to a sort of rule-worship, and an implicit moral admiration for order, regardless of its injustices.

In the seventeenth century, Thomas Hobbes first articulated legal positivism in support of the consolidation of state power. Virtually all human societies have resolved disputes by granting authority to people not involved in the disputes. Such courts are not necessarily directly connected with either state power or the more general directions of public policy. Our own legal system is a descendent of a system in which nobles held courts of their own in addition to the royal courts. In the English-speaking world, religious courts remained a separate center of legal power well into the nineteenth century. Similar systems of adjudication can be found today in the form of disciplinary procedures in workplaces and universities. The idea that the state should be the only lawmaking institution is thus comparatively new.

On Hobbes's view, law cannot be understood as anything but the command of a sovereign. If courts lie outside the direct control of the state, judges are making law rather than applying it. The result is divided sovereignty and conflict. A century and a half later, Jeremy Bentham offered a different version of positivism in support of a forward-looking version of public policy. The role of law is to provide incentives to behavior, and laws must have coercive sanctions attached to them in order to qualify as laws. For both Hobbes and Bentham, courts can only properly apply the law if judges follow clear instructions from the state.

Recent versions of positivism have had less of a tone of political urgency about them. H.L.A. Hart's influential development of positivism emphasizes the role of rules in a legal system. According to Hart, a legal system must contain both "primary" rules regulating behavior and "secondary" rules regulating the changing of the primary rules. In order to govern behavior effectively, these rules must be largely accepted by both the population they govern and the officials applying them. For Hart, any such system of rules will face cases to which they do not straightforwardly apply. In such circumstances, the judge will have no choice but to exercise discretion, making law rather than simply applying it. Hart maintains that these distinctions are descriptive and conceptual, but politically important, because keeping them in mind enables us to evaluate existing law with an open mind, rather than seeing it as either a nightmare of power politics or a noble dream of perfect justice.

The readings explore the political charges made by both positivists and their critics. Those issues come to a head in the issue of wicked legal systems. Whether the example is Nazi law, South African law under Apartheid, or slavery in the United States, positivists insist that wicked legal systems must nonetheless be seen as involving law. Opponents of positivism have two options: some insist that such systems are not legal systems at all; others insist that precisely because they are legal systems, they cannot consistently enforce their unjust dictates. According to the anti-positivist, positivist judges serve unjust regimes when they suppose that their choices are to either enforce the wishes of their political masters or give up on being judges.

The debate about whether the law is an instrument of justice carries over into recent feminist scholarship about the law. The readings approach the same set of issues in light of recent feminist scholarship. Historically, the law has treated women badly. At common law, women were not allowed to own property, husbands were allowed to beat their wives, and victims of sexual assault were presumed to have consented. Feminist scholarship has criticized these implicit (sometimes explicit) biases. Some feminist scholarship has supposed that the law can nonetheless be reclaimed for feminist purposes; other feminists take a less optimistic view.

The selections in this opening chapter look at the traditional jurisprudential question, "What is law?" Both positivists and anti-positivists agree that law is a distinctive type of social ordering, but disagree about what makes it distinctive. Positivists suppose that law can be identified solely by its sources, while their critics suppose it must be identified by its particular moral content.

Thomas Hobbes
Leviathan (1651)

Hobbes is widely regarded as the greatest of the English political philosophers. He is also plausibly credited with being the founder of modern legal philosophy. Various forms of dispute resolution, legislation, and punishment have been found in all human societies. In early modern England, the church had its own laws and courts, as did various nobles, just as universities and workplaces have analogous disciplinary practices to this day. Hobbes, writing at the dawn of the modern age, was the first philosopher to identify law as a type of order exercised above all by the state. Thus, Hobbes understands legal order in terms of its sources, rather than its particular content. The selections included here set the context for Hobbes's view of law with his description of what he calls "the natural condition of mankind." Hobbes views the state as the solution to a practical problem of order. Laws provide predictability, and are backed with threats. As a result, they change the structure of social life from one of opposition and distrust to one of coordination. For Hobbes, such coordination is only possible if there is a single sovereign charged with making, applying, and enforcing law. Anything else, including any kind of moral limitation on the sovereign, risks controversy and eventual war. As a result, law must be identified with whatever the sovereign commands.

CHAPTER 5

And as in Arithmetique, unpractised men must, and Professors themselves may often erre, and cast up false; so also in any other subject of

Reasoning, the ablest, most attentive, and most practised men, may deceive themselves, and inferre false Conclusions; Not but that Reason it selfe is always Right Reason, as well as Arithmetique is a certain and infallible Art: But no one mans Reason, nor the Reason of any one number of men, makes the certaintie; no more than an account is therefore well cast up, because a great many men have unanimously approved it. And therefore, as when there is a controversy in [19] an account, the parties must by their own accord, set up for right Reason, the Reason of some Arbitrator, or Judge, to whose sentence they will both stand, or their controversie must either come to blowes, or be undecided, for want of a right Reason constituted by Nature; so is it also in all debates of what kind soever: And when men that think themselves wiser than all others, clamor and demand right Reason for judge; yet seek no more, but that things should be determined, by no other mens reason but their own, it is as intolerable in the society of men, as it is in play after trump is turned, to use for trump on every occasion, that suite whereof they have most in their hand. For they do nothing els, that will have every of their passions, as it comes to bear sway in them, to be taken for right Reason, and that in their own controversies: bewraying their want of right Reason, by the claym they lay to it.

CHAPTER 6

But whatsoever is the object of any mans Appetite or Desire; that is it, which he for his part calleth *Good*: And the object of his Hate, and Aversion, *Evill*; And of his Contempt, *Vile*, and *Inconsiderable*. For these words of Good, Evill, and Contemptible, are ever used with relation to the person that useth them: There being nothing simply and absolutely so; nor any common Rule of Good and Evill, to be taken from the nature of the objects themselves; but from the Person of the man (where there is no Common-wealth;) or, (in a Common-wealth,) from the Person that representeth it; or from an Arbitrator or Judge, whom men disagreeing shall by consent set up, and make his sentence the Rule thereof.

CHAPTER 13: *OF THE* NATURALL CONDITION *OF* MANKIND, *AS CONCERNING THEIR* FELICITY, *AND* MISERY

Nature hath made men so equall, in the faculties of body, and mind; as that though there bee found one man sometimes manifestly stronger in body, or of quicker mind then another; yet when all is reckoned to-gether, the difference between man, and man, is not so considerable, as that one man can thereupon claim to himselfe any benefit, to which another may not pretend, as well as he. For as to the strength of body, the weakest has strength enough to kill the strongest, either by secret machination, or by confederacy with others, that are in the same danger with himselfe.

And as to the faculties of the mind, (setting aside the arts grounded upon words, and especially that skill of proceeding upon generall, and infallible rules, called Science; which very few have, and but in few things; as being not a native faculty, born with us; nor attained, (as Prudence,) while we look after somewhat els,) I find yet a greater equal-ity amongst men, than that of strength. For Prudence, is but Experience; which equall time, equally bestowes on all men, in [61] those things they equally apply themselves unto. That which may perhaps make such equality incredible, is but a vain conceipt of ones owne wisdome, which almost all men think they have in a greater degree, than the Vulgar; that is, than all men but themselves, and a few others, whom by Fame, or for concurring with themselves, they approve. For such is the nature of men, that howsoever they may acknowledge many others to be more witty, or more eloquent, or more learned; Yet they will hardly believe there be many so wise as themselves: For they see their own wit at hand, and other mens at a distance. But this proveth rather that men are in that point equall, than unequall. For there is not ordinarily a greater signe of the equall distribution of any thing, than that every man is contented with his share.

From this equality of ability, ariseth equality of hope in the attaining of our Ends. And therefore if any two men desire the same thing, which neverthelesse they cannot both enjoy, they become enemies; and in the way to their End, (which is principally their owne conservation, and sometimes their delectation only,) endeavour to destroy, or subdue one an other. And from hence it comes to passe, that where an Invader hath no more to feare, than an other mans single power; if one plant, sow, build, or possesse a convenient Seat, others may probably be expected to come prepared with forces united, to dispossesse, and deprive him, not only of the fruit of his labour, but also of his life, or liberty. And the Invader again is in the like danger of another.

And from this diffidence of one another, there is no way for any man to secure himselfe, so reasonable, as Anticipation; that is, by force, or wiles, to master the persons of all men he can, so long, till he see no other power great enough to endanger him: And this is no more than his own conservation requireth, and is generally allowed. Also because there be some, that taking pleasure in contemplating their own power in the acts of conquest, which they pursue farther than their security requires; if others, that otherwise would be glad to be at ease within modest bounds, should not by invasion increase their power, they would not be able, long time, by standing only on their defence, to subsist. And by consequence, such augmentation of dominion over men, being necessary to a mans conservation, it ought to be allowed him.

Againe, men have no pleasure, (but on the contrary a great deale of griefe) in keeping company, where there is no power able to over-awe them all. For every man looketh that his companion should value him, at the same rate he sets upon himselfe: And upon all signes of contempt, or undervaluing, naturally endeavours, as far as he dares (which amongst them that have no common power, to keep them in quiet, is far enough to make them destroy each other,) to extort a greater value from his contemners, by dommage; and from others, by the example.

So that in the nature of man, we find three principall causes of quarrell. First, Competition; Secondly, Diffidence; Thirdly, Glory.

[62] The first, maketh men invade for Gain; the second, for Safety; and the third, for Reputation. The first use Violence, to make themselves Masters of other mens persons, wives, children, and cattell; the second, to defend them; the third, for trifles, as a word, a smile, a different opinion, and any other signe of undervalue, either direct in their Persons, or by reflexion in their Kindred, their Friends, their Nation, their Profession, or their Name.

Hereby it is manifest, that during the time men live without a common Power to keep them all in awe, they are in that condition which is called Warre; and such a warre, as is of every man, against every man. For Warre, consisteth not in Battell onely, or the act of fighting; but in a tract of time, wherein the Will to contend by Battell is sufficiently known: and therefore the notion of *Time*, is to be considered in the nature of Warre; as it is in the nature of Weather. For as the nature of Foule weather, lyeth not in a showre or two of rain; but in an inclination thereto of many days together: So the nature of War, consisteth not in actuall fighting; but in the known disposition thereto, during all the time there is no assurance to the contrary. All other time is Peace.

Whatsoever therefore is consequent to a time of Warre, where every man is Enemy to every man; the same is consequent to the time, wherein men live without other security, than what their own strength, and their own invention shall furnish them withall. In such condition, there is no place for Industry; because the fruit thereof is uncertain: and consequently no Culture of the Earth; no Navigation, nor use of the commodities that may be imported by Sea; no commodious Building; no Instruments of moving, and removing such things as require much force; no Knowledge of the face of the Earth; no account of Time; no Arts; no Letters; no Society; and which is worst of all, continuall feare, and danger of violent death; And the life of man, solitary, poore, nasty, brutish, and short.

It may seem strange to some man, that has not well weighed these things; that Nature should thus dissociate, and render men apt to invade, and destroy one another: and he may therefore, not trusting to this Inference, made from the Passions, desire perhaps to have the same confirmed by Experience. Let him therefore consider with himselfe, when taking a journey, he armes himselfe, and seeks to go well accompanied; when going to sleep, he locks his dores; when even in his house he locks his chests; and this when he knows there bee Lawes, and publike Officers, armed, to revenge all injuries shall bee done him; what opinion he has of his fellow subjects, when he rides armed; of his fellow Citizens, when he locks his dores; and of his children, and servants, when he locks his chests. Does he not there as much accuse mankind by his actions, as I do by my words? But neither of us accuse mans nature in it. The Desires, and other Passions of man, are in themselves no Sin. No more are the Actions, that proceed from those Passions, till they know a Law that forbids them: which till Lawes be made they cannot know: nor can any Law be made, till they have agreed upon the Person that shall make it.

[63] It may peradventure be thought, there was never such a time, nor condition of warre as this; and I believe it was never generally so, over all the world: but there are many places, where they live so now. For the savage people in many places of *America*, except the government of small Families, the concord whereof dependeth on naturall lust, have no government at all; and live at this day in that brutish manner, as I said before. Howsoever, it may be perceived what manner of life there would be, where there were no common Power to feare; by the manner of life, which men that have formerly lived under a peacefull government, use to degenerate into, in a civill Warre.

But though there had never been any time, wherein particular men were in a condition of warre one against another; yet in all times, Kings, and Persons of Soveraigne authority, because of their Independency, are in continuall jealousies, and in the state and posture of Gladiators; having their weapons pointing, and their eyes fixed on one another;

that is, their Forts, Garrisons, and Guns upon the Frontiers of their Kingdomes; and continuall Spyes upon their neighbours; which is a posture of War. But because they uphold thereby, the Industry of their Subjects; there does not follow from it, that misery, which accompanies the Liberty of particular men.

To this warre of every man against every man, this also is consequent; that nothing can be Unjust. The notions of Right and Wrong, Justice and Injustice have there no place. Where there is no common Power, there is no Law: where no Law, no Injustice. Force, and Fraud, are in warre the two Cardinall vertues. Justice, and Injustice are none of the Faculties neither of the Body, nor Mind. If they were, they might be in a man that were alone in the world, as well as his Senses, and Passions. They are Qualities, that relate to men in Society, not in Solitude. It is consequent also to the same condition, that there be no Propriety, no Dominion, no *Mine* and *Thine* distinct; but onely that to be every mans that he can get; and for so long, as he can keep it. And thus much for the ill condition, which man by meer Nature is actually placed in; though with a possibility to come out of it, consisting partly in the Passions, partly in his Reason.

The Passions that encline men to Peace, are Feare of Death; Desire of such things as are necessary to commodious living; and a Hope by their Industry to obtain them. And Reason suggesteth convenient Articles of Peace, upon which men may be drawn to agreement. These Articles, are they, which otherwise are called the Lawes of Nature: whereof I shall speak more particularly, in the two following Chapters. [64]

CHAPTER 14: *OF THE FIRST AND SECOND* NATURALL LAWES, *AND OF* CONTRACTS

The Right of Nature, which Writers commonly call *Jus Naturale*, is the Liberty each man hath, to use his own power, as he will himselfe, for the preservation of his own Nature; that is to say, of his own Life; and consequently, of doing any thing, which in his own Judgement, and Reason, hee shall conceive to be the aptest means thereunto.

By Liberty, is understood, according to the proper signification of the word, the absence of externall Impediments: which Impediments, may oft take away part of a mans power to do what hee would; but cannot hinder him from using the power left him, according as his judgement, and reason shall dictate to him.

A Law of Nature, (*Lex Naturalis*,) is a precept, or generall Rule, found out by Reason, by which a man is forbidden to do, that, which is destructive of his life, or taketh away the means of preserving the same; and to omit, that, by which he thinketh it may be best preserved. For though they that speak of this subject, use to confound *Jus*, and *Lex*, *Right* and *Law*; yet they ought to be distinguished; because RIGHT, consisteth in liberty to do, or to forbeare; Whereas LAW, determineth, and bindeth to one of them: so that Law, and Right, differ as much, as Obligation, and Liberty; which in one and the same matter are inconsistent.

And because the condition of Man, (as hath been declared in the precedent Chapter) is a condition of Warre of every one against every one; in which case every one is governed by his own Reason; and there is nothing he can make use of, that may not be a help unto him, in preserving his life against his enemyes; It followeth, that in such a condition, every man has a Right to every thing; even to one anothers body. And therefore, as long as this naturall Right of every man to every thing endureth, there can be no security to any man, (how strong or wise soever he be,) of living out the time, which Nature ordinarily alloweth men to live. And consequently it is a precept, or generall rule of Reason, *That every man, ought to endeavour Peace, as farre as he has hope of obtaining it; and when he cannot obtain it, that he may seek, and use, all helps, and advantages of Warre.* The first branch of which Rule, containeth the first, and Fundamentall Law of Nature; which is, *to seek Peace, and follow it.* The Second, the summe of the Right of Nature; which is, *By all means we can, to defend our selves.*

From this Fundamentall Law of Nature, by which men are commanded to endeavour Peace, is derived this second Law; *That a man be willing, when others are so too, as farre-forth, as for Peace, and* [65] *defence of himselfe he shall think it necessary, to lay down this right to all things; and be contented with so much liberty against other men, as he would allow other men against himselfe.* For as long as every man holdeth this Right, of doing any thing he liketh; so long are all men in the condition of Warre. But if other men will not lay down their Right, as well as he; then there is no Reason for any one, to devest himselfe of his: For that were to expose himselfe to Prey, (which no man is bound to) rather than to dispose himselfe to Peace. This is that Law of the Gospell; *Whatsoever you require that others should do to you, that do ye to them.* And that Law of all men, *Quod tibi fieri non vis, alteri ne feceris ...*

A Covenant not to defend my selfe from force, by force, is alwayes voyd. For (as I have shewed before) no man can transferre, or lay down his Right to save himselfe from Death, Wounds, and Imprisonment, (the avoyding whereof is the onely End of laying [70] down any Right, and therefore the promise of not resisting force, in no Covenant transferreth any right; nor is obliging. For though a man may Covenant thus, *Unlesse I do so, or so, kill me*; he cannot Covenant thus, *Unlesse I do so, or so, I will not resist you, when you come to kill me.* For man by nature chooseth the lesser evill, which is danger of death in resisting; rather than the greater, which is certain and present death in not resisting. And this is granted to be true by all men, in that they lead Criminals to Execution, and Prison, with armed men, notwithstanding that such Criminals have consented to the Law, by which they are condemned.

CHAPTER 15: OF OTHER LAWES OF NATURE

From that law of Nature, by which we are obliged to transferre to another, such Rights, as being retained, hinder the peace of Mankind, there followeth a Third; which is this, *That men performe their Covenants made*: without which, Covenants are in vain, and but Empty words; and the Right of all men to all things remaining, wee are still in the condition of Warre.

And in this law of Nature, consisteth the Fountain and Originall of Justice. For where no Covenant hath preceded, there hath no Right been transferred, and every man has right to every thing; and consequently, no action can be Unjust. But when a Covenant is made, then to break it is *Unjust*: And the definition of Injustice, is no other than *the not Performance of Covenant*. And whatsoever is not Unjust, is *Just* ...

Also if *a man be trusted to judge between man and man*, it is a precept of the Law of Nature, *that he deale Equally between them*. For without that, the Controversies of men cannot be determined but by Warre. He therefore that is partiall in judgment, doth what in him lies, to deterre men from the use of Judges, and Arbitrators; and consequently, (against the fundamentall Lawe of Nature) is the cause of Warre.

The observance of this law, from the equall distribution to each man, of that which in reason belongeth to him, is called EQUITY, and (as I have sayd before) distributive Justice ...

[94] But a man may here object, that the Condition of Subjects is very miserable; as being obnoxious to the lusts, and other irregular passions of him, or them that have so unlimited a Power in their hands. And commonly they that live under a Monarch, think it the fault of Monarchy; and they that live under the government of Democracy, or other Soveraign Assembly, attribute all the inconvenience to that forme of Common-wealth; whereas the Power in all formes, if they be perfect enough to protect them, is the same; not considering that the estate of

Man can never be without some incommodity or other; and that the greatest, that in any forme of Government can possibly happen to the people in generall, is scarce sensible, in respect of the miseries, and horrible calamities, that accompany a Civill Warre; or that dissolute condition of masterlesse men, without subjection to Lawes, and a coërcive Power to tye their hands from rapine, and revenge: nor considering that the greatest pressure of Soveraign Governours, proceedeth not from any delight, or profit they can expect in the dammage, or weakening of their Subjects, in whose vigor, consisteth their own strength and glory; but in the restiveness of themselves, that unwillingly contributing to their own defence, make it necessary for their Governours to draw from them what they can in time of Peace, that they may have means on any emergent occasion, or sudden need, to resist, or take advantage on their Enemies. For all men are by nature provided of notable multiplying glasses, (that is their Passions and Self-love,) through which, every little payment appeareth a great grievance; but are destitute of those prospective glasses, (namely Morall and Civill Science,) to see a farre off the miseries that hang over them, and cannot without such payments be avoyded. ...

CHAPTER 21

... To resist the Sword of the Common-wealth, in defence of another man, guilty, or innocent, no man hath Liberty; because such Liberty, takes away from the Soveraign, the means of Protecting us; and is therefore destructive of the very essence of Government. But in case a great many men together, have already resisted the Soveraign Power unjustly, or committed some Capitall crime, for which every one of them expecteth death, whether have they not the Liberty then to joyn together, and assist, and defend one another? Certainly they have: For they but defend their lives, which the Guil[113]ty man may as well do, as the Innocent. There was indeed injustice in the first breach of their duty; Their bearing of Arms subsequent to it, though it be to maintain what they have done, is no new unjust act. And if it be onely to defend their persons, it is not unjust at all. But the offer of Pardon taketh from them, to whom it is offered, the plea of self-defence, and maketh their perseverance in assisting, or defending the rest, unlawfull.

As for other Lyberties, they depend on the silence of the Law. In cases where the Soveraign has prescribed no rule, there the Subject hath the liberty to do, or forbeare, according to his own discretion. And therefore such Liberty is in some places more, and in some lesse; and in some times more, in other times lesse, according as they that have the Soveraignty shall think most convenient. As for Example, there was a time, when in *England* a man might enter in to his own Land, (and dispossesse such as wrongfully possessed it) by force. But in after-times, that Liberty of Forcible entry, was taken away by a Statute made (by the King) in Parliament. And in some places of the world, men have the Liberty of many wives; in other places, such Liberty is not allowed.

CHAPTER 25

Command is, where a man saith, *Doe this*, or *Doe not this*, without expecting other reason than the Will of him that sayes it. From this it followeth manifestly, that he that Commandeth, pretendeth thereby his own Benefit: For the reason of his Command is his own [132] Will onely, and the proper object of every mans Will, is some Good to himselfe.

Counsell, is where a man saith, *Doe*, or *Doe not this*, and deduceth his reasons from the benefit that arriveth by it to him to whom he saith it. And from this it is evident, that he that giveth Counsell, pretendeth onely (whatsoever he intendeth) the good of him, to whom he giveth it ...

CHAPTER 26: *OF CIVILL LAWES*

By Civill Lawes, I understand the Lawes, that men are therefore bound to observe, because they are Members, not of this, or that Commonwealth in particular, but of a Common-wealth. For the knowledge of particular Lawes [137] belongeth to them, that professe the study of the Lawes of their severall Countries; but the knowledge of Civill Law in generall, to any man. The antient Law of *Rome* was called their *Civil Law*, from the word *Civitas*, which signifies a Common-wealth: And those Countries, which having been under the Roman Empire, and governed by that Law, retaine still such part thereof as they think fit, call that part the Civill Law, to distinguish it from the rest of their own Civill Lawes. But that is not it I intend to speak of here; my designe being not to shew what is Law here, and there; but what is Law; as *Plato, Aristotle, Cicero,* and divers others have done, without taking upon them the profession of the study of the Law.

And first it is manifest, that Law in generall, is not Counsell, but Command; nor a Command of any man to any man; but only of him, whose Command is addressed to one formerly obliged to obey him. And as for Civill Law, it addeth only the name of the person Commanding, which is *Persona Civitatis*, the Person of the Common-wealth.

Which considered, I define Civill Law in this manner. Civill Law, *Is to every Subject, those Rules, which the Common-wealth hath Commanded him, by Word, Writing, or other sufficient Sign of the Will, to make use of, for the Distinction of Right, and Wrong; that is to say, of what is contrary, and what is not contrary to the Rule.*

In which definition, there is nothing that is not at first sight evident. For every man seeth, that some Lawes are addressed to all the Subjects in generall; some to particular Provinces; some to particular Vocations; and some to particular Men; and are therefore Lawes, to every of those to whom the Command is directed; and to none else. As also, that Lawes are the Rules of Just, and Unjust; nothing being reputed Unjust, that is not contrary to some Law. Likewise, that none can make Lawes but the Common-wealth; because our Subjection is to the Common-wealth only: and that Commands, are to be signified by sufficient Signs; because a man knows not otherwise how to obey them. And therefore, whatsoever can from this definition by necessary consequence be deduced, ought to be acknowledged for truth. Now I deduce from it this that followeth.

1. The Legislator in all Common-wealths, is only the Soveraign, be he one Man, as in a Monarchy, or one Assembly of men, as in a Democracy, or Aristocracy. For the Legislator, is he that maketh the Law. And the Common-wealth only, præscribes, and commandeth the observation of those rules, which we call Law: Therefore the Common-wealth is the Legislator. But the Common-wealth is no Person, nor has capacity to doe any thing, but by the Representative, (that is, the Soveraign;) and therefore the Soveraign is the sole Legislator. For the same reason, none can abrogate a Law made, but the Soveraign; because a Law is not abrogated, but by another Law, that forbiddeth it to be put in execution.

2. The Soveraign of a Common-wealth, be it an Assembly, or one Man, is not Subject to the Civill Lawes. For having power to [138] make, and repeale Lawes, he may when he pleaseth, free himselfe from that subjection, by repealing those Lawes that trouble him, and making of new; and consequently he was free before. For he is free, that can be free when he will: Nor is it possible for any person to be bound to himselfe; because he that can bind, can release; and therefore he that is bound to himselfe onely, is not bound.

3. When long Use obtaineth the authority of a Law, it is not the Length of Time that maketh the Authority, but the Will of the Soveraign signified by his silence, (for Silence is sometimes an argument of Consent;) and it is no longer Law, then the Soveraign shall be silent therein. And therefore if the Soveraign shall have a question of Right grounded, not upon his present Will, but upon the Lawes formerly made; the Length of Time shal bring no prejudice to his Right; but the question shal be judged by Equity. For many unjust Actions, and unjust Sentences, go uncontrolled a longer time, than any man can remember. And our Lawyers account no Customes Law, but such as are reasonable, and that eville Customes are to be abolished: But the Judgement of what is reasonable, and of what is to be abolished, belongeth to him that maketh the Law, which is the Soveraign Assembly, or Monarch.

4. The Law of Nature, and the Civill Law, contain each other, and are of equall extent. For the Lawes of Nature, which consist in Equity, Justice, Gratitude, and other morall Vertues on these depending, in the condition of meer Nature (as I have said before in the end of the 15th Chapter,) are not properly Lawes, but qualities that dispose men to peace, and to obedience. When a Common-wealth is once settled, then are they actually Lawes, and not before; as being then the commands of the Common-wealth; and therefore also Civill Lawes: For it is the Soveraign Power that obliges men to obey them. For in the differences of private men, to declare, what is Equity, what is Justice, and what is morall Vertue, and to make them binding, there is need of the Ordinances of Soveraign Power, and Punishments to be ordained for such as shall break them; which Ordinances are therefore part of the Civill Law. The Law of Nature therefore is a part of the Civill Law in all Common-wealths of the world. Reciprocally also, the Civill Law is a part of the Dictates of Nature. For Justice, that is to say, Performance of Covenant, and giving to every man his own, is a Dictate of the Law of Nature. But every subject in a Common-wealth, hath convenanted to obey the Civill Law, (either one with another, as when they assemble to make a common Representative, or with the Representative it selfe one by one, when subdued by the Sword they promise obedience, that they may receive life;) And therefore Obedience to the Civill Law is part also of the Law of Nature. Civill, and Naturall Law are not different kinds, but different parts of Law; whereof one part being written, is called Civill, the other unwritten, Naturall. But the Right of Nature, that is, the naturall Liberty of man, may by the Civill Law be abridged, and re-

strained: nay, the end of making Lawes, is no other, but such Restraint; without the which there cannot possibly be any Peace. And Law was brought into the world for nothing else, [139] but to limit the naturall liberty of particular men, in such manner, as they might not hurt, but assist one another, and joyn together against a common Enemy.

5. If the Soveraign of one Common-wealth, subdue a People that have lived under other written Lawes, and afterwards govern them by the same Lawes, by which they were governed before; yet those Lawes are the Civill Lawes of the Victor, and not of the Vanquished Common-wealth. For the Legislator is he, not by whose authority the Lawes were first made, but by whose authority they now continue to be Lawes. And therefore where there be divers Provinces, within the Dominion of a Common-wealth, and in those Provinces diversity of Lawes, which commonly are called the Customes of each severall Province, we are not to understand that such Customes have their force, onely from Length of Time; but that they were antiently Lawes written, or otherwise made known, for the Constitutions, and Statutes of their Soveraigns; and are now Lawes, not by vertue of the Præscription of time, but by the Constitutions of their present Soveraigns. But if an unwritten Law, in all the Provinces of a Dominion, shall be generally observed, and no iniquity appear in the use thereof; that Law can be no other but a Law of Nature, equally obliging all man-kind.

6. Seeing then all Lawes, written, and unwritten, have their Authority, and force, from the Will of the Common-wealth; that is to say, from the Will of the Representative; which in a Monarchy is the Monarch, and in other Common-wealths the Soveraign Assembly; a man may wonder from whence proceed such opinions, as are found in the Books of Lawyers of eminence in several Commonwealths, directly, or by consequence making the Legislative Power depend on private men, or subordinate Judges. As for example, *That the Common Law, hath no Controuler but the Parlament*; which is true onely where a Parlament has the Soveraign Power, and cannot be assembled, not dissolved, but by their own discretion. For if there be a right in any else to dissolve them, there is a right also to controule them, and consequently to controule their controulings. And if there be no such right, then the Controuler of Lawes is not *Parlamentum*, but *Rex in Parlamento*. And where a Parlament is Soveraign, if it should assemble never so many, or so wise men, from the Countries subject to them, for whatsoever cause; yet there is no man will believe, that such an Assembly hath thereby acquired to themselves a Legislative Power. *Item*, that the two arms of a Common-wealth,

are *Force, and Justice; the first whereof is in the King; the other deposited in the hands of the Parlament.* As if a Common-wealth could consist, where the Force were in any hand, which Justice had not the Authority to command and govern.

7. That Law can never be against Reason, our Lawyers are agreed; and that not the Letter, (that is every construction of it,) but that which is according to the Intention of the Legislator, is the Law. And it is true: but the doubt is, of whose Reason it is, that shall be received for Law. It is not meant of any private Reason; for [140] then there would be as much contradiction in the Lawes, as there is in the Schooles; nor yet, (as Sr. *Ed. Coke* makes it,) an *Artificiall perfection of Reason, gotten by long study, observation, and experience,* (as his was.) For it is possible long study may encrease, and confirm erroneous Sentences: and where men build on false grounds, the more they build, the greater is the ruine: and of those that study, and observe with equall time, and diligence, the reasons and resolutions are, and must remain discordant: and therefore it is not that *Juris prudentia,* or wisedome of subordinate Judges; but the Reason of this our Artificiall Man the Common-wealth, and his Command, that maketh Law: And the Common-wealth being in their Representative but one Person, there cannot easily arise any contradiction in the Lawes; and when there doth, the same Reason is able, by interpretation, or alteration, to take it away. In all Courts of Justice, the Soveraign (which is the Person of the Common-wealth,) is he that Judgeth: The subordinate Judge, ought to have regard to the reason, which moved his Soveraign to make such Law, that his Sentence may be according thereunto; which then is his Soveraigns Sentence; otherwise it is his own, and an unjust one.

8. From this, that the Law is a Command, and a Command consisteth in declaration, or manifestation of the will of him that commandeth, by voyce, writing, or some other sufficient argument of the same, we may understand, that the Command of the Common-wealth, is Law onely to those, that have means to take notice of it. Over naturall fooles, children, or mad-men there is no Law, no more than over brute beasts; nor are they capable of the title of just, or unjust; because they had never power to make any covenant, or to understand the consequences thereof; and consequently never took upon them to authorise the actions of any Soveraign, as they must do that make to themselves a Common-wealth. And as those from whom Nature, or Accident hath taken away the notice of all Lawes in generall; so also every man, from whom any accident, not proceeding from his own default, hath taken away the

means to take notice of any particular Law, is excused, if he observe it not; And to speak properly, that Law is no Law to him. It is therefore necessary, to consider in this place, what arguments, and signes be sufficient for the knowledge of what is the Law; that is to say, what is the will of the Soveraign, as well in Monarchies, as in other formes of government.

And first, if it be a Law that obliges all the Subjects without exception, and is not written, nor otherwise published in such places as they may take notice thereof, it is a Law of Nature. For whatsoever men are to take knowledge of for Law, not upon other mens words, but every one from his own reason, must be such as is agreeable to the reason of all men; which no Law can be, but the Law of Nature. The Lawes of Nature therefore need not any publishing, nor Proclamation; as being contained in this one Sentence, approved by all the world, *Do not that to another, which thou thinkest unreasonable to be done by another to thy selfe.*

[I4I] Secondly, if it be a Law that obliges only some condition of men, or one particular man, and be not written, nor published by word, then also it is a Law of Nature; and known by the same arguments, and signs, that distinguish those in such a condition, from other Subjects. For whatsoever Law is not written, or some way published by him that makes it Law, can be known no way, but by the reason of him that is to obey it; and is therefore also a Law not only Civill, but Naturall. For Example, if the Soveraign employ a Publique Minister, without written Instructions what to doe; he is obliged to take for Instructions the Dictates of Reason; As if he make a Judge, The Judge is to take notice, that his Sentence ought to be according to the reason of his Soveraign, which being alwaies understood to be Equity, he is bound to it by the Law of Nature: Or if an Ambassador, he is (in all things not conteined in his written Instructions) to take for Instruction that which Reason dictates to be most conducing to his Soveraigns interest; and so of all other Ministers of the Soveraignty, publique and private. All which Instructions of naturall Reason may be comprehended under one name of *Fidelity*; which is a branch of naturall Justice ...

Nor is it enough the Law be written, and published; but also that there be manifest signs, that is proceedeth from the will of the Soveraign. For private men, when they have, or think they have force enough to secure their unjust designes, and convoy them safely to their ambitious ends, may publish for Lawes what they please, without, or against the Legislative Authority. There is therefore requisite, not only a Declaration of the Law, but also sufficient signes of the Author, and Authority. The Author, or Legislator is supposed in every Common-wealth to be evident, because he is the Soveraign, who having been Constituted by the consent of every one, is supposed by every one to be sufficiently known. And though the ignorance, and security of men be such, for the most part, as that when [142] the memory of the first Constitution of their Common-wealth is worn out, they doe not consider, by whose power they use to be defended against their enemies, and to have their industry protected, and to be righted when injury is done them; yet because no man that considers, can make question of it, no excuse can be derived from the ignorance of where the Soveraignty is placed. And it is a Dictate of Naturall Reason, and consequently an evident Law of Nature, that no man ought to weaken that power, the protection whereof he hath himself demanded, or wittingly received against others. Therefore of who is Soveraign, no man, but by his own fault, (whatsoever evill men suggest,) can make any doubt. The difficulty consisteth in the evidence of the Authority derived from him; The removing whereof, dependeth on the knowledge of the publique Registers, publique Counsels, publique Ministers, and publique Seales; by which all Lawes are sufficiently verified; Verifyed, I say, not Authorised: for the Verification, is but the Testimony and Record; not the Authority of the Law; which consisteth in the Command of the Soveraign only.

If therefore a man have a question of Injury, depending on the Law of Nature; that is to say, on common Equity; the Sentence of the Judge, that by Commission hath Authority to take cognisance of such causes, is a sufficient Verification of the Law of Nature in that individuall case. For though the advice of one that professeth the study of the Law, be usefull for the avoyding of contention; yet it is but advice: tis the Judge must tell men what is Law, upon the hearing of the Controversy.

But when the question is of injury, or crime, upon a written Law; every man by recourse to the Registers, by himself, or others, may (if he will) be sufficiently enformed, before he doe such injury, or commit the crime, whither it be an injury, or not: Nay he ought to doe so: For when a man doubts whether the act he goeth about, be just, or injust; and may informe himself, if he will; the doing is unlawfull. In like manner, he that supposeth himself injured, in a case determined by the written Law, which he may by himself, or others see and consider; if he complaine before he consults with the Law, he does unjustly, and bewrayeth a disposition rather to vex other men, than to demand his own right.

If the question be of Obedience to a publique Officer; To have seen his Commission, with the Publique Seale, and heard it read; or to have had the means to be informed of it, if a man would, is a sufficient

Verification of his authority. For every man is obliged to doe his best endeavour, to informe himself of all written Lawes, that may concerne his own future actions.

The Legislator known; and the Lawes, either by writing, or by the light of Nature, sufficiently published; there wanteth yet another very materiall circumstance to make them obligatory. For it is not the Letter, but the Intendment, or Meaning; that is to say, the authentique Interpretation of the Law (which is the sense of the Legislator,) in which the nature of the Law consisteth; And therefore [143] the Interpretation of all Lawes dependeth on the Authority Soveraign; and the Interpreters can be none but those, which the Soveraign, (to whom only the Subject oweth obedience) shall appoint. For else, by the craft of an Interpreter, the Law may be made to beare a sense, contrary to that of the Soveraign; by which means the Interpreter becomes the Legislator.

All Laws, written, and unwritten, have need of Interpretation. The unwritten Law of Nature, though it be easy to such, as without partiality, and passion, make use of there naturall reason, and therefore leaves the violaters thereof without excuse; yet considering there be very few, perhaps none, that in some cases are not blinded by self love, or some other passion, it is now become of all Laws the most obscure; and has consequently the greatest need of able Interpreters. The written Laws, if they be short, are easily mis-interpreted, from the divers significations of a word, or two: if long, they be more obscure by the diverse significations of many words: in so much as no written Law, delivered in few, or many words, can be well understood, without a perfect understanding of the finall causes, for which the Law was made; the knowledge of which finall causes is in the Legislator. To him therefore there can not be any knot in the Law, insoluble; either by finding out the ends, to undoe it by; or else by making what ends he will, (as *Alexander* did with his sword in the Gordian Knot,) by the Legislative power; which no other Interpreter can doe.

The Interpretation of the Lawes of Nature, in a Common-wealth, dependeth not on the books of Morall Philosophy. The Authority of writers, without the Authority of the Common-wealth, maketh not their opinions Law, by they never so true. That which I have written in this Treatise, concerning the Morall Vertues, and of their necessity, for the procuring, and maintaining peace, though it bee evident Truth, is not therefore presently Law; but because in all Common-wealths in the world, it is part of the Civill Law: For though it be naturally reasonable;

yet it is by the Soveraigne Power that it is Law: Otherwise, it were a great errour, to call the Lawes of Nature unwritten Law; whereof wee see so many volumes published, and in them so many contradictions of one another, and of themselves.

The Interpretation of the Law of Nature, is the Sentence of the Judge constituted by the Soveraign Authority, to heare and determine such controversies, as depend thereon; and consisteth in the application of the Law to the present case. For in the act of Judicature, the Judge doth no more but consider, whither the demand of the party, be consonant to naturall reason, and Equity; and the Sentence he giveth, is therefore the Interpretation of the Law of Nature; which Interpretation is Authentique; not because it is his private Sentence; but because he giveth it by Authority of the Soveraign, whereby it becomes the Soveraigns Sentence; which is Law for that time, to the parties pleading.

[144] But because there is no Judge Subordinate, nor Soveraign, but may erre in a Judgement of Equity; if afterward in another like case he find it more consonant to Equity to give a contrary Sentence, he is obliged to doe it. No mans error becomes his own Law; nor obliges him to persist in it. Neither (for the same reason) becomes it a Law to other Judges, though sworn to follow it. For though a wrong Sentence given by authority of the Soveraign, if he know and allow it, in such Lawes as are mutable, be a constitution of a new Law, in cases, in which every little circumstance is the same; yet in Lawes immutable, such as are the Lawes of Nature, they are no Lawes to the same, or other Judges, in the like cases for ever after. Princes succeed one another; and one Judge passeth, another commeth; nay, Heaven and Earth shall passe; but not one title of the Law of Nature shall passe; for it is the Eternall Law of God. Therefore all the Sentences of precedent Judges that have ever been, cannot all altogether make a Law contrary to naturall Equity: Nor any Examples of former Judges, can warrant an unreasonable Sentence, or discharge the present Judge of the trouble of studying what is Equity (in the case he is to Judge,) from the principles of his own naturall reason. For example sake, 'Tis against the Law of Nature, *To punish the innocent*; and Innocent is he that acquitteth himselfe Judicially, and is acknowledged for Innocent by the Judge. Put the case now, that a man is accused of a capitall crime, and seeing the power and malice of some enemy, and the frequent corruption and partiality of Judges, runneth away for feare of the event, and afterwards is taken, and brought to a legall triall, and maketh it sufficiently appear, he was not guilty of the

crime, and being thereof acquitted, is neverthelesse condemned to lose his goods; this is a manifest condemnation of the Innocent. I say therefore, that there is no place in the world, where this can be an interpretation of a Law of Nature, or be made a Law by the Sentences of precendent Judges, that had done the same. For he that judged it first, judged unjustly; and no Injustice can be a pattern of Judgement to succeeding Judges. A written Law may forbid innocent men to fly, and they may be punished for flying: But that flying for feare of injury, should be taken for presumption of guilt, after a man is already absolved of the crime Judicially, is contrary to the nature of a Presumption, which hath no place after Judgement given. Yet this is set down by a great Lawyer for the common Law of *England. If a man* (saith he) *that is Innocent, be accused of Felony, and for feare flyeth for the same; albeit he judicially acquitteth himselfe of the Felony; yet if it be found that he fled for the Felony, he shall notwithstanding his Innocency, Forfeit all his goods, chattells, debts, and duties. For as to the Forfeiture of them, the Law will admit no proofe against the Presumption in Law, grounded upon his flight.* Here you see, *An Innocent man, Judicially acquitted, notwithstanding his Innocency,* (when no written Law forbad him to fly) after his acquittall, *upon a Presumption in Law,* condemned to lose all the goods he hath. If the Law ground upon his flight a Presumption of the fact, (what was Capitall,) the Sen[145]tence ought to have been Capitall: if the Presumption were not of the Fact, for what then ought he to lose his goods? This therefore is no Law of *England;* nor is the condemnation grounded upon a Presumption of Law, but upon the Presumption of the Judges. It is also against Law, to say that no Proofe shall be admitted against a Presumption of Law. For all Judges, Soveraign and subordinate, if they refuse to heare Proofe, refuse to do Justice: for though the Sentence be Just, yet the Judges that condemn without hearing the Proofes offered, are Unjust Judges; and their Presumption is but Prejudice; which no man ought to bring with him to the Seat of Justice, whatsoever precedent judgements, or examples he shall pretend to follow. There be other things of this nature, wherein mens Judgements have been perverted, by trusting to Precedents: but this is enough to shew, that though the Sentence of the Judge, be a Law to the party pleading, yet it is no Law to any Judge, that shall succeed him in that Office.

In like manner, when question is of the Meaning of written Lawes, he is not the Interpreter of them, that writeth a Commentary upon them. For Commentaries are commonly more subject to cavill, than the Text;

and therefore need other Commentaries; and so there will be no end of such Interpretation. And therefore unlesse there be an Interpreter authorised by the Soveraign, from which the subordinate Judges are not to recede, the Interpreter can be no other than the ordinary Judges, in the same manner, as they are in cases of the unwritten Law; and their Sentences are to be taken by them that plead, for Lawes in that particular case; but not to bind other Judges, in like cases to give like judgements. For a Judge may erre in the Interpretation even of written Lawes; but no errour of a subordinate Judge, can change the Law, which is the generall Sentence of the Soveraigne.

In written Lawes, men use to make a difference between the Letter, and the Sentence of the Law: And when by the Letter, is meant whatsoever can be gathered from the bare words, 'tis well distinguished. For the significations of almost all words, are either in themselves, or in the metaphoricall use of them, ambiguous; and may be drawn in argument, to make many senses; but there is onely one sense of the Law. But if by the Letter, be meant the literall sense, then the Letter, and the Sentence or intention of the Law, is all one. For the literall sense is that, which the Legislator intended, should by the letter of the Law be signified. Now the Intention of the Legislator is always supposed to be Equity: For it were a great contumely for a Judge to think otherwise of the Soveraigne. He ought therefore, if the Word of the Law doe not fully authorise a reasonable Sentence, to supply it with the Law of Nature; or if the case be difficult, to respit Judgement till he have received more ample authority. For Example, a written Law ordaineth, that he which is thrust out of his house by force, shall be restored by force: It happens that a man by negligence leaves his house empty, and returning is kept out by force, in which case there is no speciall Law ordained. It is evi[146]dent, that this case is contained in the same Law: for else there is no remedy for him at all; which is to be supposed against the Intention of the Legislator. Again, the word of the Law, commandeth to Judge according to the Evidence: A man is accused falsly of a fact, which the Judge saw himself done by another; and not by him that is accused. In this case neither shall the Letter of the Law be followed to the condemnation of the Innocent, nor shall the Judge give Sentence against the evidence of the Witnesses; because the Letter of the Law is to the contrary: but procure of the Soveraign that another be made Judge, and himselfe Witnesse. So that the incommodity that follows the bare words of a written Law, may lead him to the Intention of the Law, whereby to interpret the same the better; though no Incommodity can warrant a Sentence against the Law. For every Judge of Right, and Wrong, is not Judge of what is Commodious, or Incommodious to the Common-wealth.

The abilities required in a good Interpreter of the Law, that is to say, in a good Judge, are not the same with those of an Advocate; namely the study of the Lawes. For a Judge, as he ought to take notice of the Fact, from none but the Witnesses; so also he ought to take notice of the Law, from nothing but the Statutes, and Constitutions of the Soveraign, alledged in the pleading, or declared to him by some that have authority from the Soveraign Power to declare them; and need not take care before-hand, what hee shall Judge; for it shall bee given him what hee shall say concerning the Fact, by Witnesses; and what hee shall say in point of Law, from those that shall in their pleadings shew it, and by authority interpret it upon the place. The Lords of Parlament in *England* were Judges, and most difficult causes have been heard and determined by them; yet few of them were much versed in the study of the Lawes, and fewer had made profession of them: and though they consulted with Lawyers, that were appointed to be present there for that purpose; yet they alone had the authority of giving Sentence. In like manner, in the ordinary trialls of Right, Twelve men of the common People, are the Judges, and give Sentence, not onely of the Fact, but of the Right; and pronounce simply for the Complaynant, or for the Defendant; that is to say, are Judges not onely of the Fact, but also of the Right: and in a question of crime, not onely determine whether done, or not done; but also whether it be *Murder, Homicide, Felony, Assault*, and the like, which are determinations of Law: but because they are not supposed to know the Law of themselves, there is one that hath Authority to enforme them of it, in the particular case they are to Judge of. But yet if they judge not according to that he tells them, they are not subject thereby to any penalty; unlesse it be made appear, they did it against their consciences, or had been corrupted by reward.

The things that make a good Judge, or good Interpreter of the Lawes, are, first, *A right understanding* of that principall Law of Nature called *Equity*; which depending not on the reading of other mens Writings, but on the goodnesse of a mans own naturall [147] Reason, and Meditation, is presumed to be in those most, that have had most leisure, and had the most inclination to meditate thereon. Secondly, *Contempt of unnecessary Riches*, and Preferments. Thirdly, *To be able in judgement to devest himselfe of all feare, anger, hatred, love*, and *compassion*. Fourthly, and lastly, *Patience to heare; diligent attention in hearing; and memory to retain, digest and apply what he hath heard* ...

CHAPTER 29

Another infirmity of a Common-wealth, is the immoderate greatnesse of a Town, when it is able to furnish out of its own Circuit, the number, and expence of a great Army: As also the great number of Corporations; which are as it were many lesser Common-wealths in the bowels of a greater, like wormes in the entrayles of a naturall man. To which may be added, the Liberty of Disputing against absolute Power, by pretenders to Politicall Prudence; which though bred for the most part in the Lees of the people; yet animated by False Doctrines, are perpetually medling with the Fundamentall Lawes, to the molestation of the Common-wealth; like the little Wormes, which Physicians call *Ascarides*.

CHAPTER 37

A private man has alwaies the liberty, (because thought is free,) to beleeve, or not beleeve in his heart, those acts that have been given out for Miracles, according as he shall see, what benefit can accrew by mens belief, to those that pretend, or countenance them, and thereby conjecture, whether they be Miracles, or Lies. But when it comes to confession of that faith, the Private Reason must submit to the Publique; that is to say, to Gods Lieutenant.

CONCLUSION

And thus I have brought to an end my Discourse of Civill and Ecclesiasticall Government, occasioned by the disorders of the present time, without partiality, without application, and without other designe, than to set before mens eyes the mutuall Relation be[396]tween Protection and Obedience;

READING QUESTIONS ON HOBBES

1 How realistic is Hobbes's view of the "Natural Condition of Mankind"? (Don't ask yourself if Hobbes accurately describes your motives; ask instead if he describes other people you know.)
2 Can the Hobbesian sovereign appeal to moral considerations?
3 What is the role of judges in Hobbes's theory? Could someone actually carry out the task of judging as Hobbes describes it?

4 Hobbes reserves individual freedoms of conscience and rights to
   self-defence even against the sovereign. Is this consistent with his
   view of the importance of legal order and stability?
5 Hobbes appeals to ideas of equity in deciding cases. How is this
   related to his more general positivism? Is there a tension in his view?
   Can you think of any way it might be resolved?

H.L.A. Hart
"Positivism and the Separation of Law and Morals" (1983);
The Concept of Law (1961)

Jurisprudence had lain moribund for close to half a century before Hart's
classic essay. Hart's aim is to offer a rigorous statement of legal positivism, the
view that law and morality are distinct modes of social ordering. Hart's essay
is important both for its historical place and because of its emphasis on the
importance, both moral and conceptual, of keeping law and morality apart. In
The Concept of Law, Hart elaborates his idea of a fundamental rule which has to
be accepted by legal officials.

Positivism and the Separation of Law and Morals

... I shall present the subject as part of the history of an idea ...

Bentham's general recipe for life under the government of laws was
simple: it was *"to obey punctually; to censure freely."*[1] But Bentham was
especially aware, as an anxious spectator of the French revolution, that
this was not enough: the time might come in any society when the law's
commands were so evil that the question of resistance had to be faced,
and it was then essential that the issues at stake at this point should
neither be oversimplified nor obscured.[2] Yet this was precisely what the
confusion between law and morals had done, and Bentham found that
the confusion had spread symmetrically in two different directions. On
the one hand Bentham had in mind the anarchist who argues thus:
"This ought not to be the law, therefore it is not and I am free not
merely to censure but to disregard it." On the other hand he thought of

the reactionary who argues: "This is the law, therefore it is what it ought to be", and thus stifles criticism at its birth. Both errors, Bentham thought, were to be found in Blackstone: there was his incautious statement that human laws were invalid if contrary to the law of God, and "that spirit of obsequious *quietism* that seems constitutional in our Author" which "will scarce ever let him recognise a difference" between what is and what ought to be.[3] This indeed was for Bentham the occupational disease of lawyers: "[I]n the eyes of lawyers – not to speak of their dupes – that is to say, as yet, the generality of non-lawyers – the *is* and the *ought to be* ... were one and indivisible."[4] There are therefore two dangers between which insistence on this distinction will help us to steer: the danger that law and its authority may be dissolved in man's conceptions of what law ought to be and the danger that the existing law may supplant morality as a final test of conduct and so escape criticism.

In view of later criticisms it is also important to distinguish several things that the Utilitarians did not mean by insisting on their separation of law and morals. They certainly accepted many of the things that might be called "the intersection of law and morals". First, they never denied that, as a matter of historical fact, the development of legal systems had been powerfully influenced by moral opinion, and, conversely, that moral standards had been profoundly influenced by law, so that the content of many legal rules mirrored moral rules or principles. It is not in fact always easy to trace this historical causal connection, but Bentham was certainly ready to admit its existence; so too Austin spoke of the "frequent coincidence" of positive law and morality and attributed the confusion of what law is with what law ought to be to this very fact.

Secondly, neither Bentham nor his followers denied that by explicit legal provisions moral principles might at different points be brought into a legal system and form part of its rules, or that courts might be legally bound to decide in accordance with what they thought just or best. Bentham indeed recognized, as Austin did not, that even the supreme legislative power might be subjected to legal restraints by a constitution and would not have denied that moral principles, like those of the Fifth Amendment, might form the content of such legal constitutional restraints. Austin differed in thinking that restraints on the supreme legislative power could not have the force of law, but would remain merely political or moral checks; but of course he would have recognized that a statute, for example, might confer a delegated legislative power and restrict the area of its exercise by reference to moral principles.

What both Bentham and Austin were anxious to assert were the following two simple things: first, in the absence of an expressed constitutional or legal provision, it could not follow from the mere fact that a rule violated standards of morality that it was not a rule of law; and, conversely, it could not follow from the mere fact that a rule was morally desirable that it was a rule of law ...

So much for the doctrine in the heyday of its success. Let us turn now to some of the criticisms. Undoubtedly, when Bentham and Austin insisted on the distinction between law as it is and as it ought to be, they had in mind *particular* laws, the meanings of which were clear and so not in dispute, and they were concerned to argue that such laws, even if morally outrageous, were still laws. It is, however, necessary, in considering the criticisms which later developed, to consider more than those criticisms which were directed to this particular point if we are to get at the root of the dissatisfaction felt; we must also take account of the objection that, even if what the Utilitarians said on this particular point were true, their insistence on it, in a terminology suggesting a general cleavage between what is and ought to be law, obscured the fact that at other points there is an essential point of contact between the two. So in what follows I consider not only criticisms of the particular point which the Utilitarians had in mind, but also the claim that an essential connection between law and morals emerges if we examine how laws, the meanings of which are in dispute, are interpreted and applied in concrete cases; and that this connection emerges again if we widen our point of view and ask, not whether every particular rule of law must satisfy a moral minimum in order to be a law, but whether a system of rules which altogether failed to do this could be a legal system.

There is, however, one major initial complexity by which criticism has been much confused. We must remember that the Utilitarians combined with their insistence on the separation of law and morals two other equally famous but distinct doctrines. One was the important truth that a purely analytical study of legal concepts, a study of the meaning of the distinctive vocabulary of the law, was as vital to our understanding of the nature of law as historical or sociological studies, though of course it could not supplant them. The other doctrine was the famous imperative theory of law – that law is essentially a command.

These three doctrines constitute the utilitarian tradition in jurisprudence; yet they are distinct doctrines. It is possible to endorse the separation between law and morals and to value analytical inquiries into the meaning of legal concepts and yet think it wrong to conceive of law as essentially a command. One source of great confusion in the criticism of the separation of law and morals was the belief that the falsity of any one of these three doctrines in the utilitarian tradition showed the other two to be false; what was worse was the failure to see that there were three quite separate doctrines in this tradition. The indiscriminate use of the label "positivism" to designate ambiguously each one of these three separate doctrines (together with some others which the Utilitarians never professed) has perhaps confused the issue more than any other single factor ... [5]

The famous theory that law is a command was a part of a wider and more ambitious claim. Austin said that the notion of a command was "the *key* to the sciences of jurisprudence and morals", and contemporary attempts to elucidate moral judgments in terms of "imperative" or "prescriptive" utterances echo this ambitious claim. But the command theory, viewed as an effort to identify even the quintessence of law, let alone the quintessence of morals, seems breathtaking in its simplicity and quite inadequate. There is much, even in the simplest legal system, that is distorted if presented as a command. Yet the Utilitarians thought that the essence of a legal system could be conveyed if the notion of a command were supplemented by that of a habit of obedience. The simple scheme was this: What is a command? It is simply an expression by one person of the desire that another person should do or abstain from some action, accompanied by a threat of punishment which is likely to follow disobedience. Commands are laws if two conditions are satisfied: first, they must be general; second they must be commanded by what (as both Bentham and Austin claimed) exists in every political society whatever its constitutional form, namely, a person or a group of persons who are in receipt of habitual obedience from most of the society but pay no such obedience to others. These persons are its sovereign. Thus law is the command of the uncommanded commanders of society – the creation of the legally untrammelled will of the sovereign who is by definition outside the law.

It is easy to see that this account of a legal system is threadbare. One can also see why it might seem that its inadequacy is due to the omission of some essential connection with morality. The situation which the simple trilogy of command, sanction, and sovereign avails to describe, if you take these notions at all precisely, is like that of a gunman saying to his victim, "Give me your money or your life." The only difference is that in the case of a legal system the gunman says it to a large number of people who are accustomed to the racket and habitually surrender to it. Law surely is not the gunman situation writ large, and legal order is surely not to be thus simply identified with compulsion.

This scheme, despite the points of obvious analogy between a statute and a command, omits some of the most characteristic elements of law. Let me cite a few. It is wrong to think of a legislature (and *a fortiori* an electorate) with a changing membership as a group of persons habitually obeyed: this simple idea is suited only to a monarch sufficiently long-lived for a "habit" to grow up. Even if we waive this point, nothing which legislators do makes law unless they comply with fundamental accepted rules specifying the essential law-making procedures. This is true even in a system having a simple unitary constitution like the British. These fundamental accepted rules specifying what the legislature must do to legislate are not commands habitually obeyed, nor can they be expressed as habits of obedience to persons. They lie at the root of a legal system, and what is most missing in the utilitarian scheme is an analysis of what it is for a social group and its officials to accept such rules. This notion, not that of a command as Austin claimed, is the "key to the science of jurisprudence", or at least one of the keys.

Again, Austin, in the case of a democracy, looked past the legislators to the electorate as "the sovereign" (or in England as part of it). He thought that in the United States the mass of the electors to the state and federal legislatures were the sovereign whose commands, given by their "agents" in the legislatures, were law. But on this footing the whole notion of the sovereign outside the law being "habitually obeyed" by the "bulk" of the population must go: for in this case the "bulk" obeys the bulk, that is, it obeys itself. Plainly the general acceptance of the authority of a law-making procedure, irrespective of the changing individuals who operate it from time to time, can be only distorted by an analysis in terms of mass habitual obedience to certain persons who are by definition outside the law, just as the cognate but much simpler phenomenon of the general social acceptance of a rule, say of taking off the hat when entering a church, would be distorted if represented as habitual obedience by the mass to specific persons.

Other critics dimly sensed a further and more important defect in the command theory, yet blurred the edge of an important criticism by assuming that the defect was due to the failure to insist upon some important connection between law and morals. This more radical defect is as follows. The picture that the command theory draws of life under law is essentially a simple relationship of the commander to the commanded, of superior to inferior, of top to bottom; the relationship is vertical between the commanders or authors of the law conceived of as essentially outside the law and those who are commanded and subject to the law. In this picture no place, or only an accidental or subordinate place, is afforded for a distinction between types of legal rules which are in fact radically different. Some laws require men to act in certain ways or to abstain from acting whether they wish to or not. The criminal law consists largely of rules of this sort: like commands they are simply "obeyed" or "disobeyed". But other legal rules are presented to society in quite different ways and have quite different functions. They provide facilities more or less elaborate for individuals to create structures of rights and duties for the conduct of life within the coercive framework of the law. Such are the rules enabling individuals to make contracts, wills, and trusts, and generally to mould their legal relations with others. Such rules, unlike the criminal law, are not factors designed to obstruct wishes and choices of an antisocial sort. On the contrary, these rules provide facilities for the realization of wishes and choices. They do not say (like commands) "do this whether you wish it or not", but rather "if you wish to do this, here is the way to do it". Under these rules we exercise powers, make claims, and assert rights. These phrases mark off characteristic features of laws that confer rights and powers; they are laws which are, so to speak, put at the disposition of individuals in a way in which the criminal law is not. Much ingenuity has gone into the task of "reducing" laws of this second sort to some complex variant of laws of the first sort. The effort to show that laws conferring rights are "really" only conditional stipulations of sanctions to be exacted from the person ultimately under a legal duty characterizes much of Kelsen's work.[6] Yet to urge this is really just to exhibit dogmatic determination to suppress one aspect of the legal system in order to maintain the theory that the stipulation of a sanction, like Austin's command, represents the quintessence of law. One might as well urge that the rules of baseball were "really" only complex conditional directions to the scorer and that this showed their real or "essential" nature.

One of the first jurists in England to break with the Austinian tradition, Salmond, complained that the analysis in terms of commands left the notion of a right unprovided with a place.[7] But he confused the point. He argued first, and correctly, that if laws are merely commands it is inexplicable that we should have come to speak of legal rights and powers as conferred or arising under them, but then wrongly concluded that the rules of a legal system must necessarily be connected with moral rules or principles of justice and that only on this footing could the phenomenon of legal rights be explained. Otherwise, Salmond thought, we would have to say that a mere "verbal coincidence" connects the concepts of legal and moral right. Similarly, continental critics of the Utilitarians, always alive to the complexity of the notion of a subjective right, insisted that the command theory gave it no place. Hägerström insisted that if laws were merely commands the notion of an individual's right was really inexplicable, for commands are, as he said, something which we either obey or we do not obey; they do not confer rights. But he, too, concluded that moral, or, as he put it, common-sense, notions of justice must therefore be necessarily involved in the analysis of any legal structure elaborate enough to confer rights.

Yet, surely these arguments are confused. Rules that confer rights, though distinct from commands, need not be moral rules or coincide with them. Rights, after all, exist under the rules of ceremonies, games, and in many other spheres regulated by rules which are irrelevant to the question of justice or what the law ought to be. Nor need rules which confer rights be just or morally good rules. The rights of a master over his slaves show us that. "Their merit or demerit", as Austin termed it, depends on how rights are distributed in society and over whom or what they are exercised. These critics indeed revealed the inadequacy of the simple notions of command and habit for the analysis of law; at many points it is apparent that the social acceptance of a rule or standard of authority (even if it is motivated only by fear or superstition or rests on inertia) must be brought into the analysis and cannot itself be reduced to the two simple terms. Yet nothing in this showed the utilitarian insistence on the distinction between the existence of law and its "merits" to be wrong.

III

I now turn to a distinctively American criticism of the separation of the law that is from the law that ought to be. It emerged from the critical study of the judicial process with which American jurisprudence has been on the whole so beneficially occupied. The most sceptical of these critics – the loosely named "Realists" of the 1930s – perhaps too naïvely accepted the conceptual framework of the natural sciences as adequate for the characterization of law and for the analysis of rule-guided action of which a living system of law at least partly consists. But they opened men's eyes to what actually goes on when courts decide cases, and the contrast they drew between the actual facts of judicial decision and the traditional terminology for describing it as if it were a wholly logical operation was usually illuminating; for in spite of some exaggeration the Realists made us acutely conscious of one cardinal feature of human language and human thought, emphasis on which is vital not only for the understanding of law but in areas of philosophy far beyond the confines of jurisprudence. The insight of this school may be presented in the following example. A legal rule forbids you to take a vehicle into the public park. Plainly this forbids an automobile, but what about bicycles, roller skates, toy automobiles? What about aeroplanes? Are these, as we say, to be called "vehicles" for the purpose of the rule or not? If we are to communicate with each other at all, and if, as in the most elementary form of law, we are to express our intentions that a certain type of behaviour be regulated by rules, then the general words we use – like "vehicle" in the case I consider – must have some standard instance in which no doubts are felt about its application. There must be a core of settled meaning, but there will be, as well, a penumbra of debatable cases in which words are neither obviously applicable nor obviously ruled out. These cases will each have some features in common with the standard case; they will lack others or be accompanied by features not present in the standard case. Human invention and natural processes continually throw up such variants on the familiar, and if we are to say that these ranges of facts do or do not fall under existing rules, then the classifier must make a decision which is not dictated to him, for the facts and phenomena to which we fit our words and apply our rules are as it were *dumb*. The toy automobile cannot speak up and say, "I am a vehicle for the purpose of this legal rule", nor can the roller skates chorus,"We are not a vehicle." Fact situations do not await us neatly labelled, creased, and folded; nor is their legal classification written on them to be simply read off by the judge. Instead, in applying legal rules, someone must take the responsibility of deciding that words do or do not cover some case in hand, with all the practical consequences involved in this decision.

We may call the problems which arise outside the hard core of standard instances or settled meaning "problems of the penumbra"; they are always with us whether in relation to such trivial things as the regulation of the use of the public park or in relation to the multidimensional generalities of a constitution. If a penumbra of uncertainty must surround all legal rules, then their application to specific cases in the penumbral area cannot be a matter of logical deduction, and so deductive reasoning, which for generations has been cherished as the very perfection of human reasoning, cannot serve as a model for what judges, or indeed anyone, should do in bringing particular cases under general rules. In this area men cannot live by deduction alone. And it follows that if legal arguments and legal decisions of penumbral questions are to be rational, their rationality must lie in something other than a logical relation to premises. So if it is rational or "sound" to argue and to decide that for the purposes of this rule an aeroplane is not a vehicle, this argument must be sound or rational without being logically conclusive. What is it then that makes such decisions correct or at least better than alternative decisions? Again, it seems true to say that the criterion which makes a decision sound in such cases is some concept of what the law ought to be; it is easy to slide from that into saying that it must be a moral judgment about what law ought to be. So here we touch upon a point of necessary "intersection between law and morals" which demonstrates the falsity or, at any rate, the misleading character of the Utilitarians' emphatic insistence on the separation of law as it is and ought to be. Surely, Bentham and Austin could only have written as they did because they misunderstood or neglected this aspect of the judicial process, because they ignored the problems of the penumbra.

The misconception of the judicial process which ignores the problems of the penumbra and which views the process as consisting pre-eminently in deductive reasoning is often stigmatized as the error of "formalism" or "literalism". My question now is, how and to what extent does the demonstration of this error show the utilitarian distinction to be wrong or misleading? Here there are many issues which have been confused, but I can only disentangle some. The charge of formalism has been levelled both at the "positivist" legal theorist and at the courts, but of course it must be a very different charge in each case. Levelled at the legal theorist, the charge means that he has made a theoretical mistake about the character of legal decision; he has thought of the reasoning involved as consisting in deduction from premises in which the judges' practical choices or decisions play no part. It would be easy to show that Austin was guiltless of this error; only an entire misconception of what analytical jurisprudence is and why he thought it important has led to the view that he, or any other analyst, believed that the law was a closed logical system in which judges deduced their decisions from premises. On the contrary, he was very much alive to the character of language, to its vagueness or open character; he thought that in the penumbral situation judges must necessarily legislate, and, in accents that sometimes recall those of the late Judge Jerome Frank, he berated the common-law judges for legislating feebly and timidly and for blindly relying on real or fancied analogies with past cases instead of adapting their decisions to the growing needs of society as revealed by the moral standard of utility. The villains of this piece, responsible for the conception of the judge as an automaton, are not the utilitarian thinkers. The responsibility, it if is to be laid at the door of any theorist, is with thinkers like Blackstone and, at an earlier stage, Montesquieu. The root of this evil is preoccupation with the separation of powers and Blackstone's "childish fiction" (as Austin termed it) that judges only "find", never "make", law.

But we are concerned with "formalism" as a vice not of jurists but of judges. What precisely is it for a judge to commit this error, to be a "formalist", "automatic", a "slot machine"? Curiously enough the literature, which is full of the denunciation of these vices, never makes this clear in concrete terms; instead we have only descriptions which cannot mean what they appear to say; it is said that in the formalist error courts make an excessive use of logic, take a thing to "a dryly logical extreme", or make an excessive use of analytical methods. But just how in being a formalist does a judge make an excessive use of logic? It is clear that the essence of his error is to give some general term an interpretation which is blind to social values and consequences (or which is in some other way stupid or perhaps merely disliked by critics). But logic does not prescribe interpretation of terms; it dictates neither the stupid nor intelligent interpretation of any expression. Logic only tells you hypothetically that *if* you give a certain term a certain interpretation then a certain conclusion follows. Logic is silent on how to classify particulars – and this is the heart of a judicial decision. So this reference to logic and to logical extremes is a misnomer for something else, which must be this. A judge has to apply a rule to a concrete case – perhaps the rule that one may not take a stolen "vehicle" across State lines, and in this case an aeroplane has been taken.[8] He either does not see or pretends not to see that the general terms of this rule are susceptible of different interpretations and that he has a choice left open uncontrolled by linguistic conventions. He ignores, or is blind to, the fact that he is in the area of the penumbra and is not dealing with a standard case. Instead of choosing in the light of social aims the judge fixes the meaning in a different way. He either takes the meaning that the word most obviously suggests in its ordinary non-legal context to ordinary men, or one which the word has been given in some other legal context, or, still worse, he thinks of a standard case and then arbitrarily identifies certain features in it – for example, in the case of a vehicle, (1) normally used on land, (2) capable of carrying a human person, (3) capable of being self-propelled – and treats these three as always necessary and always sufficient conditions for the use in all contexts of the word "vehicle", irrespective of the social consequences of giving it this interpretation. This choice, not "logic", would force the judge to include a toy motor car (if electrically propelled) and to exclude bicycles and the aeroplane. In all this there is possibly great stupidity, but no more "logic", and no less, than in cases in which the interpretation given to a general term and the consequent application of some general rule to a particular case is consciously controlled by some identified social aim.

Decisions made in a fashion as blind as this would scarcely deserve the name of decisions; we might as well toss a penny in applying a rule of law. But it is at least doubtful whether any judicial decisions (even in England) have been quite as automatic as this. Rather, either the interpretations stigmatized as automatic have resulted from the conviction that it is fairer in a criminal statute to take a meaning which would jump to the mind of the ordinary man at the cost even of defeating other values, and this itself is a social policy (though possibly a bad one); or much more frequently, what is stigmatized as "mechanical" and "automatic" is a determined choice made indeed in the light of a social aim but of a conservative social aim. Certainly many of the Supreme Court decisions at the turn of the century which have been so stigmatized represent clear choices in the penumbral area to give effect to a policy of a conservative type. This is peculiarly true of Mr Justice Peckham's opinions defining the spheres of police power and due process.

But how does the wrongness of deciding cases in an automatic and mechanical way and the rightness of deciding cases by reference to social purposes show that the utilitarian insistence on the distinction between what the law is and what it ought to be is wrong? I take it that no one who wished to use these vices of formalism as proof that the distinction between what is and what ought to be is mistaken would deny that the decisions stigmatized as automatic are law; nor would he deny that the system in which such automatic decisions are made is a legal system. Surely he would say that they are law, but they are bad law; they ought not to be law. But this would be to use the distinction, not to refute it; and of course both Bentham and Austin used it to attack judges for failing to decide penumbral cases in accordance with the growing needs of society.

Clearly, if the demonstration of the errors of formalism is to show the utilitarian distinction to be wrong, the point must be drastically re-stated. The point must be not merely that a judicial decision to be rational must be made in the light of some conception of what ought to be, but that the aims, the social policies and purposes to which judges should appeal if their decisions are to be rational, are themselves to be considered as part of the law in some suitably wide sense of "law" which is held to be more illuminating than that used by the Utilitarians. This restatement of the point would have the following consequence: instead of saying that the recurrence of penumbral questions shows us that legal rules are essentially incomplete, and that, when they fail to determine decisions, judges must legislate and so exercise a creative choice between alternatives, we shall say that the social policies which guide the judges' choice are in a sense there for them to discover; the judges are only "drawing out" of the rule what, if it is properly under-stood, is "latent" within it. To call this judicial legislation is to obscure some essential continuity between the clear cases of the rule's applica-tion and the penumbral decisions. I shall question later whether this way of talking is salutary, but I wish at this time to point out something obvious, but likely, if not stated, to tangle the issues. It does not follow that, because the opposite of a decision reached blindly in the formalist or literalist manner is a decision intelligently reached by reference to some conception of what ought to be, we have a junction of law and morals. We must, I think, beware of thinking in a too simple-minded fashion about the word "ought". This is not because there is no distinc-tion to be made between law as it is and ought to be. Far from it. It is because the distinction should be between what is and what from many different points of view ought to be. The word "ought" merely reflects the presence of some standard of criticism; one of these standards is a moral standard, but not all standards are moral. We say to our neighbour, "You ought not to lie", and that may certainly be a moral judgment, but we should remember that the baffled poisoner may say, "I ought to have given her a second dose". The point here is that intelligent deci-sions which we oppose to mechanical or formal decisions are not neces-sarily identical with decisions defensible on moral grounds. We may say of many a decision: "Yes, that is right; that is as it ought to be", and we may mean only that some accepted purpose or policy has been thereby advanced; we may not mean to endorse the moral propriety of the policy or the decision. So the contrast between the mechanical decision and the intelligent one can be reproduced inside a system dedicated to the pursuit of the most evil aims. It does not exist as a contrast to be found only in legal systems which, like our own, widely recognize principles of justice and moral claims of individuals.

An example may make this point plainer. With us the task of sentencing in criminal cases is the one that seems most obviously to demand from the judge the exercise of moral judgment. Here the factors to be weighed seem clearly to be moral factors: society must not be exposed to wanton attack; too much misery must not be inflicted on either the victim or his dependants; efforts must be made to enable him to lead a better life and regain a position in the society whose laws he has violated. To a judge striking the balance among these claims, with all the discretion and perplexities involved, his task seems as plain an example of the exercise of moral judgment as could be; and it seems to be the polar opposite of some mechanical application of a tariff of penalties fixing a sentence careless of the moral claims which in our system have to be weighed. So here intelligent and rational decision is guided however uncertainly by moral aims. But we have only to vary the example to see that this need not necessarily be so and surely, if it need not necessarily be so, the utilitarian point remains unshaken. Under the Nazi regime men were sentenced by courts for criticism of the regime. Here the choice of sentence might be guided exclusively by consideration of what was needed to maintain the state's tyranny effectively. What sentence would both terrorize the public at large and keep the friends and family of the prisoner in suspense so that both hope and fear would cooperate as factors making for subservience? The prisoner of such a system would be regarded simply as an object to be used in pursuit of these aims. Yet, in contrast with a mechanical decision, decision on these grounds would be intelligent and purposive, and from one point of view the decision would be as it ought to be. Of course, I am not unaware that a whole philosophical tradition has sought to demonstrate the fact that we cannot correctly call decisions or behaviour truly rational unless they are in conformity with moral aims and principles. But the example I have used seems to me to serve at least as a warning that we cannot use the errors of formalism as something which *per se* demonstrates the falsity of the utilitarian insistence on the distinction between law as it is and law as *morally* it ought to be.

We can now return to the main point. If it is true that the intelligent decision of penumbral questions is one made not mechanically but in the light of aims, purposes, and policies, though not necessarily in the light of anything we would call moral principles, is it wise to express this important fact by saying that the firm utilitarian distinction between what the law is and what it ought to be should be dropped? Perhaps the claim that it is wise cannot be theoretically refuted, for it is, in effect, an *invitation* to revise *our conception* of what a legal rule is. We are invited to include in the "rule" the various aims and policies in the light of which its penumbral cases are decided on the ground that these aims have, because of their importance, as much right to be called law as the core of legal rules whose meaning is settled. But though an invitation cannot be refuted, it may be refused, and I would proffer two reasons for refusing this invitation. First, everything we have learned about the judicial process can be expressed in other less mysterious ways. We can say laws are incurably incomplete and we must decide the penumbral cases rationally by reference to social aims. I think Holmes, who had such a vivid appreciation of the fact that "general propositions do not decide concrete cases", would have put it that way. Secondly, to insist on the utilitarian distinction is to emphasize that the hard core of settled meaning is law in some centrally important sense and that even if there are borderlines, there must first be lines. If this were not so the notion of rules controlling courts' decisions would be senseless, as some of the "Realists" – in their most extreme moods, and, I think, on bad grounds – claimed.

By contrast, to soften the distinction, to assert mysteriously that there is some fused identity between law as it is and as it ought to be, is to suggest that all legal questions are fundamentally like those of the penumbra. It is to assert that there is no central element of actual law to be seen in the core of central meaning which rules have, that there is nothing in the nature of a legal rule inconsistent with *all* questions being open to reconsideration in the light of social policy. Of course, it is good to be occupied with the penumbra. Its problems are rightly the daily diet of the law schools. But to be occupied with the penumbra is one thing, to be preoccupied with it another. And preoccupation with the penumbra is, if I may say so, as rich a source of confusion in the American legal tradition as formalism in the English. Of course we might abandon the notion that rules have authority; we might cease to attach force or even meaning to an argument that a case falls clearly within a rule and the scope of a precedent. We might call all such reasoning "automatic" or "mechanical", which is already the routine invective of the courts. But until we decide that this *is* what we want, we should not encourage it by obliterating the utilitarian distinction ...

I have endeavoured to show that, in spite of all that has been learned and experienced since the Utilitarians wrote, and in spite of the defects of other parts of their doctrine, their protest against the confusion of what is and what ought to be law has a moral as well as an intellectual value. Yet it may well be said that, though this distinction is valid and important if applied to any particular law of a system, it is at least misleading if we attempt to apply it to "law", that is, to the notion of a legal system, and that if we insist, as I have, on the narrower truth (or truism), we obscure a wider (or deeper) truth. After all, it may be urged, we have learned that there are many things which are untrue of laws taken separately, but which are true and important in a legal system considered as a whole. For example, the connection between law and sanctions and between the existence of law and its "efficacy" must be understood in this more general way. It is surely not arguable (without some desperate extension of the word "sanction" or artificial narrowing of the word "law") that every law in a municipal legal system must have a sanction, yet it is at least plausible to argue that a legal system must, to be a legal system, provide sanctions for certain of its rules. So too, a rule of law may be said to exist though enforced or obeyed in only a minority of cases, but this could not be said of a legal system as a whole. Perhaps the differences with respect to laws taken separately and a legal system as a whole are also true of the connection between moral (or some other) conceptions of what law ought to be and law in this wider sense.

This line of argument, found (at least in embryo form) in Austin, where he draws attention to the fact that every developed legal system contains certain fundamental notions which are "necessary" and "bottomed in the common nature of man",[9] is worth pursuing – up to a point – and I shall say briefly why and how far this is so.

We must avoid, if we can, the arid wastes of inappropriate definition, for, in relation to a concept as many-sided and vague as that of a legal system, disputes about the "essential" character, or necessity to the whole, of any single element soon begin to look like disputes about whether chess could be "chess" if played without pawns. There is a wish, which may be understandable, to cut straight through the question whether a legal system, to be a legal system, must measure up to some moral or other standard with simple statements of fact: for example, that no system which utterly failed in this respect has ever existed or could endure; that the normally fulfilled assumption that a legal system aims at some form of justice colours the whole way in which we interpret specific rules in particular cases, and if this normally fulfilled assumption were not fulfilled no one would have any reason to obey except fear (and probably not that), and still less, of course, any moral obligation to obey. The connection between law and moral standards and principles of justice is therefore as little arbitrary and as "necessary" as the connection between law and sanctions, and the pursuit of the question whether this necessity is logical (part of the "meaning" of law) or merely factual or causal can safely be left as an innocent pastime for philosophers.

Yet in two respects I should wish to go further (even though this involves the use of a philosophical fantasy) and show what could intelligibly be meant by the claim that certain provisions in a legal system are "necessary". The world in which we live, and we who live in it, may one day change in many different ways; and if this change were radical enough not only would certain statements of fact now true be false and vice versa, but whole ways of thinking and talking which constitute our present conceptual apparatus, through which we see the world and each other, would lapse. We have only to consider how the whole of our social, moral, and legal life, as we understand it now, depends on the contingent fact that though our bodies do change in shape, size, and other physical properties they do not do this so drastically nor with such quicksilver rapidity and irregularity that we cannot identify each other as the same persistent individual over considerable spans of time. Though this is but a contingent fact which may one day be different, on it at present rest huge structures of our thought and principles of action and social life. Similarly, consider the following possibility (not because it is more than a possibility but because it reveals why we think certain things necessary in a legal system and what we mean by this): suppose that men were to become invulnerable to attack by each other, were clad perhaps like giant land crabs with an impenetrable carapace, and could extract the food they needed from the air by some internal chemical process. In such circumstances (the details of which can be left to science fiction) rules forbidding the free use of violence and rules constituting the minimum form of property – with its rights and duties sufficient to enable food to grow and be retained until eaten – would not have the necessary non-arbitrary status which they have for us, constituted as we are in a world like ours. At present, and until such radical changes supervene, such rules are so fundamental that if a legal system did not have them there would be no point in having any other rules at all. Such rules overlap with basic moral principles vetoing murder, violence, and theft; and so we can add to the factual statement that all legal systems in fact coincide with morality at such vital points, the statement that this is, in this sense, necessarily so. And why not call it a "natural" necessity?

Of course even this much depends on the fact that in asking what content a legal system must have we take this question to be worth asking only if we who consider it cherish the humble aim of survival in close proximity to our fellows. Natural-law theory, however, in all its protean guises, attempts to push the argument much further and to assert that human beings are equally devoted to and united in their conception of aims (the pursuit of knowledge, justice to their fellow men) other than that of survival and these dictate a further necessary content to a legal system (over and above my humble minimum) without which it would be pointless. Of course we must be careful not to exaggerate the differences among human beings, but it seems to me that above this minimum the purposes men have for living in society are too conflicting and varying to make possible much extension of the argument that some fuller overlap of legal rules and moral standards is "necessary" in this sense.

Another aspect of the matter deserves attention. If we attach to a legal system the minimum meaning that it must consist of general rules – general both in the sense that they refer to courses of action, not single actions and to multiplicities of men, not single individuals – this meaning connotes the principle of treating like cases alike, though the criteria of when cases are alike will be, so far, only the general elements specified in the rules. It is, however, true that *one* essential element of the concept of justice is the principle of treating like cases alike. This is justice in the administration of the law, not justice of the law. So there is, in the very notion of law consisting of general rules, something which prevents us from treating it as if morally it is utterly neutral, without any necessary contact with moral principles. Natural procedural justice consists therefore of those principles of objectivity and impartiality in the administration of the law which implement just this aspect of law and which are designed to ensure that rules are applied only to what are genuinely cases of the rule or at least to minimize the risks of inequalities in this sense.

These two reasons (or excuses) for talking of a certain overlap between legal and moral standards as necessary and natural, of course, should not satisfy anyone who is really disturbed by the utilitarian or "positivist" insistence that law and morality are distinct. This is so because a legal system that satisfied these minimum requirements might apply, with the most pedantic impartiality as between the persons affected, laws which were hideously oppressive, and might deny to a vast rightless slave population the minimum benefits of protection from violence and theft. The stink of such society is, after all, still in our nostrils, and to argue that they have (or had) no legal system would only involve the repetition of the argument. Only if the rules failed to provide these essential benefits and protection for anyone – even for a slave-owning group – would the minimum be unsatisfied and the system sink to the status of a set of meaningless taboos. Of course no one denied those benefits would have any reason to obey except fear and would have every moral reason to revolt ...

When rules are recognized as applying to instances beyond any that legislators did or could have considered, their extension to such new cases often presents itself not as a deliberate choice or fiat on the part of those who so interpret the rule. It appears neither as a decision to give the rule a new or extended meaning nor as a guess as to what legislators, dead perhaps in the eighteenth century, would have said had they been alive in the twentieth century. Rather, the inclusion of the new case under the rule takes its place as a natural elaboration of the rule, as something implementing a "purpose" which it seems natural to attribute (in some sense) to the rule itself rather than to any particular person dead or alive. The utilitarian description of such interpretative extension of old rules to new cases as judicial legislation fails to do justice to this phenomenon; it gives no hint of the differences between a deliberate fiat or decision to treat the new case in the same way as past cases and a recognition (in which there is little that is deliberate or even voluntary) that inclusion of the new case under the rule will implement or articulate a continuing and identical purpose, hitherto less specifically apprehended.

Perhaps many lawyers and judges will see in this language something that precisely fits their experience; others may think it a romantic gloss on facts better stated in the utilitarian language of judicial "legislation" or in the modern American terminology of "creative choice".

To make the point clear Professor Fuller uses a non-legal example from the philosopher Wittgenstein which is, I think, illuminating.

Someone says to me: "Show the children a game." I teach them gaming with dice and the other says "I did not mean that sort of game." Must the exclusion of the game with dice have come before his mind when he gave me the order?[10]

Something important does seem to me to be touched on in this example. Perhaps there are the following (distinguishable) points. First, we normally do interpret not only what people are trying to do but what they say in the light of assumed common human objectives, so that unless the contrary were expressly indicated we would not interpret an instruction to show a young child a game as a mandate to introduce him to gambling even though in other contexts the word "game" would be naturally so interpreted. Secondly, very often, the speaker whose words are thus interpreted might say: "Yes, that's what I mean [or "that's what I meant all along"] though I never thought of it until you put this particular case to me." Third, when we thus recognize, perhaps after argument or consultation with others, a particular case not specifically envisaged beforehand as falling within the ambit of some vaguely expressed instruction, we may find this experience falsified by description of it as a mere decision on our part so to treat the particular case, and that we can only describe this faithfully as coming to realize and to articulate what we "really" want or our "true purpose" – phrases which Professor Fuller uses later in the same article.

I am sure that many philosophical discussions of the character of moral argument would benefit from attention to cases of the sort instanced by Professor Fuller. Such attention would help to provide a corrective to the view that there is a sharp separation between "ends" and "means" and that in debating "ends" we can only work on each other non-rationally, and that rational argument is reserved for discussion of "means". But I think the relevance of his point to the issue whether it is correct or wise to insist on the distinction between law as it is and law as it ought to be is very small indeed. Its net effect is that in interpreting legal rules there are some cases which we find after reflection to be so natural an elaboration or articulation of the rule that to think of and refer to this as "legislation", "making law", or a "fiat" on our part would be misleading. So, the argument must be, it would be misleading to distinguish in such cases between what the rule is and what it ought to be – at least in some sense of ought. We think it ought to include the new case and come to see after reflection that it really does. But even if this way of presenting a recognizable experience as an example of a fusion between is and ought to be is admitted, two caveats must be borne in mind. The first is that "ought" in this case need have nothing to do with morals for the reasons explained already in section III: there may be just the same sense that a new case will implement and articulate the purpose of a rule in interpreting the rules of a game or some hideously immoral code of oppression whose immorality is appreciated by those called in to interpret it. They too can see what the "spirit" of the game they are playing requires in previously unenvisaged cases. More important is this: after all is said and done we must remember how rare in the law is the phenomenon held to justify this way of talking, how exceptional is this feeling that one way of deciding a case is imposed upon us as the only natural or rational elaboration of some rule. Surely it cannot be doubted that, for most cases of interpretation, the language of choice between alternatives, "judicial legislation" or even "fiat" (though not arbitrary fiat), better conveys the realities of the situation.

Within the framework of relatively well-settled law there jostle too many alternatives too nearly equal in attraction between which judge and lawyer must uncertainly pick their way to make appropriate here language which may well describe those experiences which we have in interpreting our own or others' principles of conduct, intention, or wishes, when we are not conscious of exercising a deliberate choice, but rather of recognizing something awaiting recognition. To use in the description of the interpretation of laws the suggested terminology of a fusion or inability to separate what is law and ought to be will serve (like earlier stories that judges only find, never make, law) only to conceal the facts, that here if anywhere we live among uncertainties between which we have to choose, and that the existing law imposes only limits on our choice and not the choice itself.

NOTES

1 Bentham, *A Fragment on Government*, in I *Works* 221, 230 (preface, 16th para.).
2 See Bentham, "Principles of Legislation", in *The Theory of Legislation* I, 65n.*
   (Ogden edn. 1931) (c. XII, 2d para. n.*). "Here we touch upon the most difficult of questions. If the law is not what it ought to be; if it openly

combats the principle of utility; ought we to obey it? Ought we to violate it? Ought we to remain neuter between the law which commands an evil, and morality which forbids it?" See also Bentham, *A Fragment on Government*, in I *Works* 221, 287–8 (c. IV, 20th–25th paras.).

3 Bentham, *A Fragment on Government*, in I *Works* 221, 294 (c. V, 10th para.).

4 Bentham, *A Commentary on Humphreys' Real Property Code*, in 5 *Works* 389.

5 It may help to identify five (there may be more) meanings of "positivism" bandied about in contemporary jurisprudence:

(1) the contention that laws are commands of human beings; see ... *infra*;

(2) the contention that there is no necessary connection between law and morals or law as it is and ought to be; see ... *supra*;

(3) the contention that the analysis (or study of the meaning) of legal concepts is (a) worth pursuing and (b) to be distinguished from historical inquiries into the causes or origins of laws, from sociological inquiries into the relation of law and other social phenomena, and from the criticism or appraisal of law whether in terms of morals, social aims, "functions", or otherwise; see ... *infra*;

(4) the contention that a legal system is a "closed logical system" in which correct legal decisions can be deduced by logical means from predetermined legal rules without reference to social aims, policies, moral standards; see ... *infra*, and

(5) the contention that moral judgments cannot be established or defended, as statements of facts can, by rational argument, evidence, or proof ("noncognitivism" in ethics); see ... *infra*.

Bentham and Austin held the views described in (1), (2), and (3), but not those in (4) and (5). Opinion (4) is often ascribed to analytical jurists; see .... *infra*, but I know of no "analyst" who held this view.

6 See, e.g., Kelsen, *General Theory of Law and State* 58–61, 143–4 (1945). According to Kelsen, all laws, not only those conferring rights and powers, are reducible to such "primary norms" conditionally stipulating sanctions.

7 Salmond, *The First Principles of Jurisprudence* 97–8 (1893). He protested against "the creed of what is termed the English school of jurisprudence", because it "attempted to deprive the idea of law of that ethical significance which is one of its most essential elements". Ibid. at 9, 10.

8 See *McBoyle v United States*, 283 US 25 (1931).

9 Austin, "Uses of the Study of Jurisprudence," in *The Province of Jurisprudence Determined* 365, 373, 367–9 (Library of Ideas edn. 1954).

10 Fuller, "Human Purpose and Natural Law", 53 *J Philos* 697, 700 (1956).

The Concept of Law

The Elements of Law

It is, of course, possible to imagine a society without a legislature, courts or officials of any kind. Indeed, there are many studies of primitive communities which not only claim that this possibility is realized but depict in detail the life of a society where the only means of social control is that general attitude of the group towards its own standard modes of behaviour in terms of which we have characterized rules of obligation. A social structure of this kind is often referred to as one of "custom"; but we shall not use this term, because it often implies that the customary rules are very old and supported with less social pressure than other rules. To avoid these implications we shall refer to such a social structure as one of primary rules of obligation. If a society is to live by such primary rules alone, there are certain conditions which, granted a few of the most obvious truisms about human nature and the world we live in, must clearly be satisfied. The first of these conditions is that the rules must contain in some form restrictions on the free use of violence, theft, and deception to which human beings are tempted but which they must, in general, repress, if they are to coexist in close proximity to each other. Such rules are in fact always found in the primitive societies of which we have knowledge, together with a variety of others imposing on individuals various positive duties to perform services or make contributions to the common life. Secondly, though such a society may exhibit the tension, already described, between those who accept the rules and those who reject the rules except where fear of social pressure induces them to conform, it is plain that the latter cannot be more than a minority, if so loosely organized a society of persons, approximately equal in physical strength, is to endure: for otherwise those who reject the rules would have too little social pressure to fear. This too is confirmed by what we know of primitive communities where, though there are dissidents and malefactors, the majority live by the rules seen from the internal point of view.

More important for our present purpose is the following consideration. It is plain that only a small community closely knit by ties of kinship, common sentiment, and belief, and placed in a stable environment, could live successfully by such a régime of unofficial rules. In any other conditions such a simple form of social control must prove defective and will require supplementation in different ways. In the first place, the rules by which the group lives will not form a system, but will simply be a set of separate standards, without any identifying or common mark, except of course that they are the rules which a particular group of human beings accepts. They will in this respect resemble our own rules of etiquette. Hence if doubts arise as to what the rules are or as to the precise scope of some given rule, there will be no procedure for settling this doubt, either by reference to an authoritative text or to an official whose declarations on this point are authoritative. For, plainly, such a procedure and the acknowledgement of either authoritative text or persons involve the existence of rules of a type different from the rules of obligation or duty which *ex hypothesi* are all that the group has. This defect in the simple social structure of primary rules we may call its *uncertainty*.

A second defect is the *static* character of the rules. The only mode of change in the rules known to such a society will be the slow process of growth, whereby courses of conduct once thought optional become first habitual or usual, and then obligatory, and the converse process of decay, when deviations, once severely dealt with, are first tolerated and then pass unnoticed. There will be no means, in such a society, of deliberately adapting the rules to changing circumstances, either by eliminating old rules or introducing new ones: for, again, the possibility of doing this presupposes the existence of rules of a different type from the primary rules of obligation by which alone the society lives. In an extreme case the rules may be static in a more drastic sense. This, though never perhaps fully realized in any actual community, is worth considering because the remedy for it is something very characteristic of law. In this extreme case, not only would there be no way of deliberately changing the general rules, but the obligations which arise under the rules in particular cases could not be varied or modified by the deliberate choice of any individual. Each individual would simply have fixed obligations or duties to do or abstain from doing certain things. It might indeed very often be the case that others would benefit from the performance of these obligations; yet if there are only primary rules of obligation they would have no power to release those bound from performance or to transfer to others the benefits which would accrue from performance. For such operations of release or transfer create changes

in the initial positions of individuals under the primary rules of obligation, and for these operations to be possible there must be rules of a sort
different from the primary rules.

The third defect of this simple form of social life is the *inefficiency* of
the diffuse social pressure by which the rules are maintained. Disputes
as to whether an admitted rule has or has not been violated will always
occur and will, in any but the smallest societies, continue interminably,
if there is no agency specially empowered to ascertain finally, and authoritatively, the fact of violation. Lack of such final and authoritative
determinations is to be distinguished from another weakness associated
with it. This is the fact that punishments for violations of the rules, and
other forms of social pressure involving physical effort or the use of
force, are not administered by a special agency but are left to the individuals affected or to the group at large. It is obvious that the waste of
time involved in the group's unorganized efforts to catch and punish
offenders, and the smouldering vendettas which may result from self
help in the absence of an official monopoly of "sanctions", may be
serious. This history of law does, however, strongly suggest that the
lack of official agencies to determine authoritatively the fact of violation
of the rules is a much more serious defect; for many societies have
remedies for this defect long before the other.

The remedy for each of these three main defects in this simplest form
of social structure consists in supplementing the *primary* rules of obligation with *secondary* rules which are rules of a different kind. The introduction of the remedy for each defect might, in itself, be considered a
step from the pre-legal into the legal world; since each remedy brings
with it many elements that permeate law: certainly all three remedies
together are enough to convert the régime of primary rules into what is
indisputably a legal system. We shall consider in turn each of these
remedies and show why law may most illuminatingly be characterized
as a union of primary rules of obligation with such secondary rules.
Before we do this, however, the following general points should be
noted. Though the remedies consist in the introduction of rules which
are certainly different from each other, as well as from the primary
rules of obligation which they supplement, they have important features in common and are connected in various ways. Thus they may all
be said to be on a different level from the primary rules, for they are all
about such rules; in the sense that while primary rules are concerned
with the actions that individuals must or must not do, these secondary
rules are all concerned with the primary rules themselves. They specify

the ways in which the primary rules may be conclusively ascertained, introduced, eliminated, varied, and the fact of their violation conclusively determined.

The simplest form of remedy for the *uncertainty* of the régime of primary rules is the introduction of what we shall call a "rule of recognition". This will specify some feature or features possession of which by a suggested rule is taken as a conclusive affirmative indication that it is a rule of the group to be supported by the social pressure it exerts. The existence of such a rule of recognition may take any of a huge variety of forms, simple or complex. It may, as in the early law of many societies, be no more than that an authoritative list or text of the rules is to be found in a written document or carved on some public monument. No doubt as a matter of history this step from the pre-legal to the legal may be accomplished in distinguishable stages, of which the first is the mere reduction to writing of hitherto unwritten rules. This is not itself the crucial step, though it is a very important one: what is crucial is the acknowledgement of reference to the writing or inscription as *authoritative*, i.e. as the *proper* way of disposing of doubts as to the existence of the rule. Where there is such an acknowledgement there is a very simple form of secondary rule: a rule for conclusive identification of the primary rules of obligation.

In a developed legal system the rules of recognition are of course more complex; instead of identifying rules exclusively by reference to a text or list they do so by reference to some general characteristic possessed by the primary rules. This may be the fact of their having been enacted by a specific body, or their long customary practice, or their relation to judicial decisions. Moreover, where more than one of such general characteristics are treated as identifying criteria, provision may be made for their possible conflict by their arrangement in an order of superiority, as by the common subordination of custom or precedent to statute, the latter being a "superior source" of law. Such complexity may make the rules of recognition in a modern legal system seem very different from the simple acceptance of an authoritative test: yet even in this simplest form, such a rule brings with it many elements distinctive of law. By providing an authoritative mark it introduces, although in embryonic form, the idea of a legal system: for the rules are now not just a discrete unconnected set but are, in a simple way, unified. Further, in the simple operation of identifying a given rule as possessing the required feature of being an item on an authoritative list of rules we have the germ of the idea of legal validity.

The remedy for the *static* quality of the régime of primary rules consists in the introduction of what we shall call "rules of change". The simplest form of such a rule is that which empowers an individual or body of persons to introduce new primary rules for the conduct of the life of the group, or of some class within it, and to eliminate old rules. As we have already argued in Chapter IV it is in terms of such a rule, and not in terms of orders back by threats, that the ideas of legislative enactment and repeal are to be understood. Such rules of change may be very simple or very complex: the powers conferred may be unrestricted or limited in various ways: and the rules may, besides specifying the persons who are to legislate, define in more or less rigid terms the procedure to be followed in legislation. Plainly, there will be a very close connexion between the rules of change and the rules of recognition: for where the former exists the latter will necessarily incorporate a reference to legislation as an identifying feature of the rules, though it need not refer to all the details of procedure involved in legislation. Usually some official certificate or official copy will, under the rules of recognition, be taken as a sufficient proof of due enactment. Of course if there is a social structure so simple that the only "source of law" is legislation, the rule of recognition will simply specify enactment as the unique identifying mark or criterion of validity of the rules. This will be the case for example in the imaginary kingdom of Rex I depicted in Chapter IV: there the rule of recognition would simply be that whatever Rex I enacts is law.

We have already described in some detail the rules which confer on individuals power to vary their initial positions under the primary rules. Without such private power-conferring rules society would lack some of the chief amenities which law confers upon it. For the operations which these rules make possible are the making of wills, contracts, transfers of property, and many other voluntarily created structures of rights and duties which typify life under law, though of course an elementary form of power-conferring rule also underlies the moral institution of a promise. The kinship of these rules with the rules of change involved in the notion of legislation is clear, and as recent theory such as Kelsen's has shown, many of the features which puzzle us in the institutions of contract or property are clarified by thinking of the operations of making a contract or transferring property as the exercise of limited legislative powers by individuals.

The third supplement to the simple régime of primary rules, intended to remedy the *inefficiency* of its diffused social pressure, consists of secondary rules empowering individuals to make authoritative determinations of the question whether, on a particular occasion, a primary rule has been broken. The minimal form of adjudication consists in such determinations, and we shall call the secondary rules which confer the power to make them "rules of adjudication". Besides identifying the individuals who are to adjudicate, such rules will also define the procedure to be followed. Like the other secondary rules these are on a different level from the primary rules: though they may be reinforced by further rules imposing duties on judges to adjudicate, they do not impose duties but confer judicial powers and a special status on judicial declarations about the breach of obligations. Again these rules, like the other secondary rules, define a group of important legal concepts: in this case the concepts of judge or court, jurisdiction and judgment. Besides these resemblances to the other secondary rules, rules of adjudication have intimate connexions with them. Indeed, a system which has rules of adjudication is necessarily also committed to a rule of recognition of an elementary and imperfect sort. This is so because, if courts are empowered to make authoritative determinations of the fact that a rule has been broken, these cannot avoid being taken as authoritative determinations of what the rules are. So the rule which confers jurisdiction will also be a rule of recognition, identifying the primary rules through the judgments of the courts and these judgments will become a "source" of law. It is true that this form of rule of recognition, inseparable from the minimum form of jurisdiction, will be very imperfect. Unlike an authoritative text or a statute book, judgments may not be couched in general terms and their use as authoritative guides to the rules depends on a somewhat shaky inference from particular decisions, and the reliability of this must fluctuate both with the skill of the interpreter and the consistency of the judges.

It need hardly be said that in few legal systems are judicial powers confined to authoritative determinations of the fact of violation of the primary rules. Most systems have, after some delay, seen the advantages of further centralization of social pressure; and have partially prohibited the use of physical punishments or violent self help by private individuals. Instead they have supplemented the primary rules of obligation by further secondary rules, specifying or at least limiting the penalties for violation, and have conferred upon judges, where they have ascertained the fact of violation, the exclusive power to direct the application of penalties by other officials. These secondary rules provide the centralized official "sanctions" of the system ...

New Questions

Once we abandon the view that the foundations of a legal system consist in a habit of obedience to a legally unlimited sovereign and substitute for this the conception of an ultimate rule of recognition which provides a system of rules with its criteria of validity, a range of fascinating and important questions confronts us. They are relatively new questions; for they were veiled so long as jurisprudence and political theory were committed to the older ways of thought. They are also difficult questions, requiring for a full answer, on the one hand a grasp of some fundamental issues of constitutional law and on the other an appreciation of the characteristic manner in which legal forms may silently shift and change. We shall therefore investigate these questions only so far as they bear upon the wisdom or unwisdom of insisting, as we have done, that a central place should be assigned to the union of primary and secondary rules in the elucidation of the concept of law.

The first difficulty is that of classification; for the rule which, in the last resort, is used to identify the law escapes the conventional categories used for describing a legal system, though these are often taken to be exhaustive. Thus, English constitutional writers since Dicey have usually repeated the statement that the constitutional arrangements of the United Kingdom consist partly of laws strictly so called (statutes, orders in council, and rules embodied in precedents) and partly of conventions which are mere usages, understandings or customs. The latter include important rules such as that the Queen may not refuse her consent to a bill duly passed by Peers and Commons; there is, however, no legal duty on the Queen to give her consent and such rules are called conventions because the courts do not recognize them as imposing a legal duty. Plainly the rule that what the Queen in Parliament enacts is law does not fall into either of these categories. It is not a convention, since the courts are most intimately concerned with it and they use it in identifying the law; and it is not a rule on the same level as the "laws strictly so called" which it is used to identify. Even if it were enacted by statute, this would not reduce it to the level of a statute; for the legal status of such an enactment necessarily would depend on the fact that the rule existed antecedently to and independently of the enactment. Moreover, as we have shown in the last section, its existence, unlike that of a statute, must consist in an actual practice.

This aspect of things extracts from some a cry of despair: how can we show that the fundamental provisions of a constitution which are surely law are really law? Others reply with the insistence that at the base of legal systems there is something which is "not law", which is "pre-legal", "meta-legal", or is just "political fact". This uneasiness is a sure sign that the categories used for the description of this most important feature in any system of law are too crude. The case for calling the rule of recognition "law" is that the rule providing criteria for the identification of other rules of the system may well be thought a defining feature of a legal system, and so itself worth calling "law"; the case for calling it "fact" is that to assert that such a rule exists is indeed to make an external statement of an actual fact concerning the manner in which the rules of an "efficacious" system are identified. Both these aspects claim attention but we cannot do justice to them both by choosing one of the labels "law" or "fact". Instead, we need to remember that the ultimate rule of recognition may be regarded from two points of view: one is expressed in the external statement of fact that the rule exists in the actual practice of the system; the other is expressed in the internal statements of validity made by those who use it in identifying the law.

A second set of questions arises out of the hidden complexity and vagueness of the assertion that a legal system *exists* in a given country or among a given social group. When we make this assertion we in fact refer in compressed, portmanteau form to a number of heterogeneous social facts, usually concomitant. The standard terminology of legal and political thought, developed in the shadow of a misleading theory, is apt to over-simplify and obscure the facts. Yet when we take off the spectacles constituted by this terminology and look at the facts, it becomes apparent that a legal system, like a human being, may at one stage be unborn, at a second not yet wholly independent of its mother, then enjoy a healthy independent existence, later decay and finally die. These half-way stages between birth and normal, independent existence and, again, between that and death, put out of joint our familiar ways of describing legal phenomena. They are worth our study because, baffling as they are, they throw into relief the full complexity of what we take for granted when, in the normal case, we make the confident and true assertion that in a given country a legal system exists.

One way of realizing this complexity is to see just where the simple, Austinian formula of a general habit of obedience to orders fails to reproduce or distorts the complex facts which constitute the minimum conditions which a society must satisfy if it is to have a legal system. We may allow that this formula does designate one necessary condition: namely, that where the laws impose obligations or duties these should be generally obeyed or at any rate not generally disobeyed. But, though essential, this only caters for what we may term the "end product" of the legal system, where it makes its impact on the private citizen; whereas its day-to-day existence consists also in the official creation, the official identification, and the official use and application of law. The relationship with law involved here can be called "obedience" only if that word is extended so far beyond its normal use as to cease to characterize informatively these operations. In no ordinary sense of "obey" are legislators obeying rules when, in enacting laws, they conform to the rules conferring their legislative powers, except of course when the rules conferring such powers are reinforced by rules imposing a duty to follow them. Nor, in failing to conform with these rules do they "disobey" a law, though they may fail to make one. Nor does the word "obey" describe well what judges do when they apply the system's rule of recognition and recognize a statute as valid law and use it in the determination of disputes. We can of course, if we wish, preserve the simple terminology of "obedience" in face of the facts by many devices. One is to express, e.g. the use made by judges of general criteria of validity in recognizing a statute, as a case of obedience to orders given by the "Founders of the Constitution", or (where there are no "Founders") as obedience to a "depsychologized command" i.e. a command without a commander. But this last should perhaps have no more serious claims on our attention than the notion of a nephew without an uncle. Alternatively we can push out of sight the whole official side to law and forgo the description of the use of rules made in legislation and adjudication, and instead, think of the whole official world as one person (the "sovereign") issuing orders, through various agents or mouthpieces, which are habitually obeyed by the citizen. But this is either no more than a convenient shorthand for complex facts which still await description, or a disastrously confusing piece of mythology.

It is natural to react from the failure of attempts to give an account of what it is for a legal system to exist, in the agreeably simple terms of the habitual obedience which is indeed characteristic of (though it does not always exhaustively describe) the relationship of the ordinary citizen to law, by making the opposite error. This consists in taking what is characteristic (though again not exhaustive) of the official activities, especially the judicial attitude or relationship to law, and treating this as an adequate account of what must exist in a social group which has a legal system. This amounts to replacing the simple conception that the bulk of society habitually obey the law with the conception that they must generally share, accept, or regard as binding the ultimate rule of recognition specifying the criteria in terms of which the validity of laws are ultimately assessed. Of course we can imagine, as we have done in Chapter III, a simple society where knowledge and understanding of the sources of law are widely diffused. There the "constitution" was so simple that no fiction would be involved in attributing knowledge and acceptance of it to the ordinary citizen as well as to the officials and lawyers. In the simple world of Rex I we might well say that there was more than mere habitual obedience by the bulk of the population to his word. There it might well be the case that both they and the officials of the system "accepted", in the same explicit, conscious way, a rule of recognition specifying Rex's word as the criterion of valid law for the whole society, though subjects and officials would have different roles to play and different relationships to the rules of law identified by this criterion. To insist that this state of affairs, imaginable in a simple society, always or usually exists in a complex modern state would be to insist on a fiction. Here surely the reality of the situation is that a great proportion of ordinary citizens – perhaps a majority – have no general conception of the legal structure or of its criteria of validity. The law which he obeys is something which he knows of only as "the law". He may obey it for a variety of different reasons and among them may often, though not always, be the knowledge that it will be best for him to do so. He will be aware of the general likely consequences of disobedience: that there are officials who may arrest him and others who will try him and send him to prison for breaking the law. So long as the laws which are valid by the system's tests of validity are obeyed by the bulk of the population this surely is all the evidence we need in order to establish that a given legal system exists.

But just because a legal system is a complex union of primary and secondary rules, this evidence is not all that is needed to describe the relationships to law involved in the existence of a legal system. It must be supplemented by a description of the relevant relationship of the officials of the system to the secondary rules which concern them as officials. Here what is crucial is that there should be a unified or shared official acceptance of the rule of recognition containing the system's criteria of validity. But it is just here that the simple notion of general obedience, which was adequate to characterize the indispensable minimum in the case of ordinary citizens, is inadequate. The point is not, or not merely, the "linguistic" one that "obedience" is not naturally used to refer to the way in which these secondary rules are respected as rules by courts and other officials. We could find, if necessary, some wider expression like "follow", "comply", or "conform to" which would characterize both what ordinary citizens do in relation to law when they report for military service and what judges do when they identify a particular statute as law in their courts, on the footing that what the Queen in Parliament enacts is law. But these blanket terms would merely mask vital differences which must be grasped if the minimum conditions involved in the existence of the complex social phenomenon which we call a legal system is to be understood.

What makes "obedience" misleading as a description of what legislators do in conforming to the rules conferring their powers, and of what courts do in applying an accepted ultimate rule of recognition, is that obeying a rule (or an order) *need* involve no thought on the part of the person obeying that what he does is the right thing both for himself and for others to do: he need have no view of what he does as a fulfilment of a standard of behaviour for others of the social group. He need not think of his conforming behaviour as "right", "correct", or "obligatory". His attitude, in other words, need not have any of that critical character which is involved whenever social rules are accepted and types of conduct are treated as general standards. He need not, though he may, share the internal point of view accepting the rules as standards for all to whom they apply. Instead, he may think of the rule only as something demanding action from *him* under threat of penalty; he may obey it out of fear of the consequences, or from inertia, without thinking of himself or others as having an obligation to do so and without being disposed to criticize either himself or others for deviations. But this merely personal concern with the rules, which is all the ordinary citizen *may* have in obeying them, cannot characterize the attitude of the courts to the rules with which they operate as courts. This is most patently the case with the ultimate rule of recognition in terms of which the validity of other rules is assessed. This, if it is to exist at all, must be regarded from the internal point of view as a public, common standard of correct judicial decision, and not as something which each judge merely obeys for his part only. Individual courts of the system though they may, on occasion, deviate from these rules must, in general, be critically concerned with such deviations as lapses from standards, which are essentially common or public. This is not merely a matter of the efficiency or health of the legal system, but is logically a necessary condition of our ability to speak of the existence of a single legal system. If only some judges acted "for their part only" on the footing that what the Queen in

Parliament enacts is law, and made no criticisms of those who did not respect this rule of recognition, the characteristic unity and continuity of a legal system would have disappeared. For this depends on the acceptance, at this crucial point, of common standards of legal validity. In the interval between these vagaries of judicial behaviour and the chaos which would ultimately ensue when the ordinary man was faced with contrary judicial orders, we would be at a loss to describe the situation. We would be in the presence of a *lusus naturae* worth thinking about only because it sharpens our awareness of what is often too obvious to be noticed.

There are therefore two minimum conditions necessary and sufficient for the existence of a legal system. On the one hand those rules of behaviour which are valid according to the system's ultimate criteria of validity must be generally obeyed, and, on the other hand, its rules of recognition specifying the criteria of legal validity and its rules of change and adjudication must be effectively accepted as common public standards of official behaviour by its officials. The first condition is the only one which private citizens *need* satisfy: they may obey each "for his part only" and from any motive whatever; though in a healthy society they will in fact often accept these rules as common standards of behaviour and acknowledge an obligation to obey them, or even trace this obligation to a more general obligation to respect the constitution. The second condition must also be satisfied by the officials of the system. They must regard these as common standards of official behaviour and appraise critically their own and each other's deviations as lapses. Of course it is also true that besides these there will be many primary rules which apply to officials in their merely personal capacity which they need only obey.

The assertion that a legal system exists is therefore a Janus-faced statement looking both towards obedience by ordinary citizens and to the acceptance by officials of secondary rules as critical common standards of official behaviour. We need not be surprised at this duality. It is merely the reflection of the composite character of a legal system as compared with a simpler decentralized pre-legal form of social structure which consists only of primary rules. In the simpler structure, since there are no officials, the rules must be widely accepted as setting critical standards for the behaviour of the group. If, there, the internal point of view is not widely disseminated there could not logically be any rules. But where there is a union of primary and secondary rules, which is, as we have argued, the most fruitful way of regarding a legal system, the acceptance of the rules as common standards for the group may be split off from the relatively passive matter of the ordinary individual acquiescing in the rules by obeying them for his part alone. In an extreme case the internal point of view with its characteristic normative use of legal language ("This is a valid rule") might be confined to the official world. In this more complex system, only officials might accept and use the system's criteria of legal validity. The society in which this was so might be deplorably sheeplike; the sheep might end in the slaughter-house. But there is little reason for thinking that it could not exist or for denying it the title of a legal system ...

READING QUESTIONS ON HART

1 What are Hart's criticisms of the command theory?
2 What is the "internal point of view"? Is there a difference between it and a moral point of view?
3 Why are secondary rules important to a legal system?

Whitely v Chapel
(1868) LR 4 QB 147

In this nineteenth-century English case, the accused had used the names of people recently deceased whose names appeared on the voting list; the issue was whether that constituted personating another for purposes of the statute. (Footnotes omitted.)

By 14 & 15 Vict. c. 105, s. 3, if any person, pending or after the election of any guardian [of the poor], shall wilfully, fraudulently, and with intent to affect the result of such election ... "personate any person entitled to vote at such election," he is made liable on conviction to imprisonment for not exceeding three months.

The appellant was charged with having personated one J. Marston, a person entitled to vote at an election of guardians for the township of Bradford; and it was proved that Marston was duly qualified as a ratepayer on the rate book to have voted at the election, but that he had died before the election. The appellant delivered to the person appointed to collect the voting papers a voting paper apparently duly signed by Marston.

The magistrate convicted the appellant.

The question for the Court was, whether the appellant was rightly convicted.

Mellish, QC (with him *McIntyre*), for the appellant. A dead person cannot be said to be "a person entitled to vote;" and the appellant therefore could not be guilty of personation under 14 & 15 Vict. c. 105, s. 3. Very possibly he was within the spirit, but he was not within the letter, of the enactment, and in order to bring a person within a penal enactment, both must concur. In Russell on Crimes (vol. ii. p. 1013, 4th ed., p. 541, 3rd ed.), under a former statute, in which the words were similar to those of 2 Wm. 4, c. 53, s. 49, which makes it a misdemeanor to personate "a person entitled or supposed to be entitled to any prize money," &c., *Brown's Case* is cited, in which it was held that the personation must be of some person prima facie entitled to prize money. In the Parliamentary Registration Act (6 Vict. c. 18), s. 83, the words are "any person who shall knowingly personate ... any person whose name appears on the register of voters, whether such person be alive or dead;" but under the present enactment the person must be entitled, that is, could have voted himself.

Crompton, for the respondent. *Brown's Case* is, in effect, overruled by the later cases of *Rex v Martin*, and *Rex v Cramp*, in which the judges decided that the offence of personating a person "supposed to be entitled" could be committed, although the person, to the knowledge or belief of the authorities, was dead. Those cases are directly in point. The gist of the offence is the fraudulently voting under another's name; the mischief is the same, whether the supposed voter be alive or dead; and the Court will put a liberal construction on such an enactment: *Reg. v Hague*.

Mellish, QC, in reply. "Supposed to be entitled" must have been held by the judges in the cases cited to mean supposed by the person personating.

Lush, J: I do not think we can, without straining them, bring the case within the words of the enactment. The legislature has not used words wide enough to make the personation of a dead person an offence. The words "a person entitled to vote" can only mean, without a forced construction, a person who is entitled to vote at the time at which the personation takes place; in the present case, therefore, I feel bound to say the offence has not been committed. In the cases of *Rex v Martin*, and *Rex v Cramp*, the judges gave no reasons for their decision; they probably held that "supposed to be entitled" meant supposed by the person personating.

Hannen, J: I regret that we are obliged to come to the conclusion that the offence charged was not proved; but it would be wrong to strain words to meet the justice of the present case, because it might make a precedent, and lead to dangerous consequences in other cases.

Hayes, J, concurred.

Lon L. Fuller
The Morality of Law (1969)

Fuller disputes Hart's claim that a legal order can take on any content whatsoever. The excerpt included here offers the example of a hypothetical tyrant, who decides to use law as a tool to enforce his wishes. Fuller argues that such a tyrant would quickly run into difficulties because the institutional structure of a legal system cannot help but include a minimal morality of fairness. He also accuses positivism of adopting an authoritarian concept of the authority of law.

THE MORALITY THAT MAKES LAW POSSIBLE

[A] law which a man cannot obey, nor act according to it, is void and no law: and it is impossible to obey contradictions, or act according to them. – Vaughan, C. J. In *Thomas v. Sorrell*, 1677

It is desired that our learned lawyers would answer these ensuing queries ... whether ever the Commonwealth, when they chose the Parliament, gave them a lawless unlimited power, and at their pleasure to walk contrary to their own laws and ordinances before they have repealed them? – Lilburne, *England's Birth-Right Justified*, 1645

This chapter will begin with a fairly lengthy allegory. It concerns the unhappy reign of a monarch who bore the convenient, but not very imaginative and not even very regal sounding name of Rex.

Eight Ways to Fail to Make Law

Rex came to the throne filled with the zeal of a reformer. He considered that the greatest failure of his predecessors had been in the field of law. For generations the legal system had known nothing like a basic reform. Procedures of trial were cumbersome, the rules of law spoke in the archaic tongue of another age, justice was expensive, the judges were slovenly and sometimes corrupt. Rex was resolved to remedy all this and to make his name in history as a great lawgiver. It was his unhappy fate to fail in this ambition. Indeed, he failed spectacularly, since not only did he not succeed in introducing the needed reforms, but he never even succeeded in creating any law at all, good or bad.

His first official act was, however, dramatic and propitious. Since he needed a clean slate on which to write, he announced to his subjects the immediate repeal of all existing law, of whatever kind. He then set about drafting a new code. Unfortunately, trained as a lonely prince, his education had been very defective. In particular he found himself incapable of making even the simplest generalizations. Though not lacking in confidence when it came to deciding specific controversies, the effort to give articulate reasons for any conclusion strained his capacities to the breaking point.

Becoming aware of his limitations, Rex gave up the project of a code and announced to his subjects that henceforth he would act as a judge in any disputes that might arise among them. In this way under the stimulus of a variety of cases he hoped that his latent powers of generalization might develop and, proceeding case by case, he would gradually work out a system of rules that could be incorporated in a code. Unfortunately the defects in his education were more deep-seated than he had supposed. The venture failed completely. After he had handed down literally hundreds of decisions neither he nor his subjects could detect in those decisions any pattern whatsoever. Such tentatives toward generalization as were to be found in his opinions only compounded the confusion, for they gave false leads to his subjects and threw his own meager powers of judgment off balance in the decision of later cases.

After this fiasco Rex realized it was necessary to take a fresh start. His first move was to subscribe to a course of lessons in generalization. With his intellectual powers thus fortified, he resumed the project of a code and, after many hours of solitary labor, succeeded in preparing a fairly lengthy document. He was still not confident, however, that he had fully overcome his previous defects. Accordingly, he announced to his subjects that he had written out a code and would henceforth be governed by it in deciding cases, but that for an indefinite future the contents of the code would remain an official state secret, known only to him and his scrivener. To Rex's surprise this sensible plan was deeply resented by his subjects. They declared it was very unpleasant to have one's case decided by rules when there was no way of knowing what those rules were.

Stunned by this rejection Rex undertook an earnest inventory of his personal strengths and weaknesses. He decided that life had taught him one clear lesson, namely, that it is easier to decide things with the aid of hindsight than it is to attempt to foresee and control the future. Not only did hindsight make it easier to decide cases, but – and this was of supreme importance to Rex – it made it easier to give reasons. Deciding to capitalize on this insight, Rex hit on the following plan. At the beginning of each calendar year he would decide all the controversies that had arisen among his subjects during the preceding year. He would accompany his decisions with a full statement of reasons. Naturally, the reasons thus given would be understood as not controlling decisions in future years, for that would be to defeat the whole purpose of the new arrangement, which was to gain the advantages of hindsight. Rex confidently announced the new plan to his subjects, observing that he was going to publish the full text of his judgments with the rules applied by him, thus meeting the chief objection to the old plan. Rex's subjects received this announcement in silence, then quietly explained through their leaders that when they said they needed to know the rules, they meant they needed to know them *in advance* so they could act on them. Rex muttered something to the effect that they might have made that point a little clearer, but said he would see what could be done.

Rex now realized that there was no escape from a published code declaring the rules to be applied in future disputes. Continuing his lessons in generalization, Rex worked diligently on a revised code, and finally announced that it would shortly be published. This announcement was received with universal gratification. The dismay of Rex's subjects was all the more intense, therefore, when his code became available and it was discovered that it was truly a masterpiece of obscurity. Legal experts who studied it declared that there was not a single sentence in it that could be understood either by an ordinary citizen or by a trained lawyer. Indignation became general and soon a picket appeared before the royal palace carrying a sign that read, "How can anybody follow a rule that nobody can understand?"

The code was quickly withdrawn. Recognizing for the first time that he needed assistance, Rex put a staff of experts to work on a revision. He instructed them to leave the substance untouched, but to clarify the expression throughout. The resulting code was a model of clarity, but as it was studied it became apparent that its new clarity had merely brought to light that it was honeycombed with contradictions. It was reliably reported that there was not a single provision in the code that was not nullified by another provision inconsistent with it. A picket again appeared before the royal residence carrying a sign that read, "This time the king made himself clear – in both directions."

Once again the code was withdrawn for revision. By now, however, Rex had lost his patience with his subjects and the negative attitude they seemed to adopt toward everything he tried to do for them. He decided to teach them a lesson and put an end to their carping. He instructed his experts to purge the code of contradictions, but at the same time to stiffen drastically every requirement contained in it and to add a long list of new crimes. Thus, where before the citizen summoned to the throne was given ten days in which to report, in the revision the time was cut to ten seconds. It was made a crime, punishable by ten years' imprisonment, to cough, sneeze, hiccough, faint or fall down in the presence of the king. It was made treason not to understand, believe in, and correctly profess the doctrine of evolutionary, democratic redemption.

When the new code was published a near revolution resulted. Leading citizens declared their intention to flout its provisions. Someone discovered in an ancient author a passage that seemed apt: "To command what cannot be done is not to make law; it is to unmake law, for a command that cannot be obeyed serves no end but confusion, fear and chaos." Soon this passage was being quoted in a hundred petitions to the king.

The code was again withdrawn and a staff of experts charged with the task or revision. Rex's instructions to the experts were that whenever they encountered a rule requiring an impossibility, it should be revised to make compliance possible. It turned out that to accomplish this result every provision in the code had to be substantially rewritten. The final result was, however, a triumph of draftsmanship. It was clear, consistent with itself, and demanded nothing of the subject that did not lie easily within his powers. It was printed and distributed free of charge on every street corner.

However, before the effective date for the new code had arrived, it was discovered that so much time had been spent in successive revisions of Rex's original draft, that the substance of the code had been seriously overtaken by events. Ever since Rex assumed the throne there had been a suspension of ordinary legal processes and this had brought about important economic and institutional changes within the country. Accommodation to these altered conditions required many changes of substance in the law. Accordingly as soon as the new code became legally effective, it was subjected to a daily stream of amendments. Again popular discontent mounted; an anonymous pamphlet appeared on the streets carrying scurrilous cartoons of the king and a leading article with the title: "A law that changes every day is worse than no law at all."

Within a short time this source of discontent began to cure itself as the pace of amendment gradually slackened. Before this had occurred to any noticeable degree, however, Rex announced an important decision. Reflecting on the misadventures of his reign, he concluded that much of the trouble lay in bad advice he had received from experts. He accordingly declared he was reassuming the judicial power in his own person. In this way he could directly control the application of the new code and insure his country against another crisis. He began to spend practically all of his time hearing and deciding cases arising under the new code.

As the king proceeded with this task, it seemed to bring to a belated blossoming his long dormant powers of generalization. His opinions began, indeed, to reveal a confident and almost exuberant virtuosity as he deftly distinguished his own previous decisions, exposed the principles on which he acted, and laid down guide lines for the disposition of future controversies. For Rex's subjects a new day seemed about to dawn when they could finally conform their conduct to a coherent body of rules.

This hope was, however, soon shattered. As the bound volumes of Rex's judgments became available and were subjected to closer study, his subjects were appalled to discover that there existed no discernible relation between those judgments and the code they purported to apply. Insofar as it found expression in the actual disposition of controversies, the new code might just as well not have existed at all. Yet in virtually every one of his decisions Rex declared and redeclared the code to be the basic law of his kingdom.

Leading citizens began to hold private meetings to discuss what measures, short of open revolt, could be taken to get the king away from the bench and back on the throne. While these discussions were going on Rex suddenly died, old before his time and deeply disillusioned with his subjects.

The first act of his successor, Rex II, was to announce that he was taking the powers of government away from the lawyers and placing them in the hands of psychiatrists and experts in public relations. This way, he explained, people could be made happy without rules.

The Consequences of Failure

Rex's bungling career as legislator and judge illustrates that the attempt to create and maintain a system of legal rules may miscarry in at least eight ways; there are in this enterprise, if you will, eight distinct routes to disaster. The first and most obvious lies in a failure to achieve rules at all, so that every issue must be decided on an ad hoc basis. The other routes are: (2) a failure to publicize, or at least to make available to the affected party, the rules he is expected to observe; (3) the abuse of retroactive legislation, which not only cannot itself guide action, but undercuts the integrity of rules prospective in effect, since it puts them under the threat of retrospective change; (4) a failure to make rules understandable; (5) the enactment of contradictory rules or (6) rules that require conduct beyond the powers of the affected party; (7) introducing such frequent changes in the rules that the subject cannot orient his action by them; and, finally, (8) a failure of congruence between the rules as announced and their actual administration.

A total failure in any one of these eight directions does not simply result in a bad system of law; it results in something that is not properly called a legal system at all, except perhaps in the Pickwickian sense in which a void contract can still be said to be one kind of contract. Certainly there can be no rational ground for asserting that a man can have a moral obligation to obey a legal rule that does not exist, or is kept secret from him, or that came into existence only after he had acted, or was unintelligible, or was contradicted by another rule of the same system, or commanded the impossible, or changed every minute. It may not be impossible for a man to obey a rule that is disregarded by those charged with its administration, but at some point obedience becomes futile – as futile, in fact, as casting a vote that will never be counted. As the sociologist Simmel has observed, there is a kind of reciprocity between government and the citizen with respect to the observance of rules. Government says to the citizen in effect, "These are the rules we expect you to follow. If you follow them, you have our assurance that they are the rules that will be applied to your conduct." When this bond of reciprocity is finally and completely ruptured by government, nothing is left on which to ground the citizen's duty to observe the rules.

The citizen's predicament becomes more difficult when, though there is no total failure in any direction, there is a general and drastic deterioration in legality, such as occurred in Germany under Hitler. A situation begins to develop, for example, in which though some laws are published, others, including the most important, are not. Though most laws are prospective in effect, so free a use is made of retrospective legislation that no law is immune to change ex post facto if it suits the convenience of those in power. For the trial of criminal cases concerned with loyalty to the regime, special military tribunals are established and these tribunals disregard, whenever it suits their convenience, the rules that are supposed to control their decisions. Increasingly the principal object of government seems to be, not that of giving the citizen rules by which to shape his conduct, but to frighten him into impotence. As such a situation develops, the problem faced by the citizen is not so simple as that of a voter who knows with certainty that his ballot will not be counted. It is more like that of the voter who knows that the odds are against his ballot being counted at all, and that if it is counted, there is a good chance that it will be counted for the side against which he actually voted. A citizen in this predicament has to decide for himself whether to stay with the system and cast his ballot as a kind of symbolic act expressing the hope of a better day. So it was with the German citizen under Hitler faced with deciding whether he had an obligation to obey such portions of the laws as the Nazi terror had left intact.

In situations like these there can be no simple principle by which to test the citizen's obligation of fidelity to law, any more than there can be such a principle for testing his right to engage in a general revolution. One thing is, however, clear. A mere respect for constituted authority must not be confused with fidelity to law. Rex's subjects, for example, remained faithful to him as king throughout his long and inept reign. They were not faithful to his law, for he never made any.

The Aspiration toward Perfection in Legality

So far we have been concerned to trace out eight routes to failure in the enterprise of creating law. Corresponding to these are eight kinds of legal excellence toward which a system of rules may strive. What appear at the lowest level as indispensable conditions for the existence of law at all, become, as we ascend the scale of achievement, increasingly demanding challenges to human capacity. At the height of the ascent we are tempted to imagine a utopia of legality in which all rules are perfectly clear, consistent with one another, known to every citizen, and never retroactive. In this utopia the rules remain constant through time, demand only what is possible, and are scrupulously observed by courts, police, and everyone else charged with their administration. For reasons that I shall advance shortly, this utopia, in which all eight of the principles of legality are realized to perfection, is not actually a useful target for guiding the impulse toward legality; the goal of perfection is much more complex. Nevertheless it does suggest eight distinct standards by which excellence in legality may be tested.

In expounding in my first chapter the distinction between the morality of duty and that of aspiration, I spoke of an imaginary scale that starts at the bottom with the most obvious and essential moral duties and ascends upward to the highest achievements open to man. I also spoke of an invisible pointer as marking the dividing line where the pressure of duty leaves off and the challenge of excellence begins. The inner morality of law, it should now be clear, presents all of these aspects. It too embraces a morality of duty and a morality of aspiration. It too confronts us with the problem of knowing where to draw the boundary below which men will be condemned for failure, but can expect no praise for success, and above which they will be admired for success and at worst pitied for the lack of it.

In applying the analysis of the first chapter to our present subject, it becomes essential to consider certain distinctive qualities of the inner morality of law. In what may be called the basic morality of social life, duties that run toward other persons generally (as contrasted with those running toward specific individuals) normally require only forbearances, or as we say, are negative in nature: Do not kill, do not injure, do not deceive, do not defame, and the like. Such duties lend themselves with a minimum of difficulty to formalized definition. That is to say, whether we are concerned with legal or moral duties, we are able to develop standards which designate with some precision – though it is never complete – the kind of conduct that is to be avoided.

The demands of the inner morality of the law, however, though they concern a relationship with persons generally, demand more than forbearances; they are, as we loosely say, affirmative in nature: make the law known, make it coherent and clear, see that your decisions as an official are guided by it, etc. To meet these demands human energies must be directed toward specific kinds of achievement and not merely warned away from harmful acts.

Because of the affirmative and creative quality of its demands, the inner morality of law lends itself badly to realization through duties, whether they be moral or legal. No matter how desirable a direction of human effort may appear to be, if we assert there is a duty to pursue it, we shall confront the responsibility of defining at what point that duty has been violated. It is easy to assert that the legislator has a moral duty to make his laws clear and understandable. But this remains at best an exhortation unless we are prepared to define the degree of clarity he must attain in order to discharge his duty. The notion of subjecting clarity to quantitative measure presents obvious difficulties. We may content ourselves, of course, by saying that the legislator has at least a moral duty to try to be clear. But this only postpones the difficulty, for in some situations nothing can be more baffling than to attempt to measure how vigorously a man intended to do that which he has failed to do. In the morality of law, in any event, good intentions are of little avail, as King Rex amply demonstrated. All of this adds up to the conclusion that the inner morality of law is condemned to remain largely a morality of aspiration and not of duty. Its primary appeal must be to a sense of trusteeship and to the pride of the craftsman.

To these observations there is one important exception. This relates to the desideratum of making the laws known, or at least making them available to those affected by them. Here we have a demand that lends itself with unusual readiness to formalization. A written constitution may prescribe that no statute shall become law until it has been given a specified form of publication. If the courts have power to effectuate this provision, we may speak of a legal requirement for the making of law. But a moral duty with respect to publication is also readily imaginable. A custom, for example, might define what kind of promulgation of laws is expected, at the same time leaving unclear what consequences attend a departure from the accepted mode of publication. A formalization of the desideratum of publicity has obvious advantages over uncanalized efforts, even when they are intelligently and conscientiously pursued. A formalized standard of promulgation not only tells the lawmaker where to publish his laws; it also lets the subject – or a lawyer representing his interests – know where to go to learn what the law is.

One might suppose that the principle condemning retroactive laws could also be very readily formalized in a simple rule that no such law should ever be passed, or should be valid if enacted. Such a rule would, however, disserve the cause of legality. Curiously, one of the most obvious seeming demands of legality – that a rule passed today should govern what happens tomorrow, not what happened yesterday – turns out to present some of the most difficult problems of the whole internal morality of law.

With respect to the demands of legality other than promulgation, then, the most we can expect of constitutions and courts is that they save us from the abyss; they cannot be expected to lay out very many compulsory steps toward truly significant accomplishment ...

Do the Principles of Legality Constitute an "Internal Morality of Law"?

The title of my second chapter, *The Morality that Makes Law Possible*, represents a thesis my four reviewers find thoroughly unacceptable. In attempting a response to their criticisms I shall strive to avoid any escalation of polemics, for the level I confront on this issue is already uncomfortably high. "Axe-grinding," "absurd," "bizarre," "grotesque" – these are some of the terms my critics find necessary in characterizing my thesis that there is such a thing as an internal morality of law.

According to my four critics the notion of an internal morality of law betrays a basic confusion between efficacy and morality. Some respect for the eight principles of legality is essential if law is to be effective, but that does not mean that these principles are moral in nature, any more than holding a nail straight in order to hit it right is a matter of morality. You won't drive the nail properly if you don't hold it straight and so also you won't achieve an effective system of law unless you give some heed to what I have called principles of legality. Neither of these exercises of common prudence has anything to do with morality.

So runs the argument of my critics. They are not content, however, with any such prosaic comparison as that offered by the driving of nails. Instead, they assert that if there is such a thing as an internal morality of law-making and law-administering, then there must also be an internal morality of even the most disreputable and censurable of human activities. Cohen asks whether there is a lapse in morality when a would-be assassin forgets to load his gun,[1] Dworkin raises a similar question about an inept attempt at blackmail.[2] As usual, Hart is at once the most eloquent and most explicit of my critics:

the author's insistence on classifying these principles of legality as a "morality" is a source of confusion both for him and his readers ... the crucial objection to the designation of these principles of good legal craftsmanship as morality, in spite of the qualification "inner," is that it perpetrates a confusion between two notions that it is vital to hold apart: the notions of purposive activity and morality. Poisoning is no doubt a purposive activity, and reflections on its purpose may show that it has its internal principles. ("Avoid poisons however lethal if they cause the victim to vomit," or "Avoid poisons however lethal if their shape, color, or size is likely to attract notice.") But to call these principles of the poisoner's art "the morality of poisoning" would simply blur the distinction between the notion of efficiency for a purpose and those final judgments about activities and purposes with which morality in its various forms is concerned.[3]

I must confess that this line of argument struck me at first as being so bizarre, and even perverse, as not to deserve an answer. Reflection has, however, convinced me that I was mistaken in this. As I now view the matter no issue in the exchange between me and my critics reveals more clearly the tacit presuppositions that each side brings to the debate; taking seriously this argument that the alleged internal morality of law is merely a matter of efficacy has helped me to clarify not only the unarticulated "starting points" of my critics, but my own as well.

That something is here involved more basic than any mere quibble about the word "morality" becomes apparent when we note the fundamental obscurity of my critics' position. Just what do they have in mind when they speak of efficacy? It is not hard to see what is meant by efficacy when you are trying to kill a man with poison; if he ends up dead, you have succeeded; if he is still alive and able to strike back, you have failed. But how do we apply the notion of efficacy to the creation and administration of a thing as complex as a whole legal system? Let me offer an example drawn from the recent history of the Soviet Union that will suggest some of the difficulties involved in answering that question.

At the beginning of the 1960s the problem of economic crimes (including illegal transactions in foreign currencies) had apparently reached such proportions in Russia that the Soviet authorities decided drastic countermeasures were in order. Accordingly in May and July of 1961 statutes were passed subjecting such crimes to the death penalty. These statutes were then applied retrospectively and convicted men were put to death for acts which, while not lawful when committed, were not then subject to the death penalty.

The purpose of the Soviet authorities was obviously to make people quit stealing from the state. Was a retrospective application of the death

penalty "inefficacious" for this purpose? One of the problems of criminal law is to convey to the prospective criminal that you are not engaged in a game of idle threats, that you mean what you say. Is there
any more effective way of conveying that message than the retrospective application of a criminal penalty? The very fact that it marks a
drastic departure from ordinary practice is, in effect, a pledge of the
earnestness of the lawgiver. Yet there were Russians who were disturbed by this action of the authorities, as my colleague Harold Berman
reports in the following passage:

I asked a leading Soviet jurist if he could explain the decision of the Supreme
Court of the Russian Republic applying the July law retroactively – in clear
violation, it seemed to me, of the 1958 Fundamental Principles of Criminal
Procedure. He replied, "We lawyers didn't like that" – a statement as
interesting for the "we lawyers" as for the "didn't like that."[4]

Now it is reasonable to suppose, I think, that the Soviet lawyer was
not asserting that the action of the authorities was an ineffective measure for combating economic crime. He was saying that it involved a
compromise of principle, an impairment of the integrity of the law. As
Berman remarks with reference to this conversation: "it is the lawyers
who understand best of all, perhaps, the integrity of law, the universality of legal standards – in other words, the threat to legality *in general*
which is posed by any *particular* infringement of legality."[5]

At this point I can imagine my critics pulling at my sleeve: "Ah, but
you have misunderstood what we meant by efficacy. We did not have
in mind short-run efficacy in meeting some passing emergency. The
Soviet action impaired the efficacy of law because it tended to undermine public confidence in legal rules generally and reduced the incentive to obey them. It achieved an immediate gain at a cost in the damage done to the institution of law generally." But plainly if my critics
begin to expand the notion of efficacy in this direction, they will soon
find themselves drifting across the boundary they have so painstak-
ingly set up to distinguish morality from efficacy. They are likely to get
themselves into the predicament of those who try to convert all morality into enlightened selfishness and who end up with so much enlightenment, and so little selfishness, that they might have saved themselves
a good deal of trouble by simply talking about morality in the first
place.

I do not think, therefore, that in discussing problems of legality any useful joinder of issue is achieved by opposing efficacy to morality; certainly nothing is attained that justifies treating the use of the word "morality" in this connection as an exercise in obfuscation. In truth, the appeal of "efficacy" does not lie in any definiteness of its meaning, but in the tough-sounding, positivistic flavor of the word; it suggests an observer clear-eyed and result-oriented, not easily misled by fuzzy concepts of purpose. In other words, my critics' preference for "efficacy" over "morality" reflects the influence of deep-seated and largely unarticulated resolutions of the mind, rather than any reasoned-out conclusion about a specific issue.

I confront therefore the most unwelcome task of demonstrating that my critics' rejection of an internal morality of law rests on premises they have not themselves brought to expression in their writings. Let me make it clear, however, that I do not purport to explore unavowed emotional biases; my efforts lie in the realm of the intellect, in the exploration of an implicit structure that shapes my critics' thought processes. If their conclusions do not imply the premises I ascribe to them, they are at liberty to set me straight.

Proceeding then to the task at hand, I perceive *two* assumptions underlying my critics' rejection of "the internal morality of law." The *first* of these is a belief that the existence or non-existence of law is, from a moral point of view, a matter of indifference. The *second* is an assumption I have already described as characteristic of legal positivism generally. This is the assumption that law should be viewed not as the product of an interplay of purposive orientations between the citizen and his government but as a one-way projection of authority, originating with government and imposing itself upon the citizen.

In the literature of legal positivism it is of course standard practice to examine at length the relations of law and morals. With respect to the influence of morals on law it is common to point out that moral conceptions may guide legislation, furnish standards for the criticism of existing law, and may properly be taken into account in the interpretation of law. The treatment of the converse influence – that of law on morality – is generally more meager, being confined chiefly to the observation that legal rules long established tend, through a kind of cultural conditioning, to be regarded as morally right.

What is generally missing in these accounts is any recognition of the role legal rules play in making possible an effective realization of morality in the actual behavior of human beings. Moral principles cannot function in a social vacuum or in a war of all against all. To live the good life requires something more than good intentions, even if they are generally shared; it requires the support of firm base lines for human interaction, something that – in modern society at least – only a sound legal system can supply ...

So when we speak of "the moral neutrality of law" we cannot mean that the existence and conscientious administration of a legal system are unrelated to a realization of moral objectives in the affairs of life. If respect for the principles of legality is essential to produce such a system, then certainly it does not seem absurd to suggest that those principles constitute a special morality of role attaching to the office of law-maker and law-administrator. In any event the responsibilities of that office deserve some more flattering comparison than that offered by the practices of the thoughtful and conscientious poisoner who never forgets to tear the chemist's label off before he hands the bottle to his victim.

To regard as morally indifferent the existence or non-existence of law is to assume that moral precepts retain the same meaning regardless of the social context into which they are projected. It thus illustrates what I have previously described as an abstraction from the social dimension; it brings to expression a distaste for phenomena of interaction characteristic of positivistic thought. This bent of mind comes openly to the fore in the second assumption underlying my critics' rejection of the notion of an internal morality of law. This is the assumption that the essential reality of law is perceived when we picture it as a one-way projection of authority originating with government and imposing itself upon the citizen. Since this assumption is shared by unreflective common sense, and finds tacit recognition in the ordinary usages of language, it will be well to examine in some detail what is wrong with it.

Let me begin by putting in opposition to one another two forms of social ordering that are often confounded. One of these is *managerial direction*, the other is *law*. Both involve the direction and control of human activity; both imply subordination to authority. An extensive vocabulary is shared by the two forms: "authority," "orders," control," "jurisdiction," "obedience," "compliance," "legitimacy," – these are but a few of the terms whose double residence is a source of confusion.

A general and summary statement of the distinction between the two forms of social ordering might run somewhat as follows: The directives issued in a managerial context are *applied* by the subordinate in order to serve a purpose set by his superior. The law-abiding citizen, on the other hand, does not *apply* legal rules to serve specific ends set by the lawgiver, but rather *follows* them in the conduct of his own affairs, the interests he is presumed to serve in following legal rules being those of society generally. The directives of a managerial system regulate primarily the relations between the subordinate and his superior and only collaterally the relations of the subordinate with third persons. The rules of a legal system, on the other hand, normally serve the primary purpose of setting the citizen's relations with other citizens and only in a collateral manner his relations with the seat of authority from which the rules proceed. (Though we sometimes think of the criminal law as defining the citizen's duties toward his government, its primary function is to provide a sound and stable framework for the interactions of citizens with one another.)

The account just given could stand much expansion and qualification; the two forms of social ordering present themselves in actual life in many mixed, ambiguous, and distorted forms. For our present purposes, however, we shall attempt to clarify the essential difference between them by presupposing what may be called "ideal types." We shall proceed by inquiring what implications the eight principles of legality (or analogues thereof) have for a system of managerial direction as compared with their implications for a legal order.

Now five of the eight principles are quite at home in a managerial context. If the superior is to secure what he wants through the instrumentality of the subordinate he must, first of all, communicate his wishes, or "promulgate" them by giving the subordinate a chance to know what they are, for example, by posting them on a bulletin board. His directives must also be reasonably clear, free from contradiction, possible of execution and not changed so often as to frustrate the efforts of the subordinate to act on them. Carelessness in these matters may seriously impair the "efficacy" of the managerial enterprise.

What of the other three principles? With respect to the requirement of generality, this becomes, in a managerial context, simply a matter of expediency. In actual practice managerial control is normally achieved by standing orders that will relieve the superior from having to give a step-by-step direction to his subordinate's performance. But the subordinate has no justification for complaint if, in a particular case, the superior directs him to depart from the procedures prescribed by some general order. This means, in turn, that in a managerial relation there is no room for a formal principle demanding that the actions of the superior conform to the rules he has himself announced; in this context the principle of "congruence between official action and declared rule" loses its relevance. As for the principle against retrospectivity, the problem simply does not arise; no manager retaining a semblance of sanity would direct his subordinate today to do something on his behalf yesterday.

From the brief analysis just presented it is apparent that the managerial relation fits quite comfortably the picture of a one-way projection of authority. Insofar as the principles of legality (or, perhaps I should say, their managerial analogues) are here applicable they are indeed "principles of efficacy"; they are instruments for the achievement of the superior's ends. This does not mean that elements of interaction or reciprocity are ever wholly absent in a managerial relation. If the superior habitually overburdens those under his direction, confuses them by switching signals too frequently, or falsely accuses them of departing from instructions they have in fact faithfully followed, the morale of his subordinates will suffer and they may not do a good job for him; indeed, if his inconsiderateness goes too far, they may end by deserting his employ or turning against him in open revolt. But this tacit reciprocity of reasonableness and restraint is something collateral to the basic relation of order-giver and order-executor.

With a legal system the matter stands quite otherwise, for here the existence of a relatively stable reciprocity of expectations between law-giver and subject is part of the very idea of a functioning legal order. To see why and in what sense this is true it is essential to continue our examination of the implications of the eight principles, turning now to their implications for a system of law. Though the principles of legality are in large measure interdependent, in distinguishing law from managerial direction the key principle is that I have described as "congruence between official action and declared rule."

Surely the very essence of the Rule of Law is that in acting upon the citizen (by putting him in jail, for example, or declaring invalid a deed under which he claims title to property) a government will faithfully apply rules previously declared as those to be followed by the citizen and as being determinative of his rights and duties. If the Rule of Law does not mean this, it means nothing. Applying rules faithfully implies, in turn, that rules will take the form of general declarations; it would make little sense, for example, if the government were today to enact a special law whereby Jones should be put in jail and then tomorrow were "faithfully" to follow this "rule" by actually putting him in jail. Furthermore, if the law is intended to permit a man to conduct his own affairs subject to an obligation to observe certain restraints imposed by superior authority, this implies that he will not be told at each turn what to do; law furnishes a baseline for self-directed action, not a detailed set of instructions for accomplishing specific objectives.

The twin principles of generality and of faithful adherence by government to its own declared rules cannot be viewed as offering mere counsels of expediency. This follows from the basic difference between law and managerial direction; law is not, like management, a matter of directing other persons how to accomplish tasks set by a superior, but is basically a matter of providing the citizenry with a sound and stable framework for their interactions with one another, the role of government being that of standing as a guardian of the integrity of this system.

I have previously said that the principle against retrospective rule-making is without significance in a context of managerial direction simply because no manager in his right mind would be tempted to direct his subordinate today to do something yesterday. Why do things stand differently with a legal system? The answer is, I believe, both somewhat complex and at the same time useful for the light it sheds on the differences between managerial direction and law.

The first ingredient of the explanation lies in the concept of legitimation. If A purports to give orders to B, or to lay down rules for his conduct, B may demand to know by what title A claims the power to exercise a direction over the conduct of other persons. This is the kind of problem Hart had in mind in formulating his Rule of Recognition. It is a problem shared by law-making and managerial direction alike, and may be said to involve a principle of *external* legitimation. But the Rule of Law demands of a government that it also legitimate its actions toward citizens by a second and *internal* standard. This standard requires that within the general area covered by law acts of government toward the citizen be in accordance with (that is, be authorized or validated by) general rules previously declared by government itself. Thus, a lawful government may be said to accomplish an internal validation of its acts by an exercise of its own legislative power. If a prior exercise of that power can effect this validation, it is easy to slip into the belief that the same validation can be accomplished retrospectively.

What has just been said may explain why retrospective legislation is not rejected out of hand as utterly nonsensical. It does not, however, explain why retrospective law-making can in some instances actually serve the cause of legality. To see why this is so we need to recall that under the Rule of Law control over the citizen's actions is accomplished, not by specific directions, but by *general* rules expressing the principle that like cases should be given like treatment. Now abuses and mishaps in the operations of a legal system may impair this principle and require as a cure retrospective legislation. The retrospective statute cannot serve as a baseline for the interactions of citizens with one another, but it can serve to heal infringements of the principle that like cases should receive like treatment. I have given illustrations of this in my second chapter. As a further example one may imagine a situation in which a new statute, changing the law, is enacted and notice of this statute is conveyed to all the courts in the country except those in *Province X*, where through some failure of communication the courts remain uninformed of the change. The courts of this province continue to apply the old law; those in the remaining portions of the country decide cases by the new law. The principle that like cases should be given like treatment is seriously infringed, and the only cure (at best involving a choice of evils) may lie in retrospective legislation. Plainly problems of this sort cannot arise in a managerial context, since managerial direction is not in principle required to act by general rule and has no occasion to legitimate specific orders by showing that they conform to previously announced general rules.

We have already observed that in a managerial context it is difficult to perceive anything beyond counsels of expediency in the remaining principles of legality – those requiring that rules or orders be promulgated, clear in meaning, noncontradictory, possible of observance, and not subject to too frequent change. One who thinks of law in terms of the managerial model will assume as a matter of course that these five principles retain the same significance for law. This is particularly apt to be true of the desideratum of clarity. What possible motive, one may ask, other than sheer slovenliness, would prompt a legislator to leave his enactments vague and indefinite in their coverage?

The answer is that there are quite understandable motives moving him in that direction. A government wants its laws to be clear enough to be obeyed, but it also wants to preserve its freedom to deal with situations not readily foreseeable when the laws are enacted. By publishing a criminal statute government does not merely issue a directive to the citizen; it also imposes on itself a charter delimiting its powers to deal with a particular area of human conduct. The loosely phrased criminal statute may reduce the citizens' chance to know what is expected of him, but it expands the powers of government to deal with forms of misbehavior which could not be anticipated in advance. If one looks at the matter purely in terms of "efficacy" in the achievement of governmental aims, one might speak of a kind of optimum position between a definiteness of coverage that is unduly restrictive of governmental discretion and a vagueness so pronounced that it will not only fail to frighten the citizen away from a general area of conduct deemed undesirable, but may also rob the statute of its power to lend a meaningful legitimation to action taken pursuant to it.

Opposing motivations of this sort become most visible in a bureaucratic context where men deal, in some measure, face to face. Often managerial direction is accompanied by, and intertwined with miniature legal systems affecting such matters as discipline and special privileges. In such a context it is a commonplace of sociological observation that those occupying posts of authority will often resist not only the clarification of rules, but even their effective publication. Knowledge of the rules, and freedom to interpret them to fit the case at hand, are important sources of power. One student in this field has even concluded that the "toleration of illicit practices actually enhances the controlling power of superiors, paradoxical as it may seem."[6] It enhances the superior's power, of course, by affording him the opportunity to obtain gratitude and loyalty through the grant of absolutions, at the same time leaving him free to visit the full rigor of the law on those he considers in need of being brought into line. This welcome freedom of action would not be his if he could not point to rules as giving significance to his actions; one cannot, for example, forgive the violation of a rule unless there is a rule to violate. This does not mean, however, that the rule has to be free from obscurity, or widely publicized, or consistently enforced. Indeed, any of these conditions may curtail the discretion of the man in control – a discretion from which he may derive not only a sense of personal power but also a sense, perhaps not wholly perverse, of serving well the enterprise of which he is a part.

It may seem that in the broader, more impersonal processes of a national or state legal system there would be lacking any impulse toward deformations or accommodations of the sort just suggested. This is far from being the case. It should be remembered, for example, that in drafting almost any statute, particularly in the fields of criminal law and economic regulation, there is likely to occur a struggle between those who want to preserve for government a broad freedom of action and those whose primary concern is to let the citizen know in advance where he stands. In confronting this kind of problem there is room in close cases for honest differences of opinion, but there can also arise acute problems of conscience touching the basic integrity of legal processes. Over wide areas of governmental action a still more fundamental question can be raised: whether there is not a damaging and corrosive hypocrisy in pretending to act in accordance with preestablished rules when in reality the functions exercised are essentially managerial and for that reason demand – and on close inspection are seen to exhibit – a rule-free response to changing conditions.

What has just been said can offer only a fleeting glimpse of the responsibilities, dilemmas, and temptations that confront those concerned with the making and administering of laws. These problems are shared by legislators, judges, prosecutors, commissioners, probation officers, building inspectors, and a host of other officials, including – above all – the patrolman on his beat. To attempt to reduce these problems to issues of "efficacy" is to trivialize them beyond recognition.

Why, then, are my critics so intent on maintaining the view that the principles of legality represent nothing more than maxims of efficiency for the attainment of governmental aims? The answer is simple. The main ingredients of their analysis are not taken from law at all, but from what has here been called managerial direction. One searches in vain in their writings for any recognition of the basic principle of the Rule of Law – that the acts of a legal authority toward the citizen must be legitimated by being brought within the terms of a previous declaration of general rules.

This omission is conspicuous throughout Hart's *Concept of Law*. His only extended treatment of the principle of generality, for example, seems plainly inspired by the managerial model:

Even in a complex large society, like that of a modern state, there are occasions when an official, face to face with an individual, orders him to do something. A policeman orders a particular motorist to stop or a particular beggar to move on. But these simple situations are not, and could not be, the standard way in which law functions, if only because no society could support the number of officials necessary to secure that every member of society was officially and separately informed of every act which he was required to do. Instead such particularized forms of control are either exceptional or reinforcements of general forms of directions which do not name, and are not addressed to, particular individuals, and do not indicate a particular act to be done. (pp. 20–21)

Other comments by Hart on the principle of generality, while less explicit, in no way qualify the statement just quoted. (See pp. 38, 121,

202, 236.) All run in terms of providing "instruments of social control" and of enabling "social control to function."

With respect to what I have called the principle requiring "congruence between official action and declared rule," Hart's comments again relate to the problem of achieving "effective control" over the citizen's actions; failure of this control is said to be illustrated when the criminal law is so laxly enforced that the public ends by ignoring it. (See pp. 23, 82, 141.) The only departure from what may be called the managerial frame of reference is found in some remarks (pp. 156, 202) about an abstract affinity between the ideal of justice and an efficiently run legal system; both are said to respect the principle that like cases should be given like treatment. Thus "we have, in the bare notion of applying a general rule of law, the germ at least of justice." There is no intimation that a government has toward the citizen any obligation to realize this "germ of justice" in the way it makes and administers laws; the point seems to be simply that if we happen to observe a well-run legal system in operation we shall discover in it a certain formal resemblance to justice.

Thus, it will be seen that Hart's concept of law, being based essentially on the managerial model,[7] contains no element inconsistent with the view that law is a one-way projection of authority. This does not mean, of course, that the lawgiver can bring a legal system into existence by himself; like the manager he requires the acquiescence and cooperation of those subject to his direction. This is recognized quite explicitly and with his usual aptness of phrasing by Hart himself:

if a system of rules is to be imposed by force on any, there must be a sufficient number who accept it voluntarily. Without their voluntary cooperation, thus creating *authority*, the coercive power of law and government cannot be established. (p. 196)

There is no suggestion here that the citizen's voluntary cooperation must be matched by a corresponding cooperative effort on the part of government. There is no recognition in Hart's analysis that maintaining a legal system in existence depends upon the discharge of interlocking responsibilities – of government toward the citizen and of the citizen toward government.

If we assume, as I do here, that an element of commitment by the lawgiver is implicit in the concept of law, then it will be well to attempt to spell out briefly in what form this commitment manifests itself. In a passage headed by his translator "Interaction in the Idea of Law," Simmel suggests that underlying a legal system is a contract between lawgiver and subject. By enacting laws government says to the citizen, "These are the rules we ask you to follow. If you will obey them, you have our promise that they are the rules we will apply to your conduct." Certainly such a construction contains at least this much truth: if the citizen knew in advance that in dealing with him government would pay no attention to its own declared rules, he would have little incentive himself to abide by them. The publication of rules plainly carries with it the "social meaning" that the rulemaker will himself abide by his own rules. On the other hand, any attempt to conceive of a legal system as resting on a contract between lawgiver and subject not only stirs inconvenient historical associations, but has a certain incongruity about it, especially when we recall that in a democratic society the same citizen may be both lawgiver and legal subject.

There is an old-fashioned legal term that may offer an escape from our predicament. This is the word "intendment." Our institutions and our formalized interactions with one another are accompanied by certain interlocking expectations that may be called intendments, even though there is seldom occasion to bring these underlying expectations across the threshold of consciousness. In a very real sense when I cast my vote in an election my conduct is directed and conditioned by an anticipation that my ballot will be counted in favor of the candidate I actually vote for. This is true even though the possibility that my ballot will be thrown in the wastebasket, or counted for the wrong man, may never enter my mind as an object of conscious attention. In this sense the institution of elections may be said to contain an intendment that the votes cast will be faithfully tallied, though I might hesitate to say, except in a mood of rhetoric, that the election authorities had entered a contract with me to count my vote as I had cast it.

NOTES

1 "The Morality of Law – A Symposium," 10 *Villanova Law Review* 631–78 (1965) at p. 651. Individual contributions were Murray, "Introduction to the Morality of Law," 624–30; Dworkin, "The Elusive Morality of Law," 631–39; Cohen, "Law, Morality and Purpose," 640–54; Fuller, "A Reply to Professors Cohen and Dworkin," 655–66; with comments by John E. Murray, Jr., 667–70; E. Russell Naughton, 671–72; Francis H. Parker, 673–75; and Donald A. Giannella, 676–78.

2 Supra n.1 at p. 634.

3 78 *Harvard Law Review* 1281–96 (1965) at pp. 1285–86.

4 Berman, "The Struggle of Soviet Jurists Against a Return to Stalinist Terror,"
   22 *Slavic Review* 314–20, at p. 315 (1963).

5 Ibid., p. 320.

6 Blau, *The Dynamics of Bureaucracy* (2d ed. 1963), p. 215.

7 It may be well at this point to mention briefly one possible source of
   misunderstanding. A reader generally familiar with Hart's *Concept of Law*
   may recall that he explicitly rejects Austin's "command theory of law." To
   one who does not have in mind just what this rejection implies, it may seem
   that in disapproving of the command theory Hart is also rejecting what I
   have here described as a managerial theory of law. This would, however, be
   to misunderstand Hart's argument. Hart rejects the command theory chiefly
   on two grounds: (1) it sees the force of law as residing in the threat of
   sanctions, rather than in an acceptance of authority; (2) Austin's theory
   presupposes direct communication between lawgiver and legal subject. But,
   plainly, effective managerial direction rests, much more obviously than does
   law, on a willingness to accept authoritative direction. Furthermore, managerial directions need not be conveyed in a face-to-face manner; they are in
   fact commonly embodied in something like a manual of operations or may
   be set forth on a bulletin board. The crucial point in distinguishing law from
   managerial direction lies in a commitment by the legal authority to abide by
   its own announced rules in judging the actions of the legal subject. I can find
   no recognition of this basic notion in *The Concept of Law*.

READING QUESTIONS ON FULLER

1 Fuller argues that at a minimum, any legal system will include
   certain procedural safeguards. How much of a morality is this?
   Could there nonetheless be an utterly wicked legal system?

2 Do you think that Fuller correctly describes the positivist concept of
   authority as "managerial"?

3 Does Hart's "internal point of view" address Fuller's concerns about
   reciprocity?

Ronald Dworkin
"Law's Ambitions for Itself" (1985); *Law's Empire* (1986)

Dworkin seeks to expand Fuller's point, arguing that fundamental values of fairness are implicated in every legal decision. Law's ambition is to work itself pure and rid itself of all morally arbitrary distinctions. Dworkin argues that positivist judges make bad decisions when they try to steer clear of making substantive judgments of fairness.

The 1984 McCorkle Lecture
Law's Ambitions for Itself

I

My title is meant to remind you of a set of metaphors that were once cherished by lawyers but now seem both old-fashioned and silly. "Law works itself pure." "There is a higher law, within and yet beyond positive law, toward which positive law grows." "Law has its own ambitions."

Three mysteries live in these metaphors; they all recognize the obvious fact that in some sense law changes through adjudication as well as explicit legislation. Judges often describe the law, that is, as different from what people had taken it to be before, and use their novel description to decide the very case in which it is announced. The first mystery argues that these changes are (or at least can be) guided by the law itself, personified, playing out an internal program or design. The second adds that changes guided in this way by the law itself are also improvements, that law purer is law better. The third is more mysterious yet: that such changes are not really changes at all, but on the contrary discoveries of an underlying identity, so that a judge who announces a novel rule may actually be describing existing law more accurately.

There are political claims in each of these mysteries; but the practical claim of the third is most evident because it figures in the political justification of what judges do in hard cases. It seems unfair for judges to change the law in the course of litigation. If change is really self-realization, however, if apparent change is only the discovery of deeper identity, then this complaint is misplaced. On the contrary judges would be acting unfairly in the way the complaint assumes – acting against the idea of legality – if they did not recognize and enforce the apparent change.

This entire set of ideas will strike many of you as not only mysterious but idiotic. It has played no important role in formal legal theory for the better part of a century. It was ridiculed and, so most academic lawyers think, destroyed by the movement that began with the legal positivists, led by Jeremy Bentham and his energetic disciple John Austin in Britain, and by the legal realists of American jurisprudence. Their attack was direct. They argued that the mysterious claims I described employ an illegitimate personification: there is no such thing as the law that can have its own ambitions, that can guide the course of its own change. There are only judges who change the law, from time to time, in order to make it better, in their own entirely human view, or simply to repair its gaps enough to decide cases at hand. We do much better, these critics said, to junk the obscurantism, and to insist that the law already in the books, with all its faults and gaps, is the only law we have. Judges do legislate when they change that law, they do apply new law retrospectively, and we must criticize and explain what they do with our eyes open to those simple facts.

This jurisprudential battle, which almost everyone thinks the positivists and the realists won, had a political dimension. Positivists and realists saw themselves as reformers. They said that the older theorists, who celebrated the metaphors and the mysteries, were formalists blind to the practical consequences of judicial decisions for the community at large, or worse, that they were conscious or unconscious agents of oppressive capitalism who protected the status quo by pretending that their political decisions were the unfolding of the law's own necessity. I mention this political dimension because the old battle has been rejoined in our time and the political alignments are now strikingly different, indeed reversed.

The battle has been rejoined mainly in a new theater: constitutional adjudication. The famous decisions of the "Warren Court" built a jurisprudence of individual constitutional rights against the state; the justices who wrote the famous opinions said these rights were created not by the bare text of the Constitution, nor by the specific, concrete intentions of its "framers," nor by their own fiat, but instead by the constitutional structure itself working itself pure. They relied, that is, on the mysteries latent in the antique metaphors. They have been attacked with the same arguments, and all the fervor and ridicule, the earlier positivists and realists used against what they called natural law; but now the attack comes from the right, not the left, of the political spectrum. Today's skeptics are conservative, not progressive or even liberal.

The nation's attention is drawn to this argument, at least languidly, every four years, because presidential elections concentrate the public's mind on the Supreme Court. Attention was greater during the recent election, because five members of the Court are now at least seventy-five years old, and also because the lawyers President Reagan is tipped to appoint to fill the coming vacancies include several who have declared their judicial philosophies with unusual candor and academic thoroughness. Some of these are former professors of law Reagan has already appointed to the federal circuit courts of appeal, like Richard Posner and Robert Bork, and it is these I have particularly in mind when I say that the banners of positivism now march with the right.

I shall later illustrate the new political alignment by describing, in some detail, a recent decision by Judge Bork in the circuit court for the District of Columbia. But I should first mention two competing explanations of the political reversal. Some of you will think it shows that jurisprudence is epiphenomenal in the following way. If people like the recent drift of law, if they want judges to continue in the spirit of the last few decades, they will be drawn to the old metaphors about law's internal ambitions. If they do not, if they think law has been moving very much in the wrong direction, they will strike realist postures and condemn the metaphors as empty and mischievous personifications. I am not myself attracted to that cynical view of the connection between jurisprudence and legal practice. (You may think I dislike it because it makes my job pointless.) I prefer an alternative explanation: that the realignment is a natural consequence of the growing attraction, to liberals, of the idea that minorities of different types have political rights against the majority. This development, I believe, itself makes the older attitude to law more attractive to liberals and the positivist attitude correspondingly more attractive to conservatives. (I return to this alternate explanation toward the end of this discussion.)

II

I shall now try to rehabilitate the old idea expressed in the metaphors and developed in the mysteries I described. The nerve of my suggestion is this: we can understand the metaphors and mysteries, and also account for their appeal, if we take them to express an *interpretive* model of adjudication. I cannot describe that model in any detail here, though I have tried to do so elsewhere.[1] I can only summarize it here with the caution that needed detail, as well as response to obvious objections, has been left out. The omissions will not, I hope, defeat my present ambition, which is to show how the mysteries I describe become less mysterious, and less vulnerable to the ridicule of the realist attack, if taken to express a model of adjudication of the general character I describe.

The model distinguishes between the positive law – the law in the books, the law declared in the clear statements of statutes and past court decisions – and the full law, which it takes to be the set of principles of political morality that taken together provide the best interpretation of the positive law. It insists on a certain understanding of the idea of interpretation: a set of principles provides the best interpretation of the positive law if it provides the best justification available for the political decisions the positive law announces. It provides the best interpretation, in other words, if it shows the positive law in the best possible light.

That will seem an odd account of interpretation to those of you who believe that interpretation, in its very nature, is the process of recovering the "intention" of the historical author of the material being interpreted. For the positive law is the product of a great many different officials at different times who were moved by very different ambitions and purposes, and retrieving these often conflicting ambitions and purposes would be a very different enterprise from the one I have just described. But the assumption that interpretation, in its very nature, is a process of recovering intentions confuses two different levels at which the character of interpretation can be studied.

Even in the case of literary interpretation, when the "author's intention" account seems most plausible, it is only one of the several competing accounts of interpretation we find in the literature. Some scholars argue, for example, that interpretation is better understood as an attempt to capture the effect a literary work has on contemporary readers. So we must try to find some description of interpretation more abstract than any of these contending theories, a description we can use to explain the argument among them; to explain, that is, both what they are disagreeing about, and how they can all be seen as theories of the same activity. The account I gave – that interpretation seeks to show the material being interpreted as the best it can be – is meant as a candidate for that more abstract description embracing, in that way, the rival theories rather than contending with them. It explains why the author's intention theory seems appealing to some critics but not others. The former believe or assume that the point of literature is essentially communicative, so that discovering an author's communicative intentions, and showing how these are realized in his or her work, is the best way of showing the value that work can properly be claimed to have. The latter hold different views about the sources of value in literature, and these different views spawn rival ideas about which techniques of interpretation show a work in its best light. This view of the matter – this account of the level at which the author's intention thesis provides a theory of interpretation – is, I believe, suggested by the work of Professor Hirsch of the University of Virginia, who is the most powerful and illuminating exponent of that thesis.

If we keep the more abstract account of interpretation in mind, that an interpretation seeks to make of the material being interpreted the best it can be, then we insist that any interpretation of any material must be tested on two dimensions. First, it must fit that material. No interpretation of the positive law can be successful unless it can justify, broadly, the judicial decisions that have actually been reached; otherwise it cannot claim to show *these* decisions in their best light. We can state that requirement by imagining what we know not to be true, that the various decisions that form the positive law were all taken by a single official. Then the first requirement tests a proposed interpretation by asking whether that single official, guided by the principles set out in the proposed interpretation, could have made those decisions. We cannot insist on an exact fit: that every actual decision be explainable in that way. But we do insist that the fit be at least general, that no fundamental or important part of the positive law run contrary to a proposed interpretation, at least if another interpretation, much more successful in this respect, is available.

The second requirement lies on the dimension of justification. An interpretation of positive law is unsuccessful unless it offers a justification of that law, and if, as will ordinarily be the case, two competing interpretations both satisfy the first requirement of fit to an adequate degree, this second requirement of justification will discriminate between them because it will prefer the interpretation that provides the better justification. In the case of law, of course, the justification in question is one of political morality. Showing positive law in its best light means showing it as the best course of statesmanship possible.

That fact will confirm, for many of you, a suspicion that must have been growing throughout this brief account of interpretation. You will think that it makes interpretation irredeemably subjective, that since two interpreters of the law may very well have different convictions about whether a particular interpretation fits well enough to succeed on the first dimension, and are very likely to have different political convictions about which provides a better justification in political morality on the second, interpretation is just a matter of opinion and no one's interpretation could claim to be "objectively" any better than any one else's. I believe that this is the wrong conclusion to draw, that this use of the troublesome distinction between "subjective" and "objective" is confused and adds nothing useful to any discussion of either interpretation or political morality. I have tried to defend that view elsewhere,[2] but I will not expand on it now, because I can continue my argument without it.

Construe, if you like, my description of the interpretive model of adjudication "subjectively." It then becomes an account of the questions a judge should put to himself and answer from his own "subjective" convictions about fit and political morality. Since these are in any case different from the questions the positivist model requires him to put to himself, and draws on a different set of "subjective" convictions, the difference between the two models will be preserved, and so will the question I shall shortly consider, which is whether we have any basis for choosing between the two models.

III

My discussion of interpretation, and of the interpretive model of adjudication, has been exceedingly abstract. I shall try to make it somewhat more concrete by showing how a judge who accepted the interpretive model would attack the problem posed by the recent case I referred to earlier, which is *Dronenburg*.[3] The facts of that case can be stated quickly enough. Dronenburg served with distinction in the Navy for many years, but was discharged when he admitted homosexual acts in a barracks. He sued the Navy claiming that his discharge for that reason violated his constitutional rights.

The interpretive model recommends the following method of studying his claim. We begin by identifying the positive law in the neighborhood of the problem. This consists, first, in the text of the constitutional clauses Dronenburg cited, and then in the past decisions of the Supreme Court under those clauses. For our illustration we may limit the positive law to the text of the Due Process Clause and the set of decisions usually called the "privacy" decisions. *Griswold*[4] decided that states may not prohibit the use of contraceptives by married couples. *Eisenstadt*[5] confirmed that the right to contraception extends to unmarried couples as well, and *Carey*[6] condemned a New York statute requiring contraceptives to be bought only from licensed pharmacists and prohibiting their sale to children under sixteen. The Court has upheld the right to "privacy" in other contexts: for example, in *Loving*,[7] which held a Virginia statute prohibiting interracial marriage unconstitutional. The most dramatic of the "privacy" decisions so far, however, is the abortion issue, *Roe v Wade*.[8] The Court cited the contraception decisions and *Loving* to justify its ruling that the states could not constitutionally prohibit abortion in the first trimester of pregnancy.

This limited description of the positive law provides our preinterpretive base, and we must now ask which set of principles would provide the best interpretation, that is to say the best justification, of it. Which political principles would satisfy the requirement of the first dimension, the requirement of fit? I can think of two principles that might well be thought to fit, and I shall consider only these, though you might well be able to think of more. First, the decisions just described could have been made by a single statesman acting to enforce a version of Mill's famous principle, which holds that the state must not prohibit acts that harm no one just because these acts are widely considered immoral or sinful. Second, they could have been made by a statesman who accepted the narrower principle that the state may not legislate to restrict liberty touching decisions about procreation.

Suppose each of these two principles does fit the decisions of the positive law.[9] It matters very much which we accept as the better interpretation of that law. If Mill's principle is a better interpretation, then the full or genuine law protects Dronenburg through the constitutional right he claims. If the second principle, limited to procreation, is superior, then it does not (unless some other principle favoring him can be found elsewhere in constitutional law) because the choice of homosexual sex cannot plausibly be treated as a choice about procreation even though it has consequences for it. So our attention shifts to the second dimension of interpretation; we must ask which of our two putative interpretations provides a better justification of the decisions from the point of view of political morality. Can there be much doubt that the first is superior? It states a recognizable ideal of moral independence that will have considerable appeal even to those who cannot accept it in full. The second principle, which declares only that the state may not intervene in personal decisions about procreation, is not really, on a second look, a principle at all. It sets out an arbitrary line unconnected to any recognizable distinction of moral importance. It offers no reason why intimate personal decisions about procreation should be protected from state regulation though other intimate decisions need not be so protected, and we have no reason at hand in either the literature or common culture of morality that could justify that distinction.

Though, as I emphasized earlier, the interpretive model will often produce different results for different people, because the convictions they bring to bear on the questions the model provides are different, *Dronenburg* strikes me as an easy case within that model.[10] Under that model the full, genuine law holds for Dronenburg. Now please reconsider, in the light of this example, the three "mysteries" I described at the beginning of this lecture.

On the surface a decision for Dronenburg, under the claim that the constitutional right of privacy extends to homosexuals, is a change in the law, because that right is not explicit in the text of the Constitution and had not before been recognized by the Supreme Court. But we can now, I hope, see the sense in the claim that if the interpretive argument justifying this change is a good argument the change was directed by the positive law itself, realizing what can sensibly be called its own ambitions. That is only a way – I agree that it is not the most pellucid way – of saying that the positive law constrains what can count as its best interpretation, and this is patently so. The second claim we found mysterious argues that a change produced through adjudication is not neutral but an improvement, that law purer is law better. This, too, can be restated as a feature of the interpretive model we have developed, for it claims only the converse of the second requirement of interpretation we distinguished. Since an interpretation is better if it provides a better justification in political morality, then a change guided by a better interpretation will for that reason alone be an improvement. Our third "mystery" insisted that change guided by the law itself is not genuine change but only clarification of law as it stands already. That is simply the contrast between positive and full law made to sound more mysterious than it is, and the practical upshot we noticed survives the demystification. For the interpretive model insists that if the best interpretation of the positive law, and therefore the most accurate statement of the full law, yields a constitutional right for Dronenburg, then denying him that right is not merely refusing to make a change in the law that would improve it, but is itself a denial of legality, an insult to the rule of law.

IV

So the interpretive model does give point to the old metaphors and does show the illuminating power of the attitudes towards adjudication and the law they expressed. The positivist assault on those attitudes rejected not a patently absurd metaphysics but a perfectly practical style of judging. I said that the positivist critique had become the weapon of conservative lawyers in their opposition to the use of our Constitution to protect individual rights against the state. The judge who actually decided *Dronenburg* is, as it happens, a self-conscious member of the school of conservative positivists, and we may therefore turn to his opinion hoping to sharpen our sense of the contrast between the two styles of adjudication we have now distinguished.

Indeed, the contrast could hardly be more complete. Judge Bork set out the positive law I have described, but only to show that it did not contain, as positive law, any explicit recognition of a constitutional right protecting homosexuals. That, for him, was decisive of whether Dronenburg already had the constitutional right he claimed. He did not. So the only question left for adjudication was whether lower-court federal judges should create a new right in his favor, and this question, for Bork, answered itself. He allowed himself to say that, in his opinion, even the justices of the Supreme Court should not create new constitutional rights because in so doing they exceed their legitimate powers as judges. But he thought it obvious that, whatever the Supreme Court should or should not do, lower-court justices should not usurp powers not rightfully theirs. He decided, on that ground alone, against Dronenburg's claim. This opinion is remarkable for its crude positivist character. The positive law is all the law there is, and any change would be a piece of legislation merely, in this case, a constitutional amendment in defiance of the amending procedures that document itself provides.

V

So we have two models for adjudication: the interpretive model that, in this instance at least, argues for improved protection of individual rights and the positivist model that argues, at least here, against that development. What grounds could we have for choosing between these two models? It is easier to describe the grounds we do *not* have for that choice.

Positivists often appeal to skepticism as a reason for rejecting the ideas that come together in the interpretive model. This is sometimes metaphysical skepticism, expressed in comments like Holmes' scornful remark that law is not a brooding omnipresence in the sky. But this form of skepticism is available only so long as positivism can treat its opponent as committed to some ghostly form of natural law. It is not appropriate when the older tradition is restated as the interpretive model. That model seems to encourage a different form of skepticism, however, which is moral skepticism in the shape of the following argument. If two lawyers disagree about which set of principles shows positive law in the best light, there can be no right answer to that question, and therefore no single answer dictated by the interpretive model. That argument seems to me a poor one, as I said; but even if it were sound it would provide no argument for positivism against interpretation as general styles of adjudication. For positivism requires judges to make controversial judgments of political morality just as often as the interpretive model does. It is true – and important – that the questions of political morality the interpretive model puts to judges are different, and invoke different convictions, from the questions of morality positivism puts, but if there can be no right answer to the former there can be none to the latter either. So moral skepticism provides as strong – or as weak – an objection to each of the two styles of adjudication, and offers no ground for choosing between them (or, indeed, between either of them and any other theory about how judges should decide hard cases).

Legal philosophers once thought that the choice between theories of adjudication could be made on semantic grounds or (what comes to much the same thing) on grounds of conceptual clarity or convenience. Positivism was supposed to capture how lawyers use the word "law", or at least to provide a superior way to use that word. But these claims foundered for two reasons. First, they are false as claims about how lawyers talk: it is not true that almost all lawyers use "law" to refer only to positive law. (Indeed, positivists have had to invent implausible epicycles of linguistic theory to explain why they do not.) Second, since our two models are substantively different – the difference is illustrated dramatically by the different consequences of the two models in *Dronenburg* – the choice we must make is between the models themselves, not how we should speak about or within them.

We can dismiss a third suggestion, about how to choose between the two models of adjudication, equally quickly. I mean the argument Bork relied on so heavily in *Dronenburg*, that the interpretive model he refused to follow is *illegitimate* in the constitutional context because judges who follow that model usurp powers of constitutional amendment. That argument simply and directly begs the question at issue, for what the constitution actually is, at any moment, depends on which model of adjudication is the proper one to use in constitutional adjudication. If the interpretive model is the right one, for us, then our Constitution already consists of what that model identifies as the full constitutional law, and then it is *Bork's* decision declining to enforce the full law that is illegitimate, that amends the Constitution by fiat.

I anticipated this point in remarking, early in this lecture, this practical consequence of the set of ideas we have now restated in the interpretive model: it makes the scope of the rule of law, and therefore the legitimate power of judges, turn on what it identifies as the full law rather than the positive law it takes as the object of interpretation. Of course it would beg the question in the opposite direction if I were to argue, on behalf of the interpretive model, that Bork's positivistic decision was a piece of illegitimate usurpation because it amended the constitution. Claims of legitimacy of illegitimacy are part of the conclusion of an argument for a model of adjudication, and so cannot themselves figure in that argument.

It is time I turned from arguments we should reject for choosing one of our two models over the other, however, to consider whether there are any we should accept. We might well be tempted to ask which model itself provides a better interpretation of our constitutional practice. It seems plain that the interpretive model fits that practice much better. It is, indeed, a large complaint of the conservative positivists that the Supreme Court has too often decided cases in the interpretive spirit. We should not rely too heavily on that observation, however, because these conservatives might reply that the positivist model fits enough of constitutional practice – or, if not, that it fits enough of legal practice in the United States more generally – to remain eligible on the dimension of fit. So we should compare the two models on the other dimension of interpretation by asking which provides a better justification, in political morality, for the practices it claims to fit. We have an even stronger reason for turning at once to that directly political question. Positivists may claim that it begs the question, in much the way I just said Bork's argument does, to argue for the interpretive model on interpretive grounds. But if we reject the interpretive test, for that reason, then the test of political morality, where the interpretive test was already leading us, would be the only remaining method of comparing the two models.

by whom

We might begin the political test by noticing that the interpretive model supposes and serves a distinct political virtue: political integrity. The model assumes that the state, as policeman, must speak with one voice in the following sense. If it relies on one set of political principles to justify its use of coercive power in one area, it must allow those principles their natural extension. If it must rely on some version of Mill's principle, for example, to justify denying the majority the decision whether people should be permitted to use contraceptives, or to marry interracially, or to have abortions in the first trimester of pregnancy, it must extend the protection of that principle to homosexuals as well.

Can we find a comparable underlying political virtue for the positivist model of constitutional adjudication expressed in Bork's opinion? I believe so: it is the virtue of economic efficiency, conceived as the goal of satisfying the preferences of the community overall, including its political and moral as well as its more narrowly economic preferences. It is no accident that the foremost academic supporters of conservative constitutional policy are also the most obdurate advocates of what is called economic analysis in other areas of the law. Their conviction that the majority's political power should be limited as little as possible – that it should be limited only by the explicit text of the Constitution or the unambiguous intentions of its framers – reflects the same unexpressed political theory as their ambition that the rules of contract, tort, and property be constructed so as to maximize social wealth. Both reflect an unrestricted utilitarianism that allows the preferences of many people to override those of a few, in some overall calculation of a social preference, and denies any constraint on the kind of preferences that must be counted in that calculation. My preferences about how you lead your life, in other words, count as much as yours.

The conflict between the underlying virtues we have now identified for our two models – integrity for the interpretive model and efficiency for the positivist model – is clear enough. Integrity is, from the point of view of efficiency, both arbitrary and irrational: arbitrary because it cannot be drawn from unrestricted utilitarianism, and irrational because it will prove, except in the rarest cases, incompatible with it. A social engineer anxious to achieve the fullest possible satisfaction of everyone's preferences in the long run could not accept integrity as a constraint, because the preferences he seeks to satisfy are unlikely themselves to be disciplined by the principled coherence integrity would impose on them. Our leading example shows this dramatically. Many people prefer that others not have contraceptives, abortions, or homosexual sex. But the phenomenological profiles of these different "external" preferences are very different: they differ in their popularity, emotional charge, and connection to other "moral" views. Perhaps the overall satisfaction of preferences would be improved, in the long run, by some constitutional constraint prohibiting temporary majorities from banning contraception. But it hardly follows that a constraint prohibiting punishing homosexuals would have the same consequence, because the mix and character of preferences, not to mention side effects, is so different in that case.

The conflict between the two virtues seems sharper still when we reflect on the ideals of community associated with each. In a community regulated by efficiency each person sees other people as resources and competitors: resources because his preferences include and are supported by preferences about how they should act, competitors because the satisfaction of their preferences is likely to impinge on the satisfaction of his. There is no sorority or fraternity in this picture of society; it is the picture of politics as commerce by other means. A society dedicated to integrity, on the contrary, aims at the most intense version of community compatible with moral diversity.

We are not a community tied together by a concrete moral settlement, by shared opinions about the details of what justice and fairness and a decent and valuable life require. (We would, I believe, be a worse community if we did achieve consensus about these matters.) We debate about justice and fairness through the institutions we have, seeking, as part of that debate, to reform these institutions as we use them, acknowledging that any institutional structure we achieve is provisional, that no decision of majority or executive or court is right just because it has been taken, or right just because it must be respected so long as it stands. We march in this way toward what we hope is a better community, fairer and more just; we march we hope forward though we all believe some steps are backward. But we nevertheless recognize community in our present diversity, and so accept, in the name of community, a special and further constraint. We march together so that the settlements of principle we reach from time to time, as plateaus for further campaigns, extend to everyone. We leave no wounded behind, no abandoned minorities of race or gender or sexual disposition, even when bringing them along delays the gains of others.

If you find that vision of community more attractive than the community of efficiency, as I do, then you will find in it the only kind of argument we can have for one conception of law over another. It points us toward the interpretive model, toward the set of ideas locked in the old metaphors about law's ambitions for itself. You may find one feature of my argument odd. You may find it odd that the lawyers' contest about styles of adjudication finally turns in the way I claim of ideals of community, that volumes of philosophy speak in the fall of every judge's gavel. It may be odd, but I'm sure it's true, and even a little thrilling ...

NOTES

1 See, e.g., R. Dworkin, "Law as Interpretation," in *A Matter of Principle*, pt. 2 (Harvard Univ. Press, 1985).

2 Ibid., p. 167.

3 *Dronenburg v Zech*, 741 F.2d 1388 (DC Cir. 1984).

4 *Griswold v Connecticut*, 381 US 479 (1965).

5 *Eisenstadt v Baird*, 405 US 438 (1971).

6 *Carey v Population Servs. Int'l*, 431 US 678 (1977).

7 *Loving v Virginia*, 388 US 1 (1967).

8 410 US 113 (1973).

9 The assumption that the first interpretation, which appeals to Mill's principle, fits the abortion decision requires the controversial further assumption that a fetus is not a person within the first trimester, and this assumption might therefore be a necessary part of any competent interpretation of the full set of privacy decisions. Or, perhaps, Mill's principle might be used to justify the other decisions in the "privacy" group and some further principle found, if any could be, to justify the abortion decision independently. In either case Mill's principle would then be *part* of an interpretation of the decisions as a whole, though not exhaustive of it.

10 I should repeat, however, that this claim is not necessary to my main purpose, which is to show the model at work and how it differs from the positivist model I shall shortly use Bork's actual decision in *Dronenburg* to illustrate.

Law's Empire

THE CHAIN OF LAW

The Chain Novel

I argued in Chapter 2 that creative interpretation takes its formal structure from the idea of intention, not (at least not necessarily) because it aims to discover the purposes of any particular historical person or group but because it aims to impose purpose over the text or data or tradition being interpreted. Since all creative interpretation shares this feature, and therefore has a normative aspect or component, we profit from comparing law with other forms or occasions of interpretation. We can usefully compare the judge deciding what the law is on some issue not only with the citizens of courtesy deciding what the tradition requires, but with the literary critic teasing out the various dimensions of value in a complex play or poem.

Judges, however, are authors as well as critics. A judge deciding *McLoughlin* or *Brown* adds to the tradition he interprets; future judges confront a new tradition that includes what he has done. Of course literary criticism contributes to the traditions of art in which authors work; the character and importance of that contribution are themselves issues in critical theory. But the contribution of judges is more direct, and the distinction between author and interpreter more a matter of different aspects of the same process. We can find an even more fruitful comparison between literature and law, therefore, by constructing an artificial genre of literature that we might call the chain novel.

In this enterprise a group of novelists writes a novel *seriatim*; each novelist in the chain interprets the chapters he has been given in order to write a new chapter, which is then added to what the next novelist receives, and so on. Each has the job of writing his chapter so as to make the novel being constructed the best it can be, and the complexity of this task models the complexity of deciding a hard case under law as integrity. The imaginary literary enterprise is fantastic but not unrecognizable. Some novels have actually been written in this way, though mainly for a debunking purpose, and certain parlor games for rainy weekends in English country houses have something of the same structure. Television soap operas span decades with the same characters and some minimal continuity of personality and plot, though they are written by different teams of authors even in different weeks. In our example, however, the novelists are expected to take their responsibilities of continuity more seriously; they aim jointly to create, so far as they can, a single unified novel that is the best it can be.

Each novelist aims to make a single novel of the material he has been given, what he adds to it, and (so far as he can control this) what his successors will want or be able to add. He must try to make this the best novel it can be construed as the work of a single author rather than, as is the fact, the product of many different hands. That calls for an overall judgment on his part, or a series of overall judgments as he writes and rewrites. He must take up some view about the novel in progress, some working theory about its characters, plot, genre, theme, and point, in order to decide what counts as continuing it and not as beginning anew. If he is a good critic, his view of these matters will be complicated and multifaceted, because the value of a decent novel cannot be captured from a single perspective. He will aim to find layers and currents of meaning rather than a single, exhaustive theme. We can, however, in our now familiar way give some structure to any interpretation he adopts, by distinguishing two dimensions on which it must be tested. The first is what we have been calling the dimension of fit. He cannot adopt any interpretation, however complex, if he believes that no single author who set out to write a novel with the various readings of character, plot, theme, and point that interpretation describes could have written substantially the text he has been given. That does not mean his interpretation must fit every bit of the text. It is not disqualified simply because he claims that some lines or tropes are accidental, or even that some events of plot are mistakes because they work against the literary ambitions the interpretation states. But the interpretation he takes up must nevertheless flow throughout the text; it must have general explanatory power, and it is flawed if it leaves unexplained some major structural aspect of the text, a subplot treated as having great dramatic importance or a dominant and repeated metaphor. If no interpretation can be found that is not flawed in that way, then the chain novelist will not be able fully to meet his assignment; he will have to settle for an interpretation that captures most of the text, conceding that it is not wholly successful. Perhaps even that partial success is unavailable; perhaps every interpretation he considers is inconsistent with the bulk of the material supplied to him. In that case he must abandon the enterprise, for the consequence of taking the interpretive attitude toward the text in question is then a piece of internal skepticism; that nothing can count as continuing the novel rather than beginning anew.

He may find, not that no single interpretation fits the bulk of the text, but that more than one does. The second dimension of interpretation then requires him to judge which of these eligible readings makes the work in progress best, all things considered. At this point his more substantive aesthetic judgments, about the importance or insight or realism or beauty of different ideas the novel might be taken to express, come into play. But the formal and structural considerations that dominate on the first dimension figure on the second as well, for even when neither of two interpretations is disqualified out of hand as explaining too little, one may show the text in a better light because it fits more of the text or provides a more interesting integration of style and content. So the distinction between the two dimensions is less crucial or profound than it might seem. It is a useful analytical device that helps us give structure to any interpreter's working theory or style. He will form a sense of when an interpretation fits so poorly that it is unnecessary to consider its substantive appeal, because he knows that this cannot outweigh its embarrassments of fit in deciding whether it makes the novel better, everything taken into account, than its rivals. This sense will define the first dimension for him. But he need not reduce his intuitive sense to any precise formula; he would rarely need to decide whether some interpretation barely survives or barely fails, because a bare survivor, no matter how ambitious or interesting it claimed the text to be, would almost certainly fail in the overall comparison with other interpretations whose fit was evident.

We can now appreciate the range of different kinds of judgments that are blended in this overall comparison. Judgments about textual coherence and integrity, reflecting different formal literary values, are interwoven with more substantive aesthetic judgments that themselves assume different literary aims. Yet these various kinds of judgments, of each general kind, remain distinct enough to check on another in an overall assessment, and it is that possibility of contest, particularly between textual and substantive judgments, that distinguishes a chain novelist's assignment from more independent creative writing. Nor can we draw any flat distinction between the stage at which a chain novelist interprets the text he has been given and the stage at which he adds his own chapter, guided by the interpretation he has settled on. When he begins to write he might discover in what he has written a different, perhaps radically different, interpretation. Or he might find it impossible to write in the tone or theme he first took up, and that will lead him to reconsider other interpretations he first rejected. In either case he returns to the text to reconsider the lines it makes eligible.

Scrooge

We can expand this abstract description of the chain novelist's judgment through an example. Suppose you are a novelist well down the chain. Suppose Dickens never wrote *A Christmas Carol*, and the text you are furnished, though written by several people, happens to be the first part of that short novel. You consider these two interpretations of the central character: Scrooge is inherently and irredeemably evil, an embodiment of the untarnished wickedness of human nature freed from the disguises of convention he rejects; or Scrooge is inherently good but progressively corrupted by the false values and perverse demands of high capitalist society. Obviously it will make an enormous difference to the way you continue the story which of these interpretations you adopt. If you have been given almost all of *A Christmas Carol* with only the very end to be written – Scrooge has already had his dreams, repented, and sent his turkey – it is too late for you to make him irredeemably wicked, assuming you think, as most interpreters would, that the text will not bear that interpretation without too much strain. I do not mean that no interpreter could possibly think Scrooge inherently evil after his supposed redemption. Someone might take that putative redemption to be a final act of hypocrisy, though only at the cost of taking much else in the text not at face value. This would be a poor interpretation, not because no one could think it a good one, but because it is in fact, on all the criteria so far described, a poor one ...

READING QUESTIONS ON DWORKIN

1 What is Dworkin's middle ground between history and moral recommendation?
2 Can Dworkin really rely on law to work itself pure? There's an old saying "garbage in, garbage out." Dworkin seems confident that any legal system starts with enough good to generate freedom and equality in the end. What features of a legal system make him so confident? Is his belief realistic?

3 Positivists have conceded that legal systems often include moral
   values, but insist those values simply reflect the views of those
   with the power to make law. How might Dworkin reply to such a
   challenge?

Riggs v Palmer (1889)

A nineteenth-century New York case involving the right of an heir to inherit
from the grandfather he had murdered. This case raises the question of the
relation between moral principles and statutory interpretation.

RIGGS ET AL. V PALMER ET AL.

(Court of Appeals of New York. Oct. 8, 1889.)

Rights of Legatees – Murder of Testator.

The Laws of New York relating to the probate of wills and the distributions of estates will not be construed so as to secure the benefit of a will
to a legatee who has killed the testator in order to prevent a revocation
of the will. Gray and Danforth, JJ, dissenting.
   Appeal from supreme court, general term, third department.
   Leslie W. Russell, for appellants. *W.M.Hawkins*, for respondents.

Earl, J: On the 13th day of August, 1880, Francis B. Palmer made his last
will and testament, in which he gave small legacies to his two daughters, Mrs Riggs and Mrs Preston, the plaintiffs in this action, and the
remainder of his estate to his grandson, the defendant Elmer E. Palmer,
subject to the support of Susan Palmer, his mother, with a gift over to
the two daughters, subject to the support of Mrs Palmer in case Elmer
should survive him and die under age, unmarried, and without any
issue. The testator, at the date of his will, owned a farm, and considerable personal property. He was a widower, and thereafter, in March,
1882, he was married to Mrs Bresee, with whom, before his marriage,
he entered into an ante-nuptial contract, in which it was agreed that in
lieu of dower and all other claims upon his estate in case she survived

him she should have her support upon his farm during her life, and such support was expressly charged upon the farm. At the date of the will, and subsequently to the death of the testator, Elmer lived with him as a member of his family, and at his death was 16 years old. He knew of the provisions made in his favor in the will, and, that he might prevent his grandfather from revoking such provisions, which he had manifested some intention to do, and to obtain the speedy enjoyment and immediate possession of his property, he willfully murdered him by poisoning him. He now claims the property, and the sole question for our determination is, can he have it?

The defendants say that the testator is dead; that his will was made in due form, and has been admitted to probate; and that therefore it must have effect according to the letter of the law. It is quite true that statutes regulating the making, proof, and effect of wills and the devolution of property, if literally construed, and if their force and effect can in no way and under no circumstances be controlled or modified, give this property to the murderer. The purpose of those statutes was to enable testators to dispose of their estates to the objects of their bounty at death, and to carry into effect their final wishes legally expressed; and in considering and giving effect to them this purpose must be kept in view ...

In 1 Bl. Comm. 91, the learned author, speaking of the construction of statutes, says: "If there arise out of them collaterally any absurd consequences manifestly contradictory to common reason, they are with regard to those collateral consequences void. * * * Where some collateral matter arises out of the general words, and happens to be unreasonable, there the judges are in decency to conclude that this consequence was not foreseen by the parliament, and therefore they are at liberty to expound the statute by equity, and only *quoad hoc* disregard it"; and he gives as an illustration, if an act of parliament gives a man power to try all causes that arise within his manor of Dale, yet, if a cause should arise in which he himself is party, the act is construed not to extend to that, because it is unreasonable that any man should determine his own quarrel. There was a statute in Bologna that whoever drew blood in the streets should be severely punished, and yet it was held not to apply to the case of a barber who opened a vein in the street. It is commanded in the decalogue that no work shall be done upon the Sabbath, and yet giving the command a rational interpretation founded upon its design the Infallible Judge held that it did not prohibit works of necessity, charity, or benevolence on that day.

What could be more unreasonable than to suppose that it was the legislative intention in the general laws passed for the orderly, peaceable, and just devolution of property that they should have operation in favor of one who murdered his ancestor that he might speedily come into the possession of his estate? Such an intention is inconceivable. We need not, therefore, be much troubled by the general language contained in the laws. Besides, all laws, as well as all contracts, may be controlled in their operation and effect by general, fundamental maxims of the common law. No one shall be permitted to profit by his own fraud, or to take advantage of his own wrong, or to found any claim upon his own iniquity, or to acquire property by his own crime. These maxims are dictated by public policy, have their foundation in universal law administered in all civilized countries, and have nowhere been superseded by statutes. They were applied in the decision of the case of Insurance Co. v. Armstrong. There it was held that the person who procured a policy upon the life of another, payable at his death, and then murdered the assured to make the policy payable, could not recover thereon ...

Here there was no certainty that this murderer would survive the testator, or that the testator would not change his will, and there was no certainty that he would get this property if nature was allowed to take its course. He therefore murdered the testator expressly to vest himself with an estate. Under such circumstances, what law, human or divine, will allow him to take the estate and enjoy the fruits of his crime? The will spoke and became operative at the death of the testator. He caused that death, and thus by his crime made it speak and have operation. Shall it speak and operate in his favor? If he had met the testator, and taken his property by force, he would have had no title to it. Shall he acquire title by murdering him? If he had gone to the testator's house, and by force compelled him, or by fraud or undue influence had induced him, to will him his property, the law would not allow him to hold it. But can he give effect and operation to a will by murder, and yet take the property? To answer these questions in the affirmative it seems to me would be a reproach to the jurisprudence of our state, and an offense against public policy ...

In the Civil Code of Lower Canada the provisions on the subject in the Code Napoleon have been substantially copied. But, so far as I can find, in no country where the common law prevails has it been deemed important to enact a law to provide for such a case. Our revisers and law-makers were familiar with the civil law, and they did not deem it important to incorporate into our statutes its provisions upon this subject. This is not a *casus omissus*. It was evidently supposed that the maxims of the common law were sufficient to regulate such a case, and that a specific enactment for that purpose was not needed. For the same reasons the defendant Palmer cannot take any of this property as heir. Just before the murder he was not an heir, and it was not certain that he ever would be. He might have died before his grandfather, or might have been disinherited by him. He made himself an heir by the murder, and he seeks to take property as the fruit of his crime. What has before been said as to him as legatee applies to him with equal force as an heir. He cannot vest himself with title by crime. My view of this case does not inflict upon Elmer any greater or other punishment for his crime than the law specifies. It takes from him no property, but simply holds that he shall not acquire property by his crime, and thus be rewarded for its commission.

Gray, J (*dissenting*): This appeal presents an extraordinary state of facts, and the case, in respect of them, I believe, is without precedent in this state. The respondent, a lad of 16 years of age, being aware of the provisions in his grandfather's will, which constituted him the residuary legatee of the testator's estate, caused his death by poison, in 1882. For this crime he was tried, and was convicted of murder in the second degree, and at the time of the commencement of this action he was serving out his sentence in the state reformatory. This action was brought by two of the children of the testator for the purpose of having those provisions of the will in the respondent's favor canceled and annulled. The appellants' argument for a reversal of the judgment, which dismissed their complaint, is that the respondent unlawfully prevented a revocation of the existing will, or a new will from being made, by his crime; and that he terminated the enjoyment by the testator of his property, and effected his own succession to it, by the same crime. They say that to permit the respondent to take the property willed to him would be to permit him to take advantage of his own wrong. To sustain their position the appellants' counsel has submitted an able and elaborate brief, and, if I believed that the decision of the question could be effected by consideration of an equitable nature, I should not hesitate to assent to views which commend themselves to the conscience. But the matter does not lie within the domain of conscience. We are bound by the rigid rules of law, which have been established by the legislature, and within the limits of which the determination of this question is confined. The question we are dealing with is whether a testamentary disposition can be altered, or a will revoked, after the testator's death, through an appeal to the courts, when the legislature has by its enactments prescribed exactly when and how wills may be made, altered, and revoked, and apparently, as it seems to me, when they have been fully complied with, has left no room for the exercise of an equitable jurisdiction by courts over such matters. Modern jurisprudence, in recognizing the right of the individual, under more or less restrictions, to dispose of his property after his death, subjects it to legislative control, both as to extent and as to mode of exercise. Complete freedom of testamentary disposition of one's property has not been and is not the universal rule, as we see from the provisions of the Napoleonic Code, from the systems of jurisprudence in countries which are modeled upon the Roman law, and from the statutes of many of our states. To the statutory restraints which are imposed upon the disposition of one's property by will are added strict and systematic statutory rules for the execution, alteration, and revocation of the will, which must be, at least substantially, if not exactly, followed to insure validity and performance. The reason for the establishment of such rules, we may naturally assume, consists in the purpose to create those safeguards about these grave and important acts which experience has demonstrated to be the wisest and surest. That freedom which is permitted to be exercised in the testamentary disposition of one's estate by the laws of the state is subject to its being exercised in conformity with the regulations of the statutes. The capacity and the power of the individual to dispose of his property after death, and the mode by which that power can be exercised, are matters of which the legislature has assumed the entire control, and has undertaken to regulate with comprehensive particularity.

The appellants' argument is not helped by reference to those rules of the civil law, or to those laws of other governments, by which the heir, or legatee, is excluded from benefit under the testament if he has been convicted of killing, or attempting to kill, the testator.

In the absence of such legislation here, the courts are not empowered to institute such a system of remedial justice. The deprivation of the heir of his testamentary succession by the Roman law, when guilty of such a crime, plainly was intended to be in the nature of a punishment imposed upon him. The succession, in such a case of guilt, escheated to the exchequer. See Dom. Civil Law, pt. 2, bk. 1, tit. 1, s. 3. I concede that rules of law which annul testamentary provisions made for the benefit of those who have become unworthy of them may be based on principles of equity and of natural justice. It is quite reasonable to suppose that a testator would revoke or alter his will, where his mind has been so angered and changed as to make him unwilling to have his will executed as it stood. But these principles only suggest sufficient reasons for the enactment of laws to meet such cases.

The statutes of this state have prescribed various ways in which a will may be altered or revoked; but the very provision defining the modes of alteration and revocation implies a prohibition of alteration or revocation in any other way. The words of the section of the statute are: "No will in writing, except in the cases hereinafter mentioned, nor any part thereof, shall be revoked or altered otherwise," etc. Where, therefore, none of the cases mentioned are met by the facts, and the revocation is not in the way described in the section, the will of the testator is unalterable. I think that a valid will must continue as a will always, unless revoked in the manner provided by the statutes. Mere intention to revoke a will does not have the effect of revocation.

READING QUESTIONS ON RIGGS V PALMER

1 Earl, J says that the law will not allow a man to profit from his own wrongdoing. Where does he find this principle? Can you think of exceptions to it? If so, in what sense is it supposed to be binding?
2 Putting aside the question of Riggs's wrongdoing and the appropriate punishment for it, do you find Grey, J's view of the judicial role more appealing?

2

Adjudication

The core of Dworkin's argument against positivism is that positivism is not, in fact, a theory of law as it purports to be, but rather a theory of adjudication. As a theory of adjudication, it leads to bad decisions. The readings in this section explore that charge by looking in part at some horrendous decisions that judges have claimed to have been compelled to make by the positive law. The final selection offers a sophisticated version of positivism that is not supposed to be vulnerable to such charges.

Patriation Reference 25 DLR 3d 1

In this case, the Supreme Court was called upon to decide whether the federal government had the constitutional power to repatriate the constitution without first securing the consent of the provinces. The case amalgamated appeals from a number of provincial courts, and also combined questions from those cases with slightly different wording. The Court held that there was no legal requirement of provincial consent, but that there was a conventional requirement. The case is philosophically important because it raises questions about the sources of law, and the nature and role of legal conventions. The case also illustrates the dispute between legal positivists and their critics. Where positivists suppose that conventions are not binding, anti-positivists such as Dworkin suppose entrenched practices that have not been authoritatively enacted can nonetheless create legal rights.

ON THE APPEAL FROM THE QUEBEC COURT OF APPEAL

A. If the Canada Act and the Constitution Act 1981 should come into force and if they should be valid in all respects in Canada would they affect:
(i) the legislative competence of the provincial legislatures in virtue of the Canadian Constitution?
(ii) the status or role of the provincial legislatures or governments within the Canadian Federation?

ON QUESTION 1 FROM THE MANITOBA AND NEWFOUNDLAND REFERENCES AND QUESTION A FROM THE QUEBEC REFERENCE

Per curiam: Under the terms of the enactments proposed in the Resolution, the legislative powers of the provincial Legislatures would be limited by the Charter of Rights and Freedoms. The limitations of the proposed Charter of Rights and Freedoms on legislative power apply both at the federal level and the provincial level. This does not, however, alter the fact that there is an intended suppression of provincial legislative power. Moreover, the enhancement of provincial legislative authority under some provisions of the proposed enactment, as, for example, in respect of resource control, including interprovincial export (albeit subject to federal paramountcy), and in respect of taxing power, does not alter the fact that there is an effect on existing federal-provincial relationships under these and other provisions of the draft statute intended for submission to enactment by the Parliament of the United Kingdom.

ON QUESTION 2 FROM THE MANITOBA AND NEWFOUNDLAND REFERENCES AND THE CONVENTIONAL ASPECT OF QUESTION B FROM THE QUEBEC REFERENCE

2. Is it a constitutional convention that the House of Commons and Senate of Canada will not request Her Majesty the Queen to lay before the Parliament of the United Kingdom of Great Britain and Northern Ireland a measure to amend the Constitution of Canada affecting federal-provincial relationships or the powers, rights or privileges granted or secured by the Constitution of Canada to the provinces, their legislatures or governments without first obtaining the agreement of the provinces?

Per Martland, Ritchie, Dickson, Beetz, Chouinard and Lamer, JJ: A substantial part of the rules of the Canadian Constitution is written. They are contained not in a single document called a "Constitution" but in a great variety of statutes some of which have been enacted by the Parliament of Westminster, such as the British North America Act, 1867, or by the Parliament of Canada, such as the Alberta Act, 1905 (Can.), c. 3, the Saskatchewan Act, 1905 (Can.), c. 42, and the Senate and House of Commons Act, R.S.C. 1970, c. S-8, or by the provincial Legislatures, such as the provincial electoral Acts. They are also to be found in Orders in Council like the Imperial Order in Council of May 16, 1871, admitting British Columbia into the Union, and Imperial Order in Council of June 26, 1873, admitting Prince Edward Island into the Union. Another part of the Constitution of Canada consists of the rules of the common law. These are rules which the Courts have developed over the centuries in the discharge of their judicial duties. An important portion of these rules concerns the prerogative of the Crown. Those parts of the Constitution of Canada that are composed of statutory rules and common law rules are generically referred to as the law of the Constitution. In cases of doubt or dispute it is the function of the Court to declare what the law is, and since the law is sometimes breached it is generally the function of the Courts to ascertain whether it has in fact been breached in specific instances and, if so, to apply such sanctions as are contemplated by the law, whether they be punitive sanctions or civil sanctions such as a declaration of nullity. Thus, when a federal or a provincial statute is found by the Court to be in excess of the legislative competence of the Legislature that has enacted it, it is declared null and void and the Courts refuse to give effect to it. In this sense it can be said that the law of the Constitution is administered or enforced by the Courts.

Many important parts of the Constitution of Canada, with which people are most familiar because they are directly involved when they exercise their right to vote at federal and provincial elections, are nowhere to be found in the law of the constitution. For instance, it is a fundamental requirement of the Constitution that if the Opposition obtains the majority at the polls the Government must tender its resignation forthwith. But fundamental as it is, this requirement of the Constitution does not form part of the law of the Constitution. Such essential rules of the Constitution are called conventions of the Constitution. They are the principles and rules of responsible government, which were developed in Great Britain by way of custom and precedent during the nineteenth century and were exported to such British colonies as were granted self-government. A federal constitution provides for the distribution of powers between various Legislatures and Govern-

ments and may also constitute a fertile ground for the growth of constitutional conventions between those Legislatures and Governments. It is
conceivable for instance that usage and practice might give birth to
conventions in Canada relating to the holding of federal-provincial conferences, the appointment of Lieutenant-Governors, the reservation and
disallowance of provincial legislation. The main purpose of constitutional conventions is to ensure that the legal framework of the Constitution will be operated in accordance with the prevailing constitutional
values or principles of the period. Being based on custom and precedent, constitutional conventions are usually unwritten rules. Some of
them, however, may be reduced to writing and expressed in the proceedings and documents of Imperial conferences, or in the preamble of
statutes such as the Statute of Westminster, 1931 (U.K.), c. 4, or in the
proceedings and documents of federal-provincial conferences. They are
often referred to and recognized in statements made by members of
Governments. The conventional rules of the Constitution present one
striking peculiarity: in contradistinction to the laws of the Constitution,
they are not enforced by the Courts. One reason for this situation is
that, unlike common law rules, conventions are not Judge-made rules.
They are not based on judicial precedents but on precedents established
by the institutions of government themselves. Nor are they in the nature of statutory commands which it is the function and duty of the
Courts to obey and enforce. Furthermore, to enforce them would mean
to administer some formal sanction when they are breached. But the
legal system from which they are distinct does not contemplate formal
sanctions for their breach. The main reason that conventional rules cannot be enforced by the Courts is that they are generally in conflict with
the legal rules that they postulate and the Courts are bound to enforce
the legal rules. The conflict is not of a type that would entail the commission of any illegality. It results from the fact that legal rules create
wide powers, discretions and rights which conventions prescribe should
be exercised only in a certain limited manner, if at all. This conflict
between convention and law which prevents the Courts from enforcing
conventions also prevents conventions from crystallizing into laws, unless it be by statutory adoption. It is because the sanctions of convention rest with the institutions of government other than Courts, such as
the Governor General or the Lieutenant-Governor, or the Houses of
Parliament, or with public opinion and, ultimately, with the electorate
that it is generally said that they are political. It should be borne in
mind, however, that, while they are not laws, some conventions may be

more important than some laws. Their importance depends on that of the value or principle which they are meant to safeguard. They form an integral part of the Constitution and of the constitutional system. That is why it is appropriate to say that to violate a convention is to do something which is unconstitutional although it entails no direct legal consequence. But the words "constitutional" and "unconstitutional" may also be used in a strict legal sense, for instance, with respect to a statute that is found ultra vires or unconstitutional. All this may be summarized in an equation: constitutional conventions plus constitutional law equal the total Constitution of the country ...

In determining whether a convention has been established three questions must be asked: first, what are the precedents; secondly, did the actors in the precedents believe that they were bound by a rule; and thirdly, is there a reason for the rule? A single precedent with a good reason may be enough to establish the rule. A whole string of precedents without such a reason will be of no avail, unless it is perfectly certain that the persons concerned regarded themselves as bound by it. As far as the precedents are concerned, no amendment changing provincial legislative powers has been made since Confederation when agreement of a Province whose legislative powers would have been changed was withheld. The accumulation of these precedents does not of itself suffice in establishing the existence of the convention, but it points in its direction. If the precedents stood alone, it might be argued that unanimity is required. As far as the actors in the precedents are concerned there is a recognition that the requirement of provincial agreement is a constitutional rule. However, while the precedents taken alone point at unanimity, the unanimity principle cannot be said to have been accepted by all the actors in the precedents ... Nor can it be said that this lack of precision is such as to prevent the principle from acquiring the constitutional status of a conventional rule. If a consensus had emerged on the measure of provincial agreement, an amending formula would quickly have been enacted. To demand as much precision as if this were the case and as if the rule were a legal one is tantamount to denying that this area of the Canadian Constitution is capable of being governed by conventional rules. It would not be appropriate for the Court to devise in the abstract a specific formula which would indicate in positive terms what measure of provincial agreement is required for the convention to be complied with. Conventions by their nature develop in the political field and it will be for the political actors, not the Court, to determine the degree of provincial consent required. It is sufficient for the Court to decide that at least a substantial measure of provincial consent is required and to decide further whether the situation before the Court meets with this requirement. The situation is one where Ontario and New Brunswick agree with the proposed amendments whereas the eight other Provinces oppose it. By no conceivable standard could this situation be thought to pass muster. It does not disclose a sufficient measure of provincial agreement. The reason for the rule is the federal principle. Canada is a federal union. The federal principle cannot be reconciled with a state of affairs where the modification of provincial legislative powers could be obtained by the unilateral action of the federal authorities. The purpose of this conventional rule is to protect the federal character of the Canadian Constitution and prevent the anomaly that the House of Commons and Senate could obtain by simple resolutions what they could not validly accomplish by statute.

Per Laskin, CJC, Estey and McIntyre, JJ: While we are in agreement with much of what has been said by the majority, as to the general nature of conventions, we cannot agree with any suggestion that the non-observance of a convention can properly be termed unconstitutional in any strict or legal sense, or that its observance could be, in any sense, a constitutional requirement within the meaning of Question 3 of the Manitoba and Newfoundland References. In a federal State where the essential feature of the Constitution must be the distribution of powers between the two levels of Government, each supreme in its own legislative sphere, constitutionality and legality must be synonymous, and conventional rules will be accorded less significance than they may have in a unitary State such as the United Kingdom.

Can it be said that any convention having a clear definition and acceptance concerning provincial participation in the amendment of the Canadian Constitution has developed? The answer must be "no". The degree of provincial participation in constitutional amendments has been a subject of controversy in Canadian political life for generations. No view on this subject has become so clear and so broadly accepted as to constitute a constitutional convention. The convention sought to be advanced here would truncate the functioning of the executive and legislative branches at the federal level. This would impose a limitation on the sovereign body itself within the Constitution. Such a convention would require for its recognition, even in the non-legal, political sphere, the clearest signal from the plenary unit intended to be bound, and not simply a plea from the majority of the beneficiaries of such a convention, the provincial plenary units. Since confederation Canada has grown from a group of four somewhat hesitant colonies into a modern, independent State, vastly increased in size, power and wealth, and having a social and governmental structure unimagined in 1867. Vast change has occurred in Dominion-Provincial relations over that period. Many factors have influenced this process and the amendments to the British North America Act, 1867 have played a significant part. All must receive consideration in resolving this question. Only in four cases has full provincial consent been obtained and in many cases the federal Government has proceeded with amendments in the face of active provincial opposition. It is unrealistic to say that the convention has emerged.

3. Is the agreement of the provinces of Canada constitutionally required for amendment to the Constitution of Canada where such amendment affects federal-provincial relationships or alters the powers, rights or privileges granted or secured by the Constitution of Canada to the provinces, their legislatures or governments?

Per Laskin, CJC, Dickson, Beetz, Estey, McIntyre, Chouinard, and Lamer, JJ: There are two broad aspects to the matter which divide into a number of separate issues: (1) the authority of the two federal Houses to proceed by Resolution where provincial powers and federal-provincial relationships are thereby affected, and (2) the role or authority of the Parliament of the United Kingdom to act on the Resolution. The first point concerns the need of legal power to initiate the process in Canada; the second concerns legal power or want of it in the Parliament of the United Kingdom to act on the Resolution when it does not carry the consent of the Provinces. The proposition was advanced on behalf of the Attorney-General of Manitoba that a convention may crystallize into law and that the requirement of provincial consent, although in origin political, has become a rule of law. This is not so. No instance of an explicit recognition of a convention as having matured into a rule of law was produced. The nature of a convention, as political in inception and as depending on a consistent course of political recognition by those for whose benefit and to whose detriment (if any) the convention developed over a considerable period of time, is inconsistent with its legal enforcement. There is no limit in law, either in Canada or in the United Kingdom (having regard to s. 18 of the British North America

Act, 1867, as enacted by 1875 (U.K.), c. 38, s. 1, which ties the privileges, immunities and powers of the federal Houses to those of the British House of Commons), to the power of the Houses to pass resolutions. Under s. 18 the federal Parliament may by statute define those privileges, immunities and powers so long as they do not exceed those held and enjoyed by the British House of Commons at the time of the passing of the federal statute. It is said, however, that where the Resolution touches provincial powers, there is a limitation on federal authority to pass it on to the Queen unless there is provincial consent. If there is such a limitation, it arises not from any limitation on the power to adopt resolutions but from an external limitation based on other considerations. The legal question is whether this Court can enact, by what would be judicial legislation, a formula of unanimity to initiate the amending process which would be binding not only in Canada but also on the Parliament of the United Kingdom with which amending authority would still remain.

The challenge to the competency in law of the federal Houses to seek enactment by the Parliament of the United Kingdom of the statutes embodied in the Resolution is based on the recognized supremacy of provincial Legislatures in relation to the powers conferred upon them under the British North America Act, 1867, a supremacy vis-à-vis the federal Parliament. Reinforcement, or the foundation, of this supremacy is said to lie in the nature or character of Canadian federalism. What is put forward by the Provinces that oppose the forwarding of the address without provincial consent is that external relations with Great Britain in this respect must take account of the nature and character of Canadian federalism. It is contended that a legal underpinning of their position is to be found in the Canadian federal system, as reflected in historical antecedents, in the pronouncements of leading political figures and in the preamble to the British North America Act, 1867. The arguments from history do not lead to any consistent view or any single view of the nature of the British North America Act, 1867. History cannot alter the fact that in law there is a British statute to construe and apply in relation to a matter, fundamental as it is, that is not provided for by the statute. So too with pronouncements by political figures or persons in other branches of public life. What is stressed in the preamble to the British North America Act, 1867 is the desire of the named Provinces "to be federally united with a Constitution similar in principle to that of the United Kingdom". The preamble speaks also of union into "one Dominion" and of the establishment of the Union "by authority of Parliament", that is, the United Kingdom Parliament. What, then, is to be drawn from the preamble as a matter of law? A preamble has no enacting force, but it can be called in aid to illuminate provisions of the statute in which it appears. Federal union "with a constitution similar in principle to that of the United Kingdom" may well embrace responsible government and some common law aspects of the United Kingdom's unitary constitutionalism, such as the rule of law and Crown prerogatives and immunities. There is an internal contradiction in speaking of federalism in the light of the invariable principle of British parliamentary supremacy. The resolution of this contradiction lies in the scheme of distribution of legislative power, but this owes nothing to the preamble, resting rather on its own exposition in the substantive terms of the British North America Act, 1867. It is the allocation of legislative power as between the central Parliament and the provincial Legislatures that the Provinces rely on as precluding unilateral federal action to seek amendments to the British North America Act, 1867 that affect, whether by limitation or extension, provincial legislative authority. The Attorney-General of Canada was forced to answer affirmatively the theoretical question whether in law the federal Government could procure an amendment to the British North America Act, 1867 that would turn Canada into a unitary State. That is not what the present Resolution envisages because the essential federal character of the country is preserved under the enactments proposed by the Resolution. That, it is argued, is no reason for conceding unilateral federal authority to accomplish, through invocation of legislation by the United Kingdom Parliament, the purposes of the Resolution. There is here, however, an unprecedented situation in which the one constant since the enactment of the British North America Act in 1867 has been the legal authority of the United Kingdom Parliament to amend it. The law knows nothing of any requirement of provincial consent, either to a resolution of the federal Houses or as a condition of the exercise of United Kingdom legislative power.

Per Martland and Ritchie, JJ: We are not concerned with the matter of legality or illegality in the sense of determining whether or not the passage of the Resolution under consideration involves a breach of the law. The issue is as to the existence of a power to do that which is proposed to be done. The question is whether it is intra vires of the Senate and the House of Commons to cause the proposed amendments to the British North America Act, 1867 to be made by the Imperial

Parliament in the absence of provincial agreement. This issue is unique because in the 114 years since Confederation the Senate and House of Commons of Canada have never sought, without the consent of the Provinces, to obtain such an amendment; nor has that possibility ever been contemplated. The enactment of the British North America Act, 1867 created a federal constitution of Canada which confided the whole area of self-government within Canada to the Parliament of Canada and the provincial Legislatures, each being supreme within its own defined sphere and area. It can fairly be said, therefore, that the dominant principle of Canadian constitutional law is federalism. Neither level of government should be permitted to encroach on the other, either directly or indirectly. The political compromise achieved as a result of the Quebec and London Conferences preceding the passage of the British North America Act, 1867 would be dissolved unless there were substantive and effective limits on unconstitutional action. The issue is whether the established incompetence of the federal Government to encroach on provincial powers can be avoided through the use of the resolution procedure to effect a constitutional amendment passed at the behest of the federal Government by the Parliament of the United Kingdom. In no instance in the past has an amendment to the British North America Act, 1867 been enacted which directly affected federal-provincial relationships, in the sense of changing provincial legislative powers, in the absence of federal consultation with and the consent of all the Provinces. The history of amendments reveals the operation of constitutional constraints. While the choice of the resolution procedure is itself a matter of internal parliamentary responsibility, the making of the addresses to the Sovereign falls into two areas. Resolutions concerning the federal juristic unit and federal powers were made without reference to any but the members of the federal Houses. Resolutions abridging provincial authority have never been passed without the concurrence of the Provinces. In other words, the normal constitutional principles recognizing the inviolability of separate and exclusive legislative powers were carried into, and considered an integral part of, the operation of the resolution procedure.

In order to pass the Resolution now under consideration the Senate and the House of Commons must purport to exercise a power. The source of that power must be found in s. 4(a) of the Senate and House of Commons Act, RSC 1970, c. s-8, since there has been no legislation enacted to date, other than s. 4(a), which actually defines the privileges, immunities and powers of the two Houses of Parliament. The Resolution now before us was passed for the purpose of obtaining an amendment to the British North America Act, 1867, the admitted effect of which is to curtail provincial legislative powers under s. 92 of that Act. That power is not consistent with the British North America Act, 1867 but is repugnant to it. It is a power which is out of harmony with the very basis of the Act. Therefore para. (a) of s. 4, because of the limitations which it contains, does not confer that power. The Senate and the House of Commons are purporting to exercise a power that they do not possess. The two Houses of Parliament lack legal authority, of their own motion, to obtain constitutional amendments which would strike at the very basis of the Canadian federal system, i.e., the complete division of legislative powers between the Parliament of Canada and the provincial Legislatures. It is the duty of the Court to consider this assertion of rights with a view to the preservation of the Constitution. The federal Parliament is attempting to accomplish indirectly that which it is legally precluded from doing directly by perverting the recognized resolution method of obtaining constitutional amendments by the Imperial Parliament for an improper purpose. Since it is beyond the power of the federal Parliament to enact such an amendment, it is equally beyond the power of its two Houses to effect such an amendment through the agency of the Imperial Parliament.

READING QUESTIONS ON PATRIATION REFERENCE

1 Laskin et al. say that the arguments from history "do not lead to any consistent view or any single view" of the British North America Act. How is this related to their unwillingness to engage in "judicial legislation"?
2 Laskin et al. maintain that the fundamental federal character of the country would be unchanged if the federal Parliament unilaterally amended the constitution. Why is this fact relevant to their argument? Would they object if the federal government unilaterally rejected federalism?
3 Martland et al. read more significance than do the majority into the fact that there has never been a case of a unilateral amendment by Parliament. Why do they consider it significant?
4 Martland et al. justify their position by arguing that their fundamental role is to preserve the basis of the constitution. Do you suppose that Laskin would deny that their role is preserving the constitution? If not, what explains the difference?

5 Peter Hogg, one of Canada's leading constitutional lawyers, says in the *Constitutional Law of Canada* (Toronto: Carswell, 1992) that the convention question in the Patriation reference "raised no legal issues." Does his view presuppose legal positivism?

6 Hogg also maintains that because the court is not an elected body, it ought not to have answered questions about conventions, as the conclusion that there was a convention, even if not legally binding, made it politically impossible for the federal government to ignore it. Do you agree?

Herman Melville
Billy Budd, Sailor (1929)

Melville's novella tells the story of a sailor who strikes a superior officer who has severely provoked him. The officer dies from a blow almost anyone would have survived. The central drama of the story comes when the Captain, who has witnessed the death, decides that Budd must be executed, despite the fact he is morally innocent. Vere feels compelled to enforce the law, though he regards it as profoundly unjust.

The court was held in the same cabin where the unfortunate affair had taken place. This cabin, the commander's, embraced the entire area under the poop deck. Aft, and on either side, was a small stateroom, the one now temporarily a jail and the other a dead-house, and a yet smaller compartment, leaving a space between expanding forward into a goodly oblong of length coinciding with the ship's beam. A skylight of moderate dimension was overhead, and at each end of the oblong space were two sashed porthole windows easily convertible back into embrasures for short carronades.

All being quickly in readiness, Billy Budd was arraigned, Captain Vere necessarily appearing as the sole witness in the case, and as such temporarily sinking his rank, though singularly maintaining it in a matter apparently trivial, namely, that he testified from the ship's weather side, with that object having caused the court to sit on the lee side. Concisely he narrated all that had led up to the catastrophe, omitting nothing in Claggart's accusation and deposing as to the manner in which the prisoner had received it. At this testimony the three officers glanced with no little surprise at Billy Budd, the last man they would have suspected either of the mutinous design alleged by Claggart or the undeniable deed he himself had done. The first lieutenant, taking judicial primacy and turning toward the prisoner, said, "Captain Vere has spoken. Is it or is it not as Captain Vere says?"

In response came syllables not so much impeded in the utterance as might have been anticipated. They were these: "Captain Vere tells the truth. It is just as Captain Vere says, but it is not as the master-at-arms said. I have eaten the King's bread and I am true to the King."

"I believe you, my man," said the witness, his voice indicating a suppressed emotion not otherwise betrayed.

"God will bless you for that, your honor!" not without stammering said Billy, and all but broke down. But immediately he was recalled to self-control by another question, to which with the same emotional difficulty of utterance he said, "No, there was no malice between us. I never bore malice against the master-at-arms. I am sorry that he is dead. I did not mean to kill him. Could I have used my tongue I would not have struck him. But he foully lied to my face and in presence of my captain, and I had to say something, and I could only say it with a blow, God help me!"

In the impulsive aboveboard manner of the frank one the court saw confirmed all that was implied in words that just previously had perplexed them, coming as they did from the testifier to the tragedy and promptly following Billy's impassioned disclaimer of mutinous intent – Captain Vere's words, "I believe you, my man."

Next it was asked of him whether he knew of or suspected aught savoring of incipient trouble (meaning mutiny, though the explicit term was avoided) going on in any section of the ship's company.

The reply lingered. This was naturally imputed by the court to the same vocal embarrassment which had retarded or obstructed previous answers. But in main it was otherwise here, the question immediately recalling to Billy's mind the interview with the afterguardsman in the forechains. But an innate repugnance to playing a part at all approaching that of an informer against one's own shipmates – the same erring sense of uninstructed honor which had stood in the way of his reporting the matter at the time, though as a loyal man-of-war's man it was incumbent on him, and failure so to do, if charged against him and proven, would have subjected him to the heaviest of penalties; this, with the blind feeling now his that nothing really was being hatched, prevailed with him. When the answer came it was a negative.

"One question more," said the officer of marines, now first speaking and with a troubled earnestness. "You tell us that what the master-at-arms said against you was a lie. Now why should he have so lied, so maliciously lied, since you declare there was no malice between you?"

At that question, unintentionally touching on a spiritual sphere wholly obscure to Billy's thoughts, he was nonplussed, evincing a confusion indeed that some observers, such as can readily be imagined, would have construed into involuntary evidence of hidden guilt. Nevertheless, he strove some way to answer, but all at once relinquished the vain endeavor, at the same time turning an appealing glance towards Captain Vere as deeming him his best helper and friend. Captain Vere, who had been seated for a time, rose to his feet, addressing the interrogator. "The question you put to him comes naturally enough. But how can he rightly answer it? – or anybody else, unless indeed it be he who lies within there," designating the compartment where lay the corpse. "But the prone one there will not rise to our summons. In effect, though, as it seems to me, the point you make is hardly material. Quite aside from any conceivable motive actuating the master-at-arms, and irrespective of the provocation to the blow, a martial court must needs in the present case confine its attention to the blow's consequence, which consequence justly is to be deemed not otherwise than as the striker's deed."

This utterance, the full significance of which it was not at all likely that Billy took in, nevertheless caused him to turn a wistful interrogative look toward the speaker, a look in its dumb expressiveness not unlike that which a dog of generous breed might turn upon his master, seeking in his face some elucidation of a previous gesture ambiguous to the canine intelligence. Nor was the same utterance without marked effect upon the three officers, more especially the soldier. Couched in it seemed to them a meaning unanticipated, involving a prejudgment on the speaker's part. It served to augment a mental disturbance previously evident enough.

The soldier once more spoke, in a tone of suggestive dubiety addressing at once his associates and Captain Vere: "Nobody is present – none of the ship's company, I mean – who might shed lateral light, if any is to be had, upon what remains mysterious in this matter."

"That is thoughtfully put," said Captain Vere; "I see your drift. Ay, there is a mystery; but, to use a scriptural phrase, it is a 'mystery of iniquity,'" a matter for psychologic theologians to discuss. But what has a military court to do with it? Not to add that for us any possible investigation of it is cut off by the lasting tongue-tie of – him – in yonder,' again designating the mortuary stateroom. "The prisoner's deed – with that alone we have to do."

To this, and particularly the closing reiteration, the marine soldier, knowing not how aptly to reply, sadly abstained from saying aught. The first lieutenant, who at the outset had not unnaturally assumed primacy in the court, now overrulingly instructed by a glance from Captain Vere, a glance more effective than words, resumed that primacy. Turning to the prisoner, "Budd," he said, and scarce in equable tones, "Budd, if you have aught further to say for yourself, say it now."

Upon this the young sailor turned another quick glance toward Captain Vere; then, as taking a hint from that aspect, a hint confirming his own instinct that silence was now best, replied to the lieutenant, "I have said all, sir."

The marine – the same who had been the sentinel without the cabin door at the time that the foretopman, followed by the master-at-arms, entered it – he, standing by the sailor throughout these judicial proceedings, was now directed to take him back to the after compartment originally assigned to the prisoner and his custodian. As the twain disappeared from view, the three officers, as partially liberated from some inward constraint associated with Billy's mere presence, simultaneously stirred in their seats. They exchanged looks of troubled indecision, yet feeling that decide they must and without long delay. For Captain Vere, he for the time stood – unconsciously with his back toward them, apparently in one of his absent fits – gazing out from a sashed porthole to windward upon the monotonous blank of the twilight sea. But the court's silence continuing, broken only at moments by brief consultations, in low earnest tones, this served to arouse him and energize him. Turning, he to-and-fro paced the cabin athwart; in the returning ascent to windward climbing the slant deck in the ship's lee roll, without knowing it symbolizing thus in his action a mind resolute to surmount difficulties even if against primitive instincts strong as the wind and the sea. Presently he came to a stand before the three. After scanning their faces he stood less as mustering his thoughts for expression than as one inly deliberating how best to put them to well-meaning men not intellectually mature, men with whom it was necessary to demonstrate certain principles that were axioms to himself. Similar impatience as to talking is perhaps one reason that deters some minds from addressing any popular assemblies.

When speak he did, something, both in the substance of what he said and his manner of saying it, showed the influence of unshared studies modifying and tempering the practical training of an active career. This, along with his phraseology, now and then was suggestive of the grounds whereon rested that imputation of a certain pedantry socially alleged against him by certain naval men of wholly practical cast, captains who nevertheless would frankly concede that His Majesty's navy mustered no more efficient officer of their grade than Starry Vere.

What he said was to this effect: "Hitherto I have been but the witness, little more; and I should hardly think now to take another tone, that of your coadjutor for the time, did I not perceive in you – at the crisis too – a troubled hesitancy, proceeding, I doubt not, from the clash of military duty with moral scruple – scruple vitalized by compassion. For the compassion, how can I otherwise than share it? But, mindful of paramount obligations, I strive against scruples that may tend to enervate decision. Not, gentlemen, that I hide from myself that the case is an exceptional one. Speculatively regarded, it well might be referred to a jury of casvists. But for us here, acting not as casvists or moralists, it is a case practical, and under martial law practically to be dealt with.

"But your scruples: do they move as in a dusk? Challenge them. Make them advance and declare themselves. Come now; do they import something like this: If, mindless of palliating circumstances, we are bound to regard the death of the master-at-arms as the prisoner's deed, then does that deed constitute a capital crime whereof the penalty is a mortal one. But in natural justice is nothing but the prisoner's overt act to be considered? How can we adjudge to summary and shameful death a fellow creature innocent before God, and whom we feel to be so? – Does that state it aright? You sign sad assent. Well, I too feel that, the full force of that. It is Nature. But do these buttons that we wear attest that our allegiance is to Nature? No, to the King. Though the ocean, which is inviolate Nature primeval, though this be the element where we move and have our being as sailors, yet as the King's officers lies our duty in a sphere correspondingly natural? So little is that true, that in receiving our commissions we in the most important regards ceased to be natural free agents. When war is declared are we the commissioned fighters previously consulted? We fight at command. If our judgments approve the war, that is but coincidence. So in other particulars.

So now. For suppose condemnation to follow these present proceedings. Would it be so much we ourselves that would condemn as it would be martial law operating through us? For that law and the rigor of it, we are not responsible. Our vowed responsibility is in this: That however pitilessly that law may operate in any instances, we nevertheless adhere to it and administer it.

"But the exceptional in the matter moves the hearts within you. Even so too is mine moved. But let not warm hearts betray heads that should be cool. Ashore in a criminal case, will an upright judge allow himself off the bench to be waylaid by some tender kinswoman of the accused seeking to touch him with her tearful plea? Well, the heart here, sometimes the feminine in man, is as that piteous woman, and hard though it be, she must here be ruled out."

He paused, earnestly studying them for a moment; then resumed.

"But something in your aspect seems to urge that it is not solely the heart that moves in you, but also the conscience, the private conscience. But tell me whether or not, occupying the position we do, private conscience should not yield to that imperial one formulated in the code under which alone we officially proceed?"

Here the three men moved in their seats, less convinced than agitated by the course of an argument troubling but the more the spontaneous conflict within.

Perceiving which, the speaker paused for a moment; then abruptly changing his tone, went on.

"To steady us a bit, let us recur to the facts. – In wartime at sea a man-of-war's man strikes his superior in grade, and the blow kills. Apart from its effect the blow itself is, according to the Articles of War, a capital crime. Furthermore –"

"Ay, sir," emotionally broke in the officer of marines, "in one sense it was. But surely Budd proposed neither mutiny nor homicide."

"Surely not, my good man. And before a court less arbitrary and more merciful than a martial one, that plea would largely extenuate. At the Last Assizes it shall acquit. But how here? We proceed under the law of the Mutiny Act. In feature no child can resemble his father more than that Act resembles in spirit the thing from which it derives – War. In His Majesty's service – in this ship, indeed – there are Englishmen forced to fight for the King against their will. Against their conscience, for aught we know. Though as their fellow creatures some of us may appreciate their position, yet as navy officers what reck we of it? Still less recks the enemy. Our impressed men he would fain cut down in the same swath with our volunteers. As regards the enemy's naval conscripts, some of whom may even share our own abhorrence of the regicidal French Directory, it is the same on our side. War looks but to the frontage, the appearance. And the Mutiny Act, War's child, takes after the father. Budd's intent or non-intent is nothing to the purpose.

"But while, put to it by those anxieties in you which I cannot but respect, I only repeat myself – while thus strangely we prolong proceedings that should be summary – the enemy may be sighted and an engagement result. We must do; and one of two things must we do – condemn or let go."

"Can we not convict and yet mitigate the penalty?" asked the sailing master, here speaking, and falteringly, for the first.

"Gentlemen, were that clearly lawful for us under the circumstances, consider the consequences of such clemency. The people" (meaning the ship's company) "have native sense; most of them are familiar with our naval usage and tradition; and how would they take it? Even could you explain to them – which our official position forbids – they, long molded by arbitrary discipline, have not that kind of intelligent responsiveness that might qualify them to comprehend and discriminate. No, to the people the foretopman's deed, however it be worded in the announcement, will be plain homicide committed in a flagrant act of mutiny. What penalty for that should follow, they know. But it does not follow. *Why?* they will ruminate. You know what sailors are. Will they not revert to the recent outbreak at the Nore? Ay. They know the well-founded alarm – the panic it struck throughout England. Your clement sentence they would account pusillanimous. They would think that we flinch, that we are afraid of them – afraid of practicing a lawful rigor singularly demanded at this juncture, lest it should provoke new troubles. What shame to use such a conjecture on their part, and how deadly to discipline. You see then, whither, prompted by duty and the law, I steadfastly drive. But I beseech you, my friends, do not take me amiss. I feel as you do for this unfortunate boy. But did he know our hearts, I take him to be of that generous nature that he would feel even for us on whom in this military necessity so heavy a compulsion is laid."

With that, crossing the deck he resumed his place by the sashed porthole, tacitly leaving the three to come to a decision. On the cabin's opposite side the troubled court sat silent. Loyal lieges, plain and practical, though at bottom they dissented from some points Captain Vere had put to them, they were without the faculty, hardly had the inclination, to gainsay one whom they felt to be an earnest man, one too not less their superior in mind than in naval rank. But it is not improbable that even such of his words as were not without influence over them, less came home than his closing appeal to their instinct as sea officers: in the forethought he threw out as to the practical consequences to discipline, considering the unconfirmed tone of the fleet at the time, should a man-of-war's man's violent killing at sea of a superior in grade be allowed to pass for aught else than a capital crime demanding prompt infliction of the penalty.

Not unlikely they were brought to something more or less akin to that harassed frame of mind which in the year 1842 actuated the commander of the U.S. brig-of-war *Somers* to resolve, under the so-called Articles of War, Articles modelled upon the English Mutiny Act, to resolve upon the execution at sea of a midshipman and two sailors as mutineers designing the seizure of the brig. Which resolution was carried out though in a time of peace and within not many days' sail of home. An Act vindicated by a naval court of inquiry subsequently convened ashore. History, and here cited without comment. True, the circumstances on board the *Somers* were different from those on board the *Bellipotent*. But the urgency felt, well-warranted or otherwise, was much the same.

Says a writer whom few know, "Forty years after a battle it is easy for a noncombatant to reason about how it ought to have been fought. It is another thing personally and under fire to have to direct the fighting while involved in the obscuring smoke of it. Much so with respect to other emergencies involving considerations both practical and moral, and when it is imperative promptly to act. The greater the fog the more it imperils the steamer, and speed is put on though at the hazard of running somebody down. Little ween the snug card players in the cabin of the responsibilities of the sleepless man on the bridge."

In brief, Billy Budd was formally convicted and sentenced to be hung at the yardarm in the early morning watch, it being now night. Otherwise, as is customary in such cases, the sentence would forthwith have been carried out. In wartime on the field or in the fleet, a mortal punishment decreed by a drumhead court – on the field sometimes decreed by but a nod from the general – follows without delay on the heel of conviction, without appeal.

...

Of a series of incidents with a brief term rapidly following each other, the adequate narration may take up a term less brief, especially if explanation or comment here and there seem requisite to the better understanding of such incidents. Between the entrance into the cabin of him who never left it alive, and him who when he did leave it left it as one condemned to die; between this and the closeted interview just given, less than an hour and a half had elapsed. It was an interval long enough, however, to awaken speculations among no few of the ship's company.

READING QUESTIONS ON BILLY BUDD

1 Did Captain Vere really have no other option but to convict Billy? What argument might he have used to acquit him?
2 Captain Vere seems less concerned about whether or not the sailors will mutiny than about the duties of his office. He says that if he condemns Billy and the sailors mutiny, it will not be his responsibility. What view of law does this suggest?

Robert Cover
"Of Creon and Captain Vere" (1976)

Cover explores the similarities between Captain Vere's plight and that of Lemuel Shaw, an abolitionist judge in nineteenth-century Massachusetts, who felt compelled to enforce the *Fugitive Slave Acts*. Shaw's situation raised deep puzzles for theories of law. Like Captain Vere, he sees himself as torn between moral and legal duties. On the one hand, he believes slavery is immoral. On the other, he believes he is bound to uphold the rule of law. The two duties come into conflict because the United States Constitution explicitly allowed each state to decide whether or not to allow slavery. Shaw's commitment to the rule of law did not stand in the way of him campaigning for the legislative abolition of slavery in states that still allowed it. Nor did it prevent him from preventing slaveowners forcibly returning slaves they had voluntarily brought into states that did not allow slavery. In cases involving the return of escaped slaves, Shaw had a more difficult time. The *Fugitive Slave Acts* required their return to their owners; in so doing it also seemed to require that free states participate in a system of slavery.

PRELUDE: OF CREON AND CAPTAIN VERE

I

Antigone's star has shown brightly through the millennia. The archetype for civil disobedience has claimed a constellation of first-magnitude emulators. The disobedient – whether Antigone, Luther, Gandhi, King, or Bonhoeffer – exerts a powerful force upon us. The singular act, the risk, the dramatic appeal to a juster justice, all contribute to the high drama of the moment and the power of the actor's role. No wonder then, that such men and women are celebrated in literature and history. No wonder that a great psychiatrist like Erikson, upon embarking on a venture in history and biography, chose Luther and Gandhi as his first subjects.

Yet, in a curious way, to focus upon the disobedient and the process of disobedience is to accept the perspective of the established order. It is a concession that it is the man who appeals beyond law that is in need of explanation. With the sole exception of Nazi atrocities, the phenomenon of complicity in oppressive legal systems (oppressive from the actor's own perspective) has seldom been studied. Thus, Creon is present only as a foil for Antigone, not himself the object of the artist's study of human character. In *Antigone* note the curious one-dimensional character of the King. How he comes to make his law and at what cost in psychic terms is not treated at all. Indeed, Creon's first conflict is not between right and law, but between his son and his pride. And even in the midst of that conflict he betrays his singular obtuseness to the complexity of the situation he created by crying filial impiety and anarchy in one breath. He is astounded by the possibility of Haemon's sympathy to an affront to authority. Much of the simplicity of Creon lies in the choice of a tyrant as model for legal system. The making of law and its applications are wholly confined to a single will unconstrained by any but the most personal of considerations such as the feelings and actions of a son.

Melville's Captain Vere in *Billy Budd* is one of the few examples of an attempt to portray the conflict patterns of Creon or Creon's minions in a context more nearly resembling the choice situations of judges in modern legal systems. Billy Budd, radical innocence personified, is overwhelmed by a charge of fomenting mutiny, falsely levied against him by the first mate Claggart. Claggart seems to personify dark and evil forces. Struck dumb by the slanderous charges, Billy strikes out and kills the mate with a single blow. Captain Vere must instruct a drumhead court on the law of the Mutiny Act as it is to be applied to Billy Budd – in some most fundamental sense "innocent," though perpetrator of the act of killing the first mate. In what must be, for the legal scholar, the high point of the novella, Vere articulates the "scruples" of the three officers (and his own) and rejects them.

How can we adjudge to summary and shameful death a fellow creature innocent before God, and whom we feel to be so? – Does that state it aright? You sign sad assent. Well, I too feel that, the full force of that. It is Nature. But do these buttons that we wear attest that our allegiance is to Nature? No, to the King.

And, but a few paragraphs farther on, Vere asks the three whether "occupying the position we do, private conscience should not yield to that imperial one formulated in the code under which alone we officially proceed."

In Vere's words we have a positivist's condensation of a legal system's formal character. Five aspects of that formalism may be discerned and specified: First, there is explicit recognition of the role character of the judges – a consciousness of the formal element. It is a uniform, not nature, that defines obligation. Second, law is distinguished from both the transcendent and the personal sources of obligation. The law is neither nature nor conscience. Third, the law is embodied in a readily identifiable source which governs transactions and occurrences of the sort under consideration: here an imperial code of which the Mutiny Act is a part. Fourth, the will behind the law is vague, uncertain, but *clearly not* that of the judges. It is here "imperial will" which, in (either eighteenth- or) nineteenth-century terms as applied to England, is not very easy to describe except through a constitutional law treatise. But, in any event, it is not the will of Vere and his three officers. Fifth, a corollary of the fourth point, the judge is not responsible for the content of the law but for its straightforward application.

For that law and the rigor of it, we are not responsible. Our vowed responsibility is in this: That however pitilessly that law may operate in any instances, we nevertheless adhere to it and administer it.

These five elements are part of Vere's arguments. But *Billy Budd* is a literary work and much that is most interesting about Vere is not in what he says but in what he is, in overtones of character. For example, we have intimations from the outset of a personality committed to fearful symmetries. His nickname, derived from Marvell's lines

Under the discipline severe
Of Fairfax and the starry Vere

suggests an impersonal and unrelaxed severity. And his intellectual bent, too, reinforces this suggestion of rigidity. He eschewed innovations "disinterestedly" and because they seemed "insusceptible of embodiment in lasting institutions." And he lacked "companionable quality." A man emerges who is disposed to approach life institutionally, to avoid the personal realm even where it perhaps ought to hold sway, to be inflexibly honest, righteous, and duty bound.

It is this man who, seeing and appreciating Bud's violent act, exclaimed, "Struck dead by an angel of God! Yet the angel must hang." And, characteristically, it is Vere who assumes the responsibility of conveying the dread verdict to the accused. Melville's speculations on that "interview" are revealing. He stresses the likelihood that Vere revealed his own full part in the "trial". He goes on to speculate that Vere might well have assumed a paternal stance in the manner of Abraham embracing Isaac "on the brink of resolutely offering him up in obedience to the exacting behest." Such a religious conviction of duty characterizes our man. Neither conventional morality, pity, nor personal agony could bend him from a stern duty. But in Vere's case the master is not God but the King. And the King is but a symbol for a social order.

Righteous men, indeed, suffer the agonies of their righteousness. Captain Vere betrayed just such agony in leaving his meeting with Billy Budd. But there is no indication that Vere suffered the agony of doubt about his course. When Billy died uttering "God Bless Captain Vere," there is no intimation that the Captain sensed any irony (whether intended or not) in the parting benediction. If Captain Vere is Abraham, he is the biblical version, not Kierkegaard's shadow poised achingly at the chasm.

Melville has been astonishingly successful in making his readers ask dreadful questions of Vere and his behavior. What deep urge leads a man to condemn unworldly beauty and innocence? To embrace, personally, the opportunity to do an impersonal, distasteful task? How reconcile the flash of recognition of "the angel must die" and the seizing of the opportunity to act Abraham, with declared protestations, unquestionably sincere, that only plain and clear duty overcomes his sense of the victim's cosmic innocence? We have so many doubts about a man who hears and obeys the voice of the Master so quickly, and our doubts are compounded when it is a harsh social system that becomes the Lord.

I venture to suggest that Melville had a model for Captain Vere that may bring us very close to our main story. Melville's father-in-law was Chief Justice Lemuel Shaw of the Massachusetts Supreme Judicial Court. A firm, unbending man of stern integrity, Shaw dominated the Massachusetts judicial system very much as Captain Vere ran his ship. The Chief Justice was a noted, strong opponent to slavery and expressed his opposition privately, in print, and in appropriate judicial opinions. Yet, in the great causes célèbres involving fugitive slaves, Shaw came down hard for an unflinching application of the harsh and summary law. The effort cost Shaw untold personal agony. He was villified by abolitionists. I cannot claim that Vere is Lemuel Shaw (though he might be), for there is no direct evidence. I can only say that it would be remarkable that in portraying a man caught in the horrible conflict between duty and conscience, between role and morality, between nature and positive law, Melville would be untouched by the figure of his father-in-law in the *Sims Case*, the Latimer affair, or the Burns controversy. We know Melville's predilection to the ship as microcosm for the social order. He used the device quite plainly with respect to slavery in *Benito Cereno*.

The fugitive slave was very Budd-like, though he was as black as Billy was blonde. The Mutiny Act admitted of none of the usual defenses, extenuations, or mitigations. If the physical act was that of the defendant, he was guilty. The Fugitive Slave Act similarly excluded most customary sorts of defenses. The alleged fugitive could not even plead that he was not legally a slave so long as he was the person *alleged* to be a fugitive. The drumhead court was a special and summary proceeding; so was the fugitive rendition process. In both proceedings the fatal judgment was carried out immediately. There was no appeal.

More important, Billy's fatal flaw was his innocent dumbness. He struck because he could not speak. So, under the Fugitive Slave Acts, the alleged fugitive had no right to speak. And, as a rule, slaves had no capacity to testify against their masters or whites, generally. Billy Budd partakes of the slave, generalized. He was seized, impressed, from the ship *Rights of Man* and taken abroad the *Bellipotent*. Aboard the *Bellipotent* the Mutiny Act and Captain Vere held sway. The Mutiny Act was justified because of its necessity for the order demanded on a ship in time of war. So the laws of slavery, often equally harsh and unbending, were justified as necessary for the social order in antebellum America. Moreover, the institution itself was said to have its origin in war.

But most persuasive is Vere and his dilemma – the subject matter of this book. For, if there was a single sort of case in which judges during Melville's lifetime struggled with the moral-formal dilemma, it was slave cases. In these cases, time and again, the judiciary paraded its helplessness before the law; lamented harsh results; intimated that in a more perfect world, or at the end of days, a better law would emerge, but almost uniformly, marched to the music, steeled themselves, and hung Billy Budd.

Of course, *Billy Budd*, like any great work of literature, exists on many levels. I would not deny the theology in the work, nor the clash of elemental good and elemental evil in Budd and Claggart. But the novella is also about a judgment, within a social system, and about the man, who, dimly perceiving the great and abstract forces at work, bears responsibility for that judgment. It is about starry-eyed Vere and Lemuel Shaw.

2

The rest of this book is not about literature, but about Lemuel Shaw and many judges like him. It is the story of earnest, well-meaning pillars of legal respectability and of their collaboration in a system of oppression – Negro slavery. I have chosen to analyze at length only the dilemma of the antislavery judge – the man who would, in some sense, have agreed with my characterization of slavery as oppression. It was he who confronted Vere's dilemma, the choice between the demands of role and the voice of conscience. And it was he who contributed so much to the force of legitimacy that law may provide, for he plainly acted out of impersonal duty.

In a static and simplistic model of law, the judge caught between law and morality has only four choices. He may apply the law against his conscience. He may apply conscience and be faithless to the law. He may resign. Or he may cheat: He may state that the law is not what he believes it to be and, thus preserve an appearance (to others) of conformity of law and morality. Once we assume a more realistic model of law and of the judicial process, these four positions become only poles setting limits to a complex field of action and motive. For in a dynamic model, law is always becoming. And the judge has a legitimate role in determining what it is that the law will become. The flux in law means also that the law's content is frequently unclear. We must speak of direction and of weight as well as of position. Moreover, this frequent lack of clarity makes possible "ameliorist" solutions. The judge may introduce his own sense of what "ought to be" interstitially, where no "hard" law yet exists. And, he may do so without committing the law to broad doctrinal advances (or retreats).

In a given historical context the way in which judges are likely to respond to the moral-formal dilemma is going to be determined by a wide variety of intellectual and institutional variables. Judges, more than most men, are conscious of the baggage of the past. Thus, the traditions that they inherit will be important. For both slavery and the judicial role in antebellum America the judge had a library of works that influenced the idiom in which he thought. The nature of that intellectual tradition is my first inquiry. I shall examine the natural law tradition on slavery as it stood in the late eighteenth century. I shall then explore the actual uses of principled preferences for liberty in the first thirty or forty years of the nineteenth century. This exploration will delineate the areas of accepted usage of preference for liberty in judicial opinion and the areas where the judge could move the law in the direction of freedom. I shall then explore the sorts of demands that were made upon the judiciary to go beyond those accepted areas and the judicial refusal to do so. That refusal will be traced on the cognitive level to carefully formulated ideas about the judicial function that are themselves the products of a heritage of conflict over the values that ought to govern judging. The dialectical context for the judge's response was not constant, and it is necessary to examine responses to many demands varying, in part, with the ideology of the lawyers and the movements they represented.

Finally, I shall confront directly the question of personality. With Captain Vere we have the sense that it is not logic alone that leads him to his response. So, with Lemuel Shaw, John McLean, Joseph Story, and others, we must inquire into the internal forces that produced an almost uniform response of role fidelity. The theory of cognitive dissonance provides a suggestive framework for integrating the uniform response, the personalities of these men, and the professional and intellectual milieu in which they worked.

Make no mistake. The judges we shall examine really squirmed; were intensely uncomfortable in hanging Billy Budd. But they did the job. Like Vere, they were Creon's faithful minions. We must understand them – as much as Antigone – if we are to understand the processes of injustice.

Commonwealth v Aves 35 Mass. 193 (1836)

A case decided by Shaw, which holds that a slave brought into a free state by his owner is thereby set free. Shaw argues that the alternative would be to allow slave states to export their slavery to free ones.

... The precise question presented by the claim of the respondent is, whether a citizen of any one of the United States, where negro slavery is established by law, coming into this State, for any temporary purpose of business or pleasure, staying some time, but not acquiring a domicil here, who brings a slave with him as a personal attendant, may restrain such slave of his liberty during his continuance here, and convey him out of this State on his return, against his consent. It is not contended that a master can exercise here any other of the rights of a slave owner, than such as may be necessary to retain the custody of the slave during his residence, and to remove him on his return.

Until this discussion, I had supposed that there had been adjudged cases on this subject in this Commonwealth; and it is believed to have been a prevalent opinion among lawyers, that if a slave is brought voluntarily and unnecessarily within the limits of this State, he becomes free, if he chooses to avail himself of the provisions of our laws; not so much because his coming within our territorial limits, breathing our air, or treading on our soil, works any alteration in his *status*, or his condition, as settled by the law of his domicil, as because by the operation of our laws, there is no authority on the part of the master, either to restrain the slave of his liberty, whilst here, or forcibly to take him into custody in order to his removal. There seems, however, to be no decided case on the subject reported ...

Without pursuing this inquiry farther, it is sufficient for the purposes of the case before us, that by the constitution adopted in 1780, slavery was abolished in Massachusetts, upon the ground that it is contrary to natural right and the plain principles of justice. The terms of the first article of the declaration of rights are plain and explicit. "All men are born free and equal, and have certain natural, essential, and unalienable rights, which are, the right of enjoying and defending their lives and liberties, that of acquiring, possessing, and protecting property." It would be difficult to select words more precisely adapted to the abolition of negro slavery. According to the laws prevailing in all the States, where slavery is upheld, the child of a slave is not deemed to be born free, a slave has no right to enjoy and defend his own liberty, or to acquire, possess, or protect property. That the description was broad enough in its terms to embrace negroes, and that it was intended by the framers of the constitution to embrace them, is proved by the earliest contemporaneous construction, by an unbroken series of judicial decisions, and by a uniform practice from the adoption of the constitution to the present time. The whole tenor of our policy, of our legislation and jurisprudence, from that time to the present, has been consistent with this construction, and with no other.

Such being the general rule of law, it becomes necessary to inquire how far it is modified or controlled in its operation; either,

1. By the law of other nations and states, as admitted by the comity of nations to have a limited operation within a particular state; or
2. By the constitution and laws of the United States ...

Upon a general review of the authorities, and upon an application of the well established principles upon this subject, we think they fully maintain the point stated, that though slavery is contrary to natural right, to the principles of justice, humanity and sound policy, as we adopt them and found our own laws upon them, yet not being contrary to the laws of nations, if any other state or community see fit to establish and continue slavery by law, so far as the legislative power of that country extends, we are bound to take notice of the existence of those laws, and we are not at liberty to declare and hold an act done within those limits, unlawful and void, upon our views of morality and policy, which the sovereign and legislative power of the place has pronounced to be lawful. If, therefore, an unwarranted interference and wrong is done by our citizens to a foreigner, acting under the sanction of such laws, and within their proper limits, that is, within the local limits of the power by whom they are thus established, or on the high seas, which each and every nation has a right in common with all others to occupy, our laws would no doubt afford a remedy against the wrong done. So, in pursuance of a well known maxim, that in the construction of contracts, the *lex loci contractus* shall govern, if a person, having in other respects a right to sue in our courts, shall bring an action against another, liable in other respects to be sued in our courts, upon a contract made upon the subject of slavery in a state where slavery is allowed by law, the law here would give it effect. As if a note of hand made in New Orleans were sued on here, and the defence should be, that it was on a bad consideration, or without consideration, because given for the price of a slave sold, it may well be admitted, that such a defence could not prevail, because the contract was a legal one by the law of the place where it was made.

This view of the law applicable to slavery, marks strongly the distinction between the relation of master and slave, as established by the local law of particular states, and in virtue of that sovereign power and independent authority which each independent state concedes to every other, and those natural and social relations, which are everywhere and by all people recognized, and which, though they may be modified and regulated by municipal law, are not founded upon it such as the relation of parent and child, and husband and wife. Such also is the principle upon which the general right of property is founded, being in some form universally recognized as a natural right, independently of municipal law.

This affords an answer to the argument drawn from the maxim, that the right of personal property follows the person, and therefore, where by the law of a place a person there domiciled acquires personal property, by the comity of nations the same must be deemed his property everywhere. It is obvious, that if this were true, in the extent in which the argument employs it, if slavery exists anywhere, and if by the laws of any place a property can be acquired in slaves, the law of slavery must extend to every place where such slaves may be carried. The maxim, therefore, and the argument can apply only to those commodities which are everywhere, and by all nations, treated and deemed subjects of property. But it is not speaking with strict accuracy to say, that a property can be acquired in human beings, by local laws. Each state may, for its own convenience, declare that slaves shall be deemed property, and that the relations and laws of personal chattels shall be deemed to apply to them; as, for instance, that they may be bought and sold, delivered, attached, levied upon, that trespass will lie for an injury done to them, or trover for converting them. But it would be a perversion of terms to say, that such local laws do in fact make them personal property generally; they can only determine, that the same rules of law shall apply to them as are applicable to property, and this effect will follow only so far as such laws *proprio vigore* can operate ...

Sims's Case 7 Cush. 285 (1851)

Another Shaw case, which holds that a fugitive slave must be returned to his master, just as a fugitive from justice must be. The issue is presented in terms of the powers of the commissioner who is charged with deciding whether an alleged fugitive is to be returned. The commissioner's decision is conclusive. Part of the argument in the case concerned whether the commissioner's appointment was an unconstitutional exercise of judicial power; part turned on the fact that fugitive slaves were not entitled to a jury trial. (By contrast, fugitives from justice could only be returned for trial by a jury.) Shaw makes short work of these arguments, arguing instead that the *Fugitive Slave Act* is prerequisite to the stability of the nation. The report includes an *obiter dictum* on the injustice of slavery.

... Shaw, CJ: This is a petition for a writ of *habeas corpus* to bring the petitioner before this court, with a view to his discharge from imprisonment, upon the grounds stated in the petition. We were strongly urged to issue the writ, without inquiry into its cause, and to hear an argument upon the petitioner's right to a discharge, on the return of the writ. This we declined to do, on grounds of principle, and common and well settled practice. Before a writ of *habeas corpus* is granted, sufficient probable cause must be shown; but when it appears upon the party's own showing that there is no sufficient ground *prima facie* for his discharge, the court will not issue the writ ...

The evils existing immediately before the adoption of the constitution, and the greater and more appalling evils in prospect, indicated the absolute necessity of forming a more perfect union, in order to secure the peace and prosperity of all the states. This could only be done by the several states renouncing and relinquishing a portion of their powers of sovereignty; and these were the right of war and peace, the right of making treaties with foreign powers and with each other, and the right of exercising absolute power and dominion over all persons and things within their own territories respectively. In order to form this more perfect union, delegates from the several states met together. It was obvious that the renunciation of some of the powers of sovereignty, at least to the extent above mentioned, was the first step to be taken, and was absolutely essential to the success of any scheme of union. Still, it could not but be perceived that the great difference in the condition of the states in regard to the institution of slavery, and the prospect that many of the states would soon become free, from causes then in operation, constituted a difference in their relative condition, which must first be provided for. So long as the states remained sovereign, they could assert their rights in regard to fugitive slaves by war or treaty; and, therefore, before renouncing and surrendering such sovereignty, some substitute, in the nature of a treaty or compact, must necessarily be devised and agreed to. The clause above cited from the constitution seems to have been, in character, precisely such a treaty. It was a solemn compact, entered into by the delegates of states then sovereign and independent, and free to remain so, on great deliberation, and on the highest considerations of justice and policy, and reciprocal benefit, and in order to secure the peace and prosperity of all the states. It carries with it, therefore, all the sanction which can belong to it, either as an international or a social compact, made by parties invested with full powers to deliberate and act; or as a fundamental law, agreed on as the basis of a government, irrepealable, and to be changed only by the power that made it, in the form prescribed by it.

Such being the circumstances, under which this provision of the constitution was adopted; such the relations of the several states to each other; such the manifest object which the framers of the constitution had in view; we are to look at the clause in question, to ascertain its true meaning and effect. We think it was intended to guaranty to the owner of a slave, living within the territory of a state in which slavery is permitted, the rights conferred upon such owner, by the laws of such state; and that no state should make its own territory an asylum and sanctuary for fugitive slaves, by any law or regulation, by which a slave, who had escaped from a state where he owed labor or service into such state or territory, should avoid being reclaimed; it was designed also to provide a practicable and peaceable mode, by which such fugitive, upon the claim of the person to whom such labor or service should be due, might be delivered up ...

And the theory of the general government is, that these subjects, in their full extent and entire details, being placed under the jurisdiction of the general government, are necessarily withdrawn from the jurisdiction of the state, and the jurisdiction of the general government therefore becomes exclusive. And this is necessary to prevent constant collision and interference; and it is obvious that it must be so, because two distinct governments cannot exercise the same power, at the same time, on the same subject matter. This is not left to mere implication. It is expressly declared, in art. 1, s. 8, that congress shall have power to make all laws which shall be necessary and proper, for carrying into execution all the powers vested by the constitution in the government of the United States, or in any department or officer thereof. And by art. 6, "this constitution, and the laws of the United States which shall be made in pursuance thereof, and all treaties made, or which shall be made, under the authority of the United States, shall be the supreme law of the land; and the judges in every state shall be bound thereby, any thing in the constitution or laws of any state to the contrary notwithstanding." All such laws made by the general government, upon the rights, duties and subjects, specially enumerated and confided to their jurisdiction, are necessarily exclusive and supreme, as well by express provision, as by necessary implication. And the general government is provided with its executive, legislative and judicial departments, not only to make laws regulating the rights, duties and subjects thus confided to them, but to administer right and justice respecting them in a regular course of judicature, and cause them to be carried into full execution, by its own powers, without dependence upon state authority, and without any let or restraint imposed by it.

It was, as we believe, under this view of the right of regaining specifically the custody of one from whom service or labor is due by the laws of one state, and who has escaped into another, and under this view of the powers of the general government, and the duty of congress, that the law of February 12, 1793, was passed ...

The manifest intent of this act of congress was, to regulate and give effect to the right given by the constitution. It secured to the claimant the aid and assistance of certain magistrates and officers, to enable him to exercise his right in a more regular and orderly manner, and without being chargeable with a breach of the peace. It obviously contemplated a prompt and summary proceeding, adapted to the exigency of the occasion, in aid of a power, in terms conferred by the constitution on the claimant. It vested the power of inquiry, (whether regarded as judicial or otherwise,) the same power which is now drawn in question, in magistrates of counties, cities or towns corporate. As to the mode of trial contemplated by this act, it is described by Mr Justice McLean, in his opinion in *Prigg v Pennsylvania*, 16 Peters, 539, 667, in these terms: "Both the constitution and the act of 1793 require the fugitive from labor to be delivered up on claim being made by the party, or his agent, to whom the service is due. Not that a suit should be regularly instituted. The proceeding authorized by the law is summary and informal. The fugitive is seized and taken before a judge or magistrate within the state, and on proof, parol or written, that he owes labor to the claimant, it is made the duty of the judge or magistrate to give the certificate, which authorizes the removal of the fugitive to the state from whence he absconded" ...

We have thought it important thus to inquire into the validity and constitutionality of the act of 1793, because it appears to be decisive of that in question. In the only particular in which the constitutionality of the act of congress of 1850 is now called in question, that of 1793 was obnoxious to the same objection, viz., that of authorizing a summary proceeding before officers and magistrates not qualified under the constitution to exercise the judicial powers of the general government. Congress may have thought it necessary to change the preëxisting law, not in principle but in detail, because, as we have seen in the case of *Prigg v Pennsylvania*, some of the judges were of opinion that state magistrates could not act under the authority conferred on them by the act of 1793, when prohibited from doing so by the laws of their own state, and some states had in fact passed such prohibitory laws. The present fugitive slave law may vary in other respects, and provide other and more rigorous means for carrying its provisions into effect, but these are not made grounds of objection to its constitutionality.

We do not mean to say that this court will in no case issue a writ of *habeas corpus* to bring in a party, held under color of process from the courts of the United States, or whose services, and the custody of whose person, are claimed under authority derived from the laws of the United States. This is constantly done, in cases of soldiers and sailors, held by military and naval officers, under enlistments complained of as illegal and void. But it is manifest that this ought to be done only in a clear case, and in a case where it is necessary to the security of personal liberty from illegal restraint.

Since the argument in court, this morning, I am reminded by one of the counsel for the petitioner, that the law in question ought to be regarded as unconstitutional, because it makes no provision for a trial by jury. We think that this cannot vary the result. The law of 1850 stands, in this respect, precisely on the same ground with that of 1793, and the same grounds of argument which tend to show the unconstitutionality of one apply with equal force to the other; and the same answer must be made to them.

The principle of adhering to judicial precedent, especially that of the supreme court of the United States, in a case depending upon the constitution and laws of the United States, and thus placed within their special and final jurisdiction, is absolutely necessary to the peace, union and harmonious action of the state and general governments. The preservation of both, with their full and entire powers, each in its proper sphere, was regarded by the framers of the constitution, and has ever since been regarded, as essential to the peace, order and prosperity of all the United States.

If this were a new question, now for the first time presented, we should desire to pause and take time for consideration. But though this act, the construction of which is now drawn in question, is recent, and this point, in the form in which it is now stated, is new, yet the solution of the question depends upon reasons and judicial decisions, upon legal principles and a long course of practice, which are familiar, and which have often been the subject of discussion and deliberation.

Considering, therefore, the nature of the subject, the urgent necessity for a speedy and prompt decision, we have not thought it expedient to delay the judgment. I have, therefore, to state, in behalf of the court, under the weighty responsibility which rests upon us, and as the unanimous opinion of the court, that the writ of *habeas corpus* prayed for cannot be granted ...

Writ refused.

By the received laws of nations, it seems to be well established, that however odious we may consider slavery and the slave trade, however abhorrent to the dictates of humanity and the plainest principles of justice and natural right, yet each nation has a right, in this respect, to judge for itself, and to allow or prohibit slavery by its own laws, at its own will; and that whenever slavery is thus established by positive law within the limits of such state, all other nations and people are bound to respect it, and cannot rightfully interfere, either by forcibly seizing, or artfully enticing away slaves, within the limits of the territory of the nation establishing it, or on the high seas, which are the common highway of nations. In the case cited, the language of this court is this: "In considering the law of nations, we may assume that the law of this state is analogous to the law of England in this respect; that while slavery is considered as unlawful and inadmissible in both, because contrary to natural right, and the laws designed for the security of personal liberty, yet, in both, the existence of slavery in other countries is recognized, and the claims of foreigners, growing out of that condition, are, to a certain extent, respected." In *Sommersett's case*, before Lord Mansfield, in 1771, 20 Howells's State Trials, 1, 82, which is the leading case on this subject, and establishes the doctrine of the natural right to personal liberty in its fullest extent, we find a clear intimation of the principle above stated. Slavery, said Lord Mansfield, "is of such a nature that it is incapable of being introduced on any reasons, moral or political, but only by positive law." "It is so odious, that nothing can be suffered to support it, but positive law." But this is a clear admission, and indeed this is manifest throughout his opinion, that although odious and contrary to natural right, it may exist by force of positive law. And this may be mere customary law, as well as the enactment of a statute. The term "positive law," in this sense, may be understood to designate those rules, established by long and tacit acquiescence, or by the legislative act of any state, and which derive their force and effect as law from such acquiescence or legislative enactment, and are acted upon as such, whether conformable to the dictates of natural justice or otherwise.

The principle is, that although slavery and the slave trade are contrary to justice and natural right, yet each nation, in this respect, may establish its own law, within its own territory. And even the slave trade is not regarded as piracy, even by those states who regard it in the abstract as unjust, except when it has been declared so by statute, which can only operate within its own limits; or except when it has been so declared by treaty between two or more powers, in which case it may be so regarded as between such powers, their citizens and subjects. This is confirmed by the English and American authorities, although the governments of both the United States and England have made strong declarations and passed very severe laws against the slave trade ...

If then these states, prior to the adoption of the constitution, would have been sovereign and independent, these views of the established and recognized laws of nations indicate clearly what would have been their relative condition, and their respective rights. Slavery was likely to subsist in some states, and to be abolished in others. Each would have been clothed with certain rights, and bound to the performance of certain duties, which each would have a right to defend and enforce by war, to which there would be a constant temptation; and this could only have been avoided by treaty, regulating and providing for the enjoyment and security of such rights. It would have been in vain to say, that slavery being founded in wrong and injustice, any treaty tending to assent to, uphold and sanction it, would be itself immoral and wrong, and so could not conscientiously be made. Nations cannot elect the subjects on which they will treat; treaties are often made under great exigencies, as the best alternative which can be resorted to in order to avoid greater evils. In the infancy of our commerce and of our political power, we thought it not wrong to make treaties with the Algerines, and other piratical powers of the coast of Barbary, who had committed depredations on our commerce, and carried our citizens into captivity. We made treaties for ransoming our citizens held in slavery, and paid tribute to these acknowledged pirates, to induce them to forbear plundering our commerce, although such payments contributed directly to the upholding and encouragement of robbery and piracy. Having made such treaties, nobody would doubt that it was our duty to fulfil them to the letter, any more than they would doubt our perfect right to refuse renewing them, the moment we were able to defend our own rights by our own strength. No; in making a treaty, we must take our relations with others as we find them; and make the best provision for our rights which is practicable under the circumstances. The question is, in adopting or rejecting a proposed mutual stipulation, not whether it is the most desirable on general grounds of expediency, but whether it is preferable to that which is the inevitable alternative if this is rejected.

But if no binding treaty could be made on the subject of slavery, what would have been the necessary alternative? It would have been a state of things in which acknowledged rights were in constant danger of being drawn into conflict between neighboring states, leading to a war likely to be perpetual, or perhaps to a still more disastrous result – that of some states being subjugated by others of superior physical strength, in a contest in which right and wrong would be disregarded, and violence and brute force would supersede the government of law and the reign of peace. Can this be regarded as an inflamed or exaggerated view of the condition of these states, as independent, but without compact with each other, if the views of the laws of nations above stated are correct? The states were equal in right, but unequal in power. In view of the laws of nations, there was no difference between Rhode Island

and Virginia, or Pennsylvania and Delaware. With equal rights, constantly in danger of being brought into conflict, with radical differences of opinion and views, both of justice and policy, on the subject of slavery, the danger of hostile collision was imminent. What alternative was there, but either a general treaty of alliance or a league, or a union under one government, to whom should be confided all these subjects of common and mutual interest. The latter expedient was adopted. The several states agreed to renounce their rights of sovereignty to a limited extent; among other subjects, the regulation of their intercourse with foreign powers, with the Indian tribes and with each other; the right of war and peace, and that of making treaties either with foreign powers or with each other. Certain other subjects of common interest were also surrendered, and placed under the exclusive control and jurisdiction of the common government. Instead of enforcing their rights, as they could have done before, only by war, it was agreed to establish a general government, furnished with full and complete legislative, judicial and executive powers, to take cognizance of these rights, to provide by law for the regulation of them, to declare and apply them in an orderly course of judicature, and to carry them into full effect. On coming to this arrangement, it could not be kept out of view, that some states had large numbers of slaves, and were disposed to uphold and sanction the existence of slavery by their laws; whilst others denounced it and held it in abhorrence, as unjust and criminal, alike opposed to natural right and to good policy. It could not, however, but be known to the framers of the constitution, that in the states where slavery was allowed by law, certain rights attached to its citizens, which were recognized by the laws of nations, and which could not be taken away without their consent. They therefore provided for the limited enjoyment of that right, as it existed before, so as to prevent persons owing service under the laws of one state, and escaping therefrom into another, from being discharged by the laws of the latter; and authorized the general government to prescribe means for their restoration. This is the *casus fœderis*; to this extent the states are bound by their compact, but no further. Slavery was not created, established or perpetuated by the constitution. It existed before; it would have existed if the constitution had not been made. The framers of the constitution could not abrogate slavery, or the qualified rights claimed under it; they took it as they found it, and regulated it to a limited extent. The constitution, therefore, is not responsible for the origin or continuance of slavery. The provision it contains was the best adjustment which could be made of conflicting rights and claims, and was absolutely necessary to effect what may now be considered as the general pacification, by which harmony and peace should take the place of violence and war. These were the circumstances, and this the spirit, in which the constitution was made; the regulation of slavery so far as to prohibit states by law from harboring fugitive slaves, was an essential element in its formation; and the union intended to be established by it was essentially necessary to the peace, happiness and highest prosperity of all the states. In this spirit, and with these views steadily in prospect, it seems to be the duty of all judges and magistrates to expound and apply these provisions in the constitution and laws of the United States; and in this spirit it behooves all persons, bound to obey the laws of the United States, to consider and regard them.

The duties and relations of the states to each other, by the laws of nations, anterior to the making of the constitution, and the qualified but acknowledged right arising from the establishment of slavery in some states, and its exclusion in others, having been alluded to briefly in the opinion of the court, it was thought advisable, in this note, to expand the argument somewhat, arising from that consideration, but more especially to state the judicial authorities upon which it rests.

READING QUESTIONS ON SHAW

1 How can Shaw reach what seem to be opposite conclusions in the two cases?
2 Charles-Henri Sanson was appointed executioner of Paris by Louis XVI, and served him faithfully. After the French Revolution he served new political masters, and became the king's executioner in a new sense. In the counter-terror, he beheaded another former employer, Robespierre. Sanson insisted on professional detachment at his task, and is said to have argued that were he to have refused to execute those he thought unworthy, he would have been no better than a murderer for those he did behead. Compare his situation with those of Judge Shaw and Captain Vere.

Anthony Sebok
"Judging the Fugitive Slave Acts" (1991)

Sebok argues that Judge Shaw could have decided Sims's case differently had he reasoned in the way that Dworkin recommends.

Robert Cover argues in *Justice Accused* that the *Fugitive Slave Acts* created a "moral/formal" dilemma for Northern judges. As judges, these men had sworn to uphold the Constitution and the laws of the United States. It seemed apparent to many judges that the federal government's intentions were clear, that the Acts had been passed by valid majorities in Congress, and that they were sanctioned by the Constitution. But, as Northern elites, many of them held strong abolitionist beliefs and considered slavery (and, by extension, the capture of Blacks for return to a life of slavery) evil. These judges lived in a world where, with increasing frequency, many politicians, state judges, and other legal elites were arguing for the rejection of the *Fugitive Slave Acts*. The dilemma, then, lay between the judges' moral beliefs and their formal legal obligations ...

Cover's conclusion is that the leading legal theory of the age – legal positivism – so dominated these judges that they could see but not act upon the appeals made from natural law in their courtrooms. Cover concludes that it was the very same technical skill that led these men to be judges that barred them from acting on their beliefs and rejecting the slave laws. The conscientious application of positivism led to "cognitive dissonance" amongst many judges of 1850. Cover suggests that these judges responded in two ways. First, they exaggerated the mechanical operation of the law, so as to deny to themselves any discretion and thereby excuse their failure to act. Second, they "raised the formal stakes" in the cases before them by claiming that if political or moral values were introduced into the process of adjudication, the authority of the state over all citizens would be eroded. Put most starkly, Cover depicts the Northern federal judges of 1850 as saying that in such morally charged cases as those concerning fugitive slaves, adjudication did not require moral judgment, and worse, moral judgment would imperil the state's authority.

Cover implicitly reaffirms the dichotomy ... natural law (normative communal vision) on the one side; positivism (bureaucracy and order) on the other. Cover thus finds the moral/formal dilemma a necessary element of American constitutional interpretation. To rebut Cover's view of adjudication, one would either have to dissolve the moral/formal dichotomy or show why the dichotomy is in fact not a dilemma ...

Dworkin believes that the moral/formal dilemma embraced by Cover is a trap set up by the positivist in order to make positivism attractive. The trap creates two artificial categories which bear little relation to legal practice: legal positivism ("which insists that law and morals are made wholly distinct by ... rules everyone accepts for using `law'") and natural law ("which insists, on the contrary, that [law and morality] are united"). The false dichotomy poses a choice between positivism and natural law, or between setting out the judge's responsibility as searching for what the law "is" as opposed to what it "ought to be" ...

With the exception of some Constitutional Utopians, few argued that the Constitution, with its implicit references to slavery, did not actually permit slavery in some parts of the country. Further, it would have been hard for someone to argue in 1840 that the Constitution actively forbade slavery. Slavery was a matter of state law, and it is unlikely that Dworkin could generate not only a federal prohibition against slavery, but also some theory of federal common law or federal rights applicable to the states to enforce that prohibition. The Constitution did not approve of slavery, nor did it disapprove of it: its three mentions of the institution regulated a practice which the text could have outlawed but did not (until the Thirteenth Amendment) ...

A combination of these two prongs rebuts the objections to Dworkin's arguments by offering the following claim: the *Fugitive Slave Act* of 1850 was not constitutional because its application, given the conditions of 1850, violated the principle of comity that allowed the free states to tolerate slavery without compromising the demands of their own legal practices ...

Little information exists about the intentions and purposes of the Framers of the fugitive slave clause. As we saw above, however, Dworkin argues that the goal of constitutional interpretation is not to describe the specific state of affairs the Framers intended, but rather to describe the general principle they hoped to build into the Constitution. Just as Dworkin was able to describe a general principle of the Fourteenth Amendment that was "correctly" instantiated by different theories of racial equality at different times, he can do the same with the principle expressed by the fugitive slave clause. The Clause required – most generally – that each state respect the laws of its neighbor; more specifically, it required the states that forbid slavery to deliver runaway slaves to the states that had slavery. But as with the "principle" of racial equality contained in the Fourteenth Amendment, this "principle" of fugitive comity could have had many different theoretical instantiations. One theory Dworkin could advance is as follows: The Constitution, in order to leave questions of the treatment of Blacks within their borders up to each state, could not replace the laws governing the internal regulation of Blacks with federal laws that, in effect, substituted the laws of another state.

If the Clause is read to refer to this theory, then Dworkin's attack on the 1850 Act can be made on two fronts. First, the Clause, which at root was concerned with the states' obligation to return runaways, cannot be read as having granted the federal courts the power to invalidate state processes simply because they were slow or – in the eyes of other states – obstructionist. Thus, the Clause should never have been read to forbid state governments from making fundamental choices about the process necessary for a slave to be "delivered up" to a slave state. Second, the due process clause of the Fifth Amendment limited the sort of processes the federal government could erect to ensure the return of runaway slaves. Unless the process due an accused Black was at least equal to that of the state in which the federal proceeding took place, the "home" state's "pro-Black" processes were being derogated in favor of a Southern state's "anti-Black" processes. These two issues, however, are merely logical extensions of the same central issue, which is: what limits did the fugitive slave clause place on the federal government's power to decide how alleged slaves were to be treated within the Northern states' territory?

The theory of interstate comity available to judges in the 1790s and the early nineteenth century may have been something like the following: In order to respect each state's views on slavery, federal law guarantees the slave states their citizens' property rights in slaves in the United States. This theory assumes that the protection of Southern property rights would not conflict with Northern states' domestic law. This assumption may have been credible when Northern states had no body of domestic law designed to address the treatment of accused slaves by domestic or foreign actors. If the laws of Northern states did not conflict with the extraterritorial claims of residents of Southern states, and federal law went no further than to enforce Southern claims, then the principle of comity described above would be consistent with the 1793

Act. A change in conditions – in both the nature of the Northern states' relation to slave-catching and the attitude of Northern governments toward slave-catching – made the Clause's principle of comity incompatible with either Act, however.

The principle of comity changed between 1793 and 1850 as the world changed. In the early years of the 1793 Act there were few Northern laws about slave-catching to conflict with Southern laws. There was simply much less reason for the Northern states to legislate on the issue of fugitives: the lack of an organized abolition movement meant fewer slaves coming across the border and less popular outrage at the slave-catchers who would enter Northern towns and forcibly remove Blacks to Southern states and inevitably to bondage. The gradual transformation in Northern political morality is illustrated by the rise of "personal liberty" laws, as well as an increase in both the frequency and severity of Northern reaction to the use of the 1793 Act by Southern slaveowners.

In the face of this changing political morality in the North, the Clause forced judges into an inescapable dilemma. On the one hand, the Clause specifically called upon states to cooperate in the return of slaves; one could see this federal instruction as a commitment on the part of the federal government to ensure that conflicts over slaves were regulated by more than the usual "interstate comity" rules that governed choice of law disputes. On the other hand, as Northern states passed more laws regulating how slaves were to be caught within their territory, the federal involvement in slave-catching necessarily had to express a preference in upholding either the North's or the South's conception of how slaves were to be caught. Since the activity always took place in the North, to uphold the Southern conception would increasingly void Northern laws regulating conduct within their own borders.

[F]or Northern states to curb their personal liberty laws (or to choose not to pass them out of regard for the Clause) would have violated the Clause's commitment to the principle of comity described above. It would be misleading to say that the free states were, in any significant way, adopting a view about the treatment of Blacks simply by omitting to act in a way that opposed a slave state's interests. However, once the free states developed and articulated a view – upon which they based positive state action – about how alleged slaves should be treated, then each time they curbed their sense of what process was due, and acted because of the slave state's interests, they were coerced into choosing the Southern regime over their own. That is why Dworkin can say that the change in the political morality and actions in the North made demands on the Clause that exposed its incompatibility with the Acts. Once that point was reached, to the extent that the Northern states were obliged to act because of the Constitution, the Constitution was not just protecting the slaveholders interest in his slave, but forcing the North to respect that interest through procedures infected with the assumptions of slavery.

Northern states had begun to develop a coherent policy as to the treatment of fugitive slaves such that in regulating civil life within their territory, these states were taking positive steps toward preventing slave-catching. The Court's optimism that federal law could coexist with state inactivity became untenable as soon as state regulation with regard to the due process necessary to remove a fugitive slave began to look more and more like Pennsylvania's unconstitutional antikidnapping law.

[B] THE CLAUSE AND DUE PROCESS

... [B]y 1850, the Clause could not have been read to allow unconstrained federal regulation of slave-catching. A related and important point is that even if the Clause were viewed as giving the federal government the power to enforce the Northern states' obligations as set out in the Clause (to "deliver up" slaves), this still does not mean that the federal process used could violate contemporary state standards of due process. A conflict still remained concerning the extent to which the federal rules should reflect the Northern states' belief that any Black brought before a court in the North should enjoy the presumption that she was free until proven otherwise, and the Southern belief that proceedings in the North were little more than summary extradition hearings, where the presumption was reversed, and that any alleged slave could get a full and fair hearing once they were returned to the state of their alleged master.

We should recall what we determined to be the Clause's general principle: comity between the states with regard to how Blacks were to be treated within their borders. Until 1850, there was no special federal procedure for slave-catching, since there were no special federal officers like commissioners. Until 1850, federal judges (if they ever heard a runaway case) applied the procedure of the state in which they sat. This reflected the Clause's general commitment to comity. Under the pre-1850 scheme, as conceptions of due process changed in a Northern state, the federal procedure, which relied on state procedure, thus changed accordingly. Until 1850, a Dworkinian interpreter could claim that the Clause did not permit a person domiciled in Pennsylvania to receive federal procedural protections so thin that, in effect, that person's only real hearing was in South Carolina, with South Carolina "procedure." The denial of this interpretation would provide slave-catchers with guaranteed access to Southern slave law in every fugitive slave case: upon seizing a Black in the North, they then would need only to invoke a shred of federal procedure in order legitimately to introduce Southern law. On the other hand, obedience to the principle of comity would, according to our Dworkinian interpretation, require that federal due process treat Blacks with at least that process they would have received in the state in which they were seized ...

Dworkin's specific argument about the 1850 Act suggests that Cover's depiction of adjudication in hard cases is a misdescription with serious political consequences. If adjudication in hard cases requires estrangement from one's political commitments, then Cover simultaneously discourages people with political commitments from choosing to become, or remain, judges, while licensing those who remain judges to discount the role of political commitment in the interpretation of the Constitution. Cover's pessimistic view of adjudication is not necessarily correct. Judges in 1850 were not trapped between the formalism of following evil rules or the moral commands of their consciences.

READING QUESTIONS ON SEBOK

1 Summarize Sebok's argument in your own words. What steps in the argument might a positivist reject?
2 Suppose the *Fugitive Slave Act* had been designed to block the response Sebok suggests. What then?

W.J. Waluchow
"Charter Challenges: A Test Case for Theories of Law?" (1991)

Waluchow provides an introduction to legal reasoning under the *Charter*. At the same time, he argues that, despite the deeply moral nature of that reasoning, it is consistent with legal positivism's views about the nature of law.

Does the existence of valid, positive law ever depend on moral considerations? To this question, defenders of Natural Law Theory (NLT) are
thought emphatically to answer "Yes, and necessarily so. An unjust law
seems to be no law at all." Defenders of Legal Positivism (LP), by contrast, are thought to answer with a resounding "No, and necessarily so.
The existence of law is one thing, its merit or demerit quite another. The
existence of a valid, positive law is entirely a function of its pedigree,
that is, by the manner in which it becomes law."

In recent years, this conventional approach has met with serious challenge. John Finnis argues that "a theory of natural law need not have as
its principal concern, either theoretical or pedagogical, the affirmation
that "unjust laws are not laws'."[1] Others suggest that LP is in no way
wedded to a denial that moral standards can ever serve as criteria for
determining the existence or the content of positive law. They argue
that moral considerations sometimes figure in arguments purporting to
establish or challenge legal validity, or in arguments intended to determine the scope, extent, or meaning of positive law. On earlier occasions, I joined the ranks of those eager to substantiate these latter suggestions regarding LP. I argued that it is consistent with LP to suggest
that the identification of a standard as valid, positive law can depend
on substantive moral arguments. As an example, it was urged that a
legal positivist's ultimate criteria for legal validity (for instance, H.L.A.
Hart's rule of recognition) might well incorporate distinctly moral tests.
Were this true, then according to LP, the actual validity of a purportedly valid law might, on some occasion, be a function of its "moral
merit." The simple fact of its enactment by Parliament, for example,
would be insufficient to determine the standard's validity. One might
further be required to decide whether it passes the appropriate moral
tests. What permits us to view such tests as compatible with LP is that
their existence is in no way necessary for law. Rather, their existence is
contingent upon social practice. Moral tests exist as constraints on legal
validity, only if, as a matter of social fact, they have the appropriate
pedigree, such as being explicitly incorporated into a constitutional charter or bill of rights.

Another of my arguments was that versions of LP which recognize
the possibility (indeed the frequent existence) of "pedigreed," or legally
accepted, moral tests for legal validity are theoretically preferable to
NLT or any version of LP which denies that possibility. In an attempt to

support this claim, I pointed to challenges to legal validity under documents like the *Canadian Charter of Rights and Freedoms*. I suggested that these *Charter* challenges typically involve substantive moral arguments. It is mistaken to view such arguments as anything but attempts to demonstrate either that pedigreed criteria for legal validity have not been satisfied, and that what seems to be valid law is in fact no law at all, or that a law must be understood or interpreted in such a way that it does not infringe upon a pedigreed moral right protected by the *Charter*. In the former instance, morality figures in arguments purporting to establish or challenge the existence of valid law. In the latter case, it figures in arguments purporting to establish the content of valid law, the law contained within the instruments (for example, the statutes or precedents) employed for its expression. If my construal of *Charter* challenges is correct, then it follows that the existence and content of law does indeed sometimes depend on moral factors. It further follows that any version of LP which accepts this as a theoretical possibility is, on that account alone, superior to one which does not. In this essay, I shall refer to the first kind of LP as "Inclusive Legal Positivism" (ILP) and the second as "Exclusive Legal Positivism" (ELP). According to ILP, moral standards are included within the possible grounds a legal system might adopt for determining the existence and content of valid law. ELP, by contrast, logically excludes the adoption of such grounds.

My primary objective in the present paper is to develop further the argument that ILP is a sounder theory of law than ELP because it offers a better theoretical account of *Charter* challenges. A secondary objective is to show that the choice between ILP and ELP (or between one of them and some third competitor) is not an idle curiosity. The choice is an important one, not merely for traditional debates within philosophy concerning the nature of law, but ultimately for legal practice as well. It is tempting to think, contra Bentham and Hart, that traditional theories concerning the nature of law have little if any bearing upon the actual practice of law. Whether they espouse legal realism, legal positivism, or natural law theory, indeed whether they have anything remotely like a theory of law at all, judges will go about their business in the usual manner. For example, when faced with a seriously unfair but binding precedent, the judge adopting NLT will argue, "This is unfair and not law; therefore, I should perhaps not apply it in this case, even if it does satisfy all the legally recognized tests of validity." The judge adopting LP, on the other hand, will argue, "Though this is law because it satisfies all the legally recognized tests of validity, it may none the less be too unfair for me to apply in this case." In each instance, the same steps will probably be taken and the end result will likely be the same (the precedent is overridden instead of applied); this occurs despite the different descriptions under which those steps are taken and the end result conceived. If the two judges do differ in their solutions to the dilemma posed, it will not be because of any differences they might have concerning the respective merits of LP versus NLT.

The same will be true, it might be thought, in situations where the law is unsettled, perhaps because the meaning or implication of a statute is unclear. The judge adopting NLT will look to his moral theory for help in deciding what the law really requires in the case before him. Human law, on his view, is a vehicle for the expression and implementation of the moral law, and when for some reason it fails to express that higher law, it is incumbent upon a judge to appeal directly to the higher source. As for the judge adopting LP, she too may repair to moral theory to help solve the riddle left by positive law. There is little reason to think that her answer will necessarily be any different from the one provided by her NLT counterpart. It is likely, though, that she will conceive the process of finding that answer somewhat differently. She will view that process, not as the discovery of pre-existing, higher law, but as the discretionary creation of new law in fulfilment of her quasi-legislative, judicial responsibility to fill in gaps left by positive law.

We should resist the tempting view that philosophical reflection about the nature of law offers legal practice nothing except different descriptions of what judges do. My secondary aim, then, will be to give some credence to this claim. I shall do so by relating my investigation of the merits of ILP over ELP to current disputes in constitutional theory about the nature, justification, and proper extent of judicial review. More specifically, I will consider briefly various views regarding the interpretation of charters or bills of rights; whether, as the jargon has it, interpretation should be confined to "the four corners" of the document or whether a more liberal approach is the better course. It is obvious that much of practical importance hinges on how these particular disputes are settled. It takes little imagination to see how a court more firmly wedded to a narrow, literalist approach to constitutional adjudication might have decided *Roe v Wade* or *R. v Morgentaler*.[2] It may not be so clear, however, how philosophical thought about the nature of law could have any serious bearing on how these cases were or could have been decided. But as we shall see, there are indeed important theoretical and pragmatic connections here which can have a profound bearing on practice. Depending on her theory of law, a judge may view a liberal approach to *Charter* challenges as the naked usurpation of the legislative role, or alternatively, a simple attempt to interpret and determine the scope of existing law, something judges do all the time and which requires no special justification.

II ILP VS ELP

The overall objective of this section is to show that ILP provides a better theoretical account of the moral argument which sometimes takes place in *Charter* challenges. Our first order of business, then, must be to substantiate the premise that moral argument does indeed sometimes take place in such cases. Without this premise, the argument cannot even begin to get off the ground.

It might seem obvious that *Charter* challenges rely on moral arguments. After all, in listing fundamental rights and freedoms, the *Charter* uses terminology which figures prominently in virtually all modern moral theories. The right to equality (section 15), for instance, is a paradigm moral right. So too is the right not to be deprived of liberty except in accordance with fundamental justice (section 7). But the mere use of terms which admit of moral meanings is, in itself, clearly insufficient to establish our premise. From the fact that two normative systems share a certain common vocabulary, it fails to follow that their common terms have identical referents or that they have identical or even similar meanings. This is obviously true in the case of law and morals. The interpretation given to a legal term is often quite different from the corresponding moral term. One who plea bargains a murder charge down to manslaughter may yet be morally condemned as a murderer. What is legally judged to be fair business practice may quite properly be assessed as morally unfair, and so on. So the mere use of moral terminology within the *Charter* is itself of little argumentative force.

Yet, perhaps it is not the terminology itself which is of importance, but rather the way the judiciary has come to approach and understand it. As should now be clear, most Canadian judges have been willing to adopt a non-legalistic, broad, purposive, or liberal approach to the *Charter*. In *Big M Drug Mart*, for instance, the then Chief Justice of the Canadian Supreme Court, Brian Dickson, had this to say concerning the proper method of *Charter* adjudication:

In *Hunter v Southam Inc.*, [1984] 2 SCR 145, this Court expressed the view that the proper approach to the definition of the rights and freedoms guaranteed by the *Charter* was a purposive one. The meaning of a right or freedom guaranteed by the *Charter* was to be ascertained by an analysis of the purpose of such a guarantee; it was to be understood, in other words, in the light of the interests it was meant to protect ... The interpretation should be, as the judgement in *Southam* emphasizes, a generous rather than a legalistic one, aimed at fulfilling the purpose of the guarantee and securing for individuals the full benefit of the *Charter's* protection. At the same time it is important not to overshoot the actual purpose of the right or freedom in question, but to recall that the *Charter* was not enacted in a vacuum, and must therefore, as this Court's decision in *Law Society of Upper Canada v Skapinker*, [1984] SCR 357 illustrates, be placed in its proper linguistic, philosophic and historical contexts.[3]

According to Dickson, then, interpretations of the *Charter* should be generous rather than legalistic, aimed at fulfilling the interests or objects that document was meant to protect. These objects are to play a far more central role in its interpretation than is typically the case with many other types of legal standards and instruments like tax laws or administrative regulations. It is this fact, no doubt, which led one legal commentator to remark that the "*Charter* imposes substantive new responsibilities on the courts. It requires not only that they deal with new issues but that they reconsider traditional methods of reasoning."[4] They must eschew a narrow legalistic approach to *Charter* adjudication in favour of a much broader one which more firmly focuses on the interests or objects that the *Charter* sets out to protect. Of course, these objects are often none other than those fundamental rights and freedoms of political morality to which the *Charter* gives legal protection.

It is reasonably clear, then, that the Supreme Court of Canada believes that the interpretation of the *Charter* should be governed by the objects or interests it was meant to protect. If so, then it is also reasonably clear that moral argument will often figure in *Charter* challenges. If one must interpret the *Charter* in light of its objects, and those objects are often moral rights and freedoms, then it follows that one cannot determine what the *Charter* means, and thus the conditions upon legal validity which it imposes, without determining the nature and extent of the rights of political morality it seeks to guarantee. Yet, one cannot do this without engaging in substantive moral argument. This argument will of course be sensitive to the linguistic, philosophic, and historical context in which the *Charter* is to be placed. This, however, is not an objection to the point being made here, since such sensitivity is precisely what one would expect of responsible reflection concerning moral entitlements. It would be a serious mistake to think that reasoning about moral rights and freedoms, whether private or public, can take place independently of contextual considerations. What one is entitled to expect from government, other public institutions, and indeed from other private citizens, depends in large part upon shared understandings, expectations, historical circumstances, and so on – in short, on the linguistic, philosophic and historical context in which all moral arguments must take place.

So, the manner in which Canadian judges approach their task of interpreting and applying the *Charter* seems to offer some basis for the premise that moral argument is often involved in *Charter* adjudication. But more support is obviously needed, if only because the evidentiary value of judicial testimony in these matters may be open to question. Consider a parallel with the philosophy of science. Many philosophers of science adopt the methodological principle that it is better to look at what scientists actually do, rather than to what they say about what they do, when looking to support or question theories about the nature of science or of scientific methodology and reasoning. One obvious reason for this principle is the simple fact that being a good scientist in no way guarantees that one is a good philosopher, no more than being a good philosopher means one can do elementary-particle physics. Richard Feynman, the celebrated physicist and Nobel prize winner, had the following to say concerning the suggestion that scientists should give more consideration to social problems, in particular, that they should be more responsible in considering the impact of science on society: "I believe that a scientist looking at non-scientific problems is just as dumb as the next guy – and when he talks about a non-scientific matter, he sounds as naive as anyone untrained in the matter.[5]

Perhaps Feynman's point, made only partly in jest, can be generalized to other non-scientific questions, such as the proper philosophical characterization of science and scientific reasoning. If so, then we must accept the theoretical possibility that scientists generally misconceive what it is they are up to when they set out to construct scientific hypotheses and theories. They may think, for instance, that they are discovering objective, theory-independent facts, when in reality their so-called objective facts are thoroughly theory laden ... If such instances of widespread misconception are possible within science, then why not in law? Is it not possible that Canadian judges simply misconceive the fundamental nature of the enterprise in which they are engaged? If so, then they may all think that they are sometimes engaged in substantive moral argument in *Charter* challenges when in fact they are not, just as they may think that in hard cases, their decisions are discretionary, when in fact they are attempts to enforce pre-existing legal rights.

In answer to this radically sceptical objection to reliance on judicial testimony, the following may well suffice. While we must accept the theoretical possibility that Canadian courts are generally confused about what it is they are about in *Charter* cases, the burden of proof is surely on one who wishes seriously to urge this possibility as a sufficient reason to dismiss judicial characterizations of judicial practice. If those who participate in legal adjudication believe their practice requires X, then barring any good reason to the contrary, we philosophers who seek to provide theoretical accounts of the law, are surely justified in accepting that the practice really does require X. Yet the purely theoretical possibility of widespread misconception is clearly not reason enough; we should not be Cartesian sceptics in such cases, sceptics for whom the mere logical possibility of error precludes acceptance of the obvious.

Assume, however, that I am wrong about this and that the way the judges view what they do has absolutely no probative force whatsoever because they could be wrong – just as most everyone was at one time wrong in thinking that the Earth is flat. If this is true, then our only avenue for determining whether the judges are right in thinking that moral argument does sometimes figure prominently in *Charter* cases is to look ourselves at what they actually do, how they actually decide *Charter* cases. Fortunately, this task poses little difficulty. A careful reading of virtually any *Charter* challenge reveals that moral argument does play a vital role. I shall conclude my defence of the premise that moral argument plays a role in *Charter* adjudication by briefly examining one such case, *Andrews v Law Society of B.C.*[6]

This appeal was heard before the B.C. Court of Appeal and raised the issue of whether a requirement of Canadian citizenship as a prerequisite to the practice of law was in violation of section 15 of the *Charter*. Section 15 falls under the title "Equality Rights" and reads as follows:

15(1) Every individual is equal before and under the law and has the right to the equal protection and equal benefit of the law without discrimination and, in particular, without discrimination based on race, national or ethnic origin, colour, religion, sex, age or mental or physical disability.

Section 15 makes it unconstitutional for any law or other legal instrument to discriminate against persons, unless such discrimination can be justified under section 1 of the *Charter*.[7] Section 1 states that:

1. The *Canadian Charter of Rights and Freedoms* guarantees the rights and freedoms set out in it subject only to such reasonable limits prescribed by law as can be demonstrably justified in a free and democratic society.

The question whether section 1 could be used to override section 15 was crucial to the case.

The major issue before the Court was whether the citizenship requirement imposed by the Law Society of British Columbia amounted to discrimination. This question led to another more basic issue of both moral and philosophical importance: how does one define discrimination for purposes of interpreting section 15? It is in answering this latter question that we see the first signs of substantive moral argument. Three basic answers were proposed. First, there was the definition proposed by the Law Society which had been accepted by the trial judge.

D1: L is discriminatory if and only if "it draws an irrational or irrelevant distinction between people based on some irrelevant personal characteristic for the purpose, or having the effect of imposing on certain of them, a penalty, disadvantage or indignity, or denying them an advantage."[8]

The key here is the notion of rationality; a law is discriminatory only if there is no rational basis for it. It might be highly objectionable in many other ways, but so long as any distinction it draws is rational in light of what the law sets out to do, then the law is not discriminatory. This is a fairly weak definition in the sense that it employs means-end rationality as its criterion for discrimination. Regardless of the ends sought, or the effect upon people of the means used in realizing those ends, a law is not discriminatory so long as it really does work effectively towards its ends. The result, as the B.C. Court well realized, is that many laws which ruthlessly but effectively help to realize morally objectionable ends, or which serve to victimize innocent parties, will be judged non-discriminatory. As a consequence, the Court rejected D1. This definition is surely not what "equality" and "freedom from discrimination" mean.

A second definition was proposed by Andrews:

D2: L is discriminatory if it draws any adverse distinction on the basis of a personal characteristic or category.

The Court was equally unhappy with this definition. Were it to be adopted, a vast number of existing laws, which necessarily draw adverse distinctions among people based on personal characteristics, would be deemed discriminatory and thus in violation of section 15. This consequence in itself was sufficient reason, in the Court's mind, for thinking that D2 is unacceptable, though it went on to list several other reasons why the definition had to be rejected.[9]

A third possibility was accepted by the Appeal Court and used as their basis for finding in favour of the appellant:

D3: L is discriminatory if it draws any unreasonable or unfair distinctions, distinctions which are unduly prejudicial.[10]

There are some important observations to be made regarding D3. In the view of the Court, the test under D3 must be objective, that is, based on whether the law is in fact discriminatory, not on whether the lawmakers, or those who might have acted under its authority, sincerely believed that it was discriminatory. Were the test subjective, then perhaps one would be required to establish only non-moral, empirical facts about what people's moral beliefs actually are or were. But an objective test clearly means that the Court must itself determine whether L, in actual fact, does draw unreasonable or unfair distinctions. This determination cannot be made independent of moral deliberation:

[T]he question to be answered under S.15 should be whether the impugned distinction is reasonable or fair, having regard to the purposes and aims and its effect on persons adversely affected. I include the word "fair" as well as "reasonable" to emphasize that the test is not one of pure rationality [as with D1] but one connoting the treatment of persons in ways which are not unduly prejudicial to them. This test must be objective, and the discrimination must be proved on the balance of probabilities ... The ultimate question is whether a fair-minded person, weighing the purposes of legislation against its effects on the individuals adversely affected, and giving due weight to the right of the Legislature to pass laws for the good of all, would conclude that the legislative means adopted are unreasonable or unfair.[11]

Plainly, this test for discrimination requires moral deliberation. Indeed, the parallel between the test proposed – what a fair-minded person would conclude – and what is required by "ideal observer theories" of morality is striking.[12] The Court is clear in its view that the test is neither subjective, nor based on pure means-end rationality. On the contrary, it is objective, and based on what is fair and reasonable.

Upon adopting D3 as the criterion of discrimination, the Court went on to apply it to the *Andrews* situation. They ruled that the Law Society's citizenship requirement was indeed discriminatory, and thus in violation of section 15, because it was neither fair nor reasonable for someone in Andrews' position to be denied a licence to practice law. The Court rejected the Society's contention that lawyers, because they are involved in the processes or structures of government, should be citizens, and not merely residents, of Canada:

While lawyers clearly play an important role in our society, it cannot be contended that the practice of law involves performing a state or government function. In this respect the role of lawyers may be distinguished from that of legislators, judges, civil servants and policemen.[13]

In addition, the Court ruled that authority and the persuasive precedent of other jurisdictions support the unreasonableness of the citizenship requirement:

The fact is that citizenship was not seen as essential to the practice of law in this province prior to 1971. It is still not viewed as such in most jurisdictions; only two other provinces require lawyers to be citizens. In the tradition of the British Commonwealth, citizenship has never been a requirement for the right to practise law. These facts belie the contention that citizenship is vitally and integrally connected with the lawyer's role in society.[14]

After putting all these moral, philosophic, and historical factors together, the Court was prepared to rule that discrimination – unfair and unreasonable adverse treatment on the basis of a personal characteristic – had indeed occurred and that section 15 had therefore been infringed.

Of course, the violation of a *Charter* right does not in itself entail that the offending measure is unconstitutional and therefore invalid. It may yet be justified under section 1, which validates infringements under certain conditions. The question therefore arose whether a citizenship requirement, acknowledged to be unfair and therefore discriminatory, could nonetheless be justified in a free and democratic society. A second question arose too, which had to be answered first: How does one go about answering the first question? What standards, if any, apply? Fortunately an answer to this second question had already been provided in authoritative precedent. In *Regina v Oakes*,[15] the Supreme Court of Canada had enunciated several principles to govern the application of section 1. These may be summarized as follows:

1. The onus of proving that a limitation on any *Charter* right is reasonable and demonstrably justified in a free and democratic society rests upon the party seeking to uphold the limitation [in this instance, the Law Society].
2. The presumption is that *Charter* rights are guaranteed unless the party invoking section 1 can bring itself within the exceptional criteria justifying their being limited.
3. The standard of proof under section 1 is [as it is under section 15] the preponderance of probabilities.
4. It must be proven that the objectives to be served by the measures limiting a *Charter* right are sufficiently important to warrant overriding a constitutionally protected right or freedom. At a minimum, the objectives must be shown to relate to societal concerns which are pressing and substantial in a free and democratic society.
5. It must be shown that the means chosen – the offending provisions – are reasonable and demonstrably justified. This, the B.C. Court noted, involves three components:
   i. The measures must be fair and not arbitrary – they must be carefully designed to achieve the objective in question and rationally connected to it.
   ii. The means should impair the right as little as possible.
   iii. There must be proportionality between the effects of the limiting measure and the objective – the more severe the prejudicial effects of a measure, the more important the objective must be [the "proportionality test"].

Having set out the appropriate standards to be applied, the Court went on to argue that section 1 could not be utilized to justify the Law Society's discriminatory citizenship requirement. The apparent objectives of the requirement could not be said to relate, in any reasonably clear way, to societal concerns which are pressing and substantial. The effects of the means chosen were not proportional to the importance of the objectives sought, and were in fact not rationally related to them: citizenship is in no way a necessary condition of being a good lawyer.

The appeal was therefore granted. The citizenship requirement was invalid owing to its unconstitutionality.

Judging from the above analysis, it is apparent that answering the questions posed by section 1 will often require appeal to pure means-end rationality of the sort discussed above in relation to D1. In addition, it will invariably require a certain amount of historical investigation into the political morality of other democratic jurisdictions. But as with section 15, it is also clear that section 1 sometimes demands a degree of moral deliberation. One simply cannot determine whether a measure is fair without contemplating moral premises. One cannot determine proportionality without considering the moral and political importance of the various objectives and concerns which find support in the *Charter* and in the offending measures. One cannot determine whether a limit can be demonstrably justified in a free and democratic society without engaging in substantive arguments of political morality. As Peter Hogg notes,

[T]he phrase "demonstrably justified" calls for normative judgment by the court as to the legitimacy and necessity in a free and democratic society of the impugned restriction on liberty and that judgment cannot depend wholly upon what has seemed acceptable to legislative bodies in Canada and elsewhere. For good or ill, the *Charter* clearly contemplates that the majoritarian judgment of a legislative body, or even many legislative bodies, be subject to review on *Charter* grounds by the courts.[16]

Surely what is required in all these instances is not the kind of reasoning which strives to be neutral with respect to, or totally detached from, concerns of political morality. What is required is normative, moral judgment which tackles the tricky issues involved whenever one is called upon to strike a reasonable balance between competing moral and political interests. Section 1, then, requires a significant measure of moral reasoning.

If the arguments of the preceding sections are sound, we seem entitled to accept the premise that *Charter* cases sometimes involve moral argument. Even if one totally discounts the evidentiary value of the judges' own reflections about their reasoning on the *Charter*, we have ample evidence of how they actually carry out that task – in what they do as opposed to what they say they do. Our examination of *Andrews* illustrates that moral reasoning does occur, as it does in many other cases as well, cases like *Morgentaler* and *Oakes*. Indeed, if the analysis of

Andrews is correct, then application of sections 15 and 1 will almost invariably be guided, in part, by moral considerations.

So moral deliberation does figure in *Charter* cases. Our next step must be to show that it figures in the right way. That is, if our findings are to provide support for choosing ILP over ELP, it must be established that the moral standards employed in *Charter* cases sometimes function as tests for the existence and content of valid law. Without this additional premise, we have no basis for preferring ILP to ELP.

Once again, it seems *prima facie* obvious that moral standards do serve the role ILP admits but ELP conceives as impossible. In *Morgentaler*, for instance, we have what functioned for over twenty years as valid law being declared to have been unconstitutional and thus of no force or effect. The ground for this declaration was violation of section 7 of the *Charter* which recognizes a right to life, liberty, and security of the person – a right which cannot be denied except in accordance with the principles of fundamental justice. As the courts made plain, "fundamental justice" is to be understood as including substantive, not merely procedural, justice. And whatever one's view about the need for moral reasoning in determining the nature of procedural justice, it is clear that need is present when substantive justice is at issue. To determine the requirements of substantive justice (one of the interests or objects of section 7, in terms of which that section is to be understood), one must engage in moral reflection. If so, we seem to have legal rights, whose content depends upon moral considerations, being used to demonstrate the invalidity of a statutory instrument (section 251 of the *Criminal Code of Canada*).[17] This, of course, is a possibility well recognized by ILP.

But it is not a possibility recognized by ELP. If we accept that theory, the above account, which will be called the "Inclusive Account" (IA) just has to be wrong. If the existence and content of a legal right can never in any way be a function of moral considerations, then we are inexorably led to the following conclusions. When the Supreme Court of Canada considered whether the proper interpretation of section 7 of the *Charter* rendered it in conflict with section 251 of the *Criminal Code*, they could not conceivably have been trying to determine the existence or content of valid law. Similarly, when the B.C. Court of Appeal considered whether section 15 must be understood in such a way that it was unjustifiably infringed by the Law Society's citizenship requirement, they could not conceivably have been determining the existence or content of valid law. They could not have been attempting to understand and apply legal tests for legal validity, because, for example, the crucial test of discrimination, (and hence violation of section 15) is whether people are being treated unreasonably or unfairly – and this test, as we have seen it, is, at least sometimes, partly a moral one.

Yet if the courts were not attempting to determine the existence and content of valid law in these cases, what were they doing? Let us focus on *Andrews* once again. What could the B.C. Court of Appeal have been doing when it addressed the question whether the citizenship requirement was invalid because it violated section 15, and that section 15 was violated because the requirement was unfair to Andrews? There would seem to be only one possibility according to ELP. If the Court was not attempting to determine the existence and content of valid law, then it must have been attempting to determine the existence and content of something other than law, and applying that something else, in some way or other, to undermine the validity of the citizenship requirement. In applying its fairness test, the Court must have been relying on non-legal, moral standards, not to determine that the citizenship requirement was invalid owing to its conflict with superior law, but to make it invalid by declaring it to be so.

It is important to be clear how exactly the *Charter* is to be conceived on this alternative account, which will be referred to as the "Exclusive Account" (EA). According to EA, section 15 does not itself constitute or contain a legal criterion for validity. Rather, it makes reference to an extra-legal, moral criterion to which judges are required or at liberty to appeal in *Charter* challenges. Section 15 directs them to step outside of law and to seek guidance from an external source of non-pedigreed norms, namely, the norms of political morality. A useful parallel is perhaps to be found in foreign law. Courts are sometimes required to make reference to, and indeed to apply, the law of foreign legal systems in deciding cases. According to EA, the *Charter* requires (or permits?) much the same. It requires (or permits?) Canadian judges to make reference to and apply the standards of what amounts to a different kind of foreign system. And just as we would not accept that foreign law becomes part of our legal system just because our judges are required sometimes to apply it in their decisions, we should not think that standards of political morality are thereby incorporated into Canadian law as legal tests for legal validity, just because our judges must (or may) sometimes (as in *Andrews*) make reference to them when deciding *Charter* cases.

On EA, then, the Court in *Andrews* did not, when it based its decision on the unfairness of the citizenship requirement, enforce an existing legal right (to equality) against a measure (the citizenship requirement) which would be valid were it not for the conflict with section 15. On the contrary, it exercised its duty (or liberty), imposed (or granted) by section 15 to make unconstitutional what otherwise would have and had been perfectly valid law. The Court did not discover a legal conflict. It discovered a conflict between law and political morality, and by its decision settled the conflict in favour of the latter. Of course, it is consistent with EA to claim that the Court's decision, though it was based on the enforcement of a moral right, created a new legal right. The effect of the decision in *Andrews* would have been to grant a new legal right to lawyers not to be subject to a citizenship requirement. The Court's decision, as an authoritative act with the appropriate pedigree, was quite capable of creating such a legal right – just as decisions of Parliament, which are themselves often based on moral reasons, are quite obviously capable of creating new legal rights.

This, then, is the alternative account of *Charter* adjudication to which ELP seems to lead. Our next step must be to consider whether the account is an acceptable one. There are several reasons for thinking it is not.

First, EA is simply counter-intuitive. It seems quite at odds with our ordinary understanding of a constitutional document like the *Charter*. The latter is commonly conceived as a measure which creates fundamental legal rights Canadians possess against governments and government agencies. It flouts that understanding to suggest that the *Charter* does not in fact serve this role at all, but instead only makes reference to non-legal, moral rights upon the basis of which judges are empowered to create new legal rights by invalidating what would otherwise be valid legal measures. Insofar as it is part of the fundamental law of Canada, the Canadian *Charter of Rights and Freedoms* is quite naturally viewed as itself creating legal rights. And pointing out the fact that moral deliberation is sometimes required for determining the content of these legal rights does not in any way disturb that natural understanding.

Of course, it is also part of our common understanding that standards of political morality such as one finds in the *Charter* are subject to various kinds of indeterminacy. In cases where indeterminacy figures, judges are thought to play a leading role in shaping the contours of the political morality expressed in the *Charter*. They do so, as they do in any other area of law where indeterminacy is encountered, by exercising their discretion. The *Charter*'s regions of indeterminacy are perhaps greater than in many other areas of law where more closely textured terms are used, terms like "vehicle," "radio telegraph," and "assault." But terms like "equality," "discrimination," and "liberty" are not so open textured as to admit of no determinate meaning whatsoever. If so, then to the extent that the *Charter* provisions employing such terms do admit of determinate meaning, they do create fundamental legal rights Canadians possess against government and government agencies.

To view *Charter* rights as analogous to foreign law, then, comes close to an absurdity. Another factor weighing against EA is the language chosen by Parliament to characterize the *Charter*. Unlike its predecessor, the *Canadian Bill of Rights*, the *Charter* is a constitutional document. As such it has a special force, clearly described in section 52 (1) of the *Constitution Act, 1982*:

52. (1) The Constitution of Canada is the supreme law of Canada, and any law that is inconsistent with the provisions of the Constitution is, to the extent of the inconsistency, of no force or effect.

Taken literally, this provision flatly contradicts EA, and we have yet to see any good reason not to construe it literally. Section 52 does not say that upon judicial declaration that a legal measure is inconsistent with a (foreign) right referred to (but not granted by) the *Charter*, the measure shall from that moment on be of no force and effect. Rather, it says that any measure which is in conflict with a *Charter* provision is, to the extent of the inconsistency, of no force or effect. Of course, inconsistencies do not begin to exist only when judges declare that they exist. On the contrary, judges rule that the inconsistencies exist only because they believe that the legal conflicts already do exist by virtue of the *Charter* and its various provisions. Those provisions include, of course, sections 7 and 15.

Any legal measure, such as section 251 or the Law Society's citizenship requirement, which is inconsistent with either of these provisions is, independently of a judge's decision in a *Charter* challenge, of no force and effect. Yet as we have seen, the contents of sections 15 and 7 are partly determined by considerations of political morality. It seems to follow from the plain language of the *Charter*, then that some moral standards are a part of Canada's accepted conditions for legal validity, something Canadian judges seem to recognize in their decisions.

However, there are further reasons for rejecting EA. For example, it does not easily explain certain features of *Charter* challenges. At the very least, any explanation it suggests is less consonant with these features than IA, which adopts the view that judges are indeed attempting to determine the existence and content of valid law when they hear *Charter* challenges, despite their partial reliance on moral standards. One such feature is that the legal system treats a measure declared invalid as though it were invalid at the time that the actions giving rise to litigation occurred.

Consider *Morgentaler* for example: when section 251 was finally struck down, the obvious fact that Morgentaler had violated section 251 was no longer an acceptable basis for prosecution. All legal action against Morgentaler consequently ceased. The main reason, of course, is that in declaring section 251 unconstitutional, the Court ruled that section 251 had been of no force or effect when the acknowledged violations occurred. The effect of the Court's decision was the recognition that Morgentaler had been within his legal rights. He had not in fact performed actions which were illegal at the time. Were EA accepted, on the other hand, illegal acts would indeed have occurred. It was, by this reasoning, only upon declaration of invalidity by the Court that section 251 became invalid. Prior to that time the legislation had force and effect, and actions in violation of it would have indeed been illegal, criminal acts. But if so, would not prosecution still have been in order? And if not, what is the explanation?

With IA, of course, we have a ready and obvious explanation. The Court discovered a conflict in law between section 251 and a more authoritative legal provision. It discovered that section 7 was in conflict with section 251 and that the latter therefore had been of no force and effect at the time Morgentaler and his colleagues were procuring abortions. In short, the Court discovered that Morgentaler had at all times been acting within his legal rights. The legal obligations purportedly imposed by section 251 did not in fact exist when they acted.

EA offers no ready explanation for why prosecution is so clearly out of order. There was no recognition by the Court that its declaration had retroactive effect, that it was declaring to have been invalid what was in fact valid at the time, nor was there any acknowledgement that this highly unusual step – for which a very special type of justification would surely have been in order – was the reason why prosecution would have to cease. Furthermore, there was no sense that the legal system was granting Morgentaler and his colleagues a favour by no longer prosecuting them for their previous crimes. On the contrary, it was now clear that prosecution was, and always had been (subsequent to the enactment of the *Charter*), ruled out legally, owing to the fact that the criminal law of abortion had been of no force and effect.

A second, related source of difficulty for EA lies in section 24 (1) which reads as follows:

Anyone whose rights or freedoms, as guaranteed by this *Charter*, have been infringed or denied may apply to a court of competent jurisdiction to obtain such remedy as the court considers appropriate and just in the circumstances.

Charter infringement, then, is recognized as a viable ground for legal remedy. If EA is accurate, however, it is not at all obvious why such a remedy should be forthcoming following a successful *Charter* challenge. And the reason is simple: no legal rights would have been violated. Any legal rights as might exist would come into being only with the court's decision. Barring retroactivity, which again seems not at all to have been contemplated, activities pursued under the authority of a law later rendered invalid by a court would have been quite legal prior to that decision. But if so, then why should a remedy be forthcoming? The offending party violated no one's legal rights! He may have violated a moral right, but surely it is not the task of the judiciary to enforce non-legal moral rights against perfectly valid legal rights.

On the other hand, if, as IA insists, the *Charter* does create legal rights which exist antecedently to, and independently of, judicial decisions in cases like *Andrews*, then remedies seem quite appropriate. If the B.C. Court was correct in its interpretation of section 15, Andrews' legal rights had been violated by the Law Society. He should, therefore, have been entitled to an appropriate legal remedy.

Putting all these points together, we seem to have a fairly strong case for rejecting EA in favour of IA. It provides a much more coherent account of *Charter* cases. According to IA, the *Charter* creates legal rights whose content is partly dependent on moral considerations, and judges in cases like *Andrews* and *Morgentaler* are required to determine what these rights are and to apply them against less authoritative, offending measures. Insofar as ILP, but not ELP, is consistent with IA, we seem to have an important argument in its favour.

But perhaps I have been uncharitable in characterizing the account to which ELP seems committed. Perhaps the defender of ELP can offer a modified account, according to which the moral standards to which the Courts appeal in cases like *Andrews* and *Morgentaler* are indeed foreign to the legal system, but nevertheless serve, in virtue of their recognition within the *Charter*, as criteria for legal validity. If so, then to the extent that legal measures (for example, section 251 of the *Criminal Code* or the Law Society's citizenship requirement) are in conflict with these foreign standards, they are legally invalid; this can be so even before the court declares that there is a conflict in a *Charter* case.

Were this modified exclusive account (MEA) adopted, the defenders of ELP would face fewer of the difficulties discussed above. Indeed, their account would be virtually identical to IA, except for the fact that the latter does not view the standards to which appeal must be made in determining the content of *Charter* provisions as equivalent to foreign law. In their view, the standards of fairness to which appeal must be made in determining violations of section 15 are part of the content of that section, and therefore part of the law. So unlike the proponents of IA, the defenders of MEA would still want to maintain that invalidity is based on conflicts with foreign standards. But their account would share all the other desirable features of IA. It would be consonant with the language used in section 52(1) of the *Charter*, and with the various other features of *Charter* challenges examined above. For instance, it too would have a ready explanation for why legal remedies seem an appropriate response in some successful *Charter* challenges.

Attractive as it may be, MEA is clearly a position which the defender of ELP cannot accept. And the reason should now be fairly obvious. It is true, on this account, that the content of a *Charter* provision is not a function of moral reflection. But the same cannot be said for the validity of measures such as the Law Society's citizenship requirement or section 251 of the *Criminal Code*. Whether the moral standards in terms of which the validity of these measures is partly to be established are foreign or not, the fact remains that, on MEA, legal validity is determined in part by moral standards whose understanding requires moral deliberation. If MEA is advanced by the defenders of ELP, they will be forced to admit that the conditions for legal validity accepted within the Canadian legal system include moral conditions. They will be forced to concede, for example, that a condition for the validity of any legal measure within Canada is that it does not unfairly discriminate against individuals in a way which cannot be justified in a free and democratic society. But if this is so, then the existing conditions for valid Canadian laws include moral conditions, a possibility the defenders of ELP is most anxious to deny. Whether those moral conditions are foreign or not seems really beside the point.

So the defenders of ELP appear truly committed to the original account of EA. But we have seen ample reason to reject it in favour of IA. If so, then we are entitled to conclude that ILP provides a much better theoretical account of *Charter* adjudication than ELP. On that account, then, it is a superior theory of law.

NOTES

1 J. Finnis, *Natural Law and Natural Rights* (Oxford: Clarendon Press, 1980) at 351.

2 *Roe v Wade*, 410 US 113 (1973); *R. v Morgentaler* (1986), 52 OR (2d) 353 (CA), aff'd [1988] 1 SCR 30 (SCC) [hereinafter *Morgentaler* cited to SCR].

3 *R. v Big M Drug Mart*, [1958] 1 SCR 295 at 344 [hereinafter *Big M Drug Mart*].

4 W.W. Black, "Canadian Charter of Rights and Freedoms" in J.E. Magnet, ed., *Constitutional Law of Canada*, 3d ed. (Toronto: Carswell, 1987) at 2.

5 R.P. Feynman, *"What Do You Care What Other People Think?" – Further Adventures of a Curious Character* (New York: W.W. Norton, 1988) at 240.

6 *Andrews v Law Society of B.C.*, [1986] 4 WWR 242 (BCCA) [hereinafter *Andrews*]. The Court of Appeal's decision was later upheld (3 to 2) by the Supreme Court of Canada. See *Law Society of B.C. v Andrews*, [1989] 56 DLR(4th) 1. Though there are some important differences between the reasoning of the two Courts, they do not affect the argument of this paper and will be ignored. I will concentrate exclusively on the elegant judgment of McLachlin, JA (as she then was).

7 For reasons of simplicity, and because it in no way affects the arguments of this paper, we shall ignore the possibility of a section 33 override. The latter empowers Parliament or the legislature of a province to "expressly declare in an Act of Parliament or of the legislature, as the case may be, that the Act or a provision thereof shall operate notwithstanding a provision included within section 2 or sections 7 to 15 of [the *Charter*]." Section 33 also provides that a declaration made under its terms "shall cease to have effect five years after it comes into force or on such earlier date as may be specified in the declaration" and that re-enactment is possible.

8 *Andrews, supra,* note 16 at 246.

9 Ibid. at 249.

10 Ibid. at 250–52.

11 Ibid. at 252–53.

12 Ideal observer theories vary, but generally they make a claim similar to the following: "If we want to know whether something is morally right,

the question is: 'Would it be permitted by the moral code which an omnipercipient, disinterested, dispassionate [or benevolent] but otherwise normal person would most strongly tend to support as the moral code for a society in which he expected to live?'"

13 *Andrews, supra,* note 6 at 257.
14 Ibid. at 258.
15 *R. v Oakes,* [1986] 1 SCR 103, 50 CR (3d) 1 [hereinafter *Oakes* cited to SCR].
16 P. Hogg, *Constitutional Law of Canada,* 2d ed. (Toronto: Carswell, 1985) at 689.
17 RSC 1985, c. C-46 [hereinafter the *Criminal Code*].

READING QUESTIONS ON WALUCHOW

1 Would Fuller regard Waluchow's positivism as an example of what he calls "managerial authority"? Or would he regard it as not being authentically positivist?
2 Could Waluchow help Judge Shaw?

John Finnis
"Natural Law and Legal Reasoning" (1994)

Finnis, the leading contemporary exponent of natural law theory, argues that natural law theory provides a sound basis for legal reasoning.

Moral reasoning, legal reasoning, and their interrelationships can scarcely be understood reflectively without attention to two different sources of ambiguity. The source is, in each case, well known: the distinction between reasons and feelings; and the distinction between doing (the shaping of one's own "existence" by one's choices) and making (the exercise of technique by activity on some form of "cultural" object or method). But the distinctions are commonly not well understood, and the traps they lay for the analysis of morality and adjudication are usually neglected.

I

We are animals, but intelligent. Our actions all have an emotional motivation, involve our feelings and imagination and other aspects of our bodiliness, and can all be observed (if only, in some cases, by introspection) as pieces of behaviour. But rationally motivated actions also have an intelligent motivation – seek to realize (protect, promote) an intelligible good.

So our purposes, the states of affairs we seek to bring about, typically have a double aspect: the goal which we imagine and which engages our feelings, and the intelligible benefit which appeals to our rationality by promising to instantiate, either immediately or instrumentally, some basic human good. While some of the purposes we employ intelligence to pursue may be motivated ultimately by nothing more than feeling, others are motivated ultimately by (an understanding of) a basic human good. The idiom in which "reason" refers to purposes – "the reason he did that", equivalent to "his purpose in doing that" – fails to mark this distinction. But none of common speech's related terms – "purpose", "goal", "intention" – is free from the same ambiguity. So I stipulate that when I speak of "reasons" in this chapter, I refer (except when discussing technical reasons) to reason(s) as giving ground for intelligent action motivated ultimately by a basic human good (more precisely, by the intelligible benefit promised by the instantiation of a basic good).

An account of basic reasons for action should not be rationalistic. Human flourishing is not to be portrayed in terms only of exercising capacities to reason. As animals, we are organic substances part of whose well-being is *bodily life*, maintained in health, vigour, and safety, and transmitted to new human beings. To regard human life as a basic reason for action is to understand it as a good in which indefinitely many beings can participate in indefinitely many ways, going far beyond any goal or purpose which anyone could envisage and pursue, but making sense of indefinitely many purposes, and giving rational support to indefinitely many goals.

This sense of "(basic) reason for action" holds for all the other basic human goods: *knowledge* of reality (including aesthetic appreciation of it); *excellence in work and play* whereby one transforms natural realities to express meanings and serve purposes; *harmony between individuals and groups* of persons (peace, neighbourliness, and friendship); *harmony between one's feelings and one's judgements and choices* (inner peace); *harmony between one's choices and judgements and one's behaviour* (peace of conscience and authenticity in the sense of consistency between one's self and its expression); and *harmony between oneself and the wider reaches of reality* including the reality constituted by the world's dependence on *a more-than-human source of meaning and value.*

Such a statement of the basic human goods entails an account of human nature. But it does not presuppose such an account. It is not an attempt to deduce reasons for action from some preexisting theoretical conception of human nature. Such an attempt would vainly defy the logical truth (well respected by the ancients) that "ought" cannot be deduced from "is" – a syllogism's conclusion cannot contain what is not in its premises. Rather, a full account of human nature can only be given by one who understands the human goods practically, i.e., as reasons for choice and action, reasons which make full sense of supporting feelings and spontaneities.

An account of practical reasonableness can be called a theory of "natural law" because practical reasoning's very first principles are those basic reasons which identify the basic human goods as ultimate reasons for choice and action – reasons for actions which will instantiate and express human nature precisely because participating in those goods, i.e. instantiating (actualizing, realizing) those ultimate aspects of human flourishing.

II

To the extent that legal reasoning derives from and participates in practical reasonableness, a sound theory of legal reasoning must differ from some theories now current ...

But, in reality, it is the diversity of *rationally* appealing human goods which makes free choice both possible and frequently necessary. Like every other term concerning human activity, "choice" is afflicted, in common idiom, by ambiguities originating particularly in the distinction between reason and feeling. In its strong, central sense, free choice is the adoption of one amongst two or more rationally appealing and incompatible, alternative options, such that nothing but the choosing itself settles which option is chosen and pursued. Many aspects of individual and social life, and many individual and social obligations, are structured by choice between rationally appealing options whose rational appeal can be explained only in terms, ultimately, of basic human opportunities understood to be objectively good (though variously realizable). No sound sense can be made of "objectivity" and "truth", here or elsewhere, otherwise than in terms of rational judgement, open to all relevant questions.

But if the basic human goods, for all their objectivity and truth, open up so much to free choice, what can be the basis for identifying choices which, though rational, ought to be rejected because unreasonable, wrong, immoral?

Moral thought is simply rational thought at full stretch, integrating emotions and feelings but *undeflected* by them. Practical rationality's fundamental principle is: take as a premiss at least one of the basic reasons for action, and follow through to the point at which you somehow bring about the instantiation of that good in action. Do not act pointlessly. The fundamental principle of moral thought is simply the demand to be fully rational: in so far as it is in your power, allow nothing but the basic reasons for action to shape your practical thinking as you find, develop, and use your opportunities to pursue human flourishing through your chosen actions. Be entirely reasonable. Aristotle's phrase *orthos logos*, and his later followers' *recta ratio*, right reason, should simply be understood as "unfettered reason", reason undeflected by emotions and feelings. And so undeflected reason, and the morally good will, are guided by the first moral principle: that one ought to choose (and otherwise will) those and only those possibilities whose willing is compatible with a will towards the fulfilment of all human persons in all the basic goods, towards the ideal of integral human fulfilment.

Take a simple, paradigmatic form of immorality. Emotion may make one wish to destroy or damage the good life in someone one hates, or the good of knowledge; so one kills or injures, or deceives, that person just out of feelings of aversion. It is immoral, because hereabouts there is a general, so to speak methodological, moral principle intermediate between the most basic principles of practical reason (the basic goods or reasons for action, and the first moral principle) and particular moral norms against killing or lying. This intermediate moral principle, which some call a mode of responsibility, will exclude meeting injury with injury, or responding to one's own weakness or setbacks with self-destructiveness.

Perhaps more immediately relevant to political and legal theory is the intermediate moral principle requiring that one act fairly: that one not limit one's concern for basic human goods simply by one's feelings of self-preference or preference for those who are near and dear. Fairness (and its paradigmatic formulation in the Golden Rule) does not exclude treating different persons differently; it requires only that the differential treatment be justified either by inevitable limits on one's action or by intelligible requirements of the basic goods themselves. I shall say more (VII below) about the legitimate role of feelings in making fair choices in which one prioritizes goods (or instantiations of basic goods) by one's feelings without prioritizing persons simply by feelings.

There are other intermediate moral principles. Very important to the structuring of legal thought is the principle which excludes acting against a basic reason by choosing to destroy or damage any basic good in any of its instantiations in any human person (VI below). A basic human good always is a reason for action and always gives a reason *not* to choose to destroy, damage, or impede some instantiation of that good; but since the instantiations of human good at stake in any morally significant choice are not commensurable by *reason* prior to choice, there can never be a sufficient reason not to take that reason-not-to as decisive for choice. Only emotional factors such as desire or aversion could motivate a choice rejecting it.

Of course, the basic reasons for action, as the phrase suggests, present one with many reasons for choice and action, many reasons to ... And since one is finite, one's choice of any purpose, however far-reaching, will inevitably have as a side-effect some negative impact on (minimally, the non-realization of) other possible instantiations of this and other basic goods. In that sense, every choice is "against some basic reason". But only as a side-effect. In the choices which are excluded by the intermediate moral principle now in question, the damaging or destruction or impeding of an instantiation of a basic good – the harming of some basic aspect of someone's existence and well-being – is chosen, as a means, i.e., *as part* of the description of the option adopted by choice. Whereas the first intermediate principle excludes making such damage or destruction one's end, the present principle excludes making it one's means. The concepts of (the) end and means (defining an option) come together in the conception so fundamental to our law: intention.

III

Even so rapid a sketch begins to make clear that a theory of natural law, while primarily a theory of human goods as principles of practical reasoning, must accommodate within its account – as practical reasoning itself must take into account – certain features of our world.

Among these features are the reality of free choice, and the significance of choices as lasting in the character of the chooser beyond the time of the behaviour which executes them; and the distinction between what is chosen as end or means (i.e., as intended) and what is foreseen and accepted as a side-effect (i.e., an unintended effect). Again, there are such basic facts as that which Robert Nozick overlooked in declaring that (virtually) everything comes into the world already attached to someone having an entitlement over it – the reality, being, on the contrary, that the natural resources from which everything made has been made pre-exist all entitlements and "came into the world" attached to nobody in particular; the world's resources are fundamentally common and no theory of entitlements can rightly appropriate any resource to one person so absolutely as to negate that original communality of the world's stock.[1]

A further feature of the world to be accommodated by a sound natural law theory is the distinction between the orders of reality with which human reason is concerned. In attending to this set of distinctions, we shall be noticing the second of the two sources of ambiguity I mentioned at the outset.

Almost any interesting human state of affairs instantiates the four orders of reality with which human reason is concerned. Consider, for example, a lecture. (1) One hears the *sounds* produced by the speaker's vocal chords: there is an order of nature which we in no way establish by our understanding but which we can investigate by our understanding, as in the natural sciences or (as right now) in metaphysics. (2) One hears the speaker's *expositions, arguments, and explanations* and brings one's understanding into line with them (if only to the extent necessary to reject them as mistaken): there is an order which one can bring into one's own enquiries, understanding, and reasoning, the order studied by logic, methodology, and epistemology. (3) One hears *the lecturer*, who (like the audience) is freely engaging in an activity and thereby participating in a human relationship: there is an order which one can bring into one's own dispositions, choices, and actions – one's *praxis*, one's doing, one's *Existenz* – the 'existential' order studied by some parts of psychology, by biography and the history of human affairs, and by moral and political philosophy. (4) One hears the *English language* and statements ordered by an expository or rhetorical technique, making and decoding the formalized symbols of a language and the less formalized but still conventional symbols and expressive routines of a cultural form and technique: the order one can intelligently bring into matter which is subject to our power, so as to make objects such as phonemes, words, poems, boats, software, ballistic missiles and their inbuilt trajectories – the order of *poiesis*, of making, of culture – studied in the arts and technologies, and in linguistics and rhetoric. (Corresponding to these four orders are four irreducibly distinct senses of "hearing".)

Almost every form of reductionist deformation in social (say, political) theory, and many destructive misunderstandings in almost every aspect of, say, legal theory, can be traced to oversight of the complexities and ambiguities created by the irreducible distinctions between these four orders – whose irreducibility to one another is disguised by the fact that each in a sense includes all the others.

The distinction particularly relevant to legal theory is that between the third (existential, moral) order and the fourth (cultural, technical) order. Few morally significant choices can be carried out without employing some culturally formed technique; and no technique can be put to human use without some morally significant choice. But every technique has an integral, fourth-order intelligibility which can be fully explicated without referring to the morally significant choices by which it might be put to use and the moral principles of practical reasonableness pertinent to such choices.

Amongst the ambiguities created by the distinctions between the third and fourth orders is the ambiguity of the term "rational choice". It has (at least) three important, distinct senses:

1. choice which is fully reasonable, complies with all the requirements of practical reasonableness, and is thus morally upright;
2. choice which is rationally motivated in the sense that its object has been shaped by practical intelligence and has rational appeal, even if it is in some respect(s) motivated ultimately by feeling rather than reason, feelings which have to some extent fettered and instrumentalized reason, and is therefore unreasonable and immoral, though rational;
3. decision and action which is technically (technologically) right, i.e. is identifiable according to some art or technique as the most effective for attaining the relevant technical objective – typically, the decision for which there is, within this technique (e.g., this game), a dominant reason which can be commensurated with the reasons for alternative options and which includes all that these offer and some more.

Sense 3 is the only sense in which economists and exponents of "game" or "decision" theory commonly use the phrase "rational choice". I have used the terms "rational" (and its cognates) and "choice", in Section II above, in sense 2 (or senses 1 and 2) but never in sense 3. Here is rich opportunity for misunderstanding. In senses 1 and 2, what makes rational choice necessary is the incommensurability of the intelligible goods and bads involved in alternative options; if options were fully commensurable, alternatives could be identified as unqualifiedly superior and inferior, and the unqualifiedly inferior would lose its rational appeal, fall out of rational deliberation; rational choice would be unnecessary and, in a significant sense, impossible (VI below). But in sense 3, rational choice is possible *only* when one option can be identified as unqualifiedly superior.

IV

Legal reasoning and rationality has, I suggest, its distinctiveness and its peculiar elusiveness because, in the service of a third-order, existential, moral, and chosen purpose – of living together in a just order of fair and right relationships – there has been and is being constructed a fourth-order object, "the law" (as in "the law of England"). This is a vastly complex cultural object, comprising a vocabulary with many artfully assigned meanings, rules identifying permitted and excluded arguments and decision, and correspondingly very many technical routines or processes (such as pleading, trial, conveyancing, etc.) constituted and regulated according to those formulae, their assigned meanings, and the rules of argument and decision.

This cultural object, constructed or (as we say) posited by creative human choices, is an instrument, a technique adopted for a moral purpose, and adopted because there is no other available way of agreeing over significant spans of time about precisely how to pursue the moral project well. Political authority in all its manifestations, including legal institutions, is a technique for doing without unanimity in making social choices – where unanimity would almost always be unattainable or temporary – in order to secure practical (near-)unanimity about how to coordinate the actions (including forbearances) of members of the society.

Legal reasoning, then, is (at least in large part) technical reasoning – not moral reasoning. Like all technical reasoning, it is concerned to achieve a particular purpose, a definite state of affairs attainable by efficient dispositions of means to end. The particular end here is the resolution of disputes (and other allegations of misconduct) by the provision of a directive sufficiently definite and specific to identify one party as right (in-the-right) and the other as wrong (not-in-the-right).

Hence the law's distinctive devices: defining terms, and specifying rules, with sufficient and necessarily artificial clarity and definiteness to establish the 'bright lines' which make so many real-life legal questions *easy questions*. Legal definitions and rules are to provide the citizen, the legal adviser, and the judge with an algorithm for deciding as many questions as possible – in principle every question – yes (or no), this course of action would (or would not) be lawful; this arrangement is valid; this contract is at an end; these losses are compensable in damages and those are not; and so forth. As far as it can, the law is to provide sources of reasoning – statutes and statute-based rules, common law rules, and customs – capable of ranking (commensurating) alternative dispute-resolutions as right or wrong, and thus better and worse.

Lawyers' tools of trade – their ability to find and use the authoritative sources – are means in the service of a purpose sufficiently definite to constitute a technique, a mode of technical reasoning. The purpose, again, is the unequivocal resolution of every dispute (and other question for just decision) which can be in some way foreseen and provided for. Still, this quest for certainty, for a complete set of uniquely correct answers, is itself in the service of a wider good which, like all basic human goods, is not reducible to a definite goal but is rather an open-ended good which persons and their communities can participate in without ever capturing or exhausting the good of just harmony. This good is a moral good just in so far as it is itself promoted and respected as one aspect of the ideal of integral human fulfilment. As a moral good its implications are specified by all the moral principles which could bear upon it.

Thus there emerges the tension around which Ronald Dworkin's work on legal reasoning revolves.

V

Dworkin seeks to resolve the tension between law's and legal reasoning's character as a culturally specified technique of attaining predictable answers to problems of social co-ordination and its character as, in each of its decisive legislative, executive and judicial moments, a moral act participating in justice (or injustice). His attempted resolution fails, I think, to grasp the real nature and implications of that tension.

In judicial reasoning as portrayed by Dworkin, two criteria of judgement are in use; as we shall see, there is between these two criteria a kind of incommensurability analogous to the incommensurability between the human goods involved in morally significant, rationally motivated choices. One of these criteria or dimensions belongs to what I have called the third (moral) order or rationality, and the other to the fourth (technical) order. The first dimension Dworkin calls "fit": coherence with the existing legal "materials" created by past political decisions, i.e., with legislation and authoritative judicial decision (precedent). The second dimension he now calls "justification".[2] And he tries to show that a *uniquely* correct ("the right") answer is available in "most" hard cases.

One can deny this last thesis without committing oneself to any scepticism about the objectivity of human good(s) or of correct judgements about right and wrong. Nor need one's denial be predicated on the popular argument which Dworkin is rightly concerned to scorn and demolish – the argument that disagreement is endemic and ineradicable. (For disagreement is a mere fact about people, and is logically irrelevant to the merits of any practical or other interpretative claim.) Nor need a denial of Dworkin's one-right-answer thesis rest on the fact that no one has the "superhuman" powers of Dworkin's imaginary judge.

Even an ideal human judge, with superhuman powers, could not sensibly search for a uniquely correct answer to a hard case (as lawyers in sophisticated legal systems use the term "hard case"). For in such a case, the search for the one right answer is practically incoherent and senseless, in much the same way as a search for the English novel which is "most romantic and shortest" (or "funniest and best", or "most English and most profound").

Assuming with Dworkin that there are two "dimensions" or criteria of judicial assessment, we can say that a case for judicial decision is hard (not merely novel) when not only is there more than one answer which is not in evident violation of an applicable rule, but also the answers which are in that sense available can be ranked in different orders along each of the relevant criteria of evaluation: for novels, their brevity and their Englishness (or humour, or profundity, or ...); for judicial judgements their fit with previous legislation and precedent, and – let us grant (not concede) to Dworkin – their *inherent* moral soundness. In such a case there is found what theorists of "rational choice" (in sense 3) call "intransitivity", a phenomenon which such theories confessedly cannot really handle: solution A is better than solution B on the scale of legal fit, and B than C, but C is better than A on the scale of "moral soundness"; so there is no sufficient reason to declare A, or B, or C the overall "best judicial decision". If the rank order was the same on both dimensions, of course, the case was not a hard one at all, and the legal system already had what one always desires of it: a uniquely correct answer.

In his works before *Law's Empire*, Dworkin tried to overcome this incommensurability of the dimensions or criteria of assessment by proposing a kind of lexicographical (in Rawls's terminology "lexical") ordering. Candidates for the "best account" of the law of England in 1980 must fit the then existing English legal materials adequately, and of those which satisfy this threshold criterion, that which ranks highest on the other criterion (moral soundness) is overall, absolutely, "the best", even though it fits less well than (an)other(s). But this solution was empty, since he identified no criteria, however sketchy or 'in principle', for specifying when fit is "adequate", i.e., for locating the threshold (of fit) beyond which the criterion of soundness would prevail. (It was like being told to search for the funniest novel among those that are "short enough".) Presumably, candidates for the one right answer to the question "When is fit adequate?" would themselves be ranked in terms both of fit and of soundness. An infinite regress, of the vicious sort which nullifies purported rational explanations, was well under way.

In *Law's Empire*, Dworkin abandons the simple picture of a lexical ordering between these two criteria. We are left with little more than a metaphor: "balance" – as in "the general balance of political virtues" embodied in competing interpretations or accounts of the law (of England (in 1990)). But in the absence of any metric which could commensurate the different criteria, the instruction to balance (or, earlier, to weigh) can legitimately mean no more than "Bear in mind, conscientiously, all the relevant factors, and *choose*." Or, in the legal sphere, "Hear the arguments, sitting in the highest court, and then *vote*."

In understanding practical rationality in all its forms, one should notice a feature of the experience of choice. *After* one has chosen, the factors favouring the chosen option will usually seem to outweigh, overbalance, those favouring the rejected alternative options. The option chosen – to do x, to adopt rule or interpretation y – will commonly seem (to the person who chose, if not to onlookers) to have a supremacy, a unique rightness. But this sense of the supremacy, the rightness of one (the chosen) option will not alter the truth that the choice was not rationally determined, i.e., was not guided by an identification of one option or answer as "the right one". (And this does not mean that it was irrational; it was between rationally appealing options.) Rather, the choice established the "right" answer – i.e., established it in, and by reference ultimately to, the dispositions and sentiments of the chooser. When the choice in a hard case is made by (the majority in the) highest appeal court (a mere brute fact), the unique rightness of the answer is established not only by and for the attitude of those who have chosen it, but also for the legal system or community for which it has thus been authoritatively decided upon, and laid down as or in a *rule*.

VI

The incommensurability of Dworkin's two dimensions or criteria for judicial judgement has significant similarities to the incommensurability of the goods (and reasons) at stake in alternative options available for morally significant choice in any context. The moral and political rationality which underpins (though does not exhaust) legal rationality cannot be understood without an understanding of incommensurability.

Incommensurability, the absence of any *rationally* identified metric for measuring, or scale for "weighing", the goods and bads in issue, is much more pervasive and intense than one would imagine from the simple Dworkinian picture of legal reasoning along the two dimensions of legal fit and moral soundness. One meets incommensurability in humble contexts, such as having to choose between going to a lecture, reading a good book, going to the cinema, and talking to friends. One meets it in relation to grand social choices, such as whether to reject or renounce a nuclear deterrent: exploring such a choice will amply illustrate the impotence of all forms of aggregative reasoning towards morally significant choice – choice outside the purely technical or technological task of identifying the most cost-efficient means to a single limited goal.

The reasoning most characteristic of technical rationality is "cost-benefit analysis", comparing the costs of alternative options with the probable benefits. This can be carried through with full rationality only when *(a)* goals are well defined, *(b)* costs can be compared with some definite unit (e.g., money), *(c)* benefits can also be quantified in a way that renders them commensurable with one another, and *(d)* differences among means, other than their efficiency, measurable costs, and measurable benefits, are not counted as significant. None of these conditions is fulfilled in moral reasoning.

Indeed, morally significant choice would be unnecessary and, with one qualification, impossible if one option could be shown to be *the best* on a single scale which, as all aggregative reasoning does, ranks options in a single, transitive order. If there were a reason (for doing x) which some rational method of comparison (e.g., aggregation of goods and bads in a complete cost-benefit analysis) identified as rationally preferable, the alternative reason (against doing x), being thus identified as rationally inferior, would cease to be rationally appealing in that situation of choice. The reason thus identified as dominant, as unqualifiedly preferable, and the option favoured by that reason, would be rationally unopposed. There would remain *no choice* of the sort that moral theories seek to guide. For, the morally significant choices which moral theories seek to guide are between alternative options which have rational appeal.

To identify options as morally wrong does not entail identifying one option as (morally) uniquely right. Indeed, even when one option can be judged the only (morally) right option for a given person (a moral judgement which only that person's prior commitments and dispositions will make possible), this entails only that the alternative, immoral options are not fully reasonable. It in no way entails that these alternative options are irrational, i.e., lack rational appeal in terms of genuine, intelligible human goods which would be secured by the immoral options and sacrificed by the morally upright option. Thus rationally motivated, morally significant choice remains possible – indeed characteristic of the human situation – even in the perhaps relatively uncommon case of the moral "one right answer (option)".

But when technical reasonings identify one option as uniquely correct, i.e., as dominant, they do so by demonstrating that it offers *all that the other options offer and some more*; it is unqualifiedly better. The other options then lack *rational* appeal. Such deliberation ends not in choice – in the rich, central sense of that ambiguous term – but rather in insight, "decision" (not choice, but rationally compelled judgement), and action.

One of morality's principles, I have said (II above), excludes acting against a basic reason by choosing to destroy or damage any basic human good in any of its instantiations in any human person. For these instantiations are nothing other than aspects of human persons, present and future, and human persons cannot rationally be reduced to the commensurable factors captured by technical reasoning. These instantiations of human good constitute *reasons against* any option which involves choosing (intending) to destroy or damage any of them. The significance of the incommensurability of goods involved in such morally significant options is that no reason *for* such an option can be rationally preferable to such a reason against. And the same is true of the *reason against* an option which is constituted by that option's unfairness.

What, it may be asked, are the grounds for regulating one's choice according to the reason-*against* rather than by any reason *for*? Once again, they cannot be stated without reference to some features of our world, the fundamental context of all human choosing. Options which there are reasons *for* my choosing are infinite in number. Being finite, I simply cannot do everything, cannot choose every option for which there are reasons. But I can refrain from doing anything; I can respect every serious reason-against. So, an unconditional or absolute affirmative duty (duty *to* ...) would impose an impossible burden and be irrational; but negative moral absolutes (duties *not* to ...), if correctly stated with attention to the distinction between intention and side-effect, can all be adhered to in any and every circumstance.

Moreover, many human goods (e.g., the lives of others) are gifts, givens, which we can destroy or damage, but cannot create. Here, too, is a ground of the intelligible asymmetry between reasons-for and reasons-against. Nor does the priority, within their ambit, of reasons-against give morality as a whole a negative case, or elevate "moral purity" to the rank of a supreme goal. The first limb of practical reason's first principle remains that human good is to be done and pursued. Its second limb is that evil is to be avoided. But a full respect for and adherence to the absolute duties to forbear from evil leaves open a wide field of (more numerous) individual and social positive responsibilities.

VII

The moral absolutes give legal reasoning its backbone: the exclusion of intentional killing, of intentional injury to the person and even the economic interests of the person, of deliberate deception for the sake of securing desired results, of enslavement which treats a human person as an object of a lower rank of being than the autonomous human subject. These moral absolutes, which *are* rationally determined and essentially determinate, constitute the most basic human rights, and the foundations of the criminal law and the law of intentional torts or delicts, not to mention all the rules, principles, and doctrines which penalize intentional deception, withdraw from it all direct legal support, and exclude it from the legal process.

The rationality of all these moral and legal norms depends upon the incommensurability of the human goods and bads at stake in morally significant options for choice. This incommensurability has further implications of importance to legal reasoning.

The core of the moral norm of fairness is the Golden Rule: 'Do to others as you would have them do to you; do not impose on others what you would not want to be obliged by them to accept.' This has two aspects. First: practical rationality, outside the limited technical context of competitive games, includes a rational norm of impartiality. This norm excludes not all forms and corresponding feelings of preference for oneself and those who are near and dear, but rather all those forms of preference which are motivated only by desires, aversions, or hostilities which do not correspond to intelligible aspects of the real *reasons* for action, the basic human goods realizable in the lives of other human beings as in the lives of oneself or those close to one's heart.

The Golden Rule's second aspect is this. Although fairness is thus a rational norm requiring one to transcend all rationally unintegrated feelings, its concrete application in personal life presupposes a commensuration of benefits and burdens which reason is impotent to commensurate. For, to apply the Golden Rule one must know what burdens one considers too great to accept. And this knowledge, constituting a pre-moral commensuration, cannot be by rational commensuration. Therefore, it can only be one's intuitive awareness, one's discernment, of one's own differentiated *feelings* towards various goods and bads as concretely remembered, experienced, or imagined. This, I repeat, is not a rational and objective commensuration of goods and bads; but once established in one's feelings and identified in one's self-awareness, it enables one to measure one's options by a rational and objective standard of inter-personal impartiality.

Analogously, in the life of a community, the preliminary commensuration of rationally incommensurable factors is accomplished not by rationally determined judgements, but by *decisions* (choices). Is it fair to impose on others the risks inherent in driving at more than 10 m.p.h.? Yes, in our community, since our community has by custom and law *decided* to treat those risks and harms as *not too great*. Have we a rational critique of a community which decided to limit road traffic to 10 m.p.h. and to accept all the economic and other costs of that decision? Or not to have the institution of trusts, or constructive trusts? No, we have no rational critique of such a community. But we do have a rational critique of someone who drives at 60 m.p.h. but who, when struck by another, complains and alleges that the mere fact that the other's speed exceeded 10 m.p.h. established that other's negligence. Or of someone willing to receive the benefits (e.g., the tax benefits) of trusts but not willing to accept the law's distinction between trust and contract in his bankruptcy.

And, in general, we have a rational critique of one who accepts the benefits of this and other communal decisions but rejects the burdens as they bear on him and those in whom he feels interested. In short, the decision to permit road traffic to proceed faster than 10 m.p.h., or to define trusts just as English law does, was rationally underdetermined. (That is not to say that it was or is wholly unguided by reason; the good of human bodily life and integrity is a genuine reason always practically relevant, and the rational demand for consistency with our individual and communal tolerance or intolerance of other – non-traffic – threats to that good provides some rational criteria for decision. And similarly with the trust, whose rationality defied many legislative attempts, for centuries, to suppress this peculiar double ownership.) Still, though rationally underdetermined, the decision to permit fast-moving traffic, once made, provides an often fully determinate rational standard for treating those accused of wrongful conduct or wrongfully inflicting injury. Likewise with trusts, in bankruptcy.

In the working of the legal process, much turns on the principle – a principle of fairness – that litigants (and others involved in the process) should be treated by judges (and others with power to decide) *impartially*, in the sense that they are as nearly as possible to be treated by each judge as they would be treated by every other judge. It is this above all, I believe, that drives the law towards the artificial, the *techne* rationality of laying down and following a set of positive norms identifiable as far as possible simply by their "sources" (i.e., by the fact of their enactment or other constitutive event) and applied so far as possible according to their publicly stipulated meaning, itself elucidated with as little as possible appeal to considerations which, because not controlled by facts about sources (constitutive events), are inherently likely to be appealed to differently by different judges. This drive to insulate legal from moral reasoning can never, however, be complete.

Incommensurability has further, related implications for legal reasoning. It rules out the proposed technique of legal reasoning known as Economic Analysis of Law. For it is central to that technique that every serious question of social order can be resolved by aggregating the overall net good promised by alternative options, in terms of a simple commensurating factor (or maximand), namely wealth measured in terms of the money which relevant social actors would be willing and able to pay to secure their preferred option. Equally central to Economic Analysis is the assumption, or thesis, that there is no difference of principle between buying the right to inflict injury intentionally and buying the right not to take precautions which would eliminate an equivalent number of injuries caused accidentally. A root and branch critique of Economic Analysis of Law will focus on these two features of it.

Less fundamental critiques, such as Dworkin's (helpful and worth while though it is), leave those features untouched. Indeed, Dworkin's own distinction between rights and collective goals (the latter being proposed by Dworkin as the legitimate province of legislatures) is a distinction which uncritically assumes that collective goals can rationally be identified and preferred to alternatives by aggregation of value, without regard to principles of distributive fairness and other aspects of justice – principles which themselves constitute rights, and which cannot be traded off, according to some rational methodology, against measurable quantities of value.

VIII

In sum: much academic theory about legal reasoning greatly exaggerates the extent to which reason can settle what is greater good and lesser evil. At the same time, such theory minimizes the need for authoritative sources. Such sources, so far as they are clear, and respect the few absolute moral rights and duties, are to be respected as the only reasonable basis for judicial reasoning and decision, in relation to those countless issues which do not directly involve those absolute rights and duties. A natural law theory in the classical tradition makes no pretence that natural reason can identify the one right answer to those countless questions which arise for the judge who finds the sources unclear.

In the classical view, expressed by Aquinas with a clear debt to Aristotle, there are many ways of going wrong and doing wrong; but in very many, perhaps most situations of personal and social life there are a number of incompatible *right* (i.e., not-wrong) options. Prior personal choice(s) or authoritative social decision-making can greatly reduce this variety of options for the person who has made that commitment or the community which accepts that authority. Still, those choices and decisions, while rational and reasonable, were in most cases not required by reason. They were not preceded by any rational judgement that *this* option is *the* right answer, or the best solution.

NOTES

1 Robert Nozick, *Anarchy, State and Utopia* (Oxford: Blackwell, 1974), 160.
2 See Ronald Dworkin, *Law's Empire* (Cambridge, Mass.: Harvard University Press, 1986), 255. This term seems confusing, since both dimensions are, on his account, necessary to justify a judicial decision. His previous name for the second dimension (inherent substantive moral), "soundness", was better: see Dworkin, *Taking Rights Seriously* (Cambridge, Mass.: Harvard University Press, 1978), 340–1. Still, the labels adopted by Dworkin have the merit of making it clear that fit, although relevant precisely because a necessary condition for securing certain moral and political goods and requirements such as community and integrity, is itself a matter of historical fact, namely, the facts about what judgements and decisions have been made by the relevant institutions in a given span of time, and the extent to which some actual or hypothetical judgement or decision corresponds in content to earlier judgements and decisions.

READING QUESTIONS ON FINNIS

1 Do you find Finnis's account of the incommensurability of values a convincing basis for his critique of Dworkin?
2 How does Finnis's critique of Dworkin relate to Hart's account of discretion? If there is a relationship, does this bring Finnis's natural law project closer to positivism than to Dworkin's understanding of the moral basis of law?

3

Feminist Approaches to the Rule of Law

Feminist scholars and lawyers have made important contributions to legal thought and legal change in the past two decades. There are many different strands in contemporary feminist thought about law. Some feminists are critical of the detachment to which law claims to aspire, others of its implicit bias against women, still others of its emphasis on rights and the separateness of persons rather than their connectedness. These selections are not meant to be representative of all of these trends. Instead, they touch on some of the issues already considered about the general relation between morality and the rule of law. Later sections include feminist engagements with particular issues.

Catharine A. MacKinnon
"The Liberal State" (1989)

MacKinnon sees the law as a potentially powerful medium of progressive change, one that has historically not been in women's hands and has largely sided against women.

The difference between the judges and Sir Isaac [Newton] is that a mistake by Sir Isaac in calculating the orbit of the earth would not send it spinning around the sun with an increased velocity ... while if the judges ... come to a wrong result, it is none the less law.
– John Chipman Gray (1909)

Political revolutions aim to change political institutions in ways that those institutions themselves prohibit.
– Thomas Kuhn (1962)

Feminism has no theory of the state. Just as feminism has a theory of power but lacks a specific theory of its state form, marxism has a theory of value which (through the organization of work in production) becomes class analysis, but also a problematic theory of the state. Marx himself did not address the state much more explicitly than he addressed women. Women were substratum, the state epiphenomenon. He termed the state "a concentrated expression of economics," a reflection of the real action, which occurred elsewhere; it was "the official résumé of society," a unity of ruptures; it, or its "executive," was "but a committee for managing the common affairs of the whole bourgeoisie." Engels frontally analyzed women and the state, and together. But just as he presumed the subordination of women in every attempt to reveal its roots, he presupposed something like the state, or statelike society, in every attempt to find its origins.

Marx tended to use the term *political* narrowly to refer to the state or its laws, criticizing as exclusively political interpretations of the state's organization or behavior which took them as sui generis, as if they were to be analyzed apart from economic conditions. He termed "political power" as embodied in the modern state "the official expression of antagonism in civil society." Changes on this level could, therefore, emancipate the individual only within the framework of the existing social order, termed "civil society." Revolution on this level was "partial, merely political revolution." Accordingly, until recently, most marxist theory has tended to consider as political that which occurs between classes and the state as the instrument of the economically dominant class. That is, it has interpreted the political in terms of the marxist view of social inequality and the state in terms of the class that controls it. The marxist theory of social inequality has been its theory of politics. The state as such was not seen as furthering particular interests through its form. This theory does not so much collapse the state into society (although it goes far in that direction) as conceive the state as determined by the totality of social relations of which the state is one determined and determining part – without specifying which, or how much, is which.

After 1848, having seen the bourgeoisie win revolutions but then not exercise state power directly, Marx tried to understand how states could plainly serve the bourgeoisie's interest yet not represent it as a class. His attempts form the basis for much contemporary marxist work that has tried to grasp the specificity of the institutional state: how it wields class power or operates within class strictures or supplements or moderates class rule or transforms class society or responds to approach by a left aspiring to rulership or other changes. While much liberal theory has seen the state as emanating power, and traditional marxism has seen the state as expressing power constituted elsewhere, recent marxism, much of it structuralist, has tried to analyze state power as specific to the state as a form, yet integral to a determinate social whole understood in class terms.

Politics becomes "an autonomous phenomenon that is constrained by economics but not reducible to it." This state is found "relatively autonomous", that is, the state, expressed through its functionaries, has a definite class character, is definitely capitalist or socialist, but also has its own interests, which are to some degree independent of those of the ruling class and even of the class structure. The state as such, in this view, has a specific power and interest, termed "the political," such that class power, class interest expressed by and in the state, and state behavior, though inconceivable in isolation from one another, are nevertheless not linearly linked or strictly coextensive. Thus Jon Elster argues that Marx saw that the bourgeoisie perceived their interests best furthered "if they remain outside politics." Much of this work locates "the specificity of the political" in a mediate "region" between the state and its own ground of power (which alone, as in the liberal conception, would set the state above or apart from class) and the state as possessing no special supremacy or priority in terms of power, as in the more orthodox marxist view. For Nicos Poulantzas, for example, the "specific autonomy which is characteristic of the function of the state ... is the basis of the specificity of the political" – whatever that means.

The idea that the state is relatively autonomous, a kind of first among equals of social institutions, has the genius of appearing to take a stand on the issue of reciprocal constitution of state and society while straddling it. Is the state essentially autonomous of class but partly determined by it, or is it essentially determined by class but not exclusively so? Is it relatively constrained within a context of freedom or relatively free within a context of constraint? As to who or what fundamentally moves and shapes the realities and instrumentalities of domination, and where to go to do something about it, what qualifies what is as ambiguous as it is crucial. When this work has investigated law as a particular form of state expression, it has served to relieve the compulsion to find all law – directly or convolutedly, nakedly or clothed in unconscious or devious rationalia – to be simply "bourgeois," without undercutting the notion that it, with all state emanations, is determinately driven by interest.

Feminism has not confronted, on its own terms, the relation between the state and society within a theory of social determination specific to sex. As a result, it lacks a jurisprudence, that is, a theory of the substance of law, its relation to society, and the relationship between the two. Such a theory would comprehend how law works as a form of state power in a social context in which power is gendered. It would answer the questions: What is state power? Where, socially, does it come from? How do women encounter it? What is the law for women? How does law work to legitimate the state, male power, itself? Can law do anything for women? Can it do anything about women's status? Does how the law is used matter?

In the absence of answers, feminist practice has oscillated between a liberal theory of the state on the one hand and a left theory of the state on the other. Both theories treat law as the mind of society: disembodied reason in liberal theory, reflection of material interest in left theory. In liberal moments, the state is accepted on its own terms as a neutral arbiter among conflicting interests. The law is actually or potentially principled, meaning predisposed to no substantive outcome, or manipulable to any ends, thus available as a tool that is not fatally twisted. Women implicitly become an interest group within pluralism, with specific problems of mobilization and representation, exit and voice, sustaining incremental gains and losses. In left moments, the state becomes a tool of dominance and repression, the law legitimating ideology, use of the legal system a form of utopian idealism or gradualist reform, each apparent gain deceptive or cooptive, and each loss inevitable.

Liberalism applied to women has supported state intervention on behalf of women as abstract persons with abstract rights, without scrutinizing the content and limitations of these notions in terms of gender. Marxism applied to women is always on the edge of counseling abdication of the state as an arena altogether – and with it those women whom the state does not ignore or who are in no position to ignore it. As a result, feminism has been left with these tacit alternatives: either the state is a primary tool of women's betterment and status transformation, without analysis (hence strategy) of it as male; or women are left to civil society, which for women has more closely resembled a state of nature. The state, and with it the law, have been either omnipotent or impotent: everything or nothing. The feminist posture toward the state has therefore been schizoid on issues central to women's status. Rape, abortion, pornography, and sex discrimination are examples. To grasp the inadequacies for women of liberalism on the one hand and marxism on the other is to begin to comprehend the role of the liberal state and liberal legalism within a post-marxist feminism of social transformation.

Gender is a social system that divides power. It is therefore a political system. That is, over time, women have been economically exploited, relegated to domestic slavery, forced into motherhood, sexually objectified, physically abused, used in denigrating entertainment, deprived of a voice and authentic culture, and disenfranchised and excluded from public life. Women, by contrast with comparable men, have systematically been subjected to physical insecurity; targeted for sexual denigration and violation; depersonalized and denigrated; deprived of respect, credibility, and resources; and silenced – and denied public presence, voice, and representation of their interests. Men as men have generally not had these things done to them; that is, men have had to be Black or gay (for instance) to have these things done to them as men. Men have done these things to women. Even conventional theories of power – the more individuated, atomistic, and decisional approaches of the pluralists, as well as the more radical theories, which stress structural, tacit, contextual, and relational aspects of power – recognize such conditions as defining positions of power and powerlessness. If one defines politics with Harold Lasswell, who defines a political act as "one performed in power perspectives," and with Robert Dahl, who defines a political system as "any persistent pattern of human relationships that involves, to a significant extent, power, rule, or authority," and with Kate Millett, who defines political relationships as "power structured relationships," the relation between women and men is political.

Unlike the ways in which men systematically enslave, violate, dehumanize, and exterminate other men, expressing political inequalities among men, men's forms of dominance over women have been accomplished socially as well as economically, prior to the operation of law, without express state acts, often in intimate contexts, as everyday life. So what is the role of the state in sexual politics? Neither liberalism nor marxism grants women, as such, a specific relation to the state. Feminism has described some of the state's treatment of the gender difference but has not analyzed the state's role in gender hierarchy. What, in gender terms, are the state's norms of accountability, sources of power, real constituency? Is the state to some degree autonomous of the interests of men or an integral expression of them? Does the state embody and serve male interests in its form, dynamics, relation to society, and specific policies? Is the state constructed upon the subordination of women? If so, how does male power become state power? Can such a state be made to serve the interests of those upon whose powerlessness its power is erected? Would a different relation between state and society, such as may exist under socialism, make a difference? If not, is masculinity inherent in the state form as such, or is some other form of state, or some other way of governing, distinguishable or imaginable? In the absence of answers to these questions, feminism has been caught between giving more power to that state in each attempt to claim it for women and leaving unchecked power in the society to men. Undisturbed, meanwhile, like the assumption that women generally consent to sex, is the assumption that women consent to this government. The question for feminism is: what is this state, from women's point of view?

The state is male in the feminist sense: the law sees and treats women the way men see and treat women. The liberal state coercively and authoritatively constitutes the social order in the interest of men as a gender – through its legitimating norms, forms, relation to society, and substantive policies. The state's formal norms recapitulate the male point of view on the level of design. In Anglo-American jurisprudence, morals (value judgments) are deemed separable and separated from politics (power contests), and both from adjudication (interpretation). Neutrality, including judicial decision making that is dispassionate, impersonal, disinterested, and precedential, is considered desirable and descriptive. Courts, forums without predisposition among parties and with no interest of their own, reflect society back to itself resolved. Government of laws, not of men, limits partiality with written constraints and tempers force with reasonable rule-following.

At least since Langdell's first casebook in 1871, this law has aspired to be a science of rules and a science with rules, a science of the immanent generalization subsuming the emergent particularity, of prediction and control of social regularities and regulations, preferably codified. The formulaic "tests" of "doctrine" aspire to mechanism, classification to taxonomy, legislators to Linnaeus. Courts intervene only in properly "factualized" disputes, cognizing social conflicts as if collecting empirical data; right conduct becomes rule-following. But these demarcations between morals and politics, science and politics, the personality of the judge and the judicial role, bare coercion and the rule of law, tend to merge in women's experience. Relatively seamlessly they promote the dominance of men as a social group through privileging the form of power – the perspective on social life – which feminist consciousness reveals as socially male. The separation of form from substance, process from policy, adjudication from legislation, judicial role from theory or practice, echoes and reechoes at each level of the regime its basic norm: objectivity.

Formally, the state is male in that objectivity is its norm. Objectivity is liberal legalism's conception of itself. It legitimates itself by reflecting its view of society, a society it helps make by so seeing it, and calling that view, and that relation, rationality. Since rationality is measured by point-of-viewlessness, what counts as reason is that which corresponds to the way things are. Practical rationality, in this approach, means that which can be done without changing anything. In this framework, the task of legal interpretation becomes "to perfect the state as mirror of the society." Objectivist epistemology is the law of law. It ensures that the law will most reinforce existing distributions of power when it most closely adheres to its own ideal of fairness. Like the science it emulates, this epistemological stance cannot see the social specificity of reflexion as method or its choice to embrace that which it reflects. Such law not only reflects a society in which men rule women; it rules in a male way insofar as "the phallus means everything that sets itself up as a mirror." Law, as words in power, writes society in state form and writes the state onto society. The rule form, which unites scientific knowledge with state control in its conception of what law is, institutionalizes the objective stance as jurisprudence.

The state is male jurisprudentially, meaning that it adopts the standpoint of male power on the relation between law and society. This stance is especially vivid in constitutional adjudication, thought legitimate to the degree it is neutral on the policy content of legislation. The foundation for its neutrality is the pervasive assumption that conditions that pertain among men on the basis of gender apply to women as well – that is, the assumption that sex inequality does not really exist in society. The Constitution – the constituting document of this state society – with its interpretations assumes that society, absent government intervention, is free and equal; that its laws, in general, reflect that; and that government need and should right only what government has previously wronged. This posture is structural to a constitution of abstinence: for example, "Congress shall make no law abridging the freedom of ... speech." Those who have freedoms like equality, liberty, privacy, and speech socially keep them legally, free of governmental intrusion. No one who does not already have them socially is granted them legally.

In this light, once gender is grasped as a means of social stratification, the status categories basic to medieval law, thought to have been superseded by liberal regimes in aspirational nonhierarchical constructs of abstract personhood, are revealed deeply unchanged. Gender as a status category was simply assumed out of legal existence, suppressed into a presumptively pre-constitutional social order through a constitutional structure designed not to reach it. Speaking descriptively rather than functionally or motivationally, the strategy is first to constitute society unequally prior to law; then to design the constitution, including the law of equality, so that all its guarantees apply only to those values that are taken away by law; then to construct legitimating norms so that the state legitimates itself through noninterference with the status quo. Then, so long as male dominance is so effective in society that it is unnecessary to impose sex inequality through law, such that only the most superficial sex inequalities become *de jure*, not even a legal guarantee of sex equality will produce social equality.

The posture and presumptions of the negative state, the view that government best promotes freedom when it stays out of existing social arrangements, reverberates throughout constitutional law. Doctrinally, it is embodied in rubrics like the "state action" requirement of equal protection law, in the law of freedom of speech, and in the law of privacy. The "state action" requirement restricts the Constitution to securing citizens' equality rights only from violations by governments, not by other citizens. The law of the First Amendment secures freedom of speech only from governmental deprivation. In the law of privacy, governmental intervention itself is unconstitutional.

In terms of judicial role, these notions are defended as the "passive virtues": courts should not (and say they do not) impose their own substantive views on constitutional questions. Judges best vindicate the Constitution when they proceed as if they have no views, when they reflect society back to itself from the angle of vision at which society is refracted to them. In this hall of mirrors, only in extremis shall any man alter what any other man has wrought. The offspring of proper passivity is substancelessness. Law produces its progeny immaculately, without messy political intercourse.

Philosophically, this posture is expressed in the repeated constitutional invocation of the superiority of "negative freedom" – staying out, letting be – over positive legal affirmations. Negative liberty gives one the right to be "left to do or be what [he] is able to do or be, without interference from other persons." The state that pursues this value promotes freedom when it does not intervene in the social status quo. Positive freedom, freedom to do rather than to keep from being done to, by distinction, gives one the right to "control or ... determine someone to do, or be, this rather than that." If one group is socially granted the positive freedom to do whatever it wants to another group, to determine that the second group will be and do this rather than that, no amount of negative freedom legally guaranteed to the second group will make it the equal of the first. For women, this has meant that civil society, the domain in which women are distinctively subordinated and deprived of power, has been placed beyond reach of legal guarantees. Women are oppressed socially, prior to law, without express state acts, often in intimate contexts. The negative state cannot address their situation in any but an equal society – the one in which it is needed least.

This posture is enforced through judicial methodology, the formative legal experience for which is *Lochner v New York*, a case that arose out of the struggle of the working class to extract livable working conditions from a capitalist state through legislated reform. Invalidating legislation that would have restricted the number of hours bakers could work on grounds of freedom of contract, the Supreme Court sided with capitalism over workers. The dissenters' view, ultimately vindicated, was that the majority had superimposed its own views on the Constitution; they, by contrast, would passively reflect the Constitution by upholding the legislation. Soon after, in *Muller v Oregon*, the Supreme Court upheld restrictive hours legislation for women only. The opinion distinguished *Lochner* on the basis that women's unique frailty, dependency, and breeding capacity placed her "at a disadvantage in the struggle for subsistence." A later ruling, *West Coast Hotel v Parrish*, generally regarded as ending the *Lochner* era, also used women as a lever against capitalism. Minimum-wage laws were upheld for women because "the exploitation of a class of workers who are in an unequal position with respect to bargaining power and are thus relatively defenseless against the denial of a living wage ... casts a direct burden for their support upon the community."

Concretely, it is unclear whether these special protections, as they came to be called, helped or hurt women. These cases did do something for some workers (female) concretely; they also demeaned all women ideologically. They did assume that women were marginal and second-class members of the workforce; they probably contributed to keeping women marginal and second-class workers by keeping some women from competing with men at the male standard of exploitation. This benefited both male workers and capitalists. These rulings supported one sector of workers against all capitalists by benefiting male workers at the expense of female workers. They did help the working class by setting precedents that eventually supported minimum-wage and maximum-hours laws for all workers. They were a victory against capitalism and for sexism, for some women perhaps at the expense of all women (maybe including those they helped), for the working class perhaps at women's expense, at least so long as they were "women only."

The view of women in *Muller* and *West Coast Hotel* was that of the existing society: demeaning, paternalistic, and largely unrealistic; as with most pedestalization, its concrete benefits were equivocal at best. The view of workers in *Lochner* left capitalism unchecked and would have precluded most New Deal social reforms men wanted. (Protecting all workers was not considered demeaning by anyone.) For these reasons, these cases have come to stand for a critique of substantivity in adjudication as such. But their methodological solution – judicial neutrality – precludes from constitutional relief groups who are socially abject and systematically excluded from the usual political process. Despite universal rejections of "Lochnering," this substantive approach in neutral posture has continued to be incorporated in constitutional method, including in the law of equality. If over half the population has no voice in the Constitution, why is upholding legislation to give them a voice impermissibly substantive and activist, while striking down such legislation is properly substanceless and passive? Is permitting such an interpretation of, for example, the equality principle in a proper case activism, while not permitting it is properly nonsubstantive? Overruling *Lochner* was at least as judicially active as *Lochner* itself was. Further, why are legislation and adjudication regarded as exercises of state power, but passivity in the face of social inequality – even under a constitutional equality principle – is not? The result is, substantivity and activism and hunted down, flailed, and confined, while their twins, neutrality and passivity, roam at large.

To consider the "passive virtues" of judicial restraint as a tool for social change suggests that change for workers was constitutional only because workers were able to get power in legislatures. To achieve such changes by constitutional principle before achieving them socially and politically would be to engage in exactly the kind of substantive judicial activism that those who supported the changes said they opposed. The reasoning was: if courts make substantive decisions, they will express their prejudices, here, exploitive of workers, demeaning and unhelpful of women. The alternatives have been framed, then, as substantive adjudication that demeans and deprives on the one hand, or as substanceless adjudication that, passively virtuous, upholds whatever power can get out of the political process as it is.

The underlying assumption of judicial neutrality is that a status quo exists which is preferable to judicial intervention – a common law status quo, a legislative status quo, an economic status quo, or a gender status quo. For women, it also tends to assume that access to the conventional political realm might be available in the absence of legal rights. At the same time it obscures the possibility that a substantive approach to women's situation could be adequate to women's distinctive social exploitation – ground a claim to civil equality, for example – and do no more to license judicial arbitrariness than current standards do. From women's point of view, adjudications are already substantive; the view from nowhere already has content. *Lochner* saw workers legally the way capitalists see workers socially: as free agents, bargaining at arm's length. *Muller* saw women legally the way men see women socially: as breeders, marginal workers, excludable. If one wants to claim no more for a powerless group than what can be extracted under an established system of power, one can try to abstract them into entitlement by blurring the lines between them and everyone else. Neutrality as pure means makes some sense. If, however, the claim is against the definition and distribution of power itself, one needs a critique not so much of the substantivity of cases like *Lochner* and *Muller*, but of their substance. Such a critique must also include that aspect of the liberal tradition in which one strategy for dominance has been substancelessness.

If the content of positive law is surveyed more broadly from women's point of view, a pattern emerges. The way the male point of view frames an experience is the way it is framed by state policy. Over and over again, the state protects male power through embodying and ensuring existing male control over women at every level – cushioning, qualifying, or *de jure* appearing to prohibit its excesses when necessary to its normalization. *De jure* relations stabilize de facto relations. Laws that touch on sexuality provide illustrations of this argument. As in society, to the extent possession is the point of sex, rape in law is sex with a woman who is not yours, unless the act is so as to make her yours. Social and legal realities are consistent and mutually determinate: since law has never effectively interfered with men's ability to rape women on these terms, it has been unnecessary to make this an express rule of law. Because part of the kick of pornography involves eroticizing the putatively prohibited, obscenity law putatively prohibits pornography enough to maintain its desirability without ever making it unavailable or truly illegitimate. Because the stigma of prostitution is the stigma of sexuality is the stigma of the female gender, prostitution may be legal or illegal, but so long as women are unequal to men and that inequality is sexualized, women will be bought and sold as prostitutes, and law will do nothing about it.

Women as a whole are kept poor, hence socially dependent on men, available for sexual or reproductive use. To the extent that abortion exists to control the reproductive consequences of intercourse, hence to facilitate male sexual access to women, access to abortion will be controlled by "a man or The Man." So long as this is effectively done socially, it is unnecessary to do it by law. Law need merely stand passively by, reflecting the passing scene. The law of sex equality stays as far away as possible from issues of sexuality. Rape, pornography, prostitution, incest, battery, abortion, gay and lesbian rights: none have been sex equality issues under law. In the issues the law of sex discrimination does treat, male is the implicit reference for human, maleness the measure of entitlement to equality. In its mainstream interpretation, this law is neutral: it gives little to women that it cannot also give to men, maintaining sex inequality while appearing to address it. Gender, thus elaborated and sustained by law, is maintained as a division of power. The negative state views gender and sexual relations as neutrally as *Lochner* viewed class relations.

The law on women's situation produced in this way views women's situation from the standpoint of male dominance. It assumes that the conditions that pertain among men on the basis of sex – consent to sex, comparative privacy, voice in moral discourse, and political equality on the basis of gender – apply to women. It assumes on the epistemic level that sex inequality in society is not real. Rape law takes women's usual response to coercion – acquiescence, the despairing response to hopelessness to unequal odds – and calls that consent. Men coerce women; women "consent." The law of privacy treats the private sphere as a sphere of personal freedom. For men, it is. For women, the private is the distinctive sphere of intimate violation and abuse, neither free nor particularly personal. Men's realm of private freedom is women's realm of collective subordination. The law of obscenity treats pornography as "ideas." Whether or not ideas are sex for men, pornography certainly is sex for men. From the standpoint of women, who live the sexual abuse in pornography as everyday life, pornography is reality. The law of obscenity treats regulation of pornography from the standpoint of what is necessary to protect it: as regulation of morals, as some men telling other men what they may not see and do and think and say about sex. From the standpoint of women, whose torture pornography makes entertainment, pornography is the essence of a powerless condition, its effective protection by the state the essence of sexual politics. Obscenity law's "moral ideas" are a political reality of women's subordination. Just as, in male law, public oppression masquerades as private freedom and coercion is guised as consent, in obscenity law real political domination is presented as a discourse in ideas about virtue and vice.

Rape law assumes that consent to sex is as real for women as it is for men. Privacy law assumes that women in private have the same privacy men do. Obscenity law assumes that women have the access to speech men have. Equality law assumes that women are already socially equal to men. Only to the extent women have already achieved social equality does the mainstream law of equality support their inequality claims. The laws of rape, abortion, obscenity, and sex discrimination show how the relation between objectification, understood as the primary process of the subordination of women, and the power of the state is the relation between the personal and the political at the level of government. These laws are not political because the state is presumptively the sphere of politics. They are integral to sexual politics because the state, through law, institutionalizes male power over women through institutionalizing the male point of view in law. Its first state act is to see women from the standpoint of male dominance; its next act is to treat them that way. This power, this state, is not a discrete location, but a web of sanctions throughout society which "control[s] the principal means of coercion" that structures women's everyday lives. The Weberian monopoly on the means of legitimate coercion, thought to distinguish the state as an entity, actually describes the power of men over women in the home, in the bedroom, on the job, in the street, throughout social life. It is difficult, actually, to find a place it does not circumscribe and describe. Men are sovereign in society in the way Austin describes law as sovereign: a person or group whose commands are habitually obeyed and who is not in the habit of obeying anyone else. Men are the group that has had the authority to make law, embodying H.L.A. Hart's "rule of recognition" that, in his conception, makes law authoritative. Distinctively male values (and men) constitute the authoritative interpretive community that makes law distinctively lawlike to the likes of Ronald Dworkin. If one combines "a realistic conception of the state with a revolutionary theory of society," the place of gender in state power is not limited to government, nor is the rule of law limited to police and courts. The rule of law and the rule of men are one thing, indivisible, at once official and unofficial – officially circumscribed, unofficially not. State power, embodied in law, exists throughout society as male power at the same time as the power of men over women throughout society is organized as the power of the state.

Perhaps the failure to consider gender as a determinant of state behavior has made the state's behavior appear indeterminate. Perhaps the objectivity of the liberal state has made it appear autonomous of class. Including, but beyond, the bourgeois in liberal legalism, lies what is male about it. However autonomous of class the liberal state may appear, it is not autonomous of sex. Male power is systemic. Coercive, legitimated, and epistemic, it *is* the regime.

READING QUESTIONS ON MACKINNON

1 What exactly is the tension MacKinnon identifies in the law?
2 Can the tension she identifies form the basis of a progressive legal strategy?

Martha Minow
"Foreword [to The Supreme Court 1986 Term]:
Justice Engendered" (1987)

Minow examines legal assumptions about what is and is not normal, and explores opportunities to better realize law's ambitions.

I   INTRODUCTION

A   *What's the Difference?*

The use of anesthesia in surgery spread quickly once discovered. Yet the nineteenth-century doctors who adopted anesthesia selected which patients needed it and which deserved it. Both the medical literature and actual medical practices distinguished people's need for pain-killers based on race, gender, ethnicity, age, temperament, personal habits, and economic class. Some people's pain was thought more serious than others; some people were thought to be hardy enough to withstand pain. Doctors believed that women, for example, needed painkillers more than men and that the rich and educated needed painkillers more than the poor and uneducated. How might we, today, evaluate these examples of discrimination? What differences between people should matter, and for what purposes? ...

The dilemma of difference appears unresolvable. The risk of non-neutrality – the risk of discrimination – accompanies efforts both to ignore and to recognize difference in equal treatment and special treatment; in color- or gender-blindness and in affirmative action; in governmental neutrality and in governmental preferences; and in decisionmakers' discretion and in formal constraints on discretion. Yet the dilemma is not as intractable as it seems. What makes it seem so difficult are unstated assumptions about the nature of difference. Once articulated and examined, these assumptions can take their proper place among other choices about how to treat difference. I will explore here the assumptions underlying the dilemma of difference, assumptions that usually go without saying.

First, we often assume that "differences" are intrinsic, rather than viewing them as expressions of comparisons between people. We are all different from one another in innumerable ways. Each of these differences is an implicit comparison we draw. And the comparisons themselves depend upon and reconfirm socially constructed meanings about what traits should matter for purposes of comparison.

Second, typically we adopt an unstated point of reference when assessing others. From the point of reference of this norm, we determine who is different and who is normal. Women are different in relation to the unstated male norm. Blacks, Mormons, Jews, and Arabs are different in relation to the unstated white, Christian norm. Handicapped persons are different in relation to the unstated norm of able-bodiedness, or, as some have described it, the vantage point of the "Temporarily Able Persons." The unstated point of comparison is not neutral, but particular, and not inevitable, but only seemingly so when left unstated. A notion of equality that demands disregarding a "difference" calls for assimilation to an unstated norm. To strip away difference, then, often is to remove or ignore a feature distinguishing an individual from a presumed norm – like a white, able-bodied Christian man – but leaving that norm in place as the measure for equal treatment.

Third, we treat the perspective of the person doing the seeing or judging as objective, rather than as subjective. Although a person's perspective does not collapse into his or her demographic characteristics, no one is free from perspective, and no one can see fully from another's point of view.

Fourth, we assume that the perspectives of those being judged are either irrelevant or are already taken into account through the perspective of the judge. That is, we regard a person's self-conception or world view as unimportant to our treatment of that person.

Finally, there is an assumption that the existing social and economic arrangements are natural and neutral. We presume that individuals are free to form their own preferences and act upon them. In this view, any departure from the status quo risks non-neutrality and interference with free choice.

These related assumptions, once made explicit, must contend with some contrary ones. Consider these alternative starting points. Difference is relational, not intrinsic. Who or what should be taken as the point of reference for defining differences is debatable. There is no single, superior perspective for judging questions of difference. No perspective asserted to produce "the truth" is objective, but rather will obscure the power of the person attributing a difference while excluding important competing perspectives. Social arrangements can be changed: maintaining the status quo is not neutral and cannot be justified by the claim that everyone has freely chosen it.

A   THE FIVE UNSTATED ASSUMPTIONS

1   *Assumption 1: Difference Is Intrinsic, Not Relational.*

[M]any of us have never conceived of ourselves only as somebody's other.
– Barbara Christian

Can and should the questions about who is different be resolved by a process of discovering intrinsic differences? Is difference an objective, verifiable matter rather than something constructed by social attitudes? By posing legal claims through the difference dilemma, litigants and judges treat the problem of difference as what society or a given decisionmaker should do about the "different person" – a formulation that implicitly assigns the label of difference to that person.

The difference inquiry functions by pigeonholing people into sharply distinguished categories based on selected facts and features. Categorization helps people cope with complexity and understand each other. The legal analyst tends to treat the difference question as one of discovery rather than of choice. The judge asks: "Into what category does a given person or feature belong?" The categories then determine the significance of the persons or features situated within them. The distinguishing features behind critical perceptions and behind the categories themselves appear natural rather than chosen. It is hard, if not impossible, to find commonalities across differences, and to argue for the same treatment across difference. Responsibility for the consequences of identifying difference, then, is dispersed through the process of perception and categorization, even as the process of categorization itself can create new perceptions and realities.

Legal analysis of difference, and its focus on categorization, bears much similarity to legal analysis in general. Legal analysis, cast in a judicial mode, typically addresses whether a given situation "fits" in a category defined by a legal rule or instead belongs outside of it. Many questions presented to the Supreme Court, for example, take the form, "Is this a that?" A leading expositor of the nature of legal reasoning explains the three steps involved: "similarity is seen between cases; next the rule of law inherent in the first case is announced; then the rule of law is made applicable to the second case ... The finding of similarity or difference is the key step in the legal process." Again, as critics have noted for nearly a century, these patterns of legal analysis imply that legal reasoning yields results of its own accord, beyond human control.

For both legal difference and difference in general, a difference "discovered" is more aptly a statement of a relationship, expressing one person's deviation from an unstated norm assumed by the other. But where do these criteria for comparison come from, and why do they seem so natural that they escape debate? Especially when legal analysis overlaps with social analysis of difference, the criteria for comparison may express perceptions and prejudices of those with the power to define and name others.

In some cases, members of the Court have acknowledged that differences are not intrinsic but socially constructed, which implies in turn that the criteria for comparison are not "real" but humanly chosen. Thus, in *School Board v Arline*, the Court concluded that co-workers' perceptions of an individual's contagious disease actually help constitute the handicap, impairment, or difference, triggering legal protection. The Court thereby acknowledged that much of what is called disability is created by social attitudes that are themselves mutable. Similarly, many of the stereotypes we often associate with differences of race or sex are also changeable social constructs, rather than intrinsic traits.

Yet the Court has not entirely abandoned the assumption that at least some differences are intrinsic and verifiable. In *Arline*, the Court emphasized that the Rehabilitation Act protects only persons who are both "handicapped *and* otherwise qualified" and called for individualized review of persons who claim that their contagious disease constitutes a handicap. The Court thus sharpened the judicial tools for challenging mistaken attributions of difference, without abandoning the idea that people have real, objective differences.

The Court also acknowledged the socially and historically contingent construction of difference in *Shaare Tefila* and *Saint Francis*. The Court reasoned that objective, scientific sources could not resolve whether Arabs and Jews represent distinct races for the purposes of civil rights statutes. In essence, the Court acknowledged that racial identity is socially constrained and yet, oddly, the Justices turned to middle and late nineteenth-century notions of racial identity, prevalent when the remedial statutes were adopted, rather than examining contemporary assumptions and current prejudices.

In both *Shaare Tefila* and *Saint Francis*, members of minority groups sought to obtain protection by reinvoking the categories that had been used to denigrate them. As the cases thus illustrate, groups that seek to challenge socially assigned stigmas and stereotypes run into this dilemma: "How do you protest a socially imposed categorization, except by organizing around the category?" Although some people have resisted and challenged the meanings assigned to them, recipients of labels are often unable to control the many layers of negative association those labels carry. The web of negative associations assigned to the outsider complicates any effort to resist the denigration implied by difference.

What *Shaare Tefila* and *Saint Francis College* neglect to state is that attributions of difference reflect choices by those in power about what characteristics should matter. Ann Scales has noted: "To characterize similarities and differences among situations is a key step in legal judgments. That step, however, is not a mechanistic manipulation of essences. Rather, that step always has a moral crux." Some have argued that the assignment of differences in Western thought entails not just relationships and comparisons but also imposition of hierarchies. To explore this idea, we need the next unstated assumption: the implicit norm or reference point for the comparisons through which difference is assigned.

2   Assumption 2: The Unstated Norm ...

To treat someone as different means to accord them treatment that is different from treatment of someone else; to describe someone as "the same" implies "the same as" someone else. When differences are discussed without explicit reference to the person or trait on the other side of the comparison, an unstated norm remains. Usually, this default reference point is so powerful and well-established that it need not be specified.

Some remedial statutes explicitly state the norm: in 42 USC section 1981, the norm is "white citizens" – with an emphasis on both terms, implicitly establishing the terms of sameness and difference in this very statement of the norm. Claimants invoking the statute must show themselves to be relatively similar to "white citizens." Hence, these cases focus on whether the claimant is a member of a race.

When women argue for rights, the implicit reference point used in discussions of sameness and difference is the privilege accorded some males. This reference point can present powerful arguments for overcoming the exclusion of women from activities and opportunities available to men. For example, reform efforts on behalf of women during both the nineteenth and the twentieth centuries asserted women's fundamental similarities to privileged, white men as a tactic for securing equal treatment. Unfortunately for the reformers, embracing the theory of "sameness" meant that any sign of difference between women and men could be used to justify treating women differently from men. Men remained the unstated norm.

A prominent "difference" assigned to women, by implicit comparison with men, is pregnancy, especially as experienced by women working for pay outside their homes. The Supreme Court's treatment of issues concerning pregnancy and the workplace highlights the power of the unstated male norm in analyses of problems of difference. In 1975, the Court accepted the similarity of women to the male norm in striking down a Utah statute that disqualified a woman from receiving unemployment compensation for a specified period surrounding child-birth, even if her reasons for leaving work were unrelated to the pregnancy.[1] Although the capacity to become pregnant is a difference between women and men, this fact alone did not justify treating women and men differently on matters unrelated to pregnancy. Using men as the norm, the Court reasoned that any woman who can perform like a man can be treated like a man. A woman could not be denied unemployment compensation for different reasons than a man would.

What, however, is equal treatment for the woman who is correctly identified within the group of pregnant persons, not simply stereotyped as such, and who is different from nonpregnant persons in ways that are relevant to the workplace? The Court first grappled with these issues in two cases that posed the question of whether discrimination on the basis of pregnancy amounted to discrimination on the basis of sex. In both instances, the Court answered negatively, arguing that pregnancy marks a division between the groups of pregnant and nonpregnant persons and that women fall into both categories.[2] Congress responded by enacting the Pregnancy Discrimination Act (PDA), which amended title VII to include discrimination on the basis of pregnancy within the range of impermissible sex discrimination. Yet even under these new statutory terms, the power of the unstated male norm persists in debates over the definition of discrimination ...

The dissenters, on the other hand, countered by emphasizing that the PDA's commitment to equal treatment bans preferential treatment on the basis of pregnancy. The dissenters persisted in using the male norm as the measure for equal treatment in the workplace.

By contrast, the Court in *Wimberly*[3] used just such an implicit male standard in concluding that the federal law against discriminating on the basis of pregnancy in unemployment compensation provides no check against states that refuse to provide compensation for a broad range of situations, including pregnancy. In a work world designed without pregnancy in mind, requiring women to be treated like men means that there is no discrimination when women, as well as men, receive no benefits for unemployment due to pregnancy.[4] At a doctrinal level, the Court's holding that a state need not provide unemployment compensation to a woman who left her job because of pregnancy rested on the conclusion that the state treated pregnant women the same as all other persons who left for reasons unconnected with work. There was no discrimination when pregnancy was not singled out for detrimental treatment. The federal antidiscrimination statute did not demand "preferential treatment," and thus did not require that benefits be provided for pregnant persons when they would not be provided for others.

Wimberly is not an illogical ruling; a plausible theory of equality would call for a comparison between pregnant persons and other similarly situated persons. But what, exactly, is a situation similar to pregnancy? Unlike in *CalFed*, where the Court used a statute prohibiting pregnancy discrimination to establish the pregnant person as the point of comparison, the Court in *Wimberly* laid a neutral nondiscrimination demand on top of a workplace world and a state statute modeled without pregnancy in mind. Missing altogether was the equality norm that combined the work and family worlds and called for no difference in the abilities of men and women to work and have a family ...

Similar, unstated reference points appear in many other contexts. These implicit norms often work subtly, through the categories manifested in language. Reasoning processes tend to treat categories as clear, bounded, and sharp-edged; a given item either fits within the category or it does not. Instead of considering the entire individual, we often select one characteristic as representative of the whole. George Lakoff illustrates this phenomenon with the term "mother." Although "mother" appears to be a general category, with subcategories like working mother and unwed mother, the very need for modifying adjectives demonstrates an implicit prototype of the married housewife. The unstated prototype structures expectations about and valuations of members of the general category, yet treats these expectations and valuations as mere reflections of reality ...

Legal language seeks universal applicability, regardless of the particular traits of an individual. Yet abstract universalism often "takes the part for the whole, the particular for the universal and essential, the present for the eternal."[5] Making explicit the unstated points of reference is the first step in addressing this problem; the next is challenging the presumed neutrality of the observer who in fact sees from an unacknowledged perspective.

3   Assumption 3: The Observer Can See without a Perspective ...

If differences are intrinsic, then anyone can see them; if there is an objective reality, then any impartial observer can make judgments unaffected and untainted by his or her own perspective or experience. Once rules are selected, regardless of disputes over the rules themselves, a distinct aspiration is that they will be applied even-handedly. This aspiration to impartiality, however, is just that – an aspiration rather than a description – because it may suppress the inevitability of the existence of a perspective and thus make it harder for the observer, or anyone else, to challenge the absence of objectivity.

What interests us, given who we are and where we stand, affects our ability to perceive. Philosophers such as A.J. Ayer and W.V. Quine note that although we can alter the theory we use to frame our perceptions of the world, we cannot see the world unclouded by preconceptions. The impact of the observer's perspective may be crudely oppressive. Yet, we continue to believe in neutrality.

For example, in *Johnson v Transportation Agency*, in which the Court upheld an affirmative action plan for women, the press reported that the employer promoted a woman less qualified than a man, even though their scores differed by merely two points after a first interview. Johnson, the male applicant, earned the second highest score (with another applicant), whereas Joyce, the female applicant, had the next highest score. A second interview was conducted by three agency supervisors, two of whom had either harassed or made sexist comments to Joyce. Based on all the evidence and the recommendation of the affirmative action office, the employer promoted Joyce. To treat this as a case of a less qualified woman getting the job over a more qualified man perpetuates the mythology of neutral observers. The Court itself criticized this myth, noting that for unexceptional middle-level craft positions, final selection decisions are inevitably subjective, once a pool of fully qualified candidates is assembled ...

4   Assumption 4: The Irrelevance of Other Perspectives ...

Glimpsing contrasting perspectives helps resolve problems of difference. Several of the Justices have tried, on different occasions, to glimpse the point of view of a minority group or a person quite different from themselves; some have articulated eloquently the difficulty or even impossibility of knowing another's perspective, and have developed legal positions that take into account this difficulty. Others have rejected as irrelevant or relatively unimportant the experience of "difference" people and have denied their own partiality, often by using stereotypes as though they were real.

Justice Powell's majority opinion in *McCleskey v Kemp*[6] for example, ignored its own partial perspective in upholding the death penalty against a black defendant, despite strong statistical evidence of racial discrimination in capital sentencing generally. The petitioner, explained Justice Powell, failed to show that the decisionmakers in *his* case acted with a discriminatory purpose. This formulation takes seriously the vantage point of decisionmakers like the reviewing court and the jury, but not the perspective of the criminal defendant. From the black defendant's point of view, however, proof of the intent of the individual jury is much less important than the disproportionate risk of the death penalty.

The rarity of glimpses of such minority perspectives is underscored by their power when taken seriously. For example, consider Justice Brennan's dissent in *McCleskey*. Perhaps knowing that neither he nor many of his readers could fully grasp the defendant's perspective, Justice Brennan in his dissent tried to look through the eyes of the defense attorney who is asked by the black defendant about the chances of a death sentence. Adopting that viewpoint, Justice Brennan concluded that "counsel would feel bound to tell McCleskey that defendants charged with killing white victims in Georgia are 4.3 times as likely to be sentenced to death as defendants charged with killing blacks" and that "there was a significant chance that race would play a prominent role in determining if he lived or died." From the defendant's angle, Justice Powell's concluding fears about the unmanageability of more challenges to the criminal sentencing process should McCleskey prevail look strikingly confined by his perspective, prompting the question, unmanageable for whom? ...

Thus, some Justices, on some occasions, have tried to see beyond the dominant perspective and reach an alternative construction of reality. In many other instances, however, the Justices presume that the perspective they adopt is either universal or superior to others. A perspective may go unstated because it is so powerful and pervasive that it may be presumed without defense; it may also go unstated because it is so unknown to those in charge that they do not recognize it as a perspective. Presumptions about whose perspective matters ultimately may be embedded in the final, typically unstated assumption: when in doubt, the status quo is preferred, and is indeed presumed natural and free from coercion.

5   Assumption 5: The Status Quo Is Natural, Uncoerced, and Good ...

Connected with many of the other assumptions is the idea that critical features of the status quo – general social and economic arrangements – are natural and desirable. From this assumption follow three propositions: first, the goal of governmental neutrality demands the status quo because existing societal arrangements are assumed to be neutral. Second, governmental actions that change the status quo have a different status than omissions, or failures to act, that maintain the status quo. Third, prevailing social and political arrangements are not forced on anyone. Individuals are free to make choices and to assume responsibility for those choices. These propositions are rarely stated, both because they are deeply entrenched and because they view the status quo as good, natural, and freely chosen ...

Judges operating under the assumption that the world is neutral do not find discrimination unless it is specifically proven. In *McCleskey v Kemp*, for example, the Court refused to find discrimination in the case before it, despite strong statistical evidence that the race of the victim and of the defendant often determines who receives the death penalty. ...

For the most part, unstated assumptions work in subtle and complex ways. Assumptions fill the basic human need to simplify and to make our world familiar and unsurprising. Yet, by their very simplification, assumptions exclude contrasting views. Moreover, they contribute to the dilemma of difference by frustrating legislative and constitutional commitments to change the treatment of differences in race, gender, ethnicity, religion, and handicap. Before justice can be done, judges need to hear and understand contrasting points of view about the treatment of difference.

IV   PERSPECTIVES ON PERSPECTIVES ...

The difference dilemma seems paralyzing if framed by the unstated assumptions described in Part III. Those assumptions so entrench one point of view as natural and orderly that any conscious decision to notice or to ignore difference breaks the illusion of a legal world free of perspective. The assumptions make it seem that departures from unstated norms violate commitments to neutrality. Yet adhering to the unstated norms undermines commitments to neutrality – and to equality. Is it possible to proceed differently, putting these assumptions into question?

I will suggest that it is possible, even if difficult, to move beyond the constricting assumptions.

NOTES

1 The case was decided on due process grounds. See *Turner v Department of Employment Sec.*, 423 US 44 (1975) (per curiam); see also *Cleveland Bd. of Educ. v LaFleur*, 414 US 632 (1974) (invalidating a local school board rule requiring

pregnant teachers to take unpaid maternity leaves as a violation of due process).

2 See *General Electric Co v Gilbert*, 429 US 125 (1976) (title VII); *Geduldig v Aiello*, 417 US 484 (1974) (equal protection).

3 *Wimberly v Labor & Indus. Relations Comm'n*, 107 SCt 821 (1987).

4 See *General Elec. Co v Gilbert*, 429 US 125 (1976); *Geduldig v Aiello*, 417 US 484 (1974). One could seriously debate whether a man's prostate surgery or fatherhood is comparable to pregnancy and maternity.

5 Gould, "The Woman Question: Philosophy of Liberation and the Liberation of Philosophy," in *Women and Philosophy: Toward a Theory of Liberation* 21 (C. Gould & M. Wartofsky, eds. 1976).

6 107 SCt 1756 (1987).

READING QUESTIONS ON MINOW

1 What are the five assumptions Minow questions? What do they share?
2 Is there a relation between Minow's project and Dworkin's idea of the law "working itself pure"?

Patricia Williams
The Alchemy of Race and Rights (1991)

Williams's narrative tells of the importance for the oppressed of a certain formality to law.

Some time ago, Peter Gabel and I taught a contracts class together. (He was one of the first to bring critical theory to legal analysis and so is considered a "founder" of Critical Legal Studies.) Both recent transplants from California to New York, each of us hunted for apartments in between preparing for class. Inevitably, I suppose, we got into a discussion of trust and distrust as factors in bargain relations. It turned out that Peter had handed over a $900 deposit in cash, with no lease, no exchange of keys, and no receipt, to strangers with whom he had no ties other than a few moments of pleasant conversation. He said he didn't need to sign a lease because it imposed too much formality. The handshake and the good vibes were for him indicators of trust more binding than a form contract. At the time I told Peter he was mad, but his faith paid off. His sublessors showed up at the appointed time, keys in hand, to welcome him in. There was absolutely nothing in my experience to prepare me for such a happy ending. (In fact I remain convinced that, even if I were of a mind to trust a lessor with this degree of informality, things would not have worked out so successfully for me: many Manhattan lessors would not have trusted a black person enough to let me in the door in the first place, paperwork, references, and credit check notwithstanding.)

I, meanwhile, had friends who found me an apartment in a building they owned. In my rush to show good faith and trustworthiness, I signed a detailed, lengthily negotiated, finely printed lease firmly establishing me as the ideal arm's-length transactor.

As Peter and I discussed our experiences, I was struck by the similarity of what each of us was seeking, yet with such polar approaches. We both wanted to establish enduring relationships with the people in whose houses we would be living; we both wanted to enhance trust of ourselves and to allow whatever closeness was possible. This similarity of desire, however, could not reconcile our very different relations to the tonalities of law. Peter, for example, appeared to be extremely self-conscious of his power potential (either real or imagistic) as white or male or lawyer authority figure. He therefore seemed to go to some lengths to overcome the wall that image might impose. The logical ways of establishing some measure of trust between strangers were an avoidance of power and a preference for informal processes generally.

On the other hand, I was raised to be acutely conscious of the likelihood that no matter what degree of professional I am, people will greet and dismiss my black femaleness as unreliable, untrustworthy, hostile, angry, powerless, irrational, and probably destitute. Futility and despair are very real parts of my response. So it helps me to clarify boundary; to show that I can speak the language of lease is my way of enhancing trust of me in my business affairs. As black, I have been given by this society a strong sense of myself as already too familiar, personal, subordinate to white people. I am still evolving from being treated as three-fifths of a human, a subpart of the white estate. I grew up in a neighborhood where landlords would not sign leases with their poor black tenants, and demanded that rent be paid in cash; although superficially resembling Peter's transaction, such informality in most white-on-black situations signals distrust, not trust. Unlike Peter, I am still engaged in a struggle to set up transactions at arm's length, as legitimately commercial, and to portray myself as a bargainer of separate worth, distinct power, sufficient *rights* to manipulate commerce.

Peter, I speculate, would say that a lease or any other formal mechanism would introduce distrust into his relationships and he would suffer alienation, leading the commodification of his being and the degradation of his person to property. For me, in contrast, the lack of formal relation to the other would leave me estranged. It would risk a figurative isolation from that creative commerce by which I may be recognized as whole, by which I may feed and clothe and shelter myself, by which I may be seen as equal – even if I am stranger. For me, stranger-stranger relations are better than stranger-chattel.

READING QUESTION ON WILLIAMS

1 Does Williams's argument support or undermine what either MacKinnon or Minow have to say about the nature of law?

Lavallée v The Queen [1990] 555 CCC (3d) 97

Lynn Lavallée killed her abusive spouse and successfully argued that she was defending herself. The case, decided by the Supreme Court of Canada, reveals ways in which the law has attempted to integrate the sort of concerns raised by MacKinnon and Minow.

Wilson, J: – The narrow issue raised on this appeal is the adequacy of a trial judge's instructions to the jury regarding expert evidence. The broader issue concerns the utility of expert evidence in assisting a jury confronted by a plea of self-defence to a murder charge by a common law wife who had been battered by the deceased.

1. THE FACTS

The appellant, who was 22 years old at the time, had been living with Kevin Rust for some three to four years. Their residence was the scene of a boisterous party on August 30, 1986. In the early hours of August 31, after most of the guests had departed, the appellant and Rust had an argument in the upstairs bedroom which was used by the appellant.

Rust was killed by a single shot in the back of the head from a .303 calibre rifle fired by the appellant as he was leaving the room.

The appellant did not testify but her statement made to police on the night of the shooting was put in evidence. Portions of it read as follows:

Me and Wendy argued as usual and I ran in the house after Kevin pushed me. I was scared, I was really scared. I locked the door. Herb was downstairs with Joanne and I called for Herb but I was crying when I called him. I said, "Herb come up here please." Herb came up to the top of the stairs and I told him that Kevin was going to hit me actually beat on me again. Herb said he knew and that if I was his old lady things would be different, he gave me a hug. OK, we're friends, there's nothing between us. He said, "Yeah, I know" and he went outside to talk to Kevin leaving the door unlocked. I went upstairs and hid in my closet from Kevin. I was so scared ... My window was open and I could hear Kevin asking questions about what I was doing and what I was saying. Next thing I know he was coming up the stairs for me. He came into my bedroom and said, "Wench, where are you?" And he turned on my light and he said, "Your purse is on the floor," and he kicked it. OK then he turned and he saw me in the closet. He wanted me to come out but I didn't want to come out because I was scared. I was so scared. [The officer who took the statement then testified that the appellant started to cry at this point and stopped after a minute or two.] He grabbed me by the arm right there. There's a bruise on my face also where he slapped me. He didn't slap me right then. First he yelled at me then he pushed me and I pushed him back and he hit me twice on the right-hand side of my head. I was scared. All I thought about was all the other times he used to beat me, I was scared, I was shaking as usual. The rest is a blank, all I remember is he gave me the gun and a shot was fired through my screen. This is all so fast. And then the guns were in another room, and he loaded it the second shot and gave it to me. And I was going to shoot myself. I pointed it to myself, I was so upset. OK and then he went and I was sitting on the bed and he started going like this with his finger [the appellant made a shaking motion with an index finger] and said something like "You're my old lady and you do as you're told" or something like that. He said, "Wait till everybody leaves, you'll get it then," and he said something to the effect of "either you kill me or I'll get you" that was what it was. He kind of smiled and then he turned around. I shot him but I aimed out. I thought I aimed above him and a piece of his head went that way.

... The relationship between the appellant and Rust was volatile and punctuated by frequent arguments and violence. They would apparently fight for two or three days at a time or several times a week.

Considerable evidence was led at trial indicating that the appellant was frequently a victim of physical abuse at the hands of Rust. Between 1983 and 1986, the appellant made several trips to hospital for injuries including severe bruises, a fractured nose, multiple contusions and a black eye. One of the attending physicians, Dr Dirks testified that he disbelieved the appellant's explanation on one such occasion that she had sustained her injuries by falling from a horse.

A friend of the deceased, Robert Ezako, testified that he had witnessed several fights between the appellant and the deceased and that he had seen the appellant point a gun at the deceased twice and threaten to kill him if he ever touched her again. Under cross-examination Ezako admitted to seeing or hearing the deceased beat up the appellant on several occasions and, during the preliminary inquiry, described her screaming during one such incident like "a pig being butchered"...

At one point on the night of his death Rust chased the appellant outside the house and a mutual friend, Norman Kolish, testified that the appellant pleaded with Rust to "leave me alone" and sought Kolish's protection by trying to hide behind him. A neighbour overheard Rust and the appellant arguing and described the tone of the former as "argumentative" and the latter as "scared." Later, between the first and second gunshot, he testified that he could hear that "somebody was beating up somebody" and the screams were female. Another neighbour testified to hearing noises like gunshots and then a woman's voice sounding upset saying, "Fuck. He punched me in the face. He punched me in the face." He looked out the window and saw a woman matching the description of the appellant.

... [T]he appellant was seen visibly shaken and upset and was heard to say, "Rooster [the deceased] was beating me so I shot him," and, "You know how he treated me, you've got to help me." The arresting officer testified that en route to the police station the appellant made various comments in the police car, including, "He said if I didn't kill him first he would kill me. I hope he lives. I really love him," and, "He told me he was gonna kill me when everyone left."

The police officer who took the appellant's statement testified to seeing a red mark on her arm where she said the deceased had grabbed her. When the coroner who performed an autopsy on the deceased was shown pictures of the appellant (who had various bruises), he testified that it was "entirely possible" that bruises on the deceased's left hand were occasioned by an assault on the appellant. Another doctor noted an injury to the appellant's pinkie finger consistent with those sustained by the adoption of a defensive stance.

... The expert evidence which forms the subject-matter of the appeal came from Dr Fred Shane, a psychiatrist with extensive professional experience in the treatment of battered wives. At the request of defence counsel Dr Shane prepared a psychiatric assessment of the appellant. The substance of Dr Shane's opinion was that the appellant had been terrorized by Rust to the point of feeling trapped, vulnerable, worthless, and unable to escape the relationship despite the violence. At the same time, the continuing pattern of abuse put her life in danger. In Dr Shane's opinion the appellant's shooting of the deceased was a final desperate act by a woman who sincerely believed that she would be killed that night:

I think she felt, she felt in the final tragic moment that her life was on the line, that unless she defended herself, unless she reacted in a violent way that she would die. I mean he made it very explicit to her, from what she told me and from the information I have from the material that you forwarded to me, that she had, I think, to defend herself against his violence.

Dr Shane stated that his opinion was based on four hours of formal interviews with the appellant, a police report of the incident (including the appellant's statement), hospital reports documenting eight of her visits to emergency departments between 1983 and 1985, and an interview with the appellant's mother. In the course of his testimony Dr Shane related many things told to him by the appellant for which there was no admissible evidence. They were not in the appellant's statement to the police, and she did not testify at trial. For example, Dr Shane mentioned several episodes of abuse described by the appellant for which there were no hospital reports. He also related the appellant's disclosure to him that she had lied to doctors about the cause of her injuries. Dr Shane testified that such fabrication was typical of battered women. The appellant also recounted to Dr Shane occasions on which Rust would allegedly beat her, then beg her forgiveness, and ply her with flowers and temporary displays of kindness. Dr Shane was aware of the incidents described by Ezako about the appellant's pointing a gun at Rust on two occasions and explained it as "an issue for trying to defend herself. She was afraid that she would be assaulted." The appellant denied to Dr Shane that she had homicidal fantasies about Rust and mentioned that she had smoked some marijuana on the night in question. These facts were related by Dr Shane in the course of his testimony.

... The appellant was acquitted by a jury but the verdict was overturned by a majority of the Manitoba Court of Appeal and the case sent back for retrial ...

3.   RELEVANT LEGISLATION

Criminal Code, RSC 1985, c. C-46:

34(2) Every one who is unlawfully assaulted and who causes death or
grievous bodily harm in repelling the assault is justified if
(a) he causes it under reasonable apprehension of death or grievous bodily
harm from the violence with which the assault was originally made or with
which the assailant pursues his purposes, and
(b) he believes on reasonable and probable grounds, that he cannot otherwise
preserve himself from death or grievous bodily harm.

4.   ISSUES ON APPEAL

It should be noted that two bases for ordering a new trial are implicit in
the reasons of the majority of the Court of Appeal. In finding that
"absent the evidence of Dr Shane, it is unlikely that the jury, properly
instructed, would have accepted the accused's plea of self-defence" the
Court of Appeal suggests that the evidence of Dr Shane ought to have
been excluded entirely. The alternative ground for allowing the Crown's
appeal was that Dr Shane's testimony was properly admitted but the
trial judge's instructions with respect to it were deficient. Thus, the
issues before this court are as follows:

1. Did the majority of the Manitoba Court of Appeal err in concluding
   that the jury should have considered the plea of self-defence absent
   the expert evidence of Dr Shane?
2. Did the majority of the Manitoba Court of Appeal err in holding that
   the trial judge's charge to the jury with respect to Dr Shane's expert
   evidence did not meet the requirements set out by this court in
   Abbey, thus warranting a new trial?

5.   ANALYSIS

(i) Admissibility of Expert Evidence

In *Kelliher v Smith*, this court adopted the principle that in order for
expert evidence to be admissible "the subject-matter of the inquiry must

be such that ordinary people are unlikely to form a correct judgment about it, if unassisted by persons with special knowledge." More recently, this court addressed the admissibility of expert psychiatric evidence in criminal cases in *R v Abbey, supra.* At p. 409 of the unanimous judgment Dickson J (as he then was) stated the rule as follows:

With respect to matters calling for special knowledge, an expert in the field
may draw inferences and state his opinion. An expert's function is precisely
this: to provide the judge and jury with a ready-made inference which
the judge and jury, due to the technical nature of the facts, are unable to
formulate ...

Where expert evidence is tendered in such fields as engineering or pathology, the paucity of the layperson's knowledge is uncontentious. The long-standing recognition that psychiatric or psychological testimony also falls within the realm of expert evidence is predicated on the realization that in some circumstances the average person may not have sufficient knowledge of or experience with human behaviour to draw an appropriate inference from the facts before him or her.

The need for expert evidence in these areas can, however, be obfuscated by the belief that judges and juries are thoroughly knowledgeable about "human nature" and that no more is needed. They are, so to speak, their own experts on human behaviour. This, in effect, was the primary submission of the Crown to this court.

The bare facts of this case, which I think are amply supported by the evidence, are that the appellant was repeatedly abused by the deceased but did not leave him (although she twice pointed a gun at him), and ultimately shot him in the back of the head as he was leaving her room. The Crown submits that these facts disclose all the information a jury needs in order to decide whether or not the appellant acted in self-defence. I have no hesitation in rejecting the Crown's submission.

Expert evidence on the psychological effect of battering on wives and common law partners must, it seems to me, be both relevant and necessary in the context of the present case. How can the mental state of the appellant be appreciated without it? The average member of the public (or of the jury) can be forgiven for asking: Why would a woman put up with this kind of treatment? Why should she continue to live with such a man? How could she love a partner who beat her to the point of requiring hospitalization? We would expect the woman to pack her bags and go. Where is her self-respect? Why does she not cut loose and make a new life for herself? Such is the reaction of the average person confronted with the so-called battered wife syndrome. We need help to understand it and help is available from trained professionals.

The gravity, indeed, the tragedy of domestic violence can hardly be overstated. Greater media attention to this phenomenon in recent years has revealed both its prevalence and its horrific impact on women from all walks of life.

... Laws do not spring out of a social vacuum. The notion that a man has a right to "discipline" his wife is deeply rooted in the history of our society. The woman's duty was to serve her husband and to stay in the marriage at all costs "till death do us part" and to accept as her due any "punishment" that was meted out for failing to please her husband. One consequence of this attitude was that "wife battering" was rarely spoken of, rarely reported, rarely prosecuted, and even more rarely punished. Long after society abandoned its formal approval of spousal abuse, tolerance of it continued and continues in some circles to this day.

Fortunately, there has been a growing awareness in recent years that no man has a right to abuse any woman under any circumstances. Legislative initiatives designed to educate police, judicial officers, and the public, as well as more aggressive investigation and charging policies all signal a concerted effort by the criminal justice system to take spousal abuse seriously. However, a woman who comes before a judge or jury with the claim that she has been battered and suggests that this may be a relevant factor in evaluating her subsequent actions still faces the prospect of being condemned by popular mythology about domestic violence. Either she was not as badly beaten as she claims or she would have left the man long ago. Or, if she was battered that severely, she must have stayed out of some masochistic enjoyment of it.

(ii) The Relevance of Expert Testimony to the Elements of Self-Defence

In my view, there are two elements of the defence under s. 34(2) of the *Code* which merit scrutiny for present purposes. The first is the temporal connection in s. 34(2)(a) between the apprehension of death or grievous bodily harm and the act allegedly taken in self-defence. Was the appellant "under reasonable apprehension of death or grievous bodily harm" from Rust as he was walking out of the room? The second is the assessment in s. 34(2)(b) of the magnitude of the force used by the accused. Was the accused's belief that she could not "otherwise preserve herself from death or grievous bodily harm" except by shooting the deceased based "on reasonable grounds"?

The feature common to both para. (a) and para. (b) of s. 34(2) is the imposition of an objective standard of reasonableness on the apprehension of death and the need to repel the assault with deadly force ...

If it strains credulity to imagine what the "ordinary man" would do in the position of a battered spouse, it is probably because men do not typically find themselves in that situation. Some women do, however. The definition of what is reasonable must be adapted to circumstances which are, by and large, foreign to the world inhabited by the hypothetical "reasonable man."

... I turn now to a consideration of the specific components of self-defence under s. 34(2) of the *Criminal Code*.

A.   *Reasonable Apprehension of Death*

Section 34(2)(a) requires that an accused who intentionally causes death or grievous bodily harm in repelling an assault is justified if he or she does so "under reasonable apprehension of death or grievous bodily harm." In the present case, the assault precipitating the appellant's alleged defensive act was Rust's threat to kill her when everyone else had gone.

It will be observed that s. 34(2)(a) does not actually stipulate that the accused apprehend imminent danger when he or she acts. Case-law has, however, read that requirement into the defence. The sense in which "imminent" is used conjures up the image of "an uplifted knife" or a pointed gun. The rationale for the imminence rule seems obvious. The law of self-defence is designed to ensure that the use of defensive force is really necessary. It justifies the act because the defender reasonably believed that he or she had no alternative but to take the attacker's life. If there is a significant time interval between the original unlawful assault and the accused's response, one tends to suspect that the accused was motivated by revenge rather than self-defence. In the paradigmatic case of a one-time bar-room brawl between two men of equal size and strength, this inference makes sense. How can one feel endangered to the point of firing a gun at an unarmed man who utters a death threat, then turns his back and walks out of the room? One cannot be certain of the gravity of the threat or his capacity to carry it out. Besides, one can always take the opportunity to flee or to call the police. If he comes back and raises his fist, one can respond in kind if need be. These are the tacit assumptions that underlie the imminence rule.

... According to the testimony of Dr Shane these assaults [by the deceased] were not entirely random in their occurrence ... Dr Shane acknowledged his debt to Dr [Lenore] Walker in the course of establishing his credentials as an expert at trial. Dr Walker first describes the cycle in the book *The Battered Woman* (1979). In her 1984 book, *The Battered Woman Syndrome*, Dr Walker reports the results of a study involving 400 battered women. Her research was designed to test empirically the theories expounded in her earlier book. At pp. 95–6 of *The Battered Woman Syndrome*, she summarizes the Cycle Theory as follows:

A second major theory that was tested in this project is the Walker Cycle Theory of Violence (Walker, 1979). This tension reduction theory states that there are three distinct phases associated in a recurring battering cycle: (1) tension building, (2) the acute battering incident, and (3) loving contrition. During the first phase, there is a gradual escalation of tension displayed by discrete acts causing increased friction such as name-calling, other mean intentional behaviors, and/or physical abuse. The batterer expresses dissatisfaction and hostility but not in an extreme or maximally explosive form. The woman attempts to placate the batterer, doing what she thinks might please him, calm him down, or at least, what will not further aggravate him. She tries not to respond to his hostile actions and uses general anger reduction techniques. Often she succeeds for a little while which reinforces her unrealistic belief that she can control this man ...

The tension continues to escalate and eventually she is unable to continue controlling his angry response pattern. "Exhausted from the constant stress, she usually withdraws from the batterer, fearing she will inadvertently set off an explosion. He begins to move more oppressively toward her as he observes her withdrawal ... Tension between the two becomes unbearable" (Walker, 1979, p. 59). The second phase, the acute battering incident, becomes inevitable without intervention. Sometimes, she precipitates the inevitable explosion so as to control where and when it occurs, allowing her to take better precautions to minimize her injuries and pain.

"Phase two is characterized by the uncontrollable discharge of the tensions that have built up during phase one" (p. 59). The batterer typically unleashes a barrage of verbal and physical aggression that can leave the woman severely shaken and injured. In fact, when injuries do occur it usually happens during this second phase. It is also the time police become involved, if they are called at all. The acute battering phase is concluded when the batterer stops, usually bringing with its cessation a sharp physiological reduction in tension. This in itself is naturally reinforcing. Violence often succeeds because it does work.

In phase three which follows, the batterer may apologize profusely, try to assist his victim, show kindness and remorse, and shower her with gifts and/or promises. The batterer himself may believe at this point that he will never allow himself to be violent again. The woman wants to believe the batterer and, early in the relationship at least, may renew her hope in his ability to change. This third phase provides the positive reinforcement for remaining in the relationship, for the woman. In fact, our results showed that phase three could also be characterized by an absence of tension or violence, and no observable loving-contrition behaviour, and still be reinforcing for the woman.

Given the relational context in which the violence occurs, the mental state of an accused at the critical moment she pulls the trigger cannot be understood except in terms of the cumulative effect of months or years of brutality. As Dr Shane explained in his testimony, the deterioration of the relationship between the appellant and Rust in the period immediately preceding the killing led to feelings of escalating terror on the part of the appellant:

But their relationship some weeks to months before was definitely escalating in terms of tension and in terms of the discordant quality about it. They were sleeping in separate bedrooms. Their intimate relationship was lacking and things were building and building and to a point, I think, where it built to that particular point where she couldn't – she felt so threatened and so overwhelmed that she had to – that she reacted in a violent way because of her fear of survival and also because, I think because of her, I guess, final sense that she was – that she had to defend herself and her own sense of violence towards this man who had really desecrated her and damaged her for so long.

... Another aspect of the cyclical nature of the abuse is that it begets a degree of predictability to the violence that is absent in an isolated violent encounter between two strangers. This also means that it may in fact be possible for a battered spouse to accurately predict the onset of violence before the first blow is struck, even if an outsider to the relationship cannot. Indeed, it has been suggested that a battered woman's knowledge of her partner's violence is so heightened that she is able to anticipate the nature and extent (though not the onset) of the violence by his conduct beforehand.

Where evidence exists that an accused is in a battering relationship, expert testimony can assist the jury in determining whether the accused had a "reasonable" apprehension of death when she acted by explaining the heightened sensitivity of a battered woman to her partner's acts. Without such testimony I am skeptical that the average fact-finder would be capable of appreciating why her subjective fear may have been reasonable in the context of the relationship. After all, the hypothetical "reasonable man" observing only the final incident may have been unlikely to recognize the batterer's threat as potentially lethal. Using the case at bar as an example the "reasonable man" might have thought, as the majority of the Court of Appeal seemed to, that it was unlikely that Rust would make good on his threat to kill the appellant that night because they had guests staying overnight.

The issue is not, however, what an outsider would have reasonably perceived but what the accused reasonably perceived, given her situation and her experience.

... Even accepting that a battered woman may be uniquely sensitized to danger from her batterer, it may yet be contended that the law ought to require her to wait until the knife is uplifted, the gun pointed, or the fist clenched before her apprehension is deemed reasonable. This would allegedly reduce the risk that the woman is mistaken in her fear, although the law does not require her fear to be correct, only reasonable. In response to this contention, I need only point to the observation made by Huband JA that the evidence showed that when the appellant and Rust physically fought, the appellant "invariably got the worst of it." I do not think it is an unwarranted generalization to say that due to their size, strength, socialization, and lack of training, women are typically no match for men in hand-to-hand combat. The requirement imposed in *Whynot* that a battered woman wait until the physical assault is "under way" before her apprehensions can be validated in law would, in the words of an American court, be tantamount to sentencing her to "murder by installment":

B. Lack of Alternatives to Self-Help

Section 34(2) requires an accused who pleads self-defence to believe "on reasonable grounds" that it is not possible to otherwise preserve him or herself from death or grievous bodily harm. The obvious question is if the violence was so intolerable, why did the appellant not leave her abuser long ago? This question does not really go to whether she had an alternative to killing the deceased at the critical moment. Rather, it plays on the popular myth already referred to that a woman who says she was battered yet stayed with her batterer was either not as badly beaten as she claimed or else she liked it. Nevertheless, to the extent that her failure to leave the abusive relationship earlier may be used in support of the proposition that she was free to leave at the final moment, expert testimony can provide useful insights. Dr Shane attempted to explain in his testimony how and why, in the case at bar, the appellant remained with Rust:

> She had stayed in this relationship, I think, because of the strange, almost unbelievable, but yet it happens, relationship that sometimes develops between people who develop this very disturbed, I think, very disturbed quality of a relationship. Trying to understand it, I think, isn't always easy and there's been a lot written about it recently, in the recent years, in psychiatric literature. But basically it involves two people who are involved in what appears to be an attachment which may have sexual or romantic or affectionate overtones.
>
> And the one individual, and it's usually the women in our society, but there have been occasions where it's been reversed, but what happens is the spouse who becomes battered, if you will, stays in the relationship probably because of a number of reasons.
>
> One is that the spouse gets beaten so badly – so badly – that he or she loses the motivation to react and becomes helpless and becomes powerless. And it's also been shown sometimes, you know, in – not that you can compare animals to human beings, but in laboratories, what you do if you shock an animal, after a while it can't respond to a threat of its life. It becomes just helpless and lies there in an amotivational state, if you will, where it feels there's no power and there's no energy to do anything.
>
> So in a sense it happens in human beings as well. It's almost like a concentration camp, if you will. You get paralyzed with fear.
>
> The other thing that happens often in these types of relationships with human beings is that the person who beats or assaults, who batters, often tries – he makes up and begs for forgiveness. And this individual, who basically has a very disturbed or damaged self-esteem, all of a sudden feels that he or she – we'll use women in this case because it's so much more common – the spouse feels that she again can do the spouse a favour and it can make her feel needed and boost her self-esteem for a while and make her feel worthwhile and the spouse says he'll forgive her and whatnot.

The account given by Dr Shane comports with that documented in the literature. Reference is often made to it as a condition of "learned helplessness," a phrase coined by Dr Charles Seligman, the psychologist who first developed the theory by experimenting on animals in the manner described by Dr Shane in his testimony. A related theory used to explain the failure of women to leave battering relationships is described by psychologist and lawyer Charles Patrick Ewing, in his book *Battered Women Who Kill* (1987). Ewing describes a phenomenon labelled "traumatic bonding" that has been observed between hostages and captors, battered children and their parents, concentration camp prisoners and guards, and batterers and their spouses.

The situation of the battered woman as described by Dr Shane strikes me as somewhat analogous to that of a hostage. If the captor tells her that he will kill her in three days' time, is it potentially reasonable for her to seize an opportunity presented on the first day to kill the captor or must she wait until he makes the attempt on the third day? I think the question the jury must ask itself is whether, given the history, circumstances and perceptions of the appellant, her belief that she could not preserve herself from being killed by Rust that night except by killing him first was reasonable. To the extent that expert evidence can assist the jury in making that determination, I would find such testimony to be both relevant and necessary.

In light of the foregoing discussion I would summarize as follows the principles upon which expert testimony is properly admitted in cases such as this:

1. Expert testimony is admissible to assist the fact-finder in drawing inferences in areas where the expert has relevant knowledge or experience beyond that of the layperson.
2. It is difficult for the layperson to comprehend the battered-wife syndrome. It is commonly thought that battered women are not really beaten as badly as they claim; otherwise they would have left the relationship. Alternatively, some believe that women enjoy being beaten, that they have a masochistic strain in them. Each of these stereotypes may adversely affect consideration of a battered woman's claim to have acted in self-defence in killing her mate.
3. Expert evidence can assist the jury in dispelling these myths.
4. Expert testimony relating to the ability of an accused to perceive danger from her mate may go to the issue of whether she "reasonably apprehended" death or grievous bodily harm on a particular occasion.
5. Expert testimony pertaining to why an accused remained in the

battering relationship may be relevant in assessing the nature and extent of the alleged abuse.

6. By providing an explanation as to why an accused did not flee when she perceived her life to be in danger, expert testimony may also assist the jury in assessing the reasonableness of her belief that killing her batterer was the only way to save her own life.

... In my view, the trial judge did not err in admitting Dr Shane's expert testimony in order to assist the jury in determining whether the appellant had a reasonable apprehension of death or grievous bodily harm and believed on reasonable grounds that she had no alternative but to shoot Kevin Rust on the night in question.

Obviously the fact that the appellant was a battered woman does not entitle her to an acquittal. Battered women may well kill their partners other than in self-defence. The focus is not on who the woman is, but on what she did.

(iii) Adequacy of Trial Judge's Charge to the Jury

The second issue raised in this case is the adequacy of the trial judge's charge to the jury with respect to the expert evidence furnished by Dr Shane. It appears that Dr Shane relied on various sources in formulating his opinion – his series of interviews with the appellant, an interview with her mother, a police report of the incident (including information regarding her statement to the police), and hospital records documenting eight of her visits to emergency departments between 1983 and 1986. Neither the appellant nor her mother testified at trial. The contents of their statements to Dr Shane were hearsay ...

Where the factual basis of an expert's opinion is a melange of admissible and inadmissible evidence the duty of the trial judge is to caution the jury that the weight attributable to the expert testimony is directly related to the amount and quality of admissible evidence on which it relies. The trial judge openly acknowledged to counsel the inherent difficulty in discharging such a duty in the case at bar. In my view, the trial judge performed his task adequately in this regard. A new trial is not warranted on the basis of the trial judge's charge to the jury.

I would accordingly allow the appeal, set aside the order of the Court of Appeal, and restore the acquittal.

Appeal allowed; acquittal restored.

READING QUESTIONS ON LAVALLÉE

1 Madame Justice Wilson compares Lavallée's situation to that of a hostage. In what ways are the situations parallel? Do you see any disanalogies?

2 Are there dangers connected to the idea of a "battered woman syndrome"? Does the defensibility of Lavallée's acts turn on her suffering from a condition, or can it be justified purely in light of the situation in which she finds herself?

3 Johnny Frank Buggs was attacked and threatened by members of the Crips gang, who were notorious for carrying grudges and using guns. When he saw them again shortly after the attack, he shot them. Can he claim self-defence? (*State v Buggs* 806 P. 2d 1381)

4 Nellie Eyapaise, who had been in a variety of abusive relationships, stabbed a man she barely knew when he made advances at her. Can she claim self-defence? (*R v Eyapaise* 20 CR (4th) 246 (Alta. QB) (1993)

5 In the movie *Cape Fear*, a lawyer is harassed by a recently released former client. The client threatens to kill the lawyer's family. The audience knows the convict will eventually do something terrible. Although the police tell the lawyer that he can only kill the convict during a confrontation, they cannot guarantee that they will be able to protect him. Compare this lawyer's situation to those of Lavallée, Eyapaise, and Buggs. Should the lawyer be allowed to act pre-emptively?

4

Law and Values:
Law as Protector of Individual Liberty

This chapter and the following one (Chapter 5) look at a series of questions revolving around the tensions between the role of law as a protector of individual liberty and as a tool of democratic self-rule. Law has been defended as each of these, yet they are in constant tension. Individual rights are sometimes endangered by policies chosen by majorities. As a result, almost everyone supposes that some limits should be placed on majority rule. Still, profound disagreements arise about how to think about the appropriate limits. Some defenders of the rule of law insist on severe limits. They argue that the law can only protect liberty if it has clear and readily identifiable rules that enable people to plan their own affairs. This understanding of liberty has been criticized on a number of fronts. From one direction, critics have suggested that such a view of liberty sets appropriate limits to the reach of the law, but that more than the protection of liberty is needed if a society is to survive. Defenders of such views may disagree about what more is needed. Some of them suppose that what is important is that the members of the society share some conception of the good life, while others may insist that the material conditions for the meaningful exercise of liberty be guaranteed. Others argue that the very idea of negative liberty is flawed, resting on an unrealistic view of the importance of choice. From still another direction, difficulties with the idea of negative liberty have led some critics to question the very idea of the rule of law. Sometimes this criticism takes the form of a rejection of the distinction between making law and applying it, and concludes that the idea of law as a rule-governed activity makes no sense. In the eyes of these critics, law is always an exercise of power, and at best bears a contingent relation to justice and democracy.

John Stuart Mill
On Liberty (1859)

In the classic work of nineteenth-century liberalism, Mill argues that the only legitimate restrictions on individual liberty are those that will prevent harms to others.

CHAPTER I: INTRODUCTORY

The Subject of this Essay is not the so-called Liberty of the Will, so unfortunately opposed to the misnamed doctrine of Philosophical Necessity; but Civil, or Social Liberty: the nature and limits of the power which can be legitimately exercised by society over the individual. A question seldom stated, and hardly ever discussed, in general terms, but which profoundly influences the practical controversies of the age by its latent presence, and is likely soon to make itself recognised as the vital question of the future. It is so far from being new, that, in a certain sense, it has divided mankind, almost from the remotest ages; but in the stage of progress into which the more civilized portions of the species have now entered, it presents itself under new conditions, and requires a different and more fundamental treatment.

The struggle between Liberty and Authority is the most conspicuous feature in the portions of history with which we are earliest familiar, particularly in that of Greece, Rome, and England. But in old times this contest was between subjects, or some classes of subjects, and the Government. By liberty, was meant protection against the tyranny of the political rulers. The rulers were conceived (except in some of the popular governments of Greece) as in a necessarily antagonistic position to the people whom they ruled. They consisted of a governing One, or a governing tribe or caste, who derived their authority from inheritance or conquest, who, at all events, did not hold it at the pleasure of the governed, and whose supremacy men did not venture, perhaps did not desire, to contest, whatever precautions might be taken against its oppressive exercise. Their power was regarded as necessary, but also as highly dangerous; as a weapon which they would attempt to use against their subjects, no less than against external enemies. To prevent the weaker members of the community from being preyed upon by innumerable vultures, it was needful that there should be an animal of prey stronger than the rest, commissioned to keep them down. But as the king of the vultures would be no less bent upon preying on the flock than any of the minor harpies, it was indispensable to be in a perpetual attitude of defence against his beak and claws. The aim, therefore, of patriots was to set limits to the power which the ruler should be suffered to exercise over the community; and this limitation was what they meant by liberty. It was attempted in two ways. First, by obtaining a recognition of certain immunities, called political liberties or rights, which it was to be regarded as a breach of duty in the ruler to infringe, and which, if he did infringe, specific resistance, or general rebellion, was held to be justifiable. A second, and generally a later expedient, was the establishment of constitutional checks, by which the consent of the community, or of a body of some sort, supposed to represent its interests, was made a necessary condition to some of the more important acts of the governing power. To the first of these modes of limitation, the ruling power, in most European countries, was compelled, more or less, to submit. It was not so with the second; and, to attain this, or when already in some degree possessed, to attain it more completely, became everywhere the principal object of the lovers of liberty. And so long as mankind were content to combat one enemy by another, and to be ruled by a master, on condition of being guaranteed more or less efficaciously against his tyranny, they did not carry their aspirations beyond this point.

A time, however, came, in the progress of human affairs, when men ceased to think it a necessity of nature that their governors should be an independent power, opposed in interest to themselves. It appeared to them much better that the various magistrates of the State should be their tenants or delegates, revocable at their pleasure. In that way alone, it seemed, could they have complete security that the powers of government would never be abused to their disadvantage. By degrees this new demand for elective and temporary rulers became the prominent object of the exertions of the popular party, wherever any such party existed; and superseded, to a considerable extent, the previous efforts to limit the power of rulers. As the struggle proceeded for making the ruling power emanate from the periodical choice of the ruled, some persons began to think that too much importance had been attached to the limitation of the power itself. *That* (it might seem) was a resource against rulers whose interests were habitually opposed to those of the people. What was now wanted was, that the rulers should be identified with the people; that their interest and will should be the interest and will of the nation. The nation did not need to be protected against its own will. There was no fear of its tyrannizing over itself. Let the rulers be effectually responsible to it, promptly removable by it, and it could afford to trust them with power of which it could itself dictate the use to be made. Their power was but the nation's own power, concentrated, and in a form convenient for exercise. This mode of thought, or rather perhaps of feeling, was common among the last generation of European liberalism, in the Continental section of which it still apparently predominates. Those who admit any limit to what a government may do, except in the case of such governments as they think ought not to exist, stand out as brilliant exceptions among the political thinkers of the Continent. A similar tone of sentiment might by this time have been prevalent in our own country, if the circumstances which for a time encouraged it, had continued unaltered.

But, in political and philosophical theories, as well as in persons, success discloses faults and infirmities which failure might have concealed from observation. The notion, that the people have no need to limit their power over themselves, might seem axiomatic, when popular government was a thing only dreamed about, or read of as having existed at some distant period of the past. Neither was that notion necessarily disturbed by such temporary aberrations as those of the French Revolution, the worst of which were the work of an usurping few, and which, in any case, belonged, not to the permanent working of popular institutions, but to a sudden and convulsive outbreak against monarchical and aristocratic despotism. In time, however, a democratic republic came to occupy a large portion of the earth's surface, and made itself felt as one of the most powerful members of the community of nations; and elective and responsible government became subject to the observations and criticisms which wait upon a great existing fact. It was now perceived that such phrases as "self-government," and "the power of the people over themselves," do not express the true state of the case. The "people" who exercise the power are not always the same people with those over whom it is exercised; and the "self-government" spoken of is not the government of each by himself, but of each by all the rest. The will of the people, moreover, practically means the will of the most numerous or the most active *part* of the people; the majority, or those who succeed in making themselves accepted as the majority; the people, consequently, *may* desire to oppress a part of their number; and precautions are as much needed against this as against any other abuse of power. The limitation, therefore, of the power of government over individuals loses none of its importance when the holders of power are regularly accountable to the community, that is, to the strongest party therein. This view of things, recommending itself equally to the intelligence of thinkers and to the inclination of those important classes in European society to whose real or supposed interests democracy is adverse, has had no difficulty in establishing itself; and in political speculations "the tyranny of the majority" is now generally included among the evils against which society requires to be on its guard.

Like other tyrannies, the tyranny of the majority was at first, and is still vulgarly, held in dread, chiefly as operating through the acts of the public authorities. But reflecting persons perceived that when society is itself the tyrant – society collectively, over the separate individuals who compose it – its means of tyrannizing are not restricted to the acts which it may do by the hands of its political functionaries. Society can and does execute its own mandates: and if it issues wrong mandates instead of right, or any mandates at all in things with which it ought not to meddle, it practises a social tyranny more formidable than many kinds of political oppression, since, though not usually upheld by such extreme penalties, it leaves fewer means of escape, penetrating much more deeply into the details of life, and enslaving the soul itself. Protection, therefore, against the tyranny of the magistrate is not enough: there needs protection also against the tyranny of the prevailing opinion and feeling; against the tendency of society to impose, by other means than civil penalties, its own ideas and practices as rules of conduct on those who dissent from them; to fetter the development, and, if possible, prevent the formation, of any individuality not in harmony with its ways, and compel all characters to fashion themselves upon the model of its own. There is a limit to the legitimate interference of collective opinion with individual independence: and to find that limit, and maintain it against encroachment, is as indispensable to a good condition of human affairs, as protection against political despotism.

But though this proposition is not likely to be contested in general terms, the practical question, where to place the limit — how to make the fitting adjustment between individual independence and social control — is a subject on which nearly everything remains to be done. All that makes existence valuable to any one, depends on the enforcement of restraints upon the actions of other people. Some rules of conduct, therefore, must be imposed, by law in the first place, and by opinion on many things which are not fit subjects for the operation of law. What

these rules should be, is the principal question in human affairs; but if
we except a few of the most obvious cases, it is one of those which least
progress has been made in resolving. No two ages, and scarcely any
two countries, have decided it alike; and the decision of one age or
country is a wonder to another. Yet the people of any given age and
country no more suspect any difficulty in it, than if it were a subject on
which mankind had always been agreed. The rules which obtain among
themselves appear to them self-evident and self-justifying. This all but
universal illusion is one of the examples of the magical influence of
custom, which is not only, as the proverb says, a second nature, but is
continually mistaken for the first. The effect of custom, in preventing
any misgiving respecting the rules of conduct which mankind impose
on one another, is all the more complete because the subject is one on
which it is not generally considered necessary that reasons should be
given, either by one person to others, or by each to himself. People are
accustomed to believe, and have been encouraged in the belief by some
who aspire to the character of philosophers, that their feelings, on subjects of this nature, are better than reasons, and render reasons unnecessary. The practical principle which guides them to their opinions on the
regulation of human conduct, is the feeling in each person's mind that
everybody should be required to act as he, and those with whom he
sympathizes, would like them to act. No one, indeed, acknowledges to
himself that his standard of judgment is his own liking; but an opinion
on a point of conduct, not supported by reasons, can only count as one
person's preference; and if the reasons, when given, are a mere appeal
to a similar preference felt by other people, it is still only many people's
liking instead of one. To an ordinary man, however, his own preference, thus supported, is not only a perfectly satisfactory reason, but the
only one he generally has for any of his notions of morality, taste, or
propriety, which are not expressly written in his religious creed; and
his chief guide in the interpretation even of that. Men's opinions, accordingly, on what is laudable or blameable, are affected by all the
multifarious causes which influence their wishes in regard to the conduct of others, and which are as numerous as those which determine
their wishes on any other subject. Sometimes their reason – at other
times their prejudices or superstitions: often their social affections, not
seldom their antisocial ones, their envy or jealousy, their arrogance or
contemptuousness: but most commonly, their desires or fears for themselves — their legitimate or illegitimate self-interest. Wherever there is
an ascendant class, a large portion of the morality of the country ema-

nates from its class interests, and its feelings of class superiority. The morality between Spartans and Helots, between planters and negroes, between princes and subjects, between nobles and roturiers, between men and women, has been for the most part the creation of these class interests and feelings: and the sentiments thus generated, react in turn upon the moral feelings of the members of the ascendant class, in their relations among themselves. Where, on the other hand, a class, formerly ascendant, has lost its ascendancy, or where its ascendancy is unpopular, the prevailing moral sentiments frequently bear the impress of an impatient dislike of superiority. Another grand determining principle of the rules of conduct, both in act and forbearance, which have been enforced by law or opinion, has been the servility of mankind towards the supposed preferences or aversions of their temporal masters, or of their gods. This servility, though essentially selfish, is not hypocrisy; it gives rise to perfectly genuine sentiments of abhorrence; it made men burn magicians and heretics. Among so many baser influences, the general and obvious interests of society have of course had a share, and a large one, in the direction of the moral sentiments: less, however, as a matter of reason, and on their own account, than as a consequence of the sympathies and antipathies which grew out of them: and sympathies and antipathies which had little or nothing to do with the interests of society, have made themselves felt in the establishment of moralities with quite as great force.

The likings and dislikings of society, or of some powerful portion of it, are thus the main thing which has practically determined the rules laid down for general observance, under the penalties of law or opinion. And in general, those who have been in advance of society in thought and feeling, have left this condition of things unassailed in principle, however they may have come into conflict with it in some of its details. They have occupied themselves rather in inquiring what things society ought to like or dislike, than in questioning whether its likings or dislikings should be a law to individuals. They preferred endeavouring to alter the feelings of mankind on the particular points on which they were themselves heretical, rather than make common cause in defence of freedom, with heretics generally. The only case in which the higher ground has been taken on principle and maintained with consistency, by any but an individual here and there, is that of religious belief: a case instructive in many ways, and not least so as forming a most striking instance of the fallibility of what is called the moral sense: for the *odium theologicum*, in a sincere bigot, is one of the

most unequivocal cases of moral feeling. Those who first broke the
yoke of what called itself the Universal Church, were in general as little
willing to permit difference of religious opinion as that church itself.
But when the heat of the conflict was over, without giving a complete
victory to any party, and each church or sect was reduced to limit its
hopes to retaining possession of the ground it already occupied; minorities, seeing that they had no chance of becoming majorities, were
under the necessity of pleading to those whom they could not convert,
for permission to differ. It is accordingly on this battle field, almost
solely, that the rights of the individual against society have been asserted on broad grounds of principle, and the claim of society to exercise authority over dissentients, openly controverted. The great writers
to whom the world owes what religious liberty it possesses, have mostly
asserted freedom of conscience as an indefeasible right, and denied
absolutely that a human being is accountable to others for his religious
belief. Yet so natural to mankind is intolerance in whatever they really
care about, that religious freedom has hardly anywhere been practically
realized, except where religious indifference, which dislikes to have its
peace disturbed by theological quarrels, has added its weight to the
scale. In the minds of almost all religious persons, even in the most
tolerant countries, the duty of toleration is admitted with tacit reserves.
One person will bear with dissent in matters of church government, but
not of dogma; another can tolerate everybody, short of a Papist or an
Unitarian; another, every one who believes in revealed religion, a few
extend their charity a little further, but stop at the belief in a God and in
a future state. Wherever the sentiment of the majority is still genuine
and intense, it is found to have abated little of its claim to be obeyed.

In England, from the peculiar circumstances of our political history,
though the yoke of opinion is perhaps heavier, that of law is lighter,
than in most other countries of Europe; and there is considerable jealousy of direct interference, by the legislative or the executive power,
with private conduct; not so much from any just regard for the independence of the individual, as from the still subsisting habit of looking
on the government as representing an opposite interest to the public.
The majority have not yet learnt to feel the power of the government
their power, or its opinions their opinions. When they do so, individual
liberty will probably be as much exposed to invasion from the government, as it already is from public opinion. But, as yet, there is a considerable amount of feeling ready to be called forth against any attempt of
the law to control individuals in things in which they have not hitherto

been accustomed to be controlled by it; and this with very little discrimination as to whether the matter is, or is not, within the legitimate sphere of legal control; insomuch that the feeling, highly salutary on the whole, is perhaps quite as often misplaced as well grounded in the particular instances of its application. There is, in fact, no recognised principle by which the propriety or impropriety of government interference is customarily tested. People decide according to their personal preferences. Some, whenever they see any good to be done, or evil to be remedied, would willingly instigate the government to undertake the business; while others prefer to bear almost any amount of social evil, rather than add one to the departments of human interests amenable to governmental control. And men range themselves on one or the other side in any particular case, according to this general direction of their sentiments; or according to the degree of interest which they feel in the particular thing which it is proposed that the government should do, or according to the belief they entertain that the government would, or would not, do it in the manner they prefer; but very rarely on account of any opinion to which they consistently adhere, as to what things are fit to be done by a government. And it seems to me that in consequence of this absence of rule or principle, one side is at present as often wrong as the other; the interference of government is, with about equal frequency, improperly invoked and improperly condemned.

The object of this Essay is to assert one very simple principle, as entitled to govern absolutely the dealings of society with the individual in the way of compulsion and control, whether the means used be physical force in the form of legal penalties, or the moral coercion of public opinion. That principle is, that the sole end for which mankind are warranted, individually or collectively, in interfering with the liberty of action of any of their number, is self-protection. That the only purpose for which power can be rightfully exercised over any member of a civilized community, against his will, is to prevent harm to others. His own good, either physical or moral, is not a sufficient warrant. He cannot rightfully be compelled to do or forbear because it will be better for him to do so, because it will make him happier, because, in the opinions of others, to do so would be wise, or even right. These are good reasons for remonstrating with him, or reasoning with him, or persuading him, or entreating him, but not for compelling him, or visiting him with any evil in case he do otherwise. To justify that, the conduct from which it is desired to deter him, must be calculated to produce evil to some one else. The only part of the conduct of any one, for which he is amenable to society, is that which concerns others. In the part which merely concerns himself, his independence is, of right, absolute. Over himself, over his own body and mind, the individual is sovereign.

It is, perhaps, hardly necessary to say that this doctrine is meant to apply only to human beings in the maturity of their faculties. We are not speaking of children, or of young persons below the age which the law may fix as that of manhood or womanhood. Those who are still in a state to require being taken care of by others, must be protected against their own actions as well as against external injury. For the same reason, we may leave out of consideration those backward states of society in which the race itself may be considered as in its nonage. The early difficulties in the way of spontaneous progress are so great, that there is seldom any choice of means for overcoming them; and a ruler full of the spirit of improvement is warranted in the use of any expedients that will attain an end, perhaps otherwise unattainable. Despotism is a legitimate mode of government in dealing with barbarians, provided the end be their improvement, and the means justified by actually effecting that end. Liberty, as a principle, has no application to any state of things anterior to the time when mankind have become capable of being improved by free and equal discussion. Until then, there is nothing for them but implicit obedience to an Akbar or a Charlemagne, if they are so fortunate as to find one. But as soon as mankind have attained the capacity of being guided to their own improvement by conviction or persuasion (a period long since reached in all nations with whom we need here concern ourselves), compulsion, either in the direct form or in that of pains and penalties for non-compliance, is no longer admissible as a means to their own good, and justifiable only for the security of others.

It is proper to state that I forego any advantage which could be derived to my argument from the idea of abstract right, as a thing independent of utility. I regard utility as the ultimate appeal on all ethical questions; but it must be utility in the largest sense, grounded on the permanent interests of man as a progressive being. Those interests, I contend, authorize the subjection of individual spontaneity to external control, only in respect to those actions of each, which concern the interest of other people. If any one does an act hurtful to others, there is a *primâ facie* case for punishing him, by law, or, where legal penalties are not safely applicable, by general disapprobation. There are also many positive acts for the benefit of others, which he may rightfully be compelled to perform; such as, to give evidence in a court of justice; to bear his fair share in the common defence, or in any other joint work necessary to the interest of the society of which he enjoys the protection; and to perform certain acts of individual beneficence, such as saving a fellow-creature's life, or interposing to protect the defenceless against ill-usage, things which whenever it is obviously a man's duty to do, he may rightfully be made responsible to society for not doing. A person may cause evil to others not only by his actions, but by his inaction, and in either case he is justly accountable to them for the injury. The latter case, it is true, requires a much more cautious exercise of compulsion than the former. To make any one answerable for doing evil to others, is the rule; to make him answerable for not preventing evil, is, comparatively speaking, the exception. Yet there are many cases clear enough and grave enough to justify that exception. In all things which regard the external relations of the individual, he is *de jure* amenable to those whose interests are concerned, and if need be, to society as their protector. There are often good reasons for not holding him to the responsibility; but these reasons must arise from the special expediencies of the case: either because it is a kind of case in which he is on the whole likely to act better, when left to his own discretion, than when controlled in any way in which society have it in their power to control him; or because the attempt to exercise control would produce other evils, greater than those which it would prevent. When such reasons as these preclude the enforcement of responsibility, the conscience of the agent himself should step into the vacant judgment seat, and protect those interests of others which have no external protection; judging himself all the more rigidly, because the case does not admit of his being made accountable to the judgment of his fellow-creatures.

But there is a sphere of action in which society, as distinguished from the individual, has, if any, only an indirect interest; comprehending all that portion of a person's life and conduct which affects only himself, or if it also affects others, only with their free, voluntary, and undeceived consent and participation. When I say only himself, I mean directly, and in the first instance: for whatever affects himself, may affect others through himself; and the objection which may be grounded on this contingency, will receive consideration in the sequel. This, then, is the appropriate region of human liberty. It comprises, first, the inward domain of consciousness; demanding liberty of conscience, in the most comprehensive sense; liberty of thought and feeling; absolute freedom of opinion and sentiment on all subjects, practical or speculative, scientific, moral, or theological. The liberty of expressing and publishing opinions may seem to fall under a different principle, since it belongs to that part of the conduct of an individual which concerns other people; but, being almost of as much importance as the liberty of thought itself, and resting in great part on the same reasons, is practically inseparable from it. Secondly, the principle requires liberty of tastes and pursuits; of framing the plan of our life to suit our own character; of doing as we like, subject to such consequences as may follow: without impediment from our fellow-creatures, so long as what we do does not harm them, even though they should think our conduct foolish, perverse, or wrong. Thirdly, from this liberty of each individual, follows the liberty, within the same limits, of combination among individuals; freedom to unite, for any purpose not involving harm to others: the persons combining being supposed to be of full age, and not forced or deceived.

No society in which these liberties are not, on the whole, respected, is free, whatever may be its form of government; and none is completely free in which they do not exist absolute and unqualified. The only freedom which deserves the name, is that of pursuing our own good in our own way, so long as we do not attempt to deprive others of theirs, or impede their efforts to obtain it. Each is the proper guardian of his own health, whether bodily, or mental and spiritual. Mankind are greater gainers by suffering each other to live as seems good to themselves, than by compelling each to live as seems good to the rest.

Though this doctrine is anything but new, and, to some persons, may have the air of a truism, there is no doctrine which stands more directly opposed to the general tendency of existing opinion and practice. Society has expended fully as much effort in the attempt (according to its lights) to compel people to conform to its notions of personal, as of social excellence. The ancient commonwealths thought themselves entitled to practise, and the ancient philosophers countenanced, the regulation of every part of private conduct by public authority, on the ground that the State had a deep interest in the whole bodily and mental discipline of every one of its citizens; a mode of thinking which may have been admissible in small republics surrounded by powerful enemies, in constant peril of being subverted by foreign attack or internal commotion, and to which even a short interval of relaxed energy and self-command might so easily be fatal, that they could not afford to wait for the salutary permanent effects of freedom. In the modern world, the greater size of political communities, and above all, the separation between spiritual and temporal authority (which placed the direction of men's consciences in other hands than those which controlled their worldly affairs), prevented so great an interference by law in the details of private life; but the engines of moral repression have been wielded more strenuously against divergence from the reigning opinion in self-regarding, than even in social matters; religion, the most powerful of the elements which have entered into the formation of moral feeling, having almost always been governed either by the ambition of a hierarchy, seeking control over every department of human conduct, or by the spirit of Puritanism. And some of those modern reformers who have placed themselves in strongest opposition to the religions of the past, have been noway behind either churches or sects in their assertion of the right of spiritual domination: M. Comte, in particular, whose social system, as unfolded in his *Système de Politique Positive*, aims at establishing (though by moral more than by legal appliances) a despotism of society over the individual, surpassing anything contemplated in the political ideal of the most rigid disciplinarian among the ancient philosophers.

Apart from the peculiar tenets of individual thinkers, there is also in the world at large an increasing inclination to stretch unduly the powers of society over the individual, both by the force of opinion and even by that of legislation: and as the tendency of all the changes taking place in the world is to strengthen society, and diminish the power of the individual, this encroachment is not one of the evils which tend spontaneously to disappear, but, on the contrary, to grow more and more formidable. The disposition of mankind, whether as rulers or as fellow-citizens, to impose their own opinions and inclinations as a rule of conduct on others, is so energetically supported by some of the best and by some of the worst feelings incident to human nature, that it is hardly ever kept under restraint by anything but want of power; and as the power is not declining, but growing, unless a strong barrier of moral conviction can be raised against the mischief, we must expect, in the present circumstances of the world, to see it increase.

It will be convenient for the argument, if, instead of at once entering upon the general thesis, we confine ourselves in the first instance to a single branch of it, on which the principle here stated is, if not fully, yet to a certain point, recognised by the current opinions. This one branch is the Liberty of Thought: from which it is impossible to separate the cognate liberty of speaking and of writing. Although these liberties, to some considerable amount, form part of the political morality of all countries which profess religious toleration and free institutions, the grounds, both philosophical and practical, on which they rest, are perhaps not so familiar to the general mind, nor so thoroughly appreciated by many even of the leaders of opinion, as might have been expected. Those grounds, when rightly understood, are of much wider application than to only one division of the subject, and a thorough consideration of this part of the question will be found the best introduction to the remainder. Those to whom nothing which I am about to say will be new, may therefore, I hope, excuse me, if on a subject which for now three centuries has been so often discussed, I venture on one discussion more.

CHAPTER II: OF THE LIBERTY OF THOUGHT AND DISCUSSION

The time, it is to be hoped, is gone by, when any defence would be necessary of the "liberty of the press" as one of the securities against corrupt or tyrannical government. No argument, we may suppose, can now be needed, against permitting a legislature or an executive, not identified in interest with the people, to prescribe opinions to them, and determine what doctrines or what arguments they shall be allowed to hear. This aspect of the question, besides, has been so often and so triumphantly enforced by preceding writers, that it needs not be specially insisted on in this place. Though the law of England, on the subject of the press, is as servile to this day as it was in the time of the Tudors, there is little danger of its being actually put in force against political discussion, except during some temporary panic, when fear of insurrection drives ministers and judges from their propriety; and, speaking generally, it is not, in constitutional countries, to be apprehended, that the government, whether completely responsible to the people or not, will often attempt to control the expression of opinion, except when in doing so it makes itself the organ of the general intolerance of the public. Let us suppose, therefore, that the government is entirely at one with the people, and never thinks of exerting any power of coercion unless in agreement with what it conceives to be their voice. But I deny the right of the people to exercise such coercion, either by themselves or by their government. The power itself is illegitimate. The best government has no more title to it than the worst. It is as noxious, or more noxious, when exerted in accordance with public opinion, than when in opposition to it. If all mankind minus one, were of one opinion, and only one person were of the contrary opinion, mankind would be no more justified in silencing that one person, than he, if he had the power, would be justified in silencing mankind. Were an opinion a personal possession of no value except to the owner; if to be obstructed in the enjoyment of it were simply a private injury, it would make some difference whether the injury was inflicted only on a few persons or on many. But the peculiar evil of silencing the expression of an opinion is, that it is robbing the human race; posterity as well as the existing generation; those who dissent from the opinion, still more than those who hold it. If the opinion is right, they are deprived of the opportunity of exchanging error for truth: if wrong, they lose, what is almost as great a benefit, the clearer perception and livelier impression of truth, produced by its collision with error.

It is necessary to consider separately these two hypotheses, each of which has a distinct branch of the argument corresponding to it. We can never be sure that the opinion we are endeavouring to stifle is a false opinion; and if we were sure, stifling it would be an evil still.

First: the opinion which it is attempted to suppress by authority may possibly be true. Those who desire to suppress it, of course deny its truth; but they are not infallible. They have no authority to decide the question for all mankind, and exclude every other person from the means of judging. To refuse a hearing to an opinion, because they are sure that it is false, is to assume that *their* certainty is the same thing as *absolute* certainty. All silencing of discussion is an assumption of infallibility. Its condemnation may be allowed to rest on this common argument, not the worse for being common.

Unfortunately for the good sense of mankind, the fact of their fallibility is far from carrying the weight in their practical judgment, which is always allowed to it in theory; for while every one well knows himself to be fallible, few think it necessary to take any precautions against their own fallibility, or admit the supposition that any opinion, of which they feel very certain, may be one of the examples of the error to which they acknowledge themselves to be liable. Absolute princes, or others who are accustomed to unlimited deference, usually feel this complete confidence in their own opinions on nearly all subjects. People more happily situated, who sometimes hear their opinions disputed, and are not wholly unused to be set right when they are wrong, place the same unbounded reliance only on such of their opinions as are shared by all who surround them, or to whom they habitually defer: for in proportion to a man's want of confidence in his own solitary judgment, does he usually repose, with implicit trust, on the infallibility of "the world" in general. And the world, to each individual, means the part of it with which he comes in contact; his party, his sect, his church, his class of society: the man may be called, by comparison, almost liberal and large-minded to whom it means anything so comprehensive as his own country or his own age. Nor is his faith in this collective authority at all shaken by his being aware that other ages, countries, sects, churches, classes, and parties have thought, and even now think, the exact reverse. He devolves upon his own world the responsibility of being in the right against the dissentient worlds of other people; and it never troubles him that mere accident has decided which of these numerous worlds is the object of his reliance, and that the same causes which make him a Churchman in London, would have made him a Buddhist or a Confucian in Pekin. Yet it is as evident in itself, as any amount of argument can make it, that ages are no more infallible than individuals; every age having held many opinions which subsequent ages have deemed not only false but absurd; and it is as certain that many opinions, now general, will be rejected by future ages, as it is that many, once general, are rejected by the present.

The objection likely to be made to this argument, would probably take some such form as the following. There is no greater assumption of infallibility in forbidding the propagation of error, than in any other thing which is done by public authority on its own judgment and responsibility. Judgment is given to men that they may use it. Because it may be used erroneously, are men to be told that they ought not to use it at all? To prohibit what they think pernicious, is not claiming exemption from error, but fulfilling the duty incumbent on them, although fallible, of acting on their conscientious conviction. If we were never to act on our opinions, because those opinions may be wrong, we should leave all our interests uncared for, and all our duties unperformed. An objection which applies to all conduct, can be no valid objection to any conduct in particular. It is the duty of governments, and of individuals, to form the truest opinions they can; to form them carefully, and never impose them upon others unless they are quite sure of being right. But when they are sure (such reasoners may say), it is not conscientiousness but cowardice to shrink from acting on their opinions, and allow doctrines which they honestly think dangerous to the welfare of mankind, either in this life or in another, to be scattered abroad without restraint, because other people, in less enlightened times, have persecuted opinions now believed to be true. Let us take care, it may be said, not to make the same mistake: but governments and nations have made mistakes in other things, which are not denied to be fit subjects for the exercise of authority: they have laid on bad taxes, made unjust wars. Ought we therefore to lay on no taxes, and, under whatever provocation, make no wars? Men, and governments, must act to the best of their ability. There is no such thing as absolute certainty, but there is assurance sufficient for the purposes of human life. We may, and must, assume our opinion to be true for the guidance of our own conduct: and it is assuming no more when we forbid bad men to pervert society by the propagation of opinions which we regard as false and pernicious.

I answer, that it is assuming very much more. There is the greatest difference between presuming an opinion to be true, because, with every opportunity for contesting it, it has not been refuted, and assuming its truth for the purpose of not permitting its refutation. Complete liberty of contradicting and disproving our opinion, is the very condition which justifies us in assuming its truth for purposes of action; and on no other terms can a being with human faculties have any rational assurance of being right ...

Let us now pass to the second division of the argument, and dismissing the supposition that any of the received opinions may be false, let us assume them to be true, and examine into the worth of the manner in which they are likely to be held, when their truth is not freely and openly canvassed. However unwillingly a person who has a strong opinion may admit the possibility that his opinion may be false, he ought to be moved by the consideration that however true it may be, if it is not fully, frequently, and fearlessly discussed, it will be held as a dead dogma, not a living truth.

There is a class of persons (happily not quite so numerous as formerly) who think it enough if a person assents undoubtingly to what they think true, though he has no knowledge whatever of the grounds of the opinion, and could not make a tenable defence of it against the most superficial objections. Such persons, if they can once get their creed taught from authority, naturally think that no good, and some harm, comes of its being allowed to be questioned. Where their influence prevails, they make it nearly impossible for the received opinion to be rejected wisely and considerately, though it may still be rejected rashly and ignorantly; for to shut out discussion entirely is seldom possible, and when it once gets in, beliefs not grounded on conviction are apt to give way before the slightest semblance of an argument. Waving, however, this possibility — assuming that the true opinion abides in the mind, but abides as a prejudice, a belief independent of, and proof against, argument – this is not the way in which truth ought to be held by a rational being. This is not knowing the truth. Truth, thus held, is but one superstition the more, accidentally clinging to the words which enunciate a truth.

If the intellect and judgment of mankind ought to be cultivated, a thing which Protestants at least do not deny, on what can these faculties be more appropriately exercised by any one, than on the things which concern him so much that it is considered necessary for him to hold opinions on them? If the cultivation of the understanding consists in one thing more than in another, it is surely in learning the grounds of one's own opinions. Whatever people believe, on subjects on which it is of the first importance to believe rightly, they ought to be able to defend against at least the common objections. But, some one may say, "Let them be *taught* the grounds of their opinions. It does not follow that opinions must be merely parroted because they are never heard controverted. Persons who learn geometry do not simply commit the theorems to memory, but understand and learn likewise the demonstrations; and it would be absurd to say that they remain ignorant of the grounds of geometrical truths, because they never hear any one deny, and attempt to disprove them." Undoubtedly: and such teaching suffices on a subject like mathematics, where there is nothing at all to be said on the wrong side of the question. The peculiarity of the evidence of mathematical truths is, that all the argument is on one side. There are not objections, and no answers to objections. But on every subject on which difference of opinion is possible, the truth depends on a balance to be struck between two sets of conflicting reasons. Even in natural philosophy, there is always some other explanation possible of the same facts; some geocentric theory instead of heliocentric, some phlogiston instead of oxygen; and it has to be shown why that other theory cannot be the true one: and until this is shown, and until we know how it is shown, we do not understand the grounds of our opinion. But when we turn to subjects infinitely more complicated, to morals, religion, politics, social relations, and the business of life, three-fourths of the arguments for every disputed opinion consist in dispelling the appearances which favour some opinion different from it. The greatest orator, save one, of antiquity, has left it on record that he always studied his adversary's case with as great, if not with still greater, intensity than even his own. What Cicero practised as the means of forensic success, requires to be imitated by all who study any subject in order to arrive at the truth. He who knows only his own side of the case, knows little of that. His reasons may be good, and no one may have been able to refute them. But if he is equally unable to refute the reasons on the opposite side; if he does not so much as know what they are, he has no ground for preferring either opinion. The rational position for him would be suspension of judgment, and unless he contents himself with that, he is either led by authority, or adopts, like the generality of the world, the side to which he feels most inclination. Nor is it enough that he should hear the arguments of adversaries from his own teachers, presented as they state them, and accompanied by what they offer as refutations. That is not the way to do justice to the arguments, or bring them into real contact with his own mind. He must be able to hear them from persons who actually believe them; who defend them in earnest, and do their very utmost for them. He must know them in their most plausible and persuasive form; he must feel the whole force of the difficulty which the true view of the subject has to encounter and dispose of; else he will never really possess himself of the portion of truth which meets and removes that difficulty. Ninety-nine in a hundred of what are called educated men are in this condition; even of those who can argue fluently for their opinions. Their conclusion may be true, but it might be false for anything they know: they have never thrown themselves into the mental position of whose who think differently from them, and considered what such persons may have to say; and consequently they do not, in any proper sense of the word, know the doctrine which they themselves profess. They do not know those parts of it which explain and justify the remainder; the considerations which show that a fact which seemingly conflicts with another is reconcilable with it, or that, of two apparently strong reasons, one and not the other ought to be preferred. All that part of the truth which turns the scale, and decides the judgment of a completely informed mind, they are strangers to; nor is it ever really known, but to those who have attended equally and impartially to both sides, and endeavoured to see the reasons of both in the strongest light. So essential is this discipline to a real understanding of moral and human subjects, that if opponents of all important truths do not exist, it is indispensable to imagine them, and supply them with the strongest arguments which the most skilful devil's advocate can conjure up.

CHAPTER III: OF INDIVIDUALITY, AS ONE OF THE ELEMENTS OF WELL-BEING

Such being the reasons which make it imperative that human beings should be free to form opinions, and to express their opinions without reserve; and such the baneful consequences to the intellectual, and through that to the moral nature of man, unless this liberty is either conceded, or asserted in spite of prohibition; let us next examine whether the same reasons do not require that men should be free to act upon their opinions – to carry these out in their lives, without hindrance, either physical or moral, from their fellow-men, so long as it is at their own risk and peril. This last proviso is of course indispensable. No one pretends that actions should be as free as opinions. On the contrary, even opinions lose their immunity, when the circumstances in which they are expressed are such as to constitute their expression a positive instigation to some mischievous act. An opinion that corn-dealers are starvers of the poor, or that private property is robbery, ought to be unmolested when simply circulated through the press, but may justly incur punishment when delivered orally to an excited mob assembled before the house of a corn-dealer, or when handed about among the same mob in the form of a placard. Acts, of whatever kind, which, without justifiable cause, do harm to others, may be, and in the more important cases absolutely require to be, controlled by the unfavourable sentiments, and, when needful, by the active interference of mankind. The liberty of the individual must be thus far limited; he must not make himself a nuisance to other people. But if he refrains from molesting others in what concerns them, and merely acts according to his own inclination and judgment in things which concern himself, the same reasons which show that opinion should be free, prove also that he should be allowed, without molestation, to carry his opinions into practice at his own cost. That mankind are not infallible; that their truths, for the most part, are only half-truths; that unity of opinion, unless resulting from the fullest and freest comparison of opposite opinions, is not desirable, and diversity not an evil, but a good, until mankind are much more capable than at present of recognising all sides of the truth, are principles applicable to men's modes of action, not less than to their opinions. As it is useful that while mankind are imperfect there should be different opinions, so is it that there should be different experiments of living; that free scope should be given to varieties of character, short of injury to others; and that the worth of different modes of life should be proved practically, when any one thinks fit to try them. It is desirable, in short, that in things which do not primarily concern others, individuality should assert itself. Where, not the person's own character, but the traditions or customs of other people are the rule of conduct, there is wanting one of the principal ingredients of human happiness, and quite the chief ingredient of individual and social progress ...

CHAPTER IV: OF THE LIMITS TO THE AUTHORITY OF SOCIETY OVER THE INDIVIDUAL

What, then, is the rightful limit to the sovereignty of the individual over himself? Where does the authority of society begin? How much of human life should be assigned to individuality, and how much to society?

Each will receive its proper share, if each has that which more particularly concerns it. To individuality should belong the part of life in which it is chiefly the individual that is interested; to society, the part which chiefly interests society.

Though society is not founded on a contract, and though no good purpose is answered by inventing a contract in order to deduce social obligations from it, every one who receives the protection of society owes a return for the benefit, and the fact of living in society renders it indispensable that each should be bound to observe a certain line of conduct towards the rest. This conduct consists first, in not injuring the interests of one another; or rather certain interests, which, either by express legal provision or by tacit understanding, ought to be considered as rights; and secondly, in each person's bearing his share (to be fixed on some equitable principle) of the labours and sacrifices incurred for defending the society or its members from injury and molestation. These conditions society is justified in enforcing at all costs to those who endeavour to withhold fulfilment. Nor is this all that society may do. The acts of an individual may be hurtful to others, or wanting in due consideration for their welfare, without going the length of violating any of their constituted rights. The offender may then be justly punished by opinion, though not by law. As soon as any part of a person's conduct affects prejudicially the interests of others, society has jurisdiction over it, and the question whether the general welfare will or will not be promoted by interfering with it, becomes open to discussion. But there is no room for entertaining any such question when a person's conduct affects the interests of no persons besides himself, or needs not affect them unless they like (all the persons concerned being of full age, and the ordinary amount of understanding). In all such cases there should be perfect freedom, legal and social, to do the action and stand the consequences ...

READING QUESTIONS ON MILL

1 How broadly or narrowly must harm be construed for Mill's view to provide a defence of liberty?

2 What implications does Mill's focus on social injustice, rather than the injustice of the state, have for the liberal claim that the state should be neutral?

3 How are Mill's views about freedom of expression related to his understanding of individual autonomy?

F.A. von Hayek
"Planning and the Rule of Law" (1994)

Hayek proposes a vision of the rule of law organized around the idea of negative liberty as the basic value of a liberal political and legal order. Hayek's essay prompts questions about the relationship between negative liberty and legal positivism.

Recent studies in the sociology of law once more confirm that the fundamental principle of formal law by which every case must be judged according to general rational precepts, which have as few exceptions as possible and are based on logical subsumptions, obtains only for the liberal competitive phase of capitalism.
– Karl Mannheim

Nothing distinguishes more clearly conditions in a free country from those in a country under arbitrary government than the observance in the former of the great principles known as the Rule of Law. Stripped of all technicalities, this means that government in all its actions is bound by rules fixed and announced beforehand – rules which make it possible to foresee with fair certainty how the authority will use its coercive powers in given circumstances and to plan one's individual affairs on the basis of this knowledge.[1] Though this ideal can never be perfectly achieved, since legislators as well as those to whom the administration of the law is intrusted are fallible men, the essential point, that the discretion left to the executive organs wielding coercive power should be reduced as much as possible, is clear enough. While every law restricts individual freedom to some extent by altering the means which people may use in the pursuit of their aims, under the Rule of Law the government is prevented from stultifying individual efforts by *ad hoc* action. Within the known rules of the game the individual is free to pursue his personal ends and desires, certain that the powers of government will not be used deliberately to frustrate his efforts.

The distinction we have drawn before between the creation of a permanent framework of laws within which the productive activity is guided by individual decisions and the direction of economic activity by a central authority is thus really a particular case of the more general distinction between the Rule of Law and arbitrary government. Under the first the government confines itself to fixing rules determining the conditions under which the available resources may be used, leaving to the individuals the decision for what ends they are to be used. Under the second the government directs the use of the means of production to particular ends. The first type of rules can be made in advance, in the shape of *formal rules* which do not aim at the wants and needs of particular people. They are intended to be merely instrumental in the pursuit of people's various individual ends. And they are, or ought to be, intended for such long periods that it is impossible to know whether they will assist particular people more than others. They could almost be described as a kind of instrument of production, helping people to predict the behavior of those with whom they must collaborate, rather than as efforts toward the satisfaction of particular needs.

Economic planning of the collectivist kind necessarily involves the very opposite of this. The planning authority cannot confine itself to providing opportunities for unknown people to make whatever use of them they like. It cannot tie itself down in advance to general and formal rules which prevent arbitrariness. It must provide for the actual needs of people as they arise and then choose deliberately between them. It must constantly decide questions which cannot be answered by formal principles only, and, in making these decisions, it must set up distinctions of merit between the needs of different people. When the government has to decide how many pigs are to be raised or how many busses are to be run, which coal mines are to operate, or at what prices shoes are to be sold, these decisions cannot be deduced from formal principles or settled for long periods in advance. They depend inevitably on the circumstances of the moment, and, in making such decisions, it will always be necessary to balance one against the other the interests of various persons and groups. In the end somebody's views will have to decide whose interests are more important; and these views must become part of the law of the land, a new distinction of rank which the coercive apparatus of government imposes upon the people.

The distinction we have just used between formal law or justice and substantive rules is very important and at the same time most difficult to draw precisely in practice. Yet the general principle involved is simple enough. The difference between the two kinds of rules is the same as that between laying down a Rule of the Road, as in the Highway Code, and ordering people where to go; or better still, between providing signposts and commanding people which road to take. The formal rules tell people in advance which action the state will take in certain types of situation, defined in general terms, without reference to time and place or particular people. They refer to typical situations into which anyone may get and in which the existence of such rules will be useful for a great variety of individual purposes. The knowledge that in such situations the state will act in a definite way, or require people to behave in a certain manner, is provided as a means for people to use in making their own plans. Formal rules are thus merely instrumental in the sense that they are expected to be useful to yet unknown people, for purposes for which these people will decide to use them, and in circumstances which cannot be foreseen in detail. In fact, that we do *not* know their concrete effect, that we do *not* know what particular ends these rules will further, or which particular people they will assist, that they are merely given the form most likely on the whole to benefit all the people affected by them, is the most important criterion of formal rules in the sense in which we here use this term. They do not involve a choice between particular ends or particular people, because we just cannot know beforehand by whom and in what way they will be used.

In our age, with its passion for conscious control of everything, it may appear paradoxical to claim as a virtue that under one system we shall know less about the particular effect of the measures the state takes than would be true under most other systems and that a method of social control should be deemed superior because of our ignorance of its precise results. Yet this consideration is in fact the rationale of the great liberal principle of the Rule of Law. And the apparent paradox dissolves rapidly when we follow the argument a little further.

This argument is twofold; the first is economic and can here only briefly be stated. The state should confine itself to establishing rules applying to general types of situations and should allow the individuals freedom in everything which depends on the circumstances of time and place, because only the individuals concerned in each instance can fully know these circumstances and adapt their actions to them. If the individuals are to be able to use their knowledge effectively in making plans, they must be able to predict actions of the state which may affect these plans. But if the actions of the state are to be predictable, they must be determined by rules fixed independently of the concrete circumstances which can be neither foreseen nor taken into account beforehand: and the particular effects of such actions will be unpredictable. If, on the other hand, the state were to direct the individual's actions so as to achieve particular ends, its action would have to be decided on the basis of the full circumstances of the moment and would therefore be unpredictable. Hence the familiar fact that the more the state "plans," the more difficult planning becomes for the individual.

The second, moral or political, argument is even more directly relevant to the point under discussion. If the state is precisely to foresee the incidence of its actions, it means that it can leave those affected no choice. Wherever the state can exactly foresee the effects on particular people of alternative courses of action, it is also the state which chooses between the different ends. If we want to create new opportunities open to all, to offer chances of which people can make what use they like, the precise results cannot be foreseen. General rules, genuine laws as distinguished from specific orders, must therefore be intended to operate in circumstances which cannot be foreseen in detail, and, therefore, their effect on particular ends or particular people cannot be known beforehand. It is in this sense alone that it is at all possible for the legislator to be impartial. To be impartial means to have no answer to certain questions – to the kind of questions which, if we have to decide them, we decide by tossing a coin. In a world where everything was precisely foreseen, the state could hardly do anything and remain impartial.

Where the precise effects of government policy on particular people are known, where the government aims directly at such particular effects, it cannot help knowing these effects, and therefore it cannot be impartial. It must, of necessity, take sides, impose its valuations upon people and, instead of assisting them in the advancement of their own ends, choose the ends for them. As soon as the particular effects are foreseen at the time a law is made, it ceases to be a mere instrument to be used by the people and becomes instead an instrument used by the lawgiver upon the people and for his ends. The state ceases to be a piece of utilitarian machinery intended to help individuals in the fullest development of their individual personality and becomes a "moral" institution – where "moral" is not used in contrast to immoral but describes an institution which imposes on its members its views on all moral questions, whether these views be moral or highly immoral. In this sense the Nazi or any other collectivist state is "moral," while the liberal state is not.

Perhaps it will be said that all this raises no serious problem because in the kind of questions which the economic planner would have to decide he need not and should not be guided by his individual prejudices but could rely on the general conviction of what is fair and reasonable. This contention usually receives support from those who have experience of planning in a particular industry and who find that there is no insuperable difficulty about arriving at a decision which all those immediately interested will accept as fair. The reason why this experience proves nothing is, of course, the selection of the "interests" concerned when planning is confined to a particular industry. Those most immediately interested in a particular issue are not necessarily the best judges of the interests of society as a whole. To take only the most characteristic case: when capital and labor in an industry agree on some policy of restriction and thus exploit the consumers, there is usually no difficulty about the division of the spoils in proportion to former earnings or on some similar principle. The loss which is divided between thousands or millions is usually either simply disregarded or quite inadequately considered. If we want to test the usefulness of the principle of "fairness" in deciding the kind of issues which arise in economic planning, we must apply it to some question where the gains and the losses are seen equally clearly. In such instances it is readily recognized that no general principle such as fairness can provide an answer. When we have to choose between higher wages for nurses or doctors and more extensive services for the sick, more milk for children and better wages for agricultural workers, or between employment for the unemployed or better wages for those already employed, nothing short of a complete system of values in which every want of every person or group has a definite place is necessary to provide an answer.

In fact, as planning becomes more and more extensive, it becomes regularly necessary to qualify legal provisions increasingly by reference to what is "fair" or "reasonable"; this means that it becomes necessary to leave the decision of the concrete case more and more to the discretion of the judge or authority in question. One could write a history of the decline of the Rule of Law, the disappearance of the *Rechtsstaat*, in terms of the progressive introduction of these vague formulas into legislation and jurisdiction, and of the increasing arbitrariness and uncertainty of, and the consequent disrespect for, the law and the judicature, which in these circumstances could not but become an instrument of policy. It is important to point out once more in this connection that this process of the decline of the Rule of Law had been going on steadily in Germany for some time before Hitler came into power and that a policy well advanced toward totalitarian planning had already done a great deal of the work which Hitler completed.

There can be no doubt that planning necessarily involves deliberate discrimination between particular needs of different people, and allowing one man to do what another must be prevented from doing. It must lay down by a legal rule how well off particular people shall be and what different people are to be allowed to have and do. It means in effect a return to the rule of status, a reversal of the "movement of progressive societies" which, in the famous phrase of Sir Henry Maine, "has hitherto been a movement from status to contract." Indeed, the Rule of Law, more than the rule of contract, should probably be regarded as the true opposite of the rule of status. It is the Rule of Law, in the sense of the rule of formal law, the absence of legal privileges of particular people designated by authority, which safeguards that equality before the law which is the opposite of arbitrary government.

A necessary, and only apparently paradoxical, result of this is that formal equality before the law is in conflict, and in fact incompatible, with any activity of the government deliberately aiming at material or substantive equality of different people, and that any policy aiming directly at a substantive ideal of distributive justice must lead to the destruction of the Rule of Law. To produce the same result for different people, it is necessary to treat them differently. To give different people the same objective opportunities is not to give them the same subjective chance. It cannot be denied that the Rule of Law produces economic inequality – all that can be claimed for it is that this inequality is not designed to affect particular people in a particular way. It is very significant and characteristic that socialists (and Nazis) have always protested against "merely" formal justice, that they have always objected to a law which had no views on how well off particular people ought to be,[2] and that they have always demanded a "socialization of the law," attacked the independence of judges, and at the same time given their support to all such movements as the *Freirechtsschule* which undermined the Rule of Law.

It may even be said that for the Rule of Law to be effective it is more important that there should be a rule applied always without exceptions than what this rule is. Often the content of the rule is indeed of minor importance, provided the same rule is universally enforced. To revert to a former example: it does not matter whether we all drive on the left- or on the right-hand side of the road so long as we all do the same. The important thing is that rule enables us to predict other people's behavior correctly, and this requires that it should apply to all cases – even if in a particular instance we feel it to be unjust.

The conflict between formal justice and formal equality before the law, on the one hand, and the attempts to realize various ideals of substantive justice and equality, on the other, also accounts for the widespread confusion about the concept of "privilege" and its consequent abuse. To mention only the most important instance of this abuse – the application of the term "privilege" to property as such. It would indeed be privilege if, for example, as has sometimes been the case in the past, landed property were reserved to members of the nobility. And it is privilege if, as is true in our time, the right to produce or sell particular things is reserved to particular people designated by authority. But to call private property as such, which all can acquire under the same rules, a privilege, because only some succeed in acquiring it, is depriving the word "privilege " of its meaning.

The unpredictability of the particular effects, which is the distinguishing characteristic of the formal laws of a liberal system, is also important because it helps us to clear up another confusion about the nature of this system: the belief that its characteristic attitude is inaction of the state. The question whether the state should or should not "act" or "interfere" poses an altogether false alternative, and the term "laissez faire" is a highly ambiguous and misleading description of the principles on which a liberal policy is based. Of course, every state must act and every action of the state interferes with something or other. But that is not the point. The important question is whether the individual can foresee the action of the state and make use of this knowledge as a datum in forming his own plans, with the result that the state cannot control the use made of its machinery and that the individual knows precisely how far he will be protected against interference from others, or whether the state is in a position to frustrate individual efforts. The state controlling weights and measures (or preventing fraud and deception in any other way) is certainly acting, while the state permitting the use of violence, for example, by strike pickets, is inactive. Yet it is in the first case that the state observes liberal principles and in the second that it does not. Similarly with respect to most of the general and permanent rules which the state may establish with regard to production, such as building regulations or factory laws: these may be wise or unwise in the particular instance, but they do not conflict with liberal principles so long as they are intended to be permanent and are not used to favor or harm particular people. It is true that in these instances there will, apart from the long-run effects which cannot be predicted, also be short-run effects on particular people which may be clearly known. But with this kind of laws the short-run effects are in general not (or at least ought not to be) the guiding consideration. As these immediate and predictable effects become more important compared with the long-run effects, we approach the border line where the distinction, however clear in principle, becomes blurred in practice.

The Rule of Law was consciously evolved only during the liberal age and is one of its greatest achievements, not only as a safeguard but as the legal embodiment of freedom. As Immanuel Kant put it (and Voltaire expressed it before him in very much the same terms), "Man is free if he needs to obey no person but solely the laws." As a vague ideal it has, however, existed at least since Roman times, and during the last few centuries it has never been so seriously threatened as it is today. The idea that there is no limit to the powers of the legislator is in part a result of popular sovereignty and democratic government. It has been strengthened by the belief that, so long as all actions of the state are duly authorized by legislation, the Rule of Law will be preserved. But this is completely to misconceive the meaning of the Rule of Law. This rule has little to do with the question whether all actions of government are legal in the juridical sense. They may well be and yet not conform to the Rule of Law. The fact that someone has full legal authority to act in the way he does gives no answer to the question whether the law gives him power to act arbitrarily or whether the law prescribes unequivocally how he has to act. It may well be that Hitler has obtained his unlimited powers in a strictly constitutional manner and that whatever he does is therefore legal in the juridical sense. But who would suggest for that reason that the Rule of Law still prevails in Germany?

To say that in a planned society the Rule of Law cannot hold is, therefore, not to say that the actions of the government will not be legal or that such a society will necessarily be lawless. It means only that the use of the government's coercive powers will no longer be limited and determined by pre-established rules. The law can, and to make a central direction of economic activity possible must, legalize what to all intents and purposes remains arbitrary action. If the law says that such a board or authority may do what it pleases, anything that board or authority does is legal — but its actions are certainly not subject to the Rule of Law. By giving the government unlimited powers, the most arbitrary rule can be made legal; and in this way a democracy may set up the most complete despotism imaginable.[3]

If, however, the law is to enable authorities to direct economic life, it must give them powers to make and enforce decisions in circumstances which cannot be foreseen and on principles which cannot be stated in generic form. The consequence is that, as planning extends, the delegation of legislative powers to divers boards and authorities becomes increasingly common. When before the last war, in a case to which the late Lord Hewart has recently drawn attention, Mr Justice Darling said the "Parliament had enacted only last year that the Board of Agriculture in acting as they did should be no more impeachable than Parliament itself," this was still a rare thing. It has since become an almost daily occurrence. Constantly the broadest powers are conferred on new authorities which, without being bound by fixed rules, have almost unlimited discretion in regulating this or that activity of the people.

The Rule of Law thus implies limits to the scope of legislation: it restricts it to the kind of general rules known as formal law and excludes legislation either directly aimed at particular people or at enabling anybody to use the coercive power of the state for the purpose of such discrimination. It means, not that everything is regulated by law, but, on the contrary, that the coercive power of the state can be used only in cases defined in advance by the law and in such a way that it can be foreseen how it will be used. A particular enactment can thus infringe the Rule of Law. Anyone ready to deny this would have to contend that whether the Rule of Law prevails today in Germany, Italy, or Russia depends on whether the dictators have obtained their absolute power by constitutional means.[4]

Whether, as in some countries, the main applications of the Rule of Law are laid down in a bill of rights or in a constitutional code, or whether the principle is merely a firmly established tradition, matters comparatively little. But it will readily be seen that, whatever form it takes, any such recognized limitations of the powers of legislation imply the recognition of the inalienable right of the individual, inviolable rights of man.

It is pathetic but characteristic of the muddle into which many of our intellectuals have been led by the conflicting ideals in which they believe that a leading advocate of the most comprehensive central planning like H.G. Wells should at the same time write an ardent defense of the rights of man. The individual rights which Mr Wells hopes to preserve would inevitably obstruct the planning which he desires. To some extent he seems to realize the dilemma, and we find therefore the provisions of his proposed "Declaration of the Rights of Man" so hedged about with qualifications that they lose all significance. While, for instance, his declaration proclaims that every man "shall have the right to buy and sell without any discriminatory restrictions anything which may be lawfully bought and sold," which is admirable, he immediately proceeds to make the whole provision nugatory by adding that it applies only to buying and selling "in such quantities and with such reservations as are compatible with the common welfare." But since, of course, all restrictions ever imposed upon buying or selling anything are supposed to be necessary in the interest of the "common welfare," there is really no restriction which this clause effectively prevents and no right of the individual that is safeguarded by it.

Or, to take another basic clause, the declaration states that every man "may engage in any lawful occupation" and that "he is entitled to paid employment and to a free choice whenever there is any variety of employment open to him." It is not stated, however, who is to decide whether a particular employment is "open" to a particular person, and the added provision that "he may suggest employment for himself and have his claim publicly considered, accepted or dismissed," shows that Mr Wells is thinking in terms of an authority which decides whether a man is "entitled" to a particular position – which certainly means the opposite of free choice of occupation. And how in a planned world "freedom of travel and migration" is to be secured when not only the means of communication and currencies are controlled but also the location of industries planned, or how the freedom of the press is to be safeguarded when the supply of paper and all the channels of distribution are controlled by the planning authority, are questions to which Mr Wells provides as little answer as any other planner.

In this respect much more consistency is shown by the more numerous reformers who, ever since the beginning of the socialist movement, have attached the "metaphysical" idea of individual rights and insisted that in a rationally ordered world there will be no individual rights but only individual duties. This, indeed, has become the much more common attitude of our so-called progressives, and few things are more certain to expose one to the reproach of being a reactionary than if one protests against a measure on the grounds that it is a violation of the rights of the individual. Even a liberal paper like the *Economist* was a few years ago holding up to us the example of the French, of all people, who had learned the lesson that "democratic government no less than dictatorship must always [*sic*] have plenary powers *in posse*, without sacrificing their democratic and representative character. There is no restrictive penumbra of individual rights that can never be touched by government in administrative matters whatever the circumstances. There is no limit to the power of ruling which can and should be taken by a government freely chosen by the people and can be fully and openly criticised by an opposition."

This may be inevitable in wartime, when, of course, even free and open criticism is necessarily restricted. But the "always" in the statement quoted does not suggest that the *Economist* regards it as a regrettable wartime necessity. Yet as a permanent institution this view is certainly incompatible with the preservation of the Rule of Law, and it leads straight to the totalitarian state. It is, however, the view which all those who want the government to direct economic life must hold.

How even a formal recognition of individual rights, or of the equal rights of minorities, loses all significance in a state which embarks on a complete control of economic life, has been amply demonstrated by the experience of the various Central European countries. It has been shown there that it is possible to pursue a policy of ruthless discrimination against national minorities by the use of recognized instruments of economic policy without ever infringing the letter of the statutory protection of minority rights. This oppression by means of economic policy was greatly facilitated by the fact that particular industries or activities were largely in the hands of a national minority, so that many a measure aimed ostensibly against an industry or class was in fact aimed at a national minority. But the almost boundless possibilities for a policy of discrimination and oppression provided by such apparently innocuous principles as "government control of the development of industries" have been amply demonstrated to all those desirous of seeing how the political consequences of planning appear in practice.

NOTES

1   According to the classical exposition by A.V. Dicey in *The Law of the Constitution* (8th ed.), p. 198, the Rule of Law "means, in the first place, the absolute supremacy or predominance of regular law as opposed to the influence of arbitrary power, and excludes the existence of arbitrariness, of

prerogative, or even of wide discretionary authority on the part of government." Largely as a result of Dicey's work the term has, however, in England acquired a narrower technical meaning which does not concern us here. The wider and older meaning of the concept of the rule or reign of law, which in England had become an established tradition which was more taken for granted than discussed, has been most fully elaborated, just because it raised what were new problems there, in the early nineteenth-century discussion in Germany about the nature of the *Rechtsstaat*.

2   It is therefore not altogether false when the legal theorist of National Socialism, Carl Schmitt, opposes to the liberal *Rechtstaat* (i.e., the Rule of Law) the National Socialist ideal of the *gerechte Staat* ("the just state") – only that the sort of justice which is opposed to formal justice necessarily implies discrimination between persons.

3   The conflict is thus *not*, as it has often been misconceived in nineteenth-century discussions, one between liberty and law. As John Locke had already made clear, there can be no liberty without law. The conflict is between different kinds of law – law so different that it should hardly be called by the same name: one is the law of the Rule of Law, general principles laid down beforehand, the "rules of the game" which enable individuals to foresee how the coercive apparatus of the state will be used, or what he and his fellow-citizens will be allowed to do, or made to do, in stated circumstances. The other kind of law gives in effect the authority power to do what it thinks fit to do. Thus the Rule of Law could clearly not be preserved in a democracy that undertook to decide every conflict of interests not according to rules previously laid down but "on its merits."

4   Another illustration of an infringement of the Rule of Law by legislation is the case of the bill of attainder, familiar in the history of England. The form which the Rule of Law takes in criminal law is usually expressed by the Latin tag *nulla poena sine lege* – no punishment without a law expressly prescribing it. The essence of this rule is that the law must have existed as a general rule before the individual case arose to which it is to be applied. Nobody would argue that, when in a famous case in Henry VIII's reign Parliament resolved with respect to the Bishop of Rochester's cook that "the said Richard Rose shall be boiled to death without having the advantage of his clergy," this act was performed under the Rule of Law. But while the Rule of Law had become an essential part of criminal procedure in all liberal countries, it cannot be preserved in totalitarian regimes. There, as E.B. Ashton has well expressed it, the liberal maxim is replaced by the principles *nullum crimen sine poena* – no "crime" must remain without punishment, whether the law explicitly provides for it or not. "The rights of

the state do not end with punishing law breakers. The community is entitled to whatever may seem necessary to the protection of its interests - of which observance of the law, as it stands, is only one of the more elementary requirements" (E.B. Ashton, *The Fascist, His State and Mind* [1937], p. 119). What is an infringement of "the interests of the community" is, of course, decided by the authorities.

READING QUESTIONS ON HAYEK

1 To what extent can recent political changes in North America and elsewhere be understood as expressing Hayek's views of the proper role of the state?
2 What is Hayek's argument that law loses its legal character once it is put in the service of claims about positive liberty? Do you find it convincing?
3 Can Hayek be described as a legal positivist?

Charles Taylor
"What's Wrong with Negative Liberty" (1985)

Taylor criticizes the coherence of the idea of negative liberty. In particular, he questions its usefulness to liberalism's aim of enabling individuals to flourish.

... Doctrines of positive freedom are concerned with a view of freedom which involves essentially the exercising of control over one's life. On this view, one is free only to the extent that one has effectively determined oneself and the shape of one's life. The concept of freedom here is an exercise-concept.

By contrast, negative theories can rely simply on an opportunity-concept, where being free is a matter of what we can do, of what it is open to us to do, whether or not we do anything to exercise these options. This certainly is the case of the crude, original Hobbesian concept. Freedom consists just in there being no obstacle. It is a sufficient condition of one's being free that nothing stand in the way.

But we have to say that negative theories *can* rely on an opportunity-concept, rather than that they necessarily do so rely, for we have to allow for that part of the gamut of negative theories mentioned above which incorporates some notion of self-realization. Plainly this kind of view cannot rely simply on an opportunity-concept. We cannot say that someone is free, on a self-realization view, if he is totally unrealized, if for instance he is totally unaware of his potential, if fulfilling it has never even arisen as a question for him, or if he is paralysed by the fear of breaking with some norm which he has internalized but which does not authentically reflect him. Within this conceptual scheme, some degree of exercise is necessary for a man to be thought free. Or if we want to think of the internal bars to freedom as obstacles on all fours with the external ones, then being in a position to exercise freedom, having the opportunity, involves removing the internal barriers; and this is not possible without having to some extent realized myself. So that with the freedom of self-realization, having the opportunity to be free requires that I already be exercising freedom. A pure opportunity-concept is impossible here.

But if negative theories can be grounded on either an opportunity- or an exercise-concept, the same is not true of positive theories. The view that freedom involves at least partially collective self-rule is essentially grounded on an exercise-concept. For this view (at least partly) identifies freedom with self-direction, that is, the actual exercise of directing control over one's life.

But this already gives us a hint towards illuminating the above paradox, that while the extreme variant of positive freedom is usually pinned on its protagonists by their opponents, negative theorists seem prone to embrace the crudest versions of their theory themselves. For if an opportunity-concept is not combinable with a positive theory, but either it or its alternative can suit a negative theory, then one way of ruling out positive theories in principle is by firmly espousing an opportunity-concept. One cuts off the positive theories by the root, as it were, even though one may also pay a price in the atrophy of a wide range of negative theories as well. At least by taking one's stand firmly on the crude side of the negative range, where only opportunity concepts are recognized, one leaves no place for a positive theory to grow.

Taking one's stand here has the advantage that one is holding the line around a very simple and basic issue of principle, and one where the negative view seems to have some backing in common sense. The basic institution here is that freedom is a matter of being able to do something or other, of not having obstacles in one's way, rather than being a capacity that we have to realize. It naturally seems more prudent to fight the Totalitarian Menace at this last-ditch position, digging in behind the natural frontier of this simple issue, rather than engaging the enemy on the open terrain of exercise-concepts, where one will have to fight to discriminate the good from the bad among such concepts; fight, for instance, for a view of individual self-realization, against various notions of collective self-realization, of a nation, or a class. It seems easier and safer to cut all the nonsense off at the start by declaring all self-realization views to be metaphysical hog-wash. Freedom should just be tough-mindedly defined as the absence of external obstacles.

Of course, there are independent reasons for wanting to define freedom tough-mindedly. In particular there is the immense influence of the anti-metaphysical, materialist, natural-science-oriented temper of thought in our civilization. Something of this spirit at its inception induced Hobbes to take the line that he did, and the same spirit goes marching on today. Indeed, it is because of the prevalence of this spirit that the line is so easy to defend, forensically speaking, in our society.

Nevertheless, I think that one of the strongest motives for defending the crude Hobbes-Bentham concept, that freedom is the absence of external obstacles, physical or legal, is the strategic one above. For most of those who take this line thereby abandon many of their own intuitions, sharing as they do with the rest of us in a post-Romantic civilization which puts great value on self-realization, and values freedom largely because of this. It is fear of the Totalitarian Menace, I would argue, which has led them to abandon this terrain to the enemy.

I want to argue that this not only robs their eventual forensic victory of much of its value, since they become incapable of defending liberalism in the form we in fact value it, but I want to make the stronger claim that this Maginot Line mentality actually ensures defeat, as is often the case with Maginot Line mentalities. The Hobbes–Bentham view, I want to argue, is indefensible as a view of freedom.

To see this, let us examine the line more closely, and the temptation to stand on it. The advantage of the view that freedom is the absence of external obstacles is its simplicity. It allows us to say that freedom is being able to do what you want, where what you want is unproblematically understood as what the agent can identify as his desires. By contrast an exercise-concept of freedom requires that we discriminate among motivations. If we are free in the exercise of certain capacities, then we are not free, or less free, when these capacities are in some way unfulfilled or blocked. But the obstacles can be internal as well as external. And this must be so, for the capacities relevant to freedom must involve some self-awareness, self-understanding, moral discrimination and self-control, otherwise their exercise could not amount to freedom in the sense of self-direction; and this being so, we can fail to be free because these internal conditions are not realized. But where this happens, where, for example, we are quite self-deceived, or utterly fail to discriminate properly the ends we seek, or have lost self-control, we can quite easily be doing what we want in the sense of what we can identify as our wants, without being free; indeed, we can be further entrenching our unfreedom.

Once one adopts a self-realization view, or indeed any exercise-concept of freedom, then being able to do what one wants can no longer be accepted as a sufficient condition of being free. For this view puts certain conditions on one's motivation. You are not free if you are motivated, through fear, inauthentically internalized standards, or false consciousness, to thwart your self-realization.

...

There are some considerations one can put forward straight off to show that the pure Hobbesian concept will not work, that there are some discriminations among motivations which are essential to the concept of freedom as we use it. Even where we think of freedom as the absence of external obstacles, it is not the absence of such obstacles *simpliciter*. For we make discriminations between obstacles as representing more or less serious infringements of freedom. And we do this, because we deploy the concept against a background understanding that certain goals and activities are more significant than others.

Thus we could say that my freedom is restricted if the local authority puts up a new traffic light at an intersection close to my home; so that where previously I could cross as I liked, consistently with avoiding collision with other cars, now I have to wait until the light is green. In a philosophical argument, we might call this a restriction of freedom, but not in a serious political debate. The reason is that it is too trivial, the activity and purposes inhibited here are not really significant. It is not just a matter of our having made a trade-off, and considered that a small loss of liberty was worth fewer traffic accidents, or less danger for the children; we are reluctant to speak here of a loss of liberty at all; what we feel we are trading off is convenience against safety.

By contrast a law which forbids me from worshipping according to the form I believe in is a serious blow to liberty; even a law which tried to restrict this to certain times (as the traffic light restricts my crossing of the intersection to certain times) would be seen as a serious restriction. Why this difference between the two cases? Because we have a background understanding, too obvious to spell out, of some activities and goals as highly significant for human beings and others as less so. One's religious belief is recognized, even by atheists, as supremely important, because it is that by which the believer defines himself as a moral being. By contrast my rhythm of movement through the city traffic is trivial. We do not want to speak of these two in the same breath. We do not even readily admit that liberty is at stake in the traffic light case. For *de minimis non curat libertas*.

But this recourse to significance takes us beyond a Hobbesian scheme. Freedom is no longer just the absence of external obstacle *tout court*, but the absence of external obstacle to significant action, to what is important to man. There are discriminations to be made; some restrictions are more serious than others, some are utterly trivial. About many, there is of course controversy. But what the judgement turns on is some sense of what is significant for human life. Restricting the expression of people's religious and ethical convictions is more significant than restricting their movement around uninhabited parts of the country; and both are more significant than the trivia of traffic control.

But the Hobbesian scheme has no place for the notion of significance. It will allow only for purely quantitative judgements. On the toughest-minded version of his conception, where Hobbes seems to be about to define liberty in terms of the absence of physical obstacles, one is presented with the vertiginous prospect of human freedom being measurable in the same way as the degrees of freedom of some physical object, say a lever. Later we see that this will not do, because we have to take account of legal obstacles to my action. But in any case, such a quantitative conception of freedom is a non-starter.

Consider the following diabolical defence of Albania as a free country. We recognize that religion has been abolished in Albania, whereas it hasn't been in Britain. But on the other hand there are probably far fewer traffic lights per head in Tirana than in London. (I haven't checked for myself, but this is a very plausible assumption.) Suppose an apologist for Albanian socialism were nevertheless to claim that this country was freer than Britain, because the number of acts restricted was far smaller. After all, only a minority of Londoners practise some religion in public places, but all have to negotiate their way through traffic. Those who do practise a religion generally do so on one day of the week, while they are held up at traffic lights every day. In sheer quantitative terms, the number of acts restricted by traffic lights must be greater than that restricted by a ban on public religious practice. So if Britain is considered a free society, why not Albania?

Thus the application even of our negative notion of freedom requires a background conception of what is significant, according to which some restrictions are seen to be without relevance for freedom altogether, and others are judged as being of greater and lesser importance. So some discrimination among motivations seems essential to our concept of freedom. A minute's reflection shows why this must be so. Freedom is important to us because we are purposive beings. But then there must be distinctions in the significance of different kinds of freedom based on the distinction in the significance of different purposes.

But of course, this still does not involve the kind of discrimination mentioned above, the kind which would allow us to say that someone who was doing what he wanted (in the unproblematic sense) was not really free, the kind of discrimination which allows us to put conditions on people's motivations necessary to their being free, and hence to second-guess them. All we have shown is that we make discriminations between more or less significant freedoms, based on discriminations among the purposes people have.

This creates some embarrassment for the crude negative theory, but it can cope with it by simply adding a recognition that we make judgements of significance. Its central claim that freedom just is the absence of external obstacles seems untouched, as also its view of freedom as an opportunity-concept. It is just that we now have to admit that not all opportunities are equal.

But there is more trouble in store for the crude view when we examine further what these qualitative discriminations are based on. What lies behind our judging certain purposes/feelings as more significant than others? One might think that there was room here again for another quantitative theory; that the more significant purposes are those we want more. But this account is either vacuous or false.

It is true but vacuous if we take wanting more just to mean being more significant. It is false as soon as we try to give wanting more an independent criterion, such as, for instance, the urgency or force of a desire, or the prevalence of one desire over another, because it is a matter of the most banal experience that the purposes we know to be more significant are not always those which we desire with the greatest urgency to encompass, nor the ones that actually always win out in cases of conflict of desires.

When we reflect on this kind of significance, we come up against what I have called elsewhere the fact of strong evaluation, the fact that we human subjects are not only subjects of first-order desires, but of second-order desires, desires about desires. We experience our desires and purposes as qualitatively discriminated, as higher or lower, noble or base, integrated or fragmented, significant or trivial, good and bad. This means that we experience some of our desires and goals as intrinsically more significant than others: some passing comfort is less important than the fulfilment of our life-time vocation, our *amour propre* less important than a love relationship; while we experience some others as bad, not just comparatively but absolutely: we desire not to be moved by spite, or some childish desire to impress at all costs. And these judgements of significance are quite independent of the strength of the respective desires: the craving for comfort may be overwhelming at this moment, we may be obsessed with our *amour propre*, but the judgement of significance stands.

But then the question arises whether this fact of strong evaluation doesn't have other consequences for our notion of freedom, than just that it permits us to rank freedoms in importance. Is freedom not at stake when we find ourselves carried away by a less significant goal to over-ride a highly significant one? Or when we are led to act out of a motive we consider bad or despicable?

The answer is that we sometimes do speak in this way. Suppose I have some irrational fear, which is preventing me from doing something I very much want to do. Say the fear of public speaking is preventing me from taking up a career that I should find very fulfilling, and that I should be quite good at, if I could just get over this "hang-up". It is clear that we experience this fear as an obstacle, and that we feel we are less than we would be if we could overcome it.

Or again, consider the case where I am very attached to comfort. To go on short rations, and to miss my creature comforts for a time, makes me very depressed. I find myself making a big thing of this. Because of this reaction I cannot do certain things that I should like very much to do, such as going on an expedition over the Andes, or a canoe trip in the Yukon. Once again, it is quite understandable if I experience this attachment as an obstacle, and feel that I should be freer without it.

Or I could find that my spiteful feelings and reactions which I almost cannot inhibit are undermining a relationship which is terribly important to me. At times, I feel as though I am almost assisting as a helpless witness at my own destructive behaviour, as I lash out again with my unbridled tongue at her. I long to be able not to feel this spite. As long as I feel it, even control is not an option, because it just builds up inside until it either bursts out, or else the feeling somehow communicates itself, and queers things between us. I long to be free of this feeling.

These are quite understandable cases, where we can speak of freedom or its absence without strain. What I have called strong evaluation is essentially involved here. For these are not just cases of conflict, even cases of painful conflict. If the conflict is between two desires with which I have no trouble identifying, there can be no talk of lesser freedom, no matter how painful or fateful. Thus if what is breaking up my relationship is my finding fulfilment in a job which, say, takes me away from home a lot, I have indeed a terrible conflict, but I would have no temptation to speak of myself as less free.

Even seeing a great difference in the significance of the two terms doesn't seem to be a sufficient condition of my wanting to speak of freedom and its absence. Thus my marriage may be breaking up because I like going to the pub and playing cards on Saturday nights with the boys. I may feel quite unequivocally that my marriage is much more important than the release and comradeship of the Saturday night bash. But nevertheless I would not want to talk of my being freer if I could slough off this desire.

The difference seems to be that in this case, unlike the ones above, I still identify with the less important desire, I still see it as expressive of myself, so that I could not lose it without altering who I am, losing something of my personality. Whereas my irrational fear, my being quite distressed by discomfort, my spite – these are all things which I can easily see myself losing without any loss whatsoever to what I am. This is why I can see them as obstacles to my purposes, and hence to my freedom, even though they are in a sense unquestionably desires and feelings of mine.

Before exploring further what is involved in this, let us go back and keep score. It would seem that these cases make a bigger breach in the crude negative theory. For they seem to be cases in which the obstacles to freedom are internal; and if this is so, then freedom cannot simply be interpreted as the absence of *external* obstacles; and the fact that I am doing what I want, in the sense of following my strongest desire, is not sufficient to establish that I am free. On the contrary, we have to make discriminations among motivations, and accept that acting out of some motivations, for example irrational fear or spite, or this too great need for comfort, is not freedom, is even a negation of freedom :..

Thus we can experience some desires as fetters, because we can experience them as not ours. And we can experience them as not ours because we see them as incorporating a quite erroneous appreciation of our situation and of what matters to us. We can see this again if we contrast the case of spite with that of another emotion which partly overlaps, and which is highly considered in some societies, the desire for revenge. In certain traditional societies this is far from being considered a despicable emotion. On the contrary, it is a duty of honour on a male relative to avenge a man's death. We might imagine that this too might give rise to conflict. It might conflict with the attempts of a new regime to bring some order to the land. The government would have to stop people taking vengeance, in the name of peace.

But short of a conversion to a new ethical outlook, this would be seen as a trade-off, the sacrifice of one legitimate goal for the sake of another. And it would seem monstrous were one to propose reconditioning people so that they no longer felt the desire to avenge their kin. This would be to unman them.[1]

Why do we feel so different about spite (and for that matter also revenge)? Because the desire for revenge for an ancient Icelander was his sense of a real obligation incumbent on him, something it would be dishonourable to repudiate; while for us, spite is the child of a distorted perspective on things.

We cannot therefore understand our desires and emotions as all brute, and in particular we cannot make sense of our discrimination of some desires as more important and fundamental, or of our repudiation of others, unless we understand our feelings to be import-attributing. This is essential to there being what we have called strong evaluation. Consequently the half-way position which admits strong evaluation, admits that our desires may frustrate our deeper purposes, admits therefore that there may be inner obstacles to freedom, and yet will not admit that the subject may be wrong or mistaken about these purposes — this position does not seem tenable. For the only way to make the subject's assessment incorrigible in principle would be to claim that there was nothing to be right or wrong about here; and that could only be so if experiencing a given feeling were a matter of the qualities of brute feeling. But this it cannot be if we are to make sense of the whole background of strong evaluation, more significant goals, and aims that we repudiate. This whole scheme requires that we understand the emotions concerned as import-attributing, as, indeed, it is clear that we must do on other grounds as well.

But once we admit that our feelings are import-attributing, then we admit the possibility of error, or false appreciation. And indeed, we have to admit a kind of false appreciation which the agent himself detects in order to make sense of the cases where we experience our own desires as fetters. How can we exclude in principle that there may be other false appreciations which the agent does not detect? That he may be profoundly in error, that is, have a very distorted sense of his fundamental purposes? Who can say that such people cannot exist? All cases are, of course, controversial; but I should nominate Charles Manson and Andreas Baader for this category, among others. I pick them out as people with a strong sense of some purposes and goals as incomparably more fundamental as others, or at least with a propensity to act the having such a sense so as to take in even themselves a good part of the time, but whose sense of fundamental purpose was shot through with confusion and error. And once we recognize such extreme cases, how avoid admitting that many of the rest of mankind can suffer to a lesser degree from the same disabilities?

What has this got to do with freedom? Well, to resume what we have seen: our attributions of freedom make sense against a background sense of more and less significant purposes, for the question of freedom/unfreedom is bound up with the frustration/fulfilment of our purposes. Further, our significant purposes can be frustrated by our own desires, and where these are sufficiently based on misappreciation, we consider them as not really ours, and experience them as fetters. A man's freedom can therefore be hemmed in by internal, motivational obstacles, as well as external ones. A man who is driven by spite to jeopardize his most important relationships, in spite of himself, as it were, or who is prevented by unreasoning fear from taking up the career he truly wants, is not really made more free if one lifts the external obstacles to his venting his spite or acting on his fear. Or at best he is liberated into a very impoverished freedom ...

NOTE

1. Compare the unease we feel at the reconditioning of the hero of Anthony Burgess's *A Clockwork Orange*.

READING QUESTIONS ON TAYLOR

1　What are the implications for Hayek's argument about the rule of law if, as Taylor argues, the idea of negative liberty is incoherent?
2　Does Taylor's argument give us any basis for choosing between legal positivism and Dworkin's or Fuller's alternatives to it?

Patrick Devlin
"Morals and the Criminal Law" (1965)

Devlin advocates a vision of democracy in which justice is determined by the will of the majority. He argues that a society is no less entitled to protect itself against moral decay than against treason.

I: MORALS AND THE CRIMINAL LAW

The Report of the Committee on Homosexual Offences and Prostitution, generally known as the Wolfenden Report, is recognized to be an excellent study of two very difficult legal and social problems. But it has also a particular claim to the respect of those interested in jurisprudence; it does what law reformers so rarely do; it sets out clearly and carefully what in relation to its subjects it considers the function of the law to be. Statutory additions to the criminal law are too often made on the simple principle that "there ought to be a law against it". The greater part of the law relating to sexual offences is the creation of statute and it is difficult to ascertain any logical relationship between it and the moral ideas which most of us uphold. Adultery, fornication, and prostitution are not, as the Report points out, criminal offences: homosexuality between males is a criminal offence, but between females it is not. Incest was not an offence until it was declared so by statute only fifty years ago. Does the legislature select those offences haphazardly or are there some principles which can be used to determine what part of the moral law should be embodied in the criminal? There is, for example, being now considered a proposal to make A.I.D., that is, the practice of artificial insemination of a woman with the seed of a man who is not her husband, a criminal offence; if, as is usually the case, the woman is married, this is in substance, if not in form, adultery. Ought it to be made punishable when adultery is not? This sort of question is of practical importance, for a law that appears to be arbitrary and illogical, in the end and after the wave of moral indignation that has put it on the statute book subsides, forfeits respect. As a practical question it arises more frequently in the field of sexual morals than in any other, but there is no special answer to be found in that field. The inquiry must be general and fundamental. What is the connexion between crime and sin and to what extent, if at all, should the criminal law of England concern itself with the enforcement of morals and punish sin or immorality as such?

The statements of principle in the Wolfenden Report provide an admirable and modern starting-point for such an inquiry. In the course of my examination of them I shall find matter for criticism. If my criticisms are sound, it must not be imagined that they point to any shortcomings in the Report. Its authors were not, as I am trying to do, composing a paper on the jurisprudence of morality; they were evolving a working formula to use for reaching a number of practical conclusions. I do not intend to express any opinion one way or the other about these; that would be outside the scope of a lecture on jurisprudence. I am concerned only with general principles; the statement of these in the Report illuminates the entry into the subject and I hope that its authors will forgive me if I carry the lamp with me into places where it was not intended to go.

Early in the Report the Committee put forward:

Our own formulation of the function of the criminal law so far as it concerns the subjects of this enquiry. In this field, its function, as we see it, is to preserve public order and decency, to protect the citizen from what is offensive or injurious, and to provide sufficient safeguards against exploitation and corruption of others, particularly whose who are specially vulnerable because they are young, weak in body or mind, inexperienced, or in a state of special physical, official or economic dependence.

It is not, in our view, the function of the law to intervene in the private lives of citizens, or to seek to enforce any particular pattern of behaviour, further than is necessary to carry out the purposes we have outlined.

The Committee preface their most important recommendation

that homosexual behaviour between consenting adults in private should no longer be a criminal offence, [by stating the argument] which we believe to be decisive, namely, the importance which society and the law ought to give to individual freedom of choice and action in matters of private morality. Unless a deliberate attempt is to be made by society, acting through the agency of the law, to equate the sphere of crime with that of sin, there must remain a realm of private morality and immorality which is, in brief and crude terms, not the law's business. To say this is not to condone or encourage private immorality.

Similar statements of principle are set out in the chapters of the Report which deal with prostitution. No case can be sustained, the Report says, for attempting to make prostitution itself illegal. The Committee refer to the general reasons already given and add: "We are agreed that private immorality should not be the concern of the criminal law except in the special circumstances therein mentioned." They quote with approval the report of the Street Offences Committee, which says: "As a general proposition it will be universally accepted that the law is not concerned with private morals or with ethical sanctions." It will be observed that the emphasis is on *private* immorality. By this is meant immorality which is not offensive or injurious to the public in the ways defined or described in the first passage which I quoted. In other words, no act of immorality should be made a criminal offence unless it is accompanied by some other feature such as indecency, corruption, or exploitation. This is clearly brought out in relation to prostitution: "It is not the duty of the law to concern itself with immorality as such ... it should confine itself to those activities which offend against public order and decency or expose the ordinary citizen to what is offensive or injurious."

These statements of principle are naturally restricted to the subject-matter of the Report. But they are made in general terms and there seems to be no reason why, if they are valid, they should not be applied to the criminal law in general. They separate very decisively crime from sin, the divine law from the secular, and the moral from the criminal. They do not signify any lack of support for the law, moral or criminal, and they do not represent an attitude that can be called either religious or irreligious. There are many schools of thought among those who may think that morals are not the law's business. There is first of all the agnostic or free-thinker. He does not of course disbelieve in morals, nor in sin if it be given the wider of the two meanings assigned to it in the *Oxford English Dictionary* where it is defined as "transgression against divine law or the principles of morality". He cannot accept the divine law; that does not mean that he might not view with suspicion any departure from moral principles that have for generations been accepted by the society in which he lives; but in the end he judges for himself. Then there is the deeply religious person who feels that the criminal law is sometimes more of a hindrance than a help in the sphere of morality, and that the reform of the sinner – at any rate when he injures only himself – should be a spiritual rather than a temporal work. Then there is the man who without any strong feeling cannot see why, where there is freedom in religious belief, there should not logically be freedom in morality as well. All these are powerfully allied against the equating of crime with sin.

I must disclose at the outset that I have as a judge an interest in the result of the inquiry which I am seeking to make as a jurisprudent. As a judge who administers the criminal law and who has often to pass sentence in a criminal court, I should feel handicapped in my task if I thought that I was addressing an audience which had no sense of sin or which thought of crime as something quite different. Ought one, for example, in passing sentence upon a female abortionist to treat her simply as if she were an unlicensed midwife? If not, why not? But if so, is all the panoply of the law erected over a set of social regulations? I must admit that I begin with a feeling that a complete separation of crime from sin (I use the term throughout this lecture in the wider meaning) would not be good for the moral law and might be disastrous for the criminal. But can this sort of feeling be justified as a matter of jurisprudence? And if it be a right feeling, how should the relationship between the criminal and the moral law be stated? Is there a good theoretical basis for it, or is it just a practical working alliance, or is it a bit of both? That is the problem which I want to examine, and I shall begin by considering the standpoint of the strict logician. It can be supported by cogent arguments, some of which I believe to be unanswerable and which I put as follows.

Morals and religion are inextricably joined – the moral standards generally accepted in Western civilization being those belonging to Christianity. Outside Christendom other standards derive from other religions. None of these moral codes can claim any validity except by virtue of the religion on which it is based. Old Testament morals differ in some respects from New Testament morals. Even within Christianity there are differences. Some hold that contraception is an immoral practice and that a man who has carnal knowledge of another woman while his wife is alive is in all circumstances a fornicator; others, including most of the English-speaking world, deny both these propositions. Between the great religions of the world, of which Christianity is only one, there are much wider differences. It may or may not be right for the State to adopt one of these religions as the truth, to found itself upon its doctrines, and to deny to any of its citizens the liberty to practise any other. If it does, it is logical that it should use the secular law wherever it thinks it necessary to enforce the divine. If it does not, it is illogical that it should concern itself with morals as such. But if it leaves matters of religion to private judgement, it should logically leave matters of morals also. A State which refuses to enforce Christian beliefs has lost the right to enforce Christian morals.

If this view is sound, it means that the criminal law cannot justify any of its provisions by reference to the moral law. It cannot say, for example, that murder and theft are prohibited because they are immoral or sinful. The State must justify in some other way the punishments which it imposes on wrongdoers and a function for the criminal law independent of morals must be found. This is not difficult to do. The smooth functioning of society and the preservation of order require that a number of activities should be regulated. The rules that are made for that purpose and are enforced by the criminal law are often designed simply to achieve uniformity and convenience and rarely involve any choice between good and evil. Rules that impose a speed limit or prevent obstruction on the highway have nothing to do with morals. Since so much of the criminal law is composed of rules of this sort, why bring morals into it at all? Why not define the function of the criminal law in simple terms as the preservation of order and decency and the protection of the lives and property of citizens, and elaborate those terms in relation to any particular subject in the way in which it is done in the Wolfenden Report? The criminal law in carrying out these objects will undoubtedly overlap the moral law. Crimes of violence are morally wrong and they are also offences against good order; therefore they offend against both laws. But this is simply because the two laws in pursuit of different objectives happen to cover the same area. Such is the argument.

Is the argument consistent or inconsistent with the fundamental principles of English criminal law as it exists today? That is the first way of testing it, though by no means a conclusive one. In the field of jurisprudence one is at liberty to overturn even fundamental conceptions if they are theoretically unsound. But to see how the argument fares under the existing law is a good starting-point.

It is true that for many centuries the criminal law was much concerned with keeping the peace and little, if at all, with sexual morals. But it would be wrong to infer from that that it had no moral content or that it would ever have tolerated the idea of a man being left to judge for himself in matters of morals. The criminal law of England has from the very first concerned itself with moral principles. A simple way of testing this point is to consider the attitude which the criminal law adopts towards consent.

Subject to certain exceptions inherent in the nature of particular crimes, the criminal law has never permitted consent of the victim to be used as a defence. In rape, for example, consent negatives an essential element. But consent of the victim is no defence to a charge of murder. It is not a defence to any form of assault that the victim thought his punishment well deserved and submitted to it; to make a good defence the accused must prove that the law gave him the right to chastise and that he exercised it reasonably. Likewise, the victim may not forgive the aggressor and require the prosecution to desist; the right to enter a *nolle prosequi* belongs to the Attorney-General alone.

Now, if the law existed for the protection of the individual, there would be no reason why he should avail himself of it if he did not want it. The reason why a man may not consent to the commission of an offence against himself beforehand or forgive it afterwards is because it is an offence against society. It is not that society is physically injured; that would be impossible. Nor need any individual be shocked, corrupted, or exploited; everything may be done in private. Nor can it be explained on the practical ground that a violent man is a potential danger to others in the community who have therefore a direct interest in his apprehension and punishment as being necessary to their own protection. That would be true of a man whom the victim is prepared to forgive but not of one who gets his consent first; a murderer who acts only upon the consent, and maybe the request, of his victim is no menace to others, but he does threaten one of the great moral principles upon which society is based, that is, the sanctity of human life. There is only one explanation of what has hitherto been accepted as the basis of the criminal law and that is that there are certain standards of behaviour or moral principles which society requires to be observed; and the breach of them is an offence not merely against the person who is injured but against society as a whole.

Thus, if the criminal law were to be reformed so as to eliminate from it everything that was not designed to preserve order and decency or to protect citizens (including the protection of youth from corruption), it would overturn a fundamental principle. It would also end a number of specific crimes. Euthanasia or the killing of another at his own request, suicide, attempted suicide and suicide pacts, duelling, abortion, incest between brother and sister, are all acts which can be done in private and without offence to others and need not involve the corruption or exploitation of others. Many people think that the law on some of these subjects is in need of reform, but no one hitherto has gone so far as to suggest that they should all be left outside the criminal law as matters of private morality. They can be brought within it only as a matter of moral principle. It must be remembered also that although there is much immorality that is not punished by the law, there is none that is condoned by the law. The law will not allow its processes to be used by those engaged in immorality of any sort. For example, a house may not be let for immoral purposes; the lease is invalid and would not be enforced. But if what goes on inside there is a matter of private morality and not the law's business, why does the law inquire into it at all?

I think it is clear that the criminal law as we know it is based upon moral principle. In a number of crimes its function is simply to enforce a moral principle and nothing else. The law, both criminal and civil, claims to be able to speak about morality and immorality generally. Where does it get its authority to do this and how does it settle the moral principles which it enforces? Undoubtedly, as a matter of history, it derived both from Christian teaching. But I think that the strict logician is right when he says that the law can no longer rely on doctrines in which citizens are entitled to disbelieve. It is necessary therefore to look for some other source.

In jurisprudence, as I have said, everything is thrown open to discussion and, in the belief that they cover the whole field, I have framed three interrogatories addressed to myself to answer:

1 Has society the right to pass judgement at all on matters of morals? Ought there, in other words, to be a public morality, or are morals always a matter for private judgement?
2 If society has the right to pass judgement, has it also the right to use the weapon of the law to enforce it?
3 If so, ought it to use that weapon in all cases or only in some; and if only in some, on what principles should it distinguish?

I shall begin with the first interrogatory and consider what is meant by the right of society to pass a moral judgement, that is, a judgement about what is good and what is evil. The fact that a majority of people may disapprove of a practice does not of itself make it a matter for society as a whole. Nine men out of ten may disapprove of what the tenth man is doing and still say that it is not their business. There is a case for a collective judgement (as distinct from a large number of individual opinions which sensible people may even refrain from pronouncing at all if it is upon somebody else's private affairs) only if society is affected. Without a collective judgement there can be no case at all for intervention. Let me take as an illustration the Englishman's attitude to religion as it is now and as it has been in the past. His attitude now is that a man's religion is his private affair; he may think of another man's religion that it is right or wrong, true or untrue, but not that it is good or bad. In earlier times that was not so; a man was denied the right to practise what was thought of as heresy, and heresy was thought of as destructive of society.

The language used in the passages I have quoted from the Wolfenden Report suggests the view that there ought not to be a collective judgement about immorality *per se*. Is this what is meant by "private morality" and "individual freedom of choice and action"? Some people sincerely believe that homosexuality is neither immoral nor unnatural. Is the "freedom of choice and action" that is offered to the individual, freedom to decide for himself what is moral or immoral, society remaining neutral; or is it freedom to be immoral if he wants to be? The language of the Report may be open to question, but the conclusions at which the Committee arrive answer this question unambiguously. If society is not prepared to say that homosexuality is morally wrong, there would be no basis for a law protecting youth from "corruption" or punishing a man for living on the "immoral" earnings of a homosexual prostitute, as the Report recommends. This attitude the Committee make even clearer when they come to deal with prostitution. In truth, the Report takes it for granted that there is in existence a public morality which condemns homosexuality and prostitution. What the Report seems to mean by private morality might perhaps be better described as private behaviour in matters of morals.

This view – that there is such a thing as public morality – can also be justified by *a priori* argument. What makes a society of any sort is community of ideas, not only political ideas but also ideas about the way its members should behave and govern their lives; these latter ideas are its morals. Every society has a moral structure as well as a political one: or rather, since that might suggest two independent systems, I should say that the structure of every society is made up both of politics and morals. Take, for example, the institution of marriage. Whether a man should be allowed to take more than one wife is something about which every society has to make up its mind one way or the other. In England we believe in the Christian idea of marriage and therefore adopt monogamy as a moral principle. Consequently the Christian institution of marriage has become the basis of family life and so part of the structure of our society. It is there not because it is Christian. It has got there because it is Christian, but it remains there because it is built into the house in which we live and could not be removed without bringing it down. The great majority of those who live in this country accept it because it is the Christian idea of marriage and for them the only true one. But a non-Christian is bound by it, not because it is part of Christianity but because, rightly or wrongly, it has been adopted by the society in which he lives. It would be useless for him to stage a debate designed to prove that polygamy was theologically more correct and socially preferable; if he wants to live in the house, he must accept it as built in the way in which it is.

We see this more clearly if we think of ideas or institutions that are purely political. Society cannot tolerate rebellion; it will not allow argument about the rightness of the cause. Historians a century later may say that the rebels were right and the Government was wrong and a percipient and conscientious subject of the State may think so at the time. But it is not a matter which can be left to individual judgement.

The institution of marriage is a good example for my purpose because it bridges the division, if there is one, between politics and morals. Marriage is part of the structure of our society and it is also the basis of a moral code which condemns fornication and adultery. The institution of marriage would be gravely threatened if individual judgements were permitted about the morality of adultery; on these points there must be a public morality. But public morality is not to be confined to those moral principles which support institutions such as marriage. People do not think of monogamy as something which has to be supported because our society has chosen to organize itself upon it; they think of it as something that is good in itself and offering a good way of life and that it is for that reason that our society has adopted it. I return to the statement that I have already made, that society means a community of ideas; without shared ideas on politics, morals, and ethics no society can exist. Each one of us has ideas about what is good and what is evil; they cannot be kept private from the society in which we live. If men and women try to create a society in which there is no fundamental agreement about good and evil they will fail; if, having based it on common agreement, the agreement goes, the society will disintegrate. For society is not something that is kept together physically; it is held by the invisible bonds of common thought. If the bonds were too far relaxed the members would drift apart. A common morality is part of the bondage. The bondage is part of the price of society; and mankind, which needs society, must pay its price ...

You may think that I have taken far too long in contending that there is such a thing as public morality, a proposition which most people would readily accept, and may have left myself too little time to discuss the next question which to many minds may cause greater difficulty: to what extent should society use the law to enforce its moral judgements? But I believe that the answer to the first question determines the way in which the second should be approached and may indeed very nearly dictate the answer to the second question. If society has no right to make judgements on morals, the law must find some special justification for entering the field of morality: if homosexuality and prostitution are not in themselves wrong, then the onus is very clearly on the lawgiver who wants to frame a law against certain aspects of them to justify the exceptional treatment. But if society has the right to make a judgement and has it on the basis that a recognized morality is as necessary to society as, say, a recognized government, then society may use the law to preserve morality in the same way as it uses it to safeguard anything else that is essential to its existence. If therefore the first proposition is securely established with all its implications, society has a prima facie right to legislate against immorality as such.

The Wolfenden Report, notwithstanding that it seems to admit the right of society to condemn homosexuality and prostitution as immoral, requires special circumstances to be shown to justify the intervention of the law. I think that this is wrong in principle and that any attempt to approach my second interrogatory on these lines is bound to break down. I think that the attempt by the Committee does break down and that this is shown by the fact that it has to define or describe its special circumstances so widely that they can be supported only if it is accepted that the law *is* concerned with immorality as such.

The widest of the special circumstances are described as the provision of "sufficient safeguards against exploitation and corruption of others, particularly those who are specially vulnerable because they are young, weak in body or mind, inexperienced, or in a state of special physical, official or economic dependence". The corruption of youth is a well-recognized ground for intervention by the State and for the purpose of any legislation the young can easily be defined. But if similar protection were to be extended to every other citizen, there would be no limit to the reach of the law. The "corruption and exploitation of others" is so wide that it could be used to cover any sort of immorality which involves, as most do, the co-operation of another person. Even if the phrase is taken as limited to the categories that are particularized as "specially vulnerable", it is so elastic as to be practically no restriction. This is not merely a matter of words. For if the words used are stretched almost beyond breaking-point, they still are not wide enough to cover the recommendations which the committee make about prostitution.

Prostitution is not in itself illegal and the Committee do not think that it ought to be made so. If prostitution is private immorality and not the law's business, what concern has the law with the ponce or the brothel-keeper or the householder who permits habitual prostitution? The Report recommends that the laws which make these activities criminal offences should be maintained or strengthened and brings them (so far as it goes into principle; with regard to brothels it says simply that the law rightly frowns on them) under the head of exploitation. There may be cases of exploitation in this trade, as there are or used to be in many others, but in general a ponce exploits a prostitute no more than an impressario exploits an actress. The Report finds that "the great majority of prostitutes are women whose psychological makeup is such that they choose this life because they find in it a style of living which is to them easier, freer and more profitable than would be provided by any other occupation ... In the main the association between prostitute and ponce is voluntary and operates to mutual advantage." The Committee would agree that this could not be called exploitation in the ordinary sense. They say: "It is in our view an over-simplification to think that those who live on the earnings of prostitution are exploiting the prostitute as such. What they are really exploiting is the whole complex of the relationship between prostitute and customer; they are, in effect, exploiting the human weaknesses which cause the customer to seek the prostitute and the prostitute to meet the demand."

All sexual immorality involves the exploitation of human weaknesses. The prostitute exploits the lust of her customers and the customer the moral weakness of the prostitute. If the exploitation of human weaknesses is considered to create a special circumstance, there is virtually no field of morality which can be defined in such a way as to exclude the law.

I think, therefore, that it is not possible to set theoretical limits to the power of the State to legislate against immorality. It is not possible to settle in advance exceptions to the general rule or to define inflexibly areas of morality into which the law is in no circumstances to be allowed to enter. Society is entitled by means of its laws to protect itself from dangers, whether from within or without. Here again I think that the political parallel is legitimate. The law of treason is directed against aiding the king's enemies and against sedition from within. The justification for this is that established government is necessary for the existence of society and therefore its safety against violent overthrow must be secured. But an established morality is as necessary as good government to the welfare of society. Societies disintegrate from within more frequently than they are broken up by external pressures. There is disintegration when no common morality is observed and history shows that the loosening of moral bonds is often the first stage of disintegration, so that society is justified in taking the same steps to preserve its moral code as it does to preserve its government and other essential institutions.[1] The suppression of vice is as much the law's business as the suppression of subversive activities; it is no more possible to define a sphere of private morality than it is to define one of private subversive activity. It is wrong to talk of private morality or of the law not being concerned with immorality as such or to try to set rigid bounds to the part which the law may play in the suppression of vice. There are no theoretical limits to the power of the State to legislate against treason and sedition, and likewise I think there can be no theoretical limits to legislation against immorality. You may argue that if a man's sins affect only himself it cannot be the concern of society. If he chooses to get drunk every night in the privacy of his own home, is any one except himself the worse for it? But suppose a quarter or a half of the population got drunk every night, what sort of society would it be? You cannot set a theoretical limit to the number of people who can get drunk before society is entitled to legislate against drunkenness. The same may be said of gambling. The Royal Commission on Betting, Lotteries, and Gaming took as their test the character of the citizen as a member of society. They said: "Our concern with the ethical significance of gambling is confined to the effect which it may have on the character of the gambler as a member of society. If we were convinced that whatever the degree of gambling this effect must be harmful we should be inclined to think that it was the duty of the state to restrict gambling to the greatest extent practicable."

In what circumstances the State should exercise its power is the third of the interrogatories I have framed. But before I get to it I must raise a point which might have been brought up in any one of the three. How are the moral judgements of society to be ascertained? By leaving it until now, I can ask it in the more limited form that is now sufficient for my purpose. How is the law-maker to ascertain the moral judgements of society? It is surely not enough that they should be reached by the opinion of the majority; it would be too much to require the individual assent of every citizen. English law has evolved and regularly uses a standard which does not depend on the counting of heads. It is that of the reasonable man. He is not to be confused with the rational man. He is not expected to reason about anything and his judgement may be largely a matter of feeling. It is the viewpoint of the man in the street – or to use an archaism familiar to all lawyers – the man in the Clapham omnibus. He might also be called the right-minded man. For my purpose I should like to call him the man in the jury box, for the moral judgement of society must be something about which any twelve men or women drawn at random might after discussion be expected to be unanimous. This was the standard the judges applied in the days before Parliament was as active as it is now and when they laid down rules of public policy. They did not think of themselves as making law but simply as stating principles which every right-minded person would accept as valid. It is what Pollock called "practical morality", which is based not on theological or philosophical foundations but "in the mass of continuous experience half-consciously or unconsciously accumulated and embodied in the morality of common sense". He called it also "a certain way of thinking on questions of morality which we expect to find in a reasonable civilized man or a reasonable Englishman, taken at random".[2]

Immorality then, for the purpose of the law, is what every right-minded person is presumed to consider to be immoral. Any immorality is capable of affecting society injuriously and in effect to a greater or lesser extent it usually does; this is what gives the law its *locus standi*. It cannot be shut out. But – and this brings me to the third question – the individual has a *locus standi* too; he cannot be expected to surrender to the judgement of society the whole conduct of his life. It is the old and familiar question of striking a balance between the rights and interests of society and those of the individual. This is something which the law is constantly doing in matters large and small. To take a very down-to-earth example, let me consider the right of the individual whose house adjoins the highway to have access to it; that means in these days the right to have vehicles stationary in the highway, sometimes for a considerable time if there is a lot of loading or unloading. There are many cases in which the courts have had to balance the private right of access against the public right to use the highway without obstruction. It cannot be done by carving up the highway into public and private areas. It is done by recognizing that each have rights over the whole; that if each were to exercise their rights to the full, they would come into conflict; and therefore that the rights of each must be curtailed so as to ensure as far as possible that the essential needs of each are safeguarded.

I do not think that one can talk sensibly of a public and private morality any more than one can of a public or private highway. Morality is a sphere in which there is a public interest and a private interest, often in conflict, and the problem is to reconcile the two. This does not mean that it is impossible to put forward any general statements about how in our society the balance ought to be struck. Such statements cannot of their nature be rigid or precise; they would not be designed to circumscribe the operation of the law-making power but to guide those who have to apply it. While every decision which a court of law makes when it balances the public against the private interest is an *ad hoc* decision, the cases contain statements of principle to which the court should have regard when it reaches its decision. In the same way it is possible to make general statements of principle which it may be thought the legislature should bear in mind when it is considering the enactment of laws enforcing morals.

I believe that most people would agree upon the chief of these elastic principles. There must be toleration of the maximum individual freedom that is consistent with the integrity of society. It cannot be said that this is a principle that runs all through the criminal law. Much of the criminal law that is regulatory in character – the part of it that deals with *malum prohibitum* rather than *malum in se* – is based upon the opposite principle, that is, that the choice of the individual must give way to the convenience of the many. But in all matters of conscience the principle I have stated is generally held to prevail. It is not confined to thought and speech; it extends to action, as is shown by the recognition of the right to conscientious objection in war-time; this example shows also that conscience will be respected even in times of national danger. The principle appears to me to be peculiarly appropriate to all questions of morals. Nothing should be punished by the law that does not lie beyond the limits of tolerance. It is not nearly enough to say that a majority dislike a practice; there must be a real feeling of reprobation. Those who are dissatisfied with the present law on homosexuality often say that the opponents of reform are swayed simply by disgust. If that were so it would be wrong, but I do not think one can ignore disgust if it is deeply felt and not manufactured. Its presence is a good indication that the bounds of toleration are being reached. Not everything is to be tolerated. No society can do without intolerance, indignation, and disgust; they are the forces behind the moral law, and indeed it can be argued that if they or something like them are not present, the feelings of society cannot be weighty enough to deprive the individual of freedom of choice. I suppose that there is hardly anyone nowadays who would not be disgusted by the thought of deliberate cruelty to animals. No one proposes to relegate that or any other form of sadism to the realm of private morality or to allow it to be practised in public or in private. It would be possible no doubt to point out that until a comparatively short while ago nobody thought very much of cruelty to animals and also that pity and kindliness and the unwillingness to inflict pain are virtues more generally esteemed now than they have even been in the past. But matters of this sort are not determined by rational argument. Every moral judgement, unless it claims a divine source, is simply a feeling that no right-minded man could behave in any other way without admitting that he was doing wrong. It is the power of a common sense and not the power of reason that is behind the judgements of society. But before a society can put a practice beyond the limits of tolerance there must be a deliberate judgement that the practice is injurious to society. There is, for example, a general abhorrence of homosexuality. We should ask ourselves in the first instance whether, looking at it calmly and dispassionately, we regard it as a vice so abominable that its mere presence is an offence. If that is the genuine feeling of the society in which we live, I do not see how society can be denied the right to eradicate it. Our feeling may not be so intense as that. We may feel about it that, if confined, it is tolerable, but that if it spread it might be gravely injurious; it is in this way that most societies look upon fornication, seeing it as a natural weakness which must be kept within bounds but which cannot be rooted out. It becomes then a question of balance, the danger to society in one scale and the extent of the restriction in the other. On this sort of point the value of an investigation by such a body as the Wolfenden Committee and of its conclusions is manifest.

The limits of tolerance shift. This is supplementary to what I have been saying but of sufficient importance in itself to deserve statement as a separate principle which law-makers have to bear in mind. I suppose that moral standards do not shift; so far as they come from divine revelation they do not, and I am willing to assume that the moral judgements made by a society always remain good for that society. But the extent to which society will tolerate – I mean tolerate, not approve – departures from moral standards varies from generation to generation. It may be that over-all tolerance is always increasing. The pressure of the human mind, always seeking greater freedom of thought, is outwards against the bonds of society forcing their gradual relaxation. It may be that history is a tale of contraction and expansion and that all developed societies are on their way to dissolution. I must not speak of things I do not know; and anyway as a practical matter no society is willing to make provision for its own decay. I return therefore to the simple and observable fact that in matters of morals the limits of tolerance shift. Laws, especially those which are based on morals, are less easily moved. It follows as another good working principle that in any new matter of morals the law should be slow to act. By the next generation the swell of indignation may have abated and the law be left without the strong backing which it needs. But it is then difficult to alter the law without giving the impression that moral judgement is being weakened. This is now one of the factors that is strongly militating against any alteration to the law on homosexuality.

A third elastic principle must be advanced more tentatively. It is that as far as possible privacy should be respected. This is not an idea that has ever been made explicit in the criminal law. Acts or words done or said in public or in private are all brought within its scope without distinction in principle. But there goes with this a strong reluctance on the part of judges and legislators to sanction invasions of privacy in the detection of crime. The police have no more right to trespass than the ordinary citizen has; there is no general right of search; to this extent an Englishman's home is still his castle. The Government is extremely careful in the exercise even of those powers which it claims to be undisputed. Telephone tapping and interference with the mails afford a good illustration of this. A Committee of three Privy Councillors who recently inquired into these activities found that the Home Secretary and his predecessors had already formulated strict rules governing the exercise of these powers and the Committee were able to recommend that they should be continued to be exercised substantially on the same terms. But they reported that the power was "regarded with general disfavour".

This indicates a general sentiment that the right to privacy is something to be put in the balance against the enforcement of the law. Ought the same sort of consideration to play any part in the formation of the law? Clearly only in a very limited number of cases. When the help of the law is invoked by an injured citizen, privacy must be irrelevant; the individual cannot ask that his right to privacy should be measured against injury criminally done to another. But when all who are involved in the deed are consenting parties and the injury is done to morals, the public interest in the moral order can be balanced against the claims of privacy. The restriction on police powers of investigation goes further than the affording of a parallel; it means that the detection of crime committed in private and when there is no complaint is bound to be rather haphazard and this is an additional reason for moderation. These considerations do not justify the exclusion of all private immorality from the scope of the law. I think that, as I have already suggested, the test of "private behaviour" should be substituted for "private morality" and the influence of the factor should be reduced from that of a definite limitation to that of a matter to be taken into account. Since the gravity of the crime is also a proper consideration, a distinction might well be made in the case of homosexuality between the lesser acts of indecency and the full offence, which on the principles of the Wolfenden Report it would be illogical to do.

The last and the biggest thing to be remembered is that the law is concerned with the minimum and not with the maximum; there is much in the Sermon on the Mount that would be out of place in the Ten Commandments. We all recognize the gap between the moral law and the law of the land. No man is worth much who regulates his conduct with the sole object of escaping punishment, and every worthy society sets for its members standards which are above those of the law. We recognize the existence of such higher standards when we use expressions such as "moral obligation" and "morally bound". The distinction was well put in the judgement of African elders in a family dispute: "We have power to make you divide the crops, for this is our law, and we will see this is done. But we have not power to make you behave like an upright man."[3]

It can only be because this point is so obvious that it is so frequently ignored. Discussion among law-makers, both professional and amateur, is too often limited to what is right or wrong and good or bad for society. There is a failure to keep separate the two questions I have earlier posed – the question of society's right to pass a moral judgement and the question of whether the arm of the law should be used to enforce the judgement. The criminal law is not a statement of how people ought to behave; it is a statement of what will happen to them if they do not behave; good citizens are not expected to come within reach of it or to set their sights by it, and every enactment should be framed accordingly.

The arm of the law is an instrument to be used by society, and the decision about what particular cases it should be used in is essentially a practical one. Since it is an instrument, it is wise before deciding to use it to have regard to the tools with which it can be fitted and to the machinery which operates it. Its tools are fines, imprisonment, or lesser forms of supervision (such as Borstal and probation) and – not to be ignored – the degradation that often follows upon the publication of the crime. Are any of these suited to the job of dealing with sexual immorality? The fact that there is so much immorality which has never been brought within the law shows that there can be no general rule. It is a matter for decision in each case; but in the case of homosexuality the Wolfenden Report rightly has regard to the views of those who are experienced in dealing with this sort of crime and to those of the clergy who are the natural guardians of public morals.

The machinery which sets the criminal law in motion ends with the verdict and the sentence; and a verdict is given either by magistrates or by a jury. As a general rule, whenever a crime is sufficiently serious to justify a maximum punishment of more than three months, the accused has the right to the verdict of a jury. The result is that magistrates administer mostly what I have called the regulatory part of the law. They deal extensively with drunkenness, gambling, and prostitution, which are matters of morals or close to them, but not with any of the graver moral offences. They are more responsive than juries to the ideas of the legislature; it may not be accidental that the Wolfenden Report, in recommending increased penalties for solicitation, did not go above the limit of three months. Juries tend to dilute the decrees of Parliament with their own ideas of what should be punishable. Their province of course is fact and not law, and I do not mean that they often deliberately disregard the law. But if they think it is too stringent, they sometimes take a very merciful view of the facts. Let me take one example out of many that could be given. It is an offence to have carnal knowledge of a girl under the age of sixteen years. Consent on her part is no defence; if she did not consent, it would of course amount to rape. The law makes special provision for the situation when a boy and girl are near in age. If a man under twenty-four can prove that he had reasonable cause to believe that the girl was over the age of sixteen years, he has a good defence. The law regards the offence as sufficiently serious to make it one that is triable only by a judge at assizes. "Reasonable cause" means not merely that the boy honestly believed that the girl was over sixteen but also that he must have had reasonable grounds for his belief. In theory it ought not to be an easy defence to make out but in fact it is extremely rare for anyone who advances it to be convicted. The fact is that the girl is often as much to blame as the boy. The object of the law, as judges repeatedly tell juries, is to protect young girls against themselves; but juries are not impressed.

The part that the jury plays in the enforcement of the criminal law, the fact that no grave offence against morals is punishable without their verdict, these are of great importance in relation to the statements of principle that I have been making. They turn what might otherwise be pure exhortation to the legislature into something like rules that the law-makers cannot safely ignore. The man in the jury box is not just an expression; he is an active reality. It will not in the long run work to make laws about morality that are not acceptable to him.

This then is how I believe my third interrogatory should be answered – not by the formulation of hard and fast rules, but by a judgement in each case taking into account the sort of factors I have been mentioning. The line that divides the criminal law from the moral is not determinable by the application of any clear-cut principle. It is like a line that divides land and sea, a coastline of irregularities and indentations. There are gaps and promontories, such as adultery and fornication, which the law has for centuries left substantially untouched. Adultery of the sort that breaks up marriage seems to be just as harmful to the social fabric as homosexuality or bigamy. The only ground for putting it outside the criminal law is that a law which made it a crime would be too difficult to enforce; it is too generally regarded as a human weakness not suitably punished by imprisonment. All that the law can do with fornication is to act against its worst manifestations; there is a general abhorrence of the commercialization of vice, and that sentiment gives strength to the law against brothels and immoral earnings. There is no logic to be found in this. The boundary between the criminal law and the moral law is fixed by balancing in the case of each particular crime the pros and cons of legal enforcement in accordance with the sort of considerations I have been outlining. The fact that adultery, fornication, and lesbianism are untouched by the criminal law does not prove that homosexuality ought not to be touched. The error of jurisprudence in the Wolfenden Report is caused by the search for some single principle to explain the division between crime and sin. The Report finds it in the principle that the criminal law exists for the protection of individuals; on this principle fornication in private between consenting adults is outside the law and thus it becomes logically indefensible to bring homosexuality between consenting adults in private within it. But the true principle is that the law exists for the protection of society. It does not discharge its function by protecting the individual from injury, annoyance, corruption, and exploitation; the law must protect also the institutions and the community of ideas, political and moral, without which people cannot live together. Society cannot ignore the morality of the individual any more than it can his loyalty; it flourishes on both and without either it dies.

I have said that the morals which underly the law must be derived from the sense of right and wrong which resides in the community as a whole; it does not matter whence the community of thought comes, whether from one body of doctrine or another or from the knowledge of good and evil which no man is without. If the reasonable man believes that a practice is immoral and believes also – no matter whether the belief is right or wrong, so be it that it is honest and dispassionate – that no right-minded member of his society could think otherwise, then for the purpose of the law it is immoral. This, you may say, makes immorality a question of fact – what the law would consider as self-evident fact no doubt, but still with no higher authority than any other doctrine of public policy. I think that this is so, and indeed the law does not distinguish between an act that is immoral and one that is contrary to public policy. But the law has never yet had occasion to inquire into the differences between Christian morals and those which every right-minded member of society is expected to hold. The inquiry would, I believe, be academic. Moralists would find differences; indeed they would find them between different branches of the Christian faith on subjects such as divorce and birth-control. But for the purpose of the limited entry which the law makes into the field of morals, there is no practical difference. It seems to me therefore that the free-thinker and the non-Christian can accept, without offence to his convictions, the fact that Christian morals are the basis of the criminal law and that he can recognize, also without taking offence, that without the support of the churches the moral order, which has its origin in and takes its strength from Christian beliefs, would collapse.

This brings me back in the end to a question I posed at the beginning. What is the relationship between crime and sin, between the Church and the Law? I do not think that you can equate crime with sin. The divine law and the secular have been disunited, but they are brought together again by the need which each has for the other. It is not my function to emphasize the Church's need of the secular law; it can be put tersely by saying that you cannot have a ceiling without a floor. I am very clear about the law's need for the Church. I have spoken of the criminal law as dealing with the minimum standards of human conduct and the moral law with the maximum. The instrument of the criminal law is punishment; those of the moral law are teaching, training, and exhortation. If the whole dead weight of sin were ever to be allowed to fall upon the law, it could not take the strain. If at any point there is a lack of clear and convincing moral teaching, the administration of the law suffers. Let me take as an illustration of this the law on abortion. I believe that a great many people nowadays do not understand why abortion is wrong. If it is right to prevent conception, at what point does it become sinful to prevent birth and why? I doubt if anyone who has not had a theological training would give a satisfactory answer to that question. Many people regard abortion as the next step when by accident birth-control has failed; and many more people are deterred from abortion not because they think it sinful or illegal but because of the difficulty which illegality puts in the way of obtaining it. The law is powerless to deal with abortion *per se*; unless a tragedy occurs or a "professional" abortionist is involved – the parallel between the "professional" in abortions and the "professional" in fornication is quite close – it has to leave it alone. Without one or other of these features the crime is rarely detected; and when detected, the plea *ad misericordiam* is often too strong. The "professional" abortionist is usually the unskilled person who for a small reward helps girls in trouble; the man and the girl involved are essential witnesses for the prosecution and therefore go free; the paid abortionist generally receives a very severe sentence, much more severe than that usually given to the paid assistant in immorality, such as the ponce or the brothel-keeper. The reason is because unskilled abortion endangers life. In a case in 1949[4] Lord Chief Justice Goddard said: "It is because the unskilful attentions of ignorant people in cases of this kind often result in death that attempts to produce abortion are regarded by the law as very serious offences." This gives the law a twist which disassociates it from morality and, I think, to some extent from sound sense. The act is being punished because it is dangerous, and it is dangerous largely because it is illegal and therefore performed only by the unskilled.

The object of what I have said is not to criticise theology or law in relation to abortion. That is a large subject and beyond my present scope. It is to show what happens to the law in matters of morality about which the community as a whole is not deeply imbued with a sense of sin; the law sags under a weight which it is not constructed to bear and may become permanently warped.

I return now to the main thread of my argument and summarize it. Society cannot live without morals. Its morals are those standards of conduct which the reasonable man approves. A rational man, who is also a good man, may have other standards. If he has no standards at all he is not a good man and need not be further considered. If he has standards, they may be very different; he may, for example, not disapprove of homosexuality or abortion. In that case he will not share in the common morality; but that should not make him deny that it is a social necessity. A rebel may be rational in thinking that he is right but he is irrational if he thinks that society can leave him free to rebel.

A man who concedes that morality is necessary to society must support the use of those instruments without which morality cannot be maintained. The two instruments are those of teaching, which is doctrine, and of enforcement, which is the law. If morals could be taught simply on the basis that they are necessary to society, there would be no social need for religion; it could be left as a purely personal affair. But morality cannot be taught in that way. Loyalty is not taught in that way either. No society has yet solved the problem of how to teach morality without religion. So the law must base itself on Christian morals and to the limit of its ability enforce them, not simply because they are the morals of most of us, nor simply because they are the morals which are taught by the established Church – on these points the law recognizes the right to dissent – but for the compelling reason that without the help of Christian teaching the law will fail.

NOTES

1   It is somewhere about this point in the argument that Professor Hart in *Law, Liberty and Morality* discerns a proposition which he describes as central to my thought. He states the proposition and his objection to it as follows (p. 51). "He appears to move from the acceptable proposition that *some* shared morality is essential to the existence of any society [this I take to be the proposition on p. 12] to the unacceptable proposition that a society

is identical with its morality as that is at any given moment of its history, so that a change in its morality is tantamount to the destruction of a society. The former proposition might be even accepted as a necessary rather than an empirical truth depending on a quite plausible definition of society as a body of men who hold certain moral views in common. But the latter proposition is absurd. Taken strictly, it would prevent us saying that the morality of a given society had changed, and would compel us instead to say that one society had disappeared and another one taken its place. But it is only on this absurd criterion of what it is for the same society to continue to exist that it could be asserted without evidence that any deviation from a society's shared morality threatens its existence." In conclusion (p. 82) Professor Hart condemns the whole thesis in the lecture as based on "a confused definition of what a society is".

I do not assert that *any* deviation from a society's shared morality threatens its existence any more than I assert that *any* subversive activity threatens its existence. I assert that they are both activities which are capable in their nature of threatening the existence of society so that neither can be put beyond the law.

For the rest, the objection appears to me to be all a matter of words. I would venture to assert, for example, that you cannot have a game without rules and that if there were no rules there would be no game. If I am asked whether that means that the game is "identical" with the rules, I would be willing for the question to be answered either way in the belief that the answer would lead to nowhere. If I am asked whether a change in the rules means that one game has disappeared and another has taken its place, I would reply probably not, but that it would depend on the extent of the change.

Likewise I should venture to assert that there cannot be a contract without terms. Does this mean that an "amended" contract is a "new" contract in the eyes of the law? I once listened to an argument by an ingenious counsel that a contract, because of the substitution of one clause for another, had "ceased to have effect" within the meaning of a statutory provision. The judge did not accept the argument; but if most of the fundamental terms had been changed, I daresay he would have done.

The proposition that I make in the text is that if (as I understand Professor Hart to agree, at any rate for the purposes of the argument) you cannot have a society without morality, the law can be used to enforce morality as something that is essential to a society. I cannot see why this proposition (whether it is right or wrong) should mean that morality can never be changed without the destruction of society. If morality is changed, the law can be changed. Professor Hart refers (p. 72) to the proposition as "the use of legal punishment to freeze into immobility the morality dominant at a particular time in a society's existence". One might as well say that the inclusion of a penal section into a statute prohibiting certain acts freezes the whole statute into immobility and prevents the prohibitions from ever being modified.

2   *Essays in Jurisprudence and Ethics* (1882), Macmillan, pp. 278 and 353.

3   A case in the Saa-Katengo Kuta at Lialiu, August 1942, quoted in *The Judicial Process among the Barotse of Northern Rhodesia* by Max Gluckman, Manchester University Press, 1955, p. 172.

4   *R v Tate, The Times*, 22 June 1949.

READING QUESTIONS ON DEVLIN

1 Why does Devlin suppose that "intolerance, indignation, and disgust" are important?

2 Does the toleration of things that disgust many people carry the risks that Devlin suggests?

3 In Phoenix, Arizona, it is against the law to kill a pony within the city limits. There is a Tongan tradition of roasting a pony to celebrate weddings. Should the law be enforced against Tongans living in Phoenix? What would Devlin say?

4 Does Devlin provide a way of replacing the gap left by negative liberty if Taylor is right about its incoherence?

5

Law and Values:
Law as a Tool of Democratic Self-Rule

Ronald Dworkin
"Liberty and Moralism" (1977)

Dworkin examines the relation between law and democracy, arguing that democracy requires certain limits on the types of argument that can be put forward. He challenges Devlin's understanding of a moral position.

My purpose is not to settle issues of political morality by the fiat of a dictionary, but to exhibit what I believe to be mistakes in Lord Devlin's moral sociology. I shall try to show that our conventional moral practices are more complex and more structured than he takes them to be, and that he consequently misunderstands what it means to say that the criminal law should be drawn from public morality. This is a popular and appealing thesis, and it lies near the core not only of Lord Devlin's, but of many other, theories about law and morals. It is crucial that its implications be understood.

THE CONCEPT OF A MORAL POSITION

We might start with the fact that terms like "moral position" and "moral conviction" function in our conventional morality as terms of justification and criticism, as well as of description. It is true that we sometimes speak of a group's "morals", or "morality", or "moral beliefs", or "moral positions" or "moral convictions", in what might be called an anthropological sense, meaning to refer to whatever attitudes the group displays about the propriety about human conduct, qualities or goals. We say, in this sense, that the morality of Nazi Germany was based on prejudice, or was irrational. But we also use some of these terms, particularly "moral position" and "moral conviction", in a discriminatory sense, to contrast the positions they describe with prejudices, rationalizations, matters of personal aversion or taste, arbitrary stands, and the like. One use – perhaps the most characteristic use – of this discriminatory sense is to offer a limited but important sort of justification for an act, when the moral issues surrounding that act are unclear or in dispute.

Suppose I tell you that I propose to vote against a man running for a public office of trust because I know him to be a homosexual and because I believe that homosexuality is profoundly immoral. If you disagree that homosexuality is immoral, you may accuse me of being about to cast my vote unfairly, acting on prejudice or out of a personal repugnance which is irrelevant to the moral issue. I might then try to convert you to my position on homosexuality, but if I fail in this I shall still want to convince you of what you and I will both take to be a separate point – that my vote was based on *a* moral position, in the discriminatory sense, even though one which differs from yours. I shall want to persuade you of this, because if I do I am entitled to expect that you will alter your opinion of me and of what I am about to do. Your judgment of my character will be different – you might still think me eccentric (or puritanical or unsophisticated) but these are types of character and not faults of character. Your judgment of my act will also be different, in this respect. You will admit that so long as I hold my moral position, I have a moral right to vote against the homosexual, because I have a right (indeed a duty) to vote my own convictions. You would not admit such a right (or duty) if you were still persuaded that I was acting out of a prejudice or a personal taste.

I am entitled to expect that your opinion will change in these ways, because these distinctions are a part of the conventional morality you and I share, and which forms the background for our discussion. They enforce the difference between positions we must respect, although we think them wrong, and positions we need not respect because they offend some ground rule of moral reasoning. A great deal of debate about moral issues (in real life, although not in philosophy texts) consists of arguments that some position falls on one or the other side of this crucial line.

It is this feature of conventional morality that animates Lord Devlin's argument that society has the right to follow its own lights. We must therefore examine that discriminatory concept of a moral position more closely, and we can do so by pursuing our imaginary conversation. What must I do to convince you that my position is a moral position?

(a) I must produce some reasons for it. This is not to say that I have to articulate a moral principle I am following or a general moral theory to which I subscribe. Very few people can do either, and the ability to hold a moral position is not limited to those who can. My reason need not be a principle or theory at all. It must only point out some aspect or feature of homosexuality which moves me to regard it as immoral: the fact that the Bible forbids it, for example, or that one who practices homosexuality becomes unfit for marriage and parenthood. Of course, any such reason would presuppose my acceptance of some general principle or theory, but I need not be able to state what it is, or realize that I am relying upon it.

Not every reason I might give will do, however. Some will be excluded by general criteria stipulating sorts of reasons which do not count. We might take note of four of the most important such criteria:

1. If I tell you that homosexuals are morally inferior because they do not have heterosexual desires, and so are not "real men", you would reject that reason as showing one type of prejudice. Prejudices, in general, are postures of judgment that take into account considerations our conventions exclude. In a structured context, like a trial or a contest, the ground rules exclude all but certain considerations, and a prejudice is a basis of judgment which violates these rules. Our conventions stipulate some ground rules of moral judgment which obtain even apart from such special contexts, the most important of which is that a man must not be held morally inferior on the basis of some physical, racial or other characteristic he cannot help having. Thus a man whose moral judgements about Jews, or Negroes, or Southerners, or women, or effeminate men are based on his belief that any member of these classes automatically deserves less respect, without regard to anything he himself has done, is said to be prejudiced against that group.
2. If I base my view about homosexuals on a personal emotional reaction ("they make me sick") you would reject that reason as well. We distinguish moral positions from emotional reactions, not because moral positions are supposed to be unemotional or dispassionate – quite the reverse is true – but because the moral position is supposed to justify the emotional reaction, not vice versa. If a man is

unable to produce such reasons, we do not deny the fact of his emotional involvement, which may have important social or political consequences, but we do not take this involvement as demonstrating his moral conviction. Indeed, it is just this sort of position – a severe emotional reaction to a practice or a situation for which one cannot account — that we tend to describe, in lay terms, as a phobia or an obsession.

3. If I base my position on a proposition of fact ("homosexual acts are physically debilitating") which is not only false, but is so implausible that it challenges the minimal standards of evidence and argument I generally accept and impose upon others, then you would regard my belief, even though sincere, as a form of rationalization, and disqualify my reason on that ground. (Rationalization is a complex concept, and also includes, as we shall see, the production of reasons which suggest general theories I do not accept.)

4. If I can argue for my own position only by citing the beliefs of others ("everyone knows homosexuality is a sin") you will conclude that I am parroting and not relying on a moral conviction of my own. With the possible (though complex) exception of a deity, there is no moral authority to which I can appeal and so automatically make my position a moral one. I must have my own reasons, though of course I may have been taught these reasons by others.

No doubt many readers will disagree with these thumbnail sketches of prejudice, mere emotional reaction, rationalization and parroting. Some may have their own theories of what these are. I want to emphasize now only that these are distinct concepts, whatever the details of the differences might be, and that they have a role in deciding whether to treat another's position as a moral conviction. They are not merely epithets to be pasted on positions we strongly dislike.

(b) Suppose I do produce a reason which is not disqualified on one of these (or on similar) grounds. That reason will presuppose some general moral principle or theory, even though I may not be able to state that principle or theory, and do not have it in mind when I speak. If I offer, as my reason, the fact that the Bible forbids homosexual acts, or that homosexual acts make it less likely that the actor will marry and raise children, I suggest that I accept the theory my reason presupposes, and you will not be satisfied that my position is a moral one if you believe that I do not. It may be a question of my sincerity – do I in fact believe that the injunctions of the Bible are morally binding as such, or that all men have a duty to procreate? Sincerity is not, however, the only issue, for consistency is also in point. I may believe that I accept one of these general positions, and be wrong, because my other beliefs, and my own conduct on other occasions, may be inconsistent with it. I may reject certain Biblical injunctions, or I may hold that men have a right to remain bachelors if they please or use contraceptives all their lives.

Of course, my general moral positions may have qualifications and exceptions. The difference between an exception and an inconsistency is that the former can be supported by reasons which presuppose other moral positions I can properly claim to hold. Suppose I condemn all homosexuals on Biblical authority, but not all fornicators. What reason can I offer for the distinction? If I can produce none which supports it, I cannot claim to accept the general position about Biblical authority. If I do produce a reason which seems to support the distinction, the same sorts of question may be asked about that reason as were asked about my original reply. What general position does the reason for my exception presuppose? Can I sincerely claim to accept that further general position? Suppose my reason, for example, is that fornication is now very common, and has been sanctioned by custom. Do I really believe that what is immoral becomes moral when it becomes popular? If not, and if I can produce no other reason for the distinction, I cannot claim to accept the general position that what the Bible condemns is immoral. Of course, I may be persuaded, when this is pointed out, to change my views on fornication. But you would be alert to the question of whether this is a genuine change of heart, or only a performance for the sake of the argument.

In principle there is no limit to these ramifications of my original claim, though of course no actual argument is likely to pursue very many of them.

(c) But do I really have to have a reason to make my position a matter of moral conviction? Most men think that acts which cause unnecessary suffering, or break a serious promise with no excuse, are immoral, and yet they could give no reason for these beliefs. They feel that no reason is necessary, because they take it as axiomatic or self-evident that these are immoral acts. It seems contrary to common sense to deny that a position held in this way can be a moral position.

Yet there is an important difference between believing that one's position is self-evident and just not having a reason for one's position. The former presupposes a positive belief that no further reason is necessary, that the immorality of the act in question does not depend upon its social effects, or its effects on the character of the actor, or its proscription by a deity, or anything else, but follows from the nature of the act itself. The claim that a particular position is axiomatic, in other words, does supply a reason of a special sort, namely that the act is immoral in and of itself, and this special reason, like the others we considered, may be inconsistent with more general theories I hold.

The moral arguments we make presuppose not only moral principles, but also more abstract positions about moral reasoning. In particular, they presuppose positions about what kinds of acts can be immoral in and of themselves. When I criticize your moral opinions, or attempt to justify my own disregard of traditional moral rules I think are silly, I will likely proceed by denying that the act in question has any of the several features that can make an act immoral – that it involves no breach of an undertaking or duty, for example, harms no one including the actor, is not proscribed by any organized religion, and is not illegal. I proceed in this way because I assume that the ultimate grounds of immorality are limited to some such small set of very general standards. I may assert this assumption directly or it may emerge from the pattern of my argument. In either event, I will enforce it by calling positions which can claim no support from any of these ultimate standards *arbitrary*, as I should certainly do if you said that photography was immoral, for instance, or swimming. Even if I cannot articulate this underlying assumption, I shall still apply it, and since the ultimate criteria I recognize are among the most abstract of my moral standards, they will not vary much from those my neighbors recognize and apply. Although many who despise homosexuals are unable to say why, few would claim affirmatively that one needs no reason, for this would make their position, on their own standards, an arbitrary one.

(d) This anatomy of our argument could be continued, but it is already long enough to justify some conclusions. If the issue between us is whether my views on homosexuality amount to a moral position, and hence whether I am entitled to vote against a homosexual on that ground, I cannot settle the issue simply by reporting my feelings. You will want to consider the reasons I can produce to support my belief, and whether my other views and behavior are consistent with the theories these reasons presuppose. You will have, of course, to apply your own understanding, which may differ in detail from mine, of what a prejudice or a rationalization is, for example, and of when one view is inconsistent with another. You and I may end in disagreement over whether my position is a moral one, partly because of such differences in understanding, and partly because one is less likely to recognize these illegitimate grounds in himself than in others.

We must avoid the skeptical fallacy of passing from these facts to the conclusion that there is no such thing as a prejudice or a rationalization or an inconsistency, or that these terms mean merely that the one who uses them strongly dislikes the positions he describes this way. That would be like arguing that because different people have different understandings of what jealousy is, and can in good faith disagree about whether one of them is jealous, there is no such thing as jealousy, and one who says another is jealous merely means he dislikes him very much.

LORD DEVLIN'S MORALITY

We may now return to Lord Devlin's second argument. He argues that when legislators must decide a moral issue (as by his hypothesis they must when a practice threatens a valued social arrangement), they must follow any consensus of moral position which the community at large has reached, because this is required by the democratic principle, and because a community is entitled to follow its own lights. The argument would have some plausibility if Lord Devlin meant, in speaking of the moral consensus of the community, those positions which are moral positions in the discriminatory sense we have been exploring.

But he means nothing of the sort. His definition of a moral position shows he is using it in what I called the anthropological sense. The ordinary man whose opinion we must enforce, he says, "is not expected to reason about anything and his judgment may be largely a matter of feeling." "If the reasonable man believes," he adds, "that a practice is immoral and believes so – no matter whether the belief is right or wrong, so be it that it is honest and dispassionate – that no right-minded member of his society could think otherwise, then for the purpose of the law it is immoral." Elsewhere he quotes with approval Dean Rostow's attribution to him of the view that 'the common morality of a society at any time is a blend of custom and conviction, of reason and feeling, of experience and prejudice." His sense of what a moral conviction is emerges most clearly of all from the famous remark about homosexuals. If the ordinary man regards homosexuality "as a vice so abominable that its mere presence is an offence," this demonstrates for him that the ordinary man's feelings about homosexuals are a matter of moral conviction.

His conclusions fail because they depend upon using "moral position" in this anthropological sense. Even if it is true that most men think homosexuality an abominable vice and cannot tolerate its presence, it remains possible that this common opinion is a compound of prejudice (resting on the assumption that homosexuals are morally inferior creatures because they are effeminate), rationalization (based on assumptions of fact so unsupported that they challenge the community's own standards of rationality), and personal aversion (representing no conviction but merely blind hate rising from unacknowledged self-suspicion). It remains possible that the ordinary man could produce no reason for his view, but would simply parrot his neighbor who in turn parrots him, or that he would produce a reason which presupposes a general moral position he could not sincerely or consistently claim to hold. If so, the principles of democracy we follow do not call for the enforcement of the consensus, for the belief that prejudices, personal aversions and rationalizations do not justify restricting another's freedom itself occupies a critical and fundamental position in our popular morality. Nor would the bulk of the community then be entitled to follow its own lights, for the community does not extend that privilege to one who acts on the basis of prejudice, rationalization, or personal aversion. Indeed, the distinction between these and moral convictions, in the discriminatory sense, exists largely to mark off the former as the sort of positions one is not entitled to pursue.

A conscientious legislator who is told a moral consensus exists must test the credentials of that consensus. He cannot, of course, examine the beliefs of behavior of individual citizens; he cannot hold hearings on the Clapham omnibus. That is not the point.

The claim that a moral consensus exists is not itself based on a poll. It is based on an appeal to the legislator's sense of how his community reacts to some disfavored practice. But this same sense included an awareness of the grounds on which that reaction is generally supported. If there has been a public debate involving the editorial columns, speeches of his colleagues, the testimony of interested groups, and his own correspondence, these will sharpen his awareness of what arguments and positions are in the field. He must sift these arguments and positions, trying to determine which are prejudices or rationalizations, which presuppose general principles or theories vast parts of the population could not be supposed to accept, and so on. It may be that when he has finished this process of reflection he will find that the claim of a moral consensus has not been made out. In the case of homosexuality, I expect, it would not be, and that is what makes Lord Devlin's undiscriminating hypothetical so serious a misstatement. What is shocking and wrong is not his idea that the community's morality counts, but his idea of what counts as the community's morality.

Of the course the legislator must apply these tests for himself. If he shares the popular views he is less likely to find them wanting, though if he is self-critical the exercise may convert him. His answer, in any event, will depend upon his own understanding of what our shared morality requires. That is inevitable, for whatever criteria we urge him to apply, he can apply them only as he understands them.

A legislator who proceeds in this way, who refuses to take popular indignation, intolerance and disgust as the moral conviction of his community, is not guilty of moral elitism. He is not simply setting his own educated views against those of a vast public which rejects them. He is doing his best to enforce a distinct, and fundamentally important, part of his community's morality, a consensus more essential to society's existence in the form we know it than the opinion Lord Devlin bids him follow.

No legislator can afford to ignore the public's outrage. It is a fact he must reckon with. It will set the boundaries of what is politically feasible, and it will determine his strategies of persuasion and enforcement within these boundaries. But we must not confuse strategy with justice, nor facts of political life with principles of political morality. Lord Devlin understands these distinctions, but his arguments will appeal most, I am afraid, to those who do not.

READING QUESTIONS ON DWORKIN

1 Does Dworkin's view give judges too much power? Alternatively, does he give democratic assemblies too much power?
2 Read the excerpt from King, p. 453, below. Would King's religious arguments qualify as a moral position on Dworkin's view?

Allan C. Hutchinson and Patrick Monahan
"Democracy and the Rule of Law" (1987)

Hutchinson and Monahan argue that the rule of law stands in the way of democracy. They offer two reasons for distrusting courts. They suggest that surrendering power to courts leads to apathy, and they also argue that when courts have appeared to be in the forefront of social change, the results have been more apparent than real. In place of courts and the rule of law, Hutchinson and Monahan advocate citizen juries and democracy.

The practice and theory of liberal democracy is in disarray. Condemned as utopian, ideals of full public participation and control have been pre-empted by an ethic of expertise. This contemporary orthodoxy holds that public policy should be formulated only by those properly qualified for the task; the role of the people is limited to choosing the elites who make the choices for them. The link between government policy and popular sentiment is, at best, obscure, with electoral apathy and disaffection the norm. For instance nearly a third of the Canadian electorate believe that politics either makes things worse or else has no effect in solving social problems.[1] In America, almost half the electorate does not vote in presidential elections. Public trust and confidence in government has fallen to the point where less than one-quarter of Americans believe that government is run for the "benefit of all".[2]

This is nothing new. There has never been a "golden age" of popular democracy except in the wishful thoughts of the nostalgic few. Thus the current apathy and elitism which dominates liberal democratic thinking lends scant support to critics who claim that present conditions constitute an exceptional crisis for democracy. Indeed, liberal democratic institutions have continually managed to confound critics, who have underestimated their resiliency and stamina. Representative democracy has flourished in the face of widespread citizen ennui precisely because public participation and interest are dispensable to its survival and performance. Limited public participation and apathy are even regarded in a positive light, since they minimize conflict and promote stability. Democratic politics is seen as the legitimate preserve of specialists, whose only expertise happens to be that they have made a habit of engaging in political activity.

Whether by design or default, the courts have been proclaimed by many theorists as a proxy for a genuine democratic dialogue. The American Supreme Court has long been cast in the role of the nation's moral conscience. With the advent of an entrenched Charter of Rights and Freedoms in 1982, the Supreme Court of Canada is assuming a similar mantle. No longer seen merely as a means of constraining democratic debate and argument, courts act as elite forums for the enactment and resolution of this dialogue. Judicial review celebrates the triumph of detached philosophical deliberation over heated political haggling. Although a travesty of the democratic ideal, the judiciary's elevation to the status of moral prophet is defended and extolled by many in the name of democracy itself.[3]

Thomas Paine's assertion that "in American law is king" has never been more pertinent, not only in America but in Canada as well. Long a central feature of American's self-image, respect for the Rule of Law is becoming a vaunted article of Canadian constitutional faith. Indeed, the preamble to the Canadian Charter of Rights and Freedoms states that "Canada is founded upon principles that recognize the supremacy of God and the [R]ule of [L]aw." Law has been the gavel wielded to bring to order (or silence) competing voices in the cause of justice. In recent decades, the American Supreme Court has moved to front and centre on the political stage, intervening in heated political controversies. Paradoxically, the American Court's landmark decisions in *Brown* (desegregation) and *Roe v Wade* (abortion) have worn pretty thin its claims to be acting within the bounds of constitutional propriety. Rising to the challenge, legal and political theorists have championed the relocation of political debate from the legislative crucible of communal controversy to the judicial "forum of principle". The judicialization of politics has been justified under the banner of the Rule of Law. Within this projected scenario, there is no conflict between an activist judiciary and democratic governance. Indeed, the Rule of Law is welcomed as a necessary component of a properly functioning democratic polity. Checking popular excesses, litigation is thought to provide a privileged occasion for the renewal of society's commitment to continuing moral discourse.

Notwithstanding recent valiant attempts to reconcile the Rule of Law with democratic theory, this gambit fails. The Rule of Law functions as a clear check on the flourishing of a rigorous democracy. Attempts to characterize the Rule of Law as the butler of democracy are false and misleading. Liberal legalism is premised on the same logic of expertise which has made popular control over public policy dispensable. It is simply more evidence of the demise of contestability as the touchstone of politics. The first part of the essay will trace the historical and theoretical connections between the Rule of Law and liberal democracy. The second part will offer a more searching criticism of the elite and marginal practice of constitutional adjudication. The final section reasserts the primacy of democratic over legalistic values and seeks to sketch a practical vision of democratic practice.

1.   THE BRIDLE OF POWER: LAW AND POLITICS

(a) Liberalism, Law, and Democracy

The sonorous and majestic ring of the appeal to the Rule of Law has resonated through the centuries. It has operated as a potent call to moral arms, a clarion-call for constitutional justice by a whole host of political actors and combatants. At times, the Rule of Law has been used to legitimize and galvanize a challenge to entrenched power; at others, the ruling elite has relied upon it to sanction its power and resistance to would-be usurpers. Like any ideal, it only exists in the political consciousness and conscience. But, like every other ideal, it exercises a tenacious grip on the imagination and actions of its adherents. Indeed, its ideological attraction and political durability are largely attributable to its historical plasticity, the facility to accommodate itself to changing governmental situations and political forces. In short, it is the will-o'-the-wisp of constitutional history.

Notwithstanding its protean nature, the rich historical tapestry of the Rule of Law has been loosely connected by a strong liberal thread: it has been used as a seductive slogan in the struggle to establish or preserve individual liberty and action. On many occasions, this appeal to liberty has amounted to nothing more than moralistic window-dressing for otherwise naked attempts to seize political power, a rhetorical gambit in a continuing power-play. But to reduce the appeal to the Rule of Law to simply and always an exercise in mystification is to distort the historical record; it impugns the honourable motives of many and overestimates the credulity of even more.[4] Over the last millennium, the Rule of Law has occasionally proved to be an effective principle to check the indulgent abuse of power by the few over the many. However, over the long haul, the Rule of Law has been activated as a "principled" counter in the shuffling of power among elite groups; it has served to inhibit the flourishing of any governmental system of direct democracy.

The Rule of Law is more concerned with and committed to individual liberty than democratic governance. The historical development of any kind of democracy has been the by-product of a preoccupation with private autonomy. The Rule of Law is premised on the ideal of limited government; it has stood as a constitutional barrier between the governors and the governed, between power and people. The existence and extent of democratic governance is only justified insofar as it better serves the enhanced liberty of individuals; it is a recent recruit on the proclaimed march to the truly liberal state. Indeed, universal suffrage is a decidedly twentieth century phenomenon. Even today, representative democracy only extends to about 20 per cent of the world's nations (not population) and, in many of these states, the arrangements are extremely fragile and incomplete.

The compulsion to reason within a closed system of premises is said to guarantee the enduring integrity and efficacy of the constitutional compact and insulate the judges from ideological controversy. Within this constitutional scenario, adherence to the Rule of Law has come to be synonymous with compliance with a liberal scheme of constitutional governance. Although some form of representative democracy has become a modern component of this model, the history of the Rule of Law's theory and practice reveals that it is more an optional extra than an essential condition. Indeed, the opposite often seems to be true: the Rule of Law has functioned as a clear check on the actual impact and expansion of a rigorous democracy.

(b) The Thick and the Thin

If not non-democratic in aspiration and orientation, the Rule of Law is democratically indifferent in character and scope. The enduring concerns of the Rule of Law are the limitation of state power, the maintenance of a broad sphere of private liberty and the preservation of a market-exchange economy. In its many academic manifestations, it has been connected, to greater and lesser extents, to an individualistic theory of political justice and jurisprudence. Ostensibly, there have been two versions of the Rule of Law, but they both represent a commitment to liberalism; it is simply that one tends to be more explicit and marked than the other.

The "thin" version of the Rule of Law amounts to a constitutional principle of legality. It demands that government be conducted in accordance with established and performable norms; its voice remains silent or, at best, whispered on the issue of substantive policies. Rule must be by law and not discretion. Also, and especially, the lawmaker itself must be under the law, at least until it changes the law. In this "thin" form, the Rule of Law is targeted against arbitrary government and palm-tree justice. Its critical logo is "a government of laws, not men"; its operative axioms are the generality of official rules and the faithful adherence by government to those declared standards of conduct. The modern defence of such a "thin" version is that the preferred system of governance is that in which "the law furnishes a base-line for self-directed action, not a detailed set of instructions for accomplishing specific objectives."[5]

Although far from explicit or necessarily so, its substantive tendency is clearly toward a liberal society in which the best government is the one which governs least. However, unless such a constitutional requirement of official legality is supplemented by a "thicker" theory of political justice, the Rule of Law will be a weak restraint on an ambitiously unjust regime. It might even tend to legitimate its substantive excesses under a patina of formal justice. Unrepresentative government and the Rule of Law are not mutually exclusive; democracy is an entirely dispensable feature of this form of the Rule of Law. As Herbert Hart has observed, "however great the aura of majesty or authority which the official system may have, its demands in the end must be submitted to moral scrutiny."[6] Accordingly, a full and proper defence and understanding of the Rule of Law must be based on its foundational and substantive political connections.

The "thick" version of the Rule of Law incorporates the thinner one as merely one dimension of a liberal theory of justice. This conception of the Rule of Law goes back to the Greeks and Romans, but finds its modern roots in the Enlightenment.[7] Indeed, there is an almost direct line of descent from the theory and practice of 17th century England to that of late 20th century Anglo-America. The intellectual lineage runs almost unbroken from John Locke and Thomas Hobbes to John Rawls and Ronald Dworkin, through Thomas Paine, John Stuart Mill, A.V. Dicey and Friedrich Hayek. The modern defence of this "thick" version posits the necessary connection between procedural and substantive justice. The Rule of Law demands that positive law embody a particular vision of social justice, structured around the moral rights and duties which citizens have against each other and the state as a whole.

(c) 1215 and All That

Modern scholarship and constitutional practice can be traced back to the Glorious Revolution and, even beyond that, to the Magna Carta. Before the 17th century, increased individual liberty was more an incidental cost of the political struggle than the result of any deliberate strategy. Beginning with the Magna Carta in 1215, the barons sought to restrain the monarchical monopoly by demanding that the sovereign act only *per legem terrae*. And, as early as the 13th century, jurists like Henry de Bracton argued that even the king was *sub Deo et lege*; "law is the bridle of power."[8] However, by the 15th century at latest, the Magna Carta had become an obscure and hollow proclamation, only later to be romanticised by some modern legal historians. It was not until after the Tudor Reformation, when the Stuarts sought to re-invoke the divine right of kings, that the Rule of Law came into its own as an influential and effective piece of constitutional rhetoric for curbing royal power. Within this encounter, the idea and establishment of some democratic dimension to political governance was of little consequence or concern.[9]

1610 was a banner year for the Rule of Law. Sir Edward Coke, later to be dismissed as Chief Justice and become a parliamentarian committed to reviving the memory of the Magna Carta as the great charter of English freedom, held in *Dr. Bonham's Case* that "the Common Law will controll Acts of Parliament, and sometimes adjudge them to be utterly void."[10] Also, in that year, the House of Commons presented James I with the Petition of Grievances, insisting that he continue the tradition of being "guided and governed by certain rule of law." Matters did not come to a head until 1625 when Charles I assumed the throne. As so often, the major bone of contention was the right to levy taxes. The price for Parliament's compliance with Charles' fiscal demands was royal assent to the Petition of Right. This enacted that the king would govern according to the laws and statutes of the realm; that no one could be arrested by the king's order, but only for the breach of a specific offence; that only Parliament could impose taxes; and that civilians could not be made subject to martial law.

It must not be forgotten that, although these events have been regarded by generations of constitutional lawyers as laying the foundations for the modern Rule of Law, they were motivated more by a revolutionary than a legal spirit. Nevertheless, they did establish that henceforth law was the "instrument and prize; he who would control the constitution would have first to control the law."[11] But, importantly, it has to be added that Parliament did not embark on this course of action as part of a campaign to transfer power to the general populace; the progressive tenor of the times was resoundingly libertarian and not democratic.

For the next two centuries, the English constitution remained a pragmatic melange of monarchical, aristocratic and democratic ingredients, bound together by a strong libertarian commitment ... Yet, the half century after 1628 demonstrated an important historical lesson that many societies, including our own, continue to overlook: a law is worth little more than the paper it is written on unless it is accompanied by sufficient willingness *and power* to translate its promises into practice. Indeed, after the Petition of Right, Charles almost immediately dissolved Parliament and ruled alone for 11 years. Although Parliament was briefly recalled, England was soon riven by Civil War. The country was not returned to some semblance of normality until the Glorious Revolution of 1688. Significantly, the monarch was restored, but only on terms laid down by Parliament.

A major instrument of government and statement of political intent was the Bill of Rights. While this is the closest England has ever come to adopting a written constitution, it was never more than another piece of legislation, repealable by any later Parliament. The central thrust of the legislation was to force the Crown to rule through Parliament. Its constitutional ambition was not to popularize government, but to restore and conserve "the true auntient and indubitable rights and liberties of the people." It dispensed with the Stuart's extravagant claims to rule by prerogative writ, ensuring that every parliamentarian had freedom of speech and that "cruel and unusual punishments" were prohibited. These provisions were supplemented by the Act of Settlement in 1701; a major clause was that judges no longer held office at the king's whim, but *quamdiu se bene gesserint* (during good behaviour).

The undisputed apologist for these constitutional developments was John Locke, the father of modern liberalism. In his *Second Treatise on Government*, he provided the enduring account of how people created civil society to protect better their individual rights enjoyed in a state of nature. Within such a constitutional scheme, the limited role of government was to enact law "as guards and fences to the properties of all the members of society." The Rule of Law was a pivotal principle. Laws were to be general in scope and operation; "freedom of men under government is ... not to be subject to the inconstant, unknown, arbitrary will of another man." While Locke justified the initial success, it was 18th century writers, like David Hume, Edmund Burke and William Paley, who consolidated the constitutional position of the Rule of Law. Yet, it was the Americans who were to embrace and implement most directly the Lockean teachings.

(d) The American Experiment

Although England had proceeded on the path to parliamentary supremacy, the American colonists were more inclined to resuscitate the Magna Carta and its libertarian underpinnings against a recalcitrant English Parliament. After the Revolution, America set about establishing its own constitutional order. Despite significant divisions, the preferred basis for republican government was not democracy. While, by existing standards, America was enviably more representative in governance than most nations, the Founders' rabid libertarianism was only matched by its faint-hearted commitment to popular rule. As one prominent Philadelphia Conventioneer, Elbridge Gerry, put it, "the evils we experience flow from the excess of democracy."[12] People's supposed natural rights were to be put beyond the imagined vicissitudes of majoritarian politics. In particular, private property was not to be open to governmental interference. After all, the War of Independence had been fought over this very principle. The relation between personal liberty and popular democracy has been neatly described by Martin Diamond:

... for the founding generation it was liberty that was the comprehensive good, the end against which political things had to be measured; and democracy was only a form of government which, like any other form of government, had to prove itself adequately instrumental to the security of liberty.[13]

This liberal theory of democracy has continued to dominate American constitutional life. In effect, the American Revolution only managed to replace the dominion of a foreign power with that of a domestic document.[14] Entrenched individual rights always trump any collective concerns of the democratic process. Enforcing this social compact, the courts were to function as the guardians of the Rule of Law. But, in the process, they were not to turn themselves into an independent centre of constitutional power. As John Marshall announced, "judicial power, as contradistinguished from the power of laws, has no existence. Courts are the mere instruments of the law, and can will nothing."[15] The Rule of Law demanded a scrupulously objective and formalistic judiciary.

While the upholding of the Rule of Law in the United States was being increasingly entrusted to the judicial interpreters of the written constitution, the English constitution remained proudly and defiantly unwritten. Indeed, A.V. Dicey maintained that the Constitution is not "the source, but the consequence of the rights of individuals."[16] Writing at the dusk of the Victorian laissez-faire era and at pains to check the runaway development of a collectivistically-inclined bureaucracy, he symbolized the modern attempt to reinvigorate the Rule of Law as a set of constitutional postulates devoted to safeguarding individual interests and liberty. Dicey's Rule of Law comprised "three distinct though kindred conceptions:"[17] no one can be punished except for a breach of the ordinary law, established in the ordinary legal manner before the ordinary courts; no one is above the law and everyone, especially officials, is amenable to the ordinary law; and the general principles of the constitution, protecting private rights, are the result of the ordinary laws. The combined force and design of Dicey's principles was to make the Rule of Law into a bridle for a supposedly rampant administrative arm of government.

The Diceyian tradition of Lockean conservatism has been continued by Friedrich Hayek in the contemporary debate over the Rule of Law. For him, the Rule of Law stands in unequivocal opposition to state redistribution and planning; it is the essential and most important condition of individual freedom.[18] It is not simply a constitutional principle of "legality", but comprises a substantive vision of the correct and just relations between individuals and society:

Nothing distinguishes more clearly conditions in a free country from those in a country under arbitrary government than the observance in the former of the great principles known as the [R]ule of [L]aw. Stripped of all technicalities this means that government in all its actions is bound by rules fixed and announced beforehand – rules which make it possible to see with fair certainty how the authority will use its coercive powers in given circumstances, and to plan one's individual affairs on the basis of this knowledge.[19]

Not surprisingly, Hayek identifies the inter-war years, culminating in the New Deal, as the period when America began to renege on its original constitutional compact and to subvert the Rule of Law. For him, an activist government, let alone an activist judiciary, is anathema to the Rule of Law and its libertarian foundations.

This tradition has been continued by contemporary writers. Although the emphasis has become more liberal than libertarian, democracy remains very much a secondary feature of the constitutional order. Most writers agree that the Rule of Law is a vital protective and facilitative constitutional device for a fundamental scheme of individual rights; disagreement is over the scope and character of those rights. In this sense, the protean quality of the Rule of Law has allowed it to be extended beyond civil and political rights to social and economic entitlements without sacrificing its essential nature. The product of a multinational conference, the Declaration of Delhi in 1958 stated that the Rule of Law is, apart from its traditional concerns, intended "to establish social, economic, educational and cultural conditions under which [individuals'] legitimate aspirations and dignity may be realized."[20]

(d) The Contemporary Debate: Democratizing the Rule of Law

The work of Ronald Dworkin, temporarily at least, dominates the animated contemporary debate over the judicial role under the Rule of Law. Adjudication is claimed to satisfy the Rule of Law by meeting the democratic demand for judicial objectivity and the popular need for political equity. While some rail that an activist judiciary is antithetical to democratic governance,[21] Dworkin argues that, if judges are to fulfil their democratic responsibilities under the Rule of Law, they must make political decisions, albeit not personal or partisan ones. His claim is bold and brilliant. The traditional formalistic, rule-book conception of the Rule of Law requires judges in hard cases to be unconstrainedly creative or to dissemble. Dworkin's rights conception of the Rule of Law incorporates a dimension of substantive fairness and thereby appropriately constrains and guides the judge in the resolution of hard cases. In defending such a version of the Rule of Law, Dworkin keeps himself firmly within the tradition of Locke and the constitutional priority of liberty; "the idea of individual rights ... is the zodiac sign under which America was born."[22]

For Dworkin, judges are political actors whose power is limited by a legal system's history and its liberal character. The state does not give them a blank check on which to write in the political currency of their choice; they must interpret the regnant legal materials in their best light as a theory of political morality. The judge breathes political vitality into the lifeless words of legal texts by applying the twin tests of "formal fit" and "substantive justice". Any interpretation must be able to demonstrate some plausible connection with society's legal history. However, the better theory is not necessarily the one that accounts for the most decisions or statutes; "formal fit" is only a heuristic device or rule-of-thumb. This requirement acts as a threshold and combines with the test of "substantive justice". This obliges the judge to develop a scheme of rights which a just state would establish and enforce. While this task can only be provisionally and partially performed, the conscious striving for such a perfected theory is the hallmark of adjudication under the Dworkinian conception of the Rule of Law. Accordingly, judicial power is legitimated by this commitment to uphold the existing political order of rights and only to extend it in a consistent and principled manner. In this way, law is and remains rational, just and objective.

It is to Dworkin's credit that he does not disguise his individualistic revitalization of the Rule of Law. He openly concedes that his conception might well exact a price in the development of a communitarian spirit. Yet, anxious to deflect charges of being insufficiently democratic, he reminds us that his conception of the Rule of Law "enriches democracy by adding an independent forum of principle ... [where] justice is in the end a matter of individual right, and not independently a matter of the public good."[23] He casts the Supreme Court as the central constitutional institution through which the citizenry can debate, articulate and implement its collective standards for social justice. Dworkin is not alone in elevating legal conversation to a privileged form of democratic discourse. Joined by other writers, like Owen Fiss and Laurence Tribe, Bruce Ackerman has gone so far as to suggest that:

Not that a vigorous and constructive legal dialogue can ever hope to compensate for an apathetic and muddled political debate. Yet the reverse is also true: political commitment is no substitute for legal deliberation. While the future of America depends on the American people, the future of American law depends, in a special way, on the way American lawyers interpret their calling.[24]

2.   DEMOCRATIC INDIVIDUALISM AND THE RULE OF LAW

(a) Democracy and Community

Liberalism has always been ambivalent about the significance and the desirability of the value of community. For liberal theory, all roads begin with atomic, prepolitical individuals maximizing their self-interest. Thus, social contract theorists like Hobbes and Locke justified the creation of the state by analogy to a self-interested bargain between autonomous individuals in a state of nature. There was little emphasis on the possibility of the state helping to forge communal values or common ends. The state was necessary merely as a means of establishing order in a universe in which the interests of rational maximizers inevitably collided with each other.[25] The order that resulted was always in possible jeopardy, since it depended on a delicate and even-handed resort to carrots and sticks.

This emphasis on the self-interested and autonomous individual receives its highest and most explicit expression in contemporary theories of democratic institutions and behaviour. Current analyses of "polyarchal" forms of democracy lack any genuine conception of public, communal values. Democracy is simply a mechanism for choosing governments in which sets of elites compete for the right to rule. According to some observers, there is no necessary connection between the choices made by the elites and the desires of the electorate. Instead, the elites themselves formulate and resolve the issues. The demands of the voters are not the ultimate data of the system since these demands are themselves shaped or manufactured; the public's demand for political goods "does not flow from its initiative but is being shaped, and the shaping of it is an essential part of the democratic process."[26]

Other analyses of democracy do not adopt such an impoverished conception of the community and its values. Yet even when the volitions of the electorate are seen as independent rather than manufactured, the analysis continues to be framed in market terms. Individual consumers "spend" their votes so as to maximize their individual self-interest, rather than to further the ends of the community as a whole. In fact, the invocation of the "public interest" is simply an ideological masquerade for the aggregation of private interests. Citizenship involves striking bargains in one's own interest rather than forging and debating the fundamental values of the community.[27]

Polyarchal forms of democracy reinforce the very consumer mentality they purport to serve. Because effective decision-making occurs at the elite rather than the mass level, the average citizen assumes no responsibility for shaping the values, beliefs and actions of the community. Even the act of voting, the one form of citizen participation which is sanctioned and encouraged, is a jealously guarded private activity; there is no necessity for individuals to discuss or justify their choices to others.[28] In polyarchical politics, spectacle has eclipsed substance. Given an electorate unaccustomed to participating in meaningful debate over public values, election campaigns have become prized occasions for the marketing of "leadership" rather than informed discussion and choice by citizens. To the extent that issues are discussed at all, they are framed in such abstract terms (for example, "inflation" or "the deficit") as to be virtually unintelligible and have only ephemeral impact on voter choice.[29] The stunted character of this public discourse on values calls to mind Rousseau's dictum that without informed and active citizens, you have nothing but "debased slaves, from the rulers of the state downwards."[30]

The great challenge for modern democratic theory has been to justify this elitist version of democratic practice. Most justifications centre on the "realism" of representative forms of democracy. Since citizens are largely apathetic about public affairs; it is thought to be appropriate that decision-making be left to the discretion of representative elites. It is considered utopian to require all issues of public policy to be submitted for electoral debate and decision.

Notions of law and legality have played a subsidiary but significant role in the justification of polyarchal forms of democracy. Adherents to the "thick" Rule of Law have suggested that there is no necessary tension between their proposals and democratic decision-making; the Rule of Law has an important role to play in tempering and modifying the elitism in modern liberal democracies.

This might be accomplished in a variety of ways. On one view, the Rule of Law serves as a guarantee to individuals that their rights will not be ignored by the bureaucracies of the state, the corporation or the trade union. The Rule of Law requires that fundamental issues of political morality be debated as issues of principle and not simply issues of political power. The positive effects of judicial review are thought to extend far beyond the particular case or dispute before a court. The claim is that "rights talk" is a means of uplifting and revitalizing political and moral discourse in our society generally. By forcing the political process to confront the question of individual rights, public morality will become more reflective and self-critical.[31] Cast as the high priests of moral discourse, the judiciary encourages and orchestrates meaningful public debate on moral issues.

These claims that the Rule of Law can serve as an indispensable means of popular control are profoundly mistaken. The Rule of Law sustains elitist politics, with its impoverished sense of community. It does so in at least two related, but distinct ways. First, the Rule of Law's language of rights reinforces the assumption that communities are nothing more than aggregations of private interests. Rightholders are defined in contradistinction to the community rather than as integral components of it. Second, and more significantly, a politics dominated by the Rule of Law is a politics with limited scope for popular participation and control. It cramps and compresses the ability of individuals to debate and define the conditions of their communal life. In attempting to avoid the tyranny of the majority, it mistakenly embraces a doctrine of expertise and dependency which carries with it a subtle, yet despotic dominion of its own.

(b) Citizens as Rightholders

Democratic politics is not guaranteed to produce "right answers". No matter how much debate and discussion is encouraged or exists, there is still the possibility that the community will make a choice that is mean-spirited or unenlightened. This is implicit in democratic politics. A choice for democracy means that the community has a right to be wrong. Even if a citizen vehemently disagrees with a particular democratic outcome, that outcome is still entitled to a measure of respect simply by virtue of the fact that it embodies the democratic will of the community.

The notion that decisions that are "wrong" should nevertheless be entitled to respect may seem paradoxical or unsettling.[32] Consider a case where a citizen believed not only that the community's decision was wrong-headed, but that the error could be demonstrated through appeal to an uncontroversial or "neutral" form of reasoning. In such a case, that person might find it particularly galling if the collective decision were permitted to stand. He or she might struggle to discover some way of maintaining a general commitment to democracy, while disavowing the legitimacy of the community's choice on this particular occasion.

In essence, this is the attitude of those theorists who accord a central, primary role to considerations of legality and constitutionalism. Defenders of the Rule of Law do not deny that the democratic community has the right to be wrong. They simply contend that this prerogative exists within a closely circumscribed sphere. If the democratic community strays outside its appointed area and trespasses onto prohibited turf, the appropriate response is self-evident: like antibodies attacking a foreign substance, the judiciary should move swiftly to excise the offending contagion before it spreads uncontrollably throughout the body politic.

Of course, the perennial difficulty is to define the alleged boundaries of democratic politics. Contemporary political philosophy claims to have noticed these boundaries lurking in the interstices of Kantian moral theory. The argument runs a typical course.[33] Individuals are entitled to be treated as ends in themselves, rather than as a means to someone else's ends. In order to give effect to this background political ideal, it is necessary to specify the conditions under which each individual's qualities of moral agency and personality are recognized. These political conditions form a coherent whole. They can be expressed in the form of a series of entitlements or rights which must be respected by the community if it is to be true to the notion of individual autonomy. A community cannot be said to be just or rightly ordered until and unless it recognizes and guarantees these individual rights. Such a schema represents the fixed fulcrum around which democratic politics must swing.

Although this rights theory purports to leave basic democratic principles intact, it frustrates and paralyzes them. This results as much from what is excluded as included in the theory. Significantly, a rights-based conception of the Rule of Law has an impoverished or non-existent conception of communal politics. There is very little respect and a good deal of anxiety surrounding attempts on the part of the community to define its collective identity. For the rights theorist, wherever collectivities gather together to express their moral beliefs in law, there lurks the stale, but unmistakable whiff of totalitarianism on the political breeze. Questions of morality and values are considered to be inescapably relative. Such matters of taste must be left in the hands of individuals, freed from the tyranny of the opinions of others regarding their lifestyles.

The constitutional analysis of Ronald Dworkin exemplifies this impoverished conception of community with its corresponding emphasis on the privatization of morality.[34] Dworkin's analysis is premised on the notion that everyone has the right to be treated with equal concern and respect. This concern for equality is violated when the community allows a "corrupting" element to contaminate its calculation of general welfare. The corrupting element can be identified on the basis of a distinction between personal and external preferences. Individuals' personal preferences relate to the assignment of goods or advantages to themselves, while external preferences relate to the assignment of goods or advantages to others. According to Dworkin, a utilitarianism that counts both personal and external preferences is vulgar and corrupt. External preferences do not respect the right of everyone to be treated with equal concern and respect; they suppose that a particular form of life or community is more valuable than any other. For instance, to take one of Dworkin's examples, if there is a proposal to build a swimming pool, only the votes of those who want to use the pool may properly be counted in its favour. Non-swimmers who might support the construction of the pool because they wish to promote the activity of swimming should be ignored. This is because the non-swimmers are suggesting that a certain lifestyle or activity is inherently more valuable than another.

Far from purifying utilitarian discourse, Dworkin's proposal debases it. In the guise of offering a political discourse that is neutral and egalitarian, Dworkin has simply ordained that only certain values or ideals may be tolerated in political debate and argument. The accepted ideolect is that employed by individuals bargaining in their own self interest. They are entitled to be heard only if they frame their claims in terms of what they hope to gain personally from a decision. Any appeal to the values or interests of the community as a whole is corrupting. Apparently, to invoke public as opposed to private considerations is to violate the norm of equal concern and respect.

Dworkin exhibits a profound antipathy for common consciousness amongst citizens. Politics becomes nothing more than a lackey for private interest. Pluralism and relativism are constitutionally mandated because there can be no genuine public interests. The result is an aggregate of individuals secure in their abstract rights and liberties but divorced from each other. This, of course, is entirely predictable given the background theory of personality which underlies contemporary liberal accounts of politics. The common starting point of these accounts is a fictitious choosing self, stripped of all particularity. This abstract self belongs to no particular family or community, has no set of allegiances or commitments and possesses no life plan. Although liberalism fetes the individual and celebrates personal freedom, it recommends a set of social organizing principles that rests on a pessimistic notion of human personality. By depicting individuals as indifferent to others, it establishes a ephemeral lifestyle that stifles the ameliorating potential in them; "the limits of liberal democracy are the limits of self-preoccupied imagination."[35] In a liberal regime, individuals become exiles in their own society, only united in their separateness and self-interestedness. The dominant motif of liberal society is its tendency to anomie; individuals drift with no communal connections. Bereft of any sense of community, "our society may have become so anomic that explicit occasions for mutual recognition among strangers on public streets are more feared than sought."[36]

The difficulty with this individualistic ideology is that it ignores and suppresses actual human experience.[37] Individuals are located in history, within a context of allegiances. They are not abstract or bloodless, but are in part constituted by their social context. To divorce individuals from this structure of allegiances is to rob them of the "railings to which [individuals] can cling as they walk into the mist of their social lives."[38] It stunts the possibility of developing a set of shared ends and values, a precondition to the emergence of a genuine populist democratic practice. By developing a moral sense and practical experience of community, individuals will be better able to contribute to the growth of a shared set of values and institutions in accordance with which social life could be organized. Persons might come to be respected as themselves and not as simply rightholders. In this way, society could develop a modus vivendi that encourages caring and sharing and actualizes the possibility for meaningful connection with others.

(c) Adjudication and Social Change

Notwithstanding the corrosive implications of rights-based theories for communal aspirations, the Rule of Law might still be characterized as the ally of democracy. Democratic politics is usually thought to involve a utilitarian calculus of the general welfare. There is no guarantee that this calculus will be conducted in a principled manner. Individual claims to autonomy and personhood might be ignored or bypassed simply in order to further the ephemeral interests of the community as a whole. On this view, the Rule of Law is required in order to ensure that considerations of principle and individual right enter into the societal calculus. The institution of judicial review is an attempt to transform a jungle of deals into a world of rights. As Ronald Dworkin urges, judicial review promises that "the deepest, most fundamental conflicts between individual and society will once, someplace, finally, become questions of justice."[39]

A sensitivity for individual rights might be seen as particularly apposite and necessary in contemporary society. Individual life is dominated and permeated by large and complex bureaucracies, principally the state and the business corporation. The challenge to individual rights is no longer the lynch mob crying for blood, but the coolly rational bureaucrat, armed with spread sheets and cost-benefit studies. Regard for the Rule of Law is thought to ensure that "social managers" will not trample individuals in the march toward so-called organizational progress. Yet, while bureaucracy represents one of the greatest threats to genuine democratic values, there is little reason to suppose that the Rule of Law offers any refuge from the dangers of unbridled bureaucracy.

The Rule of Law is premised on a set of beliefs about the relation between adjudication and social behaviour. It assumes that judicial decisions are a significant and positive instrument for shaping popular attitudes and social action. As an explanation of social change, the account is simplistic and lacks any empirical foundation. Indeed, the gathering of social data to ground their instrumental assumptions forms no part of the agenda of traditional jurisprudence. The limited available evidence suggests that the public is only vaguely aware of judicial activity and that there is little correlation between judicial pronouncements and societal life. For instance, numerous opinion surveys confirm that the public has only marginal awareness of legal institutions and decisions. Only half of Americans can recall any Supreme Court decision. Those who can have an unfavourable opinion of it, by a margin of at least two to one. Further, Americans have less public confidence in the Supreme Court than the Presidency or Congress.[40]

It is instructive to track the direction of public opinion over time towards visible court decisions that are thought to be liberally enlightened. In the 1960s, both the school desegregation and reapportionment decisions of the American Supreme Court were favoured by about 60 per cent of respondents, while the school prayer decisions were opposed by a margin of about three to one.[41] By the 1970s, large majorities remained opposed to the school prayer decisions. In contrast, the reapportionment decisions were no longer visible to the public, while public support for the Court's desegregation decisions had eroded drastically. Although a majority of respondents remained committed to desegregation in schools, the judicial remedy of busing was opposed by 82 per cent of whites and 33 per cent of blacks.

Not surprisingly, in view of this ignorance or hostility towards adjudication, judicial decisions have not tended to bring about large-scale social change. For instance, although only about school desegregation, *Brown* is heralded by received jurisprudential wisdom as a turning point in relations between American blacks and whites and as a victory over Southern institutional racism. Yet, for almost a decade after *Brown*, the local situation of blacks remained appalling: "the Southern caste system remained intact ... [and] the federal government's efforts on behalf of oppressed blacks were sporadic and ineffective."[42] It was not until the blacks mobilized themselves en masse in the early 1960s that their situation improved. The contribution that the *Brown* decision made to this state of affairs is moot and certainly not explained by the causally reductive accounts of Rule of Law theorists.

While racist attitudes and overt institutional practices may have improved, systemic racism persists. Some hard facts make for distressing reading. The poverty rate for black Americans is three times that of whites; non-white American men earn about 80 per cent of the wages of their white counterparts; the income gap between white and black families has widened since 1977; not only is the unemployment rate among blacks more than double that for whites, this unemployment inequality has itself doubled in the last thirty years; and while 26 per cent of young black high school graduates are unemployed, the exact same proportion of young white high school dropouts are unemployed.[43] Even in the limited area of school desegregation itself, the immediate and long-term effects of *Brown* are moot. Like Dicken's Jarndyce v. Jarndyce, the *Brown* saga "drones on" and "still drags its dreary length before the Court."[44] The gap between legal doctrine and social change is striking. The rosy picture of social life painted by the legal materials is far removed from its sombre actuality.

(d) Of Vitamins and Virtues

The reasons for discussing the impact of court decisions is not to suggest that the American Supreme Court's civil rights or school prayer decisions were somehow "wrong". Such a conclusion would be beside the point. The meaningful issue is why an elite judiciary should have responsibility for making such decisions in the first place. Reliance on the Supreme Court undermines popular control and participation in the policy-making process. Although the Supreme Court receives extensive attention in the media and the law reviews, publicity is no substitute for participation and does not overcome the exclusion of citizens from such debate. The media is dominated by much the same elite voices and institutional actors as litigation. For citizens, Supreme Court judges seem to resemble inscrutable Platonic figures who make decisions in which they have no part and of which they are largely ignorant. When a decision does come to their attention, they are likely to disagree with it. This further decreases the extent to which individuals have control over their own lives.

The citizens' role as distant spectators is exacerbated by the arcane and stylized language of constitutional litigation. As disputes move into the magnetic field of law, they are translated into the received argot. To partake of the law's special privileges and prizes, citizens must become proficient in its idioms and nuances. In this way, legal discourse enforces its own canons of relevance, rationality and reasonableness. The lawyerly sentinels of power ensure that citizens comport to the rules of constitutional grammar; those who do not are deprived of a voice and are rendered powerless. The courts' historical function has not been to express popular justice, but rather "to ensnare it, control it and to strangle it, by re-inscribing it within institutions which are typical of a state apparatus."[45]

Defenders of this "elitist" approach to the Rule of Law must inevitably rely on some version of the claim that the ends justify the means. Although the elimination of popular control might be lamentable in the abstract, in cases like *Brown* it was the only realistic means available to counter deep-rooted and widespread public prejudice. Popular control, it is argued, would have been a recipe for the continued denial of justice and equality towards blacks. As such, it was simply unacceptable.

There is a good deal of force in these arguments. Given the harsh and brutal history of discrimination in the American South, it is difficult not to welcome the intervention of the Supreme Court as an antidote to racial intolerance. The difficulty with framing the debate in these terms is that it portrays the courts as an enlightened oracle proclaiming the gospel to the stupefied masses. Such an assumption is unwarranted and ahistorical; advances in social justice have been achieved through legislative rather than judicial action. Both Canadian and American courts have been as much a source of reaction and chauvinism as of edification and enlightenment. Much of the social welfare legislation enacted by the federal government in the 1930s was ruled unconstitutional by the courts as an intrusion on provincial jurisdiction. The practical effect of these decisions, such as the *Unemployment Insurance Reference* of 1937, was to make the enactment of such legislation impossible since the provinces lacked the fiscal resources to undertake such costly programs. The judicial decision in this particular instance was overcome only after the political branches of government secured a constitutional amendment which specifically empowered the federal government to put in place an unemployment insurance scheme.

The evolution of American First Amendment doctrine provides further illustration of this. Prior to World War I, the Court ruled in favour of a free speech claimant on only one occasion.[46] In subsequent decades the Court became more sensitive to free speech issues, but it cut back or ignored these doctrines during the so-called Red Scare in the 1950s. The 1960s was a period of renewed first amendment activism by the Court, coincident with the civil rights movement. However, in recent years the first amendment has been enlisted as a potent weapon in the defence of the entrenched status of power and privilege. The ability of corporations and the wealthy to dominate the political process has been constitutionally guaranteed;[47] privately-owned public areas have been excluded from first amendment scrutiny;[48] while commercial advertising has been protected.[49] In short, while popular decision-making does not guarantee enlightened answers to political questions, neither does deference to an elite judiciary.

Even in the so-called "progressive" constitutional decisions, the difficult question is whether the elimination of popular control in favour of an elite institution like the Supreme Court will actually promote the long-term cause of justice and equality. At the institutional level, there may be a marked negative effect. Because judicial decisions tend to persuade people that things are being done, reformative energy may be frustrated and other governmental institutions may feel relieved of the pressure and responsibility to initiate and facilitate social change. Moreover, the assumption seems to be that values such as justice and freedom can be defined in some external forum, like the Supreme Court, and then simply foisted on a recalcitrant public. But the reality is precisely the opposite. Public values cannot be abstractly manufactured in some antiseptic political laboratory and administered, like vitamin tablets, to a malnourished and lethargic mass.

Values such as justice and equality are the products of politics, not its antecedents. They take root in a public that engages in debate and argument and that is given the opportunity to nurture notions of reasonableness and commonality. Deprived of such empowerment, public values corrode and civic energy dissipates. Deferring to "specialists", citizens lose the capacity to define their own values and traditions. Public morality will atrophy rather than be energized. The appointment of the judicial philosopher king exacerbates the problem it was intended to remedy.

Democracy means the greatest possible engagement by people in the greatest possible range of communal tasks and public action. As people reclaim control over their own lives, they will develop an appetite and a talent for more. This rejects the prevailing pessimism about the competence of ordinary citizens; their present apathy and disaffection is a product of their current powerlessness rather than any natural infirmity. This insight is easily forgotten in a setting in which the opportunities for meaningful popular participation are few. The central importance of participation and debate in the shaping of public morality can only be grasped by focusing on an institution which rejects values of expertise and elitism in favour of participatory self-government.

Such an institution is the jury system. To suggest that the jury system represents a paradigm of democratic practice may seem anachronistic or naïve. Critics on both the right and the left have condemned the jury as a device to legitimate bigotry, ignorance or racism. These criticisms of the jury parallel those issued against democracy in general; the basic complaints are that these institutions produce decisions that are oppressive and that individual citizens are incapable of making such decisions.

Yet, whatever the failings of individual juries, the jury system as a whole embodies to a remarkable degree values of self-government.[50] The jury system rejects rule by experts; people assume the responsibility for making important civic decisions on a rotating basis. Discussion and argument are central to the success of the institution. The jurors do not simply observe the trial and then cast their votes individually in the privacy of a polling booth. They are expected to arrive at a common verdict, through persuasion and argument. Without such debate, "the jury system as a whole would be devalued, and ... individual jurors would value their own roles less."[51] The jury system represents a commitment to the principle that the ordinary citizen is competent to debate and decide important issues in the community. As E.P. Thompson states,[52]

I can imagine better laws and I can imagine better jurors, but I cannot imagine a better system. I would like to think of the jury system as a lingering paradigm of an alternative mode of participatory self-government, a nucleus around which analogous modes might grow in our town halls, factories and streets.

With its emphasis on persuasion, argument and consensus, it is democratic rule writ small. True, the jury often acts as a rubber stamp for state values, but it can also act as a lamp of liberty which might illuminate the potential and power of ordinary people.

There is no quick fix for bigotry or prejudice. Certainly, it would be naïve to suppose that such deplorable attitudes would simply disappear with the dawn of a genuine democratic community. Democracy does not guarantee civil enlightenment. But if communal morality is to become more informed and developed, this will be achieved through more rather than less democracy. It is only through public talk that small minded or superficial attitudes might be exposed and attacked. The ambition is not to attain some romantic or utopian harmony, but a political order which facilitates individual participation in the continuing social deliberation over political ends.

Judicial musing, enforced by fiat, is no substitute for civil deliberation. Rule by judiciary supposes that the only way to deter oppression is to impose external restraints on the political process. But because such restraints deny the moral competence of citizens, they undermine the very process of reflection and self-criticism which might lead to a more mature collective morality. Elitist politics breed only a mob; the nurturing of citizens demands democratic culture.

3.   CONSTRUCTION AND CONSTRAINT

The Rule of Law democrat lives in a society bereft of community. Given its historical obsession with abstract individual rights and liberties, liberal legalism stymies the establishment of a truly communal modus vivendi in which people can satisfy their collective and personal aspirations. Within a legalistic ethic, communal ambitions are destined to remain etiolated. We have tried to free democracy from its bondage to the Rule of Law. Emancipated, it might serve rather than stifle the flourishing of communal life and fulfilled citizens.

A concrete and constructive example illustrates our claims. The way modern society defines "health" and "need" and establishes standards for health care both exposes the elitism of present arrangements and suggests the possibilities for democratic involvement. Currently, the medical and legal professions have come together in an unholy alliance to monopolize the process of health decision-making. People have become "limp and mystified voyeur[s]"[53] on the treatment of their own bodies, the passive objects of clinical therapy rather than active participants in its prescription and administration. In contrast to present practice, democracy demands that people must be fully integrated into the formulation of any preventative and rehabilitative program. All individuals must become "welfare workers"; "a society which ignores [that health care involves mutual learning, mutual help and mutual responsibility] may stave off, for a time, the effects of illness and injury, only to pave a better road to ill-health."[54]

Even the fully democratic society will have to make "tragic choices" about the allocation of scarce resources. While medical technology advances apace, its direction and nature are not open to public control. Much medical research has been devoted to the reduction of mortality, but this has meant a corresponding increase in morbidity, especially among the elderly. Choices about the treatment of defective babies, geriatrics, paraplegics and other afflicted individuals have been made in the elite forums of the medical and legal establishment; they deserve to be the subject of a more thoroughgoing democratic debate. The target must be the introduction of communal health care services which work toward a local and supportive environment for recovery or readjustment to changed health circumstances.

There must develop a greater appreciation that health and welfare are as much socially caused as individually experienced. This means the fostering of a more holistic approach to well-being. This would not merely treat individual symptoms, but would concern itself with the total environment in which people live, work, play and die. The control of risk would be of, at least, the same importance as the treatment of injury and misfortune. Whereas the democratic society takes an integrated and coherent stance on risk and well-being, the liberal society adopts a divided and contradictory position.[55]

A commitment to democracy does not mean that constraints on popular decision making must always and everywhere be condemned. It is important that the basic institutions and practices of democracy – free elections, debate and assembly – be guaranteed and extended. Further, democracy implies the necessity for general laws which do not single out particular groups or individuals for special treatment and which are applied in nondiscriminatory fashion across the whole community. But there is a distinction between constitutional safeguards which constrain democratic activity in the name of democracy and those which constrain democratic activity in the name of "right answers". The latter type of constraints seek to substitute the judgments of philosophy for those of the people simply because the popular judgments are regarded as tainted. As Michael Walzer observes,[56]

... any extensive incorporation of philosophical principles into the law ... is ... to take them out of the political arena where they properly belong. The interventions of philosophers should be limited to the gifts they bring. Else they are like Greeks bringing gifts, of whom the people should beware, for what they have in mind is the capture of the city.

Democrats should always be wary of constraints that seek to substitute the cold hand of philosophy for popular judgment, no matter how presently plausible or attractive they might appear. Of course, instances will arise in which public sentiments appear so wrong-headed that they demand instant repudiation. Even a committed democrat would likely be tempted by the siren song of the Rule of Law. But to tie oneself to the post of "principle" is to court seduction rather than salvation. Far from purifying public morality, it would merely ensure its continued debasement.

NOTES

1 See J. Cohen and J. Rogers, *On Democracy; Toward a Transformation of American Society* (1983), p. 32–35.

2 See H. Clarke et al., *Absent Mandate: The Politics of Discontent in Canada* (1984), pp. 32–33.

3 See, for example, M. Perry, *The Constitution, The Courts and Human Rights: An Inquiry into the Legitimacy of Constitutional Policymaking by the Judiciary* (1982), pp. 91–145.

4 See, for example, E.P. Thompson, *Whigs and Hunters* (1975).

5 L. Fuller, *The Morality of Law* (rev. ed., 1969), p. 210.

6 H.L.A. Hart, *The Concept of Law* (1961), p. 206.

7 For an historical introduction to these events, see H. Berman, *Law and Revolution: The Formation of the Western Legal Tradition* (1983).

8 *On The Laws and Customs of England*, vol. 2 (S. Thorne trans., 1968), p. 305.

9 For an accessible and informed account of this history, see J. Ridley, *The History of England* (1981), and E. Schnapper, "The Parliament of Wonders" (1984), 83 Colum. L. Rev. 1665.

10 (1610), 77 ER 638, 652.

11 H. Nenner, *By Colour of Law* (1977), p. xi.

12 *The Records of the Federal Convention of 1787*, vol. 1, ed. M. Farrand (1937), p. 48. Roger Sherman's response was to the democratic point. Bills of Rights were "mere paper protection"; "the only real security that you can have for all your important rights must be in the nature of your government ... If you are about to trust your liberties with people whom it is necessary to bind by stipulation ... your stipulation is not even worth the trouble of writing." "Letters of a Countryman, November 22, 1787", reprinted in *Essays on the Constitution of the United States*, ed. P. Ford (1910), p. 220.

13 "The Declaration and The Constitution: Liberty, Democracy and The Founders" in *The American Commonwealth*, ed. N. Glazer (1976), p. 47.

14 See E. Corwin, *The "Higher Law" Background of American Constitutional Law* (1965).

15 *Osborn v Bank of the United States*, 22 US 738, 866 (1824).

16 *The Law of the Constitution* (1885), p. 46. Reference will be made to the 10th ed., E. Wade (1965).

17 Ibid., at 188–203.

18 See *The Constitution of Liberty* (1960) and *The Political Ideal of the Rule of Law* (1955).

19 *The Road to Serfdom* (1946), p. 54.

20 International Commission of Jurists, The Rule of Law in a Free Society (1959), p. 3.

21 See John Hart Ely, *Democracy and Distrust* (1980), p. 67 ("we may rant until we're blue in the face that legislatures aren't wholly democratic, but that isn't going to make courts more democratic than legislatures").

22 R. Dworkin, "Political Judges and the Rule of Law" in *A Matter of Principle* (1985), p. 31.

23 Ibid., at p. 32. In his most recent book, Dworkin develops and elaborates on these themes and emphasizes that the Rule of Law is "the parent and guardian of democracy." See *Law's Empire* (1986), p. 399.

24 *Reconstructing American Law* (1984), p. 110.

25 See generally, C.B. Macpherson, *The Life and Times of Liberal Democracy* (1977) and *Democratic Theory: Essays in Retrieval* (1973).

26 Schumpeter, *Capitalism, Socialism and Democracy* (1943), p. 282. For a useful discussion of the extent to which volitions of citizens are constrained in liberal democracies, see Lindblom, *Politics and Markets* (1977), pp. 208–213.

27 For examples of this economic and interest group theory of democracy, see Anthony Downs, *An Economic Theory of Democracy* (1957); Mancur Olson Jr., *The Logic of Collective Action* (1965); Robert Dahl, *Dilemmas of Pluralist Democracy: Autonomy versus Control* (1982).

28 "... our primary electoral act, voting, is rather like using a public toilet: we wait in line with a crowd in order to close ourselves up in a small compartment where we can relieve ourselves in solitude and in privacy of our burden, pull a lever, and then, yielding to the next in line, go silently home." B. Barber, *Direct Democracy* (1984), p. 188.

29 For instance, a recent analysis of voter attitudes in Canada found that issues which were seen as central in the 1974 election were barely mentioned in the 1979 campaign. When a third election was held some nine months later in 1980, a whole new set of concerns was seen as central. This shifts in public perceptions were closely related to the agenda of discussion set by the media and the political leaders. See Clarke, *supra*, note 2 at pp. 77–99.

30 J.J. Rousseau, "A Discourse on Political Economy" in *Social Contract and Discourses*, p. 251.

31 For arguments to this effect see Ackerman, *supra*, note 24.

32 See, for example, R. Wollheim, "A Paradox in the Theory of Democracy", in P. Laslett and W.G. Runciman, eds., *Philosophy, Politics and Society* (2nd Series, 1962), pp. 71–87.

33 For instances of the line of argument described in this paragraph, see J. Rawls, *A Theory of Justice* (1971); and R. Nozick, *Anarchy, State, and Utopia* (1974).

34 See R. Dworkin, *Taking Rights Seriously* (1977).

35 Barber, *supra*, note 28 at p. 18.

36 R. Burt, *Taking Care of Strangers* (1979), p. 41.

37 For a development of this argument, see A. Hutchinson and P. Monahan, "The 'Rights' Stuff: Roberto Unger and Beyond" (1984), 62 Texas Law Review 1477 at 1534–37.

38 R. Dahrendorf, *Life Chances: Approaches to Social and Political Theory* (1979), p. 32.

39 Dworkin, *supra*, note 22 at p. 71.

40 See Adamany and Grossman, "Support for the Supreme Court as a National Policymaker" (1983), 5 Law and Policy Quarterly 405.

41 The survey data is collected and analysed in Adamany and Grossman, ibid. at 422–424.

42 S. Bachmann, "Lawyers, Law, and Social Change" (1985), 13 NY Rev. of Law & Soc. Change 1.

43 See Cohen and Rogers, *supra*, note 1 at 30–32.

44 See *Bleak House* (1853), ch. 1. See *Brown v Bd. of Ed.*, 84 FRD 383 (D. Kan. 1979) (seeking intervention in original Topeka desegregation case on behalf of class represented by Linda Brown's daughter); *Clark v Bd. of Ed.*, 705 F. 2d 265 (8th Cir. 1983) (continuation of Little Rock desegregation case).

45 M. Foucault, *Power/Knowledge: Selected Interviews and Other Writings*, ed. C. Gordon (1980), p. 1.

46 *American School of Magnetic Healing v McAnnulty*, 187 U.S. 94 (1902). For a discussion, see Rabban, "The First Amendment in Its Forgotten Years (1981), 90 Yale Law Journal 514.

47 *Buckley v Valeo*, 424 US 1 (1976).

48 *Hudgens v NLRB*, 424 US 507 (1976).

49 *Virginia Pharmacy Board v Virginia Consumer Council*, 425 US 748 (1976).

50 For discussion, see E.P. Thompson, *Writing by Candlelight* (1980), pp. 167–70; M. Walzer, *Spheres of Justice: A Defense of Pluralism and Equality* (1983), pp. 308–309.

51 Walzer, ibid., at 309.

52 Thompson, *supra*, note 50 at 170.

53 I. Illich, *Limits to Medicine*, ch. 3 (1976).

54 A.V. Campbell, *Medicine, Health and Justice: The Problem of Priorities* (1978), p. 88.

55 These ideas are developed further in A. Hutchinson, "Beyond No-Fault" (1985), 60 Cal. L. Rev. 755. See also, R. Abel, "A Socialist Approach to Risk" (1982), 41 Maryland L. Rev. 695.

56 M. Walzer, "Philosophy and Democracy" (1981), 9 Political Theory 379 at 392–93.

READING QUESTIONS ON HUTCHINSON AND MONAHAN

1 Do you think juries are more or less trustworthy than judges?
2 How does Hutchinson and Monahan's position differ from Devlin's?
3 Is their position consistent with legal positivism?

Hofer v. Hofer [1970] 13 DLR 3d 1

Members of a Hutterite colony were expelled when they converted to another religion. They sued, claiming that they were entitled to their proportionate share of the colony's land. The colony insisted that their freedom of religion entitled them to hold all land in common. The decision, by the Supreme Court of Canada, provides a clear illustration of the debate between the two models of freedom that the earlier readings in this section explore. If religious freedom is construed as a negative liberty, the community has no say over the activities of its members. As a result, a certain way of life may prove to be impossible to sustain. By contrast, if freedom of religion is seen as a positive liberty, the community will have power over its members, but the negative liberty of individuals will suffer.

Ritchie, J: – ... It will be seen from the above that, in my view, adherence to the Hutterite faith was a prerequisite to membership in the Colony which by its very nature was required to be composed exclusively of Hutterian Brethren and their families. I am also of opinion that the decision as to whether or not any individual was a Hutterian Brethren so as to be entitled to continue as a member of the community was a decision which could only be made by the Hutterite Church. In the present case, as I have indicated, the decision to expel the appellants from the Colony was made by the church, but it had the effect of making the appellants ineligible for continued membership in the Colony. It follows from this that the appellants' contention to the effect that the articles of association were not properly complied with in regard to expulsion is without merit, and in my view the alternative plea with respect to the unlimited power and control of the ministers of the church over the personal life and property, being contrary to public policy, is equally invalid.

I am also of opinion, as I have indicated, that the Interlake Colony was not a partnership in the accepted legal sense of that term.

There is no doubt that the Hutterian way of life is not that of the vast majority of Canadians, but it makes manifest a form of religious philosophy to which any Canadian can subscribe and it appears to me that if any individual either through birth within the community or by choice wishes to subscribe to such a rigid form of life and to subject himself to the harsh disciplines of the Hutterian Church, he is free to do so. I can see nothing contrary to public policy in the continued existence of these communities living as they do in accordance with their own rules and beliefs, and as I have indicated, I think it is for the church to determine who is and who is not an acceptable member of any of its communities.

For all these reasons, as well as for those so fully expressed by the learned trial Judge and the Court of Appeal, I would dismiss this appeal with costs ...

Pigeon, J (dissenting): – The appellants and the respondents were all Hutterian Brethren. They lived at and were members of the Rock Lake

Colony. In 1960, the Rock Lake Colony had grown to such size that it was decided, in accordance with established practice, to split the Colony and form a "daughter" colony at Interlake, Manitoba. The members of Rock Lake Colony divided into two groups, neither of which knew whether it would go to the new colony or stay at Rock Lake Colony. This was decided by lot. The assets of Rock Lake Colony were then divided roughly in proportion to membership and 2,080 acres of land were purchased for the new Colony at $76 per acre.

The seven parties to this action formed the group moving to the new Colony. In May, 1961, they signed a document entitled "Articles of Association of the Interlake Colony of Hutterian Brethren of the Post Office of Teulon in the Province of Manitoba, Dominion of Canada". Those articles of association include the following provisions:

2. The purposes for which the said Colony is formed are: To promote, engage in and carry on the Christian religion, Christian worship, and religious education and teachings, and to worship God according to the religious belief of the members thereof; and to engage in and carry on farming, stock-raising, milling, and all branches of these industries, and to manufacture and deal in such products and by-products as may be considered by the Directors to be in the best interests of the Colony and for the purposes aforesaid, to hold, own, and possess such real and personal property as may be necessary.

3. The Colony shall be comprised of all persons who sign these Articles. No person shall become a member of the Colony and be permitted to sign these Articles, until he or she shall have:

(a) Attained the full age of seventeen years.

(b) Become a member and communicant of the Hutterian Brethren Church.

(c) Been chosen and elected to Membership upon a majority vote of all the male members of the Colony present at any annual, general, or special meeting of the Colony.

30. All the property, real and personal, of said Colony from whomsoever, whensoever and howsoever it may have been obtained, shall forever be owned, used, occupied, controlled and possessed by the said Colony for the common use, interest, and benefit of each and all members thereof, for the purposes of said Colony.

31. All the property both real and personal, that each and every member of the said Colony has or may have, own, possess or may be entitled to at the time that he or she joins such Colony, or becomes a member thereof, and all the property both real and personal, that each and every member of the said

Colony may have, obtain, inherit, possess or be entitled to, after he or she becomes a member of the said Colony, shall be and become the property of the said Colony for the common use, interest, and benefit of each and all of the members thereof as aforesaid.

32. None of the property, either real or personal, of the said Colony shall ever be taken, held, owned, removed or withdrawn from the said Colony, or be granted, sold, transferred or conveyed otherwise than by the Board of Directors, and if any member of the said Colony shall be expelled therefrom, or cease to be a member thereof, he or she shall not have, take, withdraw, grant, sell, transfer or convey, or be entitled to any of the property of the said Colony, or any interest therein; and if any member of the said Colony shall die, be expelled therefrom, or cease to be a member thereof, he or she, or his or her representatives, heirs-at-law, legatees or devisees or creditors or any other person shall not be entitled to, or have any of the property of the said Colony, or interest therein, whether or not he or she owned, possessed or had any interest in or to any of the property of the said Colony at the time he or she became member thereof, or at any time thereafter, or had given, granted, conveyed or transferred any property or property interest to the said Colony at any time.

33. Each and every member of the said Colony shall give and devote all his or her time, labor, services, earnings and energies to the said Colony, and the purposes for which it is formed, freely, voluntarily, and without compensation or reward of any kind whatsoever, other than as herein expressed.

34. The members of the said Colony shall be entitled to have their husbands, wives and children, who are not members thereof, reside with them, and be supported, maintained, instructed and educated by the said Colony, according to the rules, regulations and requirements of the said Colony, and the Christian religion, Christian worship, religious education, teachings and belief promoted, engaged in and carried on by the said Colony, during the time and so long as they obey, abide by and conform to the rules, regulations, instructions, and requirements of the said Colony.

35. Whenever any member of the said Colony shall die then his or her husband, wife and children who are not members thereof, shall have the right to remain with, and be supported, instructed and educated by the said Colony, during the time and so long as they give and devote all of their time, labor, services, earnings, and energies to the said Colony, and the purposes thereof, and obey and conform to the rules, regulations and requirements of the said Colony, the same as if the said member had lived.

37. The Community, or Association, or Colony hereby created shall not be dissolved without the consent of all of the members thereof.

The parties with their families moved to the Interlake Colony on December 20, 1961. Benjamin Hofer, one of the appellants, had by that time begun to be attracted by the teachings of the Radio Church of God and by March, 1964, he and David Hofer, another appellant, had both become converted to the beliefs of that church. These differed from those of the Hutterite Church in many respects. For instance, the Radio Church of God did not regard community of property as a part of its faith. It did not believe in the Christian festivals as observed by the Hutterian Brethren and it condemned the eating of pork. The two dissidents became subscribers to a monthly magazine published by the Radio Church of God and entitled "The Plain Truth".

On March 3, 1964, no less than 20 ministers of the Hutterite Church came from other colonies to Interlake and talked to the two dissidents in an attempt to re-establish their faith. A second and unavailing effort was made on March 13th, when 24 ministers came from other colonies and the two dissidents were asked if they did accept a church penalty of "unfrieden". Both dissidents refused and challenged the authority of the ministers to impose it. The penalty was, however, imposed and meant that the two dissidents were shunned by the rest of the Colony and their families were subjected to various indignities.

On June 13, 1964, the two dissidents, Benjamin and David Hofer, were expelled.

A year later, it became apparent that the other two appellants, John Hofer and Joseph Hofer, had also abandoned the Hutterite faith in favour of the Radio Church of God. Attempts to bring them back to the Hutterian faith were unsuccessful and in the end they were also expelled.

By their action, the appellants sought a declaration that they were still members of the Interlake Colony together with an order for the winding-up of its affairs, the appointment of a receiver, an accounting of its assets and liabilities, and a direction that its assets should be distributed equally among each of the appellants and respondents. The respondents counterclaimed for a declaration that the appellants are no longer members of the Colony, and are not entitled to any portion of its property and directing them to vacate the real property owned by the Colony and deliver up possession of all personal property owned by it which may have come into their possession.

Appellants' action was dismissed and respondents' counterclaim was allowed by Dickson, J [59 DLR (2d) 723], and this judgment was affirmed by the Court of Appeal of Manitoba [65 DLR (2d) 607].

In my view, the first question to be considered is the legal nature of the Colony. Having heard a great deal of evidence respecting the beliefs of the Hutterian Brethren Church, the trial Judge found as a fact that the Interlake Colony is a congregation of that church. I have no doubt that if the question is approached as the trial Judge did, namely, by looking how the matter is considered according to the teachings of the Hutterians, this is the correct conclusion. However, it appears to me that this is not the manner in which the question must be approached for legal purposes. What is religion, what is a church in the eyes of the law does not depend on the religious beliefs of any confession, at least under a regime of freedom of religion.

In *Walter et al. v A.-G. Alta.*, 3 DLR (3d) 1, [1969] SCR 383, 66 WWR 513, this Court decided that the fact that Hutterites consider as part of their religion the holding of land as communal property does not mean that legislation controlling such holding is in relation to religion. Martland, J, said for the Court (at p. 9):

The fact that a religious group upholds tenets which lead to economic views in relation to land holding does not mean that a provincial Legislature, enacting land legislation which may run counter to such views, can be said, in consequence, to be legislating in respect of religion and not in respect of property.

Religion, as the subject-matter of legislation, wherever the jurisdiction may lie, must mean religion in the sense that it is generally understood in Canada. It involves matters of faith and worship, and freedom of religion involves freedom in connection with the profession and dissemination of religious faith and the exercise of religious worship.

In *Robertson and Rosetanni v The Queen*, 41 DLR (2d) 485, [1964] 1 CCC 1, [1963] SCR 651, Ritchie, J, said for the majority (at p. 494):

It is said on behalf of the appellants that freedom of religion means "freedom to enjoy the freedom which my own religion allows without being confined by restrictions imposed by Parliament for the purpose of enforcing the tenets of a faith to which I do not subscribe". It is further pointed out that Orthodox Jews observe Saturday as the Sabbath and as a day of rest from their labours, whereas Friday is the day so observed by the members of the Mohammedan faith, and it is said that the *Lord's Day Act* imposes an aspect of the Christian faith, namely, the observance of Sunday on some citizens who do not subscribe to that faith.

My own view is that the *effect* of the *Lord's Day Act* rather than its *purpose* must be looked to in order to determine whether its application involves the abrogation, abridgment or infringement of religious freedom, and I can see nothing in that statute which in any way affects the liberty of religious thought and practice of any citizen of this country. Nor is the "untrammelled affirm-ations of religious belief and its propagation" in any curtailed.

The practical result of this law on those whose religion requires them to observe a day of rest other than Sunday, is a purely secular and financial one in that they are required to refrain from carrying on or conducting their business on Sunday as well as on their own day of rest. In some cases this is no doubt a business inconvenience, but it is neither an abrogation nor an abridg-ment nor an infringement of religious freedom, and the fact that it has been brought about by reason of the existence of a statute enacted for the purpose of preserving the sanctity of Sunday, cannot, in my view, be construed as attaching some religious significance to an effect which is purely secular in so far as non-Christians are concerned.

If the evidence respecting the operations of the Colony is considered on the basis that the legal nature of that association is to be determined by reference to generally accepted principles and not by reference to the tenets of the Hutterians, it becomes evident that it is a commercial undertaking, not a church. The land is used essentially for growing crops and raising livestock and while some part of the production is consumed by the members of the Colony and their families, the major part is sold in the same manner as the product of any similar undertak-ing whether owned by an individual, a joint stock company or a co-operative association. Of course, some small part of the land is used for a place of worship but it is clear that looking at the matter according to ordinary principles, this is only an extremely minor part. For legal pur-poses, it can no more be controlling than the use of two small rooms, one for the chaplain's office, the other for board meetings, in a large building otherwise occupied for commercial purposes could be consid-ered as putting a property in the class of "properties occupied by a youth association" in *L'Association Catholique de la Jeunesse Canadienne-Francaise v Chicoutimi*, [1940] 4 DLR 348, [1940] SCR 510.

It must also be noted that if the articles of association rather than the teachings and theories of the Hutterian Church are examined, it becomes apparent that two distinct purposes are enumerated in art. 2: religion and industry, the industrial purpose being described in the following way:

... to engage in and carry on farming, stock-raising, milling, and all branches of these industries, and to manufacture and deal in such products and by-products as may be considered by the Directors to be in the best interest of the Colony.

It is therefore contrary to the articles of association to say that the Colony was set up as a church. The articles of association as well as the facts properly considered show that the Colony was set up both for a religious purpose and the object of operating a communal farm. In respect of the agricultural operations, the Colony cannot be considered otherwise than as a secular undertaking; it is not a charitable undertaking. Because it has among its purposes an object that cannot be classified as charitable, it follows that it must in law be treated as a commercial undertaking.

With great deference to the trial Judge and the Judges of the Court of Appeal, it was wrong to decide the case by the application of rules of law governing churches. In my view, the situation from the point of view of religion must be said to be that the members of the Colony and their families formed a congregation of the Hutterian Brethren Church. This distinction between the church and the Colony is fully recognized in the articles of association. One of the qualifications for becoming a member of the Colony is to have "(b) Become a member and communicant of the Hutterian Brethren Church." It is clear that the church in this provision of the articles means the unincorporated religious community. This is not to be identified with the Hutterian Brethren Church, a corporation incorporated by the Parliament of Canada (1950–51 (Can.), c. 77).

From a religious point of view, the dissenting tendencies of Benjamin and David Hofer were obviously of concern to the whole church and not merely to the Interlake congregation and that may explain why a large number of ministers of other congregations together with the local minister concerned themselves with the situation, and in fact made the decision first to impose a church penalty and ultimately, when the appellants did not repent from their dissent, to expel them from the church.

Before considering the effect of that decision with respect to the subsequent expulsion from the Colony, it seems convenient to examine the status of churches in Canada. It is clear that the basic principle is freedom of religion. I see no reason for not applying in Manitoba the following statement of the legal situation in Quebec that was made by the Privy Council in *Despatie v Tremblay*, 58 DLR 27 at pp. 37–8 [1921] 1 AC 702, 47 Que. KB 305:

The religious position in the Province of Quebec in 1774, was therefore that every individual had the right to profess and practise the Catholic religion without let or hindrance. But it must be borne in mind that this is a privilege granted to the individual. There is no legislative compulsion of any kind whatever. He may change his religion at will. If he remains in the Roman Catholic community he may, so far as the law is concerned, choose to be orthodox or not, subject to the inherent power of any voluntary community, such as the Roman Catholic Church, to decide the conditions on which he may remain a member of that community unless that power has been limited in some way by the past acts of the community itself. In other words, each member of the Roman Catholic community in Quebec possessed the same privileges as any other citizen so far as religious freedom is concerned, save that he was not subject to any of the disabilities which then and, for a long time after, attached to Protestant dissenters. The Legislature did not put over him as a citizen any ecclesiastical jurisdiction. The decisions of the ecclesiastical Courts that existed in the Roman Church bound him solely as a matter of conscience. The Legislature gave to their decrees no civil effect nor bound any of its subjects to obey them. Indeed, the Act in art. 17 expressly reserves to His Majesty the power to set up Courts of ecclesiastical jurisdiction in the Province and to appoint Judges thereof, although that power seems never to have been acted upon. But what has just been said must not be misunderstood. The law did not interfere in any way with the jurisdiction of any ecclesiastical Courts of the Roman Catholic religion over the members of that communion so far as questions of conscience were concerned. But it gave to them no civil operation. Whether the persons affected chose to recognize those decrees or not was a matter of individual choice which might, or might not, affect their continuance as members of that religious communion. But that was a matter which concerned themselves alone.

It will be noted that freedom of religion includes the right for each individual to change his religion at will. While churches are otherwise free like other voluntary associations to establish whatever rules they may see fit, freedom of religion means that they cannot make rules having the effect of depriving their members of this fundamental freedom. In my view, this is precisely what these Hutterians have been attempting to do. With respect to the indignities suffered by appellants and their families, the learned trial Judge said [59 DLR (2d) 723 at p. 731]:

The application of pressures upon a deviant, through shunning, deprivation of privileges, and the like, follows Hutterian custom and was intended to make the non-conforming deviant once more conform. Some of the indignities and mistreatment suffered by plaintiffs and members of their families appear strange and repellant, and on occasion excessive, although there can be no doubt that within a religious community stern discipline must be observed if the community is to survive.

With deference, it appears to me that the learned Judge's comments are based on a misconception of the extent of the power that may properly be exercised by church authorities on communicants. He is clearly assuming that this may be whatever the rules of a church provide for. In other words, the decision in the Courts below proceeds on the assumption that religion extends to whatever a particular congregation may choose to include in it and that the religious authority is coextensive with such definition. This is contrary to the proper legal conception of religion whereby its scope is limited to what is commonly so considered and the extent of religious authority is limited to what is consistent with freedom of religion as properly understood, that is freedom for the individual not only to adopt a religion but also to abandon it at will.

The evidence shows that the rules and practices of this religious group make it as nearly impossible as can be for those who are born in it to do otherwise than embrace its teachings and remain forever within it. As the trial Judge has noted, it is unusual for Hutterian children to be allowed to go beyond Grade 8 education. They have no right at any time in their life to leave the Colony where they are living unless they abandon literally everything. Even the clothes they are wearing belong to the Colony and, according to the judgments below, they are to be returned to it as its property by anyone who ceases to be a member of the church.

Such a construction of the contractual relationship between the members of the Colony means that they really cannot exercise their right of freedom of religion. If the rights of the church and of the Colony are fully enforceable as the Courts below have held them to be, it is really legally impossible for them to leave because to do so they must do what the respondents did not hesitate to characterize as "stealing from the Church", in other words committing a crime (*Criminal Code*, ss. 2, 37, 269, 280). It does not seem to me that it is a proper answer to say that these rights will not be enforced to the limit. This is precisely what the British Court of Appeal refused to admit with respect to a contract with a money-lender that was not nearly as harsh as the contract embodied in the articles of association: *Horwood v Millar's Timber & Trading Co. Ltd.*, [1917] 1 KB 305. In that case, the Master of the Rolls [Lord Cozens-Hardy] said (at p. 311):

Is it open for a man in consideration of a sum of cash to bind himself not to leave the house where he is, not to sell any of his furniture and effects in the house or in any future house he may move into, which furniture is not the subject of any charge in favour of the mortgagee; is it open to him to say "Whatever property I may have I will not give any kind of security upon it for any sum of money or for any debt which legally or morally I may desire to pay"? Such a covenant would prevent the man from employing a doctor or a surgeon in the case of illness in his family, and would prevent him from raising money for the maintenance of his wife and children, or for the education of the latter. I think this is a deed which the law must recognize as bad on grounds of public policy of the most well-established kind.

He had previously stated the applicable principle in the following words (at p. 311):

It seems to me that if as a matter of construction I come to the conclusion that the contract is one which puts the covenantor in the position – I cannot think of a better word at the moment to express my view – of adscriptus glebae, as the villein used to be called in mediaeval times, on the ground of public policy the law will not recognize such a thing. No one has a right so to deal with a man's liberty of action as well as his property, and the law says it is contrary to public policy.

In the present case, through the articles of association if construed and applied as embodying therein the rules of the Hutterian Church, each of the appellants was literally made *adscriptus glebae* and, in my view, such a result is contrary to public policy ...

I cannot agree that on their proper construction the articles of association provide for automatic expulsion of any member who is expelled from the church. Such expulsion would be in the nature of a forfeiture of the whole of appellants' worldly possessions and would divest them without compensation of an important share in very valuable assets. Under ordinary rules of construction this could not be inferred, explicit words would be required which I cannot find. In any event, I am of the opinion that such a provision would be unenforceable as contrary to freedom of religion and also contrary to public policy in the context of such an association or partnership as these colonies existing for commercial purposes as opposed to church bodies or other religious or charitable organizations that may be subject to the rules applicable to churches and as to which no opinion is expressed.

In the Court of Appeal, Freedman, JA, said [65 DLR (2d) at p. 613]:

Here, however, the vital point is that Benjamin and his brothers had by their own free and voluntary act precluded themselves, so long as they continued to be members of the Colony, from the luxury of adopting or espousing doctrines alien to Hutterianism. Outside the Hutterian Brethren Church, and not as members of the Colony, they possessed (and still possess) the ordinary rights of free citizens to follow any religious beliefs they might desire, or indeed no religious beliefs, if that should be their inclination. But within the Colony they were Hutterites, pledged by solemn obligation and specific covenants to adhere to the religion of the Hutterian Brethren Church. Their rejection of that religion and their acceptance in its place of the doctrines of the Church of God could only be a disruptive influence in a close-knit and united Colony.

With respect, I fail to see on what basis freedom of religion can be so circumscribed. Of course, inside a church no one can be allowed to disrupt services by challenging the tenets of the religion according to which they are conducted. But, as this Court in effect held in the *Barickman Colony* case, the Colony is a farm, not a Church. No one can contract out of freedom of religion, no one can by acquiring a large tract of land establish one religion over that area and exclude freedom of religion therefrom. The authorities already cited make it abundantly clear that such freedom is a matter of public policy.

It is of some significance that in Manitoba the *Religious Societies' Lands Act*, RSM 1940, c. 180 [RSM 1954, c. 225], limits the land that a religious society may hold to a maximum area that is small by comparison with that which is held by the Interlake Colony. The following provisions of that Act are to be noted:

2 (1) In this Act,
   (c) "religious society" means a religious society, church, or congregation, of
      Christians or Jews in Manitoba.
3 (1) A religious society may, in the name of trustees subject to this Act hold
   (a) land not exceeding three hundred acres to be used for the site of a
      church, chapel, meeting house, residence of a minister, or for the support
      of public worship and the propagation of Christian knowledge or for
      other like religious or congregational purposes;
   (b) lands not exceeding twenty acres to be used [subject to subsection (2)]
      for a cemetery.

Those provisions show that if the Colony was considered as a church it would be holding land largely in excess of the maximum area fixed by law. I do not find it necessary to consider what the legal consequences would be in that view because I agree with Freedman, JA, that the proper rule to apply in the instant case is that which was enunciated by Wynn-Parry, J, in the case of *Re Hartley Baird Ltd.*, [1955] Ch. 143 at p. 146, as follows:

In the interpretation of such a commercial document as articles of association, the maxim ut res magis valeat quam pereat [it is better for a thing to have effect than to be made void] should certainly be applied, and I propose to interpret these articles in the light of that maxim.

It appears to me that the application of that rule supports the view already expressed that the Colony is a farmers' association, not a church, and that members are not subject to expulsion for the reason that they cease to be members of the Hutterian Church. It follows that the resolutions whereby the appellants were expelled should be declared void and they should be declared to be members.

Because, in the opinion of the majority, this appeal fails, it becomes unnecessary to consider what further remedies should be allowed.

As to costs, this is a case where all parties throughout appear to have acted in accordance with their sincere view of what their respective religious beliefs required. I would therefore order the costs of all parties in all Courts to be paid out of the assets of the Colony.

Appeal dismissed.

READING QUESTIONS ON HOFER V HOFER

1 Do you think that the court reaches the right balance between individual and group freedoms?
2 Suppose that the Hutterites, like many agrarian religious communities, held land individually. Would the tension between the two understandings of freedom of religion still arise? To what extent is the tension between competing views of property, rather than about religious freedom?

PART TWO

SOME CONTEMPORARY ISSUES

6

Defining Family

Family structure is sometimes said to be a purely private matter. Yet the state has always played some role in enabling some intimate arrangements and discouraging others. For example, certain benefits are conferred on only married couples, such as the ability to gain landed immigrant status for a spouse, or the right to adopt the biological children of one's spouse, or to receive survivor benefits of the spouse's pension plan. In addition, various employment benefits, such as dental plans and bereavement leaves, typically apply only to family members. While these are not government benefits *per se*, human rights codes require that they not be enforced in a discriminatory fashion. As a result, questions arise about whether a government can draw a distinction, or allow employers to draw one, between traditional and non-traditional families. Even if the state does not act to directly outlaw non-traditional families, issues of fairness may arise concerning their treatment under the law.

In Canada, these questions have been the subject of recent litigation concerning the rights of same-sex couples. Some of the issues are related to Devlin's claim that a majority is entitled to enforce its moral understandings simply because it is a majority. Thus, Devlin would presumably have no complaint about the result in *Bowers v Hardwick*, below, in which an American court upheld a law prohibiting homosexual sodomy. Other issues are tied to Dworkin's idea of the law "working itself pure" by getting rid of arbitrary distinctions. The difficult question is which distinctions count as arbitrary. Are distinctions based on sexual orientation arbitrary?

Canada (Attorney General) v Mossop [1993] 1 SCR 554

A gay federal government employee applied for bereavement leave when his lover's father died. The employee and his lover had known each other for more than ten years and owned their home together. The collective agreement between the government and Mossop's union limited bereavement leave to the death of a member of an employee's "immediate family." That included a common-law spouse but the agreement restricted the definition of "common-law spouse" to persons of the opposite sex. As a result, Mossop's request was denied. When his subsequent grievance failed, he filed a complaint with the Canadian Human Rights Commission. The Commission concluded that he had been the victim of a discriminatory practice committed contrary to the *Canadian Human Rights Act (CHRA)* which prohibited discrimination on the basis of "family status." It ordered that the day of the funeral be designated as a day of bereavement leave, and that the collective agreement be amended so as to include persons of the same sex in the definition of common-law spouse if they satisfy the definition in all other respects. The government appealed this decision, and the issue eventually reached the Supreme Court, which held that "family status" had to be understood in terms of the implicit legislative decision to exclude homosexuals from the protection of the Human Rights Act. (Note that the complainant did not argue that the agreement was contrary to the *Charter*. Rather, he claimed that if the phrase "family status" in the collective agreement was interpreted in the spirit of the *Charter*, it clearly would not permit excluding gay couples.)

Lamer, CJ: – ... The appellant chose not to take this approach [of a constitutional challenge to the section], however, and insisted that this Court dispose of its action solely on the basis of the meaning of "family status." In these circumstances ... I can do no more than to dispose of this appeal on the basis of the law as it stood at the time of the events in question. Accordingly, the issue to be determined, on the facts of this case, is whether there was discrimination on the basis of Mr Mossop's "family status" under the *CHRA* as it stood at the time the events occurred.

When Mr Mossop was denied bereavement leave in June 1985, the *CHRA* did not prohibit discrimination on the basis of sexual orientation. In my opinion, this fact is a highly relevant part of the context in which the phrase "family status" in the Act must be interpreted. It is interesting to note in this regard that there was a recommendation by the Canadian Human Rights Commission that sexual orientation be made a prohibited ground of discrimination. Nevertheless, at the time of the 1983 amendments to the *CHRA*, no action was taken to implement this recommendation.

It is thus clear that when Parliament added the phrase "family status" to the English version of the *CHRA* in 1983, it refused at the same time to prohibit discrimination on the basis of sexual orientation in that Act. In my opinion, this fact is determinative. I find it hard to see how Parliament can be deemed to have intended to cover the situation now before the Court in the *CHRA* when we know that it specifically excluded sexual orientation from the list of prohibited grounds of discrimination contained in the Act. In the case at bar, Mr Mossop's sexual orientation is so closely connected with the grounds which led to the refusal of the benefit that this denial could not be condemned as discrimination on the basis of "family status" without indirectly introducing into the *CHRA* the prohibition which Parliament specifically decided not to include in the Act, namely, the prohibition of discrimination on the basis of sexual orientation.

While, with respect, I am not in agreement with all of Marceau, JA's judgment [in the Court of Appeal], I believe that he correctly identified the relationship which exists between sexual orientation and the discrimination at issue in this case (at p. 37):

... should it be admitted that a homosexual couple constitutes a family in the same manner as a husband and wife, it then becomes apparent that the disadvantage that may result to it by a refusal to treat it as a heterosexual couple is inextricably related to the sexual orientation of its members. It is sexual orientation which has led the complainant to enter with Popert into a "familial relationship" (to use the expression of the expert sociologist) and sexual orientation, therefore, which has precluded the recognition of his family status with regard to his lover and that man's father. So in final analysis, sexual orientation is really the ground of discrimination involved.

While it may be argued that the discrimination here applies to homosexual couples through their familial relationship or in their "family status" and does not apply to the sexual orientation of Mr Mossop as an individual as such, I am not persuaded by this distinction. I cannot conclude that by omitting sexual orientation from the list of prohibited grounds of discrimination contained in the *CHRA*, Parliament intended to exclude from the scope of that Act only discrimination on the basis of the sexual orientation of individuals. If such an interpretation were to be given to the *CHRA*, the result would be somewhat surprising: while homosexuals who are not couples would receive no protection under the Act, those who are would be protected.

Whatever may be my personal views in that regard, I find that Parliament's clear intent throughout the *CHRA*, before and at the time of the amendment of 1983, was to not extend to anyone protection from discrimination based on sexual orientation.

Absent a *Charter* challenge of its constitutionality, when Parliamentary intent is clear, courts and administrative tribunals are not empowered to do anything else but to apply the law. If there is some ambiguity as to its meaning or scope, then the courts should, using the usual rules of interpretation, seek out the purpose of the legislation and if more than one reasonable interpretation consistent with that purpose is available, that which is more in conformity with the *Charter* should prevail.

But, I repeat, absent a *Charter* challenge, the *Charter* cannot be used as an interpretative tool to defeat the purpose of the legislation or to give the legislation an effect Parliament clearly intended it not to have.

Of course, if the effect of the legislation is in violation of the *Charter*, and a challenge of the constitutionality of the law is made before the courts, then the courts are commanded under s. 52 of the *Constitution Act*, 1982 to declare the section inoperative or to amend it when permissible ...

Before concluding, I should add that this does not mean that the hypothesis of overlapping grounds of discrimination should be ruled out in other contexts. Indeed, in this case, if Parliament had decided to include sexual orientation in the list of prohibited grounds of discrimination, my interpretation of the phrase "family status" might have been entirely different and I might perhaps then have concluded that Mr Mossop's situation included both his sexual orientation and his "family status." For the reasons I have given, however, and in particular as there is no challenge under the *Charter*, I am unable to come to such a conclusion in the case at bar.

Nor should this decision be interpreted as meaning that homosexual couples cannot constitute a "family" for the purposes of legislation other than the *CHRA*. In this regard, each statute must be interpreted in its own context.

IV CONCLUSION

For these reasons, I would dismiss the appeal.

L'Heureux-Dube, J (dissenting): – It is well established in the jurisprudence of this Court that human rights legislation has a unique quasi-constitutional nature, and that it is to be given a large, purposive, and liberal interpretation ... This long line of cases mandates that courts interpret human rights legislation in a manner consistent with its overarching goals ... In interpreting a statute, *Charter* values must not be ignored ...

The respondent Attorney General of Canada argued that, although the Act should be interpreted as remedial legislation, the ordinary rules of interpretation should apply ... I would agree that the rules of interpretation which have guided the courts to this day have not been set aside, and that they continue to play a role in the interpretation of legislation, including constitutional and quasi-constitutional documents ...

The Court has repeatedly warned of the dangers of strict or legalistic approaches which would restrict or defeat the purpose of quasi-constitutional documents ... In short, though traditional interpretational tools ought not be ignored, they must be applied in the context of a broad and purposive approach.

2. PURPOSE OF THE ACT

The purpose of the Act, set out in s. 2 recited earlier, is to ensure that people have an equal opportunity to make for themselves the life that they are able and wish to have without being hindered by discriminatory practices. The social cost of discrimination is insupportably high, and these insidious practices are damaging not only to the individuals who suffer the discrimination, but also to the very fabric of our society. This Court decried the multiple harms caused by discrimination in the context of hate promotion in *R v Keegstra*, [1990] 3 SCR 697. Dickson, CJ remarked, at pp. 746–47, that the consequences of such discriminatory practices "bear heavily in a nation that prides itself on tolerance and the fostering of human dignity through, among other things, respect for the many racial, religious and cultural groups in our society" ... The Act, in prohibiting certain forms of discrimination, has the express purpose of promoting the value of equality which lies at the centre of a free and democratic society. Our society is one of rich diversity, and the Act fosters the principle that all members of the community deserve to be treated with dignity, concern, respect, and consideration, and are entitled to a community free from discrimination.

The Tribunal did not fail to appreciate these factors, and understood the importance of interpreting the Act in light of its purpose ...

Against this framework, I would like to briefly address the arguments advanced before us that, in its interpretation, the Tribunal failed to adequately consider both textual context and legislative intent, and that this failure constituted an error of law.

3. TEXTUAL INTERPRETATION

It was argued that a correct interpretive approach would warrant that a textual interpretation be determinative, and that the coupling of the terms "family" and "status" in the English text of s. 3 of the Act required the Tribunal to construe "family status" as including only those families who have recognizable status at law. This is the way that the Court of Appeal approached the matter. Leaving aside for the moment the broad and purposive approach which, in my view, should guide the interpretation of human rights legislation, even if one were to take a textual approach to the interpretation of s. 3 of the Act, the result of such an interpretive exercise would not lead to the conclusions of the Court of Appeal, but rather would, in my view, support the Tribunal's findings.

First, the word "status" is capable of bearing several meanings. The *Concise Oxford Dictionary*, 7th ed., provides the following definition:

1. social position, rank, relation to others, relative importance; ...
2. (Law). person's relation to others as fixed by law. 3. position of affairs;

While the term "status" may be used to indicate status at law, it may indicate more factual matters of rank, social position, or relation to others. The use of the term "status" is not sufficient by itself to restrict the notion of "family status" to only those families that are recognized at law. Reference to the French version of the term, "situation de famille" is warranted here. *Le Petit Robert* provides the following definitions of the term "situation":

1. Le fait d'être en un lieu; manière dont une chose est disposée, située ou orientée.
2. Ensemble des circonstances dans lesquelles une personne se trouve.

3. Emploi, post rémunérateur régulier et stable ...

"Situation" is not a legal term, is broader than the English term "status," and encompasses a host of meanings. When the meaning of the French term is considered, it is apparent that the scope of "family status" has potential to be very broad. In French, the term "situation de famille" would not be used to express a legal notion. "État matrimonial" would.

As noted in the Court of Appeal reasons, until 1983, the French text of the Act prohibited discrimination on the basis of "situation de famille," while the English text of the Act prohibited discrimination on the basis of "marital status." In 1983 the Act was amended, the French text to include both "situation de famille" and "état matrimonial," the English text to include both "marital status" and "family status." The amendment did not simply modify the existing terms, but in fact expanded the Act. Had the intention been to narrow the scope of protection, it would have been simple to use one term or the other. In my view the purpose of the amendment could only have been to envelop the two notions. Furthermore, if both terms "situation de famille" and "état matrimonial," "marital status" and "family status," in the French or in the English texts, were similar, there would have been no need to juxtapose them. One such expression would have been sufficient as the legislator is not presumed to use meaningless words (P.A. Côté, *The Interpretation of Legislation in Canada* (2nd ed. 1992), at p. 232).

In any event, I have difficulty with the Court of Appeal's proposition that the meaning of "family status" and its French equivalent can be determined through reference to what it found to be the more restrictive English term. First, as I have noted above, the English term is not necessarily more restrictive. Second, even if it could be said that "family status" encompassed only families with legal status, it would be highly inappropriate to interpret the term by relying on the more narrow meaning of the French and English texts. It is an established principle of interpretation in Canada that French and English texts of legislation are deemed to be equally authoritative (*R v Turpin*, [1989] 1 SCR 1296), and where there is a discrepancy between the two, it is the meaning which furthers the purpose of the legislation which must prevail ... In this case, given that the purpose of the Act is to prevent discrimination and provide an equal opportunity to make the type of life one wishes, the broader of the two meanings should prevail.

A textual interpretation seems to me to support the conclusion of the Tribunal that "family status" should not be restricted to a narrow legal meaning. Nothing in the textual context indicates that the protection of the Act is to be extended only to certain types of legally validated families. On the contrary, the term "family status" suggests a broader protection that would prohibit discrimination against individuals on the basis on the internal structuring of their families. But, as I said above, a strict textual interpretation is not warranted here. That leaves then the argument concerning legislative intent.

4.   PURPOSE AND INTENT

[H]ad Parliament intended that the protection for families be restricted to legally recognized families, the amendment to the Act could have made this clear. However, this was not done. Instead, the amendment increased the scope of protection by adding a new ground of discrimination to each text: both "marital status" and "family status" became prohibited grounds. As the terms are juxtaposed, it is reasonable to conclude that "family status" must be something other than "marital status," just as "situation de famille" must be something other than "état matrimonial." Since "état matrimonial" is closer to a legal notion, "situation de famille" or "family status" can only be broader. It was, of course, open to Parliament to define the concept of "family status" within the Act. It did not choose to do so, even in the face of debate about the meaning of the term. Instead, Parliament determined that the task of dealing with any ambiguity in any concepts in the Act should be left to the administrative board charged with the task of implementing the Act ... Though the members of Parliament may perhaps not at that precise moment have envisaged that "family status" would be interpreted by the Tribunal so as to extend to same-sex couples, the decision to leave the term undefined is evidence of clear legislative intent that the meaning of "family status," like the meaning of other undefined concepts in the Act, be left for the Commission and its Tribunals to define. In my view, if the legislative record helps here in the search for legislative intent, it rather supports the Tribunal's wide and broad discretion in the interpretation of the provisions of its own Act.

An interpretation of a human rights document, or for that matter any legislation, that may not conform with Parliament's intention can be easily cured by Parliament itself. Because legislation can be amended more readily than a Constitution, legislatures who find the interpretations given by administrative tribunals inconsistent with legislative intent can always amend the legislation, or pass new legislation in order to modify that interpretation ...

Even if Parliament had in mind a specific idea of the scope of "family status," in the absence of a definition in the Act which embodies this scope, concepts of equality and liberty which appear in human rights documents are not bounded by the precise understanding of those who drafted them. Human rights codes are documents that embody fundamental principles, but which permit the understanding and application of these principles to change over time. These codes leave ample scope for interpretation by those charged with that task. The "living-tree" doctrine, well understood and accepted as a principle of constitutional interpretation, is particularly well suited to human rights legislation. The enumerated grounds of discrimination must be examined in the context of contemporary values, and not in a vacuum. As with other such types of legislation, the meaning of the enumerated grounds in s. 3 of the Act is not "frozen in time," and the scope of each ground may evolve.

Textual context should not detract from the purposive approach mandated by human rights documents, and legislative intent is best inferred from the legislation itself. Any ambiguities as to the exact boundaries of the enumerated grounds of discrimination were specifically left to the Tribunal's interpretation. Consequently, the Tribunal cannot be reproached for having applied recognized principles of interpretation of human rights legislation, in light of the particular purpose of its Act

...

That being said, I turn now to the Tribunal's actual interpretation of "family status" in s. 3. of the Act, to determine whether, according to the proper standard of review, it was patently unreasonable.

5. THE MEANING OF "FAMILY STATUS"

Across the political spectrum, there is broad appreciation of the vital importance of strong, stable families ...

This "unexamined consensus" leads many to feel that the term "family" in fact has a plain meaning. This belief is reflected in the decision of the Court of Appeal where Marceau, JA asks the question, "Is it not to be acknowledged that the basic concept signified by the word has always been a group of individuals with common genes, common blood, common ancestors?" However, the unexamined consensus begins to fall apart when one is required to define the concepts which are embedded in the term "family" in the context of "family status." How are the boundaries of that status to be drawn? Is there a plain meaning for "family status"? Could it not be said that "family status" is an attribute of those who live as if they were a family, in a family relationship, caring for each other?

Those who support a formalistic or more restrictive meaning for the term "family" point out that there is a dominant conception of family that has been traditionally enforced by laws and social custom. The form taken by this dominant conception is commonly referred to as the traditional family. It is widely understood that the traditional family is one composed of a married man and woman and their children ...

The multiplicity of definitions and approaches to the family illustrates clearly that there is no consensus as to the boundaries of family, and that "family status" may not have a sole meaning, but rather may have varied meanings depending on the context or purpose for which the definition is desired. This same diversity in definition can be seen in a review of Canadian legislation affecting the "family." The law has evolved and continues to evolve to recognize an increasingly broad range of relationships. Different pieces of legislation contain more or less restrictive definitions depending on the benefit or burden of the law to be imposed. These definitions of family vary with legislative purpose, and depend on the context of the legislation. By way of example, one may be part of a family for the purpose of receiving income assistance under welfare legislation, but not for the purpose of income tax legislation.

Despite the demonstrable range of definitions for family, the respondent Attorney General of Canada took a more narrow approach, arguing that the legal status of same-sex partners, either as family or as spouses, has not received extensive judicial consideration. Furthermore, he submits that where it has been considered, courts have almost consistently rejected the proposition that the concept of spouse can include same-sex partners.

The Tribunal, of course, was not concerned here with the definition of "spouse" but rather with "family status" in the particular context of an employee benefit. Be that as it may, both legislatures and courts have long been involved in the process of defining the relationships which will or will not be recognized for various purposes. The resulting legislation and decisions have often had an impact on the ways that families structure themselves. However, the family is not merely a creation of law, and while law may affect the ways in which families behave or structure themselves, the changing nature of family relationships also has an impact on the law. A review of our own legislation reveals the extent to which laws have changed to reflect the realities of families. The treatment of common law spouses is but one example. Law and Family have long been engaged in an Escherian dialectic, each shaping the other while at the same time being shaped. Therefore, in attempting to define "family status," the Tribunal found that it would be inadequate to consider the law without examining the family itself. In this case, the Tribunal considered that the interpretation of "family status" in the Act must account not only for current legal and societal conceptions, but also for the lived experience of family.

While it is arguable that the "traditional family" has an ideological stronghold, it is clear that a large number of Canadians do not live within traditional families. One cannot ignore the fact, that, between 1970 and 1987, the divorce rate in Canada rose from 18.6% to 43.1% ... The *Statistics Canada 1990 Family and Friends* survey indicated that half of divorcees aged 30–39 and more than one-third of those aged 40–49 were living common-law (Marriage and Conjugal Life in Canada, *supra*, at p. 50). Many children do not live in nuclear families. For example, in the United States in 1982, it was reported that 25% of children under the age of 18 did not live with both biological parents ... Single-parent families, especially mother-led, are prevalent; an increasing number of parents never marry; divorce is common; as is remarriage; significant numbers of families are comprised of a husband and wife with no children at home; lesbians and homosexuals establish long-term and committed relationships, and many are involved in raising and nurturing children ...

The evidence before the Tribunal was that the traditional family form is not the only family form, but co-exists with numerous others. Though there are Canadians whose experience of family does in fact accord with the traditional model, the way many people in Canada currently experience family does not necessarily fit with this model ...

While the structure of the family may be a question of choice for some, for others the structure of family may be in part a natural response to social and political pressures. The definition of "family" is thus capable of adapting to changes in the family structure which are caused by such pressures.

In defining the scope of the protection for "family status," the Tribunal considered it essential not only look at families in the traditional sense, but also to consider the values that lie at the base of our support for families. To look beyond the specific forms a family might take is to ask what value one sees in the family and what lies at the base of society's desire to recognize the support families. In order to define "family status," it is no error to examine the underlying values of families so that, as Lisa R. Zimmer says in "Family, Marriage, and the Same-Sex Couple" (1990), 12 *Cardozo L Rev* 681, at p. 699, "actual families, rather than theoretical stereotypes, may enjoy their protected status."

There are a variety of values that may lie at the base of society's support of the family. The state focuses on the family as an organizing structure of society. It is argued that the state has an interest in family as a vehicle to promote social stability. The comments made in *Moge v Moge*, SCC, No. 21979, December 17, 1992, at p. 32, are germane here:

Many believe that marriage and the family provide for the emotional, economic, and social well-being of its members. It may be the location of safety and comfort, and it may be the place where its members have their most intimate human contact. Marriage and the family act as an emotional and economic support system as well as a forum for intimacy. In this regard, it serves vital personal interests, and may be linked to building a "comprehensive sense of personhood." Marriage and the family are a superb environment for raising and nurturing the young of our society by providing the initial environment for the development of social skills. These institutions also provide a means to pass on the values that we deem to be central to our sense of community.

The Tribunal found that these values are not exclusive to the traditional family and can be advanced in other types of families. For example, while many see marriage as an indicator of stability, it appears from the current rate of marriage breakdown that heterosexual union is not an absolute guarantee of stability ...

Stability is a desirable value, but it may be achieved in a variety of family forms ... It could certainly not have been lost on the Tribunal that long-lasting and stable relationships have been maintained outside the bounds of legal marriage, as well as within same-sex relationships.

These comments also apply to intimate and emotional relationships. These relationships are often conceptualized as heterosexual, and it is often thought that people will form their most intimate and emotionally rewarding relationships with a heterosexual partner. However, the Tribunal was of the view that many individuals have found their most fulfilling relationships outside of marriage, and even outside of sexual relationships completely. In its view, it is to be bound by myth to assume that only heterosexual couples are capable of forming loving caring stable relationships ... If there is value in encouraging individuals to form stable and emotionally intimate relationships, such relationships can be forged and maintained in a wide variety of family forms. The emotional and economic safety nets forged by same-sex couples and their families were found not to be without value to society at large.

It was argued by the intervener Focus on the Family that one of the values of the family is its importance to society in fostering procreation, and that procreation requires families to be heterosexual. The argument is that procreation is somehow necessary to the concept of family, and that same-sex couples cannot be families as they are incapable of procreation. Though there is undeniable value in procreation, the Tribunal could not have accepted that the capacity to procreate limits the boundaries of family. If this were so, childless couples and single parents would not constitute families. Further, this logic suggests that adoptive families are not as desirable as natural families. The flaws in this position must have been self-evident. Though procreation is an element in many families, placing the ability to procreate as the inalterable basis of family could result in an impoverished rather than enriched vision.

It was also argued by the interveners Focus on the Family that the traditional family provides the most favourable environment for raising children. Many people in society are still influenced by myth and stereotype concerning the ability of same-sex couples to raise and nurture the children of one or the other ... What is important is that children be nurtured. The critical factor is not the family form, nor the presence of mixed-sex role models, but the provision of a loving and nurturing environment. From this perspective, the ideal family is one which meets the needs of its members, and best attempts to realize the values that lie at the base of family ...

Families, both traditional and otherwise, have not always succeeded in the promotion of these values. As Adrienne Rich notes in "Husband-Right and Father-Right" in *On Lies, Secrets and Silence* (1979), at p. 219:

The "preservation of the family" is quoted as an abstract principle without considering the quality of life within the family, or the fact that families may be held together by force, legally sanctioned terrorism, and the threat of violence.

Not all families are or have been sites of happiness, fulfilment, and joy for their members. This Court has had many occasions to consider incidents of emotional, physical, and sexual violence within families. It goes without saying that the values that lie at the base of society's desire to protect families are not always or even necessarily met within the family.

The reality is, as Didi Herman writes, in "Are We Family?: Lesbian Rights and Women's Liberation" (1990), 28 *Osgoode Hall L J* 789, at p. 802, that families are "sites of contradiction." Some people find family life oppressive, others seek supportive family relations but cannot find them. While the family may provide emotionally satisfying experiences, it may also be the site of brutal, violent, and terrifying experiences. However, despite the very real potential for oppression within the family, most people continue to believe that the family also has the potential to be the site of our most important human connections, and that it is these intimate connections that offer the greatest possibilities for individual fulfilment. It is the connections themselves, not simply the form they take, that are important ...

Given the range of human preferences and possibilities, it is not unreasonable to conclude that families may take many forms. It is important to recognize that there are differences which separate as well as commonalities which bind. The differences should not be ignored, but neither should they be used to de-legitimize those families that are thought to be different, and as Audre Lorde puts it in "Age, Race, Class and Sex: Women Redefining Difference" in *Sister Outsider* (1984) 114 at p. 122:

We must recognize differences among [people] who are our equals, neither inferior nor superior, and devise ways to use each others' differences to enrich our visions and our joint struggles.

Though not all people structure their family relations in the same manner, it is clear that there are common problems. Today, families of all descriptions are subject to pressures that are often shattering. Changes in the economy mean that most families feel that they need the wages of two adult workers. At the same time, families must often care for the young, elderly, and ill, with little help from the larger community. Although these problems are shared by all forms of families, they are further exacerbated in families whose legitimacy is called into question. Given these pressures and responsibilities, it would seem that it is in society's interest to improve conditions to enable families to function as they can, free from discrimination.

In light of all this, it is interesting to note that, in some ways, the debate about family presents society with a false choice. It is possible to be pro-family without rejecting less traditional family forms. It is not anti-family to support protection for non-traditional families. The traditional family is not the only family form, and non-traditional family forms may equally advance true family values.

The above discussion is not intended to provide an authoritative definition of what constitutes the family, but is rather to illustrate that a purposive approach to the term "family status" can result in an interpretation that can vary depending on the specific context. In the context of the claim made by Mr Mossop, the Tribunal found that a unilateral and inflexible definition of "family status" could not accord with the purpose of the Act. As the Tribunal explained, "[t]he possibilities inherent in the term family are many and complex" (p. D/6092). Cognizant that the purpose of the Act could be subverted by an inappropriate definition, the Tribunal fully appreciated the values at the base of "family," and had a clear understanding of the need to interpret the term in a manner that would accord with the purpose of the Act ...

The Tribunal did not conclude that there is one definition which will serve for all purposes, but rather determined that the task was to find a reasonable meaning which advanced the rights contained in the Act ... On the evidence before it and in the context of the Act, the Tribunal concluded that the potential scope of the term "family status" is broad enough that it does not prima facie exclude same-sex couples. In making this finding, the Tribunal used the proper interpretational approach, considered the purpose of the Act, and the values at the base of the protection of families ... Whatever definition I myself would have adopted, I would not substitute my opinion for the Tribunal's conclusion based on its specialized field of expertise and the evidence before it. Its conclusion is in accord with the broad and purposive interpretation warranted in human rights legislation and is one that, given its purpose, the Act can bear.

READING QUESTIONS ON MOSSOP

1 In light of *Egan*, below, is the majority judgment in *Mossop* convincing when it implies that its decision might well have been different had the case been brought as a *Charter* challenge?
2 What views of the judicial role (positivist, anti-positivist, or feminist) do the majority judgment and the dissent presume? Can these views be mapped onto the different views in *Riggs v Palmer*, above?
3 To what extent do you think the different views of statutory interpretation offered by the judges are rooted in different political commitments?

Egan v Canada [1995] 2 SCR 513

A case in which the Supreme Court of Canada upheld the constitutionality of
a law that defined "spouse" in a way which excluded homosexual couples.
A narrow majority of the court held that the law did not unfairly discriminate
against homosexuals since it also excluded benefits to other cohabiting pairs
not joined in heterosexual unions, such as siblings.

La Forest, J: – This appeal concerns the constitutionality of ss. 2 and
19(1) of the *Old Age Security Act*, RSC, 1985, c. O-9, which accord to
spouses of pensioners under the Act whose income falls below a stipulated amount, an allowance when they reach the age of 60, payable
until they themselves become pensioners at age 65. The appellants maintain these provisions violate s. 15 of the *Canadian Charter of Rights and
Freedoms* as discriminating against persons living in a homosexual relationship because the effect of the definition of "spouse" in s. 2 is to
restrict the allowances to spouses in a heterosexual union, i.e., those
who are legally married or who live in a common-law relationship ...
   The provision providing for the payment of the allowance is s. 19(1),
which reads as follows:

19. (1) Subject to this Act and the regulations, for each month in any fiscal
year, a spouse's allowance may be paid to the spouse of a pensioner if the
spouse
   (a) is not separated from the pensioner;
   (b) has attained sixty years of age but has not attained sixty-five years of
   age; and
   (c) has resided in Canada after attaining eighteen years of age and prior to
   the day on which the spouse's application is approved for an aggregate
   period of at least ten years and, where that aggregate period is less than
   twenty years, was resident in Canada on the day preceding the day on
   which the spouse's application is approved.

That provision, without more, would be confined – as the term "spouse"
had been interpreted in the Act before the original enactment of s. 19(1)
in 1975 – to spouses in a legal marriage. At the time of the enactment of
s. 19(1), however, s. 2 of the Act was amended to define the term

"spouse" for the purposes of the Act to include common-law spouses described in the definition. The definition reads:

2. In this Act ...
"spouse", in relation to any person, includes a person of the opposite sex who is living with that person,
> having lived with that person for at least one year, if the two persons have publicly represented themselves as husband and wife;

The effect of this new definition was to extend the allowances to spouses living in a common-law relationship as well as those in a legal marriage.

The appellants, James Egan and John Norris Nesbit, are homosexuals who have since 1948 lived together in a relationship marked by commitment and interdependence similar to that which one expects to find in a marriage. When Egan became 65 in 1986, he began to receive old age security and guaranteed income supplements under the Act. On reaching age 60, Nesbit applied for a spousal allowance under s. 19(1), which as I mentioned is available to spouses as defined in the Act between the ages of 60 and 65 whose combined income falls below a fixed level. His application was rejected because the relationship between Nesbit and Egan did not fall within the Act.

The appellants' claim before this Court is that the Act contravenes s. 15 of the *Charter* in that it discriminates on the basis of sexual orientation. To establish that claim, it must first be determined that s. 15's protection of equality without discrimination extends to sexual orientation as a ground analogous to those specifically mentioned in the section. This poses no great hurdle for the appellants; the respondent Attorney General of Canada conceded this point. While I ordinarily have reservations about concessions of constitutional issues, I have no difficulty accepting the appellants' contention that whether or not sexual orientation is based on biological or physiological factors, which may be a matter of some controversy, it is a deeply personal characteristic that is either unchangeable or changeable only at unacceptable personal costs, and so falls within the ambit of s. 15 protection as being analogous to the enumerated grounds ...

The nature of discrimination within the meaning of s. 15(1) of the *Charter* was first discussed by this Court in the seminal case of *Andrews v Law Society of British Columbia*, [1989] 1 SCR 143. In the principal reasons in that case, McIntyre, J, at p. 175, underlined the importance in a constitutional document, which is not easily modified, of achieving a workable balance that permits government to perform effectively its function of making ongoing choices in the interests of society and the work of the courts in ensuring protection for the equality rights described in s. 15. As he stated, what we must do is "to provide a "continuing framework for the legitimate exercise of governmental power" and, at the same time, for 'the unremitting protection' of equality rights." And he warned (see p. 168), as I did in my separate reasons, that not all distinctions resulting in disadvantage to a particular group will constitute discrimination. It would bring the legitimate work of our legislative bodies to a standstill if the courts were to question every distinction that had a disadvantageous effect on an enumerated or analogous group. This would open up a s. 1 inquiry in every case involving a protected group. As I put it in *Andrews*, at p. 194, "It was never intended in enacting s. 15 that it become a tool for the wholesale subjection to judicial scrutiny of variegated legislative choices in no way infringing on values fundamental to a free and democratic society."

When then is discrimination? There are several comments in the course of McIntyre, J's remarks in *Andrews* that go a long way towards clarifying the concept. Thus, at p. 174, he stated:

I would say then that discrimination may be described as a distinction,
whether intentional or not but based on grounds relating to personal characteristics of the individual or group, which has the effect of imposing burdens,
obligations, or disadvantages on such individual or group not imposed upon
others, or which withholds or limits access to opportunities, benefits, and
advantages available to other members of society.

This statement cannot, however, be looked at in isolation. It must be read in conjunction with McIntyre, J's earlier comment, at p. 165, as follows:

In other words, the admittedly unattainable ideal [of equality] should be that a
law expressed to bind all should not because of irrelevant personal differences
have a more burdensome or less beneficial impact on one than another.

Similarly in my separate reasons, at p. 193, I observed that "the relevant question ... is ... whether the impugned provision amounts to discrimination in the sense in which my colleague has defined it, i.e., on the basis of "irrelevant personal differences" such as those listed in s. 15

... " ... As Gonthier, J has noted in *Miron v Trudel* [1995] 2 SCR 418, this involves a three-step analysis, which he puts this way (at p. 435):

The first step looks to whether the law has drawn a distinction between the claimant and others. The second step then questions whether the distinction results in disadvantage, and examines whether the impugned law imposes a burden, obligation or disadvantage on a group of persons to which the claimant belongs which is not imposed on others, or does not provide them with a benefit which it grants others (*Andrews, supra*).

The third step assesses whether the distinction is based on an irrelevant personal characteristic which is either enumerated in s. 15(1) or one analogous thereto.

There is no question that the first step is satisfied in this case. Parliament has clearly made a distinction between the claimant and others. This, of course, does not carry one very far. Parliament is in the business of making such distinctions in developing programs and policies which is the task assigned to it in our democratic system. Further ingredients must be added to warrant a distinction being discriminatory.

The second step will also, in general at least, not be of great assistance. Ordinarily decisions do result in advantages or disadvantages to individuals and groups, sometimes intentionally, sometimes unintentionally. Parliament, as I mentioned, is in the business of making choices, and this inevitably involves the distribution of benefits and burdens in our society.

In this case, however, the respondent contends that the appellants have suffered no prejudice because by being treated as individuals they have received considerably more in combined federal and provincial benefits than they would have received had they been treated as "spouses." I would simply dispose of this argument on the ground that, while this may be true in this specific instance, there is nothing to show that this is generally the case with homosexual couples, which is the point the respondent must establish ...

I turn then to the third step of the analysis described by Gonthier, J. Since it has already been accepted that "sexual orientation" is an analogous ground under s. 15(1), all that remains to be considered under this step is whether the distinction made by Parliament is relevant, what Gonthier, J describes in *Miron v Trudel*, at p. 436, as the second aspect of this third step. He there notes that in assessing relevancy for this purpose one must look at "the nature of the personal characteristic and its relevancy to the functional values underlying the law." At this stage, he adds, one must necessarily undertake a form of comparative analysis to determine whether particular facts give rise to inequality ... This proposition, too, derives from McIntyre, J's reasons in *Andrews, supra,* who, at p. 164, states:

It [equality] is a comparative concept, the condition of which may only be attained or discerned by comparison with the condition of others in the social and political setting in which the question arises. It must be recognized at once, however, that every difference in treatment between individuals under the law will not necessarily result in inequality and, as well, that identical treatment may frequently produce serious inequality.

Gonthier, J adds ... that this comparative analysis must be linked to an examination of the larger context ...

In embarking upon this comparative analysis, I shall begin with an examination of the statute with a view to determining "the functional values underlying the law." I shall then examine the personal characteristic here in issue to determine its relevancy to these functional values.

In undertaking an examination of the statute, it is now settled that one must not focus narrowly on a provision that has the effect of depriving a group of a benefit that others who initially appear to be in a similar position are accorded. This is the "similarly situated test" which has been categorically rejected by this Court ... McIntyre, J in *Andrews* immediately stated that such a fixed rule or formula cannot be accepted, and then concluded by setting forth how the relevant statute must be approached in the following remarks, at p. 168:

Consideration must be given to the content of the law, to its purpose, and its impact upon those to whom it applies, and also upon those whom it excludes from its application. The issues which will arise from case to case are such that it would be wrong to attempt to confine these considerations within such a fixed and limited formula.

It is in that spirit that I propose to examine the *Old Age Security Act.*

...

As is evident ... Parliament, in addition to providing greater benefits to the elderly in need, long ago took special account of married couples in need; as I mentioned earlier, before 1975 the term "spouse" only applied to persons who were legally married. This special interest is clearly expressed by the Minister of National Health and Welfare, the Honourable Marc Lalonde, when testifying before the *Standing Committee on Health, Welfare, and Social Affairs* in relation to the amendment adding the spousal allowance in 1975. He stated:

Its objective is clear and singular in purpose. It is to ensure that when a couple is in a situation where one of the spouses has been forced to retire, and that couple has to live on the pension of a single person, that there should be a special provision, when the breadwinner has been forced to retire at or after 65, to make sure that particular couple will be able to rely upon an income which would be equivalent to both members of the couple being retired or 60 [*sic*] years of age and over. That is the purpose of this Bill, no more than that, no less than that.

See *Minutes of Proceedings and Evidence*, June 12, 1975, at p. 25:7.

I add that other evidence of Parliament's continuing concern for the needs of married couples is the benefits for widows and widowers. To complete the picture, I repeat that in 1975 Parliament, by defining spouse as above described, extended the benefits under the Act beyond those who were legally married to common-law couples, and it is that definition that has formed the principal focus of the appellants' attack. As I earlier noted, however, it is dangerous to focus narrowly on a particular provision. A more comprehensive contextual approach must be taken to determine the relevancy of the personal characteristic in question to the functional values underlying the law. That is how I propose to proceed.

The singling out of legally married and common-law couples as the recipients of benefits necessarily excludes all sorts of other couples living together such as brothers and sisters or other relatives, regardless of sex, and others who are not related, whatever reasons these other couples may have for doing so and whatever their sexual orientation ...

What reason or purpose, then, can be assigned to the distinction made by Parliament? It seems to me that it is both obvious and deeply rooted in our fundamental values and traditions, values and traditions that could not have been lost on the framers of the *Charter*. Simply stated, what Parliament clearly had in mind was to accord support to married couples who were aged and elderly, and this for the advancement of public policy central to society. Moreover, in recognition of changing social realities, s. 2 was amended so that whenever the term "spouse" was used in the Act it was to be construed to extend beyond legal married couples to couples in a common-law marriage.

My colleague Gonthier, J in *Miron v Trudel* has been at pains to discuss the fundamental importance of marriage as a social institution, and I need not repeat his analysis at length or refer to the authorities he cites. Suffice it to say that marriage has from time immemorial been firmly grounded in our legal tradition, one that is itself a reflection of long-standing philosophical and religious traditions. But its ultimate *raison d'être* transcends all of these and is firmly anchored in the biological and social realities that heterosexual couples have the unique ability to procreate, that most children are the product of these relationships, and that they are generally cared for and nurtured by those who live in that relationship. In this sense, marriage is by nature heterosexual. It would be possible to legally define marriage to include homosexual couples, but this would not change the biological and social realities that underlie the traditional marriage.

The marital relationship has special needs with which Parliament and the legislatures and indeed custom and judge-made law have long been concerned. The legal institution of marriage exists both for the protection of the relationship and for defining the obligations that flow from entering into a legal marriage. Because of its importance, legal marriage may properly be viewed as fundamental to the stability and well-being of the family and, as such, as Gonthier, J argued in *Miron v Trudel*, Parliament may quite properly give special support to the institution of marriage. It is spouses in legal marriage who constitute the bulk of the beneficiaries of spousal allowances.

But many of the underlying concerns that justify Parliament's support and protection of legal marriage extend to heterosexual couples who are not legally married. Many of these couples live together indefinitely, bring forth children, and care for them in response to familial instincts rooted in the human psyche. These couples have need for support just as legally married couples do in performing this critical task, which is of benefit to all society. Language has long captured the essence of this relationship by the expression "common-law marriage."

Faced with the social reality that increasing numbers choose not to enter a legal marriage but live together in a common-law relationship, Parliament has elected to support these relationships. The legal institution of marriage has long been viewed as the fundamental instrument to promote the underlying values I have referred to. But Parliament cannot force people to get married, and I see no reason why it should not take the necessary means to promote the basic social interests and policies that inform the institution of legal marriage through other instrumentalities. Support of common-law relationships with a view to promoting their stability seems well devised to advance many of the underlying values for which the institution of marriage exists. For example, children brought up by single parents more often end up in poverty and impose greater burdens on society. Parliament, it seems to me, is wholly justified in extending support to heterosexual couples like this, which is not to say, however, that it is obligated to do so and may not treat married and unmarried couples differently ...

Viewed in the larger context, then, there is nothing arbitrary about the distinction supportive of heterosexual family units. And for the reasons set forth by Gonthier, J in *Miron*, I am not troubled by the fact that not all these heterosexual couples in fact have children. It is the social unit that uniquely has the capacity to procreate children and generally cares for their upbringing, and as such warrants support by Parliament to meet its needs. This is the only unit in society that expends resources to care for children on a routine and sustained basis. As counsel for the intervener the Inter-Faith Coalition on Marriage and the Family put it, whether the mother or the father leaves the paid work force or whether both parents are paying after-tax dollars for day care, this is the unit in society that fundamentally anchors other social relationships and other aspects of society. I add that I do not think the courts should attempt to require meticulous line drawing that would ensure that only couples that had children were included. This could impose on Parliament the burden of devising administrative procedures to ensure conformity that could be both unnecessarily intrusive and difficult to administer, thereby depriving Parliament of that "reasonable room to manoeuvre" which this Court has frequently recognized as necessary ... This I think is wholly consistent with the workable balance between Parliament and the courts sought to be achieved in *Andrews, supra*, to which I have earlier referred.

Neither in its purpose or effect does the legislation constitute an infringement of the fundamental values sought to be protected by the *Charter*. None of the couples excluded from benefits under the Act are capable of meeting the fundamental social objectives thereby sought to be promoted by Parliament. These couples undoubtedly provide mutual support for one another, and that, no doubt, is of some benefit to society. They may, it is true, occasionally adopt or bring up children, but this is exceptional and in no way affects the general picture. I fail to see how homosexuals differ from other excluded couples in terms of the fundamental social reasons for which Parliament has sought to favour heterosexuals who live as married couples. Homosexual couples, it is true, differ from other excluded couples in that their relationships include a sexual aspect. But this sexual aspect has nothing to do with the social objectives for which Parliament affords a measure of support to married couples and those who live in a common-law relationship.

In a word, the distinction made by Parliament is grounded in a social relationship, a social unit that is fundamental to society. That unit, as I have attempted to explain, is unique. It differs from all other couples, including homosexual couples. Other excluded couples, it is true, do not have to be described by reference to sex or sexual preferences, but this is of no moment. The distinction adopted by Parliament is relevant, indeed essential, to describe the relationship in the way the statute does so as to differentiate the couples described in the statute from all couples that do not serve the social purposes for which the legislature has made the distinction. Homosexual couples are not, therefore, discriminated against; they are simply included with these other couples.

I add that this distinction exists in a plethora of statutes, both federal and provincial, and, indeed, it directly or indirectly forms the substratum of an abundance of legal principles and rules at common law and under the civil law system. I realize, of course, that the distinction could in certain circumstances be used in a discriminatory manner, but that is not this case. It is relevant here to describe a fundamental social unit, indeed the fundamental unit in society, to which some measure of support is given. I add, interstitially, that this support does not exacerbate an historic advantage; rather it ameliorates an historic economic disadvantage, both for couples who are legally married and those who live in a common-law relationship. If the distinction is thought to be irrelevant here, this would, in my view, mean that the courts would have to embark upon a s. 1 justification every time a distinction was made on the basis of marriage, legal or common law. Moreover, it would interfere with the appropriate balance between legislative and judicial power described in *Andrews*, which I have discussed earlier in these reasons.

Had I concluded that the impugned legislation infringed s. 15 of the *Charter*, I would still uphold it under s. 1 of the *Charter* ...

I would dismiss the appeal and would answer the constitutional questions as follows:

Question 1:   Does the definition of "spouse" in s. 2 of the *Old Age Security Act*,
              RSC, 1985, c. O-9, infringe or deny s. 15(1) of the *Canadian Charter*
              of Rights and Freedoms?
Answer: No.
Question 2:   If the answer to question 1 is yes, is the infringement or denial
              demonstrably justified in a free and democratic society pursuant
              to s. 1 of the *Canadian Charter of Rights and Freedoms*?
Answer: Assuming it is an infringement, it is justifiable under s. 1 of the
              Charter.

READING QUESTIONS ON EGAN

1 How plausible do you find the court's arguments about the discrimination not being unfair?
2 Would it be more appropriate to allow any pair of people, regardless of their sexual relations (or lack thereof) to form domestic
  partnerships?
3 The *Globe and Mail* (August 17, 1995) carried a report of a decision on
  a *Charter* challenge to the constitutional validity of the crime of
  incest. The Nova Scotia Supreme Court rejected a family's claim that
  its adult members were constitutionally entitled to have sex with
  each other. The argument was that, while incest may be morally
  wrong, it is a matter of individual choice for the parties when they
  are adults and use contraception to prevent the danger of genetic
  defects in children. The Crown Attorney argued that incest strikes at
  the heart of the family and the rights of society far outweigh the
  rights of the individual. Judge Carver agreed. He said that while
  Charter rights provide an individual with the freedom to move and
  act freely within an imaginary fence: "When an individual lives in a
  society outside that fence, the legislature is free to pass legislation for
  the good of society." What do you think of this holding? Is there any
  analogy between it and the argument of the majority in *Egan*? Would
  Dworkin classify Judge Carver's argument as a moral position?

Bowers v Hardwick (1986)

A case in which the U.S. Supreme Court upheld the Georgia law outlawing consensual sodomy. The majority argues that, because homosexuality has traditionally been judged to be immoral, the state is entitled to prohibit it.

Justice White delivered the opinion of the Court: – In August 1982, respondent Hardwick (hereafter respondent) was charged with violating the Georgia statute criminalizing sodomy[1] by committing that act with another adult male in the bedroom of respondent's home. After a preliminary hearing, the District Attorney decided not to present the matter to the grand jury unless further evidence developed. Respondent then brought suit in the Federal District Court, challenging the constitutionality of the statute insofar as it criminalized consensual sodomy.[2]

This case does not require a judgment on whether laws against sodomy between consenting adults in general, or between homosexuals in particular, are wise or desirable. It raises no question about the right or propriety of state legislative decisions to repeal their laws that criminalize homosexual sodomy, or of state-court decisions invalidating those laws on state constitutional grounds. The issue presented is whether the Federal Constitution confers a fundamental right upon homosexuals to engage in sodomy and hence invalidates the laws of the many States that still make such conduct illegal and have done so for a very long time. The case also calls for some judgment about the limits of the Court's role in carrying out its constitutional mandate.

We first register our disagreement with the Court of Appeals and with respondent that the Court's prior cases have construed the Constitution to confer a right of privacy that extends to homosexual sodomy and for all intents and purposes have decided this case ...

Precedent aside, however, respondent would have us announce, as the Court of Appeals did, a fundamental right to engage in homosexual sodomy. This we are quite unwilling to do.

Striving to assure itself and the public that announcing rights not readily identifiable in the Constitution's text involves much more than the imposition of the Justices' own choice of values on the States and the Federal Government, the Court has sought to identify the nature of the rights qualifying for heightened judicial protection. In *Palko v Connecticut*, it was said that this category includes those fundamental liberties that are "implicit in the concept of ordered liberty," such that "neither liberty nor justice would exist if [they] were sacrificed." A different description of fundamental liberties appeared in *Moore v East Cleveland*, where they are characterized as those liberties that are "deeply rooted in this Nation's history and tradition."

It is obvious that neither of these formulations would extend a fundamental right to homosexuals to engage in acts of consensual sodomy. Proscriptions against that conduct have ancient roots ... Sodomy was a criminal offense at common law and was forbidden by the laws of the original 13 States when they ratified the Bill of Rights. In 1868, when the Fourteenth Amendment was ratified, all but 5 of the 37 States in the Union had criminal sodomy laws.

In fact, until 1961, all 50 States outlawed sodomy, and today, 24 States and the District of Columbia continue to provide criminal penalties for sodomy performed in private and between consenting adults ... Against this background, to claim that a right to engage in such conduct is "deeply rooted in this Nation's history and tradition" or "implicit in the concept of ordered liberty" is, at best, facetious.

Victimless crimes, such as the possession and use of illegal drugs, do not escape the law where they are committed at home ... Offered no protection for the possession in the home of drugs, firearms, or stolen goods. And if respondent's submission is limited to the voluntary sexual conduct between consenting adults, it would be difficult, except by fiat, to limit the claimed right to homosexual conduct while leaving exposed to prosecution adultery, incest, and other sexual crimes even though they are committed in the home. We are unwilling to start down that road.

... This is essentially not a question of personal "preferences" but rather of the legislative authority of the State. I find nothing in the Constitution depriving a State of the power to enact the statute challenged here.

Dissent: Justice Blackmun – This case is no more about "a fundamental right to engage in homosexual sodomy," as the Court purports to declare, than *Stanley v Georgia* was about a fundamental right to watch obscene movies, or *Katz v United States* was about a fundamental right to place interstate bets from a telephone booth. Rather, this case is about "the most comprehensive of rights and the right most valued by civilized men," namely, "the right to be let alone."

... I believe that "[it] is revolting to have no better reason for a rule of law than that so it was laid down in the time of Henry IV. It is still more revolting if the grounds upon which it was laid down have vanished long since, and the rule simply persists from blind imitation of the past."[3] I believe we must analyze respondent Hardwick's claim in the light of the values that underlie the constitutional right to privacy. If that right means anything, it means that, before Georgia can prosecute its citizens for making choices about the most intimate aspects of their lives, it must do more than assert that the choice they have made is an "abominable crime not fit to be named among Christians."

I cannot agree that either the length of time a majority has held its convictions or the passions with which it defends them can withdraw legislation from this Court's scrutiny. That certain, but by no means all, religious groups condemn the behavior at issue gives the State no license to impose their judgments on the entire citizenry. The legitimacy of secular legislation depends instead on whether the State can advance some justification for its law beyond its conformity to religious doctrine. ... Thus, far from buttressing his case, petitioner's invocation of Leviticus, Romans, St Thomas Aquinas, and sodomy's heretical status during the Middle Ages undermines his suggestion that s. 16-6-2 represents a legitimate use of secular coercive power.

NOTES

1 Georgia Code Ann. at 16-6-2 (1984) provides, in pertinent part, as follows: "(a) A person commits the offense of sodomy when he performs or submits to any sexual act involving the sex organs of one person and the mouth or anus of another ... (b) A person convicted of the offense of sodomy shall be punished by imprisonment for not less than one nor more than 20 years ..."

2 John and Mary Doe were also plaintiffs in the action. They alleged that they wished to engage in sexual activity proscribed by 16-6-2 in the privacy of their home, App. 3, and that they had been "chilled and deterred" from engaging in such activity by both the existence of the statute and Hardwick's arrest. Ibid., at 5. The District Court held, however, that because they had neither sustained, nor were in immediate danger of sustaining, any direct injury from the enforcement of the statute, they did not have proper standing to maintain the action. Ibid., at 18. The Court of

Appeals affirmed the District Court's judgment dismissing the Does' claim for lack of standing, 760 F.2d 1202, 1206–1207 (CA11 1985), and the Does do not challenge that holding in this Court.

3   Holmes, *The Path of the Law*, 10 Harv L Rev 457, 469 (1897).

Michael M. v Gerald D. [1989] 491 U.S. 110

The U.S. Supreme Court upheld a California law establishing a conclusive presumption that the husband of the mother of a child was the child's father for legal purposes. The excerpt concerns the question of how broadly or narrowly traditions are to be interpreted in addressing issues of due process.

Opinion by Scalia, J ... We do not understand why, having rejected our focus upon the societal tradition regarding the natural father's rights vis-à-vis a child whose mother is married to another man, Justice Brennan would choose to focus instead upon "parenthood." Why should the relevant category not be even more general – perhaps "family relationships"; or "personal relationships"; or even "emotional attachments in general"? Though the dissent has no basis for the level of generality it would select, we do: We refer to the most specific level at which a relevant tradition protecting, or denying protection to, the asserted right can be identified. If, for example, there were no societal tradition, either way, regarding the rights of the natural father of a child adulterously conceived, we would have to consult, and (if possible) reason from, the traditions regarding natural fathers in general. But there is such a more specific tradition, and it unqualifiedly denies protection to such a parent. One would think that Justice Brennan would appreciate the value of consulting the most specific tradition available, since he acknowledges that "[e]ven if we can agree ... that "family" and "parenthood" are part of the good life, it is absurd to assume that we can agree on the content of those terms and destructive to pretend that we do." Because such general traditions provide such imprecise guidance, they permit judges to dictate rather than discern the society's views.

Brennan, J (Dissenting): – Wherever I would begin to look for an interest "deeply rooted in the country's traditions," one thing is certain:

I would not stop (as does the plurality) at Bracton, or Blackstone, or Kent, or even the American Law Reports in conducting my search. Because reasonable people can disagree about the content of particular traditions, and because they can disagree even about which traditions are relevant to the definition of "liberty," the plurality has not found the objective boundary that it seeks. Even if we could agree, moreover, on the content and significance of particular traditions, we still would be forced to identify definition of liberty and the moment at which it becomes too obsolete to be relevant any longer.

... The plurality's interpretive method is more than novel; it is misguided. It ignores the good reasons for limiting the role of "tradition" in interpreting the Constitution's deliberately capacious language. In the plurality's constitutional universe, we may not take notice of the fact that the original reasons for the conclusive presumption of paternity are out of place in a world in which blood tests can prove virtually beyond a shadow of a doubt who sired a particular child and in which the fact of illegitimacy no longer plays the burdensome and stigmatizing role it once did. Nor, in the plurality's world, may we deny "tradition" its full scope by pointing out that the rationale for the conventional rule has changed over the years ... instead, our task is simply to identify a rule denying the asserted interest and not to ask whether the basis for that rule – which is the true reflection of the values undergirding it – has changed too often or too recently to call the rule embodying that rationale a "tradition."

READING QUESTIONS ON BOWERS AND MICHAEL M.

1 Why does the Court suppose tradition is important? How broadly or narrowly should it be interpreted? Is there a principled answer to this question?

Jody Freeman
"Defining Family in *Mossop v DSS*: The Challenge of Anti-Essentialism and Interactive Discrimination for Human Rights Litigation" (1994)

Freeman argues that the law should reflect different contemporary understandings of the family. Her article provides insight into *Charter* litigation in a progressive cause, as well as outlining a "post-modern" basis for such litigation.

INTRODUCTION

This article is a narrative about the construction of a legal argument: a close analysis of the intervenors' factum in *Mossop v DSS*, a case recently decided by the Supreme Court of Canada, in which a gay man argued that his exclusion from an employment benefit constituted discrimination on the basis of family status in contravention of the *Canadian Human Rights Act (CHRA)*. The intervention brought together a broad and diverse coalition of interests, including Equality for Gays and Lesbians Everywhere, the National Action Committee on the Status of Women, the Canadian Disability Rights Council, the National Association of Women and the Law, and the Canadian Rights and Liberties Federation. The coalition's intervention in *Mossop* can be understood from a variety of perspectives. For some, it is a gay rights test case; for others, it is an attempt to demythologize the traditional family; and for still others, it represents an attempt to infuse human rights interpretation with notions of anti-essentialism and interactive discrimination. The factum is interesting both methodologically and substantively; one of its lessons is that a self-conscious and critical process is essential to the development of a self-conscious and critical legal argument.

Collaborating on this project blurred for me the already suspect distinction between legal practice and legal scholarship. Virtually every paragraph of the factum is the product of heated debate about the appropriateness of a particular theoretical framework, the symbolic importance of a word choice, the long-term implications of one argument over another, the likelihood of persuading the audience, and the chance of "winning." Each of these debates usually led to another, deeper discussion about why theory is important in the first place, to what extent word choice or long-term considerations ought to matter, whether we really agreed about who the audience was, and what "winning" might be in the context. The experience of contributing to this factum was extraordinarily rich for me for a number of reasons: the inclusive and collaborative process established by Gwen Brodsky, the intervenors' counsel, at the outset; the combination of powerful intellects working on the factum from a variety of perspectives; and the challenges presented by the legal and social issues. *Mossop* was treated by Ms Brodsky in keeping with the tradition of her *Charter* and human rights litigation to date. She calls her procedural method "participatory litigation," by which she means that the litigation process is substantially democratized and inclusive, compared with the traditional model of solicitor/client relations: "I believe that this transformation of the litigation process is essential to the realization of the egalitarian goals that drive the equality rights movement." The factum was constructed with ongoing consultation among the five groups comprising the coalition, Ms Brodsky, and her staff. The intervenors participated in a serious and substantive way, reviewing drafts of the factum, voicing their concerns, and approving the direction of the litigation. The process facilitated a thoughtful and energetic treatment of some very complicated issues, both technical and deeply philosophical. It enabled participants, regardless of status and formal rank, to advance novel conceptual paradigms or legal arguments without fear that they would be prematurely dismissed as too risky or unreasonable. This experience, and others, have convinced me that test case litigation benefits immeasurably from a process that mirrors its substantive social vision. Not only do the participants feel that their contribution, and the litigation in general, is meaningful, but the final product is inevitably superior to one conceived and borne of a closed, non-consultative process. As I explain, elaborate upon, and then critique the factum, the link between methodology and substance should be clear.

THE PROBLEM

Although most people have an image of what constitutes a "traditional" family, neither legislation nor the common law reflects a consistent definition. In fact, the legal definition of family continues to evolve over time along with the reality of social life. And yet, the field of "family" law is implicitly based on a heterosexual norm. Although no statute explicitly defines "family" for all purposes, and despite the fact that one can find inconsistency in the definition if one searches for it, an impressive variety of legislation, legal holdings, rules, and omission, taken together, nonetheless reinforce the notion that a "normal" family comprises two heterosexual parents and their children.[1] These legal interpretations are only part of the vast array of cultural messages that are responsible for the dominance of the image of "normality" that most people draw upon when asked to define family. As part of culture, both legislation and judge-made law contribute to the social pressure to conform to a mythologized traditional family, but law is not the only, nor is it necessarily the most powerful, social force. Popular culture overwhelmingly reinforces the dominance of the "traditional" family form, as reflected in the media, advertising, television, music, and theatre. Single-parent families are represented as anomalous and unfortunate; they are held in contempt, vilified, and blamed for a number of social ills including maladjusted children and welfare dependency. Positive cultural representations of counterexamples to the traditional, heterosexual, two-parent family are relatively rare. Social institutions, to the extent that they are "family-friendly" at all, are designed to meet the needs of traditional, and not alternative, families. This broader cultural message is often most strictly enforced in the context of our own families. Who of us can claim to have been raised in an environment where remaining single, getting a divorce, or being gay would not be viewed as a failure, or where choosing not to have children would be greeted with the same enthusiasm as the announcement that one is pregnant?

In its factum, the coalition exposes this paradox – that despite inconsistent and evolving definitions of family in legislation, and a great variety of families in contemporary society, a dominant conception of the family persists. The intervenors' argument is that no single, all-purpose definition of family is accurate or defensible. Families that do not conform to the traditional model might include single-parent families, extended families, unmarried people who consider themselves family but do not meet common law criteria, and gay men and lesbians. In order to include such relationships, the intervenors advance an anti-essentialist definition of family, one that is non-discriminatory and justifiable in the light of the legislative provision or specific regulation to which the definition is linked.

The coalition makes a conscious attempt in its factum to discredit the pervasive notion that only heterosexual couples with children are families, while resisting the temptation to supply the Court with a new universal definition. In marked contrast to the appellant, the Canadian Human Rights Commission (CHRC), and in direct opposition to the respondent, the Department of the Secretary of State (DSS) and its supporting intervenors,[2] the factum challenges essentialist understandings of family in general, and socially constructed stereotypes of gay men and lesbians in particular. In addition, by asserting that sexual orientation and family status discrimination are inseparable in this case, it invites the Court to acknowledge the interactive and multiple nature of discrimination. Finally, the intervenors' factum might be viewed as an example of postmodern legal argument.[3] Although postmodernism means different things to different people, and is met with hostility by those who view its critique of modernity as potentially nihilist, a postmodern "stance" in difficult cases like *Mossop* makes it possible to see contradictions and impasses as opportunities for contesting settled meanings and suggesting creative remedies. This stance is borne out in a number of the factum's features: its insistence on the falsity of universals; its refusal to choose between dichotomized alternatives; its emphasis on the indeterminacy of interpretation; and its reliance on contextualized argument. Confronted with the confines and limitations of legal argument in general, and rights discourse in particular, lawyers and academics are sometimes tempted to abandon it entirely as a means of progressive social change, or to condemn its radical transformative potential in a fit of antirationalism. The intervenors' factum in *Mossop* resists that temptation without ignoring the critical lessons which lead to it. In my view, this factum's innovative strategies sit, albeit uncomfortably, somewhere between the scepticism of those with no faith in the liberatory potential of the legal system, and the hope of those who wish to see it transformed from within. My own justification for engaging in test case litigation is that law is a critical site of struggle over meaning, although by no means the only one. And although the factum is vulnerable to critiques that it is either too radical, too liberal, too moderate, or inadequately feminist, it represents a laudable attempt to place anti-essentialism and intersection theory at the heart of the interpretation of human rights legislation ...

THE PERSPECTIVE IN THE SUPREME COURT OF CANADA OF THE INTERVENORS

Two goals seemed to me to inform the construction of the factum during its early stages: that it perform an educative function by exposing both the variety of families currently existing in Canadian society and the ideological role that the dominant conception of family plays in our socialization; and that it demonstrate convincingly how the denial of bereavement leave was experienced by Mossop as a denial of his family, such that he suffered *both* family status discrimination and discrimination on the basis of sexual orientation. The coalition's position was supportive of Mossop's desire for legal recognition of his family, but over time, the intervenors' factum differed substantially from that of the CHRC by challenging the coherence of the conception of family itself. The coalition rejected not only the CHRC's philosophical approach, but also its analysis of the legal and ideological issues before the Court and the CHRC's choice of remedy. The CHRC adopted what could be described as a "sameness" approach to equality, arguing that Mossop's relationship with Popert was "just like" a heterosexual relationship, and that this equivalence entitled the two men to inclusion within the ground family status. If the Court were to accept this argument, an appropriate remedy would be to amend the definition of family in the collective agreement to include same-sex couples. Although such an amendment would have satisfied the order of the human rights tribunal, it would have imposed criteria on same-sex relationships that many could not meet, and the result would still amount to discrimination on the basis of family status. The remedies sought by the intervenors, to eliminate the family relationship qualification for granting bereavement leave, or to define family in an open-ended way, were also consistent with the tribunal's order. They had the advantage, as well, of eliminating entirely family status discrimination. The CHRC's remedial approach, in the end, left the ideological force of the dominant conception of family unexplored and did not fully ameliorate the discriminatory impact of the sameness strategy.

THE SOCIAL REALITY OF FAMILIES

Demographic research demonstrates that intimate relationships do not overwhelmingly fit the dominant norm for family. In fact, there is a variety of "family" forms in Canadian society: many children do not live in traditional nuclear families with two heterosexual parents; single parents with children and step-parent or step-sibling relationships are prevalent and on the rise; divorce statistics are high; and many couples are childless. There are no statistics available for how many families are non-traditional, because official census definitions reflect only the traditional model. Organizations of people into what they call their families occurs for a number of highly contingent reasons that vary with age, circumstance, religion, economics, race, and gender, among other considerations. Variety exists not only in terms of the form of relationships (some of which people can consciously alter through decisions to marry, divorce, remarry, adopt, cohabit, etc., and others of which are "inherited") but also in terms of how they function. Some families are more affectionate than others, for example, or more abusive than others. They are bound together with different degrees of emotional, intellectual, and economic dependence. Some relationships are more easily recognized as family by outsiders and by the legal regime. Although one could provide a list of features that are common to many self-regarding families, it is difficult to define the "essence" of family. Some couples have children, while others do not; some related individuals share a residence, while others do not; some married people share their finances, while others do not; and so on. In the face of this diversity, the notion of a "core" definition of family becomes increasingly unworkable.

As noted earlier, however, neither federal nor provincial legislation reflects a consistent definition of family, even if the definition of spouse is consistently heterosexual. The meaning of family varies with legislative purpose. For example, individuals may be deemed a family for the purpose of receiving income assistance under welfare legislation, but not for the purpose of income tax legislation. Further, over time, legal definitions of family have evolved, along with social attitudes. Legislative reforms, both federal and provincial, have extended the status of family to common law spouses. "Illegitimate" children are no longer denied status as equal to "legitimate" ones. Social resistance to interracial marriage has declined over time as well. In the face of this legislative and social history, in the light of the broad purpose of the *CHRA*, and given that legislative intent is neither clear nor determinative, it is remarkable that the Federal Court of Appeal and the federal government could insist that family has a single, all-purpose meaning. Family is less a fact than it is a product of legal and social regulation and ideology. Only by blinding itself both to the lack of consistency in the legal regulation of the family and to the existing diversity of people's affiliations could the Court interpret family status in the *CHRA* to be limited to heterosexuals.

A restrictive interpretation of family status would effectively freeze human rights legislation and significantly widen the gap between law and social life. The coalition's factum argues that it would exclude from the reach of the *CHRA* those who most need protection from discrimination, precisely because they have historically lacked "status." The coalition argued that this interpretation would be inconsistent with the purposes of human rights legislation, which include the amelioration of group disadvantage, the breakdown of negative stereotypes, and the recognition of the inherent dignity and value of all persons. The Supreme Court has approached the interpretation of human rights legislation purposively, with a view to furthering its goals, and it has focused on the effects of the discrimination complained of, regardless of whether it was intentional or not. Moreover, the Court has taken pains to assess the effects of discrimination in its specific context, and from the perspective of those victimized by it. The intervenors argued that it was fully consistent with the Court's recent jurisprudence to consider the meaning of family status from the perspective of those most affected by exclusion from the category, including gay men and lesbians.

Implicit in the coalition's position is the notion that a legal decision about what constitutes a family is necessarily normative, and has an important symbolic or legitimating force. Judicial decisions proclaim "truths" in the course of resolving particular disputes. Even if only indirectly or diffusely, judicial pronouncements can reinforce and alter social views. Of course, it is virtually impossible to measure the isolated impact of a single decision; but as part of the barrage of authoritative messages from the State, the Supreme Court's refusal to acknowledge the diversity of affiliative relationships and accord them human rights protection would send a powerful message to society about what an "appropriate" and "normal" family relationship looks like. Individuals are likely to internalize authoritative proclamations emanating from courts and other institutions that are seen as neutral and rational, and that have achieved a special cultural status. As a result, their impact can be hurtful personally, as well as inhibiting to movement building. An adverse decision in a case like *Mossop* could provide the legal backdrop against which oppressive actions emanating from the State, private organizations, and individuals might seem justifiable.[4]

The coalition's factum describes the increasing variety of family life and juxtaposes it with the idealized, traditional model of the two-heterosexual-parent family with children. The factum demythologizes the family, and provides the Court with a more realistic image of the diversity of affiliative relationships. Demythologizing the family meant exposing the function of family ideology and explaining how its pervasiveness insulates conventional families from criticism, helps maintain the invisibility of child and spousal abuse, reinforces heterosexuality as the only legitimate sexual identity (thereby fuelling and legitimizing homophobia), and denies non-conforming families the material and psychological benefits of recognition and legitimation.

This section of the factum relies heavily on "fact," including data collected to contradict prevailing beliefs about family, beliefs that appear to be obvious and to make "common sense" until interrogated. Here the factum contrasts the model of family that pervades our legal and political rhetoric with empirical facts about the prevalence of single-parent families, families comprising gay people both with and without children, and childless families, all of which deviate from the imagined norm. The Court's interpretation of family status in the *CHRA*, the intervenors argued, should be informed by social reality, not fiction and ideology.

The factum also provides the Court with positive images of gay men and lesbians ...

This strategy directly confronts, and seeks to correct, assumptions that often lurk in the minds of even well-intentioned people: that gay men and lesbians do not reproduce; that they are bad parents; that they do not love; or that if they do, it is a lesser love than that shared between heterosexuals. It seemed possible that the judges' subconscious views might influence their ability even to imagine family status in an inclusive way. Ideally, the factum provided judges the impetus for careful scrutiny of their own, perhaps unintentional, biases.[5]

ANTI-ESSENTIALISM

The demographic evidence made it increasingly difficult to imagine that any single definition of family could capture the diversity of relationships that regard each other as such, even if providing one might have comforted the Court. To me, the factum's educative function gave birth to its anti-essentialism. Being anti-essentialist in this context meant refusing to use an abstract and universal definition intended to capture the 'essence' of family because it would be indefensibly reductive and exclude a wide variety of affiliations.

And yet, even armed with social science evidence, reaching the rather destabilizing conclusion that family has no core meaning was a struggle for some of us working on the factum in its early stages. It seemed, intuitively, that family had to be "fundamentally" about something. Some of us agonized over this problem, trying on, and then discarding, a series of possible definitions. At one point, it seemed that the only common denominator of all families was love, and a moving paragraph to this effect was written into the factum. Although it survived several overhauls and rewrites, the love paragraph was eventually criticized as idealistic, factually wrong, and, as with many other definitions of family, essentialist. At one meeting it was even referred to as "romantic drivel." In an ideal world, love might lie at the heart of all families, but in reality, many relationships endure for a variety of reasons that have nothing to do with love. Rather, they are sustained by the desire for companionship, the needs of children, a sense of obligation, or convenience, among other things. Still, relationships held together for these reasons, rather than love, are not less worthy of respect and recognition than those that fit the romantic model. The love paragraph was, in the end, deleted.

The process of letting the love paragraph go forced me to confront my own discomfort with the idea that family eluded an essence, and perhaps any attempt at definition, a discomfort that I suspected judges might feel more intensely. It seemed to follow logically from the anti-essentialist argument that the definition of family was arbitrary, even meaningless, and that any group of people could plausibly argue that they were one. The heart of the debate was whether there should be any minimal requirements that people must meet to "qualify" for the label family. To some extent, however, getting lost in the question of what "counts" as family in general was unnecessary to resolve the problem of providing employees bereavement leave in a manner that did not discriminate on the basis of family status.

Why, many of us wondered during the construction of the factum, use the category of "family" at all? Should I not receive paid leave to attend, say, Elvis Presley's funeral, I asked at one point, if his death means more to me than the death of someone whom others would regard as a member of my "family"? Would my unrequited regard for Elvis make him a member of my family? It may be true that people take leave more often to mourn the death of those others regard as closest to them, but was the determination of who "counted most," in this way, not very subjective? The example was not meant to be funny; it raised a serious issue and forced me, and others, to think through the factum's position. The idea that there are no limits on the definition of family would likely bother any judge, and might be raised by the bench in oral argument.

The factum's response to the "Elvis Presley problem" as the concern about limits came to be known, is that the definition of family need not be meaningless or arbitrary, but should be linked to the purpose of the legislation, or the benefit at issue. For example, the purpose of bereavement leave is to acknowledge that individual's need to mourn the loss of those close to them, or support others who must mourn. Limiting the class of relationships one is entitled to mourn without losing a day's pay to an employer-imposed definition of family might undermine this purpose. The crux of the argument is that a definition of family in the context of employment benefits ought not to be limited to those whom the state, or an employer recognizes as a family member but expanded to include people the employee cares about, respects, depends upon, or with whom he or she shares a special relationship. That relationship, in my view (although this was not stated in the factum), need not even be reciprocal to be considered close enough to merit this special status. Even in many traditional family relationships, the degree of closeness is not mutual. Two remedies would solve this problem: the employer could limit the number of days of bereavement leave for all employees, to be used at their discretion, avoiding entirely the need to define family. Or, if the employer were wed to the idea of bereavement leave only for a category of people known as "family members," the employer could permit employees to supply a list of those they regarded as family, honouring the subjectivity of the definition.

Although both of these solutions would work, in the sense of fulfilling the purpose of the benefit without imposing a limited definition of family on employees, it seemed that the Elvis Presley problem would not go away. This was because it raised two questions that often became intertwined: for what deaths should employees be permitted to take bereavement leave, and, if that leave is restricted to "immediate family" members, as in the case at bar, could any relationship qualify as "immediate family" just because someone makes that claim? The first question seemed easier to answer, but the second was more important because the intervenors were accepting Mossop's contention that he and the Poperts were a family, and arguing that he had suffered discrimination on the basis of family status. If Mossop and Popert's relationship were defensible as a "family," would the Court not expect the intervenors to say why, and to set limits on what relationships would qualify? Would this not lead to a comparison between their relationship and that of conventional heterosexual couples, in effect, the approach taken by the tribunal? In the end, the factum did not supply a single definition of family but it did insist that Mossop, Popert, and Popert, Sr, were a family because Mossop regarded them as such, and it did suggest that in the context of bereavement leave, the definition of immediate family should be subjectively determined.

Thus, the Elvis Presley problem had troublesome ripple effects. Having gone down a path from anti-essentialism to meaninglessness, and back again, it seemed potentially contradictory to argue that Mossop and Popert were a family, a claim which arguably presumes the coherence and stability of the category. It was as if we had destroyed the club to which we now demanded entry. But closer analysis revealed that these two aspects of the coalition's position were not inconsistent. The point of arguing against abstract universal definitions and in favour of context-based, purposive definitions is to recognize and include families that are excluded from legal and social recognition simply because they are seen to deviate from the established norm. The argument is not that "family" is meaningless, but that its meaning is subjective and shifting. The challenge was to achieve recognition of Mossop's family, but not at the cost of reinforcing an exclusionary definition.

Despite the absence of a "core" meaning, particular definitions of family might be defensible in terms of the purpose of legislation. The prohibition on family status discrimination might have a broader reach than benefits or burdens assigned on the basis of membership in a family. For example, as counsel for the intervenors argued, government entitlements intended for children might be available only to relationships involving children. Such legislation could justifiably prevent all self-regarding families, or singles without children, from claiming the entitlement, but it need not distinguish between families on the basis of the parents' sexual orientation. This approach would at least require the government to justify their definitions of family with reference to the purpose of any given benefit. An explicitly homophobic purpose would arguably violate section 15 of the *Charter*.

There are three common reactions to this position: first, that if the meaning of family is so unstable, laws will be inconsistent, and inconsistency leads to unpredictability, which is a bad thing; second, that extending the category of family to those not traditionally thought of as family might suggest that family includes even single people, which seems ludicrous at first glance; and third, that adopting a flexible definition of family may permit "selective opting-in," where people would pick and choose when they want to be considered family, in order to claim the benefits and avoid the burdens of such a status. In response to the first point, a historical analysis reveals that instability and inconsistency already plague legislation. More importantly, however, inconsistency is far preferable to an imposed definition of family that discriminates against some families in favour of others, providing it is justifiable in the light of the purpose of the legislation.

On the second point, it seems very plausible that family status protection could extend to singles in some case, if, for example, they were excluded from employment benefits, or access to housing arbitrarily, simply because of their non-married status. Again, a particular context might require a broader or narrower definition of what constitutes a family. The factum uses the *Charter* guarantee of freedom of religion as a useful analogy here. It seems clear that atheists should be protected by the *Charter* guarantee of freedom of religion, even though one might think of them as not having a religion, and as therefore outside the scope of the right. Discrimination against atheists because they do not partake of dominant religion can still interfere with their freedom *from* religion. Singles might be thought of, then, as the atheists of familial ideology.

Finally, concerns about abuse should be confronted directly by employers, and should apply to heterosexuals as well as to gay men and lesbians. There is no evidence to support the assertion that lesbians and gay men would take more advantage of flexible bereavement leave provisions than would heterosexuals, but safeguards could be put in place if they were deemed necessary (a position the coalition did not support). An employer concerned about abuse might have to police *everyone* who claims to be a family, a practice which, although raising privacy concerns, is at least non-discriminatory. Judges might also be reluctant to accord to non-traditional families what they see as benefits, without assigning them the perceived burdens associated with marriage. Although this differs from an employee who takes advantage of flexible definitions, it might be viewed by judges as another potential form of abuse. Precisely this reasoning, even though it is deeply flawed, has been employed to prevent the recognition of same-sex marriage.

There is, in fact, no reason to believe that people who form non-traditional families want all of the advantages and none of the disadvantages of legal recognition, nor is it entirely clear what counts, or ought to count, as an advantage. Fear that the disadvantages of being deemed a family by the state will outweigh the advantages, particularly for those with lower incomes, may be one reason why some gay men and lesbians do not want recognition as family. But for those who seek legal recognition, burdens may be as welcome as benefits. Still, the question of concomitant burdens is irrelevant to whether the denial of employment benefits in this case contravened human rights legislation. The issue is not discussed in the factum because, as Ms Brodsky put it, even having to raise it would impose on the appellants an unfair burden. Those who suffer discrimination should not be required to agree to "package deals" as a condition of obtaining their rights.

Although they were not explicit in the factum, counsel in oral argument addressed the problems associated with a functional definition of family, and rejected it as both discriminatory and administratively unworkable. This approach isolated common features of the traditional family (for example, a joint bank account, a shared residence, the public holding out of the relationship) and uses them as a checklist against which people claiming to be a family are measured. The coalition rejected, on the basis of this argument, the CHRC's proposed remedy of including same-sex couples within the definition of common law spouse because it would not solve the problem of imposing discriminatory criteria on only some relationships.

Some people, gay rights advocates among them, would argue that a functional approach makes sense because some indicators of "family" are, in fact, fairly common. A checklist of features might even appear to pose less of an administrative burden than a vague, shifting notion of family. Most importantly, a functional approach may be palatable as a compromise of sorts: it introduces some flexibility into the definition of family, without conceding the idea that family cannot be objectively determined. On a narrow interpretation of the functional approach, if a gay couple functions like a heterosexual couple, that is, if they do the things families are meant to do, and look the way families are meant to look (apart from being of the same gender, of course), they ought to be recognized as a family.

Although the hurdles established by a functional test could be cleared by some gay men and lesbians, it is problematic. Embracing such an approach strikes some as requiring that gays argue they are essentially "the same" as heterosexuals; it forces them to mimic heterosexual relationships and confines them to a narrow, unimaginative conception of family life. And even if this were not a serious concern, it remains true that the most common features of the traditional family, such as a shared residence or pooled finances, are by no means universal. The checklist test is often criticized for being both internally flawed and assimilationist: internally flawed, because even married heterosexuals do not consistently meet its standards and are nonetheless assumed to be families; assimilationist, because it forces families to look the same in order for them to receive benefits heterosexuals get just because they are heterosexual.

Although in theory a broader functionalist approach might be defensible (a more creative and flexible list might include love, intimacy, respect, and the provision of care, for example, along with shared assets, mutual dependency, cohabitation, a sexual relationship, children, and so forth), its application in practice is what worries most people. Even a broad test represents an administrative morass, since it would call for inquiries into the most intimate aspects of people's lives. How would the state or an employer test for the "intention to continue to be spouses," which is required even of common law couples under the definition of "immediate family" in the collective agreement? What amounts to a public "holding out" as spouses? Would gay couples have to prove, somehow, their sexual fidelity, or their love of reach other? Would they need to pool their finances, and jointly own all property? If they had no assets, what would count as a commitment to partnership? although some gay people would certainly benefit from the application of such a test, its effect would be to create a dichotomy between "good" gay people and "bad" gay people, the former being those who behave in ways that make their relationships recognizable to heterosexuals.

Many gay men and lesbians do not share a residence, use joint bank accounts, or hold themselves out to the public as a "couple" precisely because they risk being victimized on the basis of their sexual orientation and family status. And even though many heterosexual married couples do not conform to these criteria, they are nonetheless automatically recognized as family. The question is, why should a test be applied to homosexual couples, and not to heterosexual ones? The only explanation for such differential treatment is that heterosexual couples are viewed as the norm, and as more natural than gay and lesbian couples. Thus, families that have not been legally or socially recognized must "qualify" as families by achieving the heterosexual standard. Common law couples are still routinely subject to these kinds of discriminatory tests, such as the requirement that they hold themselves out as spouses and intend to remain together. People who regard themselves as a family are no less so simply because they arrange their relationship differently from the traditional norm. A checklist of features used to determine who is "in" and who is "out" of family normalizes the dominant conception of family, and reinforces the notion that difference is deviance. Resort to such a test leaves intact the hierarchy of heterosexual over same-sex relationships. It thus preserves the exclusionary function of family, albeit with slightly adjusted boundaries.

In other words, if the recognition of gay couples as families only reinforces the already idealized conception of family without challenging it, and if inclusion in the prohibited ground family status means looking, acting, and functioning like traditional families, many lesbians and gay men would undoubtedly forgo legal and social recognition. Not that such a view is universal. Some people would be perfectly content to submit to a functional test. They would claim to be just like heterosexuals in all relevant ways and argue for similar treatment. Counsel for the CHRC effectively adopted this position in his submissions to be Supreme Court of Canada, arguing that Mossop was entitled to bereavement leave because his relationship was *analogous* to that of a traditional family. Critics would call it an assimilationist argument.

This issue provokes vigorous disagreement within gay, lesbian, and heterosexual communities, which extends to the question of what acceptance as "family" would mean. While some argue that asking for legal and social recognition as "family" reinforces the norm of the traditional family, others say that the inclusion of gay men and lesbians within the concept would necessarily change that norm. In a related debate, many gay men and lesbians staunchly oppose the idea of same-sex marriage as a tribute to a sexist and homophobic institution. It should be resisted, even dismantled, but certainly not embraced, they say. Others argue that recognizing marriage between gay men or lesbians would revolutionize its meaning. Some gay men and lesbians reject any attempt at "inclusion" on the basis that their relationships *are* different from the norm, just as they are different from each other. Proponents of this view prefer not to be compared to heterosexuals, and do not want their relationships legalized and regulated.

The intervenors' factum rejects both sides of the "inclusion/exclusion" dichotomy, and argues that recognition as family need not amount to the acceptance of its traditional meaning. Exposing the harmful, exclusionary effect of popular mythology about the family, the coalition seems to be saying, is consistent with the notion that being recognized as family for the purpose of human rights protection is important to some gay men and lesbians. In fact, legal recognition can represent significant material, psychological, and symbolic benefits. And (although the factum does not make the point, for reasons stated earlier) even if legal recognition would eventually be accompanied by the imposition of some burdens on gay couples, such as support obligations, these would be welcomed by some individuals if the result yielded a reduction in social stigma and discrimination. Some activists think concerns about assimilation are inflated and misplaced. The important thing, they say, is to win the legal argument and get the benefit desired, not to insist on an anti-assimilationist position for its own sake. The factum, however, does not support this view. Instead, it claims inclusion and attempts to alter the category of family at the same time.

INTERACTIVE DISCRIMINATION

Another critical feature of the factum is its insistence on the multiplicity and inseparability of discrimination. The intervenors claimed two things that might seem contradictory in the light of the conventional way lawyers argue about discrimination: that Mossop was denied bereavement leave because he is gay, *and* that because his family was not recognized, he experienced the denial as discrimination on the basis of his family status. The Federal Court of Appeal held that the denial of bereavement leave constituted sexual orientation discrimination, and not family status discrimination. This technique of either/or characterization allowed the Federal Court to avoid dealing with the reality of how discrimination operates and is experienced, a reality which is infinitely more complex than its reflection in the tidy categories used to delineate different grounds of discrimination in human rights legislation. More specifically, it allowed the court to avoid considering family status entirely, as if, because Mossop is gay, non-recognition of his family ceases to be an issue.

Conveying to a court how different "kinds" of discrimination overlap and intersect is an enormous challenge. Jurisprudence and legal scholarship about discrimination have not, as a rule, been geared to determining how discrimination on the basis of race and sex, for example, work together. Equality analysis has paid scant attention to the ways in which discrimination may occur on multiple grounds. And yet, people often experience discrimination in precisely this way. They are denied a benefit or an opportunity because of their gender *and* their race, or their disability *and* their sexuality, or their race *and* their class. The effects of multiple discrimination are so entangled that they seem intransigent in the face of analytical attempts to separate them. Even if judges understand additive discrimination, that is, two different kinds of discrimination added together, they may not grasp the notion of interactive or overlapping discrimination, which is qualitatively different. For example, when women of colour are systematically excluded from certain job classifications, it may not be purely because they are women, or purely because they are not white, but due to the interaction of both. Similarly, when an openly gay man living with AIDS is denied housing, one might argue that it is because he is gay, or, alternatively, because of his disability, but in fact, it might be very difficult to separate the two.

This is not to say that discrimination can always be expressed in terms of two grounds. Some forms of discrimination on the basis of sexual orientation are unrelated to family status, or less related than others. For example, if an employee is refused a job because the employer assumes he is gay, and the employer dislikes gay men because he thinks them inadequately "male," the employee would have a difficult time establishing a claim that he suffered discrimination on the basis of his family status. Here, the discrimination arguably had nothing to do with the prospective employee's relationships, but stemmed from his perceived membership in the class "homosexual." Similarly, if an HIV-positive man is refused service in a restaurant because the owner knows or suspects he has the AIDS virus, it would be difficult to characterize the denial of service as family status discrimination, as opposed to discrimination on the basis of sexual orientation and/or disability.

But even if these examples are unconvincing, and one could imagine how every example of discrimination against gay men and lesbians could *potentially* involve both family status and sexual orientation discrimination, it would be at least a stretch to describe, say, physical assault, or a denial of health care of the basis of HIV-positivity, as discrimination on the basis of "family status." The strongest case for a "family status" argument arises where the benefit or opportunity sought hinges on membership in a family. Denying gay men and lesbians a benefit that flows to people *because* of their family relationships, a benefit triggered by a definition of family, such as bereavement leave, is the clearest instance of discrimination on both grounds.

Again, as with the Elvis Presley problem, the concern that recognizing interactive discrimination will cause uncertainty, or complicate legal decisions, is a concern about abuse. Acknowledging that interactive discrimination exists does not, realistically, raise the spectre of lawyers hopping arbitrarily from one combination of prohibited grounds to another, until they hit one that works. ("Well, my Lord, if it wasn't race and sex discrimination, then how about, um, religious and family status discrimination?") Courts are capable of distinguishing between fatuous and legitimate claims. Acknowledgment likely does mean, however, that judges will begin to understand the qualitative differences between people's experience of discrimination, enabling courts to recognize harms to which until now, they have been blind. And even if the concept of a continuum of grounds of discrimination (or better yet, a three-dimensional model) did create new possibilities for successful arguments based on interactive or coexisting kinds of discrimination, that is not necessarily a bad development. It could represent an important evolution in the judicial understanding of discrimination, one that should not be stunted by a "floodgates" paranoia.

The argument about interactive discrimination answers the Federal Court of Appeal's concern that Mossop and the intervenors were attempting to amend the *CHRA* "through the back door." The court was of the view that an inclusive interpretation of family status would effectively add sexual orientation to the statute. But this is simply not true. Family status protection would not provide a remedy for gay men and lesbians who face a wide variety of discriminatory practices, many of which are unrelated to their relationships. An interpretation of "family status" that acknowledges interactive discrimination would not necessarily provide a remedy to people who are physically assaulted, fired, and denied housing, among other things, simply because they are homosexual. Those interested in protecting gay men and lesbians from the entire spectrum of public and private abuses would still press the federal and provincial governments to amend human rights legislation to include sexual orientation as a prohibited ground. They would also continue to challenge the constitutionality of legislation and other state action that discriminates on the basis of sexual orientation, in violation of the *Charter*'s equality guarantees.

The intervenors' factum admonishes judges not simply to characterize discrimination away, in an effort to avoid dealing with its felt effects. For example, if a jurisdiction were to prohibit discrimination on the ground of disability, but not sexual orientation, a court could find that the exclusion of a gay man with AIDS from housing constitutes discrimination on the basis of sexual orientation alone, which would not contravene the legislation. In *Mossop*, the easiest way out of the perplexing dilemma of defining family was to understand the discrimination as stemming solely from sexual orientation, as the Federal Court of Appeal did, since the *CHRA* does not prohibit discrimination on this ground. The simple fact is that it will always be open to courts to prefer the least problematic categorization available, without regard for how discrimination is experienced by those subjected to it.

Obviously, the categorization game, like all interpretive techniques, is highly manipulable. If sexual orientation were a prohibited ground in the *CHRA*, instead of family status, the attorney general arguing *Mossop* would undoubtedly have claimed that the definition of 'immediate family' in the collective agreement discriminates on the basis of family status, not sexual orientation. One can be homosexual as much as one wants, he would argue, pointing to the fact that the employer makes no inquiry whatsoever into an employee's sexual practices under the terms of the collective agreement. He would assert that what matters is whether an employee's formal family arrangements conform to the definition in the collective agreement, not, technically, one's sexual preferences. Confronted with this argument, the intervenors would be forced to demonstrate how disingenuous this was, and how integral sexual orientation is to one's family arrangements, again highlighting the inseparability of sexual orientation and family status discrimination in this case. And so it goes. In this reverse situation, the characterization game still enables the Court to avoid addressing the injury done to Mossop.

POSTMODERN LEGAL ARGUMENT

This case points to the possibility of postmodernism as a strategic paradigm, even if it cannot be a specific agenda or a consistent methodology. Perhaps it is best understood in this context as a sensitivity to perspective and contingency, combined with a dislike for closure, topped off with a deep scepticism about the process of naturalization. I view the factum's anti-essentialism, its critical approach to the dominant conception of family, and its acknowledgment of interactive discrimination as postmodern because it challenges the notion that what is tradition is natural and therefore good, and advances the proposition that seemingly obvious meanings suppress others. The methodology of the factum is to argue from the margins (the experience of families who have no social or legal status), in a specific context (bereavement leave), without making overreaching, universal claims (anti-essentialism). Substantively, this translated into the argument that 'family' means different things in different legislative contexts, and that legal definitions, which tend to presume static subjects and conditions, do not correspond to the realities in which people lead their lives. The best we can do in the light of the shifting models of family is to adopt a flexible approach to its definition.

Although characterization is an inevitable part of identifying the source and nature of discrimination, the intervenors' factum argued that, at a minimum, the characterization should be informed by the view of those affected by the exclusion or denial. By focusing on the effects of discrimination instead of the discriminatory intent of the perpetrator, both Canadian constitutional and human rights jurisprudence has already laid the basis for appreciating the interplay of different prohibited grounds. Rooting human rights analysis in the *impact* of the impugned behaviour may enable courts to acknowledge that discrimination can be both additive and interactive. Thus, rather than cancelling each other out, multiple grounds of discrimination reinforce each other.

I do not know whether anyone collaborating on the factum consciously tried to implement postmodern theory; certainly no one invoked it in discussion. It did lurk in the background for me, however, more as a set of related beliefs and a methodological stance than a coherent ideology. Postmodern art and architecture and poststructuralist philosophy and literary criticism expose the contingent status of dominant ideologies and suggest, implicitly, that resistance to them is possible. One critical insight is that dominant representations of reality emerge from a closed, self-referential system in which meaning is relative. For example, "deviance" has meaning only in the context of its opposite, "normality." Words and concepts have meaning, then only *in relation* to each other. In my view, this factum explores the implications of poststructuralist thought by explaining how the relationship between normality and deviance (family and not family) is hierarchical, and socially constructed.

It also challenges the rationality and integrity of legal categories and the objectivity of legal reasoning. I understand its central points as challenges to traditional legal arguments and as an attempt to stretch the limits of the form of argument itself: family cannot be defined as if it had a stable meaning, the way courts are inclined to define concepts; discrimination is not unidimensional, the way courts have historically understood it; and merely amending the definition of common law spouse is insufficient as a remedy because it leaves intact a standard to which all "deviant" families must be measured. These arguments were a critique of the Court's *approach* to problems of interpretation, as much as they were about obtaining a particular outcome. In the course of explaining how the Court of Appeal erred, the factum contests its representation of social reality and challenges the integrity of the distinctions upon which its decision relied, such as "family/not family" or "real/imitation." For example, who is family and who is not is a product of legal among other, discourses; it is not a product of nature. And what makes a family real, as opposed to an imitation, depends on what we have historically privileged as natural. This line of argument ultimately contests the very notion of the "real."

It may be possible, however, to practise litigation in a postmodern manner. After all, the coalition's submissions were packaged in familiar legal discourse, filed in a factum written according to the rules of civil procedure, and then put to the Court in oral argument which, no matter how creative and persuasive, was confined by the customs and conventions of practice, both formal and informal. One might think that regardless of the technical quality of the product and the deftness of counsel's advocacy, this deference to authority, both in substance (the pursuit of a legal remedy) and form (using the terms of legal discourse), is hardly postmodern, or that, at best, it is what one legal scholar has dubbed "postmodernism-lite." The notion of persuading a higher authority by using legal argument itself depends upon a belief in the possibility of rationality, and reinforces a hierarchical process of decision-making that ultimately establishes truths. At a minimum, however, postmodernism's central tenets, to the extent that they can be discerned at all, can provide a theoretical framework from which progressive lawyers can challenge conventional meanings, interrogate the production of "normality," and give voice to suppressed accounts of experience. Perhaps because I do not fully embrace the "version" of postmodernism that would make rationality and agency impossible, I believe in the possibility of a partial and self-conscious, if instrumental, "use" of its insights. Rather than absolute moral relativism, which is one potential product of postmodernism's hypercritical approach to settled meanings, I prefer continuous self-reflective criticism applied to goals that are always subject to revision.

CRITIQUES FROM THE RIGHT

The Perceived Assault on the Family

In both the United States and Canada, it is a time of antifeminist backlash, rising hate crimes against sexual minorities, outrageous scapegoating against the least powerful in society, and surging support for reactionary politicians. In this climate, unconventional families, and gay men and lesbians in particular, are seen as threats to an already unstable way of life. It is, to say the least, an especially bad time to be mounting what is perceived as an "attack" on the family. The intervenors' factum could undoubtedly be seen as part of an antifamily campaign.

In the last American presidential campaign "family values" became a critical battleground. Preserving traditional families was the rallying cry for the conservative right, which depicted the "liberal" left as sympathetic to deviant and immoral "life style" choices. America was in cultural crisis, and the conservative right's agenda could save the country. All of this rhetoric translated into furious "gay bashing" and self-

righteous criticism of single mothers by the Republican Party, both at
its National Convention in August 1992 and throughout the campaign
for George Bush's reelection. The Republican's unmistakable message
was that single mothers (implicitly – although erroneously – understood to be overwhelmingly African-American), and gay men and lesbians, were the enemies of the American family. Even though this performance was generally considered a failure by observers and apparently alienated many voters, that it dominated the convention at all was
shocking.

As a Canadian in the United States, I was exceedingly contemptuous
watching the discourse erupt into a national debate about who "really"
was a family and whether only traditional ones were worthy of respect.
When I returned to Canada and began working on the intervenors'
factum, this kind of rhetoric had not taken centre stage on the Canadian
political scene and I could not imagine that it would. In the last two
years, however, the family caucus of the Conservative Party has sounded
increasingly like the Republican right, going as far as proposing to
entrench the "importance of family" in a preamble to the Constitution,
and attempting to amend federal laws to include an "official definition
of the family, specifying that the couple must be male and female."[6]
Ironically, a chilling story about the caucus's accomplishments and ambitions appeared on the front page of the Toronto *Globe and Mail* the
very day the *Mossop* appeal was heard by the Supreme Court.

Whether the intervenors' argument in *Mossop* is "pro-family" or "anti-
family" depends entirely upon how family is defined. The factum is
clearly pro-family on its own terms. And attaching labels like this only
avoids the central questions: what *is* a family anyway? The argument
that Mossop and Popert are a family in the context of an employment
benefits scheme can be characterized, as argued earlier, as a claim for
inclusion, which is meant to expand, and not destroy, the concept of
family. If the factum is anti-family, it is only anti this narrow, exclusive,
rigidly heterosexual, and purely procreative family. The notion that
groups like the coalition are trying to "destroy" conventional families is
at best the product of paranoia and at worst intentional hatemongering.
It is simply not credible to claim that legal recognition of unconventional families will lead to the breakup of traditional ones, even though
this reasoning is usually implicit in arguments against homosexual marriage or progressive notions of family. The right's attempt to blame all
the problems of our troubled times (a failing economy, drugs, sexual
abuse, racial conflict) on, for example, the breakdown of the traditional

family, the feminist agenda, and sexual "deviance," instead of on ill-conceived policies, a culture of greed and violence, or a lack of political will, is just shameless scapegoating. What is really threatened here, and the reason the right is so defensive, is an ideology of superiority.

CRITIQUES FROM THE LEFT

The Radical Critique

The factum might be criticized from the left for not being radical enough. According to this view, the coalition should have approached this project as an opportunity to oppose more strenuously the idea that family status is relevant to employment or other benefits. The heart of the radical critique is a scepticism about any appeal to family, given its oppressive ideological function. Neither the state nor employers should have the power to define family, and legislation should not distinguish between "family" and "not family" for the purpose of allocating benefits and burdens. The construct itself, in other words, is the problem. Proponents of this view would, I imagine, support the allotment of a fixed number of days of bereavement leave for each employee to use at their discretion.

As noted above, the coalition did suggest this remedy to the court. Still, the factum does not argue that the concept of family should be abandoned; in fact, in oral argument, counsel took pains to make clear that its meaning should be assessed in the light of its context, the legislative purpose. The coalition may simply have not been prepared to argue that the conception of family is inherently destructive and should be abandoned for all purposes. For my part, I believed that some of the things 'family' *might* connote are good things, such as intimacy, emotional support, mutual dependence, and shared responsibility. Perhaps the state has a place encouraging these aspects of relationship under the term family, as long as it does so in a non-discriminatory way. This is essentially an argument that the category can be rehabilitated. Another concern might be that abandoning family as an organizational category and adopting a radically individualistic approach to benefits is unrealistic, because it ignores the fact that people do live constantly in relationships, and that they have responsibilities as a result.

One could also argue that the prospect of entirely eliminating the concept of family from legal and social discourse seems very remote, and that an attempt to do so in the factum might be perceived as extreme. Perhaps more significantly, even if it could be achieved, the elimination of state regulation of the family might lead to its reprivatization, a daunting prospect to the women and children who are often abused within it. Finally, as long as legal and social significance attach to "family status," and benefits or protections flow to those entitled to the label, it will be necessary, even if only from a defensive stance, to engage in the debate about what the term means. Disengaging from the struggle to define family will lead not to the abandonment of the category; instead the concept will be used by those with the power of definition to impose their categorizations on others, and further marginalize disadvantaged individuals and groups.

Finally, some critics might think that the intervenors should have focused more sharply on the connection between homophobia and the domination of women by men. The factum could have explained how a restrictive definition of family is central to the efficient policing of gender boundaries, which define women as different from and "less than" men. To some extent, the factum did this by pointing out how the idealization of the "traditional" family masks its problems. The intervenors argued, for example, that for many women and children the family is a site of gender role stereotyping, inequality, domination, physical and emotional violence, and incest. But in the end, the link between homophobia and misogyny did take a back seat to the more primary argument that the denial of bereavement leave was indeed family status discrimination. This prioritization made sense given the facts of the case; Mossop is, after all, a gay man.

THE LIBERAL CRITIQUE

Perhaps predictably, the factum is vulnerable to a number of very potent critiques from the left, including the anti-assimilation argument described earlier. Significantly, however, the factum explicitly rejects a 'similarly-situated' approach to family status precisely to avoid a comparative paradigm that would reinforce the superiority of the traditional family. It is very different to argue that people who conform to an imposed norm should be entitled to the same rights as the dominant group, than it is to throw the notion of "sameness" into question, which is what we did in this case. The factum's anti-essentialism does not fit easily with liberal legalism, and had the Court adopted the intervenors' argument, it would have marked an important step away from it.

Among those who would refer to the intervenors' position as consistent with liberal pluralism – and mean it disparagingly – another concern would be that the factum appears agnostic about the relative value of different family arrangements. If all families are equal, these critics say, on what basis could one condemn abusive families and applaud loving ones? Indeed, the factum does support diversity in and among families and declines to prefer, say, a family of heterosexual people to a family of gay people, or a family without children to one with children. But this in no way advocates tolerance of family members that abuse and neglect others. Child abuse and spousal assault are unacceptable regardless of a family's composition or the sexuality of its members, and should be penalized on that basis.

Other critics, who may or may not overlap with those concerned about assimilation, might reject the notion that human rights litigation has anything substantive to offer members of marginalized groups. They are sceptical about the possibility of deconstructing or subverting traditional meanings within the conceptual framework and discourse of rights. Material gains, they would argue, rarely flow from legal decisions. Most attempts to secure rights for marginalized individuals and groups fail, and participating in conventional litigation only reinforces the legitimacy of judges and the authority of the liberal-legal state.

I must confess my deep sympathy with many of these views. And yet, although I realize that even progressive interpretations of the *Charter* and human rights codes are not the answer to all of our social ills, I am not persuaded that test case litigation is necessarily self-defeating.[7] The symbolic power of law is potentially too enormous, and its influence on culture too profound, to abandon it as a site of dialogue, confrontation, and resistance. It makes for both good law and policy that legal decisions be informed by the reality of the social life they regulate. I simply disagree with conventional leftist wisdom about the impossibility of achieving significant social change through, among other things, rights arguments because I see them, from a historical perspective, as an indispensable part of the political strategies of social movements. I also believe that it is important to challenge established meanings within legal discourse, because representations of reality are created and fixed in the form of judicial decisions and are then absorbed into the fabric of society, with broad and unpredictable effects. Finally, I am one of those who places value on the secondary or "ripple" effects of litigation: it can create opportunities for coalition work both within and around lawsuits, and provide marginalized individuals and groups with a sense of entitlement and legitimacy that fuels their political engagement. Even adverse decisions may ultimately contribute to social change by mobilizing previously quiescent constituencies.

In addition, at least *some* material gains can result from legal decisions; gay men and lesbians stood to gain employment benefits from which they were excluded, had Mossop won his case. Granted, this may not be their most significant problem, and some people fear that the price to be paid in terms of assimilation is too onerous, but formal recognition of an entitlement can still be an important victory and change people's lives. The fact that the issue was litigated could provide the impetus for hesitant private and public employers to independently extend benefits to lesbians and gay men. The case also arguably added to the pressure on the federal government to amend the *CHRA*, and it forced an important discussion onto the public agenda by attracting media coverage. Ultimately, of course, the willingness to engage in test case litigation, and to make rights claims in particular, depends on one's personal beliefs about the scope and value of their impact, but it is a false argument to suggest that they must be embraced *in place of* some other strategy. In reality, test case litigation coexists with a number of equally problematic and potentially helpful alternatives.

To be sure, there are different arenas in which to pursue one's vision of social change, including the legal, the political, and the personal. The categories are not, however, very neatly divisible, and the power of legal discourse is ignored at our peril. In other words, were it up to me, I would rather advance the argument articulated in the intervenors' factum, discuss its risks, and admit its shortcomings, than wait for the Court to interpret the meaning of "family status" based on arguments from the CHRC and the Salvation Army. I have not decided yet whether my attitude towards legal strategies is best described as defensive cynicism, quasi-liberal optimism, or postmodern pragmatism, but it is driven by a deep scepticism about the possibility that other forums are somehow more compatible to these arguments than is law.

CONCLUSION

All of these critiques are sound to some extent and should be taken seriously. I honestly believe that most people involved in the litigation on the coalition's behalf struggled daily with just such issues. Among other things, the critiques bring into focus the premium placed by some activists and lawyers on ideology when writing a factum and pursuing legal remedies. For my part, the self-imposed need to be ideologically consistent created an enormous pressure that was not always productive. I am learning that ideological purity for its own sake may be debilitating, even if it is partly what leads people to test case litigation or political activism in the first place. It can blind advocates to strategic compromises or different forms of expression, to the possibility of achieving less than complete victories, and to making improvements on the margins and in the interstices of the existing legal regime. Whether or not it is important to insist on an ideological point, or simply to do whatever it takes to win the case, will depend on what the clients and lawyers see as their goals. Views on this may vary with the characteristics of the litigants, the lawyers, and the perceived audience. Some people are interested in short-term tangible results, and others value ideological or symbolic victories which, although not always mutually exclusive, can conflict at times. For example, if the goal is to secure employment benefits at any cost, then an "assimilationist" argument will be acceptable. It might be important to speak the familiar language of the court, to use contentional legal strategies, even if they are not ideologically consistent with the clients' or the lawyers' perspectives. By contrast, if the point is to give voice to an excluded perspective, and to give the clients a sense of having asserted their "rights," then risking a novel argument might make sense. Intervenors arguably have more latitude for both creativity and ideology.

A willingness to question the role of ideology in the context of the progressive use of litigation makes one vulnerable to aggressive (and sometimes dismissive) critiques of one's commitment to the issues at stake. One might be accused of being a minimalist, a sellout, lacking in backbone, ad hoc in approach, and empty of vision. But at least considering the possible conflicts between ideology and tactics forces public interest lawyers and their clients to ask important questions about strategy. What are the interests at stake? What are the responsibilities of advocates to the class of people ostensibly represented by the clients, but which is larger and more diverse than they are? Is the purpose of the factum to confront the court with a different picture of reality, or secure the remedy sought? These are not new questions. *Charter* litigation often involves controversial social issues and the factums usually reflect a balancing of strategic and ideological choices. But the nature of the balance is a product of the people who do the work and it cannot possibly speak to the concerns of every interested party. The only certainty that emerges from such work is the impossibility of pleasing all of the people any of the time.

I doubt that anyone involved in producing the intervenors' factum believed that a single legal decision, even from the Supreme Court, would change social attitudes and lead to the acceptance of non-conforming families. Perhaps an inclusive interpretation of family would ultimately backfire by reinforcing the dominance of the traditional model, resulting in increased "tolerance" for "alternative" families that are in some ways like "real" families. It might in time, applied more generally and beyond the employment context in which counsel sought to confine this case, deprive gay men and lesbians of an important counsel sought to confine this case, deprive gay men and lesbians of an important form of dissent from the category of family, as even those who would rather not be regarded as family find family status imposed upon them, like common law spouses. This could happen, notwithstanding the intervenors' argument that what weighs most in the determination of family, at least in the context of employment benefits, are the subjective views of the parties. Perhaps, for example, same-sex couples would be the first to lose entitlements under welfare legislation on the reasoning that they are family, and obligated to support each other. The long-term, although unintended, result could be increased state intervention into the lives of gay men and lesbians, with no concomitant amelioration of their inferior social status. The intervenors' factum alone would neither cause nor prevent this, but the negative possibilities of the litigation's ultimate impact gave me, personally, pause.

The discussion about what constitutes a family and whether marginalized groups should claim inclusion has only just begun. Even if there were consensus in the gay and lesbian communities, or the larger progressive community, on whether gay men and lesbians should or should not argue that they 'are' families (which is highly unlikely in the near future), doubts about the strategic utility of test case litigation would still exist. The attempt to argue for inclusion in an institution like the family, while simultaneously deconstructing it, is an unquestionably high-risk position. People may misunderstand the coalition's position as a purely liberal claim for equality and tolerance on the basis of sameness, while ignoring the deconstructive aspect, or may purposely simplify it, for political reasons, as dangerously threatening to 'real' families. Resorting to litigation will always be criticized by some as a doomed attempt to change the system from within.

Resisting the temptation to take an inflexible position on what can be subversive or challenging to existing notions of naturalness, rationality, objectivity, and hierarchy is a very postmodern and, to my mind, very advisable view. Thus, although I would be the first to stress the importance of carefully gauging the effects of any strategy, they will always be, at best, contingent. It is very possible that legal recognition for unconventional families under the category "family status" in human rights legislation will be simultaneously (or alternately or occasionally) liberating and assimilationist, depending on the context, the audience, and the issues at stake. There is no reliable way to test the "ultimate" meaning of the inclusion/deconstruction strategy employed by the coalition, and the notion of it having any single meaning seems hopelessly naive. Before the Supreme Court's decision was rendered, I had no idea whether the arguments about interactive discrimination and anti-essentialism would be misinterpreted, partly adopted, or completely ignored by the Court. I always understood that the result in *Mossop* might lead us towards more acceptance of unconventional families, or might prompt a backlash against them, and specifically against gay men and lesbians. But to me such uncertainty is a reason to engage in legal argument and not abandon it ...

NOTES

1 Same-sex couples are excluded from the definition of spouse in all provincial and federal legislation and are therefore deprived of the benefits and entitlements that flow to people on the basis of spousal status. Challenges to this exclusion have systematically failed.
2 These were the Salvation Army, Focus on the Family Association of Canada, REAL Women, and the Pentecostal Assemblies of Canada.
3 Postmodernism is difficult to define, but it refers generally to a movement/ critique/methodology/ideology that spans art, architecture, dance, history, literary criticism, philosophy, and a variety of other fields. Although it has different inflections in every discipline, postmodernism represents a critique of modernist rationalism, rejects the notion of objectivity and neutrality, insists that meaning is a product of perspective, stipulates that universalism and "meta-narratives" suppress different accounts of reality and truth, and understands subjectivity to be socially and discursively produced and reproduced. Needless to say, such tenets (shamelessly reduced here to mere slogans) pose a direct challenge to traditional

understandings of rationality, truth, subjectivity, and universality. See Jacques Derrida 'Structure, Sign and Play in the Discourse of Human Sciences' in *Writing and Difference* (1967; trans. 1978). Derrida is religiously cited as the pre-eminent poststructuralist philosopher and the father of deconstruction, a methodology that reveals how meaning is deferred and relative, and that inverts the dichotomies on which any intelligible reading of a text depends. Derrida's own style upsets the presumption of a stable interpretive context to which a reader can appeal for a determination of reason. The reader's desire for rationality, or for "closure," according to Derrida, represses other notions of rationality and privileges some meanings over others.

4   A good example is the aftermath of the United States Supreme Court's decision in *Bowers v Hardwick* 478 US 186 (1986) upholding a Georgia sodomy statute on the basis that sexual behaviour between two gay men in the privacy of their home is not constitutionally protected by the due process clause of the Fourteenth Amendment. This case provided a justificatory backdrop for other laws or policies that penalize gay men and lesbians. It has arguably exacerbated the difficulty of convincing the American military to repeal its ban on gay men and lesbians, and dimmed the prospects of persuading courts that homosexuality ought to be a suspect class for the purpose of equal protection analysis. The argument against including sexual orientation in anti-discrimination legislation is strengthened when gay sexual behaviour is criminal (22 states retain sodomy statutes). If the Court finds in *Mossop* that gay men and lesbians are not included in the term "family status" it could be interpreted very broadly, by traditionalists and reactionaries, to mean that gay men and lesbians are less worthy as human beings.

5   The factum also uses the term "sexual identity" along with "sexual orientation," which undermines the idea that sexuality is biologically fixed (and that whether it is fixed or not should be irrelevant to human rights protection).

6   *Globe and Mail* June 3 1992. With respect to the definition in federal laws, Don Blenkarn, MP for Mississauga South, said, "It should define a family as a male and a female, living together to raise children. And that's the only kind of family that ought to be defined." Ibid. This caucus, dating back, according to the article, to 1989, is credited with eliminating tax benefits from common law couples, scrapping a long-term Conservative commitment to a national day-care program, and introducing a targeted system of child benefits, measures which the caucus sees as encouraging women to stay home with children. The family caucus also ran a campaign against

amending the *CHRA* to prohibit discrimination against gay men and lesbians. Blenkarn stated in an interview, "You don't give privileges to homosexuals if they derogate from the family." Ibid.

7 I have been called both naive and hopelessly liberal when I espouse this point of view, but I think people who respond dismissively are not listening carefully to my understanding of useful or worthwhile litigation. They often, for their part, display an amazingly single-minded confidence in electoral politics, or in education, which I do not share. The difference is that I see *all* of these discourses as sources of domination and possible sources of liberation. I think they are related, and I believe it is a mistake to concede the territory of any one of them without a struggle.

READING QUESTION ON FREEMAN

1 Reflect back on the readings by MacKinnon, Minow, and Williams. How does Freeman's post-modernism fit with their views about law?

7

Civil Disobedience

Civil disobedience has a long and distinguished history. Henry David Thoreau wrote a classic defence of breaking the law while in prison for refusal to pay taxes that supported slavery. Thoreau argued that there were some circumstances in which the only place an honest person could feel comfortable is in jail. Mahatma Gandhi directed a massive campaign of non-violent non-cooperation in the attempt to end British rule in India. In the 1960s, Martin Luther King, Jr, organized a campaign of civil disobedience to end discrimination against African Americans.

In each of these examples, the nobility of the cause and the eloquence of its leaders makes the choice of tactics strike us as obviously appropriate (at least in retrospect). Not surprisingly, more recent opponents of what are perceived to be illegitimate government policies have engaged in activities that they too describe as civil disobedience. Opponents of everything from nuclear weapons development to Sunday closing laws have claimed the mantle of civil disobedience. At one level, the description plainly fits: in the service of what is believed to be a "higher" law, laws are broken, but violence is generally not employed. Yet if the concept of civil disobedience is to have any moral purchase, there must be some limits to its application. Not every illegal act done in the service of what is thought to be moral principle deserves either our support or the lenience of courts in sentencing. The readings in this section explore a variety of ways of thinking about civil disobedience as a moral and legal category. They seek to determine which acts are worthy of special support. They also consider whether, and when, courts should treat morally motivated disobedience differently.

John Rawls
"Civil Disobedience" (1971)

Rawls suggests that any theory of democracy and the rule of law needs to include an account of the legitimate occasions of civil disobedience. He argues that civil disobedience is justified when it serves to remind citizens of injustices in a society that is largely just.

55.   THE DEFINITION OF CIVIL DISOBEDIENCE

... The problem of civil disobedience, as I shall interpret it, arises only within a more or less just democratic state for those citizens who recognize and accept the legitimacy of the constitution. The difficulty is one of a conflict of duties. At what point does the duty to comply with laws enacted by a legislative majority (or with executive acts supported by such a majority) cease to be binding in view of the right to defend one's liberties and the duty to oppose injustice? This question involves the nature and limits of majority rule. For this reason the problem of civil disobedience is a crucial test case for any theory of the moral basis of democracy.

A constitutional theory of civil disobedience has three parts. First, it defines this kind of dissent and separates it from other forms of opposition to democratic authority. These range from legal demonstrations and infractions of law designed to raise test cases before the courts to militant action and organized resistance. A theory specifies the place of civil disobedience in this spectrum of possibilities. Next, it sets out the grounds of civil disobedience and the conditions under which such action is justified in a (more or less) just democratic regime. And finally, a theory should explain the role of civil disobedience within a constitutional system and account for the appropriateness of this mode of protest within a free society.

Before I take up these matters, a word of caution. We should not expect too much of a theory of civil disobedience, even one framed for special circumstances. Precise principles that straightway decide actual cases are clearly out of the question. Instead, a useful theory defines a perspective within which the problem of civil disobedience can be approached; it identifies the relevant considerations and helps us to assign them their correct weights in the more important instances. If a theory about these matters appears to us, on reflection, to have cleared our vision and to have made our considered judgments more coherent, then it has been worthwhile. The theory has done what, for the present, one may reasonably expect it to do: namely, to narrow the disparity between the conscientious convictions of those who accept the basic principles of a democratic society.

I shall begin by defining civil disobedience as a public, nonviolent, conscientious yet political act contrary to law usually done with the aim of bringing about a change in the law or policies of the government. By acting in this way one addresses the sense of justice of the majority of the community and declares that in one's considered opinion the principles of social cooperation among free and equal men are not being respected. A preliminary gloss on this definition is that it does not require that the civilly disobedient act breach the same law that is being protested. It allows for what some have called indirect as well as direct civil disobedience. And this a definition should do, as there are sometimes strong reasons for not infringing on the law or policy held to be unjust. Instead, one may disobey traffic ordinances or laws of trespass as a way of presenting one's case. Thus, if the government enacts a vague and harsh statute against treason, it would not be appropriate to commit treason as a way of objecting to it, and in any event, the penalty might be far more than one should reasonably be ready to accept. In other cases there is no way to violate the government's policy directly, as when it concerns foreign affairs, or affects another part of the country. A second gloss is that the civilly disobedient act is indeed thought to be contrary to law, at least in the sense that those engaged in it are not simply presenting a test case for a constitutional decision; they are prepared to oppose the statute even if it should be upheld. To be sure, in a constitutional regime, the courts may finally side with the dissenters and declare the law or policy objected to unconstitutional. It often happens, then, that there is some uncertainty as to whether the dissenters' action will be held illegal or not. But this is merely a complicating element. Those who use civil disobedience to protest unjust laws are not prepared to desist should the courts eventually disagree with them, however pleased they might have been with the opposite decision.

It should also be noted that civil disobedience is a political act not only in the sense that it is addressed to the majority that holds political power, but also because it is an act guided and justified by political principles, that is, by the principles of justice which regulate the constitution and social institutions generally. In justifying civil disobedience one does not appeal to principles of personal morality or to religious doctrines, though these may coincide with and support one's claims; and it goes without saying that civil disobedience cannot be grounded solely on group or self-interest. Instead one invokes the commonly shared conception of justice that underlies the political order. It is assumed that in a reasonably just democratic regime there is a public conception of justice by reference to which citizens regulate their political affairs and interpret the constitution. The persistent and deliberate violation of the basic principles of this conception over any extended period of time, especially the infringement of the fundamental equal liberties, invites either submission or resistance. By engaging in civil disobedience a minority forces the majority to consider whether it wishes to have its actions construed in this way, or whether, in view of the common sense of justice, it wishes to acknowledge the legitimate claims of the minority.

A further point is that civil disobedience is a public act. Not only is it addressed to public principles, it is done in public. It is engaged in openly with fair notice; it is not covert or secretive. One may compare it to public speech, and being a form of address, an expression of profound and conscientious political conviction, it takes place in the public forum. For this reason, among others, civil disobedience is nonviolent. It tries to avoid the use of violence, especially against persons, not from the abhorrence of the use of force in principle, but because it is a final expression of one's case. To engage in violent acts likely to injure and to hurt is incompatible with civil disobedience as a mode of address. Indeed, any interference with the civil liberties of others tends to obscure the civilly disobedient quality of one's act. Sometimes if the appeal fails in its purpose, forceful resistance may later be entertained. Yet civil disobedience is giving voice to conscientious and deeply held convictions; while it may warn and admonish, it is not itself a threat.

Civil disobedience is nonviolent for another reason. It expresses disobedience to law within the limits of fidelity to law, although it is at the outer edge thereof. The law is broken, but fidelity to law is expressed by the public and nonviolent nature of the act, by the willingness to accept the legal consequences of one's conduct. This fidelity to law helps to establish to the majority that the act is indeed politically conscientious and sincere, and that is intended to address the public's sense of justice. To be completely open and nonviolent is to give bond of one's sincerity, for it is not easy to convince another that one's acts are conscientious, or even to be sure of this before oneself. No doubt it is possible to imagine a legal system in which conscientious belief that the law is unjust is accepted as a defense for noncompliance. Men of great honesty with full confidence in one another might make such a system work. But as things are, such a scheme would presumably be unstable even in a state of near justice. We must pay a certain price to convince others that our actions have, in our carefully considered view, a sufficient moral basis in the political convictions of the community.

Civil disobedience has been defined so that it falls between legal protest and the raising of test cases on the one side, and conscientious refusal and the various forms of resistance on the other. In this range of possibilities it stands for that form of dissent at the boundary of fidelity to law. Civil disobedience, so understood, is clearly distinct from militant action and obstruction; it is far removed from organized forcible resistance. The militant, for example, is much more deeply opposed to the existing political system. He does not accept it as one which is nearly just or reasonably so; he believes either that it departs widely from its professed principles or that it pursues a mistaken conception of justice altogether. While his action is conscientious in its own terms, he does not appeal to the sense of justice of the majority (or those having effective political power), since he thinks that their sense of justice is erroneous, or else without effect. Instead, he seeks by well-framed militant acts of disruption and resistance, and the like, to attack the prevalent view of justice or to force a movement in the desired direction. Thus the militant may try to evade the penalty, since he is not prepared to accept the legal consequences of his violation of the law; this would not only be to play into the hands of forces that he believes cannot be trusted, but also to express a recognition of the legitimacy of the constitution to which he is opposed. In this sense militant action is not within the bounds of fidelity to law, but represents a more profound opposition to the legal order. The basic structure is thought to be so unjust or else to depart so widely from its own professed ideals that one must try to prepare the way for radical or even revolutionary change. And this is to be done by trying to arouse the public to an awareness of the fundamental reforms that need to be made. Now in certain circumstances militant action and other kinds of resistance are surely justified. I shall not, however, consider these cases. As I have said, my aim here is the limited one of defining a concept of civil disobedience and understanding its role in a nearly just constitutional regime.

56. THE DEFINITION OF CONSCIENTIOUS REFUSAL

Although I have distinguished civil disobedience from conscientious refusal, I have yet to explain the latter notion. This will now be done. It must be recognized, however, that to separate these two ideas is to give a narrower definition to civil disobedience than is traditional; for it is customary to think of civil disobedience in a broader sense as any non-compliance with law for conscientious reasons, at least when it is not covert and does not involve the use of force. Thoreau's essay is characteristic, if not definitive, of the traditional meaning. The usefulness of the narrower sense will, I believe, be clear once the definition of conscientious refusal is examined.

Conscientious refusal is noncompliance with a more or less direct legal injunction or administrative order. It is refusal since an order is addressed to us and, given the nature of the situation, whether we accede to it is known to the authorities. Typical examples are the refusal of the early Christians to perform certain acts of piety prescribed by the pagan state, and the refusal of the Jehovah's Witnesses to salute the flag. Other examples are the unwillingness of a pacifist to serve in the armed forces, or of a soldier to obey an order that he thinks is manifestly contrary to the moral law as it applies to war. Or again, in Thoreau's case, the refusal to pay a tax on the grounds that to do so would make him an agent of grave injustice to another. One's sanction is assumed to be known to the authorities, however much one might wish, in some cases, to conceal it. Where it can be covert, one might speak of conscientious evasion rather than conscientious refusal. Covert infractions of a fugitive slave law are instances of conscientious evasion.

There are several contrasts between conscientious refusal (or evasion) and civil disobedience. First of all, conscientious refusal is not a form of address appealing to the sense of justice of the majority. To be sure, such acts are not generally secretive or covert, as concealment is often impossible anyway. One simply refuses on conscientious grounds to obey a command or to comply with a legal injunction. One does not invoke the convictions of the community, and in this case conscientious refusal is not an act in the public forum. Those ready to withhold obedience recognize that there may be no basis for mutual understanding; they do not seek out occasions for disobedience as a way to state their cause. Rather, they bide their time hoping that the necessity to disobey will not arise. They are less optimistic than those undertaking civil disobedience and they may entertain no expectation of changing laws or policies. The situation may allow no time for them to make their case, or again there may not be any chance that the majority will be receptive to their claims.

Conscientious refusal is not necessarily based on political principles; it may be founded on religious or other principles at variance with the constitutional order. Civil disobedience is an appeal to a commonly shared conception of justice, whereas conscientious refusal may have other grounds. For example, assuming that the early Christians would not justify their refusal to comply with the religious customs of the Empire by reasons of justice but simply as being contrary to their religious convictions, their argument would not be political; nor, with similar qualifications, are the views of a pacifist, assuming that wars of self-defense at least are recognized by the conception of justice that underlies a constitutional regime. Conscientious refusal may, however, be grounded on political principles. One may decline to go along with a law thinking that it is so unjust that complying with it is simply out of the question. This would be the case if, say, the law were to enjoin our being the agent of enslaving another, or to require us to submit to a similar fate. These are patent violations of recognized political principles.

It is a difficult matter to find the right course when some men appeal to religious principles in refusing to do actions which, it seems, are required by principles of political justice. Does the pacifist possess an immunity from military service in a just war, assuming that there are such wars? Or is the state permitted to impose certain hardships for noncompliance? There is a temptation to say that the law must always respect the dictates of conscience, but this cannot be right. As we have seen in the case of the intolerant, the legal order must regulate men's pursuit of their religious interests so as to realize the principle of equal liberty; and it may certainly forbid religious practices such as human sacrifice, to take an extreme case. Neither religiosity nor conscientiousness suffices to protect this practice. A theory of justice must work out from its own point of view how to treat those who dissent from it. The aim of a well-ordered society, or one in a state of near justice, is to preserve and strengthen the institutions of justice. If a religion is denied its full expression, it is presumably because it is in violation of the equal liberties of others. In general, the degree of tolerance accorded opposing moral conceptions depends upon the extent to which they can be allowed an equal place within a just system of liberty.

If pacifism is to be treated with respect and not merely tolerated, the explanation must be that it accords reasonably well with the principles of justice, the main exception arising from its attitude toward engaging in a just war (assuming here that in some situations wars of self-defense are justified). The political principles recognized by the community have a certain affinity with the doctrine the pacifist professes. There is a common abhorrence of war and the use of force, and a belief in the equal status of men as moral persons. And given the tendency of nations, particularly great powers, to engage in war unjustifiably and to set in motion the apparatus of the state to suppress dissent, the respect accorded to pacifism serves the purpose of alerting citizens to the wrongs that governments are prone to commit in their name. Even though his views are not altogether sound, the warnings and protests that a pacifist is disposed to express may have the result that on balance the principles of justice are more rather than less secure. Pacifism as a natural departure from the correct doctrine conceivably compensates for the weakness of men living up to their professions.

It should be noted that there is, of course, in actual situations no sharp distinction between civil disobedience and conscientious refusal. Moreover the same action (or sequence of actions) may have strong elements of both. While there are clear cases of each, the contrast between them is intended as a way of elucidating the interpretation of civil disobedience and its role in a democratic society. Given the nature of this way of acting as a special kind of political appeal, it is not usually justified until other steps have been taken within the legal framework. By contrast this requirement often fails in the obvious cases of legitimate conscientious refusal. In a free society no one may be compelled, as the early Christians were, to perform religious acts in violation of equal liberty, nor must a soldier comply with inherently evil commands while awaiting an appeal to higher authority. These remarks lead up to the question of justification.

57.   THE JUSTIFICATION OF CIVIL DISOBEDIENCE

With these various distinctions in mind, I shall consider the circumstances under which civil disobedience is justified. For simplicity I shall limit the discussion to domestic institutions and so to injustices internal to a given society. The somewhat narrow nature of this restriction will be mitigated a bit by taking up the contrasting problem of conscientious refusal in connection with the moral law as it applies to war. I shall begin by setting out what seem to be reasonable conditions for engaging in civil disobedience, and then later connect these conditions more systematically with the place of civil disobedience in a state of near justice. Of course, the conditions enumerated should be taken as presumptions; no doubt there will be situations when they do not hold, and other arguments could be given for civil disobedience.

The first point concerns the kinds of wrongs that are appropriate objects of civil disobedience. Now if one views such disobedience as a political act addressed to the sense of justice of the community, then it seems reasonable, other things equal, to limit it to instances of substantial and clear injustice, and preferably to those which obstruct the path to removing other injustices. For this reason there is a presumption in favor of restricting civil disobedience to serious infringements of the first principle of justice, the principle of equal liberty, and to blatant violations of the second part of the second principle, the principle of fair equality of opportunity. Of course, it is not always easy to tell whether these principles are satisfied. Still, if we think of them as guaranteeing the basic liberties, it is often clear that these freedoms are not being honored. After all, they impose certain strict requirements that must be visibly expressed in institutions. Thus when certain minorities are denied the right to vote or to hold office, or to own property and to move from place to place, or when certain religious groups are repressed and others denied various opportunities, these injustices may be obvious to all. They are publicly incorporated into the recognized practice, if not the letter, of social arrangements. The establishment of these wrongs does not presuppose an informed examination of institutional effects.

By contrast infractions of the difference principle are more difficult to ascertain. There is usually a wide range of conflicting yet rational opinion as to whether this principle is satisfied. The reason for this is that it applies primarily to economic and social institutions and policies. A choice among these depends upon theoretical and speculative beliefs as well as upon a wealth of statistical and other information, all of this seasoned with shrewd judgment and plain hunch. In view of the complexities of these questions, it is difficult to check the influence of self-interest and prejudice; and even if we can do this in our own case, it is another matter to convince others of our good faith. Thus unless tax laws, for example, are clearly designed to attack or to abridge a basic equal liberty, they should not normally be protested by civil disobedience. The appeal to the public's conception of justice is not sufficiently clear. The resolution of these issues is best left to the political process provided that the requisite equal liberties are secure. In this case a reasonable compromise can presumably be reached. The violation of the principle of equal liberty is, then, the more appropriate object of civil disobedience. This principle defines the common status of equal citizenship in a constitutional regime and lies at the basis of the political order. When it is fully honored the presumption is that other injustices, while possibly persistent and significant, will not get out of hand.

A further condition for civil disobedience is the following. We may suppose that the normal appeals to the political majority have already been made in good faith and that they have failed. The legal means of redress have proved of no avail. Thus, for example, the existing political parties have shown themselves indifferent to the claims of the minority or have proved unwilling to accommodate them. Attempts to have the laws repealed have been ignored and legal protests and demonstrations have had no success. Since civil disobedience is a last resort, we should be sure that it is necessary. Note that it has not been said, however, that legal means have been exhausted. At any rate, further normal appeals can be repeated; free speech is always possible. But if past actions have shown the majority immovable or apathetic, further attempts may reasonably be thought fruitless, and a second condition for justified civil disobedience is met. This condition is, however, a presumption. Some cases may be so extreme that there may be no duty to use first only legal means of political opposition. If, for example, the legislature were to enact some outrageous violation of equal liberty, say by forbidding the religion of a weak and defenseless minority, we surely could not expect that sect to oppose the law by normal political procedures. Indeed, even civil disobedience might be much too mild, the majority having already convicted itself of wantonly unjust and overtly hostile aims.

The third and last condition I shall discuss can be rather complicated. It arises from the fact that while the two preceding conditions are often sufficient to justify civil disobedience, this is not always the case. In certain circumstances the natural duty of justice may require a certain restraint. We can see this as follows. If a certain minority is justified in engaging in civil disobedience, then any other minority in relevantly similar circumstances is likewise justified. Using the two previous conditions as the criteria of relevantly similar circumstances, we can say that, other things equal, two minorities are similarly justified in resorting to civil disobedience if they have suffered for the same length of time from the same degree of injustice and if their equally sincere and normal political appeals have likewise been to no avail. It is conceivable, however, even if it is unlikely, that there should be many groups with an equally sound case (in the sense just defined) for being civilly disobedient; but that, if they were all to act in this way, serious disorder would follow which might well undermine the efficacy of the just constitution. I assume here that there is a limit on the extent to which civil disobedience can be engaged in without leading to a breakdown in the respect for law and the constitution, thereby setting in motion consequences unfortunate for all. There is also an upper bound on the ability of the public forum to handle such forms of dissent; the appeal that civilly disobedient groups wish to make can be distorted and their intention to appeal to the sense of justice of the majority lost sight of. For one or both of these reasons, the effectiveness of civil disobedience as a form of protest declines beyond a certain point; and those contemplating it must consider these constraints.

The ideal solution from a theoretical point of view calls for a cooperative political alliance of the minorities to regulate the overall level of dissent. For consider the nature of the situation: there are many groups each equally entitled to engage in civil disobedience. Moreover they all wish to exercise this right, equally strong in each case; but if they all do so, lasting injury may result to the just constitution to which they each recognize a natural duty of justice. Now when there are many equally strong claims which if taken together exceed what can be granted, some fair plan should be adopted so that all are equitably considered. In simple cases of claims to goods that are indivisible and fixed in number, some rotation or lottery scheme may be the fair solution when the number of equally valid claims is too great. But this sort of device is completely unrealistic here. What seems called for is a political understanding among the minorities suffering from injustice. They can meet their duty to democratic institutions by coordinating their actions so that while each has an opportunity to exercise its right, the limits on the degree of civil disobedience are not exceeded. To be sure, an alliance of this sort is difficult to arrange; but with perceptive leadership, it does not appear impossible.

Certainly the situation envisaged is a special one, and it is quite possible that these sorts of considerations will not be a bar to justified civil disobedience. There are not likely to be many groups similarly entitled to engage in this form of dissent while at the same time recognizing a duty to a just constitution. One should note, however, that an injured minority is tempted to believe its claims as strong as those of any other; and therefore even if the reasons that different groups have for engaging in civil disobedience are not equally compelling, it is often wise to presume that their claims are indistinguishable. Adopting this maxim, the circumstance imagined seems more likely to happen. This kind of case is also instructive in showing that the exercise of the right to dissent, like the exercise of rights generally, is sometimes limited by others having the very same right. Everyone's exercising this right would have deleterious consequences for all, and some equitable plan is called for.

Suppose that in the light of the three conditions, one has a right to appeal one's case by civil disobedience. The injustice one protests is a clear violation of the liberties of equal citizenship, or of equality of opportunity, this violation having been more or less deliberate over an extended period of time in the face of normal political opposition, and any complications raised by the question of fairness are met. These conditions are not exhaustive; some allowance still has to be made for the possibility of injury to third parties, to the innocent, so to speak. But I assume that they cover the main points. There is still, of course, the question whether it is wise or prudent to exercise this right. Having established the right, one is now free, as one is not before, to let these matters decide the issue. We may be acting within our rights but nevertheless unwisely if our conduct only serves to provoke the harsh retaliation of the majority. To be sure, in a state of near justice, vindictive repression of legitimate dissent is unlikely, but it is important that the action be properly designed to make an effective appeal to the wider community. Since civil disobedience is a mode of address taking place in the public forum, care must be taken to see that it is understood. Thus the exercise of the right to civil disobedience should, like any other right, be rationally framed to advance one's ends or the ends of those one wishes to assist. The theory of justice has nothing specific to say about these practical considerations. In any event questions of strategy and tactics depend upon the circumstances of each case. But the theory of justice should say at what point these matters are properly raised.

Now in this account of the justification of civil disobedience I have not mentioned the principle of fairness. The natural duty of justice is the primary basis of our political ties to a constitutional regime. As we noted before (s. 52), only the more favored members of society are likely to have a clear political obligation as opposed to a political duty. They are better situated to win public office and find it easier to take advantage of the political system. And having done so, they have acquired an obligation owed to citizens generally to uphold the just constitution.

But members of subjected minorities, say, who have a strong case for civil disobedience will not generally have a political obligation of this sort. This does not mean, however, that the principle of fairness will not give rise to important obligations in their case. For not only do many of the requirements of private life derive from this principle, but it comes into force when persons or groups come together for common political purposes. Just as we acquire obligations to others with whom we have joined in various private associations, those who engage in political action assume obligatory ties to one another. Thus while the political obligation of dissenters to citizens generally is problematical, bonds of loyalty and fidelity still develop between them as they seek to advance their cause. In general, free association under a just constitution gives rise to obligations provided that the ends of the group are legitimate and its arrangements fair. This is as true of political as it is of other associations. These obligations are of immense significance and they constrain in many ways what individuals can do. But they are distinct from an obligation to comply with a just constitution. My discussion of civil disobedience is in terms of the duty of justice alone; a fuller view would note the place of these other requirements.

58.   THE JUSTIFICATION OF CONSCIENTIOUS REFUSAL

In examining the justification of civil disobedience I assumed for simplicity that the laws and policies protested concerned domestic affairs. It is natural to ask how the theory of political duty applies to foreign policy. Now in order to do this it is necessary to extend the theory of justice to the law of nations. I shall try to indicate how this can be done. To fix ideas I shall consider briefly the justification of conscientious refusal to engage in certain acts of war, or to serve in the armed forces. I assume that this refusal is based upon political and not upon religious or other principles; that is, the principles cited by way of justification are those of the conception of justice underlying the constitution. Our problem, then, is to relate the just political principles regulating the conduct of states to the contract doctrine and to explain the moral basis of the law of nations from this point of view ...

I can give only an indication of the principles that would be acknowledged. But, in any case, there would be no surprises, since the principles chosen would, I think, be familiar ones. The basic principle of the law of nations is a principle of equality. Independent peoples organized as states have certain fundamental equal rights. This principle is analogous to the equal rights of citizens in a constitutional regime. One consequence of this equality of nations is the principle of self-determination, the right of a people to settle its own affairs without the intervention of foreign powers. Another consequence is the right to self-defense against attack, including the right to form defensive alliances to protect this right. A further principle is that treaties are to be kept, provided they are consistent with the other principles governing the relations of states. Thus treaties for self-defense, suitably interpreted, would be binding, but agreements to cooperate in an unjustified attack are void *ab initio*.

These principles define when a nation has a just cause in war or, in the traditional phrase, its *jus ad bellum*. But there are also principles regulating the means that a nation may use to wage war, its *jus in bello*. Even in a just war certain forms of violence are strictly inadmissible; and where a country's right to war is questionable and uncertain, the constraints on the means it can use are all the more severe. Acts permissible in a war of legitimate self-defense, when these are necessary, may be flatly excluded in a more doubtful situation. The aim of war is a just peace, and therefore the means employed must not destroy the possibility of peace or encourage a contempt for human life that puts the safety of ourselves and of mankind in jeopardy. The conduct of war is to be constrained and adjusted to this end. The representatives of state would recognize that their national interest, as seen from the original position, is best served by acknowledging these limits on the means of war. This is because the national interest of a just state is defined by the principles of justice that have already been acknowledged. Therefore such a nation will aim above all to maintain and to preserve its just institutions and the conditions that make them possible. It is not moved by the desire for world power or national glory; nor does it wage war for purposes of economic gain or the acquisition of territory. These ends are contrary to the conception of justice that defines a society's legitimate interest, however prevalent they have been in the actual conduct of states. Granting these presumptions, then, it seems reasonable to suppose that the traditional prohibitions incorporating the natural duties that protect human life would be chosen.

Now if conscientious refusal in time of war appeals to these principles, it is founded upon a political conception, and not necessarily upon religious or other notions. While this form of denial may not be a political act, since it does not take place in the public forum, it is based upon the same theory of justice that underlies the constitution and guides its interpretation. Moreover, the legal order itself presumably recognizes in the form of treaties the validity of at least some of these principles of the law of nations. Therefore if a soldier is ordered to engage in certain illicit acts of war, he may refuse if he reasonably and conscientiously believes that the principles applying to the conduct of war are plainly violated. He can maintain that, all things considered, his natural duty not to be made the agent of grave injustice and evil to another outweighs his duty to obey. I cannot discuss here what constitutes a manifest violation of these principles. It must suffice to note that certain clear cases are perfectly familiar ...

A somewhat different question is whether one should join the armed forces at all during some particular war. The answer is likely to depend upon the aim of the war as well as upon its conduct. In order to make the situation definite, let us suppose that conscription is in force and that the individual has to consider whether to comply with his legal duty to enter military service. Now I shall assume that since conscription is a drastic interference with the basic liberties of equal citizenship, it cannot be justified by any needs less compelling than those of national security. In a well-ordered society (or in one nearly just) these needs are determined by the end of preserving just institutions. Conscription is permissible only if it is demanded for the defense of liberty itself, including here not only the liberties of the citizens of the society in question, but also those of persons in other societies as well. Therefore if a conscript army is less likely to be an instrument of unjustified foreign adventures, it may be justified on this basis alone despite the fact that conscription infringes upon the equal liberties of citizens. But in any case, the priority of liberty (assuming serial order to obtain) requires that conscription be used only as the security of liberty necessitates. Viewed from the standpoint of the legislature (the appropriate stage for this question), the mechanism of the draft can be defended only on this ground. Citizens agree to this arrangement as a fair way of sharing the burdens of national defense. To be sure, the hazards that any particular individual must face are in part the result of accident and historical happenstance. But in a well-ordered society anyway, these evils arise externally, that is, from unjustified attacks from the outside. It is impossible for just institutions to eliminate these hardships entirely. The most that they can do is to try to make sure that the risks of suffering from these imposed misfortunes are more or less evenly shared by all members of society over the course of their life, and that there is no avoidable class bias in selecting those who are called for duty.

Imagine, then, a democratic society in which conscription exists. A person may conscientiously refuse to comply with his duty to enter the armed forces during a particular war on the ground that the aims of the conflict are unjust. It may be that the objective sought by war is economic advantage or national power. The basic liberty of citizens cannot be interfered with to achieve these ends. And, of course, it is unjust and contrary to the law of nations to attack the liberty of other societies for these reasons. Therefore a just cause for war does not exist, and this may be sufficiently evident that a citizen is justified in refusing to discharge his legal duty. Both the law of nations and the principles of justice for his own society uphold him in this claim. There is sometimes a further ground for refusal based not on the aim of the war but upon its conduct. A citizen may maintain that once it is clear that the moral law of war is being regularly violated, he has a right to decline military service on the ground that he is entitled to insure that he honors his natural duty. Once he is in the armed forces, and in a situation where he finds himself ordered to do acts contrary to the moral law of war, he may not be able to resist the demand to obey. Actually, if the aims of the conflict are sufficiently dubious and the likelihood of receiving fragrantly unjust commands is sufficiently great, one may have a duty and not only a right to refuse. Indeed, the conduct and aims of states in waging war, especially large and powerful ones, are in some circumstances so likely to be unjust that one is forced to conclude that in the foreseeable future one must abjure military service altogether. So understood a form of contingent pacifism may be a perfectly reasonable position: the possibility of a just war is conceded but not under present circumstances.

What is needed, then, is not a general pacifism but a discriminating conscientious refusal to engage in war in certain circumstances. States have not been loath to recognize pacifism and to grant it a special status. The refusal to take part in all war under any conditions is an unworldly view bound to remain a sectarian doctrine. It no more challenges the state's authority than the celibacy of priests challenges the sanctity of marriage. By exempting pacifists from its prescriptions the state may even seem to display a certain magnanimity. But conscientious refusal based upon the principles of justice between peoples as they apply to particular conflicts is another matter. For such refusal is an affront to the government's pretensions, and when it becomes widespread, the continuation of an unjust war may prove impossible. Given the often predatory aims of state power, and the tendency of men to defer to their government's decision to wage war, a general willingness to resist the state's claims is all the more necessary.

59. THE ROLE OF CIVIL DISOBEDIENCE

The third aim of a theory of civil disobedience is to explain its role within a constitutional system and to account for its connection with a democratic polity. As always, I assume that the society in question is one that is nearly just; and this implies that it has some form of democratic government, although serious injustices may nevertheless exist. In such a society I assume that the principles of justice are for the most part publicly recognized as the fundamental terms of willing cooperation among free and equal persons. By engaging in civil disobedience one intends, then, to address the sense of justice of the majority and to serve fair notice that in one's sincere and considered opinion the conditions of free cooperation are being violated. We are appealing to others to reconsider, to put themselves in our position, and to recognize that they cannot expect us to acquiesce indefinitely in the terms they impose upon us.

Now the force of this appeal depends upon the democratic conception of society as a system of cooperation among equal persons. If one thinks of society in another way, this form of protest may be out of place. For example, if the basic law is thought to reflect the order of nature and if the sovereign is held to govern by divine right as God's chosen lieutenant, then his subjects have only the right of suppliants. They can plead their cause but they cannot disobey should their appeal be denied. To do this would be to rebel against the final legitimate moral (and not simply legal) authority. This is not to say that the sovereign cannot be in error but only that the situation is not one for his subjects to correct. But once society is interpreted as a scheme of cooperation among equals, those injured by serious injustice need not submit. Indeed, civil disobedience (and conscientious refusal as well) is one of the stabilizing devices of a constitutional system, although by definition an illegal one. Along with such things as free and regular elections and an independent judiciary empowered to interpret the constitution (not necessarily written), civil disobedience used with due restraint and sound judgment helps to maintain and strengthen just institutions. By resisting injustice within the limits of fidelity to law, it serves to inhibit departures from justice and to correct them when they occur. A general disposition to engage in justified civil disobedience introduces stability into a well-ordered society, or one that is nearly just ...

One distinction between medieval and modern constitutionalism is that in the former the supremacy of law was not secured by established institutional controls. The check to the ruler who in his judgments and edicts opposed the sense of justice of the community was limited for the most part to the right of resistance by the whole society, or any part. Even this right seems not to have been interpreted as a corporate act; an unjust king was simply put aside. Thus the Middle Ages lacked the basic ideas of modern constitutional government, the idea of the sovereign people who have final authority and the institutionalizing of this authority by means of elections and parliaments, and other constitutional forms. Now in much the same way that the modern conception of constitutional government builds upon the medieval, the theory of civil disobedience supplements the purely legal conception of constitutional democracy. It attempts to formulate the grounds upon which legitimate democratic authority may be dissented from in ways that while admittedly contrary to law nevertheless express a fidelity to law and appeal to the fundamental political principles of a democratic regime. Thus to the legal forms of constitutionalism one may adjoin certain modes of illegal protest that do not violate the aims of a democratic constitution in view of the principles by which such dissent is guided. I have tried to show how these principles can be accounted for by the contract doctrine.

Some may object to this theory of civil disobedience that it is unrealistic. It presupposes that the majority has a sense of justice, and one might reply that moral sentiments are not a significant political force. What moves men are various interests, the desires for power, prestige, wealth, and the like. Although they are clever at producing moral arguments to support their claims, between one situation and another their opinions do not fit into a coherent conception of justice. Rather their views at any given time are occasional pieces calculated to advance certain interests. Unquestionably there is much truth in this contention, and in some societies it is more true than in others. But the essential question is the relative strength of the tendencies that oppose the sense of justice and whether the latter is ever strong enough so that it can be invoked to some significant effect.

A few comments may make the account presented more plausible. First of all, I have assumed throughout that we have to do with a nearly just society. This implies that there exists a constitutional regime and a publicly recognized conception of justice. Of course, in any particular situation certain individuals and groups may be tempted to violate its principles but the collective sentiment in their behalf has considerable strength when properly addressed. These principles are affirmed as the necessary terms of cooperation between free and equal persons. If those who perpetrate injustice can be clearly identified and isolated from the larger community, the convictions of the greater part of society may be of sufficient weight. Or if the contending parties are roughly equal, the sentiment of justice of those not engaged can be the deciding factor. In any case, should circumstances of this kind not obtain, the wisdom of civil disobedience is highly problematic. For unless one can appeal to the sense of justice of the larger society, the majority may simply be aroused to more repressive measures if the calculation of advantages points in this direction. Courts should take into account the civilly disobedient nature of the protester's act, and the fact that it is justifiable (or may seem so) by the political principles underlying the constitution, and on these grounds reduce and in some cases suspend the legal sanction. Yet quite the opposite may happen when the necessary background is lacking. We have to recognize then that justifiable civil disobedience is normally a reasonable and effective form of dissent only in a society regulated to some considerable degree by a sense of justice.

There may be some misapprehension about the manner in which the sense of justice is said to work. One may think that this sentiment expresses itself in sincere professions of principle and in actions requiring a considerable degree of self-sacrifice. But this supposition asks too much. A community's sense of justice is more likely to be revealed in the fact that the majority cannot bring itself to take the steps necessary to suppress the minority and to punish acts of civil disobedience as the law allows. Ruthless tactics that might be contemplated in other societies are not entertained as real alternatives. Thus the sense of justice affects, in ways we are often unaware of, our interpretation of political life, our perception of the possible courses of action, our will to resist the justified protests of others, and so on. In spite of its superior power, the majority may abandon its position and acquiesce in the proposals of the dissenters; its desire to give justice weakens its capacity to defend its unjust advantages. The sentiment of justice will be seen as a more vital political force once the subtle forms in which it exerts its influence are recognized, and in particular its role in rendering certain social positions indefensible.

In these remarks I have assumed that in a nearly just society there is a public acceptance of the same principles of justice. Fortunately this assumption is stronger than necessary. There can, in fact, be considerable differences in citizens' conceptions of justice provided that these conceptions lead to similar political judgments. And this is possible, since different premises can yield the same conclusion. In this case there exists what we may refer to as overlapping rather than strict consensus. In general, the overlapping of professed conceptions of justice suffices for civil disobedience to be a reasonable and prudent form of political dissent. Of course, this overlapping need not be perfect; it is enough that a condition of reciprocity is satisfied. Both sides must believe that however much their conceptions of justice differ, their views support the same judgment in the situation at hand, and would do so even should their respective positions be interchanged. Eventually, though, there comes a point beyond which the requisite agreement in judgment breaks down and society splits into more or less distinct parts that hold diverse opinions on fundamental political questions. In this case of strictly partitioned consensus, the basis for civil disobedience no long obtains. For example, suppose those who do not believe in toleration, and who would not tolerate others had they the power, wish to protest their lesser liberty by appealing to the sense of justice of the majority which holds the principle of equal liberty. While those who accept this principle should, as we have seen, tolerate the intolerant as far as the safety of free institutions permits, they are likely to resent being reminded of this duty by the intolerant who would, if positions were switched, establish their own dominion. The majority is bound to feel that their allegiance to equal liberty is being exploited by others for unjust ends. This situation illustrates once again the fact that a common sense of justice is a great collective asset which requires the cooperation of many to maintain. The intolerant can be viewed as free-riders, as persons who seek the advantages of just institutions while not doing their share to uphold them. Although those who acknowledge the principles of justice should always be guided by them, in a fragmented society as well as in one moved by group egoisms, the conditions for civil disobedience do not exist. Still, it is not necessary to have strict consensus, for often a degree of overlapping consensus allows the reciprocity condition to be fulfilled.

There are, to be sure, definite risks in the resort to civil disobedience. One reason for constitutional forms and their judicial interpretation is to establish a public reading of the political conception of justice and an explanation of the application of its principles to social questions. Up to

a certain point it is better that the law and its interpretation be settled
than that it be settled rightly. Therefore it may be protested that the
preceding account does not determine who is to say when circumstances are such as to justify civil disobedience. It invites anarchy by
encouraging everyone to decide for himself, and to abandon the public
rendering of political principles. The reply to this is that each person
must indeed make his own decision. Even though men normally seek
advice and counsel, and accept the injunctions of those in authority
when these seem reasonable to them, they are always accountable for
their deeds. We cannot divest ourselves of our responsibility and transfer the burden of blame to others. This is true on any theory of political
duty and obligation that is compatible with the principles of a democratic constitution. The citizen is autonomous yet he is held responsible
for what he does (s. 78). If we ordinarily think that we should comply
with the law, this is because our political principles normally lead to
this conclusion. Certainly in a state of near justice there is a presumption in favor of compliance in the absence of strong reasons to the
contrary. The many free and reasoned decisions of individuals fit together into an orderly political regime.

But while each person must decide for himself whether the circumstances justify civil disobedience, it does not follow that one is to decide
as one pleases. It is not by looking to our personal interest, or to our
political allegiances narrowly construed, that we should make up our
minds. To act autonomously and responsibly a citizen must look to the
political principles that underlie and guide the interpretation of the
constitution. He must try to assess how these principles should be applied in the existing circumstances. If the comes to the conclusion after
due consideration that civil disobedience is justified and conducts himself accordingly, he acts conscientiously. And though he may be mistaken, he has not done as he pleased. The theory of political duty and
obligation enables us to draw these distinctions.

There are parallels with the common understandings and conclusions reached in the sciences. Here, too, everyone is autonomous yet
responsible. We are to assess theories and hypotheses in the light of the
evidence by publicly recognized principles. It is true that there are authoritative works, but these sum up the consensus of many persons
each deciding for himself. The absence of a final authority to decide,
and so of an official interpretation that all must accept, does not lead to
confusion, but is rather a condition of theoretical advance. Equals accepting and applying reasonable principles need have no established

superior. To the question, who is to decide? The answer is: all are to decide, everyone taking counsel with himself, and with reasonableness, comity, and good fortune, it often works out well enough.

In a democratic society, then, it is recognized that each citizen is responsible for his interpretation of the principles of justice and for his conduct in the light of them. There can be no legal or socially approved rendering of these principles that we are always morally bound to accept, not even when it is given by a supreme court or legislature. Indeed each constitutional agency, the legislature, the executive, and the court, puts forward its interpretation of the constitution and the political ideals that inform it. Although the court may have the last say in settling any particular case, it is not immune from powerful political influences that may force a revision of its reading of the constitution. The court presents its doctrine by reason and argument; its conception of the constitution must, if it is to endure, persuade the major part of the citizens of its soundness. The final court of appeal is not the court, or the executive, nor the legislature, but the electorate as a whole. The civilly disobedient appeal in a special way to this body. There is no danger of anarchy so long as there is a sufficient working agreement in citizens' conceptions of justice and the conditions for resorting to civil disobedience are respected. That men can achieve such an understanding and honor these limits when the basic political liberties are maintained is an assumption implicit in a democratic polity. There is no way to avoid entirely the danger of divisive strife, any more than one can rule out the possibility of profound scientific controversy. Yet if justified civil disobedience seems to threaten civic concord, the responsibility falls not upon those who protest but upon those whose abuse of authority and power justifies such opposition. For to employ the coercive apparatus of the state in order to maintain manifestly unjust institutions is itself a form of illegitimate force that men in due course have a right to resist.

With these remarks we have reached the end of our discussion of the content of the principles of justice. Throughout this part my aim has been to describe a scheme of institutions that satisfies these principles and to indicate how duties and obligations arise. These things must be done to see if the theory of justice put forward matches our considered judgments and extends them in an acceptable way. We need to check whether it defines a workable political conception and helps to focus our reflections on the most relevant and basic moral concerns. The account in this part is still highly abstract, but I hope to have provided some guidance as to how the principles of justice apply in practice. However, we should not forget the limited scope of the theory presented. For the most part I have tried to develop an ideal conception, only occasionally commenting on the various cases of nonideal theory. To be sure the priority rules suggest directives in many instances, and they may be useful if not pressed too far. Even so, the only question of nonideal theory examined in any detail is that of civil disobedience in the special case of near justice. If ideal theory is worthy of study, it must be because, as I have conjectured, it is the fundamental part of the theory of justice and essential for the nonideal part as well. I shall not pursue these matters further. We have still to complete the theory of justice by seeing how it is rooted in human thought and feeling, and tied in with our ends and aspirations.

READING QUESTIONS ON RAWLS

1 Why does Rawls suppose that non-violence is so important to civil disobedience?
2 Paul Magder stayed open in defiance of Ontario's Sunday closing laws, and claimed to be engaged in an act of civil disobedience. How would Rawls assess his claim? (*Paul Magder Furs Ltd v Ontario (Attorney-General)* [1993] 107 DLR 4th 634)

Ronald Dworkin
"Civil Disobedience" (1979)

Dworkin suggests that civil disobedience has an important place in a constitutional regime, because it serves to raise test cases about laws that some believe to be unjust. Because he believes that the law always has a moral content, Dworkin argues that when citizens believe a law is unjust, they may be justified in believing that it is not a law at all.

How should the government deal with those who disobey the draft laws out of conscience? Many people think the answer is obvious: The government must prosecute the dissenters, and if they are convicted it must punish them. Some people reach this conclusion easily, because they hold the mindless view that conscientious disobedience is the same as lawlessness. They think that the dissenters are anarchists who must be punished before their corruption spreads. Many lawyers and intellectuals come to the same conclusion, however, on what looks like a more sophisticated argument. They recognize that disobedience to law may be *morally* justified, but they insist that it cannot be *legally* justified, and they think that it follows from this truism that the law must be enforced. Erwin Griswold, once Solicitor General of the United States, and before that Dean of the Harvard Law School, appears to have adopted this view. "[It] is of the essence of law," he said, "that is equally applied to all, that it binds all alike, irrespective of personal motive. For this reason, one who contemplates civil disobedience out of moral conviction should not be surprised and must not be bitter if a criminal conviction ensues. And he must accept the fact that organized society cannot endure on any other basis."

The New York Times applauded that statement. A thousand faculty members of several universities had signed a *Times* advertisement calling on the Justice Department to quash the indictments of the Rev. William Sloane Coffin, Dr Benjamin Spock, Marcus Raskin, Mitchell Goodman, and Michael Ferber, for conspiring to counsel various draft offenses. The *Times* said that the request to quash the indictments "confused moral rights with legal responsibilities".

But the argument that, because the government believes a man has committed a crime, it must prosecute him is much weaker than it seems. Society "cannot endure" if it tolerates all disobedience; it does not follow, however, nor is there evidence, that it will collapse if it tolerates some. In the United States prosecutors have discretion whether to enforce criminal laws in particular cases. A prosecutor may properly decide not to press charges if the lawbreaker is young, or inexperienced, or the sole support of a family, or is repentant, or turns state's evidence, or if the law is unpopular or unworkable or generally disobeyed, or if the courts are clogged with more important cases, or for dozens of other reasons. This discretion is no license – we expect prosecutors to have good reasons for exercising it – but there are, at least *prima facie*, some good reasons for not prosecuting those who disobey the draft laws out of conscience. One is the obvious reason that they act out of better motives than those who break the law out of greed or a desire to subvert government. If motive can count in distinguishing between thieves, then why not in distinguishing between draft offenders? Another is the practical reason that our society suffers a loss if it punishes a group that includes – as the group of draft dissenters does – some of its most loyal and law-respecting citizens. Jailing such men solidifies their alienation from society, and alienates many like them who are deterred by the threat. If practical consequences like these argued for not enforcing prohibition, why do they not argue for tolerating offenses of conscience?

Those who think that conscientious draft offenders should always be punished must show that these are not good reasons for exercising discretion, or they must find contrary reasons that outweigh them. What arguments might they produce? There are practical reasons for enforcing draft laws, and I shall consider some of these later. But Dean Griswold and those who agree with him seem to rely on a fundamental moral argument that it would be unfair, not merely impractical, to let the dissenters go unpunished. They think it would be unfair, I gather, because society could not function if every disobeyed laws he disapproved of or found disadvantageous. If the government tolerates those few who will not "play the game", it allows them to secure the benefits of everyone else's deference to law, without shouldering the burdens, such as the burden of the draft.

This argument is a serious one. It cannot be answered simply by saying that the dissenters would allow everyone else the privilege of disobeying a law he believed immoral. In fact, few draft dissenters would accept a changed society in which sincere segregationists were free to break civil rights laws they hated. The majority want no such change, in any event, because they think that society would be worse off for it; until they are shown this is wrong, they will expect their officials to punish anyone who assumes a privilege which they, for the general benefit, do not assume.

There is, however, a flaw in the argument. The reasoning contains a hidden assumption that makes it almost entirely irrelevant to the draft cases, and indeed to any serious case of civil disobedience in the United States. The argument assumes that the dissenters know that they are breaking a valid law, and that the privilege they assert is the privilege to do that. Of course, almost everyone who discusses civil disobedience recognizes that in America a law may be invalid because it is unconstitutional. But the critics handle this complexity by arguing on separate hypotheses: If the law is invalid, then no crime is committed, and society may not punish. If the law is valid, then a crime has been committed, and society must punish. This reasoning hides the crucial fact that the validity of the law may be doubtful. The officials and judges may believe that the law is valid, the dissenters may disagree, and both sides may have plausible arguments for this positions. If so, then the issues are different from what they would be if the law were clearly valid or clearly invalid, and the argument of fairness, designed for these alternatives, is irrelevant.

Doubtful law is by no means special or exotic in cases of civil disobedience. On the contrary. In the United States, at least, almost any law which a significant number of people would be tempted to disobey on moral grounds would be doubtful – if not clearly invalid – on constitutional grounds as well. The constitution makes our conventional political morality relevant to the question of validity; any statute that appears to compromise that morality raises constitutional questions, and if the compromise is serious, the constitutional doubts are serious also.

The connection between moral and legal issues was especially clear in the draft cases of the last decade. Dissent was based at the time on the following moral objections: (a) The United States is using immoral weapons and tactics in Vietnam. (b) The war has never been endorsed by deliberate, considered, and open vote of the peoples' representatives. (c) The United States has no interest at stake in Vietnam remotely strong enough to justify forcing a segment of its citizens to risk death there. (d) If an army is to be raised to fight that war, it is immoral to raise it by a draft that defers or exempts college students, and thus discriminated against the economically underprivileged. (e) The draft exempts those who object to all wars on religious grounds, but not those who object to particular wars on moral grounds; there is no relevant difference between these positions, and so the draft, by making the distinction, implies that the second group is less worthy of the nation's respect than the first. (f) The law that makes it a crime to counsel draft resistance stifles those who oppose the war, because it is morally impossible to argue that the war is profoundly immoral, without encouraging and assisting those who refuse to fight it.

Lawyers will recognize that these moral positions, if we accept them, provide the basis for the following constitutional arguments: (a) The constitution makes treaties part of the law of the land, and the United States is a party to international conventions and covenants that make illegal the acts of war the dissenters charged the nation with committing. (b) The constitution provides that Congress must declare war; the legal issue of whether our action in Vietnam was a "war" and whether the Tonkin Bay Resolution was a "declaration" is the heart of the moral issue of whether the government had made a deliberate and open decision. (c) Both the due process clause of the Fifth and Fourteenth Amendments and equal protection clause of the Fourteenth Amendment condemn special burdens placed on a selected class of citizens when the burden or the classification is not reasonable; the burden is unreasonable when it patently does not serve the public interest, or when it is vastly disproportionate to the interest served. If our military action in Vietnam was frivolous or perverse, as the dissenters claimed, then the burden we placed on men of draft age was unreasonable and unconstitutional. (d) In any event, the discrimination in favor of college students denied to the poor the equal protection of the law that is guaranteed by the constitution. (e) If there is no pertinent difference between religious objection to all wars and moral objection to some wars, then the classification the draft made was arbitrary and unreasonable, and unconstitutional on that ground. The "establishment of religion" clause of the First Amendment forbids governmental pressure in favor of organized religion; if the draft's distinction coerced men in this direction, it was invalid on that count also. (f) The First Amendment also condemns invasions of freedom of speech. If the draft law's prohibition on counseling did inhibit expression of a range of views on the war, it abridged free speech.

The principal counterargument, supporting the view that the courts ought not to have held the draft unconstitutional, also involves moral issues. Under the so-called political question doctrine, the courts deny their own jurisdiction to pass on matters – such as foreign or military policy – whose resolution is best assigned to other branches of the government. The Boston court trying the Coffin, Spock case declared, on the basis of this doctrine, that it would not hear arguments about the legality of the war. But the Supreme Court has shown itself (in the reapportionment cases, for example) reluctant to refuse jurisdiction when it believed that the gravest issues of political morality were at stake and that no remedy was available through the political process. If the dissenters were right, and the war and the draft were state crimes of profound injustice to a group of citizens, then the argument that the courts should have refused jurisdiction is considerably weakened.

We cannot conclude from these arguments that the draft (or any part of it) was unconstitutional. When the Supreme Court was called upon to rule on the question, it rejected some of them, and refused to consider the others on grounds that they were political. The majority of lawyers agreed with this result. But the arguments of unconstitutionality were at least plausible, and a reasonable and competent lawyer might well think that they present a stronger case, on balance, than the counter-arguments. If he does, he will consider that the draft was not constitutional, and there will be no way of proving that he is wrong.

Therefore we cannot assume, in judging what should have been done with the draft dissenters, that they were asserting a privilege to disobey valid laws. We cannot decide that fairness demanded their punishment until we try to answer further questions: What should a citizen do when the law is unclear, and when he thinks it allows what others think it does not? I do not mean to ask, of course, what it is *legally* proper for him to do, or what his *legal* rights are – that would be begging the question, because it depends upon whether he is right or they are right. I mean to ask what his proper course is as a citizen, what, in other words, we would consider to be "playing the game". That is a crucial question, because it cannot be unfair not to punish him if he is acting as, given his opinions, we think he should.[1]

There is no obvious answer on which most citizens would readily agree, and that is itself significant. If we examine our legal institutions and practices, however, we shall discover some relevant underlying principles and policies. I shall set out three possible answers to the question, and then try to show which of these best fits our practices and expectations. The three possibilities I want to consider are these:

1. If the law is doubtful, and it is therefore unclear whether it permits someone to do what he wants, he should assume the worst, and act on the assumption that it does not. He should obey the executive authorities who command him, even though he thinks they are wrong, while using the political process, if he can, to change the law.
2. If the law is doubtful, he may follow his own judgment, that is, he may do what he wants if he believes that the case that the law permits this is stronger than the case that it does not. But he may follow his own judgment only until an authoritative institution, like a court, decides the other way in a case involving him or someone else. Once an institutional decision has been reached, he must abide by that decision, even though he thinks that it was wrong. (There are, in theory, many subdivisions of this second possibility. We may say that the individual's choice is foreclosed by the contrary decision of any court, including the lowest court in the system if the case is not appealed. Or we may require a decision of some particular court

or institution. I shall discuss this second possibility in its most liberal form, namely that the individual may properly follow his own judgment until a contrary decision of the highest court competent to pass on the issue, which, in the case of the draft, was the United States Supreme Court.)

3. If the law is doubtful, he may follow his own judgment, even after a contrary decision by the highest competent court. Of course, he must take the contrary decision of any court into account in making his judgment of what the law requires. Otherwise the judgment would not be an honest or reasonable one, because the doctrine of precedent, which is an established part of our legal system, has the effect of allowing the decision of the courts to *change* the law. Suppose, for example, that a taxpayer believes that he is not required to pay tax on certain forms of income. If the Supreme Court decides to the contrary, he should, taking into account the practice of according great weight to the decisions of the Supreme Court on tax matters, decide that the Court's decision has itself tipped the balance, and that the law now requires him to pay the tax.

Someone might think that this qualification erases the difference between the third and the second models, but it does not. The doctrine of precedent gives different weights to the decisions of different courts, and greatest weight to the decisions of the Supreme Court, but it does not make the decisions of any court conclusive. Sometimes, even after a contrary Supreme Court decision, an individual may still reasonably believe that the law is on his side; such cases are rare, but they are most likely to occur in disputes over constitutional law when civil disobedience is involved. The Court has shown itself more likely to overrule its past decisions if these have limited important personal or political rights, and it is just these decisions that a dissenter might want to challenge.

We cannot assume, in other words, that the Constitution is always what the Supreme Court says it is. Oliver Wendell Holmes, for example, did not follow such a rule in his famous dissent in the *Gitlow* case. A few years before, in *Abrams*, he had lost his battle to persuade the court that the First Amendment protected an anarchist who had been urging general strikes against the government. A similar issue was presented in *Gitlow*, and Holmes once again dissented. "It is true," he said, "that in my opinion this criterion was departed from [in *Abrams*] but the convictions that I expressed in that case are too deep for it to be possible for me as yet to believe that it ... settled the law." Holmes voted for acquitting Gitlow, on the ground that what Gitlow had done was no crime, even though the Supreme Court had recently held that it was.

Here then are three possible models for the behavior of dissenters who disagree with the executive authorities when the law is doubtful. Which of them best fits our legal and social practices?

I think it plain that we do not follow the first of these models, that is, that we do not expect citizens to assume the worst. If no court has decided the issue, and a man thinks, on balance, that the law is on his side, most of our lawyers and critics think it perfectly proper for him to follow his own judgment. Even when many disapprove of what he does – such as peddling pornography – they do not think he must desist just because the legality of his conduct is subject to doubt.

It is worth pausing a moment to consider what society would lose if it did follow the first model or, to put the matter the other way, what society gains when people follow their own judgment in cases like this. When the law is uncertain, in the sense that lawyers can reasonably disagree on what a court ought to decide, the reason usually is that different legal principles and policies have collided, and it is unclear how best to accommodate these conflicting principles and policies.

Our practice, in which different parties are encouraged to pursue their own understanding, provides a means of testing relevant hypotheses. If the question is whether a particular rule would have certain undesirable consequences, or whether these consequences would have limited or broad ramifications, then, before the issue is decided, it is useful to know what does in fact take place when some people proceed on that rule. (Much anti-trust and business regulation law has developed through this kind of testing.) If the question is whether and to what degree a particular solution would offend principles of justice or fair play deeply respected by the community, it is useful, again, to experiment by testing the community's response. The extent of community indifference to anti-contraception laws, for example, would never have become established had not some organizations deliberately flouted those laws.

If the first model were followed, we would lose the advantages of these tests. The law would suffer, particularly if this model were applied to constitutional issues. When the validity of a criminal statute is in doubt, the statute will almost always strike some people as being unfair or unjust, because it will infringe some principle of liberty or justice or fairness which they take to be built into the Constitution. If our practice were that whenever a law is doubtful on these grounds, one must act as if it were valid, then the chief vehicle we have for challenging the law on moral grounds would be lost, and over time the law we obeyed would certainly become less fair and just, and the liberty of our citizens would certainly be diminished.

We would lose almost as much if we used a variation of the first model, that a citizen must assume the worst unless he can anticipate that the courts will agree with his view of the law. If everyone deferred to his guess of what the courts would do, society and its law would be poorer. Our assumption in rejecting the first model was that the record a citizen makes in following his own judgment, together with the arguments he makes supporting that judgment when he has the opportunity, are helpful in creating the best judicial decision possible. This remains true even when, at the time the citizen acts, the odds are against his success in court. We must remember, too, that the value of the citizen's example is not exhausted once the decision has been made. Our practices require that the decision be criticized, by the legal profession and the law schools, and the record of dissent may be invaluable here.

Of course a man must consider what the courts will do when he decides whether it would be *prudent* to follow his own judgment. He may have to face jail, bankruptcy, or opprobrium if he does. But it is essential that we separate the calculation of prudence from the question of what, as a good citizen, he may properly do. We are investigating how society ought to treat him when its courts believe that he judged wrong; therefore we must ask what he is justified in doing when his judgment differs from others. We beg the question if we assume that what he may properly do depends on his guess as to how society will treat him.

We must also reject the second model, that if the law is unclear a citizen may properly follow his own judgment until the highest court has ruled that he is wrong. This fails to take into account the fact that any court, including the Supreme Court, may overrule itself. In 1940 the Court decided that a West Virginia law requiring students to salute the Flag was constitutional. In 1943 it reversed itself, and decided that such a statute was unconstitutional after all. What was the duty as citizens, of those people who in 1941 and 1942 objected to saluting the Flag on grounds of conscience, and thought that the Court's 1940 decision was wrong? We can hardly say that their duty was to follow the first decision. They believed that saluting the Flag was unconscionable, and they believed, reasonably, that no valid law required them to do so. The

Supreme Court later decided that in this they were right. The Court did not simply hold that after the second decision failing to salute would not be a crime; it held (as in a case like this it almost always would) that it was no crime after the first decision either.

Some will say that the flag-salute dissenters should have obeyed the Court's first decision, while they worked in the legislatures to have the law repealed, and tried in the courts to find some way to challenge the law again without actually violating it. That would be, perhaps, a plausible recommendation if conscience were not involved, because it would then be arguable that the gain in orderly procedure was worth the personal sacrifice of patience. But conscience was involved, and if the dissenters had obeyed the law while biding their time, they would have suffered the irreparable injury of having done what their conscience forbade them to do. It is one thing to say that an individual must sometimes violate his conscience when he knows that the law commands him to do it. It is quite another to say that he must violate his conscience even when he reasonably believes that the law does not require it, because it would inconvenience his fellow citizens if he took the most direct, and perhaps the only, method of attempting to show that he is right and they are wrong.

Since a court may overrule itself, the same reasons we listed for rejecting the first model count against the second as well. If we did not have the pressure of dissent, we would not have a dramatic statement of the degree to which a court decision against the dissenter is felt to be wrong, a demonstration that is surely pertinent to the question of whether it was right. We would increase the chance of being governed by rules that offend the principles we claim to serve.

These considerations force us, I think, from the second model, but some will want to substitute a variation of it. They will argue that once the Supreme Court has decided that a criminal law is valid, then citizens have a duty to abide by that decision until they have a reasonable belief, not merely that the decision is a bad law, but that the Supreme Court is likely to overrule it. Under this view the West Virginia dissenters who refused to salute the Flag in 1942 were acting properly, because they might reasonably have anticipated that the Court would change its mind. But once the Court held laws like the draft laws constitutional, it would be improper to continue to challenge these laws, because there would be no great likelihood that the Court would soon change its mind. This suggestion must also be rejected, however. For once we say that a citizen may properly follow his own judgment of the law, in spite of his judgment that the courts will probably find against him, there is no plausible reason why he should act differently because a contrary decision is already on the books.

Thus the third model, or something close to it, seems to be the fairest statement of a man's social duty in our community. A citizen's allegiance is to the law, not to any particular person's view of what the law is, and he does not behave unfairly so long as he proceeds on his own considered and reasonable view of what the law requires. Let me repeat (because it is crucial) that this is not the same as saying that an individual may disregard what the courts have said. The doctrine of precedent lies near the core of our legal system, and no one can make a reasonable effort to follow the law unless he grants the courts the general power to alter it by their decisions. But if the issue is one touching fundamental personal or political rights, and it is arguable that the Supreme Court has made a mistake, a man is within his social rights in refusing to accept that decision as conclusive.

One large question remains before we can apply these observations to the problems of draft resistance. I have been talking about the case of a man who believes that the law is not what other people think, or what the courts have held. This description may fit some of those who disobey the draft laws out of conscience, but it does not fit most of them. Most of the dissenters are not lawyers or political philosophers; they believe that the laws on the books are immoral, and inconsistent with their country's legal ideals, but they have not considered the question of whether they may be invalid as well. Of what relevance to their situation, then, is the proposition that one may properly follow one's own view of the law?

To answer this, I shall have to return to the point I made earlier. The Constitution, through the due process clause, the equal protection clause, the First Amendment, and the other provisions I mentioned, injects an extraordinary amount of our political morality into the issue of whether a law is valid. The statement that most draft dissenters are unaware that the law is invalid therefore needs qualification. They hold beliefs that, if true, strongly support the view that the law is on their side; the fact that they have reached that further conclusion can be traced, in at least most cases, to their lack of legal sophistication. If we believe that when the law is doubtful people who follow their own judgment of the law may be acting properly, it would seem wrong not to extend that view to those dissenters whose judgments come to the same thing. No part of the case that I made for the third model would entitle us to distinguish them from their more knowledgeable colleagues.

We can draw several tentative conclusions from the argument so far: When the law is uncertain, in the sense that a plausible case can be made on both sides, then a citizen who follows his own judgment is not behaving unfairly. Our practices permit and encourage him to follow his own judgment in such cases. For that reason, our government has a special responsibility to try to protect him, and soften his predicament, whenever it can do so without great damage to other policies. It does not follow that the government can guarantee him immunity – it cannot adopt the rule that it will prosecute no one who acts out of conscience, or convict no one who reasonably disagrees with the courts. That would paralyze the government's ability to carry out its policies; it would, moreover, throw away the most important benefit of following the third model. If the state never prosecuted, then the courts could not act on the experience and the arguments the dissent has generated. But it does follow that when the practical reasons for prosecuting are relatively weak in a particular case, or can be met in other ways, the path of fairness lies in tolerance. The popular view that the law is the law and must always be enforced refuses to distinguish the man who acts on his own judgment of a doubtful law, and thus behaves as our practices provide, from the common criminal. I know of no reason, short of moral blindness, for not drawing a distinction in principle between the two cases.

I anticipate a philosophical objection to these conclusions: that I am treating law as a "brooding omnipresence in the sky". I have spoken of people making judgments about what the law requires, even in cases in which the law is unclear and undemonstrable. I have spoken of cases in which a man might think that the law requires one thing, even though the Supreme Court has said that it requires another, and even when it was not likely that the Supreme Court would soon change its mind. I will therefore be charged with the view that there is always a "right answer" to a legal problem to be found in natural law or locked up in some transcendental strongbox.

The strongbox theory of law is, of course, nonsense. When I say that people hold views on the law when the law is doubtful, and that these views are not merely predictions of what the courts will hold, I intend no such metaphysics. I mean only to summarize as accurately as I can many of the practices that are part of our legal process.

Lawyers and judges make statements of legal right and duty, even when they know these are not demonstrable, and support them with arguments even when they know that these arguments will not appeal to everyone. They make these arguments to one another, in the professional journals, in the classrooms, and in the courts. They respond to these arguments, when others make them, by judging them good or bad or mediocre. In so doing they assume that some arguments for a given doubtful position are better than others. They also assume that the case on one side of a doubtful proposition may be stronger than the case on the other, which is what I take a claim of law in a doubtful case to mean. They distinguish, without too much difficulty, these arguments from predictions of what the courts will decide.

These practices are poorly represented by the theory that the judgments of law on doubtful issues are nonsense, or are merely predictions of what the courts will do. Those who hold such theories cannot deny the fact of these practices; perhaps these theorists mean that the practices are not sensible, because they are based on suppositions that do not hold, or for some other reason. But this makes their objection mysterious, because they never specify what they take the purposes underlying these practices to be; and unless these goals are specified, one cannot decide whether the practices are sensible. I understand these underlying purposes to be those I described earlier: the development and testing of the law through experimentation by citizens and through the adversary process.

Our legal system pursues these goals by inviting citizens to decide the strengths and weaknesses of legal arguments for themselves, or through their own counsel, and to act on these judgments, although that permission is qualified by the limited threat that they may suffer if the courts do not agree. Success in this strategy depends on whether there is sufficient agreement within the community on what counts as good or bad argument, so that, although different people will reach different judgments, these differences will be neither so profound nor so frequent as to make the system unworkable, or dangerous for those who act by their own lights. I believe there is sufficient agreement on the criteria of the argument to avoid these traps, although one of the main tasks of legal philosophy is to exhibit and clarify these criteria. In any event, the practices I have described have not yet been shown to be misguided; they therefore must count in determining whether it is just and fair to be lenient to those who break what others think is the law.

I have said that the government has a special responsibility to those who act on a reasonable judgment that a law is invalid. It should make accommodation for them as far as possible, when this is consistent with other policies. It may be difficult to decide what the government ought to do, in the name of that responsibility, in particular cases. The decision will be a matter of balance, and flat rules will not help. Still, some principles can be set out.

I shall start with the prosecutor's decision whether to press charges. He must balance both his responsibility to be lenient and the risk that convictions will rend the society, against the damage to the law's policy that may follow if he leaves the dissenters alone. In making his calculation he must consider not only the extent to which others will be harmed, but also how the law evaluates that harm; and he must therefore make the following distinction. Every rule of law is supported, and presumably justified, by a set of policies it is supposed to advance and principles it is supposed to respect. Some rules (the laws prohibiting murder and theft, for example) are supported by the proposition that the individuals protected have a moral right to be free from the harm proscribed. Other rules (the more technical anti-trust rules, for example) are not supported by any supposition of any underlying right; their support comes chiefly from the alleged utility of the economic and social policies they promote. These may be supplemented with moral principles (like the view that it is a harsh business practice to undercut a weak competitor's prices) but these fall short of recognizing a moral right against the harm in question.

The point of the distinction here is this: if a particular rule of law represents an official decision that individuals have a moral right to be free from some harm, then that is a powerful argument against tolerating violations that inflict those injuries. Laws protecting people from personal injury or the destruction of their property, for example, do represent that sort of decision, and this is a very strong argument against tolerating civil disobedience that involves violence.

It may be controversial, of course, whether a law does rest on the assumption of a moral right. The question is whether it is reasonable to suppose, from the background and administration of the law, that its authors recognized such a right. There are cases, in addition to rules against violence, where it is plain that they did; the civil rights laws are examples. Many sincere and ardent segregationists believe that the civil rights laws and decisions are unconstitutional, because they compromise principles of local government and of freedom of association. This is an arguable, though not a persuasive, view. But these laws and decisions clearly embody the view that Negroes, as individuals, have a right not to be segregated. They do not rest simply on the judgment that other national policies are best pursued by preventing racial segregation. If we take no action against the man who blocks the school house door, therefore, we violate the moral rights, confirmed by law, of the schoolgirl he blocks. The responsibility of leniency cannot go this far.

The schoolgirl's position is different, however, from that of the draftee who may be called up sooner or given a more dangerous post if draft offenders are not punished. The draft laws, taken as a whole and with an eye to their administration, cannot be said to reflect the judgment that a man has a moral right to be drafted only after certain other men or groups have been called. The draft classifications, and the order-of-call within classifications, are arranged for social and administrative convenience. They also reflect considerations of fairness, like the proposition that a mother who has lost one of two sons in war ought not to be made to risk losing the other. But they presuppose no fixed rights. The draft boards are given considerable discretion in the classification process, and the army, of course, has almost complete discretion in assigning dangerous posts. If the prosecutor tolerates draft offenders, he makes small shifts in the law's calculations of fairness and utility. These may cause disadvantage to others in the pool of draftees but that is a different matter from contradicting their moral rights.

This difference between segregation and the draft is not an accident of how the laws happen to have been written. It would run counter to a century of practice to suppose that citizens have moral rights with respect to the order in which they are called to serve; the lottery system of selection, for example, would be abhorrent under that supposition. If our history had been different, and if the community had recognized such a moral right, it seems fair to suppose that some of the draft dissenters, at least, would have modified their acts so as to try to respect these rights. So it is wrong to analyze draft cases in the same way as cases of violence or civil rights cases, as many critics do when considering whether tolerance is justified. I do not mean that fairness to others is irrelevant in draft cases; it must be taken into account, and balanced against fairness to dissenters and the long-term benefit to society. But it does not play the commanding role here that it does when rights are at stake.

Where, then, does the balance of fairness and utility lie in the case of those who counseled draft resistance? If these men had encouraged violence or otherwise trespassed on the rights of others, then there would have been a strong case for prosecution. But in the absence of such actions, the balance of fairness and utility seems to me to lie the other way, and I therefore think that the decision to prosecute Coffin, Spock, Raskin, Goodman, and Ferber was wrong. It might have been argued that if those who counsel draft resistance are free from prosecution, the number who resist induction will increase; but not, I think, much beyond the number of those who would resist in any event.

If this is wrong, and there is much greater resistance, then a sense of this residual discontent is of importance to policy makers, and it ought not to have been hidden under a ban on speech. Conscience is deeply involved – it is hard to believe that many who counseled resistance did so on any other grounds. The case is strong that the laws making counseling a crime are unconstitutional; even those who do not find the case persuasive will admit that its arguments have substance. The harm to potential draftees, both those who may have been persuaded to resist and those who may have been called earlier because others have been persuaded, was remote and speculative.

The cases of men who refused induction when drafted are more complicated. The crucial question is whether a failure to prosecute will lead to wholesale refusals to serve. It may not – there were social pressures, including the threat of career disadvantages, that would have forced many young Americans to serve if drafted, even if they knew they would not go to jail if they refused. If the number would not much have increased, then the State should have left the dissenters alone, and I see no great harm in delaying any prosecution until the effect of that policy became clearer. If the number of those who refuse induction turned out to be large, this would argue for prosecution. But it would also make the problem academic, because if there had been sufficient dissent to bring us to that pass, it would have been most difficult to pursue the war in any event, except under a near-totalitarian regime.

There may seem to be a paradox in these conclusions. I argued earlier that when the law is unclear citizens have the right to follow their own judgment, partly on the grounds that this practice helps to shape issues for adjudication; now I propose a course that eliminates or postpones adjudication. But the contradiction is only apparent. It does not follow from the fact that our practice facilitates adjudication, and renders it more useful in developing the law, that a trial should follow whenever citizens do act by their own lights. The question arises in each case whether the issues are ripe for adjudication, and whether adjudication would settle these issues in a manner that would decrease the chance of, or remove the grounds for, further dissent.

In the draft cases, the answer to both these questions was negative: there was much ambivalence about the war, and ignorance about the scope of the moral issues involved in the draft. It was far from the best time for a court to pass on these issues, and tolerating dissent for a time was one way of allowing the debate to continue until it produced something clearer. Moreover, it was plain that an adjudication of the constitutional issues would not settle the law. Those who had doubts whether the draft was constitutional had the same doubts even after the Supreme Court said that it was. This is one of those cases, touching fundamental rights, in which our practices of precedent encourage such doubts.

Even if the prosecutor does not act, however, the underlying problem will be only temporarily relieved. So long as the law appears to make acts of dissent criminal, a man of conscience will face danger. What can Congress, which shares the responsibility of leniency, do to lessen this danger?

Congress can review the laws in question to see how much accommodation can be given to dissenters. Every program a legislature adopts is a mixture of policies and restraining principles. We accept loss of efficiency in crime detection and urban renewal, for example, so that we can respect the rights of accused criminals and compensate property owners for their damages. Congress may properly defer to its responsibility toward the dissenters by adjusting or compromising other policies. The relevant questions are these: What means can be found for allowing the greatest possible tolerance of conscientious dissent while minimizing its impact on policy? How strong is the government's responsibility for leniency in this case – how deeply is conscience involved, and how strong is the case that the law is invalid after all? How important is the policy in question – is interference with that policy too great a price to pay? These questions are no doubt too simple, but they suggest the heart of the choices that must be made.

For the same reasons that those who counseled resistance should not have been prosecuted, I think that the law that makes this a crime should be repealed. The case is strong that this law abridges free speech. It certainly coerces conscience, and it probably serves no beneficial effect. If counseling would persuade only a few to resist who otherwise would not, the value of the restraint is small; if counseling would persuade many, that is an important political fact that should be known.

The issues are more complex, again, in the case of draft resistance itself. Those who believed that the war in Vietnam was itself a grotesque blunder would have favoured any change in the law that made peace more likely. But if we take the position of those who think the war was necessary, then we must admit that a policy that continued the draft but wholly exempted dissenters would have been unwise. Two less drastic alternatives should have been considered, however: a volunteer army, and an expanded conscientious objector category that included those who found the war immoral. There is much to be said against both proposals, but once the requirement of respect for dissent is recognized, the balance of principle may be tipped in their favor.

So the case for not prosecuting conscientious draft offenders, and for changing the laws in their favor, was a strong one. It would have been unrealistic to expect this policy to prevail, however, for political pressures opposed it.

We must consider, therefore, what the courts could and should have done. A court might, of course, have upheld the arguments that the draft laws were in some way unconstitutional, in general or as applied to the defendants in the case at hand. Or it might acquit the defendants because the facts necessary for conviction are not proved. I shall not argue the constitutional issues, or the facts of any particular case. I want instead to suggest that a court ought not to convict, at least in some circumstances, even if it sustains the statutes and finds the facts as charged. The Supreme Court had not ruled on the chief arguments that the draft was unconstitutional, nor had it held that these arguments raised political questions that are not within its jurisdiction, when several of the draft cases arose. There are strong reasons why a Court should acquit in these circumstances even if it does then sustain the draft. It ought to acquit on the ground that before its decision the validity of the draft was doubtful, and it is unfair to punish men for disobeying a doubtful law.

There would be precedent for a decision along these lines. The Court has several times reversed criminal convictions, on due process grounds, because the law in question was too vague. (It has overturned convictions, for example, under laws that made it a crime to charge 'unreasonable prices' or to be a member of a 'gang'.) Conviction under a vague criminal law offends the moral and political ideals of due process in two ways. First, it places a citizen in the unfair position of either acting at his peril or accepting a more stringent restriction on his life than the legislature may have authorized: As I argued earlier, it is not acceptable, as a model of social behavior, that in such cases he ought to assume the worst. Second, it gives power to the prosecutor and the courts to make criminal law, by opting for one or the other possible interpretations after the event. This would be a delegation of authority by the legislature that is inconsistent with our scheme of separation of powers.

Conviction under a criminal law whose terms are not vague, but whose constitutional validity is doubtful, offends due process in the first of these ways. It forces a citizen to assume the worst, or act at his peril. It offends due process in something like the second way as well. Most citizens would be deterred by a doubtful statute if they were to risk jail by violating it. Congress, and not the courts, would then be the effective voice in deciding the constitutionality of criminal enactments, and this also violates the separation of powers.

If acts of dissent continue to occur after the Supreme Court has ruled that the laws are valid, or that the political question doctrine applies, then acquittal on the grounds I have described is no longer appropriate. The Court's decision will not have finally settled the law, for the reasons given earlier, but the Court will have done all that can be done to settle it. The courts may still exercise their sentencing discretion, however, and impose minimal or suspended sentences as a mark of respect for the dissenters' position.

Some lawyers will be shocked by my general conclusion that we have a responsibility toward those who disobey the draft laws out of conscience, and that we may be required not to prosecute them, but rather to change our laws or adjust our sentencing procedures to accommodate them. The simple Draconian propositions, that crime must be punished, and that he who misjudges the law must take the consequences, have an extraordinary hold on the professional as well as the popular imagination. But the rule of law is more complex and more intelligent than that and it is important that it survive.

NOTES

1 I do not mean to imply that the government should always punish a man who deliberately breaks a law he knows is valid. There may be reasons of fairness or practicality, like those I listed in the third paragraph, for not prosecuting such men. But cases like the draft cases present special arguments for tolerance; I want to concentrate on these arguments and therefore have isolated these cases.

1 How are Dworkin's views about civil disobedience related to his view of law?
2 Could something qualify as civil disobedience on Dworkin's view despite being morally unjustified in the final analysis?
3 Protesters at Clayoquot sound sought to disrupt block clear-cut logging, and claimed to be engaged in civil disobedience. How would Dworkin assess their claim? (*MacMillan Bloedel Ltd v Simpson,* [1994] 89 CCC 3d 217)

Martin Luther King, Jr
"Letter from Birmingham City Jail" (1968)

Dr King argues that there is a duty to break the law under certain circumstances, when the alternative is to acquiesce to injustice.

My dear Fellow Clergymen,

While confined here in the Birmingham City Jail, I came across your recent statement calling our present activities "unwise and untimely." Seldom, If ever, do I pause to answer criticism of my work and ideas. If I sought to answer all the criticisms that cross my desk, my secretaries would be engaged in little else in the course of the day, and I would have no time for constructive work. But since I feel that you are men of genuine goodwill and your criticisms are sincerely set forth, I would like to answer your statement in what I hope will be patient and reasonable terms.

I think I should give the reason for my being in Birmingham, since you have been influenced by the argument of "outsiders coming in." I have the honor of serving as president of the Southern Christian Leadership Conference, an organization operating in every Southern state, with headquarters in Atlanta, Georgia. We have some eighty-five affiliate organizations all across the South – one being the Alabama Christian Movement for Human Rights. Whenever necessary and possible we share staff, educational and financial resources with our affiliates.

Several months ago our local affiliate here in Birmingham invited us to be on call to engage in a nonviolent direct action program if such were deemed necessary. We readily consented and when the hour came we lived up to our promises. So I am here, along with several members of my staff, because we were invited here. I am here because I have basic organizational ties here.

Beyond this, I am in Birmingham because injustice is here. Just as the eighth century prophets left their little villages and carried their "thus saith the Lord" far beyond the boundaries of their home town; and just as the Apostle Paul left his little village of Tarsus and carried the gospel of Jesus Christ to practically every hamlet and city of the Graeco-Roman world, I too am compelled to carry the gospel of freedom beyond my particular home town. Like Paul, I must constantly respond to the Macedonian call for aid.

Moreover, I am cognizant of the interrelatedness of all communities and states. I cannot sit idly by in Atlanta and not be concerned about what happens in Birmingham. Injustice anywhere is a threat to justice everywhere. We are caught in an inescapable network of mutuality, tied in a single garment of destiny. Whatever affects one directly affects all indirectly. Never again can we afford to live with the narrow, provincial "outside agitator" idea. Anyone who lives inside the United States can never be considered an outsider anywhere in this country.

You deplore the demonstrations that are presently taking place in Birmingham. But I am sorry that your statement did not express a similar concern for the conditions that brought the demonstrations into being. I am sure that each of you would want to go beyond the superficial social analyst who looks merely at effects, and does not grapple with underlying causes. I would not hesitate to say that it is unfortunate that so-called demonstrations are taking place in Birmingham at this time, but I would say in more emphatic terms that it is even more unfortunate that the white power structure of this city left the Negro community with no other alternative.

In any nonviolent campaign there are four basic steps: (1) Collection of the facts to determine whether injustices are alive. (2) Negotiation. (3) Self-purification and (4) Direct Action. We have gone through all of these steps in Birmingham. There can be no gainsaying of the fact that racial injustice engulfs this community.

Birmingham is probably the most thoroughly segregated city in the United States. Its ugly record of police brutality is known in every section of this country. Its unjust treatment of Negroes in the courts is a notorious reality. There have been more unsolved bombings of Negro homes and churches in Birmingham than any city in this nation. These are the hard, brutal and unbelievable facts. On the basis of these conditions Negro leaders sought to negotiate with the city fathers. But the political leaders consistently refused to engage in good faith negotiation.

Then came the opportunity last September to talk with some of the leaders of the economic community. In these negotiating sessions certain promises were made by the merchants – such as the promise to remove the humiliating racial signs from the stores. On the basis of these promises Rev. Shuttlesworth and the leaders of the Alabama Christian Movement for Human Rights agreed to call a moratorium on any type of demonstrations. As the weeks and months unfolded we realized that we were the victims of a broken promise. The signs remained. Like so many experiences of the past we were confronted with blasted hopes, and the dark shadow of a deep disappointment settled upon us. So we had no alternative except that of preparing for direct action, whereby we would present our very bodies as a means of laying our case before the conscience of the local and national community. We were not unmindful of the difficulties involved. So we decided to go through a process of self-purification. We started having workshops on non-violence and repeatedly asked ourselves the questions, "Are you able to accept blows without retaliating?" "Are you able to endure the ordeals of jail?" We decided to set our direct action program around the Easter season, realizing that with the exception of Christmas, this was the largest shopping period of the year. Knowing that a strong economic withdrawal program would be the by-product of direct action, we felt that this was the best time to bring pressure on the merchants for the needed changes. Then it occurred to us that the March election was ahead and so we speedily decided to postpone action until after election day. When we discovered that Mr Connor was in the run-off, we decided again to postpone action so that the demonstrations could not be used to cloud the issues. At this time we agreed to begin our nonviolent witness the day after the run-off.

This reveals that we did not move irresponsibly into direct action. We too wanted to see Mr Connor defeated; so went through postponement after postponement to aid in this community need. After this we felt that direct action could be delayed no longer.

You may well ask, "Why direct action? Why sit-ins, marches, etc.? Isn't negotiation a better path?" You are exactly right in your call for negotiation. Indeed, this is the purpose of direct action. Nonviolent direct action seeks to create such a crisis and establish such creative tension that a community that has constantly refused to negotiate is forced to confront the issue. It seeks so to dramatize the issue that it can no longer be ignored. I just referred to the creation of tension as a part of the work of the nonviolent resister. This may sound rather shocking. But I must confess that I am not afraid of the word tension. I have earnestly worked and preached against violent tension, but there is a type of constructive nonviolent tension that is necessary for growth. Just as Socrates felt that it was necessary to create a tension in the mind so that individuals could rise from the bondage of myths and half-truths to the unfettered realm of creative analysis and objective appraisal, we must see the need of having nonviolent gadflies to create the kind of tension in society that will help men to rise from the dark depths of prejudice and racism to the majestic heights of understanding and brotherhood. So the purpose of the direct action is to create a situation so crisis-packed that it will inevitably open the door to negotiation. We, therefore, concur with you in your call for negotiation. Too long has our beloved South-land been bogged down in the tragic attempt to live in monologue rather than dialogue.

One of the basic points in your statement is that our acts are untimely. Some have asked, "Why didn't you give the new administration time to act?" The only answer that I can give to this inquiry is that the new administration must be prodded about as much as the outgoing one before it acts. We will be sadly mistaken if we feel that the election of Mr Boutwell will bring the millennium to Birmingham. While Mr Boutwell is much more articulate and gentle than Mr Connor, they are both segregationists, dedicated to the task of maintaining the status quo. The hope I see in Mr Boutwell is that he will be reasonable enough to see the futility of massive resistance to desegregation. But he will not see this without pressure from the devotees of civil rights. My friends, I must say to you that we have not made a single gain in civil rights without determined legal and nonviolent pressure. History is the long and tragic story of the fact that privileged groups seldom give up their privileges voluntarily. Individuals may see the moral light and voluntarily give up their unjust posture; but as Reinhold Niebuhr has reminded us, groups are more immoral than individuals.

We know through painful experience that freedom is never voluntarily given by the oppressor; it must be demanded by the oppressed. Frankly, I have never yet engaged in a direct action movement that was "well timed," according to the timetable of those who have not suffered unduly from the disease of segregation. For years now I have heard the words "Wait!" It rings in the ear of every Negro with a piercing familiarity. This "Wait" has almost always meant "Never." It has been a tranquilizing thalidomide, relieving the emotional stress for a moment, only to give birth to an ill-formed infant of frustration. We must come to see with the distinguished jurist of yesterday that "justice too long delayed is justice denied." We have waited for more than three hundred and forty years for our constitutional and God-given rights. The nations of Asia and Africa are moving with jet-like speed toward the goal of political independence, and we still creep at horse and buggy pace toward the gaining of a cup of coffee at a lunch counter. I guess it is easy for those who have never felt the stinging darts of segregation to say, "Wait." But when have you seen vicious mobs lynch your mothers and fathers at will and drown your sisters and brothers at whim; when have you seen hate-filled policemen curse, kick, brutalize and even kill your black brothers and sisters with impunity; when you see the vast majority of your twenty million Negro brothers smothering in an airtight cage of poverty in the midst of an affluent society; when you suddenly find your tongue twisted and your speech stammering as you seek to explain to your six-year-old daughter why she can't go to the public amusement park that has just been advertised on television, and see tears welling up in her little eyes when she is told that Funtown is closed to colored children, and see the depressing clouds of inferiority begin to form in her little mental sky, and see her begin to distort her little personality by unconsciously developing a bitterness toward white people; when you have to concoct an answer for a five-year-old son asking in agonizing pathos: "Daddy, why do white people treat colored people so mean?"; when you take a cross country drive and find it necessary to sleep night after night in the uncomfortable corners of your automobile because no motel will accept you; when you are humiliated day in and day out by nagging signs reading "white" and "colored"; when your first name becomes "nigger" and your middle name becomes "boy" (however old you are) and your last name becomes "John," and when your wife and mother are never given the respected title "Mrs"; when you are harried by day and haunted at night by the fact that you are a Negro, living constantly at tip-toe stance never quite knowing what to expect next, and plagued with inner fears and outer resentments; when you are forever fighting a degenerating sense of "nobodiness"; then you will understand why we find it difficult to wait. There comes a time when the cup of endurance runs over, and men are no longer willing to be plunged into an abyss of injustice where they experience the blackness of corroding despair. I hope, sirs, you can understand our legitimate and unavoidable impatience.

You express a great deal of anxiety over our willingness to break laws. This is certainly a legitimate concern. Since we so diligently urge people to obey the Supreme Court's decision of 1954 outlawing segregation in the public schools, it is rather strange and paradoxical to find us consciously breaking laws. One may well ask, "How can you advocate breaking some laws and obeying others?" The answer is found in the fact that there are two types of laws: There are *just* and there are *unjust* laws. I would agree with Saint Augustine that "An unjust law is no law at all."

Now what is the difference between the two? How does one determine when a law is just or unjust? A just law is a man-made code that squares with the moral law or the law of God. An unjust law is a code that is out of harmony with the moral law. To put it in the terms of Saint Thomas Aquinas, an unjust law is a human law that is not rooted in eternal and natural law. Any law that uplifts human personality is just. Any law that degrades human personality is unjust. All segregation statutes are unjust because segregation distorts the soul and damages the personality. It gives the segregator a false sense of superiority, and the segregated a false sense of inferiority. To use the words of Martin Buber, the great Jewish philosopher, segregation substitutes an "I-it" relationship for the "I-thou" relationship, and ends up relegating persons to the status of things. So segregation is not only politically, economically and sociologically unsound, but it is morally wrong and sinful. Paul Tillich has said that sin is separation. Isn't segregation an existential expression of man's tragic separation, an expression of his awful estrangement, his terrible sinfulness? So I can urge man to disobey segregation ordinances because they are morally wrong.

Let us turn to a more concrete example of just and unjust laws. An unjust law is a code that a majority inflicts on a minority that is not binding on itself. This is difference made legal. On the other hand a just law is a code that a majority compels a minority to follow that it is willing to follow itself. This is sameness made legal.

Let me give another explanation. An unjust law is a code inflicted upon a minority which that minority had no part in enacting or creating because they did not have the unhampered right to vote. Who can say that the legislature of Alabama which set up the segregation laws was democratically elected? Throughout the state of Alabama all types of conniving methods are used to prevent Negroes from becoming registered voters and there are some counties without a single Negro registered to vote despite the fact that the Negro constitutes a majority of the population. Can any law set up in such a state be considered democratically structured?

These are just a few examples of unjust and just laws. There are some instances when a law is just on its face and unjust in its application. For instance, I was arrested Friday on a charge of parading without a permit. Now there is nothing wrong with an ordinance which requires a permit for a parade, but when the ordinance is used to preserve segregation and to deny citizens the First Amendment privilege of peaceful assembly and peaceful protest, then it becomes unjust.

I hope you can see the distinction I am trying to point out. In no sense did I advocate evading or defying the law as the rabid segregationist would do. This would lead to anarchy. One who breaks an unjust law must do it *openly, lovingly* (not hatefully as the white mothers did in New Orleans when they were seen on television screaming "nigger, nigger, nigger"), and with a willingness to accept the penalty. I submit that an individual who breaks a law that conscience tells him is unjust, and willingly accepts the penalty by staying in jail to arouse the conscience of the community over its injustice, is in reality expressing the very highest respect for the law.

Of course, there is nothing new about this kind of civil disobedience. It was seen sublimely in the refusal of Shadrach, Meshach and Abednego to obey the laws of Nebuchadnezzar because a higher moral law was involved. It was practised superbly by the early Christians who were willing to face hungry lions and the excruciating pain of chopping blocks, before submitting to certain unjust laws of the Roman empire. To a degree academic freedom is a reality today because Socrates practised civil disobedience.

We can never forget that everything Hitler did in Germany was "legal" and everything the Hungarian freedom fighters did in Hungary was "illegal." It was "illegal" to aid and comfort a Jew in Hitler's Germany. But I am sure that if I had lived in Germany during that time I would have aided and comforted my Jewish brothers even though it was illegal. If I lived in a Communist country today where certain principles dear to the Christian faith are suppressed, I believe I would openly advocate disobeying these anti-religious laws. I must make two honest confessions to you, my Christian and Jewish brothers. First, I must confess that over the last few years I have been gravely disappointed with the white moderate. I have almost reached the regrettable conclusion that the Negro's great stumbling block in the stride toward freedom is not the White Citizen's Council-er or the Ku Klux Klanner, but the white moderate who is more devoted to "order" than to justice; who prefers a negative peace which is the absence of tension to a positive peace which is the presence of justice; who constantly says, "I agree with you in the goal you seek, but I can't agree with your methods of direct action"; who paternalistically feels that he can set the timetable for another man's freedom; who lives by the myth of time and who constantly advises the Negro to wait until a "more convenient season." Shallow understanding from people of goodwill is more frustrating than absolute misunderstanding from people of ill will. Lukewarm acceptance is much more bewildering than outright rejection.

I had hoped that the white moderate would understand that law and order exist for the purpose of establishing justice, and that when they fail to do this they become dangerously structured dams that block the flow of social progress. I had hoped that the white moderate would understand that the present tension of the South is merely a necessary phase of the transition from an obnoxious negative peace, where the Negro passively accepted his unjust plight, to a substance-filled positive peace, where all men will respect the dignity and worth of human personality. Actually, we who engage in nonviolent direct action are not the creators of tension. We merely bring to the surface the hidden tension that is already alive. We bring it out in the open where it can be seen and dealt with. Like a boil that can never be cured as long as it is covered up but must be opened with all its pus-flowing ugliness to the natural medicines of air and light, injustice must likewise be exposed, with all of the tension its exposing creates, to the light of human conscience and the air of national opinion before it can be cured.

In your statement you asserted that our actions, even though peaceful, must be condemned because they precipitate violence. But can this assertion be logically made? Isn't this like condemning the robbed man because his possession of money precipitated the evil act of robbery? Isn't this like condemning Socrates because his unswerving commitment to truth and his philosophical delvings precipitated the misguided popular mind to make him drink the hemlock? Isn't this like condemning Jesus because His unique God-Consciousness and never-ceasing devotion to His will precipitated the evil act of crucifixion? We must come to see, as federal courts have consistently affirmed, that it is immoral to urge an individual to withdraw his efforts to gain his basic constitutional rights because the quest precipitates violence. Society must protect the robbed and punish the robber.

I had also hoped that the white moderate would reject the myth of time. I received a letter this morning from a white brother in Texas which said: "All Christians know that the colored people will receive equal rights eventually, but it is possible that you are in too great of a religious hurry. It has taken Christianity almost 2000 years to accomplish what it has. The teachings of Christ take time to come to earth." All that is said here grows out of a tragic misconception of time. It is the strangely irrational notion that there is something in the very flow of time that will inevitably cure all ills. Actually time is neutral. It can be used either destructively or constructively. I am coming to feel that the people of ill will have used time much more effectively than the people of goodwill. We will have to repent in this generation not merely for the vitriolic words and actions of the bad people, but for the appalling silence of the good people. We must come to see that human progress never rolls in on wheels of inevitability. It comes through the tireless efforts and persistent work of men willing to be co-workers with God, and without this hard work time itself becomes an ally of the forces of social stagnation. We must use time creatively, and forever realize that the time is always ripe to do right. Now is the time to make real the promise of democracy, and transform our pending national elegy into a creative psalm of brotherhood. Now is the time to lift our national policy from the quicksand of racial injustice to the solid rock of human dignity.

You spoke of our activity in Birmingham as extreme. At first I was rather disappointed that fellow clergymen would see my nonviolent efforts as those of the extremist. I started thinking about the fact that I stand in the middle of two opposing forces in the Negro community. One is a force of complacency made up of Negroes who, as a result of long years of oppression, have been so completely drained of self-respect and a sense of "somebodiness" that they have adjusted to segregation, and, of a few Negroes in the middle class who, because of a degree of academic and economic security, and because at points they profit by segregation, have unconsciously become insensitive to the problems of the masses. The other force is one of bitterness and hatred, and comes perilously close to advocating violence. It is expressed in the various black nationalist groups that are springing up over the nation, the largest and best known being Elijah Muhammad's Muslim movement. This movement is nourished by the contemporary frustration over the continued existence of racial discrimination. It is made up of people who have lost faith in America, who have absolutely repudiated Christianity, and who have concluded that the white man is an incurable "devil." I have tried to stand between these two forces, saying that we need not follow the "donothingism" of the complacent or the hatred and despair of the black nationalist. There is the more excellent way of love and non-violent protest. I'm grateful to God that, through the Negro church, the dimension of nonviolence entered our struggle. If this philosophy had not emerged, I am convinced that by now many streets of the South would be flowing with floods of blood. And I am further convinced that if our white brothers dismiss as "rabble rousers" and "outside agitators" those of us who are working through the channels of nonviolent direct action and refuse to support our nonviolent efforts, millions of Negroes, out of frustration and despair, will seek solace and security in black nationalist ideologies, a development that will lead inevitably to a frightening racial nightmare.

Oppressed people cannot remain oppressed forever. The urge for freedom will eventually come. This is what happened to the American Negro. Something within has reminded him of his birthright of freedom; something without has reminded him that he can gain it. Consciously and unconsciously, he has been swept in by what the Germans call the *Zeitgeist*, and with his black brothers of Africa, and his brown and yellow brothers of Asia, South America and the Caribbean, he is moving with a sense of cosmic urgency toward the promised land of racial justice. Recognizing this vital urge that has engulfed the Negro community, one should readily understand public demonstrations. The Negro has many pent-up resentments and latent frustrations. He has to get them out. So let him march sometime; let him have his prayer pilgrimages to the city hall; understand why he must have sit-ins and freedom rides. If his repressed emotions do not come out in these non-violent ways, they will come out in ominous expressions of violence. This is not a threat; it is a fact of history. So I have not said to my people "get rid of your discontent." But I have tried to say that this normal and healthy discontent can be channelized through the creative outlet of nonviolent direct action. Now this approach is being dismissed as extremist. I must admit that I was initially disappointed in being so categorized.

But as I continued to think about the matter I gradually gained a bit of satisfaction from being considered an extremist. Was not Jesus an extremist in love – "Love your enemies, bless them that curse you, pray for them that despitefully use you." Was not Amos an extremist for justice – "Let justice roll down like waters and righteousness like a mighty stream." Was not Paul an extremist for the gospel of Jesus Christ – "I bear in my body the marks of the Lord Jesus." Was not Martin Luther an extremist – "Here I stand; I can do none other so help me God." Was not John Bunyan an extremist – "I will stay in jail to the end of my days before I make a butchery of my conscience." Was not Abraham Lincoln an extremist – "This nation cannot survive half slave and half free." Was not Thomas Jefferson an extremist "We hold these truths to be self-evident, that all men are created equal." So the question is not whether we will be extremist but what kind of extremist will we be. Will we be extremists for hate or will we be extremists for love? Will we be extremists for the preservation of injustice – or will we be extremists for the cause of justice? In that dramatic scene on Calvary's hill, three men were crucified. We must not forget that all three were crucified for the same crime – the crime of extremism. Two were extremists for immorality, and thusly fell below their environment. The other, Jesus Christ, was an extremist for love, truth and goodness, and thereby rose above his environment. So, after all, maybe the South, the nation and the world are in dire need of creative extremists.

I had hoped that the white moderate would see this. Maybe I was too optimistic. Maybe I expected too much. I guess I should have realized that few members of a race that has oppressed another race can understand or appreciate the deep groans and passionate yearnings of those that have been oppressed and still fewer have the vision to see that injustice must be rooted out by strong, persistent and determined action. I am thankful, however, that some of our white brothers have grasped the meaning of this social revolution and committed themselves to it. They are still all too small in quantity, but they are big in quality. Some like Ralph McGill, Lillian Smith, Harry Golden and James Dabbs have written about our struggle in eloquent, prophetic and understanding terms. Others have marched with us down nameless streets of the South. They have languished in filthy roach-infested jails, suffering the abuse and brutality of angry policemen who see them as "dirty nigger lovers." They, unlike so many of their moderate brothers and sisters, have recognized the urgency of the moment and sensed the need for powerful "action" antidotes to combat the disease of segregation.

Let me rush on to mention my other disappointment. I have been so greatly disappointed with the white church and its leadership. Of course, there are some notable exceptions. I am not unmindful of the fact that each of you has taken some significant stands on this issue. I commend you, Rev. Stallings, for your Christian stand on this past Sunday, in welcoming Negroes to your worship service on a non-segregated basis. I commend the Catholic leaders of this state for integrating Springhill College several years ago.

But despite these notable exceptions I must honestly reiterate that I have been disappointed with the church. I do not say that as one of the negative critics who can always find something wrong with the church. I say it as a minister of the gospel, who loves the church; who was nurtured in its bosom; who has been sustained by its spiritual blessings and who will remain true to it as long as the cord of life shall lengthen.

I had the strange feeling when I was suddenly catapulted into the leadership of the bus protest in Montgomery several years ago that we would have the support of the white church. I felt that the white ministers, priests and rabbis of the South would be some of our strongest allies. Instead, some have been outright opponents, refusing to understand the freedom movement and misrepresenting its leaders; all too many others have been more cautious than courageous and have remained silent behind the anesthetizing security of the stained-glass windows.

In spite of my shattered dreams of the past, I came to Birmingham with the hope that the white religious leadership of this community would see the justice of our cause, and with deep moral concern, serve as the channel through which our just grievances would get to the power structure. I had hoped that each of you would understand. But again I have been disappointed. I have heard numerous religious leaders of the South call upon their worshippers to comply with a desegregation decision because it is the *law*, but I have longed to hear white ministers say, "Follow this decree because integration is morally *right* and the Negro is your brother." In the midst of blatant injustices inflicted upon the Negro, I have watched white churches stand on the sideline and merely mouth pious irrelevancies and sanctimonious trivialities. In the midst of a mighty struggle to rid our nation of racial and economic injustice, I have heard so many ministers say, "Those are social issues with which the gospel has no real concern," and I have watched so many churches commit themselves to a completely other-worldly religion which made a strange distinction between body and soul, the sacred and the secular.

So here we are moving toward the exit of the twentieth century with a religious community largely adjusted to the status quo, standing as a tail-light behind other community agencies rather than a headlight leading men to higher levels of justice.

I have traveled the length and breadth of Alabama, Mississippi and all the other southern states. On sweltering summer days and crisp autumn mornings I have looked at her beautiful churches with their lofty spires pointing heavenward. I have beheld the impressive outlay of her massive religious education buildings. Over and over again I have found myself asking: "What kind of people worship here? Who is their God? Where were their voices when the lips of Governor Barnett dripped with words of interposition and nullification? Where were they when Governor Wallace gave the clarion call for defiance and hatred? Where were their voices of support when tired, bruised and weary Negro men and women decided to rise from the dark dungeons of complacency to the bright hills of creative protest?"

Yes, these questions are still in my mind. In deep disappointment, I have wept over the laxity of the church. But be assured that my tears have been tears of love. There can be no deep disappointment where there is not deep love. Yes, I love the church; I love her sacred walls. How could I do otherwise? I am in the rather unique position of being the son, the grandson and the great-grandson of preachers. Yes, I see the church as the body of Christ. But, oh! How we have blemished and scarred that body through social neglect and fear of being nonconformists.

There was a time when the church was very powerful. It was during that period when the early Christians rejoiced when they were deemed worthy to suffer for what they believed. In those days the church was not merely a thermometer that recorded the ideas and principles of popular opinion; it was a thermostat that transformed the mores of society. Wherever the early Christians entered a town the power structure got disturbed and immediately sought to convict them for being "disturbers of the peace" and "outside agitators." But they went on with the conviction that they were "a colony of heaven," and had to obey God rather than man. They were small in number but big in commitment. They were too God-intoxicated to be "astronomically intimidated." They brought an end to such ancient evils as infanticide and gladiatorial contest.

Things are different now. The contemporary church is often a weak, ineffectual voice with an uncertain sound. It is so often the arch supporter of the status quo. Far from being disturbed by the presence of the church, the power structure of the average community is consoled by the church's silent and often vocal sanction of things as they are.

But the judgment of God is upon the church as never before. If the church of today does not recapture the sacrificial spirit of the early church, it will lose its authentic ring, forfeit the loyalty of millions, and be dismissed as an irrelevant social club with no meaning for the twentieth century. I am meeting young people every day whose disappointment with the church has risen to outright disgust.

Maybe again, I have been too optimistic. Is organized religion too inextricably bound to the status quo to save our nation and the world? Maybe I must turn my faith to the inner spiritual church, the church within the church, as the true *ecclesia* and the hope of the world. But again I am thankful to God that some noble souls from the ranks of organized religion have broken loose from the paralyzing chains of conformity and joined us as active partners in the struggle for freedom. They have left their secure congregations and walked the streets of Albany, Georgia, with us. They have gone through the highways of the South on tortuous rides for freedom. Yes, they have gone to jail with us. Some have been kicked out of their churches, and lost support of their bishops and fellow ministers. But they have gone with the faith that right defeated is stronger than evil triumphant. These men have been the leaven in the lump of the race. Their witness has been the spiritual salt that has preserved the true meaning of the Gospel in these troubled times. They have carved a tunnel of hope through the dark mountain of disappointment.

I hope the church as a whole will meet the challenge of this decisive hour. But even if the church does not come to the aid of justice, I have no despair about the future. I have no fear about the outcome of our struggle in Birmingham, even if our motives are presently misunderstood. We will reach the goal of freedom in Birmingham and all over the nation, because the goal of America is freedom. Abused and scorned though we may be, our destiny is tied up with the destiny of America. Before the pilgrims landed at Plymouth we were here. Before the pen of Jefferson etched across the pages of history the majestic words of the Declaration of Independence, we were here. For more than two centuries our foreparents labored in this country without wages; they made cotton king; and they built the homes of their masters in the midst of brutal injustice and shameful humiliation – and yet out of a bottomless vitality they continued to thrive and develop. If the inexpressible cruelties of slavery could not stop us, the opposition we now face will surely fail. We will win our freedom because the sacred heritage of our nation and the eternal will of God are embodied in our echoing demands.

I must close now. But before closing I am impelled to mention one other point in your statement that troubled me profoundly. You warmly commended the Birmingham police for keeping "order" and "preventing violence." I don't believe you would have so warmly commended the police force if you had seen its angry violent dogs literally biting six unarmed, nonviolent Negroes. I don't believe you would so quickly commend the policemen if you would observe their ugly and inhuman treatment of Negroes here in the city jail; if you would watch them push and curse old Negro women and young Negro girls; if you would see them slap and kick old Negro men and young boys; if you will observe them, as they did on two occasions, refuse to give us food because we wanted to sing our grace together. I'm sorry that I can't join you in your praise for the police department.

It is true that they have been rather disciplined in their public handling of the demonstrators. In this sense they have been rather publicly "nonviolent." But for what purpose? To preserve the evil system of segregation. Over the last few years I have consistently preached that nonviolence demands that the means we use must be as pure as the ends we seek. So I have tried to make it clear that it is wrong to use immoral means to attain moral ends. But now I must affirm that it is just as wrong, or even more so, to use moral means to preserve immoral ends. Maybe Mr Connor and his policemen have been rather publicly nonviolent, as Chief Pritchett was in Albany, Georgia, but they have used the moral means of nonviolence to maintain the immoral end of flagrant racial injustice. T.S. Eliot has said that there is no greater treason than to do the right deed for the wrong reason.

I wish you had commended the Negro sit-inners and demonstrators of Birmingham for their sublime courage, their willingness to suffer and their amazing discipline in the midst of the most inhuman provocation. One day the South will recognize its real heroes. They will be the James Merediths, courageously and with a majestic sense of purpose facing jeering and hostile mobs and the agonizing loneliness that characterises the life of the pioneer. They will be old, oppressed, battered Negro women, symbolized in a seventy-two old woman of Montgomery, Alabama, who rose up with a sense of dignity and with her people decided not to ride the segregated buses, and responded to one who inquired about her tiredness with ungrammatical profundity: "My feet is tired, but my soul is rested." They will be the young high school and college students, young ministers of the Gospel and a host of their elders courageously and nonviolently sitting-in at lunch counters and willingly going to jail for conscience's sake. One day the South will know that when these disinherited children of God sat down at lunch counters they were in reality standing up for the best in the American dream and the most sacred values in our Judeo-Christian heritage, and thusly, carrying our whole nation back to those great wells of democracy which were dug deep by the founding fathers in the formulation of the Constitution and the Declaration of Independence.

Never before have I written a letter this long (or should I say a book?). I'm afraid that it is much too long to take your precious time. I can assure you that it would have been much shorter if I had been writing from a comfortable desk, but what else is there to do when you are alone for days in the dull monotony of a narrow jail cell other than write long letters, think strange thoughts, and pray long prayers?

If I have said anything in this letter that is an overstatement of the truth and is indicative of an unreasonable impatience, I beg you to forgive me. If I have said anything in this letter that is an understatement of the truth and is indicative of my having a patience that makes me patient with anything less than brotherhood, I beg God to forgive me.

I hope this letter finds you strong in the faith. I also hope that circumstances will soon make it possible for me to meet each of you, not as an integrationist or a civil-rights leader, but as a fellow clergyman and a Christian brother. Let us all hope that the dark clouds of racial prejudice will soon pass away and the deep fog of misunderstanding will be lifted from our fear-drenched communities and in some not too distant tomorrow the radiant stars of love and brotherhood will shine over our great nation with all of their scintillating beauty.

Yours for the cause of Peace and Brotherhood,
Martin Luther King, Jr

READING QUESTIONS ON KING

1 Why is non-violence important in King's argument?
2 Under what circumstances should a court be sensitive to arguments like King's?
3 Members of a group calling itself "operation rescue" have blocked access to abortion clinics and claimed to be engaged in civil disobedience. Are King's arguments of any help to them?

8

The Limits of the Legal Order

Nelson Mandela
"Speech from the Dock" (1962)

Mandela was charged with inciting workers to act illegally and with leaving the country without a valid permit. In his statement to the court, Mandela challenges the legitimacy of the court to try people without political rights.

Your Worship, before I plead to the charge, there are one or two points I would like to raise.

CONDUCTS OWN DEFENCE

Firstly, Your Worship will recall that this matter was postponed last Monday at my request until today, to enable Counsel to make the arrangements to be available here today. Although Counsel is now available, after consultation with him and my attorneys, I have elected to conduct my own defence. Some time during the progress of these proceedings, I hope to be able to indicate that this case is a trial of the aspirations of the African people, and because of that I thought it proper to conduct my own defence. Nevertheless, I have decided to retain the services of Counsel, who will be here throughout these proceedings, and I also would like my attorney to be available in the course of these proceedings as well, but subject to that I will conduct my own defence.

RECUSAL

The second point I would like to raise is an application which is addressed to Your Worship. Now at the outset, I want to make it perfectly clear that the remarks I am going to make are not addressed to Your Worship in his personal capacity, nor are they intended to reflect upon the integrity of the Court. I hold Your Worship in high esteem and I do not for one single moment doubt your sense of fairness and justice. I must also mention that nothing I am going to raise in this application is intended to reflect against the Prosecutor in his personal capacity.

The point I wish to raise in my argument is based not on personal considerations, but on important questions that go beyond the scope of this present trial. I might also mention that in the course of this application I am frequently going to refer to the White man and the White people. I want at once to make it plain that I am no racialist, and I detest racialism, because I regard it as a barbaric thing, whether it comes from a Black man or from a White man. The terminology that I am going to employ will be compelled on me by the nature of the application I wish to make.

I want to apply for Your Worship's recusal from this case. I challenge the right of this Court to hear my case on two grounds.

I challenge it firstly because I fear that I will not be given a fair and proper trial. I challenge it in the second place because I consider myself neither legally nor morally bound to obey laws made by a Parliament in which I have no representation. In a political trial such as the present one which involves a clash of the aspirations of the African people and those of the Whites, the country's courts as presently constituted cannot be impartial and fair. In such cases Whites are interested parties. To have a White judicial officer presiding, however high his esteem, and however strong his sense of justice and fairness, is to make Whites judge their own case. It is improper and against the elementary principles of justice to entrust Whites with cases involving the denial by them of basic human rights to the African people. What sort of justice is this that enables the aggrieved to sit in judgement upon those whom they accused, a judiciary controlled entirely by Whites and enforcing laws enacted by a White Parliament in which we have no representation: laws, which in most cases are passed in the face of unanimous opposition from Africans.

By the Court: I am wondering whether I shouldn't interfere with you at this stage, Mr Mandela. Aren't we going beyond the scope of the proceedings? After all is said and done, there is only one Court today and that is the White Man's Court. There is no other Court. What purpose does it serve you to make an application when there is only one Court, as you know yourself. What Court do you wish to be tried by?

By the Accused: Well, Your Worship, firstly I would like Your Worship to bear in mind that in a series of cases our Courts have laid it down that the right of a litigant to ask for a recusal of a judicial officer is an extremely important right, which must be given full protection by the Court, as long as that right is exercised honestly. Now I honestly have apprehensions, as I am going to demonstrate just now, that this unfair discrimination throughout my life has been responsible for very grave injustices, and I am going to contend that that race discrimination which outside this Court has been responsible for all my troubles, I fear in this Court is going to do me the same injustice. Now Your Worship may disagree with that, but Your Worship is perfectly entitled, in fact, obliged to listen to me, and because of that I feel that Your Worship –

By the Court: I would like to listen, but I would like you to give me the grounds for your application for me to recuse myself.

By the Accused: Well, these are the grounds, I am developing them, sir. If Your Worship will give me time –

By the Court: I don't wish you to go out of the scope of the proceedings.

By the Accused: – Of the scope of the application. I am within the scope of the application, because I am putting forward grounds which in my opinion are likely not to give me a fair and proper trial.

By the Court: Anyway, proceed.

By the Accused: As Your Worship pleases. I was developing the point that a judiciary controlled entirely by Whites and enforcing laws enacted by a White Parliament in which we have no representation, laws which in most cases are passed in the face of unanimous opposition from Africans, cannot be regarded as an impartial tribunal in a political trial where an African stands as an accused.

The Universal Declaration of Humans Rights provides that all men are equal before the law, and are entitled without any discrimination to equal protection of the law. In May, 1951, Dr D.F. Malan, then Prime

Minister, told the Union Parliament that this provision of the Declaration applies in this country. Similar statements have been made on numerous occasions in the past by prominent Whites in this country, including Judges and Magistrates. But the real truth is that there is in fact no equality before the law whatsoever as far as our people are concerned, and statements to the contrary are definitely incorrect and misleading.

EQUALITY BEFORE THE LAW

It is true that an African who is charged in a court of law enjoys on the surface the same rights and privileges as a White accused, insofar as the conduct of his trial is concerned. He is governed by the same rules of procedure and evidence as apply to a White accused. But it will be grossly inaccurate to conclude from this fact that an African consequently enjoys equality before the law. In its proper meaning equality before the law means the right to participate in the making of the laws by which one is governed. It means a constitution which guarantees democratic rights to all sections of the population, the right to approach the Court for protection or relief in the case of the violation of the rights guaranteed in the Constitution, and the right to take part in the administration of justice as Judges, Magistrates, Attorney-General, Prosecutors, law advisers and similar positions. In the absence of these safeguards the phrase "equal before the law" insofar as it is intended to apply to us, is meaningless and misleading.

All the rights and privileges to which I have referred are monopolised in this country exclusively by Whites, and we enjoy none of them. The White Man makes all the laws, he drags us before his courts and accuses us, and he sits in judgement over us. Now it is fit and proper to ask the question, Sir, what is this rigid colour bar in the administration of justice all about? Why is it that in this Courtroom I am facing a White Magistrate, confronted by a White Prosecutor, escorted by White Orderlies? Can anybody honestly and seriously suggest that in this type of atmosphere the scales of justice are evenly balanced? Why is it that no African in the history of this country has ever had the honour of being tried by his own kith and kin, by his own flesh and blood? I will tell Your Worship why: the real purpose of this rigid colour code is to ensure that the justice dispensed by the courts should conform to the policy of the country, however much that policy might be in conflict with the norms of justice accepted in judiciaries throughout the civilised world.

I feel oppressed by the atmosphere of White domination that is around me in this Courtroom. Somehow this atmosphere recalls to mind the inhuman injustice caused to my people outside this Courtroom by the same White domination. It reminds me that I am voteless because there is a Parliament in this country that is White-controlled. I am without land because the White minority has taken the lion's share of my country, and I am forced to occupy poverty stricken reserves which are over populated and over stocked. We are ravished by starvation and disease because our country's worth –

By the Court: What has that got to do with the case, Mr Mandela?

By the Accused: With the last point, Sir, it hangs together, if Your Worship will give me the chance to develop it.

By the Court: You have been developing for quite a while now, and I feel you are going beyond the scope of your application.

By the Accused: Your Worship, this to me is an extremely important ground which the Court must consider.

By the Court: I fully realise your position, Mr Mandela, but you must confine yourself to the application and not go beyond it. I don't want to know about starvation. That in my view has got nothing to do with the case at the present moment.

By the Accused: Well, Your Worship has already raised the point that here in this country there is only a White Court. What is the purpose of all this? Now if I demonstrate to Your Worship that outside this Courtroom race discrimination has been used in such a way as to deprive me of my rights, not to treat me fairly, certainly this is a relevant fact from which to infer that wherever race discrimination is practised, this will be the same result, and this is the only reason why I am using this point.

By the Court: I am afraid that I will have to interrupt you, and you will have to confine yourself to the reasons, the real reasons for asking me to recuse myself.

By the Accused: Your Worship, the next point which I want to make is this: I raise the question, how can I be expected to believe that this same racial discrimination which has been the cause of so much injustice and suffering right through the years should now operate here to give me a fair and open trial? Is there no danger that an African accused may regard the courts not as impartial tribunals, dispensing justice without fear or favour, but as instruments used by the White man to punish those amongst us who clamour for deliverance from the fiery furnace of White rule. I have grave fears that this system of justice may enable the guilty to drag the innocent before the courts. It enables the unjust to prosecute and demand vengeance against the just. It may tend to lower the standards of fairness and justice applied in the country's courts by White judicial officers to Black litigants. This is the first ground for this application: that I will not receive a fair and proper trial.

Now the second ground for this application is that I consider myself neither morally nor legally bound to obey laws made by a Parliament in which I have no representation. That the will of the people is the basis of the authority of government is a principle universally acknowledged as sacred throughout the civilised world, and constitutes the basic foundation of freedom and justice. It is understandable why citizens who have the vote as well as the right of direct representation in the country's governing bodies should be morally and legally bound by the laws governing the country. It should be equally understandable why we as Africans should adopt the attitude that we are neither morally nor legally bound to obey laws which were not made with our consent, nor can we be expected to have confidence in courts that interpret and enforce such laws.

I am aware, Your Worship, that in many cases of this nature in the past South African courts have upheld the right of the African people to work for democratic changes. Some of our judicial officers have even openly critised the policy which refuses to acknowledge that all men are born free and equal, and fearlessly condemned the denial of opportunities to our people. But such exceptions, Your Worship, exist in spite, not because of the grotesque system of justice that has been built up in this country. These exceptions furnish yet another proof that even among the country's Whites there are honest men, whose sense of fairness and justice revolt against the cruelties perpetrated by their own White brothers to our people. The existence of genuine democratic values among some of the country's Whites in the judiciary, however slender they may be, is welcomed by me, but I have no illusions about the significance of this fact, healthy a sign as it may be. Such honest and upright men are few, and they have certainly not succeeded in convincing the vast majority of the rest of the White population that White supremacy leads to dangers and disasters.

"I HATE RACIAL DISCRIMINATION –"

Your Worship, I hate racial discrimination most intensely and in all its manifestations. I have fought it all along my life. I fight it now, and I will do so until the end of my days. I detest most intensely the set-up that surrounds me here. It makes me feel that I am a Black man in a White man's Court. This should not be. I should feel perfectly free and at ease with the assurance that I am being tried by a fellow South African who does not regard me as inferior, entitled to a special type of justice. This is not the type of atmosphere most conducive to feelings of security and confidence in the impartiality of the Court.

Now the Court might reply to this part of my argument by assuring me that it will try my case fairly and without fear or favour, that in deciding whether or not I am guilty of the offence charged by the State, the Court will not be influenced by the colour of my skin or by any improper motive. That might well be so. But such a reply will completely miss the whole point of my argument. As already indicated, my objection is not directed to Your Worship in his personal capacity, nor is it intended to reflect upon the integrity of the Court. My objection is based upon the fact that our courts as presently constituted create grave doubts in the mind of an African accused whether he will receive a fair and a proper trial. This doubt springs from objective facts relating to the practice of unfair discrimination against the Black man in the constitution of the country's courts. Such doubts cannot be allayed by mere verbal assurances from a presiding officer, however sincere such assurances may be. There is only one way, and one way only of allaying such doubts: By removing discrimination, particularly in judicial appointments. This is my first difficulty.

WHITE AND BLACK ETHICS

I have yet another difficulty about similar assurances Your Worship might give. Broadly speaking Africans and Whites in this country have no common standard of fairness, morality and ethics, and it will be very difficult for me to determine what standard of fairness and justice

Your Worship has in mind. In relationships with us, South African Whites regard as fair and just to pursue policies which have outraged the conscience of mankind, and of honest and upright men throughout the civilised world. They suppress our aspirations, bar our way to freedom and deny us opportunities in our moral and material progress, to secure ourselves from fear and want. All the good things of life are reserved for the White folk, and we Blacks are expected to be content to nourish our bodies with such pieces of food as drop from the tables of men with a White skin. This is the White man's standard of fairness and justice. Herein lies his conception of ethics. Whatever he himself may say in his defence, the White man's moral standards in this country must be judged by the extent to which he has condemned the vast majority of its citizens to serfdom and inferiority.

We, on the other hand, Your Worship, regard the struggle against colour discrimination and for the pursuit of freedom as the highest aspiration of all men. Through bitter experience we have learnt to regard the White man as a harsh and merciless type of human being, whose contempt for our rights and whose utter indifference to the promotion of our welfare makes his assurances to us absolutely meaningless and hypocritical.

I have the hope and the confidence that Your Worship will not treat this objection lightly, nor regard it as a frivolous one. I have decided to speak frankly and honestly, because the injustices I have referred to tend to undermine our confidence in the impartiality of our courts in cases of this nature, and they contain the seeds of an extremely dangerous situation for our country and people. I make no threats, Your Worship, when I say that unless these wrongs to which I have pointed are remedied without delay, we might well find that even plain talk before the country's courts is too timid a method to draw attention to our grievances.

Finally, I need only say that the courts have said that the possibility of bias and not actual bias is all that need be proved to ground an application of this nature. In this application I have merely referred to certain objective facts, from which I submit that the possibility be inferred that I will not receive a fair and proper trial.

By the Court: Mr Prosecutor, have you anything to say?

By the Prosecutor: Very briefly, Your Worship, I just wish to point out that there are certain legal grounds upon which an accused person is entitled to apply for the recusal of a judicial officer from the case in which he is to be tried. I submit that the Accused's application is not based on one of those principles, and I ask the Court to reject it.

By the Court: Your application is dismissed. Will you now plead to your charges?

By the Accused: I plead NOT GUILTY to both charges, to all the charges.

READING QUESTIONS ON MANDELA

1 How broad is the reach of Mandela's view? Does it only apply to politically motivated disobedience? Or does an illegitimate state lose its right to try people for any crimes?
2 What theory of the state is Mandela working with?
3 Reread *Lavallée*, above. Are Lavallée's duties to refrain from defending herself changed by the fact that the state has failed to protect her in the past?

Queen's University Letter (1990)

During the stand-off between the Sûreté de Québec and the Mohawk Warrior society at Oka in 1990, a number of members of the Faculty of Law at Queen's University wrote a letter to the minister of justice arguing that the Mohawk occupation was legal, so that their use of force to defend it against state intrusion was legitimate.

24 September 1990

Hon. Kim Campbell
Minister of Justice and Attorney General of Canada

Dear Ms. Campbell:
Both the federal and provincial governments have recently declared that the Rule of Law must be followed in determining the criminal liability of persons who have participated in the blockade at Kanesatake and in the stand-off that is continuing there. While we agree with this

position, we are disturbed by the inadequate conception of what is required by the Rule of Law in this context. Contrary to the position being taken by the governments of Canada and Quebec it is far from clear that the actions at Kanesatake are accountable under the provincial regime for the administration of criminal justice. This assumption, we believe, may be seriously flawed in law.

While the law on the administration of justice on reserves and with respect to native persons is not clear, it is clear that subjecting the Mohawk participants immediately to the normal provincial administrative regime would not be legally responsible.

Canadian constitutional law, the law of aboriginal rights, treaty law and international law all contain legal norms that must be reflected in the Rule of Law appropriate to this situation. For example, these factors must be taken into account in establishing the appropriate legal order:

1. Canadian courts in Charter decisions have demonstrated a commitment to understanding the content of the Charter in terms of international human rights obligations. The rapidly developing body of international law relating to indigenous peoples, supportive of autonomy for aboriginal communities, will impact on decisions under section 35 of the Constitution Act, 1982.
2. Supreme Court of Canada decisions on aboriginal rights under section 35 of the Constitution Act, 1982, draw on American precedents founded on the same Imperial law principles which govern aboriginal rights in Canada. These precedents support aboriginal autonomy with respect to elements of public administration, including the control of social deviance. See the Supreme Court's decisions in *R v Guerin* (1984), *R v Simon* (1985), *R v Sioui* (1990) and *R v Sparrow* (1990).
3. There are legal arguments in favour of the Mohawks' assertion that their aboriginal and treaty rights entitle them to exclusive policing authority over Mohawk people. The 1664 Treaty of Fort Albany under which the Mohawks first confirmed their relationship with the British Crown, contains specific undertakings on this question.
4. The actions of the federal and provincial governments and of agents acting under their authority are unconstitutional if they interfere with aboriginal or treaty rights and cannot be justified on the basis of both the purposes they serve and the methods they employ (see, *R v Sparrow*).
5. Governments bear the burden of persuading the courts that actions which violate aboriginal or treaty rights are justified (*R v Sparrow*).

Statements that "the rule of law must be applied" or that "there is only one law for all Canadians" will not suffice as legal justifications for actions which infringe aboriginal or treaty rights.

6. There are also substantial international legal issues raised in the present case. *The Western Sahara* decision of the International Court of Justice on the right of self-determination under international law has direct bearing. Further, the applicability of current work of two United Nations agencies on the rights of indigenous people cannot be ignored.

In light of these legal factors we urge you to act to form a Legal Commission to investigate the question of what would be required to comply with current Canadian and international law. As you can imagine the issues are complex and the legal principles are not easily reconcilable. A Legal Commission to investigate these issues is not only a constructive response to current legal difficulties, it is essential.

The Commission should be comprised of persons who are able to address the various legal aspects. These would include aboriginal persons, international lawyers, government lawyers, legal scholars and legal practitioners.

The undersigned are members of the Queen's Faculty of Law, concerned that present governmental policies with respect to events at Kanesatake are undermining the Rule of Law in Canada.

READING QUESTIONS ON QUEEN'S UNIVERSITY LETTER

1 The Queen's faculty argue that the Mohawks have a legitimate legal claim to their land. In such circumstances, do they also have the right to use force to repel representatives of the state contesting their claim? How does the past failure of the state to honour aboriginal claims figure in your answer to this question?

An Act Respecting the Future of Quebec (Bill 1) Introduced in the National Assembly of Quebec on September 7, 1995

This is the Bill that would have come into force if the people of Quebec had voted "Yes" in the referendum of October 30, 1995. The next two readings challenge the legitimacy of the referendum and the Bill.

THE PARLIAMENT OF QUEBEC ENACTS AS FOLLOWS

Self-Determination

1. The National Assembly is authorized, within the scope of the Act, to proclaim the sovereignty of Quebec.

The proclamation must be preceded by a formal offer of economic and political partnership with Canada.

Sovereignty

2. On the date fixed in the proclamation of the National Assembly, the Declaration of sovereignty appearing in the Preamble shall take effect and Quebec shall become a sovereign country; it shall acquire the exclusive power to pass all its laws, levy all its taxes and conclude all its treaties.

Partnership Treaty

3. The Government is bound to propose to the Government of Canada the conclusion of a treaty of economic and political partnership on the basis of the tripartite agreement of June 12, 1995 reproduced in the schedule.

The treaty must be approved by the National Assembly before being ratified.

4. A committee charged with the orientation and supervision of the negotiations relating to the partnership treaty, composed of independent personalities appointed by the Government in accordance with the tripartite agreement, shall be established.

5. The Government shall favor the establishment in the Outaouais region of the seat of the institutions created under the partnership treaty.

New Constitution

6. A draft of a new constitution shall be drawn up by a constituent commission established in accordance with the prescriptions of the National Assembly. The commission, consisting of an equal number of men and women, shall be composed of a majority of non-parliamentarians, and shall include Quebecers of various origins and from various backgrounds.

The proceedings of the commission must be organized so as to ensure the fullest possible participation of citizens in all regions of Quebec, notably through the creation of regional sub-commissions, if necessary.

The commission shall table the draft constitution before the National Assembly, which shall approve the final text. The draft constitution shall be submitted to a referendum and shall, once approved, become the fundamental law of Quebec.

7. The new constitution shall state that Quebec is a French-speaking country and shall impose upon the Government the obligation of protecting Quebec culture and ensuring its development.

8. The new constitution shall affirm the rule of law, and shall include a charter of human rights and freedoms. It shall also affirm that citizens have responsibilities towards their fellow citizens.

The new constitution shall guarantee the English-speaking community that its identity and institutions will be preserved. It shall also recognize the right of the aboriginal nations to self-government on lands over which they have full ownership and their right to participate in the development of Quebec; in addition, the existing constitutional rights of the aboriginal nations shall be recognized in the constitution. Such guarantee and such recognition shall be exercised in a manner consistent with the territorial integrity of Quebec.

Representatives of the English-speaking community and of each of the aboriginal nations must be invited by the constituent commission to take part in the proceedings devoted to defining their rights. Such rights shall not be modified otherwise than in accordance with a specific procedure.

9. The new constitution shall affirm the principle of decentralization. Specific powers and corresponding fiscal and financial resources shall be attributed by law to local and regional authorities.

Territory

10. Quebec shall retain its boundaries as they exist within the Canadian federation on the date on which Quebec becomes a sovereign country. It shall exercise its jurisdiction over the land, air and water forming its territory and over the areas adjacent to its coast, in accordance with the rules of international law.

Citizenship

11. Every person who, on the date on which Quebec becomes a sovereign country, holds Canadian citizenship and is domiciled in Quebec acquires Quebec citizenship.

Every person born in Quebec who, on the date on which Quebec becomes a sovereign country, is domiciled outside Quebec and who claims Quebec citizenship also acquires Quebec citizenship.

In the two years following the date on which Quebec becomes a sovereign country, any person holding Canadian citizenship who settles in Quebec or who has established a substantial connection with Quebec without being domiciled in Quebec may claim Quebec citizenship.

12. Quebec citizenship may be obtained, once Quebec has become a sovereign country, in the cases and on the conditions determined by law. The law must provide, in particular, that Quebec citizenship shall be granted to every person born in Quebec, or born outside Quebec to a father or mother holding Quebec citizenship.

13. Quebec citizenship may be held concurrently with Canadian citizenship or that of any other country.

Currency

14. The currency having legal tender in Quebec shall remain the Canadian dollar.

Treaties and International Organizations and Alliances

15. In accordance with the rules of International law, Quebec shall assume the obligations and enjoy the rights set forth in the relevant treaties and international conventions and agreements to which Canada or Quebec is a party on the date on which Quebec becomes a sovereign country, in particular in the North American Free Trade Agreement.

16. The Government is authorized to apply for the admission of Quebec to the United Nations Organization and its specialized agencies. It shall take the necessary steps to ensure the participation of Quebec in the World Trade Organization, the Organization of American States, the Organization for Economic Co-operation and Development, the Organization for Security and Co-operation in Europe, the Franco-phonie, the Commonwealth and other international organizations and conferences.

17. The Government shall take the necessary steps to ensure the continuing participation of Quebec in the defence alliances of which Canada is a member. Such participation must, however, be compatible with Quebec's desire to give priority to the maintenance of work peace under the leadership of the United Nations Organization.

Continuity of Laws, Pensions, Benefits, Licences and Permits, Contracts and Courts of Justice

18. The Acts of the Parliament of Canada and the regulations thereunder that apply in Quebec on the date on which Quebec becomes a sovereign country shall be deemed to the laws and regulations of Quebec. Such legislative and regulatory provisions shall be maintained in force until they are amended, replaced or repealed.

19. The Government shall ensure the continuity of the unemployment insurance and child tax benefit programs and the payment of the other benefits paid by the Government of Canada to individuals domiciled in Quebec on the date on which Quebec becomes a sovereign country. Pensions and supplements payable to the elderly and to veterans shall continue to be paid by the Government of Quebec according to the same terms and conditions.

20. Permits, licences and other authorizations issued before October 30, 1995 under an Act of the Parliament of Canada that are in force in Quebec on the date on which Quebec becomes a sovereign country shall be maintained. Those issued or renewed on or after October 30, 1995 shall also be maintained unless they are denounced by the Government within one month following the date on which Quebec becomes a sovereign country.

Permits, licences and other authorizations that are so maintained will be renewable according to law.

21. Agreements and contracts entered into before October 30, 1995 by the Government of Canada or its agencies or organizations that are in force in Quebec on the date on which Quebec becomes a sovereign country shall be maintained, with the Government of Quebec substituted, where required, for the Canadian party. Those entered into on or after October 30, 1995 shall also be maintained, with the Government of Quebec substituted, where required, for the Canadian party, unless they are denounced by the Government within one month following the date on which Quebec becomes a sovereign country.

22. The courts of justice shall continue to exist after the date on which Quebec becomes a sovereign country. Cases pending may be continued until judgment. However, the law may provide that cases pending before the Federal Court or before the Supreme Court shall be transferred to the Quebec jurisdiction it determines.

The Court of Appeal shall become the court of highest jurisdiction until a Supreme Court is established under the new constitution, unless otherwise provided for by law.

Judges appointed by the Government of Canada before October 30, 1995 who are in office on the date on which Quebec becomes a sovereign country shall be confirmed in their functions and shall retain their jurisdiction. The judges of the Federal Court and of the Supreme Court of Canada who were members of the Quebec Bar shall become, if they so wish, judges of the Superior Court and the Court of Appeal respectively.

Federal Public Servants and Employees

23. The Government may, in accordance with the conditions prescribed by law, appoint the necessary personnel and take appropriate steps to facilitate the application of the Canadian laws that continue to apply in Quebec pursuant to section 18. The sums required for the application of such laws shall be taken out of the consolidated revenue fund.

The government shall ensure that the public servants and other employees of the Government of Canada and of its agencies and organizations, appointed before October 30, 1995 and domiciled in Quebec on the date on which Quebec becomes a sovereign country, shall become, if they so wish, public servants or employees of the Government of Quebec. The government may, for that purpose, conclude agreements with any association of employees or any other person in order to facilitate such transfers. The Government may also set up a program of voluntary retirement; it shall honor any retirement or voluntary departure arrangement made with a transferred person.

Interim Constitution

24. The Parliament of Quebec may adopt the text of an interim constitution which will be in force from the date on which Quebec becomes a sovereign country until the coming into force of the new constitution of Quebec. The interim constitution must ensure the continuity of the democratic institutions of Quebec and of the constitutional rights existing on the date on which Quebec becomes a sovereign country, in particular those relating to human rights and freedoms, the English-speaking community, access to English-language schools, and the aboriginal nations.

Until the coming into force of the interim constitution, the laws, rules and conventions governing the internal constitution of Quebec shall remain in force.

Other Agreements

25. In addition to the partnership treaty, the Government is authorized to conclude with the Government of Canada any other agreement to facilitate the application of this Act, in particular with respect to the equitable apportionment of the assets and liabilities of the Government of Canada.

Coming into Force

26. The negotiations relating to the conclusion of the partnership treaty must not extend beyond October 30, 1996, unless the National Assembly decides otherwise.

The proclamation of sovereignty may be made as soon as the partnership treaty has been approved by the National Assembly or as soon as the latter, after requesting the opinion of the orientation and supervision committee, has concluded that the negotiations have proved fruitless.

27. This Act comes into force on the day on which it is assented to.

Sovereign Injustice: Forcible Inclusion of James Bay Crees and Cree Territory into a Sovereign Québec, **Grand Council of the Crees (1995)**

These excerpts contain part of the argument of the Cree Nation about the illegitimacy of the Quebec referendum on secession.

A MESSAGE REGARDING THE RIGHTS OF THE CREES AND OTHER ABORIGINAL PEOPLES IN CANADA

We are *Eeyouch*. We are a people. We have our own land, *Eeyou Astchee*. We are an organized society of Aboriginal people forming part of the community of the world's indigenous peoples. We are the original inhabitants of our territory, and have occupied our land and governed ourselves for the past 9000 years.

At least four times – in 1670, 1870, 1898, and 1912 – *Eeyou Astchee*, our traditional lands and waters, have changed status, purportedly, transferred between kings as gifts, or deeded between colonial companies and governments, all without our knowledge, and certainly without our consent. It has always been assumed that we the James Bay Crees, the actual owners and occupants, simply passed with the land, without voice, without the right to determine or even know what was being done with us.

Now in 1995, although we live in a modern and democratic state, protected by the Canadian Constitution with its Charter of Rights and Freedoms, our people and our territory may once again be transferred from sovereign to sovereign, this time from Canada to what may become the newly independent state of Québec. And although there is now a United Nations, with a Universal Declaration of Human Rights and a vast array of international human rights instruments that should protect us, a process has been set in motion that would forcibly remove the Crees from Canada, and incorporate us and our lands in this new state.

What is our remedy against this threat to deprive us of our rights, status, and interests – to hand a whole people over against its democratic will to another state? What action can we, the Crees, take now to prevent this assault on democracy and human rights?

This book holds part of the answer. Herein we set out our rights as the Cree people, as one of the world's indigenous peoples, as citizens of Canada and residents of Québec, as a people with internationally protected human rights. This is a timely call to avoid the tragic repetition of history, to invoke fairly and democratically, the principles of equality and non-discrimination and to respect the Crees' right to self-determination.

Although this book has its origins in the possible separation of Québec from Canada, its scope extends far beyond the Québec referendum into the future of the Crees in Canada as a self-governing people. It explores our rights as a people bound to Canada by a treaty and the land itself, and it examines our right of self-determination as it pertains to our aspirations and our rights to share equally in the development of our country.

The myth persists in Québec and elsewhere in Canada, that this country consists of two founding nations or peoples. This fiction constitutes a practical denial of our presence, our rights and status, and our role in the history, economy, and well-being of this country.

Now as Canada debates its own possible disintegration, many would prefer once again to conduct this debate without facing the troubling and far-reaching questions regarding our rights as an Aboriginal people.

Many Aboriginal peoples would also prefer to stay in the background and allow the "non-natives" to fight this out among themselves.

For the Crees this is no longer possible. It is our people and our own land that is being threatened, and the Crees must be heard or we may become the victims of our own silence, passed along with the land.

It will become clear when you read this book that we have been making extensive preparations to defend ourselves. We know our rights, and we can reply strongly to every one of the many false arguments that have been made by those who consider it in their own interest to deny our rights.

This debate will continue in Canada – the need to recognize and respect the rights of the Crees and other Aboriginal peoples in order to advance the well-being of all of its citizens, to strengthen its democracy, its respect for human rights, and its future as a country that includes Aboriginal peoples in its own vision of itself.

That has not yet happened. Perhaps the unity debate, and the examination of Cree rights and status that it brings into focus, will help to bring this about. That is certainly one of our goals, and perhaps the most important reason to read this study.

In any case, this is certain: The Crees will be here. We are not going anywhere. Nothing will be done with us, now or in the future, without our informed consent.

Grand Chief Matthew Coon Come
Nemaska, *Eeyou Astchee* – October 1995

INTRODUCTION

For thousands of years, the James Bay Crees have used and occupied the James Bay and Hudson Bay area in and beyond northern Québec. We have always lived in harmony with our physical environment. Presently, the James Bay Cree people (Eeyouch) is comprised of the Nemaska, Mistissini, Oujé-Bougoumou, Waswanipi, Waskaganish, Whapmagoostui, Chisabi, Wemindji and Eastmain communities of James Bay, Canada.

The Cree Nation is an organized society and includes approximately 12,000 aboriginal people of Cree ancestry. The Grand Council of the Crees is a corporation of the Cree Nation and enjoys consultative status (roster) with the United Nations Economic and Social Council.

The present analysis is an elaborate update to an earlier Submission made in February 1992 by the Grand Council of the Crees to the United

Nations Commission on Human Rights in Geneva. On behalf of the James Bay Cree Nation in Québec, the Grand Council tabled an extensive brief entitled, *Status and Rights of the James Bay Crees in the Context of Québec's Secession From Canada*. This first Submission served to inform the international community of political developments in Québec. In particular, we highlighted the threat of Québec secession and the unjust refusal of the Québec government to recognize the right of the Crees and other Aboriginal peoples in Québec to determine their own future.

At that time, the Québec government had enacted a law (Bill 150)[1] to hold a consultative referendum, possibly in regard to establishing a sovereign Québec state. However, no referendum on Québec independence was held in 1992. Instead, a constitutional agreement known as the Charlottetown Accord was negotiated by federal and provincial governments and national Aboriginal organizations. Consequently, a referendum was held in Québec and elsewhere in Canada on the contents of the draft legal text accompanying the Accord. Both a majority of Quebecers and of Canadians in general refused to support the constitutional compromises reached in the Accord.

In 1994, following the election of the separatist Parti Québécois (PQ) government in Québec, concrete measures to create an independent Québec were taken by the new provincial government. For the first time in Québec and Canadian history, a draft Bill[2] was made public calling for a unilateral declaration of independence (UDI). The sole prerequisite to this far-reaching action would be an affirmative majority vote by Quebecers in a provincial referendum. Should that occur, the National Assembly would be required to proceed with a UDI, within a maximum period of one year.

When support for this draft Bill waned among the Québec population, an *Act respecting the future of Québec* (Bill 1)[3] was introduced in the National Assembly. This Bill requires that "a formal offer of economic and political partnership" be made with Canada,[4] before any UDI could be proclaimed by Québec's legislative assembly. Presently, the threat of Québec secession is a most serious one, since the Québec referendum on separation has been formally announced by Premier Parizeau to be held on October 30, 1995.

The PQ government's Bill 1, if adopted, has already been declared by Québec's Superior Court to be unconstitutional.[5] However, the separatist government in Québec takes the position that constitutional or legal questions are largely irrelevant. Rather, the PQ government claims that a simple majority vote in a province-wide referendum would confer on Quebecers a legitimate and democratic "right" to secede from Canada. The territorial integrity of Canada or the integrity of Aboriginal territories is of little consequence. Further, despite legal opinion to the contrary, the government continues to claim that Québec can separate from Canada with its present borders intact.

In the opinion of this present Study, the PQ government's current political and legislative strategy towards secession of Québec from Canada has no legal validity. It also lacks legitimacy from either a Canadian or international perspective. Moreover, should Québec secession proceed, it would seriously impinge upon other peoples' fundamental status, rights and interests – including those of the James Bay Crees.

Throughout Canada's history, Quebecers have established an impressive reputation as producing some of the best constitutional jurists in the country. This strong tradition and participation in constitutional affairs have served to safeguard and advance the interests of Québec. It would be unfortunate if these skills in the constitutional arena are now cast aside, along with the rule of law, in favour of unilateralism.

To date, basic matters regarding Aboriginal peoples' right to self-determination are being denied or ignored by the PQ government and its separatist ally at the federal level, the Bloc Québécois (BQ).[6] In regard to Aboriginal peoples, questions pertaining to their legal status and rights are intrinsically related to questions of legitimacy and democracy. Despite the claims of the PQ government or BQ leaders, issues concerning legitimacy and democracy cannot be severed from those relating to Aboriginal peoples' status and legal rights.

The PQ government and the Bloc Québécois are not facing and resolving critical questions in any appropriate manner. These include:

- *Aboriginal peoples as "peoples" with the right to self-determination.* Who are "people" with the right to self-determination? Are the James Bay Crees a distinct "people"? Can the PQ government force Aboriginal peoples to be a part of the "Quebec people" for purposes of self-determination and secession? On what basis does the PQ government justify its denial of Aboriginal self-determination in the current secession debate?
- *Undermining the functioning of Canada.* If the PQ government is acting in a manner to undermine the functioning of the Canadian federa-

tion, how can the government turn around and declare that Canada is not working? Such action hardly legitimizes secession. Moreover, as the National Assembly's own studies confirm, Quebecers presently enjoy self-determination within Canada.

- *Effective control and use of force.* The PQ government is claiming that an independent Québec state can achieve international recognition by achieving effective control over the whole of the present territory of the province. However, what will the Québec government do if Aboriginal peoples and others continue to respect and apply the laws of Canada, including maintenance of their territories within Canada and implementation of Canadian programs and services? Will the Québec government resort to the use of force against Aboriginal peoples?

- *Territorial integrity.* On what basis can the PQ claim that Canada is divisible, but not the territory of a secessionist Québec? How is it that the integrity of the traditional or historical territories of Aboriginal peoples is so easily dismissed by separatists?

- *Vulnerability of Québec's borders.* Have the potential risks to Québec's current provincial borders been adequately evaluated? Can the PQ government legitimately impose Québec's "territorial integrity" on Aboriginal peoples?

- *Denial of Aboriginal referendums.* On what basis can the PQ government and its separatist supporters believe that they can deny Aboriginal peoples the right to hold their own referendums to decide their own future?[7] Should Aboriginal referendums establish that the Aboriginal peoples concerned wish to remain in Canada, do not these results significantly limit the potential impact of any Yes vote in the Québec referendum?

- *Inadequacies of simple majority vote.* In the Canada/Québec/Aboriginal context where other rights and interests are involved, is a simple majority vote by Quebecers truly legitimate and democratic? Also, how can it be said that an affirmative Québec referendum vote on independence is legitimate or adequate, in the absence of a proposed Constitution and other fundamental arrangements for Quebecers to consider?

- *Unilateral alteration of Aboriginal treaties.* Existing land claims treaties provide for a permanent federalist arrangement and include federal and Quebec governments (as well as Aboriginal peoples) as parties. How can the PQ government claim it would be legal or legitimate for a secessionist Québec to unilaterally alter existing treaties with Aboriginal peoples in Québec? On what basis could Québec claim it can simply take over existing federal treaty obligations and unilaterally determine that the Canadian government would no longer be a party to the treaties concerned?

- *Failure to consider impacts on Aboriginal peoples.* What are the potential impacts of Québec secession on Aboriginal peoples in Québec? If Aboriginal peoples choose not to subject themselves to such impacts, how can a secessionist Québec government forcibly include them and their territories in a separate new state?

It is astounding that the above questions remain inadequately addressed or completely unanswered, as we approach the eve of the Québec referendum debate. This is especially surprising since the Québec National Assembly's Committee on Sovereignty emphasized that "prior agreement" with Aboriginal peoples in Québec is essential if additional problems are to be avoided:

... the testimony of aboriginal representatives leads the Committee to the conclusions that, unless there is prior agreement with the aboriginal peoples, Québec's accession to sovereignty will generate more problems in relations with the aboriginal nations and the rest of Québec society.[8]

The increase in problems referred to by the Committee on Sovereignty are symptomatic of a continuation of colonial attitudes by governments that have been repeatedly imposed on Aboriginal peoples for centuries. If the same unilateral approaches are perpetuated, the relationship with non-Aboriginal governments will deteriorate, the healing process among Aboriginal peoples will be severely impeded, and injustice will continue to result. This must not be the legacy of Québec's attempts to secede from Canada. As E.-I. Daes recently stated on the occasion of *International Day of the World's Indigenous People:*

For healing to begin, *there must be some clear recognition of the legitimacy of the victim's claims to justice.* We must acknowledge the wrong that has been done. *We must place responsibility where it truly belongs, on the oppressor and not the victim* ... Facts and feelings must be faced, squarely, before we can move beyond them. Denying pain and anger does not make these emotions go away; they grow deeper, and more bitter.[9] [Emphasis added.]

In the following pages, this Study deals with the above questions and others that are central to the issue of Québec secession and its threats to the rule of law, genuine democracy, and respect for fundamental human rights. Hopefully, the Study will contribute to a peaceful debate on key substantive issues, prior to any actions being taken by Québec separatists against Aboriginal peoples, contrary to international, Canadian and Aboriginal[10] law.

In the context of any secessionist attempts by Québec, the right of the James Bay Crees and other Aboriginal peoples in the province to make free choices in determining their own future must be assured. The message we bring relating to Aboriginal self-determination and its current denial is intended for all Canadians, including Quebecers, many of whom we are grateful to for their ongoing support. Ultimately, it is the people of any society that demand accountability and compel its government to act fairly and respectfully towards the rights of others.

This Study is equally intended to inform the international community – the United Nations, member states, political observers, human rights organizations, and academics – of the status and rights of the James Bay Crees and other Aboriginal peoples in Québec who face a secessionist threat. We believe the current issues have important international dimensions. These entail a significant measure of responsibility and appropriate international response.

Further, the international community may wish to devote careful, sober thought to the potentially far-reaching implications of a unilateral secession by Québec, based on a simple majority vote. It would be clearly counterproductive to ongoing international efforts towards peace, stability and respect for human rights, if a UDI in Québec were to establish some form of adverse precedent – a precedent to ignore the human right of self-determination of indigenous peoples, as well as break up an existing democratic state ...

Québec's Unilateral Secession Process – Is It Legitimate or Democratic?

81. In the absence of any lawful authority, the PQ government is declaring that it can unilaterally secede from Canada based on arguments of "legitimacy" and "democracy". However, to date, neither legitimacy nor democracy has been adequately demonstrated by the separatist government in Québec.

82. In particular, the PQ government takes the position that a simple majority vote in a Québec referendum would constitute a demo-

cratic expression of the will of the population in Québec. Consequently, it is argued that such an affirmative vote alone would provide "legitimacy" for a unilateral declaration of independence by the Québec government.

83. Legitimacy is not simply determined by a majority vote by Quebecers in a single referendum. In order to ensure legitimacy, numerous factors would have to be equitably considered and implemented. This is especially important when the rights of other peoples, such as Aboriginal peoples in Québec, are directly and most fundamentally affected.

84. Even in cases where secession is based on the right to self-determination (which is not the case in Québec), the rights of others must be taken into account. Moreover, there exist competing legitimacies that must be fully considered. Aside from Aboriginal peoples in Québec, the rest of Canada has an immense interest in the current debate in light of the foreseeable and profound impacts on the country's future.

85. Issues of democracy, human rights and the rule of law are closely interrelated. They are also of international concern. The PQ government cannot ignore the human rights to self-determination of others, as well as the rule of law, yet claim its referendum process is legitimate and democratic. While circumstances sometimes exist where the rule of law lacks legitimacy or democracy, this is not the situation affecting Quebecers.

86. For the PQ government to suggest that all people in Québec, including Aboriginal peoples, must vote (if at all) in a single referendum is coercive and devoid of legitimacy. Similarly, to forcibly include Aboriginal peoples in a secessionist Québec is fundamentally wrong, undemocratic and illegitimate. Such an approach of inequality and forced dominance can best be described as yet another version of colonialism for the 1990s. It is the antithesis of a democratic process.

87. In addition, it is undemocratic to ask Québec voters to approve the PQ government's bill on Québec independence, without knowing the precise contents of a new Québec constitution or the results of negotiations with the rest of Canada. In this regard, it is highly inappropriate for voters to provide the government with a "blank cheque" through a referendum.

88. Aside from the brief description of a future offer of economic and political union with Canada in the Agreement of June 12, 1995

(among separatist leaders), few details are known of the PQ government's possible offer to Canada. Moreover, it appears that Quebecers are being asked to pronounce on Québec's future in a referendum even before the PQ government has fully worked out its own position.

89. In addition, the absence of any detailed information makes it extremely difficult for the James Bay Crees and other Aboriginal peoples to assess the impacts on them of any future offer of a Canada-Québec union by the PQ government. However, what appears to be clear is that there is no role contemplated by the PQ government in any of the new proposed Canada-Québec institutions for the Aboriginal peoples concerned.

Limitations of Québec's Upcoming Referendum

90. According to Canadian law, referendums are not legally binding, but are consultative in nature. Referendum processes can only have a binding effect on governments and the adoption of constitutional laws, if these processes would be so recognized in Canada's Constitution.

91. Unlike Québec referendum procedures in the past which were solely of an advisory nature, the original draft Bill on sovereignty of the PQ government would have attempted to have a permanently binding effect on all parties concerned. It would have required the National Assembly of Québec to unilaterally declare the independence of Québec within a maximum of one year in the event of an affirmative vote in its upcoming referendum.

92. However, apparently as a result of the decision in the *Bertrand* case, the PQ government tabled a new Bill that does not expressly require the National Assembly to adopt legislation proclaiming a UDI, in the event of a simple majority vote in the 1995 Québec referendum. In fact, the draft *Act respecting the future of Québec* makes no mention of any referendum. Therefore, from a strictly legal viewpoint, it appears that the 1995 referendum to be held by the PQ government is consultative and not legally binding.

93. In the event of a YES vote in the Québec referendum, the PQ government is intending to proceed with the adoption of the draft *Act respecting the future of Québec*. This Act, which purports to authorize the National Assembly to unilaterally establish an

independent state, includes a number of provisions whose unconstitutionality and illegality are apparent.

94. Unconstitutional provisions in the current draft Act include: (i)
unilateral declaration of independence; (ii) adoption of a constitution for a new state; (iii) unilateral determination of Québec's
borders, including offshore areas; (iv) unilateral assumption of
Canadian government obligations in treaties; and (v) unilateral
ousting of the jurisdiction of the Supreme Court of Canada.

95. Even if there were to be an affirmative vote in a referendum on
secession, a referendum does not determine the terms or conditions
for separation. One of the inherent limitations of a YES vote in a
Québec referendum would be that it could not settle any of the
conditions for separation nor fairly address the self-determination
of Aboriginal peoples.

Undemocratic Nature of a Simple Majority Vote in Québec

96. True democracy is not always achieved by a simple majority vote.
If a simple majority vote were always definitive, a pan-Canadian
referendum could determine the future of Quebecers.

97. The decision to secede from an independent state is markedly
different from an election or a vote to become a member of a
supranational body, such as the European Community. Unilateral
secession not only entails more far-reaching consequences, but also
includes a notion of finality that would be most difficult to reverse.

98. In other secession situations internationally, referendum results
have demonstrated exceedingly high majorities. For example, the
registered affirmative votes in two of the republics of former
Yugoslavia exceeded eighty or ninety percent. Similarly, high
support was registered in the Ukraine vote on independence in
1991, the Baltic states in 1991, and the case of Norway in 1905.
Based on such examples, it cannot be concluded that there is any
legitimacy to the claim that a simple majority would be a sufficient
indication of popular political will by Quebecers to secede in
Québec.

99. Even jurists who are supportive of Québec sovereignty have called
for "incontestable majorities", "massive support," "absolute majorities" (of all registered voters), or "double majorities" that would
require support from numerous distinct regions in the province.

Also, most people in Québec express the view that a simple majority vote is insufficient to begin the separation process. Yet the PQ government shows no inclination to shape its "legitimacy" and "democracy" arguments to reflect the views of the Québec population.[12]

NOTES

1 *An Act respecting the process for determining the political and constitutional future of Québec*, SQ 1991, c 34, assented to on June 20, 1991 by the National Assembly, First Session, 34th Legislature.

2 *An Act respecting the sovereignty of Québec* (Draft Bill), Québec National Assembly, First Sess., 35th Legisl., 1994, made public by Premier Jacques Parizeau on December 6, 1994. This "avant-projet de loi" was never tabled as a bill in the National Assembly.

3 *An Act respecting the future of Québec* (Bill 1), Québec National Assembly, First Sess., 35th Legisl., tabled by Premier Jacques Parizeau on September 7, 1995.

4 Ibid., s. 1.

5 *Bertrand v A.G. Québec*, Québec Superior Court, Québec city, No. 200-05-002117-955, decision rendered on September 8, 1995 by Mr. Justice Robert Lesage. At p. 44 of the decision, Lesage J. declares that the draft Act (Bill 1) of the PQ government constitutes a serious threat to the rights and freedoms of the plaintiff Bertrand guaranteed in the *Canadian Charter of Rights and Freedoms*, since the draft Act purports to confer on the Québec National Assembly the power to proclaim Québec a sovereign country without following the amendment procedure in the *Constitution Act, 1982*. For a brief discussion of the circumstances surrounding this case and the judge's decision, see notes 248, *et seq.* and accompany text *infra*.

6 This Study refers for the most part to the PQ and BQ. However, it is worth noting that a fledgling new party, the Action démocratique du Québec, with a single elected member in Québec, has also joined the separatists in working towards an independent Québec state.

7 The Parti Québécois government takes the position that Aboriginal peoples can hold referendums if they wish, but the government will not respect the results of their referendums.

8 Committee to Examine Matters Relating to the Accession of Québec to Sovereignty, *Draft Report* (Québec: Bibliothèque nationale du Québec, 1992), at 33. It would appear that this Draft Report was never finalized, since it was difficult for Liberal and Parti Québécois members on the Committee on

Sovereignty to reach consensus on the precise contents of the Report. For an official French version of the Draft Report, see Commission d'étude des questions afférentes à l'accession du Québec à la souveraineté, *Projet de rapport* (Québec: Bibliothèque nationale du Québec, 1992).

9 E.-I. Daes, *International Day of the World's Indigenous People*, Speaking Notes of Erica-Irene Daes, Chairperson, Working Group, Palais des Nations, Geneva, August 9, 1995, at 2.

10 This Study necessarily focuses primarily on international and Canadian law and practice. However, it should be emphasized that any diminution or denial of Cree status and rights would be viewed by the James Bay Crees as wholly contrary to their own laws, customs and practices. In regard to the expansive multi-disciplinary approach taken in Aboriginal law, see testimony in Royal Commission into Aboriginal Deaths in Custody, *National Report* (Australia: 1991), vol. 5, at 361: "What [Aboriginal] people mean when they talk about their Law, is a cosmology, a worldview which is a religious, philosophic, poetic and normative explanation of how the natural, human and supernatural domains work." See also draft *U.N. Declaration on the Rights of Indigenous Peoples*, sixth preambular para.: " ... [indigenous peoples'] rights to their lands, territories and resources, which derive from political, economic and social structures and from their cultures, spiritual traditions, histories and philosophies".

11 In Canada, there are ample precedents for requiring substantially more than a simple majority vote if the latter would be unjust, undemocratic or impractical. For example, amendments to the Canadian Constitution require, as a general rule, approval of the federal Parliament along with two-thirds of the provincial legislatures. In other cases, where national institutions may be affected in a critical manner, unanimity is needed.

12 Regardless of what level of vote (higher than a simple majority) might be deemed to be legitimate or democratic in the current context, this does not change the reality that an affirmative vote can only serve as one factor towards legitimacy. Such a vote in itself cannot legitimize a UDI by Québec, especially if it purported to forcibly include Aboriginal peoples and territories.

READING QUESTIONS ON SOVEREIGN INJUSTICE

1 What conception of democracy underpins the Cree people's arguments?
2 Would the Cree people's demands be satisfied merely by requiring, say, a two-thirds majority in the referendum?

3 What is the relation between the Cree people's argument and the arguments of the Native Women's Association, below?

Bertrand v Quebec [1995] 127 DLR (4th) 408

Bertrand sought to halt the Quebec referendum by challenging its legality under Section 24(1) of the *Canadian Charter of Rights and Freedoms.*

BERTRAND V ATTORNEY GENERAL OF QUEBEC ET AL.; JOHNSON ET AL., MIS EN CAUSE

Lesage, J: ... The plaintiff, whose standing was not challenged, affirms in his statement of claim (para. 14) that [translation] "the conduct of the Quebec government, and its deeds and actions in regard to the draft bill respecting sovereignty and the June 12, 1995 agreement, constitute a veritable parliamentary and constitutional *coup d'état,* a fraud on the Canadian Constitution, and a misappropriation of authority the consequence of which will be the violation and denial of the rights and freedoms of the plaintiff and of all Quebec taxpayers".

The draft bill respecting the sovereignty of Quebec is a document tabled by Prime Minister Parizeau in the National Assembly on December 6, 1994, accompanied by a message to all citizens of Quebec, calling on them [translation] "to study, criticize or change this draft bill in a great exercise of democratic participation" and to "imagine together" the "declaration of sovereignty to Quebec" that is to serve as a recital to the eventual bill.

The agreement of June 12, 1995, is an agreement between the representatives of three political parties, the Parti québécois, the Bloc québécois and the Action démocratique du Québec, concerning "a common project to be submitted in the referendum" that is contemplated in the draft bill. It refers to this referendum as "the Fall 1995 referendum" and states that: "The elements of this common project will be integrated in the bill that will be tabled in the Fall." The objective is stated as follows [translation]":

To achieve sovereignty for Quebec and a formal proposal for a new economic and political partnership with Canada, aimed among other things at consolidating the existing economic space.

Both the action for a declaratory judgment and the motion for an injunction seek relief under s. 24 of the *Canadian Charter of Rights and Freedoms*, s-s. (1) of which states:

Enforcement of guaranteed rights and freedoms
24(1) Anyone whose rights or freedoms, as guaranteed by this Charter, have been infringed or denied may apply to a court of competent jurisdiction to obtain such remedy as the court considers appropriate and just in the circumstances. ...

The Evidence

The plaintiff's affidavit and his deposition at the hearing are not contested. I make a distinction, of course, between the statement of a fact and the analysis the plaintiff might make of it in his affirmations.

The plaintiff was led to institute the present proceedings after the tabling in the National Assembly, on December 6, 1994, by Prime Minister Parizeau on behalf of the Government of Quebec, of a draft bill respecting the sovereignty of Quebec. Section 1 of this draft bill states:

1. Quebec is a sovereign country.

The draft bill is preceded by explanatory notes indicating that it is a political project of the Quebec government, a project that is described in the following terms:

It is proposed that Québec become a sovereign country through the democratic process. The accession to full sovereignty has been defined by the National Assembly as "the accession of Québec to a position of exclusive jurisdiction, through its democratic institutions, to make laws and levy taxes in its territory and to act on the international scene for the making of agreements and treaties of any kind with other independent States and participating in various international organizations."*

An economic association with Canada would be maintained in order to preserve and further develop the free circulation of goods and services, of capital and of persons that is currently prevailing. To the same end, Québec would continue to adhere to the North American Free Trade Agreement and the General Agreement on Tariffs and Trade. The Canadian dollar would continue to be the legal currency of Québec.

* *Act respecting the process for determining the political and constitutional future of Québec* (S.Q. 1991, c. 34).

A new constitution would be drafted following a procedure to be defined by the National Assembly. This new constitution would include a charter of human rights and freedoms and provide guarantees, in a manner consistent with Québec's territorial integrity, to the English-speaking community and to the Aboriginal nations. It would also provide for the decentralization of specific powers to local and regional authorities, together with sufficient resources.

Provisions are made as to the territory of a sovereign Québec, Québec citizenship and the continuity of treaties, international alliances and laws. In this respect, the Government of Québec would be authorized to take over, from the Government of Canada, all services and transfer payments currently provided to Québec citizens by the Canadian government.

Several other transitional measures are provided for, including the conclusion of an agreement on the apportionment of the property and debts of Canada.

The explanatory notes also describe the process that the government intends to follow in making Quebec a distinct country. This process comprises six stages, described as follows:

1. publication of the draft bill;
2. a period of information and participation for the purposes of improving the bill and drafting the "Declaration of Sovereignty" which will form the preamble to the bill;
3. discussion of the bill respecting the sovereignty of Québec, and passage by the National Assembly;
4. approval of the Act by the population in a referendum;
5. a period of discussions with Canada on the transitional measures to be set in place, particularly as regards the apportionment of property and debts; during this period the new Québec constitution will be drafted;
6. the accession of Québec to sovereignty.

The first two stages are already completed or in the process of being completed. Government Orders in Council were adopted in January and February, 1995, to create various regional commissions "on the future of Quebec" and two commissions addressed to seniors and young people, with an overarching "national" commission that includes the Prime Minister.

The plaintiff says he has been informed that $5 million of public funds have already been spent on the establishment and operation of these commissions and that several hundred thousand dollars were spent on commissioning studies on Quebec sovereignty and conducting propaganda in support of this option.

The plaintiff appeared before one of these commissions. He points out that the official opposition refused to participate in these commissions on sovereignty, calling them [translation] "mock commissions".

The Commission nationale sur l'avenir du Québec [National commission on the future of Quebec] submitted its report to the Prime Minister on April 19, 1995. This was followed on June 12, 1995, by an agreement between the Prime Minister, representing the Parti québécois, Lucien Bouchard, representing the Bloc québécois and Mario Dumont, representing the Action démocratique du Québec; this agreement, the parameters of which are to be incorporated within the projected bill, was referred to at the beginning of this judgment.

The plaintiff argues that the government's action and all the expenditures of public funds with a view to achieving Quebec's secession are illegal, as they are made in the context of a project that proposes, in fraudulent violation of the Constitution of Canada [translation], "to separate Quebec from Canada without complying with the amending formula provided in the *Constitution Act, 1982*". He states that the Quebec government is acting anarchically, in violation of public order, placing itself above the supreme law of the land, and that it is preparing to use its majority in the National Assembly to bring about a veritable constitutional *coup d'état*, in which it is involving the population without informing it of its fraud on the Constitution. He pleads bad faith on the part of the defendants and compares their actions to a conspiracy against the state. He characterizes the proceedings undertaken by the Government of Quebec as a constitutional revolution that has no justification under international law.

The plaintiff applies to the court, as the guardian of the Constitution, asking it to protect his rights and freedoms, which are seriously threatened [translation] "by the strategy, deeds and actions of the government of Québec as substantiated in the draft bill respecting the sovereignty of Québec and in the text of the agreement between the Parti québécois, the Bloc québécois and the Action démocratique du Québec" (para. 102 of the statement of claim). He submits that the Quebec government is seriously violating public order instead of governing in accordance with the rule of law.

In his testimony at the hearing, the plaintiff elaborated on the affirmations in this statement of claim to the effect that his rights and freedoms guaranteed by the *Canadian Charter of Rights and Freedoms* are dangerously threatened, and in particular:

- his freedom of thought, opinion and expression, as conceived and applied by Canadian courts, particularly the Supreme Court of Canada;
- his Canadian citizenship, and his right to vote and to run in federal elections;
- his right to enter, remain in and leave Canada as he wishes;
- his right to move to and take up residence wherever he wishes in Canada and to pursue the gaining of a livelihood therein;
- his right to liberty and security in the event of disruption of the legal order;
- his right to equality without discrimination in relation to other Canadians;
- his right to rely on the *Canadian Charter of Rights and Freedoms* and the Supreme Court of Canada's interpretations in order to obtain redress for violations of the Charter which, he alleges, would deprive him of the very possibility of engaging in the present proceedings.

He argues forcefully that once sovereignty is proclaimed, he will have lost the assistance of the court in protecting his fundamental rights and freedoms.

The plaintiff says he is acting in the interests of both himself and millions of Quebecers.

In fact, the plaintiff's situation is not unlike that of other Quebecers, which is not to say that he is barred from seeking the protection of the courts to enforce his constitutional rights and freedoms. He seeks relief on that very basis.

On the other hand, the government's position, upheld by the representations of its counsel, is that the democratic principle of the popular vote is the applicable principle. In my opinion, it is worth reviewing a few concepts of constitutional law before drawing some conclusions.

Some Principles

A society's political organization is derived from the sociological and historical wellsprings of the nation. The state is a product of the political organization. Not all states necessarily exercise full sovereignty over their territory and the people that inhabit it. We have the example of the provinces in our federal system, as in any federation. International recognition is a factor in establishing a country's sovereignty.

The constitution of a sovereign country – the set of rules governing the institutions that make up its political organization – is not always written. The constitution is not a statute, in the sense that it does not emanate from the legislative authority of the country, although it may take the form of a statute. Still less may the constitution be contingent upon a statute. A statute must be consistent with the constitution, and not the converse. That is why the Constitution of Canada is characterized as the "supreme law of Canada" in the *Constitution Act, 1982* (s. 52).

The legal system is a manifestation of state sovereignty which must pass muster with the judiciary. In societies that recognize the supremacy of the law, the judiciary exists to enforce the rule of law and, pre-eminently, the laws enacted by the legislature. In a federal system, the legal system includes some rules that govern the distribution of powers between the central state and the federated states. These rules are enforceable by the courts.

The judiciary does not create the law, still less the constitution of which it is an emanation. It interprets them. It is distinguished as well from the executive authority, the government which alone has the duty and responsibility to act on behalf of the state. The role of the judiciary is circumscribed by the existence of rules of law, which are normally contained in statutes. Now, it is recognized that some constitutional usages, referred to as conventions, are not rules enforceable by the courts: *Reference re Amendment of the Constitution of Canada (Nos. 1, 2, and 3) (1981), 125 DLR (3d) 1, [1981] 1 SCR 753 sub nom. Re: Resolution to Amend the Constitution, [1981] 6 WWR 1 sub nom. Attorney General of Manitoba v Attorney General of Canada*. Contrary to a convention, a *coup d'état* or revolution may occur, breaking the continuity of the legal order, and the courts are powerless to intervene.

A country's sovereignty is, in effect, based on the *de facto* exercise of authority over a territory and the people who inhabit it. This exercise is secured through the voluntary or involuntary acceptance of the rules, including the constitution, that govern the relationships between the state and its citizens. These rules may be altered in accordance with the procedure provided by the existing legal system, i.e., by following the path of legality, but they might also be altered by a declaration by some authority that places itself over and above the existing constitution and ensures its physical control of the territory and acceptance by the population occupying that territory.

This latter course is not legal. A new legal order can arise only after the *fait accompli*. This was the experience in Southern Rhodesia. As Professor Peter Hogg relates in his *Constitutional Law of Canada*, 2nd ed. (Toronto: Carswell, 1985), pp. 104–5:

> In assessing the legality of a regime established by revolution – meaning any break in legal continuity – the issue for the courts is simply whether or not the revolution has been successful. As de Smith says, "legal theorists have no option but to accommodate their concepts to the facts of political life".* In *Madzimbamuto v Lardner-Burke* (1969),† the Privy Council had to decide whether validity should be accorded to the acts of the legislature and government of Southern Rhodesia after the "unilateral declaration of independence" (UDI) from Britain. Their lordships held that the post-UDI acts were not valid, because it could not be said "with certainty" that the break-away government was in effective control of the territory which it claimed the right to govern. Their lordships pointed out that Britain was still claiming to be the lawful government and was taking steps to regain control. In a later case, the Appellate Division of the High Court of Rhodesia decided that, having regard to developments since the decision in *Madzimbamuto*, it could "now predict with certainty that sanctions will not succeed in their objective overthrowing the present government and of restoring the British government to the control of the government of Rhodesia".‡ The Court accordingly held that the existing Rhodesian government was the legal government, and the post-UDI constitution was the only valid constitution.§

In *Blackburn v Attorney-General*, [1971] 2 All ER 1380, which involved an attempt to block the negotiations on the United Kingdom's entry

* de Smith, 76.

† [1969] 1 AC 645.

‡ *R v Ndhlovu*, [1968] 4 SALR 515, 532. The decision was never appealed to the Privy Council, probably because the Rhodesian government did not recognize the authority of the Privy Council (the government was not represented before the Privy Council in *Madzimbamuto*) and an appeal would have been futile.

§ Subsequent events suggested that this conclusion was premature. Guerilla war led the break-away government to seek a constitutional settlement with the United Kingdom (as well as with the blacks of Southern Rhodesia). A settlement was agreed upon at a conference in London in 1979, and independence and a new constitution (under which the white minority no longer held power) was granted to the state, now called Zimbabwe, by imperial statute: Zimbabwe Act 1979 (UK), c 60; Zimbabwe Constitution Order 1979 (UK), SI 1979, No. 1600.

into the European Common Market (a judgment referred to by the Supreme Court of Canada in the Patriation Reference: *Reference re Amendment of the Constitution of Canada, supra*). Lord Denning MR of the UK Court of Appeal, after stating that the courts cannot intervene in the negotiation of international treaties, cites with approval a statement by Professor H.W.R. Wade, in (1954–55), Cambridge LJ 196: "'sovereignty is a political fact for which no purely legal authority can be constituted'" [at p. 1383].

We hasten to add that the English Court of Appeal decision had its source in the supremacy of Parliament, which is unlimited in the unitary regime of the United Kingdom, while in Canada there is a distribution of sovereignty between the federal government and the provinces, and this distribution is subject to interpretation by the courts.

The Matter at Issue

Our task is, in the first place, to assess the right claimed by the plaintiff, namely, whether the government's action violates his rights and freedoms under the *Canadian Charter of Rights and Freedoms*.

Freedoms

The Charter, introduced by the *Constitution Act, 1982*, is part of the Constitution of Canada. It undeniably applies to Quebec. The Supreme Court of Canada was clear about this in *Quebec (Attorney-General) v Canada (Attorney-General)* (1982), 140 DLR (3d) 385 at pp. 395–6 [1982] 2 SCR 793, 45 NR 317:

The *Constitution Act, 1982*, is now in force. Its legality is neither challenged nor assailable. It contains a new procedure for amending the Constitution of Canada which entirely replaces the old one in its legal as well as in its conventional aspects. Even assuming therefore that there was a conventional requirement for the consent of Quebec under the old system, it would no longer have any object or force.

The legitimation or forced imposition of a new legal order can in no way be considered a contingency that a court should take into account.

The supremacy of law is recognized by the Constitution of Canada (preamble of the *Canadian Charter of Rights and Freedoms*) and our superior courts have stated many times that the courts are the guardians of the Constitution. We know of no authority to the contrary.

Section 24(1) is the appropriate remedy for redress of a violation of Charter rights and freedoms (*BCGEU v British Columbia (Attorney-General)* (1988), 53 DLR (4th) 1 at p. 12, 44 CCC (3d) 289, [1988] 2 SCR 214). The Charter applies not only to the Parliament and Government of Canada in respect of all matters within the authority of Parliament, but also to the legislature and government of each province in respect of all matters within the authority of the legislature of each province (s. 32 of the *Constitution Act, 1982*). It cannot be maintained, as was suggested to us, that governmental acts that create no obligation do not attract the supervision and control of the courts under the Charter. This would limit the operation of the Charter to rules of law, which can be declared of no force or effect under s. 52 of the *Constitution Act, 1982*. The Charter applies to any government action if such action violates the rights and freedoms it guarantees ...

All of the actions taken by the Quebec government, and the procedure described in the draft bill, indicate that the government, through the Prime Minister and other Cabinet ministers, has undertaken, on behalf of Quebec, to proceed with a unilateral declaration of independence and to obtain Quebec's recognition as a state distinct from Canada.

It is manifest, if not expressly stated, that the Quebec government has no intention of resorting to the amending formula in the Constitution to accomplish the secession of Quebec. In this regard, the Quebec government is giving itself a mandate that the Constitution of Canada does not confer on it.

The actions taken by the Government of Quebec in view of the secession of Quebec are a repudiation of the Constitution of Canada. If such secession were to occur, the *Canadian Charter of Rights and Freedoms*, which is part of the Constitution of Canada, would cease to apply to Quebec and the plaintiff would no longer be able to demand compliance therewith.

It is not my job to pass judgment on the degree of probability that the government's objective will be achieved. It is enough to note that its efforts affect the very foundations of Canada's political institutions and deny the plaintiff Bertrand, like the other citizens of Quebec, the protection that the Constitution of Canada gives them for the enforcement of their fundamental rights and freedoms. The promise to substitute a charter of human rights and freedoms in a forthcoming constitution is not equivalent to the constitutional guarantee that each Canadian presently enjoys.

The constitutional change proposed by the Government of Quebec would result in a break in continuity in the legal order, which is manifestly contrary to the Constitution of Canada. It does not follow that the measures sought by the plaintiff in the numerous conclusions to his motion must be granted. It should not be forgotten that it is fundamental rights and freedoms that are guaranteed by the Charter and not forms of relief ...

The government's patently unlawful exercise does, however, point to the conclusion that the plaintiff in entitled to the remedy that the court considered "appropriate and just in the circumstances". This remedy will ultimately have to determined by the judge who hears the action on its merits.

Irreparable Harm

The plaintiff argues that in the event of a "yes" vote in the referendum, he will have lost the protection of the rights and freedoms guaranteed to him by the Canadian Charter. At the same time, he predicts legal chaos, and points to the federal government's duty to defend those citizens of Quebec who would be unwilling to accept the new legal order. These two propositions are contradictory, to say the least.

The court cannot prevent the political forces from operating. On the other hand, it cannot approve a violation of the constitutional order. The events that have been set in motion by the Government of Quebec may lead to such a violation. This is not pure speculation. The government is going to very great lengths to get its way. Using its political authority and public moneys, it is seeking to overthrow the constitutional order. The plaintiff is opposed to this process. The tension that he and other citizens are experiencing can only increase day by day. The threat is a serious one. Similar considerations apply in the case of public order. The harm is irreparable.

Preponderance of Inconvenience

The plaintiff urges us to grant at the interlocutory stage the entire panoply of remedies that he is seeking. Among these remedies, the injunction against the holding of the referendum has blown the dispute out of proportion. A simple court proceeding is now being interpreted as an interference by the judiciary in the affairs of the National Assembly.

A referendum, by its nature, is consultative: *Haig v Canada* (1993), 105 DLR (4th) 577 at p. 601, [1993] 2 SCR 995, 16 CRR (2d) 193. It does not offend the legal or constitutional order. The plaintiff has stated many times that he is not opposed to the holding of a purely consultative referendum. What he objects to is the effect that would be given by an Act similar to the draft bill proposed by the government to the approval by referendum of a declaration of sovereignty.

What is contemplated is the imposition of a new legal order and a transitional period during which negotiations would be undertaken with the rest of Canada. Parallel to this, measures would be taken to enact a new constitution for Quebec.

We take judicial notice (art. 2808, *Civil Code of Quebec*, SQ 1991, c. 64 (CCQ)) of Bill 1 of the 35th legislature, entitled an *Act respecting the future of Quebec*, tabled on September 7, 1995, which states (in s. 6) that a constituent commission will be established to draw up a draft of a new constitution. This new constitution would then be submitted to popular consultation in a further referendum. In the intervening period, of undetermined duration, an interim constitution would be adopted by the Parliament of Quebec. Section 26 authorizes the National Assembly to make the proclamation of sovereignty at any time after the Act has been assented to if, in the opinion of the committee charged with the orientation and supervision of the negotiations with the Government of Canada, these negotiations prove fruitless.

In this scenario, the stability of the legal order is compromised. The preponderance of inconvenience unquestionably dictates that, in the public interest, I prescribe forthwith some practical and effective relief.

Parliamentary privileges cannot place the National Assembly over and above the Constitution of Canada. The MNAs may discuss any topic and adopt any provision, even one that is invalid and illegal, but there is a limit: they cannot impugn the Constitution from which they derive their powers. It is a function of the courts to denounce an unconstitutional measure.

The National Assembly of Quebec does not have the powers of the Parliament of Westminster.

The plaintiff is asking me to issue a series of injunctions against the defendants and the Government of Quebec, as well as certain injunctions addressed to the chief electoral officer. The court cannot, of course, paralyze the functioning of the National Assembly or prohibit it from debating the issue. That would be an infringement of parliamentary privileges. Moreover, it is preferable that the public discussion be held with full knowledge of the facts.

As to prohibiting the use of public funds for the promotion of the government's constitutional project, no injunction can be issued since no legal provision controlling these types of expenditures, which are made on behalf of the Crown, was drawn to my attention.

However, I take judicial notice that neither the official opposition in Quebec nor the federal government intends to block the holding of the referendum. It must be understood that the people wish to express themselves. To issue an injunction against the holding of the referendum would risk creating a greater wrong than the wrong that it is sought to prevent.

However, a declaratory judgment may be just as if not more effective than an injunction. Moreover, it is the remedy favoured by the courts in constitutional matters, for a variety of reasons. The declaration is not an intrusion into the functioning of the executive or the legislature. It does not open the door to execution proceedings that might appear odious. On the contrary, it allows governments to conceive of ways in which to satisfy the judicial declaration, and thus helps to maintain the balance in our democratic institutions.

Furthermore, the declaratory remedy is more adapted to a preventive form of justice. These are among the considerations canvassed by Kent Roach, of the Ontario Bar, in his work *Constitutional Remedies in Canada* (Aurora, Ont.: Canada Law Book Inc., 1994).

Conclusions

To ensure that the plaintiff's remedy is not completely ineffective once judgment becomes final, the only declaration that would, in my opinion, constitute effective relief is to state, as the plaintiff is asking, that a bill that reiterates the terms of the agreement ratified and executed on June 12, 1995, by Messrs. Jacques Parizeau, Lucien Bouchard and Mario Dumont, that would grant the National Assembly of Quebec the capacity or power to declare the sovereignty of Quebec without following the amending procedure provided for in the Constitution of Canada, constitutes a serious threat to the rights or freedoms of the plaintiff guaranteed by the *Canadian Charter of Rights and Freedoms*, particularly in ss. 2, 3, 6, 7, 15 and 24(1).

Since the Bill respecting the future of Quebec is included in this application, it would be appropriate to adapt this declaration by referring specifically to that bill. Any other declaratory judgment would risk misconstruing the nature of the issue that is before the court.

In the circumstances, the operative part of this judgment will not be addressed to the chief electoral officer, who appeared through counsel and noted that he reports directly to the National Assembly and not the government.

By These Reasons: –

Declares that Bill 1, entitled an *Act respecting the future of Quebec*, introduced by Prime Minister Jacques Parizeau in the National Assembly on September 7, 1995, which would grant the National Assembly of Quebec the power to proclaim that Quebec will become a sovereign country without the need to follow the amending procedure provided for in Part V of the *Constitution Act, 1982*, constitutes a serious threat to the rights and freedoms of the plaintiff guaranteed by the *Canadian Charter of Rights and Freedoms*, in particular in ss. 2, 3, 6, 7, 15 and 24(1) ...

Application granted in part.

READING QUESTIONS ON BERTRAND

1 What does the decision tell you about the judicial role in defending legal order? With which conception of judicial role (positivism's, Dworkin's, Fuller's, Devlin's, Hutchinson and Monahan's) does the judgment best fit?
2 What are the implications of the judgment for a citizen of Quebec had the vote in the referendum been a mandate to negotiate secession?

9

Speech, Hate Propaganda, and Pornography

Freedom of expression is a central value in a free and democratic society. Indeed, it is so important that some people have suggested that it is entirely without exceptions. Despite its high-minded tone, such a view is probably unrealistic. As the American judge Oliver Wendell Holmes famously put it, even the most stringent protection of free speech will not extend to the person falsely shouting "fire" in a crowded theatre. There are plainly exceptions to free expression; the problem for philosophers is to come up with a principled way of thinking about them. Unfortunately, much of the public debate about free expression consists in exaggerated claims about the harmful effects of either speech or censorship. The readings in this section offer some more sophisticated accounts of the basis and limits of the protection of expression.

Joel Feinberg
"Pornography and the Criminal Law" (1979)

Feinberg argues that offensive material should be treated as a private matter. As a result, regulations are only legitimate if they aim to protect those who are offended from materials that bother them.

When the possession, use, or display of sexually explicit materials is prohibited by law, and violations are punished by fine or imprisonment, many thousands of persons are prevented from doing what they would otherwise freely choose to do. Such forceful interference in private affairs seems morally outrageous, unless, of course, it is supported by special justifying reasons. In the absence of appropriate reasons, the coercive use of governmental power, based ultimately on guns and clubs, is merely arbitrary and as such is always morally illegitimate. Criminal prohibitions, of course, are sometimes backed by appropriate reasons, and when that is the case, they are not morally illicit uses of force but rather reasonable regulations of our social activities.

What then are "appropriate reasons" for criminal prohibitions? Surely the need to prevent harm or injury to persons other than the one interfered with is one kind of legitimate reason. Some actions, however, while harmless in themselves, are great nuisances to those who are affected by them, and the law from time immemorial has provided remedies, some civil and some criminal, for actions in this category. So a second kind of legitimate reason for prohibiting conduct is the need to protect others from certain sorts of offensive, irritating, or inconveniencing experiences. Extreme nuisances can actually reach the threshold of harm, as when noises from the house next door prevent a student from studying at all on the evening before an examination, or when an obstructed road causes a person to be late for an important appointment. But we are not very happy with nuisances even when they do not harm our interests, but only cause irritations to our senses, or inconvenient detours from our normal course. The offending conduct produces unpleasant or uncomfortable experiences – affronts to sense or sensibility, disgust, shock, shame, embarrassment, annoyance, boredom, anger, or humiliation – from which one cannot escape without unreasonable inconvenience or even harm.

We demand protection from nuisances when we think of ourselves as *trapped* by them, and we think it unfair that we should pay the cost in inconvenience that is required to escape them. In extreme cases, the offending conduct commandeers our attention from the outside, forcing us to relinquish control of our inner states, and drop what we were doing in order to cope, when it is greatly inconvenient to do so. That is why laws prohibiting nuisances are sometimes said to protect our interest in "privacy."

What distinguishes the "liberal position" on this question is the insistence that the need to prevent harm to others and the need to prevent offensive nuisances to others between them exhaust all the types of reasons which may appropriately support criminal prohibitions. Insofar as a criminal statute is unsupported by reasons of either of these two kinds, it tends to be arbitrary and hence morally illicit. In this respect certain commonly proffered reasons are no better than no reasons at all. The need to protect either the interests or the character of the actor himself from his own folly, does not, according to the liberal, confer moral legitimacy on a criminal statute, nor does the need to prevent inherently sinful or immoral conduct as such. Liberalism so construed does not purport to be a guide to useful public policy for the utilitarian legislator, nor does it claim to provide a key to the interpretation of the American, or any other, constitution. (It is entirely possible that the moral restrictions liberalism would place on legislative discretion are not always socially useful, and also that the Constitution itself allows some morally illegitimate statutes to remain as valid laws.) Instead liberalism purports to indicate to the legislator where the moral limits to government coercion are located.

Let me state from the outset that I am a committed liberal, in this sense, on the question of the legal regulation of pornography. Like the late Herbert Packer, I believe that pornography, at its worst, is not so much a menace as a nuisance, and that the moral right of legislatures to restrict it derives from, and is limited by, the same principles that morally entitle the state to command owners of howling dogs to stop their racket, to punish owners of fertilizing plants for letting odors escape over a whole town, to prohibit indecent exposure and public defecation, and so on. It is absurd to punish nuisances as severely as harmful or injurious conduct, however, and unless certain well-understood conditions are satisfied, it may be illegitimate to punish a given nuisance at all. For that reason it may be useful, before looking at the pornography problem, to examine the restrictions recognized by legislatures and courts on the proper regulation of harmless but offensive nuisances.

I

The most interesting aspect of the law of nuisance is its version of the unavoidable legal balancing act. Both legislatures, when they formulate statutes that define public nuisances, and courts, when they adjudicate conflicts between neighboring landowners in "private nuisance" cases, must weigh opposing considerations. Establishing that one person's conduct is or would be a nuisance to someone else is by no means sufficient to warrant legal interference. First one must compare carefully the magnitude of the nuisance to the one against the reasonableness of the conduct of the other, and the necessity "that all may get on together."[1] William Prosser, describing the various factors that weigh on one side of the scale, tells us that the magnitude of the nuisance (or "seriousness of the inconvenience") to the plaintiff in a private nuisance action depends upon (1) the extent, duration, and character of the interference, (2) the social value of the use the plaintiff makes of his land, and (3) the extent to which the plaintiff can, without undue burden or hardship, avoid the offense by taking precautions against it.[2] These three factors yield the weight to be assigned to the seriousness of the inconvenience. They must be weighed against the reasonableness of the defendant's conduct, which is determined by (1) "the social value of its ultimate purpose, (2) the motive of the defendant [in particular its character as innocent or spiteful], and (3) whether the defendant by taking reasonable steps can avoid or reduce the inconvenience to the plaintiff without undue burden or inconvenience to himself."[3] Finally Prosser would have us throw on to the scale the interests of the "public at large," in particular its interest in "the nature of the locality" where the nuisance occurred – to "what paramount use it is already devoted" – and given that background, "the suitability of the use made of the land by both plaintiff and defendant."[4] In sum, the more extended, durable, and severe the inconvenience to the plaintiff, and the greater the social value of the land uses interfered with, then the greater is the magnitude of the nuisance, while the greater the ease with which the plaintiff can avoid the nuisance, the smaller its magnitude. Similarly, the greater the social value of the defendant's conduct[5] and the freer his motives of spite toward the plaintiff, the more reasonable is his conduct, despite its inconvenience to the plaintiff, while the easier it is for him to achieve his goals by means that do not inconvenience the plaintiff, the less reasonable is his offending conduct. Finally, the prevalent character of the neighborhood weighs heavily, so that a householder who takes up residence in a manufacturing district cannot complain, as a plaintiff in a private nuisance suit, of the noise, dust, or vibration, whereas the same amount of disturbance caused by a factory in a primarily residential district, will be declared a nuisance to the landowners in its vicinity.

If, as I recommend, we think of pornographic exhibitions and publications as nuisances which may properly be controlled by the law under certain very strict conditions, we shall have to posit a similar set of conflicting considerations to be weighed carefully, not only by juries in private tort suits, but also by legislatures in their deliberations over the wording of criminal statutes designed to prohibit and punish pornography. Let me suggest that legislators who are impressed by the model of "public nuisance" should weigh, in the case of each main category and context of pornography, the seriousness of the offense caused to unwilling witnesses against the reasonableness of the offender's conduct. The magnitude of the offensiveness would be determined by (1) the intensity and durability of the repugnance the material produces, and the extent to which repugnance could be anticipated to be the general reaction of strangers to the conduct displayed or represented (conduct offensive only to persons with an abnormal susceptibility to offense would not count as *very* offensive), (2) the ease with which unwilling witnesses can avoid the offensive displays, and (3) whether or not the witnesses have willingly assumed the risk of being offended either through curiosity or the anticipation of pleasure. (The maxim *volenti non fit injuria* applies to offense as well as to harm.) We can refer to these norms, in order, as "the extent of offense standard" (with its "exclusion of abnormal susceptibility corollary"), "the reasonable avoidability standard," and "the *volenti* standard."

These factors would be weighed as a group against the reasonableness of the pornographers' conduct as determined by (1) its personal importance to the exhibitors themselves and its social value generally, remembering always the enormous social utility of unhampered expression (in those cases where expression is involved), (2) the availability of alternative times and places where the conduct in question would cause less offense, (3) the extent if any to which the offense is caused by spiteful motives. In addition, the legislature would examine the prior established character of various neighborhoods, and consider establishing licensed zones in areas where the conduct in question is known to be already prevalent, so that people inclined to be offended are not likely to stumble on it to their surprise.

A legislature, of course, does not concern itself with judging specific actions and specific offended states after they have occurred. Rather its eyes are to the future, and it must weigh against one another, or authorize courts to weigh against one another, generalized *types* of conduct and offense. In hard cases this balancing procedure can be very complex and uncertain, but there are some cases that fall clearly within one or another standard in such a way as to leave no doubt how they must be decided. Thus, the *volenti* standard, for example, preempts all the others when it clearly applies. Film exhibitors cannot reasonably be charged with criminally offensive conduct when they have seen to it that the only people who witness their films are those adults who voluntarily purchased tickets to do so, knowing full well what sort of film they were about to see. One cannot be *wrongfully* offended by that to which one fully consents. Similarly, bans on *books* must fail to be morally legitimate in view of the ease with which offense at printed passages can be avoided. Since potential readers are not "captive audiences," here the reasonable avoidability standard is preemptive. So also do inoffensively expressed political or theological opinions fail to qualify as "criminal nuisances," by virtue of their personal and social importance as "free expression." On the other side, purely spiteful motives in the offender can be a preemptive consideration weighting the balance scale decisively on the side of unreasonableness.

In some cases, no one standard is preemptive, but nevertheless all applicable standards pull together towards one inevitable decision. The public eating of excrement (coprophagia) fully and unambiguously satisfies the extent of offense standard. One doesn't have to be abnormally squeamish to be offended by the very sight of it. If it is done (say) on a public bus, it definitely fails to win the support of the reasonable avoidability and *volenti* standards, which is to say that is causes intense disgust to captive observers. Hence, by *all* the relevant criteria, it is seriously offensive. By all the criteria for weighing reasonableness, public coprophagia does poorly too. It cannot be very important to the neurotic person who does it (not as important, for example, as earning a living, or eating fresh food); it has a definitely limited social utility; it is not the expression in language of an opinion, nor does it fall into a recognized genre of aesthetic expression; and it could as well be done in private. Hence it is both seriously offensive and unredeemed by independent "reasonableness." It would not of course be called "pornography," but its criminal proscription under another name would be morally legitimate in principle, even though in practice it might be unwise, uneconomical, or unnecessary.

NOTES

1 Practically all human activities, unless carried on in a wilderness, interfere to some extent with others or involve some risk of interference, and these interferences range from mere trifling annoyances to serious harms. It is an obvious truth that each individual in a community must put up with a certain amount of annoyance, inconvenience and interference, and must take a certain amount of risk in order that all may get on together. The very existence of organized society depends upon the principle of "give and take, live and let live," and therefore the law of torts does not attempt to impose

liability or shift the loss in every case where one person's conduct has some detrimental effect on another. Liability is imposed only in those cases where the harm or risk [or inconvenience or offense] to one is greater than he ought to be required to bear under the circumstances ... Restatement of Torts s. 822, comment j (1939).

2 W. Prosser, *Handbook of the Law of Torts* 597 (4th ed. 1971).

3 Ibid., at 597–99.

4 Ibid., at 599–600.

5 "The world must have factories, smelters, oil refineries, noisy machinery, and blasting, as well as airports, even at the expense of some inconvenience to those in the vicinity, and the plaintiff may be required to accept and tolerate some not unreasonable discomfort for the general good ... On the other hand, a foul pond, or a vicious or noisy dog, will have little if any social value, and relatively slight annoyance from it may justify relief." Ibid. at 597–98 (footnotes omitted).

READING QUESTIONS ON FEINBERG

1 Feinberg seems to suppose that the liberal commitment to individual autonomy survives confining one's expression of important aspects of one's personality to the private. Is this adequate, or do you suppose that public expression is sometimes important to autonomy?

2 As you go through the readings below, think about the implications of Feinberg's distinction between offence and harm. How should such a distinction be drawn in particular cases?

T.M. Scanlon
"A Theory of Freedom of Expression" (1972)

Scanlon argues that the need to protect freedom of expression follows from the importance of individual autonomy. The state must treat citizens as capable of making up their own minds. As a result, it cannot hold one person responsible for something that others do because of reasons they have offered them.

... Typically, the acts of expression with which a theory of "free speech" is concerned are addressed to a large (if not the widest possible) audience,

and express propositions or attitudes thought to have a certain generality of interest. This accounts, I think, for our reluctance to regard as an
act of expression in the relevant sense the communication between the
average bank robber and the teller he confronts. This reluctance is diminished somewhat if the note the robber hands the teller contains, in
addition to the usual threat, some political justification for his act and
an exhortation to others to follow his example. What this addition does
is to broaden the projected audience and increase the generality of the
message's interest. The relevance of these features is certainly something which an adequate theory of freedom of expression should explain, but it will be simpler at present not to make them part of the
definition of the class of acts of expression.

Almost everyone would agree, I think, that the acts which are protected by a doctrine of freedom of expression will all be acts of expression in the sense I have defined. However, since acts of expression can
be both violent and arbitrarily destructive, it seems unlikely that anyone would maintain that as a class they were immune from legal restrictions. Thus the class of protected acts must be some proper subset
of this class. It is sometimes held that the relevant subclass consists of
those acts of expression which are instances of "speech" as opposed to
"action." But those who put forward such a view have generally wanted
to include within the class of protected acts some which are not speech
in any normal sense of the word (for instance, mime and certain forms
of printed communication) and to exclude from it some which clearly
are speech in the normal sense (talking in libraries, falsely shouting
"fire" in crowded theatres etc.). Thus if acts of speech are the relevant
subclass of acts of expression, then "speech" is here functioning as a
term of art which needs to be defined. To construct a theory following
these traditional lines we might proceed to work out a technical corre-
late to the distinction between speech and action which seemed to fit
our clearest intuitions about which acts do and which do not qualify for
protection.[1]

To proceed in this way seems to me, however, to be a serious mistake. It seems clear that the intuitions we appeal to in deciding whether
a given restriction infringes freedom of expression are not intuitions
about which things are properly called speech as opposed to action,
even in some refined sense of "speech." The feeling that we must look
for a definition of this kind has its roots, I think, in the view that since
any adequate doctrine of freedom of expression must extend to some
acts a privilege not enjoyed by all, such a doctrine must have its theo-

retical basis in some difference between the protected acts and others, i.e., in some definition of the protected class. But this is clearly wrong. It could be, and I think is, the case that the theoretical bases of the doctrine of freedom of expression are multiple and diverse, and while the net effect of these elements taken together is to extend to some acts a certain privileged status, there is no theoretically interesting (and certainly no simple and intuitive) definition of the class of acts which enjoys this privilege. Rather than trying at the outset to carve out the privileged subset of acts of expression, then, I propose to consider the class as a whole and to look for ways in which the charge of irrationality brought against the doctrine of freedom of expression might be answered without reference to a single class of privileged acts.

As I mentioned at the start, this charge arises from the fact that under any nontrivial form of the doctrine there will be cases in which acts of expression are held to be immune from legal restriction despite the fact that they give rise to undoubted harms which would in other cases be sufficient to justify such restriction. (The "legal restriction" involved here may take the form either of the imposition of criminal sanctions or of the general recognition by the courts of the right of persons affected by the acts to recover through civil suits for damages.) Now it is not in general sufficient justification for a legal restriction on a certain class of acts to show that certain harms will be prevented if this restriction is enforced. It might happen that the costs of enforcing the restriction outweigh the benefits to be gained, or that the enforcement of the restriction infringes some right either directly (e.g., a right to the unimpeded performance of exactly those acts to which the restriction applies) or indirectly (e.g., a right which under prevailing circumstances can be secured by many only through acts to which the restriction applies). Alternatively, it may be that while certain harms could be prevented by placing legal restrictions on a class of acts, those to whom the restriction would apply are not responsible for those harms and hence cannot be restricted in order to prevent them.

Most defences of freedom of expression have rested upon arguments of the first two of these three forms. In arguments of both these forms factors which taken in isolation might have been sufficient to justify restrictions on a given class of acts are held in certain cases to be overridden by other considerations. As will become clear later, I think that appeals both to rights and to the balancing of competing goals are essential components of a complete theory of freedom of expression. But I want to begin by considering arguments which, like disclaimers of responsibility, have the effect of showing that what might at first seem to be reasons for restricting a class of acts cannot be taken as such reasons at all.

My main reason for beginning in this way is this: it is easier to say what the classic violations of freedom of expression have in common than it is to define the class of acts which is protected by that doctrine. What distinguishes these violations from innocent regulation of expression is not the character of the acts they interfere with but rather what they hope to achieve – for instance, the halting of the spread of heretical notions. This suggests that an important component of our intuitions about freedom of expression has to do not with the illegitimacy of certain restrictions but with the illegitimacy of certain justifications for restrictions. Very crudely, the intuition seems to be something like this: those justifications are illegitimate which appeal to the fact that it would be a bad thing if the view communicated by certain acts of expression were to become generally believed; justifications which are legitimate, though they may sometimes be overridden, are those that appeal to features of acts of expression (time, place, loudness) other than the views they communicate.

As a principle of freedom of expression this is obviously unsatisfactory as it stands. For one thing, it rests on a rather unclear notion of "the view communicated" by an act of expression; for another, it seems too restrictive, since, for example, it appears to rule out any justification for laws against defamation. In order to improve upon this crude formulation, I want to consider a number of different ways in which acts of expression can bring about harms, concentrating on cases where these harms clearly can be counted as reasons for restricting the acts that give rise to them. I will then try to formulate the principle in a way which accommodates these cases. I emphasize at the outset that I am not maintaining in any of these cases that the harms in question are always sufficient justification for restrictions on expression, but only that they can always be taken into account.

1. Like other acts, acts of expression can bring about injury or damage as a direct physical consequence. This is obviously true of the more bizarre forms of expression mentioned above, but no less true of more pedestrian forms: the sound of my voice can break glass, wake the sleeping, trigger an avalanche, or keep you from paying attention to something else you would rather hear. It seems clear that when harms brought about in this way are intended by the person

performing an act of expression, or when he is reckless or negligent with respect to their occurrence, then no infringement of freedom of expression is involved in considering them as possible grounds for criminal penalty or civil action.

2. It is typical of the harms just considered that their production is in general quite independent of the view which the given act of expression is intended to communicate. This is not generally true of a second class of harms, an example of which is provided by the common-law notion of assault. In at least one of the recognized senses of the term, an assault (as distinct from a battery) is committed when one person intentionally places another in apprehension of imminent bodily harm. Since assault in this sense involves an element of successful communication, instances of assault may necessarily involve expression. But assaults and related acts can also be part of larger acts of expression, as for example when a guerrilla theatre production takes the form of a mock bank robbery which starts off looking like the real thing, or when a bomb scare is used to gain attention for a political cause. Assault is sometimes treated as inchoate battery, but it can also be viewed as a separate offence which consists in actually bringing about a specific kind of harm. Under this analysis, assault is only one of a large class of possible crimes which consist in the production in others of harmful or unpleasant states of mind, such as fear, shock, and perhaps certain kinds of offence. One may have doubts as to whether most of these harms are serious enough to be recognized by the law or whether standards of proof could be established for dealing with them in court. In principle, however, there seems to be no alternative to including them among the possible justifications for restrictions on expression.

3. Another way in which an act of expression can harm a person is by causing others to form an adverse opinion of him or by making him an object of public ridicule. Obvious examples of this are defamation and interference with the right to a fair trial.

4. As Justice Holmes said, "The most stringent protection of free speech would not protect a man in falsely shouting fire in a theatre and causing a panic."[2]

5. One person may through an act of expression contribute to the production of a harmful act by someone else, and at least in some cases the harmful consequences of the latter act may justify making the former a crime as well. This seems to many people to be the case

when the act of expression is the issuance of an order or the making of a threat or when it is a signal or other communication between confederates.

6. Suppose some misanthropic inventor were to discover a simple method whereby anyone could make nerve gas in his kitchen out of gasoline, table salt, and urine. It seems just as clear to me that he could be prohibited by law from passing out his recipe on handbills or broadcasting it on television as that he could be prohibited from passing out free samples of his product in aerosol cans or putting it on sale at Abercrombie and Fitch. In either case his action would bring about a drastic decrease in the general level of personal safety by radically increasing the capacity of most citizens to inflict harm on each other. The fact that he does this in one case through an act of expression and in the other through some other form of action seems to me not to matter.

It might happen, however, that a comparable decrease in the general level of personal safety could be just as reliably predicted to result from the distribution of a particularly effective piece of political propaganda which would undermine the authority of the government, or from the publication of a theological tract which would lead to a schism and a bloody civil war. In these cases the matter seems to me to be entirely different, and the harmful consequence seems clearly not to be a justification for restricting the acts of expression.

What I conclude from this is that the distinction between expression and other forms of action is less important than the distinction between expression which moves others to act by pointing out what they take to be good reasons for action and expression which gives rise to action by others in other ways, e.g., by providing them with the means to do what they wanted to do anyway. This conclusion is supported, I think, by our normal views about legal responsibility.

If I were to say to you, an adult in full possession of your faculties, "What you ought to do is rob a bank", and you were subsequently to act on this advice, I could not be held legally responsible for your act, nor could my act legitimately be made a separate crime. This remains true if I supplement my advice with a battery of arguments about why banks should be robbed or even about why a certain bank in particular should be robbed and why you in particular are entitled to rob it. It might become false – what I did might legitimately be made a crime – if certain further conditions held: for example, if you were a child, or so weak-minded as to be legally incompetent, and I knew this or ought to have known it; or if you were my subordinate in some organization and what I said to you was not advice but an order, backed by the discipline of the group; or if I went on to make further contributions to your act, such as aiding you in preparations or providing you with tools or giving you crucial information about the bank.

The explanation for these differences seems to me to be this. A person who acts on reasons he has acquired from another's act of expression acts on what *he* has come to believe and has judged to be a sufficient basis for action. The contribution to the genesis of his action made by the act of expression is, so to speak, superseded by the agent's own judgment. This is not true of the contribution made by an accomplice, or by a person who knowingly provides the agent with tools (the key to the bank) or with technical information (the combination of the safe) which he uses to achieve his ends. Nor would it be true of my contribution to your act if, instead of providing you with reasons for thinking bank robbery a good thing, I issued orders or commands backed by threats, thus changing your circumstances so as to *make* it a (comparatively) good thing for you to do.

It is a difficult matter to say exactly when legal liability arises in these cases, and I am not here offering any positive thesis about what constitutes being an accessory, inciting, conspiring, etc. I am interested only in maintaining the negative thesis that whatever these crimes involve, it has to be something more than merely the communication of persuasive reasons for action (or perhaps some special circumstances, such as diminished capacity of the person persuaded).

I will now state the principle of freedom of expression which was promised at the beginning of this section. The principle, which seems to me to be a natural extension of the thesis Mill defends in Chapter II of *On Liberty*, and which I will therefore call the Millian Principle, is the following:

There are certain harms which, although they would not occur but for certain acts of expression, nonetheless cannot be taken as part of a justification for legal restrictions on these acts. There harms are: (a) harms to certain individuals which consist in their coming to have false beliefs as a result of those acts of expression; (b) harmful consequences of acts performed as a result of those acts of expression, where the connection between the acts of expression and the subsequent harmful acts consists merely in the fact that the act of expression led the agents to believe (or increased their tendency to believe) these acts to be worth performing.

I hope it is obvious that this principle is compatible with the examples of acceptable reasons for restricting expression presented in 1 through 6 above. (One case in which this may not be obvious, that of the man who falsely shouts "fire", will be discussed more fully below.) The preceding discussion, which appealed in part to intuitions about legal responsibility, was intended to make plausible the distinction on which the second part of the Millian Principle rests and, in general, to suggest how the principle could be reconciled with cases of the sort included in 5 and 6. But the principle itself goes beyond questions of responsibility. In order for a class of harms to provide a justification for restricting a person's act it is not necessary that he fulfil conditions for being legally responsible for any of the individual acts which actually produce those harms. In the nerve-gas case, for example, to claim that distribution of the recipe may be prevented one need not claim that a person who distributed it could be held legally responsible (even as an accessory) for any of the particular murders the gas is used to commit. Consequently, to explain why this case differs from sedition it would not be sufficient to claim that providing means involves responsibility while providing reasons does not.

I would like to believe that the general observance of the Millian Principle by governments would, in the long run, have more good consequences than bad. But my defence of the principle does not rest on this optimistic outlook. I will argue in the next section that the Millian Principle, as a general principle about how governmental restrictions on the liberty of citizens may be justified, is a consequence of the view, coming down to us from Kant and others, that a legitimate government is one whose authority citizens can recognize while still regarding themselves as equal, autonomous, rational agents. Thus, while it is not a principle about legal responsibility, the Millian Principle has its origins in a certain view of human agency from which many of our ideas about responsibility also derive.

Taken by itself, the Millian Principle obviously does not constitute an adequate theory of freedom of expression. Much more needs to be said about when the kinds of harmful consequences which the principle allows us to consider can be taken to be sufficient justification for restrictions on expression. Nonetheless, it seems to me fair to call the

Millian Principle the basic principle of freedom of expression. This is so, first, because a successful defence of the principle would provide us with an answer to the charge of irrationality by explaining why certain of the most obvious consequences of acts of expression cannot be appealed to as a justification for legal restrictions against them. Second, the Millian Principle is the only plausible principle of freedom of expression I can think of which applies to expression in general and makes no appeal to special rights (e.g., political rights) or to the value to be attached to expression in some particular domain (e.g., artistic expression or the discussion of scientific ideas). It thus specifies what is special about acts of expression as opposed to other acts and constitutes in this sense the usable residue of the distinction between speech and action.

I will have more to say in Section IV about how the Millian Principle is to be supplemented to obtain a full account of freedom of expression. Before that, however, I want to consider in more detail how the principle can be justified.

III

As I have already mentioned, I will defend the Millian Principle by showing it to be a consequence of the view that the powers of a state are limited to those that citizens could recognize while still regarding themselves as equal, autonomous, rational agents. Since the sense of autonomy to which I will appeal is extremely weak, this seems to me to constitute a strong defence of the Millian Principle as an exceptionless restriction on governmental authority. I will consider briefly in section V, however, whether there are situations in which the principle should be suspended.

To regard himself as autonomous in the sense I have in mind a person must see himself as sovereign in deciding what to believe and in weighing competing reasons for action. He must apply to these tasks his own canons of rationality, and must recognize the need to defend his beliefs and decisions in accordance with these canons. This does not mean, of course, that he must be perfectly rational, even by his own standard of rationality, or that his standard of rationality must be exactly ours. Obviously the content of this notion of autonomy will vary according to the range of variation we are willing to allow in canons of rational decision. If just anything counts as such a canon then the requirements I have mentioned will become mere tautologies: an autonomous man believes what he believes and decides to do what he decides to do. I am sure I could not describe a set of limits on what can count as canons of rationality which would secure general agreement, and I will not try, since I am sure that the area of agreement on this question extends far beyond anything which will be relevant to the applications of the notion of autonomy that I intend to make. For present purposes what will be important is this. An autonomous person cannot accept without independent consideration the judgment of others as to what he should believe or what he should do. He may rely on the judgment of others, but when he does so he must be prepared to advance independent reasons for thinking their judgment likely to be correct, and to weigh the evidential value of their opinion against contrary evidence.

The requirements of autonomy as I have so far described them are extremely weak. They are much weaker than the requirements Kant draws from essentially the same notion,[3] in that being autonomous in my sense (like being free in Hobbes's) is quite consistent with being subject to coercion with respect to one's actions. A coercer merely changes the considerations which militate for or against a certain course of action; weighing these conflicting considerations is still up to you.

An autonomous man may, if he believes the appropriate arguments, believe that the state has a distinctive right to command him. That is, he may believe that (within certain limits, perhaps) the fact that the law requires a certain action provides him with a very strong reason for performing that action, a reason which is quite independent of the consequences, for him or others, of his performing it or refraining. How strong this reason is – what, if anything, could override it – will depend on his view of the arguments for obedience to law. What is essential to the person's remaining autonomous is that in any given case his mere recognition that a certain action is required by law does not settle the question of whether he will do it. That question is settled only by his own decision, which may take into account his current assessment of the general case for obedience and the exceptions it admits, consideration of his other duties and obligations, and his estimate of the consequences of obedience and disobedience in this particular case.[4]

Thus, while it is not obviously inconsistent with being autonomous to recognize a special obligation to obey the commands of the state, there are limits on the *kind* of obligation which autonomous citizens could recognize. In particular, they could not regard themselves as being under an "obligation" to believe the decrees of the state to be correct, nor could they concede to the state the right to have its decrees obeyed without deliberation. The Millian Principle can be seen as a refinement of these limitations.

The apparent irrationality of the doctrine of freedom of expression derives from its apparent conflict with the principle that it is the prerogative of a state – indeed, part if its duty to its citizens – to decide when the threat of certain harms is great enough to warrant legal action, and when it is, to make laws adequate to meet this threat. (Thus Holmes's famous reference to "substantive evils that Congress has a right to prevent."[5]) Obviously this principle is not acceptable in the crude form in which I have just stated it; no one thinks that Congress can do *anything* it judges to be required to save us from "substantive evils". The Millian Principle specifies two ways in which this prerogative must be limited if the state is to be acceptable to autonomous subjects. The argument for the first part of the principle is as follows.

The harm of coming to have false beliefs is not one that an autonomous man could allow the state to protect him against through restrictions on expression. For a law to provide such protection it would have to be in effect and deterring potential misleaders while the potentially misled remained susceptible to persuasion by them. In order to be protected by such a law a person would thus have to concede to the state the right to decide that certain views were false and, once it had so decided, to prevent him from hearing them advocated even if he might wish to. The conflict between doing this and remaining autonomous would be direct if a person who authorized the state to protect him in this way necessarily also bound himself to accept the state's judgment about which views were false. The matter is not quite this simple, however, since it is conceivable that a person might authorize the state to act for him in this way while still reserving to himself the prerogative of deciding, on the basis of the arguments and evidence left available to him, where the truth was to be found. But such a person would be "deciding for himself" only in an empty sense, since in any case where the state exercised its prerogative he would be "deciding" on the basis of evidence preselected to include only that which supported one conclusion. While he would not be under an obligation to accept the state's judgment as correct, he would have conceded to the state the right to deprive him of grounds for making an independent judgement.

The argument for the second half of the Millian Principle is parallel to this one. What must be argued against is the view that the state, once it has declared certain conduct to be illegal, may when necessary move to prevent that conduct by outlawing its advocacy. The conflict between this thesis and the autonomy of citizens is, just as in the previous one, slightly oblique. Conceding to the state the right to use this means to secure compliance with its laws does not immediately involve conceding to it the right to require citizens to believe that what the law says ought not to be done ought not to be done. None the less, it is a concession that autonomous citizens could not make, since it gives the state the right to deprive citizens of the grounds for arriving at an independent judgement as to whether the law should be obeyed.

These arguments both depend on the thesis that to defend a certain belief as reasonable a person must be prepared to defend the grounds of his belief as not obviously skewed or otherwise suspect. There is a clear parallel between this thesis and Mill's famous argument that if we are interested in having truth prevail we should allow all available arguments to be heard.[6] But the present argument does not depend, as Mill's may appear to, on an empirical claim that the truth is in fact more likely to win out if free discussion is allowed. Nor does it depend on the perhaps more plausible claim that, given the nature of people and governments, to concede to governments the power in question would be an outstandingly poor strategy for bringing about a situation in which true opinions prevail.

It is quite conceivable that a person who recognized in himself a fatal weakness for certain kinds of bad arguments might conclude that everyone would be better off if he were to rely entirely on the judgment of his friends in certain crucial matters. Acting on this conclusion, he might enter into an agreement, subject to periodic review by him, empowering them to shield him from any sources of information likely to divert him from their counsel on the matters in question. Such an agreement is not obviously irrational, nor, if it is entered into voluntarily, for a limited time, and on the basis of the person's own knowledge of himself and those he proposes to trust, does it appear to be inconsistent with his autonomy. The same would be true if the proposed trustees were in fact the authorities of the state. But the question we have been considering is quite different: Could an autonomous individual regard the state as having, not as part of a special voluntary agreement with him but as part of its normal powers *qua* state, the power to put such an arrangement into effect without his consent whenever *it* (i.e., the legislative authority) judged that to be advisable? The answer to this question seems to me to be quite clearly no.

Someone might object to this answer on the following grounds. I have allowed for the possibility that an autonomous man might accept a general argument to the effect that the fact that the state commands a certain thing is in and of itself a reason why that thing should be done. Why couldn't he also accept a similar argument to the effect that the state *qua* state is in the best position to decide when certain counsel is best ignored?

I have already argued that the parallel suggested here between the state's right to command action and a right to restrict expression does not hold. But there is a further problem with this objection. What saves temporary, voluntary arrangements of the kind considered above from being obvious violations of autonomy is the fact that they can be based on a firsthand estimation of the relative reliability of the trustee's judgment and that of the "patient". Thus the person whose information is restricted by such an arrangement has what he judges to be good grounds for thinking the evidence he does receive to be a sound basis for judgment. A principle which provided a corresponding basis for relying on the state *qua* state would have to be extremely general, applying to all states of a certain kind, regardless of who occupied positions of authority in them, and to all citizens of such states. Such a principle would have to be one which admitted variation in individual cases and rested its claim on what worked out best "in the long run". Even if some generalization of this kind were true, it seems to me altogether implausible to suppose that it could be rational to rely on such a general principle when detailed knowledge of the individuals involved in a particular case suggested a contrary conclusion.

A more limited case for allowing states the power in question might rest not on particular virtues of governments but on the recognized fact that under certain circumstances individuals are quite incapable of acting rationally. Something like this may seem to apply in the case of the man who falsely shouts "fire" in a crowded theatre. Here a restriction on expression is justified by the fact that such acts would lead others (give them reason) to perform harmful actions. Part of what makes the restriction acceptable is the idea that the persons in the theatre who react to the shout are under conditions that diminish their capacity for rational deliberation. This case strikes us as a trivial one. What makes it trivial is, first, the fact that only in a very far-fetched sense is a person who is prevented from hearing the false shout under such circumstances prevented from making up his own mind about some question. Second, the diminished capacity attributed to those in the theatre is extremely brief, and applies equally to anyone under the relevant conditions. Third, the harm to be prevented by the restriction is not subject to any doubt or controversy, even by those who are temporarily "deluded". In view of all these facts, the restriction is undoubtedly one which would receive unanimous consent if that were asked.[7]

This is not true, however, of most of the other exceptions to the Millian Principle that might be justified by appeal to "diminished rationality". It is doubtful, for example, whether any of the three conditions I have mentioned would apply to a case in which political debate was to be suspended during a period of turmoil and impending revolution. I cannot see how nontrivial cases of this kind could be made compatible with autonomy.

The arguments I have given may sound like familiar arguments against paternalism, but the issue involved is not simply that. First, a restriction on expression justified on grounds contrary to the Millian Principle is not necessarily paternalistic, since those who are to be protected by such a restriction may be other than those (the speaker and his audience) whose liberty is restricted. When such a restriction is paternalistic, however, it represents a particularly strong form of paternalism, and the arguments I have given are arguments against paternalism only in this strong form. It is quite consistent with a person's autonomy, in the limited sense I have employed, for the law to restrict his freedom of action "for his own good", for instance by requiring him to wear a helmet while riding his motorcycle. The conflict arises only if compliance with this law is then promoted by forbidding, for example, expression of the view that wearing a helmet isn't worth it, or is only for sissies.

It is important to see that the argument for the Millian Principle rests on a limitation of the authority of states to command their subjects rather than on a right of individuals. For one thing, this explains why this particular principle of freedom of expression applies to governments rather than to individuals, who do not have such authority to begin with. There are surely cases in which individuals have the right not to have their acts of expression interfered with by other individuals, but these rights presumably flow from a general right to be free from arbitrary interference, together with considerations which make certain kinds of expression particularly important forms of activity.

If the argument for the Millian Principle were thought to rest on a right, "the right of citizens to make up their own minds", then that argument might be thought to proceed as follows. Persons who see themselves as autonomous see themselves as having a right to make up their own minds, hence also a right to whatever is necessary for them to do this; what is wrong with violations of the Millian Principle is that they infringe this right.

A right of this kind would certainly support a healthy doctrine of freedom of expression, but it is not required for one. The argument given above was much more limited. Its aim was to establish that the authority of governments to restrict the liberty of citizens in order to prevent certain harms does not include authority to prevent these harms by controlling people's sources of information to ensure that they will maintain certain beliefs. It is a long step from this conclusion to a right which is violated whenever someone is deprived of information necessary for him to make an informed decision on some matter that concerns him.

There are clearly cases in which individuals have a right to the information necessary to make informed choices and can claim this right against the government. This is true in the case of political decisions, for example, when the right flows from a certain conception of the relation between a democratic government and its citizens. Even where there is no such right, the provision of information and other conditions for the exercise of autonomy is an important task for states to pursue. But these matters take us beyond the Millian Principle.

IV

The Millian Principle is obviously incapable of accounting for all of the cases that strike us as infringements of freedom of expression. On the basis of this principle alone we would raise no objection against a government that banned all parades or demonstrations (they interfere with traffic), outlawed posters and handbills (too messy), banned public meetings of more than 10 people (likely to be unruly), and restricted newspaper publication to one page per week (to save trees). Yet such policies surely strike us as intolerable. That they so strike us is a reflection of our belief that free expression is a good which ranks above the maintenance of absolute peace and quiet, clean streets, smoothly flowing traffic, and rock-bottom taxes.

Thus there is a part of our intuitive view of freedom of expression which rests upon a balancing of competing goods. By contrast with the Millian Principle, which provides a single defence for all kinds of expression, here it does not seem to be a matter of the value to be placed on expression (in general) as opposed to other goods. The case seems to be different for, say, artistic expression than for the discussion of scientific matters, and different still for expression of political views.

Within certain limits, it seems clear that the value to be placed on having various kinds of expression flourish is something which should be subject to popular will in the society in question. The limits I have in mind here are, first, those imposed by considerations of distributive justice. Access to means of expression for whatever purposes one may have in mind is a good which can be fairly or unfairly distributed among the members of a society, and many cases which strike us as violations of freedom of expression are in fact instances of distributive injustice. This would be true of a case where, in an economically inegalitarian society, access to the principal means of expression was controlled by the government and auctioned off by it to the highest bidders, as is essentially the case with broadcasting licences in the United States today. The same might be said of a parade ordinance which allowed the town council to forbid parades by unpopular groups because they were too expensive to police.

But to call either of these cases instances of unjust distribution tells only part of the story. Access to means of expression is in many cases a necessary condition for participation in the political process of the country, and therefore something to which citizens have an independent right. At the very least the recognition of such rights will require governments to ensure that means of expression are readily available through which individuals and small groups can make their views on political issues known, and to ensure that the principal means of expression in the society do not fall under the control of any particular segment of the community. But exactly what rights of access to means of expression follow in this way from political rights will depend to some extent on the political institutions in question. Political participation may take different forms under different institutions, even under equally just institutions.

The theory of freedom of expression which I am offering, then, consists of at least four distinguishable elements. It is based upon the Millian Principle, which is absolute but serves only to rule out certain justifications for legal restrictions on acts of expression. Within the limits set by this principle the whole range of governmental policies affecting opportunities for expression, whether by restriction, positive intervention, or failure to intervene, are subject to justification and criticism on a number of diverse grounds. First, on grounds of whether they reflect an appropriate balancing of the value of certain kinds of expression relative to other social goods; second, whether they ensure equitable distribution of access to means of expression throughout the society; and third, whether they are compatible with the recognition of certain special rights, particularly political rights.

This mixed theory is somewhat cumbersome, but the various parts seem to me both mutually irreducible and essential if we are to account for the full range of cases which seem intuitively to constitute violations of "free speech".

V

The failure of the Millian Principle to allow certain kinds of exceptions may seem to many the most implausible feature of the theory I have offered. In addition to the possibility mentioned earlier, that exceptions should be allowed in cases of diminished rationality, there may seem to be an obvious case for allowing deviations from the principle in time of war or other grave emergency.

It should be noticed that because the Millian Principle is much narrower than, say, a blanket protection of "speech", the theory I have offered can already accommodate some of the restrictions on expression which wartime conditions may be thought to justify. The Millian Principle allows one, even in normal times, to consider whether the publication of certain information might present serious hazards to public safety by giving people the capacity to inflict certain harms. It seems likely that risks of this kind which are worth taking in time of peace in order to allow full discussion of, say, certain scientific questions, might be intolerable in wartime.

But the kind of emergency powers that governments feel entitled to invoke often go beyond this and include, for example, the power to cut off political debate when such debate threatens to divide the country or otherwise to undermine its capacity to meet a present threat. The obvious justification for such powers is clearly disallowed by the Millian Principle, and the theory I have offered provides for no exceptions of this kind.

It is hard for me at the present moment to conceive of a case in which I would think the invocation of such powers by a government right. I am willing to admit that there might be such cases, but even if there are I do not think that they should be seen as "exceptions" to be incorporated within the Millian Principle.

That principle, it will be recalled, does not rest on a right of citizens but rather expresses a limitation on the authority governments can be supposed to have. The authority in question here is that provided by a particular kind of political theory, one which has its starting point in the question: How could citizens recognize a right of governments to command them while still regarding themselves as equal, autonomous, rational agents? The theory is normally thought to yield the answer that this is possible if, but only if, that right is limited in certain ways, and if certain other conditions, supposed to ensure citizen control over government, are fulfilled. I have argued that one of the necessary limitations is expressed by the Millian Principle. If I am right, then the claim of a government to rule by virtue of this particular kind of authority is undermined, I think completely, if it undertakes to control its citizens in the ways that the Millian Principle is intended to exclude.

This does not mean, however, that it could not in an extreme case be right for certain people, who normally exercised the kind of authority held to be legitimate by democratic political theory, to take measures which this authority does not justify. These actions would have to be justified on some other ground (e.g. utilitarian), and the claim of their agents to be obeyed would not be that of a legitimate government in the usual (democratic) sense. None the less most citizens might, under the circumstances, have good reason to obey.

There are a number of different justifications for the exercise of coercive authority. In a situation of extreme peril to a group, those in the group who are in a position to avert disaster by exercising a certain kind of control over the others may be justified in using force to do so, and there may be good reason for their commands to be obeyed. But this kind of authority differs both in justification and extent from that which, if democratic political theory is correct, a legitimate democratic government enjoys. What I am suggesting is that if there are situations in which a general suspension of civil liberties is justified – and, I repeat, it is not clear to me that there are such – these situations constitute a shift from one kind of authority to another. The people involved will probably continue to wear the same hats, but this does not mean that they still rule with the same title.

It should not be thought that I am here giving governments licence to kick over the traces of constitutional rule whenever this is required by the "national interest". It would take a situation of near catastrophe to justify a move of the kind I have described, and if governments know what they are doing it would take such a situation to make a move of this sort inviting. For a great deal is given up in such a move, including any notion that the commands of government have a claim to be obeyed which goes beyond the relative advantages of obedience and disobedience.

When the situation is grave and the price of disorder enormous, such utilitarian considerations may give the government's commands very real binding force. But continuing rule on this basis would be acceptable only for a society in permanent crisis or for a group of people who, because they could see each other only as obedient servants or as threatening foes, could not be ruled on any other.

NOTES

1 This task is carried out by Thomas Emerson in *Toward a General Theory of the First Amendment* (New York, 1966). See esp. pp. 60–2.
2 In *Schenck v United States*, 249 US 47 (1919).
3 Kant's notion of autonomy goes beyond the one I employ in that for him there are special requirements regarding the reasons which an autonomous being can act on. (See the second and third sections of *Foundations of the Metaphysics of Morals*.) While his notion of autonomy is stronger than mine, Kant does not draw from it the same limitations on the authority of states (see *Metaphysical Elements of Justice*, sections 46–9).
4 I am not certain whether I am here agreeing or disagreeing with Robert Paul Wolff (*In Defense of Anarchism*, New York, 1970). At any rate I would not call what I am maintaining anarchism. The limitation on state power I have in mind is that described by John Rawls in the closing paragraphs of "The Justification of Civil Disobedience", in *Civil Disobedience: Theory and Practice*, ed. Hugo Bedau (New York, 1969).
5 In *Schenck v United States*.
6 In Ch. II of *On Liberty*.
7 This test is developed as a criterion for justifiable paternalism by Gerald Dworkin in his essay "Paternalism", in *Morality and the Law*, ed. Richard Wasserstrom (Belmont, Calif., 1971).

READING QUESTIONS ON SCANLON

1 Does Scanlon's argument apply to all types of speech that claims to offer reasons?
2 Do all forms of speech purport to offer reasons to be evaluated? Think about pornography and hate speech.

3 Reread Mill's discussion of speech, above. How is Scanlon's view
  related to Mill's?

Mayo Moran
"Talking about Hate Speech: A Rhetorical Analysis of
American and Canadian Approaches to the Regulation
of Hate Speech" (1994)

Moran contrasts the visions of the state which distinguish American and
Canadian jurisprudence on free speech.

THE CONTEXT

As is apparent in American cases, much depends upon the context in
which the court chooses to situate the problem of hate speech. The
Keegstra majority selected a very different context in which to analyze
the problem of hate speech than that chosen in the American cases. It is
telling that Chief Justice Dickson, speaking for the majority, begins his
analysis of the constitutionality of the legislation by focusing on why
the legislature thought regulation of this speech was important. Since
the legislation was developed following the Second World War and the
discovery of the horrors of Nazi Germany, the historical analysis naturally leads into a discussion of discrimination, racial and religious relations, and the violent activities of hate groups, including the Ku Klux
Klan. This in turns leads to a discussion of the harms of hate speech.

Several things are accomplished by situating hate speech in this context. Linking hate speech to a history of genocide and discrimination
makes the speech appear violent and dangerous, rather than innocuous. However, it does more than this. The conflict made visible by
situating hate speech in the context of racial and religious discrimination is not the conflict between the individual and the state, but rather
between private individuals within society. The relevant source of danger is not the coercive state but violent individuals. Describing civil
society in this way also allows for the possibility of casting the state in
the benevolent role of attempting to ensure a society in which the vulnerable as well as the powerful can be free.

CHARACTERS

As with the American cases, the choice of context has an important bearing not merely on how the characters are depicted but even more fundamentally on what characters are depicted. Given the significantly different context chosen by the Canadian majority, it is unsurprising that these characterizations are very different from those found in the American cases.

The most significant and far-reaching difference is the treatment of the state. The American discourse characterizes the state as the ominous police power, acting arbitrarily and clumsily overreaching its constitutional confines. In sharp contrast to this is the Canadian majority's vision of the state. This state appears calm and deliberative rather than unwieldy and threatening. It is conscientiously pursuing public good, not placating narrow factional interests. And far from overreaching its constitutional limits, the state here appears to be acting upon prudent legal considerations.

The majority in *Keegstra* and the other decisions conveys the image of a restrained and prudent state in part by carefully chronicling the legal sources that both inspire and constrain official action. By emphasizing that the Holocaust was the impetus for the legislation, the Court casts the state in the role of protector rather than destroyer of individual freedom. However, the Court does not rely simply on a sympathetic rendering of history to support this characterization of the state. It also finds justifications for state action in what might be termed persuasive legal authority.

The Court finds one such legal source in international law. For example, the Court outlines the development of the internationally based obligation to prohibit the dissemination of hate propaganda. The codification of the obligation to prevent the dissemination of hate propaganda is found in the International Convention on the Elimination of All Forms of Racial Discrimination, International Covenant on Civil and Political Rights, and in documents such as the European Convention for the Protection of Human Rights and Fundamental Freedoms. These documents are used to emphasize that, in legislating against the dissemination of hate propaganda, the Canadian government was not acting rashly or out of narrow self-interest. Rather, it was proceeding on the basis of a broad consensus borne of both historical experience and of the efforts of human rights scholars over the last several decades.

The Court finds another legal argument in support of the regulation of hate speech. In the section 1 inquiry, the Court insists that a particular right or freedom should not be viewed in isolation, but rather should be seen in the context of the broader obligations which the *Charter* as a whole imposes on the state. The Court finds the equality guarantee in section 15 and the obligation to respect and enhance the multicultural heritage of Canada in section 27 particularly relevant to hate speech:

The message of [hate speech] is that members of identifiable groups are not to be given equal standing in society, and are not human beings equally deserving of concern, respect and consideration. The harms caused by this message run directly counter to the values central to a free and democratic society, and in restricting the promotion of hatred Parliament is therefore seeking to bolster the notion of mutual respect necessary in a nation which venerates the equality of all persons.[1]

By emphasizing these legal obligations, the Court advances a justification for official action that goes beyond an empathic response to the plight of the targets. The use of historical and legal precedents does more than draw attention to the moral and other-directed impetus behind the regulation of hate speech. It also makes the crucial point that in regulating hate speech the state is not unconstrained, nor is it acting arbitrarily and merely protecting its own self-interest or playing favorites. Instead, the state is seeking, within the confines of an extensive system of legal obligations, to further public good by securing the most fundamental of constitutional values.

In addition to identifying various legal motivations behind the regulation of hate speech, the Court depicts the state in a positive light in other related ways. The Court broadens the inquiry by focusing on the dialogical situation, thus recasting the question that confronted the legislature. So the issue is not simply the narrow question of how to ensure that the speaker is as free as possible, but rather the broader question of how to ensure that public debate is as free as possible. And of necessity, this broader inquiry must take into consideration the effect of hate speech on the ability of the targets to speak, act, and participate in the world.

This dialogical focus is crucial to the Court's analysis of the extent to which the traditional rationales for protecting freedom of expression justify protecting hate speech. Once the inquiry is broadened to include the target's interests as well as the speaker's, justifying tolerance of hate

speech on traditional freedom of expression rationales becomes problematic.[2] So, for instance, the Court finds that hate speech cannot be
upheld on the self-actualization rationale because its "extreme opposition" to the "process of individual self-development and human flourishing among all members of society" inhibits the targets of the speech
from being self-actualized.[3]

This broader focus also makes the hate speech's effect on the target
relevant to the analysis of the justifiability of regulation. By describing
hate speech from the target's point of view, the Court is able to identify
the distinctive harms that justify the regulation of such speech, even
according to the liberal harm principle. Thus, the Court's language associates the harms of hate speech with the most elemental aspects of
personhood. Hate speech does not simply offend sensibilities, it also
attacks "human dignity" and "an individual's sense of self-worth,"[4]
values which resonate with liberalism's emphasis on human equality
and autonomy. Including the vantage point of the target supports the
harm principle justification in another way, for it undermines the pure
speech argument by illuminating the link between racist speech and
exclusion, racial violence and even genocide.

While the Court does discuss how the liberal harm principle can
justify the regulation of hate speech, the plight of the target is not the
exclusive, or even the primary, focus of the analysis. Rather, the Court
carefully explains that in legislating against hate speech, the legislature
is not merely protecting a private party, no matter how deserving of
protection that person might be. By identifying the link between individual and collective identity, the Court illustrates how protecting particular individuals can also further constitutional interests. The Court
notes that the hate speech attack is not simply an individual affront – it
also undermines social and even constitutional values, such as the "relations between the various cultural and religious groups in Canadian
society."[5] In this way, the Court uncovers how the legislation not only
protects the dignity of individual targets, but also supports vital public
interests.

The Court finds another public interest behind the regulation by describing the regulation itself as a form of "expression" inspired by constitutional ambitions: "[T]he reaction to various types of expression by
a democratic government may be perceived as meaningful expression
on behalf of the vast majority of citizens."[6] Such regulation provides
society with an opportunity to "illustrate" and to publicize "the values
beneficial to a free and democratic society."[7] Similarly, the Court insists

that the regulation encourages "the values central to freedom of expression, while simultaneously demonstrating dislike for the vision forwarded by the hate-mongers."[8] In this way, the Court identifies expressive rights of constitutional dimension on both sides of the hate speech equation.

Throughout this discussion, the Court invokes the image of an even more important public good ensured by the regulation of hate speech. The point of hate speech regulation is not simply to fulfill various legal obligations, nor just to protect the target. Behind these aims the Court discerns and gives voice to a deeper ambition, an ambition that is at the heart of who we are as a community. It is, at bottom, an image of a certain kind of public world, a conception of democracy. This public world is not a rough and tumble place where only the loudest survive. If it is a "marketplace of ideas," it is the regulated marketplace of the late twentieth century, not the Darwinian marketplace of nineteenth-century capitalism.

However, the public world that the Supreme Court of Canada both describes and helps to create seems more aptly described in conversational or deliberative terms. For while the marketplace metaphor imagines ideal (efficient) results emerging from the wholly separate actions of self-interested individuals, the rhetoric of the Canadian Supreme Court rests on a fundamentally different notion. In this more Aristotelian public world it is the "open participation" of all persons in the processes of collective deliberation that forms the heart of the democratic ideal. This can only be achieved, the Court suggests, through observance of the fundamental tenet, the animating idea, of democracy: the notion that "all persons are equally deserving of respect and dignity."[9] Because the regulation of hate speech bolsters these democratic values, the Court is able to identify such regulation with a fundamental public interest – the protection of democracy. Thus, our treatment of the target is the barometer of the strength of our democratic convictions.[10] According to this view, democracy requires more than simply the absence of official obstacles to participation; it must also enshrine the fundamental commitment to equal respect and dignity that is the substantive heart of the democratic ideal.

The sharp contrast between how the Canadian and American states are depicted derives at least in part from the language used to describe the state. For the courts do not merely analyze, but actually recreate, the deliberations of the state. It is not coincidental that American courts convey the state's unwieldy ambitions partly through dramatic and

even feverish rhetoric in which the judges imagine an apparently end-
less array of potentially silenced speakers and threats to democracy.
Part of the sense that the state is dangerous comes precisely from this
anxious language. Conversely, the deliberative and careful terms in
which the *Keegstra* majority recreates legislative motivation and traces
out the sources and justifications for the regulation of hate speech help
to create a very different image of the state. The language is not sensa-
tional or dramatic, but calm and reasoned. It is less overtly metaphori-
cal and less figurative than the language in the American cases. The
state is depicted as careful and responsible, and the measured rhetoric
of the Court subtly reinforces this image.

But for all of this restraint, there is also rhetorical power in the Canadian Supreme Court's discussion of the state. The organic connection
between the government and the people is conveyed partly through
language that emphasizes the unity of the government and the governed. Both the Court's vision and its language refute the notion of a
state-society dichotomy, of an opposition between the people and their
government. Over and over again, the term "community" and references to "collective" values and ambitions are used to describe the
unified collectivity of state and society. Additionally, the language of
shared moral ambition is used to describe the aspirations of the legislation: the purpose of the legislation is to foster "harmonious social relations in a community dedicated to equality and multiculturalism,"[11] our
"aspirations" include "fostering a vibrant democracy where the participation of all individuals is accepted and encouraged,"[12] the ambition of
Parliament is to "bolster the notion of mutual respect necessary in a
nation which venerates the equality of all persons."[13] References to the
fundamental democratic values of equality and human dignity that we
all share also reinforce the sense of a unified and morally engaged
communal life.

The Court's extensive and laudatory discussion of the state stands in
sharp contrast to its characterization of the speaker. The speaker appears as the violent enemy of the target, partly because the Court brings
the target much more into view in discussing the speaker. When the
effect on the target is treated as a structural part of assessing the claim
that the speech deserves protection, the speaker appears less like a free-
thinking zealot and more like a threatening hate-monger. However, the
Court depicts the speaker not only as inflicting injury on the target, but
also as striving to undermine our worthy communal aspirations. Thus,
the language used to describe the proponents of hate speech draws

attention to the impact of their speech both on the targets and on the fundamental values which define our legal and political community.

Unlike the calm and deliberative language used to describe the state, the language used to describe the speaker is strong, negative and extreme. Those who promote hate speech are routinely described as "hate-mongers" who advocate their views with "inordinate vitriol."[14] The whole aim of their speech is to "subvert" and "repudiate" and "undermine" democracy, which they do with "unparalleled vigor."[15] Since their ideas are "anathemic" and "inimical" to our fundamental values, we view them with "severe reprobation."[16] In this way, the Court characterizes the speaker as the enemy of democracy, not its litmus test, a hypocrite using democracy's most cherished ideal of free speech to undermine the freedom and democracy of others.

JUDICIAL VOICE

The judicial voice that dominates the Canadian hate speech cases provides an interesting contrast with the American jurisprudence. The majority in the Canadian hate speech decisions conceives of constitutional adjudication and of the role of judges in a very different way. According to this view, good judging is a matter of defensible value choices, rather than of steering a neutral course among (or perhaps above) particular value choices. And since there is no elevated position above all value choices, the judge cannot avoid making choices. Thus, the Court must come to terms with the value conflict in all of its particularity.[17] Only in this way, the Court insists, can the normative issues inherent in the conflict properly come into view. It is partly this close scrutiny that accounts for the concerned and engaged tone of the Canadian Supreme Court.

Thus, the Canadian cases discuss the speech in great detail, focusing on its specific content. Indeed, the majority's focus on the specific message of hate speech is crucial to its conclusion that such speech is appropriately regulated. By characterizing hate speech as "deeply offensive, hurtful and damaging to target group members, misleading to ... listeners, and antithetical to the furtherance of tolerance and understanding in society," the Court helps to settle the question of the normative value of the speech. Indeed, in the companion case of *Canada (HRC) v Taylor*,[18] Chief Justice Dickson expresses a certain frustration with the dissent's abstract characterization of the speech. After noting that he "cannot ignore the setting" in which freedom of expression is raised, he continues:

It is not enough to simply balance or reconcile those interests promoted by a government objective with abstract panegyrics to the value of open expression. Rather, a contextual approach to s. 1 demands an appreciation of the extent to which a restriction of the activity at issue on the facts of the particular case debilitates or compromises the principles underlying the broad guarantee of freedom of expression.[19]

This careful inquiry into the particulars of the speech at issue is crucial to the Court's resolution of the problem. It also helps to account for the less detached tone of the *Keegstra* majority's legal analysis.

The Court's admission that it too must engage in a process of mediating different values also helps to create a more egalitarian relationship with the reader. Although the Court must try to fairly assess the conflict and understand both perspectives, it does not and indeed cannot view the conflict from a privileged, neutral position above the particular sides in the debate. So, while the American hate speech cases suggest that it is incumbent upon judges to set aside their personal assessments of the speech in favor of a more objective point of view, the rhetoric of the Canadian Supreme Court clearly illustrates that the Court's considered response to the speech is a relevant factor in determining whether the speech should be protected. Since the Court does not claim that it has a privileged perspective from which it can see what hate speech really is (although it does have an institutional tradition of fairness and even-handedness to respect), it must justify its decision on normative grounds. And this justification inevitably implicates the Court's own determinations of value, determinations which must themselves be assessed and either justified or rejected.

The Court strengthens this egalitarian relationship with the reader by exposing her to some of the difficulties inherent in the position it ultimately defends. Throughout the opinion one has a sense of intellectual struggle ... So, in considering the appropriate course of action, the Chief Justice admits that the state "cannot act to hinder or condemn a political view without to some extent harming the openness of Canadian democracy."[20] Similarly, after illustrating that no course of action can completely protect the values underlying freedom of expression, he wonders how to deal with the possibility that his ruling weakens our communal commitment to freedom of expression, albeit in a different way than does the toleration of hate speech.[21] By thus exposing the weaknesses of the position ultimately adopted,[22] the Court encourages the reader to participate in the process of thinking through the best approach to this difficult problem. And the Court refuses to allow easy equivalences to obscure the difficulty of the choices we all, judges and citizens, face:

> While we must guard carefully against judging expression according to its popularity, it is equally destructive of free expression values, as well as the other values which underlie a free and democratic society, to treat all expression as equally crucial [to the values of freedom of expression].[23]

Even the language of the Canadian Supreme Court's hate speech opinions creates the sense that the Court hopes to forge a different relationship with its audience, for the Court chooses language that reaches beyond the legal community to the citizen. These opinions, although dauntingly long, are generally written in language which makes sense to the ordinary person. There is little technical language, and when legal doctrines are discussed, they are discussed in accessible rather than esoteric language. Reading these cases, one feels that the Court was aware that it was crafting an important cultural document, creating our most basic cultural values, even as it expressed them. In its eloquent statements about Canadians' traditional beliefs in equality and tolerance, the Court not only expresses but also encourages us to strengthen those beliefs, to become more fully who we like to think we are.

COMPARATIVE JURISPRUDENCE AND THE PROBLEM OF TRANSLATION

... Naturally, we all speak languages that are largely inherited. Particularly – but by no means solely – in the field of law, the established language is powerful, ordering our existence and our relations with others, but also obscuring certain aspects of our world. Power has a way of concealing point of view and making a particular understanding of reality look simply neutral and true. And the realities our languages obscure remain invisible; the possibility of change, however necessary, seems elusive. But power cannot be exercised responsibly, nor perhaps even impartially, until this is recognized. The American discourse of hate speech that has developed in the past few decades is so powerful, so formulaic, that it indeed becomes difficult to conceive of alternative understandings. Much of it seems to insiders, even critical ones, to be so natural and inevitable as to be unquestionable. For this reason, comparing the American discourse of hate speech with the recent hate speech decisions of the Canadian Supreme Court may be a useful way of revivifying the American hate speech debate and enabling it to move forward.

Part of the potency of encountering another's way of speaking about the world is that it makes apparent the conditions on which our own language operates; it renders visible what our own languages make invisible. Clifford Geertz suggest that to grasp concepts that, for another people are "experience-near" (in the sense that they are so foundational, so un-self-conscious that they do not appear as concepts at all), may enable us to move towards a more nuanced understanding of both ourselves and others. In this comparative activity we may begin to discover not only the value of other languages, but also the strictures of our own. Our own rhetorical choices, which inevitably privilege certain points of view and make others implausible, become matters to be discussed and justified rather than simply assumed. In this process of normative justification, we engage in the ongoing human task of fashioning a language adequate to our changing world.

There is a pragmatic reason why it can be valuable to compare the way different legal systems approach a similar problem. As discussed above, the dominant American discourse on the issue of hate speech makes a persuasive rendering of the alternative perspective within the system all but impossible. For this reason, it can be helpful to those seeking to articulate a subjugated perspective to look to comparative jurisprudence. The decisions of the Canadian Supreme Court provide a useful illustration of how one might go about making a persuasive case for the constitutionality of the regulation of hate speech.

In particular, the Canadian hate speech decisions are helpful because they illustrate the kinds of sources that might be called upon to make a case for the regulation of hate speech. For example, as noted above, the Canadian Supreme Court finds several legal sources, including international human rights instruments and the equality guarantee of the *Charter*, which foster respect for the legislature's decision to prohibit hate speech. On the critical issue of how the facts of a hate speech case are constructed, it may also be helpful that the majority of the Canadian Supreme Court implicitly and explicitly challenges the use of the vagueness and overbreadth arguments to shift the focus from actual litigants to more attractive constitutional stand-ins. The decisions of the Cana-

dian Supreme Court also provide some guidance for how the regulation of hate speech might be understood to further a public interest. The
American approach to hate speech classifies the target's interest in protection as purely private. The predominant technique of critics, which
relies on story-telling and the creation of empathy, implicitly accepts
that classification and hopes to generate enough sympathy to make the
private plight a matter of public concern. But the failure to challenge
the implicit classification of that interest as purely private allows the
official discourse to characterize regulation as illegitimate favoritism
and to ignore the alternative perspectives. In contrast, the Canadian
hate speech cases find that the regulation of hate speech protects not
just the targets, but also important public interests, including equal
participation in public life, democracy and respect for human dignity
and equality. These arguments may further a richer discussion of the
potential public – as opposed to merely private – issues in the regulation of hate speech.

However, comparative jurisprudence offers more than practical benefits. In the context of hate speech, for instance, comparing the Canadian and American approaches can reveal the crucial yet unstated assumptions which underlie each discussion.

Judicial construction of the facts is one of the most decisive elements
of a legal opinion. In a sense, the war over hate speech is largely fought
on the battleground of what will be considered the relevant facts. Paradoxically, justification for any particular construction of the facts is one
of the most neglected issues in both judicial opinions and theoretical
writings. But this poverty of discussion means that the war is largely a
guerilla war – the opinions state only the bare result of any particular
battle. Judges do not tell us why they situate facts in a particular way,
nor why certain facts are relevant but others are not. Yet, comparing the
American and the Canadian descriptions of the very similar facts of a
hate speech case uncovers the vital choices judges nonetheless make in
finding the facts.[24]

Perhaps most importantly, the Canadian and American cases come to
very different conclusions on the crucial determination of how to situate the hate speech problem. While the American courts treat hate speech
as an unproblematic extension of the subversive advocacy cases, the
Canadian Supreme Court instead situates it in the context of racial and
religious discrimination. This demonstrates that although the choice of
context is indeed crucial to the resolution of the issue, hate speech can
plausibly be understood in the context of either subversive advocacy or

of racial discrimination. Comparison of the Canadian and the American discussions also uncovers a whole range of choices about how to characterize hate speech. The American cases characterize the speech in very general terms and dwell very little on its specific content. In contrast, the Canadian cases focus closely on the specific content of the speech. There is an important link between how the speech is described and the resolution of the case. Focusing on its specific content makes hate speech seem like violent harassment, so that protecting it in freedom's name seems dubious. Conversely, describing the speech in general terms as political or even philosophical speech makes any regulation of it appear unjustifiable. But there does not seem to be any objective or neutral way to choose between the various levels of specificity at which speech can be described. Nor can it plausibly be said that general descriptions are more objective, particularly when it is necessary to select among general descriptions like "racial harassment" or "political speech."

Similar choices become apparent when one compares the points of view adopted by the courts. The American hate speech cases talk about the vantage point of the judge as if it were above the messy events of history, where the judge can see what hate speech really is. When one compares this vantage point with the Canadian cases, however, the particularity of this apparently neutral perspective becomes apparent. It is point of view that seems to distinguish the context and the description of the facts adopted by the American courts from those adopted by the Canadian courts. Seeing the problem as one of subversive advocacy and political speech casts the speaker as an idealistic dissident and thus tracks his or her self-understanding. In contrast, describing the issue as racial harassment and focusing on the impact of the hate message on the target implicitly identifies the target's perspective as the normatively relevant point of view. The different treatments of democracy in the Canadian and American cases also privilege different perspectives. If, as the American cases suggest, democracy requires the unfettered airing of all ideas, then the speaker's interest in participation in the "marketplace of ideas" is privileged. In contrast, a view of democracy that protects each member's equality and dignity gives greater priority to the interests of the targets. But in what meaningful sense can one of these perspectives be said to be more neutral than the other?

The way a court describes the facts of a case always has an intimate relationship to the legal conclusion. It is partly by adopting apt descriptions of the facts that courts so often are able to plausibly invoke precedent without any discussion. So, for example, in the American cases on hate speech, the fact that the speech is described as symbolic and political speech involving philosophical ideas helps to determine whether the law of subversive advocacy or the law concerning racial harassment and civil rights will be relevant. If the speaker is described as an idealistic radical, cases about war protesters and civil rights activists naturally seem applicable. In contrast, as the Canadian cases illustrate, if the speech and the speaker are characterized in terms of discrimination and harassment, then it is precisely the precedents on discrimination and human rights that seem applicable.

This comparison also reveals an absence that is at least as relevant as the fact of these choices. Courts make crucial choices in their descriptions of the facts and invocation of precedent, but they do not justify those choices. Instead, they rely on rhetoric that makes their understanding appear natural and even inevitable – rhetoric that obscures the fact of choice and thus avoids responsibility. Comparison illustrates that these questions cannot be adjudicated simply by resort to truth claims. The issue is not whether a particular description or classification is true, but whether it is illuminating. This requires a substantive discussion of the merits of viewing hate speech in one context or another. How does it further understanding, for instance, to treat hate speech as morally and legally equivalent to the speech of idealistic anarchists like Jacob Abrams? There are at least as many discontinuities as continuities in the analogy, so the argument cannot simply be that it is the same. So why exactly do courts think that the continuities are more deserving of judicial attention? There may be good reasons why, but the hate speech cases do not divulge them. And if justification is crucial to judicial decisionmaking, then this cannot be adequate. It is also necessary to justify why any one particular perspective is a better way of viewing the problem than another, or perhaps more optimistically, whether it isn't possible to take multiple perspectives into consideration. Since one body of law cannot simply be assumed to apply, courts must explain what makes one body of law more applicable than another. Such a discussion would most certainly not only enrich decisions but might also inspire more meaningful conversations by enabling the participants to concur on what truly divides them.

Comparing the Canadian and the American discussions of hate speech is also illuminating because the rhetoric provides a window to the deepest commitments of the two discourses. The two sides in the American hate speech debate often fail to engage at all on the deepest issues that divide them. However, uncovering the fundamental assumptions that underlie the official American discourse on hate speech by contrasting that discourse with the Canadian approach may at least make discussion possible. Comparison reveals that the two discourses rest on very different understandings of the nature of the state, the concept of freedom, and even the concept of democracy itself. These understandings are "experience-near" – so fundamental that they are not mentioned, so constitutive of our ways of speaking about and living in the world that they do not seem to be assumptions at all.

The notion of the state is the most fundamental concept underlying the competing discussions of hate speech. While neither the American nor the Canadian cases explicitly discuss their views of the state, these unarticulated views profoundly inform the way the problem of hate speech is discussed. Indeed, the very unselfconsciousness of the concept is testimony to its power. Unifying much of the discussion of hate speech in the American cases is the premise that the state is profoundly dangerous. A belief that no private actor, however threatening, could ever be as dangerous as the state underlies much of both the rhetoric and the results in the American hate speech cases. The very language used to describe the state invokes this image – it is the menacing police power, exercising thought control, playing favorites, and likely to use even the most apparently innocuous regulation for its own selfish purposes. This state is characterized by pluralist politics and dominated by factions. It is this vision of the state, and of official psychology, that underlies the all too prevalent slippery slope argument, for the assumption that the state is a dangerous megalomaniac is what gives force to the concern with the precision and clarity of the legal line. This is also what makes plausible the depiction of the speaker as beleaguered. In a political culture dominated by this conception of the state, the threat one private individual poses to another inevitably appears insignificant. For this reason, courts characterize the state as the dangerous discriminator. In this sense too, the language of "mere offensiveness" and other attempts to minimize the harm of the speech can be seen as an attempt of the part of the judiciary to convince the audience that abuses of private power pale in comparison with abuses of state power. As Justice Scalia's warning against adding the First Amendment to the fire so aptly illustrates, in this discourse the state is a kind of super-individual, like other individuals in its pursuit of its own selfish ambitions, but profoundly more dangerous because of its relative power.

In contrast, the Canadian hate speech cases rest on a much more positive understanding of the state. The descriptions of the state and of official motivation in the Canadian cases convey an image of the orderly and rational pursuit of public interest. According to this view, given constitutional expression in section 1 of the *Charter*, the state is not a super-individual necessarily concerned with selfish motives. Instead, the state can be public-spirited, and, as the Court describes it, the state does indeed seem to be pursuing a conception of the public good. This conception emphasizes both the centrality of equal citizenship as well as the responsibility of the state to ensure that this kind of equality can be realized. It is to make this point that the opinions emphasize the equality-seeking and the freedom-enhancing nature of official action. And it is in part this possibility of benevolent state action that makes the dissent's slippery slope arguments ring hollow. Culturally, even if Canadians do not particularly like the government, we do not tend to see it as dangerous – foolish and bumbling, yes, but rarely dangerous.

This difference in the understanding of the state also has important implications for the concept of freedom at work in the two narratives. If the state is the fundamental threat to freedom, then freedom is secured by restraining the state and giving full play to forces in the private sphere. This classic "negative liberty"[25] view of freedom and of the state forms the conceptual underpinning of the way that hate speech is discussed in the American cases. Its implicit distinction between the freedom of civil society and the coerciveness of public authority makes plausible the notion that the courts are preserving freedom, even as they uphold the rights of groups like the Nazis and the Ku Klux Klan, for what the courts are preserving is a sphere in which individuals may act free of government interference. This view of the freedom of the private sphere is also apparent in the judicial rhetoric that identifies the speaker with the cause of freedom and the state with oppressive constraint. If government intervention is seen as an inevitable threat to liberty, then keeping government out will be seen as freedom. Preserving freedom of speech thus requires the courts to keep the meddlesome and dangerous state at a safe distance from the free interplay of ideas.

Underlying the Canadian discourse is a profoundly different vision of freedom. Indeed, it is perhaps unsurprising given the long tradition of public involvement in medical care, higher education, public broadcasting and many other areas of life, that Canadians generally embrace not only negative but also positive liberty. Since the state is not seen as necessarily threatening, freedom is not automatically equated with the state staying out. This conception of freedom has more in common with the "exercise-concept" of positive liberty, according to which freedom is not merely the absence of external constraint, but is instead the effective exercise of control over one's life.[26] Even the structure of the *Charter* is illustrative of this. If many of the guarantees of the *Charter* protect the classic negative liberties, section 1 gives expression to Canada's belief in positive liberty. This is because section 1 embodies the recognition that the state may well be *acting*, and even limiting, some *Charter* rights and freedoms, in an attempt to secure a more positive form of freedom not sufficiently safeguarded in private ordering. When seen in light of this more positive conception of liberty, section 1's reference to those limits on rights which are justified by a free and democratic society is not incoherent. Instead, it expresses the "uniquely Canadian"[27] vision of a free society – a society in which members have not merely the opportunity to be free, but also the means of exercising that freedom. This accounts for the necessity of looking at the effects of speech and of legislation in order to determine how much effective self-determination people can actually exercise in the private realm, under conditions not only of state intervention, but also of non-intervention. The Canadian Supreme Court does exactly this in the hate speech cases by describing the speaker as destructive of freedom and the regulation as supportive of it.

Perhaps most interesting of the underlying assumptions at work in the two discussions of hate speech is the vision of democracy. In both the American and Canadian cases, identification of the overwhelming public interest is crucial. Interestingly, both approaches accomplish this identification primarily through their notions of democracy. However, the visions of democracy invoked by the two courts are strikingly different.

An important part of the rationale at work in the American cases is the view that if the state is allowed to silence anyone, it will inevitably distort the processes of democracy. This embodies a certain ideal of democracy as a process by which all ideas are presented so that the populace can select among them. Like the market metaphor on which this view is based, democracy itself is a mechanism neutral as among the contending ideas. In this sense, the prevalence of the "marketplace of ideas" metaphor is anything but accidental. According to this Schumpeterean model, democracy consists purely of the unfettered process by which the people choose among contending views: "The main stipulations of this model are, first, that democracy is simply a mechanism for choosing and authorizing governments, not a kind of society nor a set of moral ends; and second, that the mechanism consists of a competition between two or more self-chosen sets of politicians ... [28]

Under this model, the purpose of democracy is not to assess but simply to register preferences, and therefore any restriction of the market options inevitably undermines democracy. Thus, judges indicate that only the protection of hate speech can safeguard democracy, for such protection ensures that the market will proffer the widest possible array of options. This model also underlies the claim that the refusal to regulate hate speech distinguishes the American way of life from totalitarian societies — that is, from societies where the state dictates what options can and cannot enter the democratic marketplace. It is this view of democracy that gives force to the normative identification of anarchists with members of the Klan and Nazis. They are equally legitimate representatives of democracy, for they bring ideas to the marketplace. Indeed, they are even plausibly the litmus test for the extent of a society's commitment to democracy, since they test its devotion to the unfettered airing of ideas and thus to democracy itself. Politics is conceived as a competition among interest groups and whoever wins rules legitimately, for the touchstone of legitimacy is the unfettered process which guarantees the citizens' ability to replace one government with another of their choice.

The Canadian view of democracy sharply contrasts with this vision. The democratic ideal that animates the Canadian hate speech decisions is at its core concerned with the substantive value commitments democracy entails, including most prominently an overriding belief in the dignity and equal worth of each human being. This model of democracy, which has John Stuart Mill and the ethical-liberal democrats of the late nineteenth and early twentieth centuries as it philosophical ancestors, aims toward a society where all people are equally free to realize their capabilities. Therefore, the democratic process must be measured against the substantive commitments to human dignity and equality which infuse the democratic ideal. For example, the Canadian Chief Justice argues that the open participation so crucial to democracy is not simply procedural, but instead relies on the substantive belief that "all persons are equally deserving of respect and dignity." It is this understanding of democracy which enables the Supreme Court of Canada to find that hate speech subverts and repudiates the democratic ideal. This focus on substantive results also underlies the distinction that the Canadian Supreme Court draws between Canada and totalitarian or undemocratic regimes. The Court points out that hate speech aims to undermine not only the democratic process but also the substantive belief in equal humanity and dignity that underlies that ideal, thus suggesting that restricting hate speech supports rather than undermines the democratic ideal.

So, there are very fundamental differences underlying the rhetoric of the American and the Canadian hate speech cases. But this may call into question whether the two discourses are in fact so divergent that the Canadian approach cannot serve as a useful means of revivifying the American debate on hate speech and suggesting some new directions. Are the differences simply too great to make comparison useful?

Canadian legal and political institutions have developed in a political culture that has imbued them with certain ideals well suited to their allotted role. And the same is true of the American institutions. Moreover, the histories of the two countries are very different despite many obvious similarities. In particular, Canada has no true equivalent of the McCarthy-era and the subversive advocacy cases which seem to be the impetus for the judicial concern with the regulation of speech. It may be the case that when it comes to political freedoms, the American state is more dangerous than the Canadian state. There may be other significant differences between the two countries that are important for the issue of hate speech regulation. For instance, it is possible that Canadians are more tolerant of certain kinds of differences. It is noteworthy, for example, that the Canadian political culture is typically described in terms of a cultural mosaic while the American political culture is described as a melting pot. While these characterizations are obviously simplistic, and probably overplay the real differences, it may nonetheless be true that there is in Canada greater tolerance for a wide range of political opinions, as well as for various cultural differences. Thus, promoting tolerance through non-regulation of hate speech may not seem as crucial to Canadians. To the extent that Canadian and American political culture differ on this point, then, the approach of the Canadian hate speech cases may not be persuasive in the American situation.

It is also important to note the very different institutional histories that inform the two judicial approaches. The rhetoric of the Canadian Supreme Court betrays some of the zeal of the newcomer to the exhilarating language which the *Charter* puts at the disposal of the courts. Until 1982, discussions of individual rights by the Canadian judiciary were lodged in the oblique language of federalism and the division of powers. Perhaps for this reason, Canadian courts, and the Supreme Court in particular, have enthusiastically embraced the more appropriate language of the *Charter*. Conversely, it is certainly of some relevance that American judicial history is much more extensive and naturally contains episodes that make contemporary courts aware of the dangers of wholeheartedly embracing an interpretive position that acknowledges that constitutional interpretation ultimately requires judges to make substantive value choices. Though Canadian courts will no doubt at some point have their own equivalent of the *Lochner* era or the subversive advocacy era, they have no such troubling judicial history under the *Charter* at this point, and this is reflected in their understanding of the judicial role.

No doubt these are but a few of the reasons why, even if one were so inclined, it would not be possible to simply transpose the Canadian approach to the regulation of hate speech to the United States. Nonetheless, comparative jurisprudence can be illuminating, perhaps most of all because it makes us aware of the most fundamental commitments we make when we invoke – as we inevitably do – an inherited way of speaking about the world. Ironically, in studying the approach that another country takes to a problem we all face, the most valuable knowledge we gain may be self-knowledge. What always seemed simple and natural becomes, through force of comparison, complex and problematic ...

Certainly we cannot simply import wholesale the approach of one country's jurisprudence into that of our own. Indeed, this would undermine the whole point of trying to shape a language adequate to one's own world. There is, in fact, no easy way around this enduring human struggle. It is no more adequate to simply transpose the approach of another country than it is to hold blindly onto inherited understandings. Like the growth and development of the old city that Wittgenstein described, revivifying our languages proceeds by means more piecemeal, more uncertain. Difficult as it is, even as we work within our own languages, we must struggle against them and question what they enable us to see of our world. In this arduous task, comparative jurisprudence can be useful. It makes visible possibilities obscured by our way of speaking about the world, makes problematic what had always seemed simple, and thus helps us to become aware of the straightjackets of our once liberating ideas. But this rediscovery of complexity and ambiguity is only the beginning. Ultimately we must ask what makes sense now, in *our* time. No matter what the outcome, this is a crucial part of each citizen's moral education.

Comparing the American and Canadian approaches to the regulation of hate speech can therefore be instructive. Uncovering some of the differences also illustrates that the construction of the state, of the private realm, and of democracy are choices about how to understand and speak about the world, not unassailable truths. This process helps to uncover – and thus enables discussion about – the complexities that the reductionist pressures of legal language work to suppress. This comparison may also be helpful in another way. The energetic American debate on freedom of speech is frustrating for several reasons, among them the fact that the contending perspectives do not seem to address each other at all. Examining another way of approaching the problem may help to uncover the invisible assumptions and therefore make it possible to identify some of the fundamental points of contention. In this way, the two sides may, at least, begin to really speak about what divides them. Such a discussion cannot help but enrich the debate, even if the result remains the same.

This process of questioning is also crucial to the democratic ideal, for, as John Dewey said, "democracy begins in conversation." Our constitutional provisions themselves can never be considered completely defined by history, for we are responsible for interpreting that history and its import for our time. Our forbearers inhabited a certain world and fashioned their ideals accordingly. Our world is in some respects the same and in some different. It is our responsibility to reexamine that world and struggle with how we can best live together. And in that process, in reexamining the way we understand and speak about the world, we begin the conversation that begins democracy.

NOTES

1 [1990] 3 SCR 697, 756 (Can.).
2 Lee Bollinger makes a similar point.
3 [1990] 3 SCR at 763.
4 Ibid. at 746.
5 Ibid. at 767.
6 Ibid. at 764–5.
7 *Keegstra*, [1990] 3 SCR at 769.
8 Ibid. at 764.
9 *Keegstra*, [1990] 3 SCR at 764.
10 Interestingly, the Court implies here that part of what makes Canada different from South Africa or Nazi Germany is the fact that the state not only does not itself engage in violent discrimination, but it also does not tolerate others doing so. The distinction that the Canadian Supreme Court implicitly makes between states such as Nazi Germany and Apartheid

South Africa on one hand, and Canada on the other, is that in Canada, individuals should never have to live under the shadow of racial hatred. In contrast, as noted above, several of the American cases suggest that what separates the U.S. from Nazi Germany is the fact that in the U.S. one can say what one thinks, while in Nazi Germany, one could not.

11 *Keegstra*, [1990] 3 SCR at 767.

12 Ibid. at 766.

13 Ibid. at 756.

14 Ibid. at 763.

15 Ibid. at 764–65.

16 Ibid. at 769.

17 So, for example, the Supreme Court has insisted that section 1 requires a contextual approach in order to "[b]ring into sharp relief the aspect of the right or freedom which is truly at stake in the case as well as the relevant aspects of any values in competition with it." *Keegstra*, [1990] 3 SCR at 737 (quoting *Edmonton Journal v Alberta*, [1989] 2 SCR 1326, 1355–56 (Can.)).

18 [1990] 3 SCR 892 (Can.).

19 Ibid. at 922.

20 *Keegstra*, [1990] 3 SCR at 764.

21 Ibid. at 766.

22 This is not to suggest, however, that the judgments are in all respects ideal. They particularly seem to fall short in their treatment of the hate speech proponent. While the Court allows the target a certain kind of personhood not granted in the American case law, it does not seem willing to go the final step and also grant the proponent of hate speech the status of personhood. Instead, he is routinely described as a violent hate-monger. There may be a fair middle ground available between the American approach, which minimizes the harm and venerates open expression, and the Canadian approach, which reduces the speaker to a violent-hate monger. Of course, these speakers may be violent hate-mongers, but they are also individuals even if they are profoundly misguided and dangerous. Watching a film like *Blood in the Face* or the trial of someone like Jim Keegstra should make anyone but the ideologue feel some sense of sorrow for people who are so racked by hatred, and some sense of concern about how we have failed them (for instance, the class dynamics of this kind of racial hatred are often troubling). Thus, I think the Canadian hate speech opinions would be strengthened by recognizing that judgments upholding the regulation of hate speech do inflict a certain amount of real suffering on the proponent of hate speech. Surely we do not have to deny this in order to say that the regulation is nonetheless justified. There is something elitist,

and even authoritarian, about the fact that courts do not seem to trust their audiences to feel some sympathy for the proponents of hate speech, and yet to feel that legislation is justified. This all too common technique of simplifying the moral equation by allowing personhood to only one party does not do us justice. A related difficulty is found in the Canadian Supreme Court's decision to uphold pornography legislation. *R v Butler*, [1992] 1 SCR 452 (Can.). In *Butler*, a unanimous Court simply dismissed far more serious problems of vagueness, and did not even address indications that the legislation had been disproportionately applied to gay bookstores. Since *Butler*, there have been continuing complaints about the unfair enforcement of pornography laws against gay and lesbian bookstores, as well as discontent about the failure to enforce the legislation against "mainstream" pornography. A lesbian bookstore in Vancouver B.C. called "The Little Sister Cooperative" has just commenced litigation in which it alleges that the practices of customs officials in enforcing the pornography provisions discriminate against lesbians. Arguments in the case concluded in the late fall of 1994.

23 *Keegstra*, [1990] 3 SCR at 760.

24 This is not to suggest that this is a conscious choice. Indeed, part of the invisible power of an established language is its ability to make choices not seem like choices, even to those who make them. Further, as noted above, there also seems to be at work a desire to minimize the sense that the decision inflicts harm, and this is achieved partly by creating sympathy for the speaker and avoiding serious discussion of the plight of the target.

25 Sir Isaiah Berlin describes negative liberty in the following terms: "By being free in this sense I mean not being interfered with by others. The wider the area of non-interference the wider my freedom." Isaiah Berlin, Two Concepts of Liberty, in *Four Essays on Liberty* 123 (1979). Berlin notes that since, as Hobbes argued, "Law is always a 'fetter,' even if it protects you from being bound in chains that are heavier than those of law," there must be a frontier "drawn between the area of private life and that of public authority." Otherwise, there will be no personal freedom. Ibid. at 124. Charles Taylor describes – and critically discusses – this "opportunity concept" of negative liberty in What's Wrong with Negative Liberty, in *Philosophy and the Human Sciences: Philosophical Papers* 2, 213 (1985).

26 Taylor, *supra* note 25, at 213.

27 *R v Keegstra*, [1990], 3 SCR 697, 743 (Can.). The Court seems to be referring to the uniqueness of section 1 as compared with the American view of rights and liberty.

28 C.B.MacPherson, *The Life and Times of Liberal Democracy* 78 (1977).

1 Moran suggests that American hate speech jurisprudence views the state with suspicion. To what extent is this an appropriate starting point for a view about regulation?
2 How are the views of democracy which Moran contrasts related to the debates about positive and negative liberty considered above?

R v Keegstra [1990] 3 SCR 697

The Supreme Court of Canada upheld the section of the *Criminal Code* outlawing the incitement of hatred. Writing for the majority, Dickson, CJC argued that the reasons for limiting expression in this case were the same as the reasons for protecting it more generally.

Dickson, CJC: This appeal ... raises a delicate and highly controversial issue as to the constitutional validity of s. 319(2) of the *Criminal Code, RSC*, 1985, c. C-46, a legislative provision which prohibits the wilful promotion of hatred, other than in private conversation, towards any section of the public distinguished by colour, race, religion or ethnic origin. In particular, the court must decide whether this section infringes the guarantee of freedom of expression found in s 2(b) of the *Canadian Charter of Rights and Freedoms* in a manner that cannot be justified under s. 1 of the *Charter*. A secondary issue arises as to whether the presumption of innocence protected in the *Charter's* s. 11(d) is unjustifiably breached by reason of s. 319(3)(a) of the *Code*, which affords a defence of "truth" to the wilful promotion of hatred, but only where the accused proves the truth of the communicated statements on the balance of probabilities.

FACTS

Mr James Keegstra was a high school teacher in Eckville, Alberta, from the early 1970s until his dismissal in 1982. In 1984, Mr Keegstra was charged under s. 319(2) (then 281.2(2)) of the *Criminal Code* with unlawfully promoting hatred against an identifiable group by communicating anti-Semitic statements to his students. He was convicted by a jury in a trial before McKenzie, J of the Alberta Court of Queen's Bench.

Mr Keegstra's teachings attributed various evil qualities to Jews. He thus described Jews to his pupils as "treacherous," "subversive," "sadistic," "money-loving," "power hungry," and "child killers." He taught his classes that Jewish people seek to destroy Christianity and are responsible for depressions, anarchy, chaos, wars, and revolution. According to Mr Keegstra, Jews "created the Holocaust to gain sympathy" and, in contrast to the open and honest Christians, were said to be deceptive, secretive, and inherently evil. Mr Keegstra expected his students to reproduce his teachings in class and on exams. If they failed to do so, their marks suffered.

Prior to his trial, Mr Keegstra applied to the Court of Queen's Bench in Alberta for an order quashing the charge on a number of grounds, the primary one being that s. 319(2) of the *Criminal Code* unjustifiably infringed his freedom of expression as guaranteed by s. 2(b) of the *Charter*. Among the other grounds of appeal was the allegation that the defence of truth found in s. 319(3)(a) of the *Code* violates the *Charter's* presumption of innocence. The application was dismissed by Quigley, J, and Mr Keegstra was thereafter tried and convicted. He then appealed his conviction to the Alberta Court of Appeal, raising the same *Charter* issues. The Court of Appeal unanimously accepted his argument, and it is from this judgment that the Crown appeals.

RELEVANT STATUTORY AND CONSTITUTIONAL PROVISIONS

The relevant legislative and *Charter* provisions are set out below:

Criminal Code
319(2) Every one who, by communicating statements, other than in private conversation, wilfully promotes hatred against any identifiable group is guilty of
(a) an indictable offence and is liable to imprisonment for a term not exceeding two years; or
(b) an offence punishable on summary conviction.

(3) No person shall be convicted of an offence under subsection (2)
(a) if he establishes that the statements communicated were true;
(b) if, in good faith, he expressed or attempted to establish by argument an opinion upon a religious subject;

(c) if the statements were relevant to any subject of public interest, the discussion of which was for the public benefit, and if on reasonable grounds he believed them to be true; or
(d) if, in good faith, he intended to point out, for the purpose of removal, matters producing or tending to produce feelings of hatred towards an identifiable group in Canada.

(6) No proceeding for an offence under subsection (2) shall be instituted without the consent of the Attorney General.

(7) In this section,
"communicating" includes communicating by telephone, broadcasting or other audible or visible means;
"identifiable group" has the same meaning as in section 318;
"public place" includes any place to which the public have access as of right or by invitation, express or implied;
"statements" includes words spoken or written or recorded electronically or electro-magnetically or otherwise, and gestures, signs or other visible representations.

318(4) In this section, "identifiable group" means any section of the public distinguished by colour, race, religion or ethnic origin.

Canadian Bill of Rights, RSC 1985, App. III

1. It is hereby recognized and declared that in Canada there have existed and shall continue to exist without discrimination by reason of race, national origin, colour, religion or sex, the following human rights and fundamental freedoms, namely, ...
(d) freedom of speech;

Canadian Charter of Rights and Freedoms

1. The Canadian *Charter* of Rights and Freedoms guarantees the rights and freedoms set out in it subject only to such reasonable limits prescribed by law as can be demonstrably justified in a free and democratic society.

2. Everyone has the following fundamental freedoms:
(b) freedom of thought, belief, opinion and expression, including freedom of the press and other media of communication;

11. Any person charged with an offence has the right
(d) to be presumed innocent until proven guilty according to law in a fair and public hearing by an independent and impartial tribunal;

15(1) Every individual is equal before and under the law and has the right to the equal protection and equal benefit of the law without discrimination and, in particular, without discrimination based on race, national and ethnic origin, colour, religion, sex, age or mental or physical disability.

27. This *Charter* shall be interpreted in a manner consistent with the preservation and enhancement of the multicultural heritage of Canadians.

THE HISTORY OF HATE PROPAGANDA CRIMES IN CANADA

While the history of attempts to prosecute criminally the libel of groups is lengthy, the *Criminal Code* provisions discussed so far do not focus specifically upon expression propagated with the intent of causing hatred against racial, ethnic, or religious groups. Even before the Second World War, however, fears began to surface concerning the inadequacy of Canadian criminal law in this regard. In the 1930s, for example, Manitoba passed a statute combatting a perceived rise in the dissemination of Nazi propaganda. Following the Second World War and revelation of the Holocaust, in Canada and throughout the world a desire grew to protect human rights, and especially to guard against discrimination. Internationally, this desire led to the landmark *Universal Declaration of Human Rights in 1948*, and, with reference to hate propaganda, was eventually manifested in two international human rights instruments ...

The Special Committee on Hate Propaganda in Canada, usually referred to as the Cohen Committee ...

The tenor of the report is reflected in the opening paragraph of its preface, which reads:

This Report is a study in the power of words to maim, and what it is that a civilized society can do about it. Not every abuse of human communication can or should be controlled by law or custom. But every society from time to time draws lines at the point where the intolerable and the impermissible coincide. In a free society such as our own, where the privilege of speech can induce ideas that may change the very order itself, there is bias weighted heavily in favour of the maximum of rhetoric whatever the cost and consequences. But that bias stops this side of injury to the community itself and to individual members or identifiable groups innocently caught in verbal crossfire that goes beyond legitimate debate.

In keeping with these remarks, the recurrent theme running throughout the report is the need to prevent the dissemination of hate propaganda without unduly infringing the freedom of expression ...

SECTION 2(B) OF THE *CHARTER* − FREEDOM OF EXPRESSION

Obviously, one's conception of the freedom of expression provides a crucial backdrop to any s. 2(b) inquiry; the values promoted by the freedom help not only to define the ambit of s. 2(b), but also come to the forefront when discussing how competing interests might co-exist with the freedom under s. 1 of the *Charter*.

In the recent past, this court has had the opportunity to hear and decide a number of freedom of expression cases ... Together, the judgments in these cases provide guidance as to the values informing the freedom of expression, and additionally indicate the relationship between ss. 2(b) and 1 of the *Charter*.

It was argued before this court that the wilful promotion of hatred is an activity the form and consequences of which are analogous to those associated with violence or threats of violence. This argument contends that Supreme Court of Canada precedent excludes violence and threats of violence from the ambit of s. 2(b), and that the reason for such exclusion must lie in the fact that these forms of expression are inimical to the values supporting freedom of speech. Indeed, in support of this view it was pointed out to us that the court in *Irwin Toy* stated that "freedom of expression ensures that we can convey our thoughts and feelings in non-violent ways without fear of censure" (p. 607). Accordingly, we were urged to find that hate propaganda of the type caught by s. 319(2), insofar as it imperils the ability of target group members themselves to convey thoughts and feelings in non-violent ways without fear of censure, is analogous to violence and threats of violence and hence does not fall within s. 2(b).

Turning specifically to the proposition that hate propaganda should be excluded from the coverage of s. 2(b), I begin by stating that the communications restricted by s. 319(2) cannot be considered as violence, which on a reading of *Irwin Toy* I find to refer to expression communicated directly through physical harm. Nor do I find hate propaganda to be analogous to violence, and through this route exclude it from the protection of the guarantee of freedom of expression. As I have explained, the starting proposition in *Irwin Toy* is that all activities conveying or attempting to convey meaning are considered expression for the purposes of s. 2(b); the content of expression is irrelevant in determining the scope of this *Charter* provision. Stated at its highest, an exception has been suggested where meaning is communicated directly via physical violence, the extreme repugnance of this form to free expression values justifying such an extraordinary step. Section 319(2) of the *Criminal Code* prohibits the communication of meaning that is repugnant, but the repugnance stems from the content of the message as opposed to its form. For this reason, I am of the view that hate propaganda is to be categorized as expression so as to bring it within the coverage of s. 2(b).

As for threats of violence, *Irwin Toy* spoke only of restricting s. 2(b) to certain forms of expression, stating at p. 607 that,

While the guarantee of free expression protects all content of expression, certainly violence as a form of expression receives no such protection. It is not necessary here to delineate precisely when and on what basis a form of expression chosen to convey a meaning falls outside the sphere of the guarantee. But it is clear, for example, that a murderer or rapist cannot invoke the freedom of expression in justification of the form of expression he has chosen.

While the line between form and content is not always easily drawn, in my opinion threats of violence can only be so classified by reference to the content of their meaning. As such, they do not fall within the exception spoken of in *Irwin Toy*, and their suppression must be justified under s. 1. As I do not find threats of violence to be excluded from the definition of expression envisioned by s. 2(b), it is unnecessary to determine whether the threatening aspects of hate propaganda can be seen as threats of violence, or analogous to such threats, so as to deny it protection under s. 2(b).

The second matter which I wish to address before leaving the s. 2(b) inquiry concerns the relevance of other *Charter* provisions and international agreements to which Canada is a party in interpreting the coverage of the freedom of expression guarantee. It has been argued in support of excluding hate propaganda from the coverage of s. 2(b) that the use of ss. 15 and 27 of the *Charter* – dealing respectively with equality and multiculturalism – and Canada's acceptance of international agreements requiring the prohibition of racist statements make s. 319(2) incompatible with even a large and liberal definition of the freedom: The general tenor of this argument is that these interpretive aids inextricably infuse each constitutional guarantee with values supporting equal societal participation and the security and dignity of all persons. Consequently, it is said that s. 2(b) must be curtailed so as not to extend to communications which seriously undermine the equality, security, and dignity of others ...

I thus conclude on the issue of s. 2(b) by finding that s. 319(2) of the *Criminal Code* constitutes an infringement of the *Charter* guarantee of freedom of expression, and turn to examine whether such an infringement is justifiable under s. 1 as a reasonable limit in a free and democratic society.

SECTION 1 ANALYSIS OF SECTION 319(2)

General Approach to Section 1

Though the language of s. 1 appears earlier in these reasons, it is appropriate to repeat its words:

1. The Canadian *Charter* of Rights and Freedoms guarantees the rights and freedoms set out in it subject only to such reasonable limits prescribed by law as can be demonstrably justified in a free and democratic society.

In *R v Oakes* (1986), 24 CCC (3d) 321, this court offered a course of analysis to be employed in determining whether a limit on a right or freedom can be demonstrably justified in a free and democratic society. Under the approach in *Oakes*, it must first be established that impugned state action has an objective of pressing and substantial concern in a free and democratic society. Only such an objective is of sufficient stature to warrant overriding a constitutionally protected right or freedom. The second feature of the *Oakes* test involves assessing the proportionality between the objective and the impugned measure. The inquiry as to proportionality attempts to guide the balancing of individual and group interests protected in s. 1, and in *Oakes* was broken down into the following three segments:

First, the measures adopted must be carefully designed to achieve the objective in question. They must not be arbitrary, unfair or based on irrational considerations. In short, they must be rationally connected to the objective. Secondly, the means, even if rationally connected to the objective in this first sense, should impair "as little as possible" the right or freedom in question ... Thirdly, there must be a proportionality between the effects of the measures which are responsible for limiting the *Charter* right or freedom, and the objective which has been identified as of "sufficient importance."

The analytical framework of *Oakes* has been continually reaffirmed by this court, yet it is dangerously misleading to conceive of s. 1 as a rigid and technical provision, offering nothing more than a last chance for the state to justify incursions into the realm of fundamental rights. From a crudely practical standpoint, *Charter* litigants sometimes may perceive s. 1 in this manner, but in the body of our nation's constitutional law it plays an immeasurably richer role, one of great magnitude and sophistication ... As this court has said before, the premier article of the *Charter* has a dual function, operating both to activate *Charter* rights and freedoms and to permit such reasonable limits as a free and democratic society may have occasion to place upon them (*Oakes*, at pp. 343–4). What seems to me to be of significance in this dual function is the commonality that links the guarantee of rights and freedoms to their limitation. This commonality lies in the phrase "free and democratic society."

Obviously, a practical application of s. 1 requires more than an incantation of the words "free and democratic society." These words require some definition, an elucidation as to the values that they invoke. To a large extent, a free and democratic society embraces the very values and principles which Canadians have sought to protect and further by entrenching specific rights and freedoms in the Constitution, although the balancing exercise in s. 1 is not restricted to values expressly set out in the *Charter*. With this guideline in mind, in *Oakes* I commented upon some of the ideals that inform our understanding of a free and democratic society, saying (at p. 346):

> The court must be guided by the values and principles essential to a free and democratic society which I believe embody, to name but a few, respect for the inherent dignity of the human person, commitment to social justice and equality, accommodation of a wide variety of beliefs, respect for cultural and group identity, and faith in social and political institutions which enhance the participation of individuals and groups in society. The underlying values and principles of a free and democratic society are the genesis of the rights and freedoms guaranteed by the *Charter* and the ultimate standard against which a limit on a right or freedom must be shown, despite its effect, to be reasonable and demonstrably justified.

Undoubtedly these values and principles are numerous, covering the guarantees enumerated in the *Charter* and more. Equally, they may well deserve different emphases, and certainly will assume varying degrees of importance depending upon the circumstances of a particular case.

It is important not to lose sight of factual circumstances in undertaking a s. 1 analysis, for these shape a court's view of both the right or freedom at stake and the limit proposed by the state; neither can be surveyed in the abstract. As Wilson, J said in *Edmonton Journal, supra,* referring to what she termed the "contextual approach" to *Charter* interpretation (at p. 584):

... a particular right or freedom may have a different value depending on the context. It may be, for example, that freedom of expression has greater value in a political context than it does in the context of disclosure of the details of a matrimonial dispute.

Though Wilson, J was speaking with reference to the task of balancing enumerated rights and freedoms, I see no reason why her view should not apply to all values associated with a free and democratic society. Clearly, the proper judicial perspective under s. 1 must be derived from an awareness of the synergetic relation between two elements: the values underlying the *Charter* and the circumstances of the particular case.

The Use of American Constitutional Jurisprudence

Having discussed the unique and unifying role of s. 1, I think it appropriate to address a tangential matter, yet one nonetheless crucial to the disposition of this appeal: the relationship between Canadian and American approaches to the constitutional protection of free expression, most notably in the realm of hate propaganda. Those who attack the constitutionality of s. 319(2) draw heavily on the tenor of First Amendment jurisprudence in weighing the competing freedoms and interests in this appeal, a reliance which is understandable given the prevalent opinion that the criminalization of hate propaganda violates the Bill of Rights ... In response to the emphasis placed upon this jurisprudence, I find it helpful to summarize the American position and to determine the extent to which it should influence the s. 1 analysis in the circumstances of this appeal.

A myriad of sources – both judicial and academic – offer reviews of First Amendment jurisprudence as it pertains to hate propaganda. Central to most discussions is the 1952 case of *Beauharnais v Illinois*, 343 US 250, where the Supreme Court of the United States upheld as constitutional a criminal statute forbidding certain types of group defamation. Though never overruled, *Beauharnais* appears to have been weakened by later pronouncements of the Supreme Court: The trend reflected in many of these pronouncements is to protect offensive, public invective as long as the speaker has not knowingly lied and there exists no clear and present danger of violence or insurrection.

In the wake of subsequent developments in the Supreme Court, on several occasions *Beauharnais* has been distinguished and doubted by lower courts.

The question that concerns us in this appeal is not, of course, what the law is or should be in the United States. But it is important to be explicit as to the reasons why or why not American experience may be useful in the s. 1 analysis of s. 319(2) of the *Criminal Code*. In the United States, a collection of fundamental rights has been constitutionally protected for over 200 years. The resulting practical and theoretical experience is immense, and should not be overlooked by Canadian courts. On the other hand, we must examine American constitutional law with a critical eye, and in this respect La Forest, J has noted:

While it is natural and even desirable for Canadian courts to refer to American constitutional jurisprudence in seeking to elucidate the meaning of *Charter* guarantees that have counterparts in the United States Constitution, they should be wary of drawing too ready a parallel between constitutions born to different countries in different ages and in very different circumstances ...

Having examined the American cases relevant to First Amendment jurisprudence and legislation criminalizing hate propaganda, I would be adverse to following too closely the line of argument that would overrule *Beauharnais* on the ground that incursions placed upon free expression are only justified where there is a clear and present danger of imminent breach of peace. Equally, I am unwilling to embrace various categorizations and guiding rules generated by American law without careful consideration of their appropriateness to Canadian constitutional theory. Though I have found the American experience tremendously helpful in coming to my own conclusions regarding this appeal, and by no means reject the whole of the First Amendment doctrine, in a number of respects I am thus dubious as to the applicability of this doctrine in the context of a challenge to hate propaganda legislation.

... [A]pplying the *Charter* to the legislation challenged in this appeal reveals important differences between Canadian and American constitutional perspectives. I have already discussed in some detail the special role of s. 1 in determining the protective scope of *Charter* rights and freedoms. Section 1 has no equivalent in the United States, a fact previously alluded to by this court in selectively utilizing American constitutional jurisprudence. Of course, American experience should never be rejected simply because the *Charter* contains a balancing provision, for it is well known that American courts have fashioned compromises between conflicting interests despite what appears to be the absolute guarantee of constitutional rights. Where s. 1 operates to accentuate a uniquely Canadian vision of a free and democratic society, however, we must not hesitate to depart from the path taken in the United States. Far from requiring a less solicitous protection of *Charter* rights and freedoms, such independence of vision protects these rights and freedoms in a different way. As will be seen below, in my view the international commitment to eradicate hate propaganda and, most importantly, the special role given equality and multiculturalism in the Canadian Constitution necessitate a departure from the view, reasonably prevalent in America at present, that the suppression of hate propaganda is incompatible with the guarantee of free expression.

Most importantly, the nature of the s. 1 test as applied in the context of a challenge to s. 319(2) may well demand a perspective particular to Canadian constitutional jurisprudence when weighing competing interests. If values fundamental to the Canadian conception of a free and democratic society suggest an approach that denies hate propaganda the highest degree of constitutional protection, it is this approach which must be employed.

Objective of Section 319(2)

I now turn to the specific requirements of the *Oakes* approach in deciding whether the infringement of s. 2(b) occasioned by s. 319(2) is justifiable in a free and democratic society. According to *Oakes*, the first aspect of the s. 1 analysis is to examine the objective of the impugned legislation. Only if the objective relates to concerns which are pressing and substantial in a free and democratic society can the legislative limit on a right or freedom hope to be permissible under the *Charter*. In examining the objective of s. 319(2), I will begin by discussing the harm caused by hate propaganda as identified by the Cohen Committee and subsequent study groups, and then review in turn the impact upon this objective of international human rights instruments and ss. 15 and 27 of the *Charter*.

What about radical politicians?

Harm Caused by Expression Promoting the Hatred of Identifiable Groups

Looking to the legislation challenged in this appeal, one must ask whether the amount of hate propaganda in Canada causes sufficient harm to justify legislative intervention of some type. The Cohen Committee, speaking in 1965, found that the incidence of hate propaganda in Canada was not insignificant (at p. 24):

... there exists in Canada a small number of persons and a somewhat larger number of organizations, extremist in outlook and dedicated to the preaching and spreading of hatred and contempt against certain identifiable minority groups in Canada. It is easy to conclude that because the number of persons and organizations is not very large, they should not be taken too seriously. The Committee is of the opinion that this line of analysis is no longer tenable after what is known to have been the result of hate propaganda in other countries, particularly in the 1930s when such material and ideas played a significant role in the creation of a climate of malice, destructive to the central values of Judaic-Christian society, the values of our civilization. The Committee believes, therefore, that the actual and potential danger caused by present hate activities in Canada cannot be measured by statistics alone.

Even the statistics, however, are not unimpressive, because while activities have centered heavily in Ontario, they nevertheless have extended from Nova Scotia to British Columbia and minority groups in at least eight Provinces have been subjected to these vicious attacks.

In 1984, the House of Commons Special Committee on Participation of Visible Minorities in Canadian Society in its report, entitled *Equality Now!*, observed that increased immigration and periods of economic difficulty "have produced an atmosphere that may be ripe for racially motivated incidents" (p. 69). With regard to the dissemination of hate propaganda, the Special Committee found that the prevalence and scope of such material had risen since the Cohen Committee made its report, stating (at p. 69):

There has been a recent upsurge in hate propaganda. It has been found in virtually every part of Canada. Not only is it anti-semitic and anti-black, as in the 1960s, but it is also now anti-Roman Catholic, anti-East Indian, anti-aboriginal people and anti-French. Some of this material is imported from the

United States but much of it is produced in Canada. Most worrisome of all is that in recent years Canada has become a major source of supply of hate propaganda that finds its way to Europe, and especially to West Germany.

As the quotations above indicate, the presence of hate propaganda in Canada is sufficiently substantial to warrant concern. Disquiet caused by the existence of such material is not simply the product of its offensiveness, however, but stems from the very real harm which it causes. Essentially, there are two sorts of injury caused by hate propaganda. First, there is harm done to members of the target group. It is indisputable that the emotional damage caused by words may be of grave psychological and social consequence. In the context of sexual harassment, for example, this court has found that words can in themselves constitute harassment: *Janzen v Platy Enterprises Ltd* (1989), 59 DLR (4th) 352. In a similar manner, words and writings that wilfully promote hatred can constitute a serious attack on persons belonging to a racial or religious group, and in this regard the Cohen Committee noted that these persons are humiliated and degraded (p. 214).

In my opinion, a response of humiliation and degradation from an individual targeted by hate propaganda is to be expected. A person's sense of human dignity and belonging to the community at large is closely linked to the concern and respect accorded the groups to which he or she belongs. The derision, hostility and abuse encouraged by hate propaganda therefore have a severely negative impact on the individual's sense of self-worth and acceptance. This impact may cause target group members to take drastic measures in reaction, perhaps avoiding activities which bring them into contact with non-group members or adopting attitudes and postures directed towards blending in with the majority. Such consequences bear heavily in a nation that prides itself on tolerance and the fostering of human dignity through, among other things, respect for the many racial, religious, and cultural groups in our society.

A second harmful effect of hate propaganda which is of pressing and substantial concern is its influence upon society at large. The Cohen Committee noted that individuals can be persuaded to believe "almost anything" (p. 30) if information or ideas are communicated using the right technique and in the proper circumstances (at p. 8):

... we are less confident in the 20th century that the critical faculties of individuals will be brought to bear on the speech and writing which is directed at them. In the 18th and 19th centuries, there was a widespread belief that man was a rational creature, and that if his mind was trained and liberated from superstition by education, he would always distinguish truth from falsehood, good from evil. So Milton, who said "let truth and falsehood grapple: who ever knew truth put to the worse in a free and open encounter."

We cannot share this faith today in such a simple form. While holding that over the long run, the human mind is repelled by blatant falsehood and seeks the good, it is too often true, in the short run, that emotion displaces reason and individuals perversely reject the demonstrations of truth put before them and forsake the good they know. The successes of modern advertising, the triumphs of impudent propaganda such as Hitler's, have qualified sharply our belief in the rationality of man. We know that under the strain and pressure in times of irritation and frustration, the individual is swayed and even swept away by hysterical, emotional appeals. We act irresponsibly if we ignore the way in which emotion can drive reason from the field.

It is thus not inconceivable that the active dissemination of hate propaganda can attract individuals to its cause, and in the process create serious discord between various cultural groups in society. Moreover, the alteration of views held by the recipients of hate propaganda may occur subtly, and is not always attendant upon conscious acceptance of the communicated ideas. Even if the message of hate propaganda is outwardly rejected, there is evidence that its premise of racial or religious inferiority may persist in a recipient's mind as an idea that holds some truth, an incipient effect not to be entirely discounted.

The threat to the self-dignity of target group members is thus matched by the possibility that prejudiced messages will gain some credence, with the attendant result of discrimination, and perhaps even violence, against minority groups in Canadian society. With these dangers in mind, the Cohen Committee made clear in its conclusions that the presence of hate propaganda existed as a baleful and pernicious element, and hence a serious problem, in Canada (at p. 59):

We believe that, given a certain set of socio-economic circumstances, such as a deepening of the emotional tensions or the setting in of a severe business recession, public susceptibility might well increase significantly. Moreover, the potential psychological and social damage of hate propaganda, both to a desensitized majority and to sensitive minority target groups, is incalculable.

As noted previously, in articulating concern about hate propaganda and its contribution to racial and religious tension in Canada, the Cohen

Committee recommended that Parliament use the *Criminal Code* in order to prohibit wilful, hate-promoting expression and underline Canada's commitment to end prejudice and intolerance ...

International Human Rights Instruments

There is a great deal of support, both in the submissions made by those seeking to uphold s. 319(2) in this appeal and in the numerous studies of racial and religious hatred in Canada, for the conclusion that the harm caused by hate propaganda represents a pressing and substantial concern in a free and democratic society. I would also refer to international human rights principles, however, for guidance with respect to assessing the legislative objective.

Generally speaking, the international human rights obligations taken on by Canada reflect the values and principles of a free and democratic society, and thus those values and principles that underlie the *Charter* itself ...:

No aspect of international human rights has been given attention greater than that focused upon discrimination ... In 1966, the United Nations adopted the international *Convention on the Elimination of All Forms of Racial Discrimination*, 1970, Can. TS, No. 28 (hereinafter *CERD*). The convention, in force since 1969 and including Canada among its signatory members, contains a resolution that states parties agree to:

... adopt all necessary measures for speedily eliminating racial discrimination in all its forms and manifestations, and to prevent and combat racist doctrines and practices in order to promote understanding between races and to build an international community free from all forms of racial segregation and racial discrimination...

Article 4 of the *CERD* is of special interest, providing that:

States Parties condemn all propaganda and all organizations which are based on ideas or theories of superiority of one race or group of persons of one colour or ethnic origin, or which attempt to justify or promote racial hatred and discrimination in any form, and undertake to adopt immediate and positive measures designed to eradicate all incitement to, or acts of, such discrimination and, to this end, with due regard to the principles embodied in the *Universal Declaration of Human Rights* and the rights expressly set forth in article 5 of this *Convention*, inter alia:

> (a) Shall declare an offence punishable by law all dissemination of ideas based on racial superiority or hatred, incitement to racial discrimination, as well as all acts of violence or incitement to such acts against any race or group of persons of another colour or ethnic origin, and also the provision of any assistance to racist activities, including the financing thereof;

Further, the *International Covenant on Civil and Political Rights*, 1966, 999 UNTS 171 (hereinafter ICCPR), adopted by the United Nations in 1966 and in force in Canada since 1976, in the following two articles guarantees the freedom of expression while simultaneously prohibiting the advocacy of hatred.

It appears that the protection provided freedom of expression by *CERD* and *ICCPR* does not extend to cover communications advocating racial or religious hatred ...

Other Provisions of the *Charter*

Significant indicia of the strength of the objective behind s. 319(2) are gleaned not only from the international arena, but are also expressly evident in various provisions of the *Charter* itself. As Wilson, J noted in *Singh v Canada (Minister of Employment and Immigration)* (1985), 17 DLR (4th) 422 at p. 468, [1985] 1 SCR 177, 14 CRR 13:

> ... it is important to bear in mind that the rights and freedoms set out in the *Charter* are fundamental to the political structure of Canada and are guaranteed by the *Charter* as part of the supreme law of our nation. I think that in determining whether a particular limitation is a reasonable limit prescribed by law which can be "demonstrably justified in a free and democratic society" it is important to remember that the courts are conducting this inquiry in light of a commitment to uphold the rights and freedoms set out in other sections of the *Charter*.

Most importantly for the purposes of this appeal, ss. 15 and 27 represent a strong commitment to the values of equality and multiculturalism, and hence underline the great importance of Parliament's objective in prohibiting hate propaganda.

[T]he effects of entrenching a guarantee of equality in the *Charter* are not confined to those instances where it can be invoked by an individual against the state. Insofar as it indicates our society's dedication to promoting equality, s. 15 is also relevant in assessing the aims of s. 319(2) of the *Criminal Code* under s. 1. In *Andrews v Law Society of British Columbia* (1989), 56 DLR (4th) 1 at p. 15, this court examined the equality guarantee of s. 15, McIntyre, J noting:

It is clear that the purpose of s. 15 is to ensure equality in the formulation and application of the law. The promotion of equality entails the promotion of a society in which all are secure in the knowledge that they are recognized at law as human beings equally deserving of concern, respect and consideration. It has a large remedial component.

... The principles underlying s. 15 of the *Charter* are thus integral to the s. 1 analysis.

In its written submission to the court, the intervenor LEAF [Women's Legal Education and Action Fund *(eds.)*] made the following comment in support of the view that the public and wilful promotion of group hatred is properly understood as a practice of inequality:

Government sponsored hatred on group grounds would violate section 15 of the *Charter*. Parliament promotes equality and moves against inequality when it prohibits the wilful public promotion of group hatred on these grounds. It follows that government action against group hate, because it promotes social equality as guaranteed by the *Charter*, deserves special constitutional consideration under section 15.

I agree with this statement. In light of the *Charter* commitment to equality, and the reflection of this commitment in the framework of s. 1, the objective of the impugned legislation is enhanced insofar as it seeks to ensure the equality of all individuals in Canadian society. The message of the expressive activity covered by s. 319(2) is that members of identifiable groups are not to be given equal standing in society, and are not human beings equally deserving of concern, respect, and consideration. The harms caused by this message run directly counter to the values central to a free and democratic society, and in restricting the promotion of hatred Parliament is therefore seeking to bolster the notion of mutual respect necessary in a nation which venerates the equality of all persons.

Section 15 is not the only *Charter* provision which emphasizes values both important to a free and democratic society and pertinent to the disposition of this appeal under s. 1. Section 27 states that:

27. This *Charter* shall be interpreted in a manner consistent with the preservation and enhancement of the multicultural heritage of Canadians.

This court has where possible taken account of s. 27 and its recognition that Canada possesses a multicultural society in which the diversity and richness of various cultural groups is a value to be protected and enhanced ... The value expressed in s. 27 cannot be casually dismissed in assessing the validity of s. 319(2) under s. 1, and I am of the belief that s. 27 and the commitment to a multicultural vision of our nation bears notice in emphasizing the acute importance of the objective of eradicating hate propaganda from society.

Hate propaganda seriously threatens both the enthusiasm with which the value of equality is accepted and acted upon by society and the connection of target group members to their community. I thus agree with the sentiments of Cory, JA who, in writing to uphold s. 319(2) in *R v Andrews* (1988), 43 CCC (3d) 193 at p. 213, said: "Multiculturalism cannot be preserved let alone enhanced if free rein is given to the promotion of hatred against identifiable cultural groups." When the prohibition of expressive activity that promotes hatred of groups identifiable on the basis of colour, race, religion, or ethnic origin is considered in light of s. 27, the legitimacy and substantial nature of the government objective is therefore considerably strengthened.

Conclusion Respecting Objective of Section 319(2)

In my opinion, it would be impossible to deny that Parliament's objective in enacting s. 319(2) is of the utmost importance ...

Proportionality

The second branch of the *Oakes* test – proportionality – poses the most challenging questions with respect to the validity of s. 319(2) as a reasonable limit on freedom of expression in a free and democratic society. It is therefore not surprising to find most commentators, as well as the litigants in the case at bar, agreeing that the objective of the provision is of great importance, but to observe considerable disagreement when it comes to deciding whether the means chosen to further the objective are proportional to the ends.

Relation of the Expression at Stake to Free Expression Values

In discussing the nature of the government objective, I have commented at length upon the way in which the suppression of hate propaganda furthers values basic to a free and democratic society. I have said little, however, regarding the extent to which these same values, including the freedom of expression, are furthered by permitting the exposition of such expressive activity. This lacuna is explicable when one realizes that the interpretation of s. 2(b) under *Irwin Toy*, *supra*, gives protection to a very wide range of expression. Content is irrelevant to this interpretation, the result of a high value being placed upon freedom of expression in the abstract. This approach to s. 2(b) often operates to leave unexamined the extent to which the expression at stake in a particular case promotes freedom of expression principles. In my opinion, however, the s. 1 analysis of a limit upon s. 2(b) cannot ignore the nature of the expressive activity which the state seeks to restrict. While we must guard carefully against judging expression according to its popularity, it is equally destructive of free expression values, as well as the other values which underlie a free and democratic society, to treat all expression as equally crucial to those principles at the core of s. 2(b).

In *Rocket v Royal College of Dental Surgeons of Ontario*, *supra*, McLachlin, J recognized the importance of context in evaluating expressive activity under s. 1, stating with regard to commercial speech (at p. 78):

While the Canadian approach does not apply special tests to restrictions on commercial expression, our method of analysis does permit a sensitive, case-oriented approach to the determination of their constitutionality. Placing the conflicting values in their factual and social context when performing the s. 1 analysis permits the courts to have regard to special features of the expression in question.

Royal College dealt with provincial limitations upon the freedom of dentists to impart information to patients and potential patients via advertisements. In these circumstances, the court found that the expression regulated was of a nature that made its curtailment something less than a most serious infringement of the freedom of expression, the limitation affecting neither participation in the political process nor the ability of the individual to achieve spiritual or artistic self-fulfilment.

Applying the *Royal College* approach to the context of this appeal is a key aspect of the s. 1 analysis. One must ask whether the expression prohibited by s. 319(2) is tenuously connected to the values underlying s. 2(b) so as to make the restriction "easier to justify than other infringements." In this regard, let me begin by saying that, in my opinion, there can be no real disagreement about the subject-matter of the messages and teachings communicated by the respondent, Mr Keegstra: it is deeply offensive, hurtful and damaging to target group members, misleading to his listeners, and antithetical to the furtherance of tolerance and understanding in society. Furthermore, as will be clear when I come to discuss in detail the interpretation of s. 319(2), there is no doubt that all expression fitting within the terms of the offence can be similarly described. To say merely that expression is offensive and disturbing, however, fails to address satisfactorily the question of whether, and to what extent, the expressive activity prohibited by s. 319(2) promotes the values underlying the freedom of expression. It is to this difficult and complex question that I now turn.

From the outset, I wish to make clear that in my opinion the expression prohibited by s. 319(2) is not closely linked to the rationale underlying s. 2(b). Examining the values identified in *Ford* and *Irwin Toy* as fundamental to the protection of free expression, arguments can be made for the proposition that each of these values is diminished by the suppression of hate propaganda. While none of these arguments is spurious, I am of the opinion that expression intended to promote the hatred of identifiable groups is of limited importance when measured against free expression values.

At the core of freedom of expression lies the need to ensure that truth and the common good are attained, whether in scientific and artistic endeavors or in the process of determining the best course to take in our political affairs. Since truth and the ideal form of political and social organization can rarely, if at all, be identified with absolute certainty, it is difficult to prohibit expression without impeding the free exchange of potentially valuable information. Nevertheless, the argument from truth does not provide convincing support for the protection of hate propaganda. Taken to its extreme, this argument would require us to permit the communication of all expression, it being impossible to know with absolute certainty which factual statements are true, or which ideas obtain the greatest good. The problem with this extreme position, however, is that the greater the degree of certainty that a statement is erroneous or mendacious, the less its value in the quest for truth. Indeed, expression can be used to the detriment of our search for truth; the state should not be the sole arbiter of truth, but neither should we overplay the view that rationality will overcome all falsehoods in the unregulated market-place of ideas. There is very little chance that statements intended to promote hatred against an identifiable group are true, or that their vision of society will lead to a better world. To portray such statements as crucial to truth and the betterment of the political and social milieu is therefore misguided.

Another component central to the rationale underlying s. 2(b) concerns the vital role of free expression as a means of ensuring individuals the ability to gain self-fulfilment by developing and articulating thoughts and ideas as they see fit. It is true that s. 319(2) inhibits this process among those individuals whose expression it limits, and hence arguably works against freedom of expression values. On the other hand, such self-autonomy stems in large part from one's ability to articulate and nurture an identity derived from membership in a cultural or religious group. The message put forth by individuals who fall within the ambit of s. 319(2) represents a most extreme opposition to the idea that members of identifiable groups should enjoy this aspect of the s. 2(b) benefit. The extent to which the unhindered promotion of this message furthers free expression values must therefore be tempered insofar as it advocates with inordinate vitriol an intolerance and prejudice which views as execrable the process of individual self-development and human flourishing among all members of society.

Moving on to a third strain of thought said to justify the protection of free expression, one's attention is brought specifically to the political realm. The connection between freedom of expression and the political process is perhaps the linchpin of the s. 2(b) guarantee, and the nature of this connection is largely derived from the Canadian commitment to democracy. Freedom of expression is a crucial aspect of the democratic commitment, not merely because it permits the best policies to be chosen from among a wide array of proffered options, but additionally because it helps to ensure that participation in the political process is open to all persons. Such open participation must involve to a substantial degree the notion that all persons are equally deserving of respect and dignity. The state therefore cannot act to hinder or condemn a political view without to some extent harming the openness of Canadian democracy and its associated tenet of equality for all.

The suppression of hate propaganda undeniably muzzles the participation of a few individuals in the democratic process, and hence detracts somewhat from free expression values, but the degree of this limitation is not substantial. I am aware that the use of strong language in political and social debate – indeed, perhaps even language intended to promote hatred – is an unavoidable part of the democratic process. Moreover, I recognize that hate propaganda is expression of a type which would generally be categorized as "political," thus putatively placing it at the very heart of the principle extolling freedom of expression as vital to the democratic process. Nonetheless, expression can work to undermine our commitment to democracy where employed to propagate ideas anathemic to democratic values. Hate propaganda works in just such a way, arguing as it does for a society in which the democratic process is subverted and individuals are denied respect and dignity simply because of racial or religious characteristics. This brand of expressive activity is thus wholly inimical to the democratic aspirations of the free expression guarantee.

Indeed, one may quite plausibly contend that it is through rejecting hate propaganda that the state can best encourage the protection of values central to freedom of expression, while simultaneously demonstrating dislike for the vision forwarded by hate-mongers. In this regard, the reaction to various types of expression by a democratic government may be perceived as meaningful expression on behalf of the vast majority of citizens. I do not wish to be construed as saying that an infringement of s. 2(b) can be justified under s. 1 merely because it is the product of a democratic process; the *Charter* will not permit even the democratically elected legislature to restrict the rights and freedoms crucial to a free and democratic society. What I do wish to emphasize, however, is that one must be careful not to accept blindly that the suppression of expression must always and unremittingly detract from values central to freedom of expression.

I am very reluctant to attach anything but the highest importance to expression relevant to political matters. But given the unparalleled vigour with which hate propaganda repudiates and undermines democratic values, and in particular its condemnation of the view that all citizens need be treated with equal respect and dignity so as to make participation in the political process meaningful, I am unable to see the protection of such expression as integral to the democratic ideal so central to the s. 2(b) rationale ... In my view, hate propaganda should not be accorded the greatest of weight in the s. 1 analysis.

As a caveat, it must be emphasized that the protection of extreme statements, even where they attack those principles underlying the freedom of expression, is not completely divorced from the aims of s. 2(b) of the *Charter*. As noted already, suppressing the expression covered by s. 319(2) does to some extent weaken these principles. It can also be argued that it is partly through a clash with extreme and erroneous views that truth and the democratic vision remain vigorous and alive. In this regard, judicial pronouncements strongly advocating the importance of free expression values might be seen as helping to expose prejudiced statements as valueless even while striking down legislative restrictions that proscribe such expression. Additionally, condoning a democracy's collective decision to protect itself from certain types of expression may lead to a slippery slope on which encroachments on expression central to s. 2(b) values are permitted. To guard against such a result, the protection of communications virulently unsupportive of free expression values may be necessary in order to ensure that expression more compatible with these values is never unjustifiably limited.

None of these arguments is devoid of merit, and each must be taken into account in determining whether an infringement of s. 2(b) can be justified under s. 1. It need not be, however, that they apply equally or with the greatest of strength in every instance ... While I cannot conclude that hate propaganda deserves only marginal protection under the s. 1 analysis, I can take cognizance of the fact that limitations upon hate propaganda are directed at a special category of expression which strays some distance from the spirit of s. 2(b), and hence conclude that "restrictions on expression of this kind might be easier to justify than other infringements of s. 2(b)": *Royal College, supra*, at p. 79.

As a final point, it should be stressed that in discussing the relationship between hate propaganda and freedom of expression values I do not wish to be taken as advocating an inflexible "levels of scrutiny" categorization of expressive activity. The contextual approach necessitates an open discussion of the manner in which s. 2(b) values are engaged in the circumstances of an appeal. To become transfixed with categorization schemes risks losing the advantage associated with this sensitive examination of free expression principles, and I would be loath to sanction such a result.

Having made some preliminary comments as to the nature of the expression at stake in this appeal, it is now possible to ask whether s.

319(2) is an acceptably proportional response to Parliament's valid objective. As stated above, the proportionality aspect of the *Oakes* test requires the court to decide whether the impugned state action: (i) is rationally connected to the objective; (ii) minimally impairs the *Charter* right or freedom at issue, and (iii) does not produce effects of such severity so as to make the impairment unjustifiable.

Rational Connection

... Doubts have been raised, however, as to whether the actual effect of s. 319(2) is to undermine any rational connection between it and Parliament's objective. As stated in the reasons of McLachlin, J, there are three primary ways in which the effect of the impugned legislation might be seen as an irrational means of carrying out the Parliamentary purpose. First, it is argued that the provision may actually promote the cause of hate-mongers by earning them extensive media attention. In this vein, it is also suggested that persons accused of intentionally promoting hatred often see themselves as martyrs, and may actually generate sympathy from the community in the role of underdogs engaged in battle against the immense powers of the state. Secondly, the public may view the suppression of expression by the government with suspicion, making it possible that such expression – even if it be hate propaganda – is perceived as containing an element of truth. Finally, it is often noted that Germany of the 1920s and 1930s possessed and used hate propaganda laws similar to those existing in Canada, and yet these laws did nothing to stop the triumph of a racist philosophy under the Nazis.

If s. 319(2) can be said to have no impact in the quest to achieve Parliament's admirable objectives, or in fact works in opposition to these objectives, then I agree that the provision could be described as "arbitrary, unfair or based on irrational considerations": (*Oakes, supra,* at p. 348). I recognize that the effect of s. 319(2) is impossible to define with exact precision – the same can be said for many laws, criminal or otherwise. In my view, however, the position that there is no strong and evident connection between the criminalization of hate propaganda and its suppression is unconvincing. I come to this conclusion for a number of reasons, and will elucidate these by answering in turn the three arguments just mentioned ...

It is undeniable that media attention has been extensive on those occasions when s. 319(2) has been used. Yet from my perspective, s. 319(2) serves to illustrate to the public the severe reprobation with which society holds messages of hate directed towards racial and religious groups. The existence of a particular criminal law, and the process of holding a trial when that law is used, is thus itself a form of expression, and the message sent out is that hate propaganda is harmful to target group members and threatening to a harmonious society: The many, many Canadians who belong to identifiable groups surely gain a great deal of comfort from the knowledge that the hate-monger is criminally prosecuted and his or her ideas rejected. Equally, the community as a whole is reminded of the importance of diversity and multiculturalism in Canada, the value of equality and the worth and dignity of each human person being particularly emphasized.

In this context, it can also be said that government suppression of hate propaganda will not make the expression attractive and hence increase acceptance of its content. Similarly, it is very doubtful that Canadians will have sympathy for either propagators of hatred or their ideas. Governmental disapproval of hate propaganda does not invariably result in dignifying the suppressed ideology. Pornography is not dignified by its suppression, nor are defamatory statements against individuals seen as meritorious because the common law lends its support to their prohibition. Again, I stress my belief that hate propaganda legislation and trials are a means by which the values beneficial to a free and democratic society can be publicized. In this context, no dignity will be unwittingly foisted upon the convicted hate-monger or his or her philosophy, and that a hate-monger might see him or herself as a martyr is of no matter to the content of the state's message.

As for the use of hate propaganda laws in pre-World War Two Germany, I am skeptical as to the relevance of the observation that legislation similar to s. 319(2) proved ineffective in curbing the racism of the Nazis. No one is contending that hate propaganda laws can in themselves prevent the tragedy of a Holocaust; conditions particular to Germany made the rise of Nazi ideology possible despite the existence and use of these laws. Rather, hate propaganda laws are one part of a free and democratic society's bid to prevent the spread of racism, and their rational connection to this objective must be seen in such a context. Certainly West Germany has not reacted to the failure of pre-war laws by seeking their removal, a new set of criminal offences having been implemented as recently as 1985: In sum, having found that the purpose of the challenged legislation is valid, I also find that the means chosen to further this purpose are rational in both theory and operation, and therefore conclude that the first branch of the proportionality test has been met.

Minimal Impairment of the Section 2(b) Freedom

The criminal nature of the impugned provision, involving the associated risks of prejudice through prosecution, conviction, and the imposition of up to two years' imprisonment, indicates that the means embodied in hate propaganda legislation should be carefully tailored so as to minimize impairment of the freedom of expression. It therefore must be shown that s. 319(2) is a measured and appropriate response to the phenomenon of hate propaganda, and that it does not overly circumscribe the s. 2(b) guarantee.

The main argument of those who would strike down s. 319(2) is that it creates a real possibility of punishing expression that is not hate propaganda. It is thus submitted that the legislation is overbroad, its terms so wide as to include expression which does not relate to Parliament's objective, and also unduly vague, in that a lack of clarity and precision in its words prevents individuals from discerning its meaning with any accuracy. In either instance, it is said that the effect of s. 319(2) is to limit the expression of merely unpopular or unconventional communications. Such communications may present no risk of causing the harm which Parliament seeks to prevent, and will perhaps be closely associated with the core values of s. 2(b). This overbreadth and vagueness could consequently allow the state to employ s. 319(2) to infringe excessively the freedom of expression or, what is more likely, could have a chilling effect whereby persons potentially within s. 319(2) would exercise self-censorship. Accordingly, those attacking the validity of s. 319(2) contend that vigorous debate on important political and social issues, so highly valued in a society that prizes a diversity of ideas, is unacceptably suppressed by the provision.

The question to be answered, then, is whether s. 319(2) indeed fails to distinguish between low value expression that is squarely within the focus of Parliament's valid objective and that which does not invoke the need for the severe response of criminal sanction.

Terms of Section 319(2)

In assessing the constitutionality of s. 319(2), especially as concerns arguments of overbreadth and vagueness, an immediate observation is that statements made "in private conversation" are not included in the criminalized expression. The provision thus does not prohibit views expressed with an intention to promote hatred if made privately, indicating Parliament's concern not to intrude upon the privacy of the individual. Indeed, that the legislation excludes private conversation, rather than including communications made in a public forum, suggests that the expression of hatred in a place accessible to the public is not sufficient to activate the legislation. This observation is supported by comparing the words of s. 319(2) with those of the prohibition against the incitement of hatred likely to lead to a breach of peace in s. 319(1). Section 319(1) covers statements communicated "in a public place," suggesting that a wider scope of prohibition was intended where the danger occasioned by the statements was of an immediate nature, while the wording of s. 319(2) indicates that private conversations taking place in public areas are not prohibited. Moreover, it is reasonable to infer a subjective *mens rea* requirement regarding the type of conversation covered by s. 319(2), an inference supported by the definition of "private communications" contained in s. 183 of the *Criminal Code*. Consequently, a conversation or communication intended to be private does not satisfy the requirements of the provision if through accident or negligence an individual's expression of hatred for an identifiable group is made public.

Is s. 319(2) nevertheless overbroad because it captures all public expression intended to promote hatred? It would appear not, for the harm which the government seeks to prevent is not restricted to certain mediums and/or locations. To attempt to distinguish between various forms and fora would therefore be incongruent with Parliament's legitimate objective.

The way in which I have defined the s. 319(2) offence, in the context of the objective sought by society and the value of the prohibited expression, gives me some doubt as to whether the *Charter* mandates that truthful statements communicated with an intention to promote hatred need be excepted from criminal condemnation. Truth may be used for widely disparate ends, and I find it difficult to accept that circumstances exist where factually accurate statements can be used for no other purpose than to stir up hatred against a racial or religious group. It would seem to follow that there is no reason why the individual who intentionally employs such statements to achieve harmful ends must under the *Charter* be protected from criminal censure.

Nevertheless, it is open to Parliament to make a concession to free expression values, whether or not such is required by the *Charter*. Deference to truth as a value central to free expression has thus led Parliament to include the defence in s. 319(3)(a), even though the accused has used truthful statements to cause harm of the type falling squarely within the objective of the legislation. When the statement contains no truth, however, this flicker of justification for the intentional promotion of hatred is extinguished, and the harmful malice of the disseminator stands alone. The relationship between the value of hate propaganda as expression and the parliamentary objective of eradicating harm, slightly altered so as to increase the magnitude of the former where the statement of the accused is truthful, thus returns to its more usual condition, a condition in which it is permissible to suppress the expression.

Because the presence of truth, though legally a defence to a charge under s. 319(2), does not change the fact that the accused has intended to promote the hatred of an identifiable group, I cannot find excessive impairment of the freedom of expression merely because s. 319(3)(a) does not cover negligent or innocent error. Whether or not a statement is susceptible to classification as true or false, my inclination is therefore to accept that such error should not excuse an accused who has wilfully used a statement in order to promote hatred against an identifiable group.

That s. 319(2) may in the past have led authorities to restrict expression offering valuable contributions to the arts, education, or politics in Canada is surely worrying. I hope, however, that my comments as to the scope of the provision make it obvious that only the most intentionally extreme forms of expression will find a place within s. 319(2). In this light, one can safely say that the incidents mentioned above illustrate not over-expansive breadth and vagueness in the law, but rather actions by the state which cannot be lawfully taken pursuant to s. 319(2). The possibility of illegal police harassment clearly has minimal bearing on the proportionality of hate propaganda legislation to legitimate parliamentary objectives, and hence the argument based on such harassment can be rejected.

Alternative Modes of Furthering Parliament's Objective

Given the stigma and punishment associated with a criminal conviction and the presence of other modes of government response in the fight against intolerance, it is proper to ask whether s. 319(2) can be said to impair minimally the freedom of expression. With respect to the efficacy of criminal legislation in advancing the goals of equality and multicultural tolerance in Canada, I agree that the role of s. 319(2) will be limited. It is important, in my opinion, not to hold any illusions about the ability of this one provision to rid our society of hate propaganda and its associated harms. Indeed, to become overly complacent, forgetting that there are a great many ways in which to address the problem of racial and religious intolerance, could be dangerous. Obviously, a variety of measures need be employed in the quest to achieve such lofty and important goals.

In assessing the proportionality of a legislative enactment to a valid governmental objective, however, s. 1 should not operate in every instance so as to force the government to rely upon only the mode of intervention least intrusive of a *Charter* right or freedom. It may be that a number of courses of action are available in the furtherance of a pressing and substantial objective, each imposing a varying degree of restriction upon a right or freedom. In such circumstances, the government may legitimately employ a more restrictive measure, either alone or as part of a larger program of action, if that measure is not redundant, furthering the objective in ways that alternative responses could not, and is in all other respects proportionate to a valid s. 1 aim.

Analysis of Section 319(2) under Section 1 of the Charter: *Conclusion*

I find that the infringement of the respondent's freedom of expression as guaranteed by s. 2(b) should be upheld as a reasonable limit prescribed by law in a free and democratic society. Furthering an immensely important objective and directed at expression distant from the core of free expression values, s. 319(2) satisfies each of the components of the proportionality inquiry. I thus disagree with the Alberta Court of Appeal's conclusion that this criminal prohibition of hate propaganda violates the *Charter*, and would allow the appeal in this respect.

McLachlin, J (dissenting): ...

Hate Propaganda and Freedom of Speech – An Overview

Before entering upon the analysis of whether s. 319(2) of the *Criminal Code* is inconsistent with the *Charter* and must be struck down, it may be useful to consider the conflicting values underlying the question of the prohibition of hate literature and how the issue has been treated in other jurisdictions.

Hate literature presents a great challenge to our conceptions about the value of free expression. Its offensive content often constitutes a direct attack on many of the other principles which are cherished by our society. Tolerance, the dignity and equality of all individuals; these and other values are all adversely affected by the propagation of hateful sentiment. The problem is not peculiarly Canadian; it is universal.

Wherever racially or culturally distinct groups of people live together, one finds people, usually a small minority of the population, who take it upon themselves to denigrate members of a group other than theirs. Canada is no stranger to this conduct. Our history is replete with examples of discriminatory communications. In their time, Canadians of Asian and East Indian descent, black, and native people have been the objects of communications tending to foster hate. In the case at bar it is the Jewish people who have been singled out as objects of calumny.

The evil of hate propaganda is beyond doubt. It inflicts pain and indignity upon individuals who are members of the group in question. Insofar as it may persuade others to the same point of view, it may threaten social stability. And it is intrinsically offensive to people – the majority in most democratic countries – who believe in the equality of all people regardless of race or creed.

For these reasons, governments have legislated against the dissemination of propaganda directed against racial groups, and in some cases this legislation has been tested in the courts. Perhaps the experience most relevant to Canada is that of the United States, since its Constitution, like ours, places a high value on free expression, raising starkly the conflict between freedom of speech and the countervailing values of individual dignity and social harmony. Like s. 2(b), the First Amendment guarantee is conveyed in broad, unrestricted language, stating that "Congress shall make no law ... abridging the freedom of speech, or of the press." The relevance of aspects of the American experience to this case is underlined by the factums and submissions, which borrowed heavily from ideas which may be traced to the United States.

The protections of the First Amendment to the U.S. Constitution, and in particular free speech, have always assumed a particular importance within the U.S. constitutional scheme, being regarded as the cornerstone of all other democratic freedoms. As expressed by Jackson, J, in *West Virginia State Board of Education v Barnette*, 319 US 624 (1943), "[i]f there is any fixed star in our constitutional constellation, it is that no official, high or petty, can prescribe what shall be orthodox in politics, nationalism, religion, or other matters of opinion or force citizens to confess by word or act their faith therein" (p. 642). The U.S. Supreme Court, particularly in recent years, has pronounced itself strongly on the need to protect speech even at the expense of other worthy competing values.

In the United States, a provision similar to s. 319(2) of the *Criminal Code* was struck down in *Collin v Smith, supra*, on the ground that is was fatally overbroad. In addition, the Seventh Circuit Court of Appeals hinted that the provision might also be void for vagueness. The ordinance in *Collin* prohibited "[t]he dissemination of any materials within the Village of Skokie which promotes and incites hatred against persons by reason of their race, national origin, or religion, and is intended to do so." The court found that the activity in question in the case – a proposed neo-Nazi demonstration in Skokie, Illinois – was a form of expression entitled to protection under the First Amendment. The ordinance, it found, was overbroad in that it "could conceivably be applied to criminalize dissemination of *The Merchant of Venice* or a vigorous discussion of the merits of reverse racial discrimination in Skokie" (p. 1207).

The *Charter* follows the American approach in method, affirming freedom of expression as a broadly defined and fundamental right, and contemplating balancing the values protected by and inherent in freedom of expression against the benefit conferred by the legislation limiting that freedom under s. 1 of the *Charter*. This is in keeping with the strong liberal tradition favouring free speech in this country – a tradition which had led to conferring quasi-constitutional status on free expression in this country prior to any bill of rights or *Charter*. At the same time, the tests are not necessarily the same as in the United States ...

The Construction Arguments

These submissions urge that s. 2(b) of the *Charter* should not be construed as extending to statements which offend s. 319(2) of the *Criminal Code*. The arguments are founded on three distinct considerations: s. 15 of the *Charter*, s. 27 of the *Charter*; and Canada's international obligations.

The Argument Based on Section 15 of the *Charter*

The first argument is that the scope of s. 2(b) is diminished by s. 15 of the *Charter*. This argument is based on the principle of construction that where possible, the provisions of a statute should be read together so as to avoid conflict. The guarantee of equality in s. 15, it is submitted, is offended by speech which denigrates a particular ethnic or religious group. The competing values reflected by the two sections might therefore be reconciled by informing the content of s. 2(b) with the values of s. 15. Accordingly, the freedom of expression guarantee should be read down to exclude from protected expression statements whose content promotes such inequality.

It is important initially to define the nature of the potential conflict between s. 2(b) and s. 15 of the *Charter*. This is not a case of the collision of two rights which are put into conflict by the facts of the case. There is no violation of s. 15 in the case at bar, since there is no law or state action which puts the guarantee of equality into issue. The right granted by s. 15 is the right to be free from inequality and discrimination effected by the state. That right is not violated in the case at bar. The conflict, then, is not between rights, but rather between philosophies ...

There are two significant considerations which militate against an acceptance of the argument based on s. 15. First, it is important to consider the nature of the two guarantees in question. On the one hand, s. 2(b) confers on each individual freedom of expression, unconstrained by state regulation or action, and subject only to a possible limitation under s. 1. On the other hand s. 15 grants the right to be free from inequality and discrimination effected by the state. Given that the protection under s. 2(b) is aimed at protecting individuals from having their expression infringed by the government, it seems a misapplication of *Charter* values to thereby limit the scope of that individual guarantee with an argument based on s. 15, which is also aimed at circumscribing the power of the state.

This conclusion is supported by a second factor which weighs against limiting the scope of freedom of expression on the basis of the guarantee of s. 15. The cases where this court has considered the meaning of s. 2(b) have expressly rejected the suggestion that certain statements should be denied the protection of the guarantee on the basis of their content. This court has repeatedly affirmed that no matter how offensive or disagreeable the content of the expression, it cannot on that account be denied protection under s. 2(b) of the *Charter*: see *Irwin Toy* and *Reference re ss. 193 and 195.1(1)(c) of the Criminal Code* (Man.), *supra*. The argument based on s. 15 is clearly opposed to this principle, as it suggests that protection be denied expression whose content conflicts with the values underlying the s. 15 guarantee.

Even if these difficulties could be surmounted, one would be faced with the prospect of cutting back a freedom guaranteed by the *Charter* on the basis that the exercise of the freedom may run counter to the philosophy behind another section of the *Charter*. The alleged breach of s. 2(b) can be placed in a factual context. But since there is no breach of s. 15, the value to be weighed on that side of the balance cannot be placed in a factual context. This would render the exercise of balancing the conflicting values extremely difficult.

I conclude that this court should not reduce the scope of expression protected by s. 2(b) of the *Charter* because of s. 15 of the *Charter*.

The Argument Based on Section 27 of the *Charter*

Section 27 states that the *Charter* shall be interpreted in a manner consistent with the preservation and enhancement of the multicultural heritage of Canadians. Similar considerations apply here as applied to the argument based on s. 15 of the *Charter*. As in the case of the s. 15 argument, there is no conflict of rights, s. 27 embodying not a right or freedom but a principle of construction. As in the case of the s. 15 argument, the submission under s. 27 amounts to advocating that certain statements be denied protection under s. 2(b) because of their content, an approach which this court has rejected. Using s. 27 to limit the protection guaranteed by s. 2(b) is likewise subject to the objection that it would leave unprotected a large area of arguably legitimate social and political debate. All this is not to mention the difficulty of weighing abstract values such as multiculturalism in the balance against freedom of speech.

Further difficulties are not hard to conjure up. Different people may have different ideas about what undermines multiculturalism. The issue is inherently vague and to some extent a matter of personal opinion. For example, it might be suggested that a statement that Canada should not permit immigration from a certain part of the world is inconsistent with the preservation and enhancement of multiculturalism. Is s. 2(b) to be cut back to eliminate protection for such a statement, given the differing opinions one might expect on such a matter? It may be argued, moreover, that a certain latitude for expression of derogatory opinion about other groups is a necessary correlative of a multicultural society, where different groups compete for limited resources.

Before leaving this point I would add that there is no evidence that the impugned legislation in fact contributes to the enhancement and preservation of multiculturalism in Canada. Reliance, therefore, on s. 27 to tailor or otherwise cut back the protection afforded by s. 2(b) risks undercutting the fundamental freedom with no guarantee of a tangible benefit in return. In my opinion, the weighing of interests and values implicit in questions such as these is better accomplished under s. 1 of the *Charter*.

The Argument Based on International Law

... Canada's international obligations, and the accords negotiated between international governments may well be helpful in placing *Charter* interpretation in a larger context. Principles agreed upon by free and democratic societies may inform the reading given to certain of its guarantees. It would be wrong, however, to consider these obligations as determinative of or limiting the scope of those guarantees. The provisions of the *Charter*, though drawing on a political and social philosophy shared with other democratic societies, are uniquely Canadian. As a result, considerations may point, as they do in this case, to a conclusion regarding a rights violation which is not necessarily in accord with those international covenants.

I should add that I am not of the view that any measures taken to implement Canada's international obligations to combat racial discrimination and hate propaganda must necessarily be unconstitutional. The obligations expressed in the *International Covenant on Civil and Political Rights* (to prohibit by law "[a]ny advocacy of national, racial or religious hatred that constitutes incitement to discrimination, hostility or violence") and the *International Convention on the Elimination of All Forms of Racial Discrimination* (to "declare an offence punishable by law all dissemination of ideas based on racial superiority or hatred") are general in nature. Details of methods to be used are not specified. Nothing in those instruments compels enactment of s. 319(2), as opposed to other provisions combating racism.

I conclude that none of the arguments which are advanced for construing s. 2(b) of the *Charter* narrowly to exclude from its protection, statements offending s. 319(2) of the *Criminal Code* can prevail.

THE ANALYSIS UNDER SECTION 1

Section 1 and the Infringement of Freedom of Expression

The court's function under s. 1 of the *Charter* is that of weighing and balancing. Before reaching s. 1, the court must already have determined that the law in question infringes a right or freedom guaranteed by the *Charter*. The infringement alone, however, does not mandate that the law must fall. If the limit the law imposes on the right infringed is "reasonable" and "can be demonstrably justified in a free and democratic society," the law is valid. The demonstration of this justification, the burden of which lies on the state, involves proving that there are other rights or interests which outweigh the right infringed in the context of that case ...

The Objective of Section 319(2) of the *Criminal Code*

The objective of s. 319(2) of the *Criminal Code* is to prevent the promotion of hatred towards identifiable groups within our society. As the Attorney-General of Canada puts it, the objective of the legislation is, "among other things, to protect racial, religious and other groups from the wilful promotion of hatred against them, to prevent the spread of hatred and the breakdown of racial and social harmony, and "to prevent the destruction of our multicultural society." These aims are subsumed in the twin values of social harmony and individual dignity.

Given the problem of racial and religious prejudice in this country, I am satisfied that the objective of the legislation is of sufficient gravity to be capable of justifying limitations on constitutionally protected rights and freedoms.

Proportionality

General Considerations

The real question in this case, as I see it, is whether the means – the criminal prohibition of wilfully promoting hatred – are proportional and appropriate to the ends of suppressing hate propaganda in order to maintain social harmony and individual dignity. The objective of the legislation is one of great significance, such significance that it is capable of outweighing the fundamental values protected by the *Charter*. The ultimate question is whether this objective is of sufficient importance to justify the limitation on free expression effected by s. 319(2) of the *Criminal Code*. In answering this question, the court must consider not only the importance of the right or freedom in question and the significance of its limitation, but whether the way in which the limitation is imposed is justifiable. How serious is the infringement of the constitutionally guaranteed freedom, in this case freedom of expression? Is the limiting measure likely to further the objective in practice? Is the limiting measure overbroad or unnecessarily invasive? In the final analysis, bearing all these things in mind, does the benefit to be derived from the legislation outweigh the seriousness of the infringement? These are the considerations relevant to the question of the proportionality of the limiting law.

I have said that the contest in this case lies between the fundamental right of free expression on the one hand, and the values of social harmony and individual liberty on the other. In approaching the difficult task of determining where the balance lies in the context of this case, it is important not to be diverted by the offensive content of much of the speech in question. As this court has repeatedly stated, even the most reprehensible or disagreeable comments are prima facie entitled to the protection of s. 2(b). It is not the statements of Mr Keegstra which are at issue in this case, but rather the constitutionality of s. 319(2) of the *Criminal Code*. That must be our focus ...

Another general consideration relevant to the balancing of values involved in the proportionality test in this case relates peculiarly to the nature of freedom of expression. Freedom of expression is unique among the rights and freedoms guaranteed by the *Charter* in two ways.

The first way in which freedom of expression may be unique was alluded to earlier in the context of the philosophical underpinnings of freedom of expression. The right to fully and openly express one's views on social and political issues is fundamental to our democracy and hence to all the other rights and freedoms guaranteed by the *Charter*. Without free expression, the vigourous debate on policies and values that underlies participatory government is lacking. Without free expression, rights may be trammelled with no recourse in the court of public opinion. Some restrictions on free expression may be necessary and justified and entirely compatible with a free and democratic society. But restrictions which touch the critical core of social and political debate require particularly close consideration because of the dangers inherent in state censorship of such debate. This is of particular importance under s. 1 of the *Charter* which expressly requires the court to have regard to whether the limits are reasonable and justified in a free and democratic society.

A second characteristic peculiar to freedom of expression is that limitations on expression tend to have an effect on expression other than that which is their target. In the United States this is referred to as the chilling effect. Unless the limitation is drafted with great precision, there will always be doubt about whether a particular form of expression offends the prohibition. There will always be limitations inherent in the use of language, but that must not discourage the pursuit of the greatest drafting precision possible. The result of a failure to do so may be to deter not only the expression which the prohibition was aimed at, but legitimate expression. The law-abiding citizen who does not wish to run afoul of the law will decide not to take the chance in a doubtful case. Creativity and the beneficial exchange of ideas will be adversely affected. This chilling effect must be taken into account in performing the balancing required by the analysis under s. 1. It mandates that in weighing the intrusiveness of a limitation on freedom of expression our consideration cannot be confined to those who may ultimately be convicted under the limit, but must extend to those who may be deterred from legitimate expression by uncertainty as to whether they might be convicted.

I make one final point before entering on the specific tests for proportionality proposed in *Oakes*. In determining whether the particular limitation of a right or freedom is justified under s. 1, it is important to consider not only the proportionality and effectiveness of the particular law in question, but alternative ways of furthering the objective. This is particularly important at stages two (minimum impairment) and three (balancing the infringement against the objective) of the proportionality analysis proposed in *Oakes*.

Against this background, I turn to the three considerations critical to determining whether the limitation on freedom of expression effected by s. 319(2) of the *Criminal Code* is reasonably and demonstrably justifiable in a free and democratic society.

Rational Connection
The first question is whether s. 319(2) of the *Criminal Code* may be seen as carefully designed or rationally connected to the objectives which it is aimed at promoting. This may be viewed in two ways.

The first is whether Parliament carefully designed s. 319(2) to meet the objectives it is enacted to promote.

Although some evidence of care in linking s. 319(2) to its objectives is clear, it has been argued that it is overbroad, an allegation which I will consider in greater detail in discussing whether s. 319(2) represents a "minimum impairment" of the right of free speech guaranteed by s. 2(b) of the *Charter*. Nevertheless it is clear that the legislation does, at least at one level, further Parliament's objectives. Prosecutions of individuals for offensive material directed at a particular group may bolster its members' beliefs that they are valued and respected in their community, and that the views of a malicious few do not reflect those of the population as a whole. Such a use of the criminal law may well affirm certain values and priorities which are of a pressing and substantial nature.

It is necessary, however, to go further, and consider not only Parliament's intention, but whether, given the actual effect of the legislation, a rational connection exists between it and its objectives. Legislation designed to promote an objective may in fact impede that objective.

Section 319(2) may well have a chilling effect on defensible expression by law-abiding citizens. At the same time, it is far from clear that it provides an effective way of curbing hate-mongers. Indeed, many have suggested it may promote their cause. Prosecutions under the *Criminal Code* for racist expression have attracted extensive media coverage. Zundel, prosecuted not under s. 319(2), but for the crime of spreading false news (s. 181), claimed that his court battle had given him "a million dollars worth of publicity": *Globe and Mail*, March 1, 1985, p. 1.

Not only does the criminal process confer on the accused publicity for his dubious causes — it may even bring him sympathy. The criminal process is cast as a conflict between the accused and the state, a conflict in which the accused may appear at his most sympathetic. Franz Kafka was not being entirely whimsical when he wrote, "If you have the right eye for these things, you can see that accused men are often attractive" (*The Trial*, 1976, p. 203).

The argument that criminal prosecutions for this kind of expression will reduce racism and foster multiculturalism depends on the assumption that some listeners are gullible enough to believe the expression if exposed to it. But if this assumption is valid, these listeners might be just as likely to believe that there must be some truth in the racist expression because the government is trying to suppress it. Theories of a grand conspiracy between government and elements of society wrongly perceived as malevolent can become all too appealing if government dignifies them by completely suppressing their utterance. It is therefore not surprising that the criminalization of hate propaganda and prosecutions under such legislation have been subject to so much controversy in this country.

Minimum Impairment

The second matter which must be considered in determining whether the infringement represented by the legislation is proportionate to its ends is whether the legislation impairs the right to the minimum extent possible.

Those supporting s. 319(2) of the *Criminal Code* point to the fact that it applies only to wilful promotion of hatred, and not to promotion of any lesser emotion. Hatred, they argue, is the most extreme and reprehensible of human emotions. They also point out that s. 319(2) provides a number of defences, including the truth of the statements made, discussion for public benefit of a subject of public importance (provided the statements were believed to be true on reasonable grounds), and good faith opinion on a religious subject. They add that s. 319(2) does no more than fulfil Canada's international obligations and that similar provisions apply in other Western democracies.

Despite the limitations found in s. 319(2), a strong case can be made that it is overbroad in that its definition of offending speech may catch many expressions which should be protected. The first difficulty lies in the different interpretations which may be placed on the word "hatred." The *Shorter Oxford English Dictionary* defines "hatred" as: "The condition or state of relations in which one person hates another; the emotion of hate; active dislike, detestation; enmity, ill-will, malevolence." The wide range of diverse emotions which the word "hatred" is capable of denoting is evident from this definition. Those who defend its use in s. 319(2) of the *Criminal Code* emphasize one end of this range – hatred, they say, indicates the most powerful of virulent emotions lying beyond the bounds of human decency and limiting s. 319(2) to extreme materials. Those who object to its use point to the other end of the range, insisting that "active dislike" is not an emotion for the promotion of which a person should be convicted as a criminal. To state the arguments is to make the case; "hatred" is a broad term capable of catching a wide variety of emotion.

It is not only the breadth of the term "hatred" which presents dangers; it is its subjectivity. "Hatred" is proved by inference – the inference of the jury or the judge who sits as trier of fact – and inferences are more likely to be drawn when the speech is unpopular. The subjective and emotional nature of the concept of promoting hatred compounds the difficulty of ensuring that only cases meriting prosecution are pursued and that only those whose conduct is calculated to dissolve the social bonds of society are convicted.

The absence of any requirement that actual harm or incitement to hatred be shown further broadens the scope of s. 319(2) of the *Criminal Code*. This, in the view of the Court of Appeal, was the section's main defect. In effect, the provision makes a crime not only of actually inciting others to hatred, but also of attempting to do so. The Court of

Appeal accepted the argument that this made the crime, at least potentially, a victimless one. In the view of Kerans, JA, while a prohibition on expression that actually spread hatred would be justified, a prohibition on attempts to spread hatred was not.

Not only is the category of speech caught by s. 319(2) defined broadly. The application of the definition of offending speech, i.e., the circumstances in which the offending statements are prohibited, is virtually unlimited. Only private conversations are exempt from state scrutiny. Section 319(2) is calculated to prevent absolutely expression of the offending ideas in any and all public forums through any and all mediums. Speeches are caught. The corner soap-box is no longer open. Books, films, and works of art – all these fall under the censor's scrutiny because of s. 319(2) of the *Criminal Code*.

The real answer to the debate about whether s. 319(2) is overbroad is provided by the section's track record. Although the section is of relatively recent origin, it has provoked many questionable actions on the part of the authorities. There have been no reported convictions, other than the instant appeals. But the record amply demonstrates that intemperate statements about identifiable groups, particularly if they represent an unpopular viewpoint, may attract state involvement or calls for police action.

The combination of overbreadth and criminalization may well lead people desirous of avoiding even the slightest brush with the criminal law to protect themselves in the best way they can – by confining their expression to non-controversial matters. Novelists may steer clear of controversial characterizations of ethnic characteristics, such as Shakespeare's portrayal of Shylock in *The Merchant of Venice*. Scientists may well think twice before researching and publishing results of research suggesting difference between ethnic or racial groups. Given the serious consequences of criminal prosecution, it is not entirely speculative to suppose that even political debate on crucial issues such as immigration, educational language rights, foreign ownership, and trade may be tempered. These matters go to the heart of the traditional justifications for protecting freedom of expression.

This brings me to the second aspect of minimum impairment. The examples I have just given suggest that the very fact of criminalization itself may be argued to represent an excessive response to the problem of hate propagation. The procedures and sanctions associated with the criminal law are comparatively severe. Given the stigma that attaches and the freedom which is at stake, the contest between the individual and the state imposed by a criminal trial must be regarded as difficult and harrowing in the extreme. The seriousness of the imprisonment which may follow conviction requires no comment. Moreover, the chilling effect of prohibitions on expression is at its most severe where they are effected by means of the criminal law. It is this branch of the law more than any other which the ordinary, law-abiding citizen seeks to avoid. The additional sanction of the criminal law may pose little deterrent to a convinced hate-monger who may welcome the publicity it brings; it may, however, deter the ordinary individual.

Moreover, it is arguable whether criminalization of expression calculated to promote racial hatred is necessary. Other remedies are perhaps more appropriate and more effective. Discrimination on grounds of race and religion is worthy of suppression. Human rights legislation, focusing on reparation rather than punishment, has had considerable success in discouraging such conduct ...

Finally, it can be argued that greater precision is required in the criminal law than, for example, in human rights legislation because of the different character of the two types of proceedings. The consequences of alleging a violation of s. 319(2) of the *Criminal Code* are direct and serious in the extreme. Under the human rights process a tribunal has considerable discretion in determining what messages or conduct should be banned and by its order may indicate more precisely their exact nature, all of which occurs before any consequences inure to the alleged violator.

In summary, s. 319(2) of the *Criminal Code* catches a broad range of speech and prohibits it in a broad manner, allowing only private conversations to escape scrutiny. Moreover, the process by which the prohibition is effected – the criminal law – is the severest our society can impose and is arguably unnecessary given the availability of alternate remedies. I conclude that the criminalization of hate statements does not impair free speech to the minimum extent permitted by its objectives.

READING QUESTIONS ON KEEGSTRA

1 What does Dickson, CJC mean in saying that the reasons for limiting expression in this case are the same as those for protecting it more generally?
2 How are Dickson's reasons related to Minow's arguments?
3 Both the majority and the dissent appeal to the consequences of the law. How are considerations of equality and consequences related in the competing arguments?

4 How are McLachlin, J's arguments about statutory construction related to Hayek's views about the rule of law?

RAV v City of St Paul 112 S Ct 2538 (1992)

The U.S. Supreme Court overturned a Minnesota ordinance prohibiting displays of racial hatred on the grounds that it advocated a particular viewpoint. In the instant case, the law would have punished white youths for burning a cross on the lawn of an African American family.

... Justice Scalia delivered the opinion of the Court.

In the predawn hours of June 21, 1990, petitioner and several other teenagers allegedly assembled a crudely-made cross by taping together broken chair legs. They then allegedly burned the cross inside the fenced yard of a black family that lived across the street from the house where petitioner was staying. Although this conduct could have been punished under any of a number of laws, one of the two provisions under which respondent city of St Paul chose to charge petitioner (then a juvenile) was the St Paul Bias-Motivated Crime Ordinance, St Paul, Minn.Legis.Code s. 292.02 (1990), which provides:

Whoever places on public or private property a symbol, object, appellation, characterization or graffiti, including, but not limited to, a burning cross or Nazi swastika, which one knows or has reasonable grounds to know arouses anger, alarm or resentment in others on the basis of race, color, creed, religion or gender commits disorderly conduct and shall be guilty of a misdemeanor.

Petitioner moved to dismiss this count on the ground that the St. Paul ordinance was substantially overbroad and impermissibly content-based and therefore facially invalid under the First Amendment. The trial court granted this motion, but the Minnesota Supreme Court reversed. That court rejected petitioner's overbreadth claim because, as construed in prior Minnesota cases, see, e.g., *In re Welfare of SLJ*, 263 NW2d 412 (Minn.1978), the modifying phrase "arouses anger, alarm or resentment in others" limited the reach of the ordinance to conduct that amounts to "fighting words," i.e., "conduct that itself inflicts injury or tends to incite immediate violence ...," *In re Welfare of RAV*, 464 NW2d 507, 510 (Minn.1991) (citing *Chaplinsky v New Hampshire*, 315 US 568, 572, 62 SCt

766, 769, 86 L.Ed 1031 (1942)), and therefore the ordinance reached only expression "that the first amendment does not protect." 464 NW2d, at 511. The court also concluded that the ordinance was not impermissibly content-based because, in its view, "the ordinance is a narrowly tailored means toward accomplishing the compelling governmental interest in protecting the community against bias-motivated threats to public safety and order." Ibid. We granted certiorari, 501 US –, 111 SCt 2795, 115 L.Ed.2d 969 (1991).

[1] In construing the St Paul ordinance ... we accept the Minnesota Supreme Court's authoritative statement that the ordinance reaches only those expressions that constitute "fighting words" within the meaning of *Chaplinsky*. 464 NW2d, at 510–511. Petitioner and his *amici* urge us to modify the scope of the *Chaplinsky* formulation, thereby invalidating the ordinance as "substantially overbroad," *Broadrick v Oklahoma*, 413 US 601, 610, 93 SCt 2908, 2914–2915, 37 L.Ed.2d 830 (1973). We find it unnecessary to consider this issue. Assuming, *arguendo*, that all of the expression reached by the ordinance is proscribable under the "fighting words" doctrine, we nonetheless conclude that the ordinance is facially unconstitutional in that it prohibits otherwise permitted speech solely on the basis of the subjects the speech addresses ...[1]

[2, 3] The First Amendment generally prevents government from proscribing speech ... From 1791 to the present, however, our society, like other free but civilized societies, has permitted restrictions upon the content of speech in a few limited areas, which are "of such slight social value as a step to truth that any benefit that may be derived from them is clearly outweighed by the social interest in order and morality." *Chaplinsky, supra*, 315 US, at 572, 62 SCt, at 762. We have recognized that the "freedom of speech" referred to by the First Amendment does not include a freedom to disregard these traditional limitations ...

[4] We have sometimes said that these categories of expression are "not within the area of constitutionally protected speech" ... or that the "protection of the First Amendment does not extend" to them ...

Such statements must be taken in context, however, and are no more literally true than is the occasionally repeated shorthand characterizing obscenity "as not being speech at all" ...

What they mean is that these areas of speech can, consistently with the First Amendment, be regulated *because of their constitutionally proscribable content* (obscenity, defamation, etc.) – not that they are categories of speech entirely invisible to the Constitution, so that they may be made the vehicles for content discrimination unrelated to their distinctively proscribable content. Thus, the government may proscribe libel; but it may not make the further content discrimination of proscribing *only* libel critical of the government ...

Our cases surely do not establish the proposition that the First Amendment imposes no obstacle whatsoever to regulation of particular instances of such proscribable expression, so that the government "may regulate [them] freely," *post*, at 2552 (White, J, concurring in judgment). That would mean that a city council could enact an ordinance prohibiting only those legally obscene works that contain criticism of the city government or, indeed, that do not include endorsement of the city government. Such a simplistic, all-or-nothing-at-all approach to First Amendment protection is at odds with common sense and with our jurisprudence as well.[2] It is not true that "fighting words" have at most a *"de minimis"* expressive content, ibid., or that their content is *in all respects* "worthless and undeserving of constitutional protection," *post*, at 2553; sometimes they are quite expressive indeed. We have not said that they constitute *"no* part of the expression of ideas," but only that they constitute "no *essential* part of any exposition of ideas." *Chaplinsky*, 315 US, at 572, 62 S Ct, at 769 (emphasis added).

The proposition that a particular instance of speech can be proscribable on the basis of one feature (e.g. obscenity) but not on the basis of another (e.g., opposition to the city government) is commonplace, and has found application in many contexts. We have long held, for example, that nonverbal expressive activity can be banned because of the action it entails, but not because of the ideas it expresses — so that burning a flag in violation of an ordinance against outdoor fires could be punishable, whereas burning a flag in violation of an ordinance against dishonoring the flag is not.

When the basis for the content discrimination consists entirely of the very reason the entire class of speech at issue is proscribable, no significant danger of idea or viewpoint discrimination exists. Such a reason, having been adjudged neutral enough to support exclusion of the entire class of speech from First Amendment protection, is also neutral enough to form the basis of distinction within the class ...

And the Federal Government can criminalize only those threats of violence that are directed against the President ... since the reasons why threats of violence are outside the First Amendment (protecting individuals from the fear of violence, from the disruption that fear engenders, and from the possibility that the threatened violence will occur) have special force when applied to the person of the President ...

But the Federal Government may not criminalize only those threats against the President that mention his policy on aid to inner cities ...

[7, 8] Applying these principles to the St Paul ordinance, we conclude that, even as narrowly construed by the Minnesota Supreme Court, the ordinance is facially unconstitutional. Although the phrase in the ordinance, "arouses anger, alarm or resentment in others," has been limited by the Minnesota Supreme Court's construction to reach only those symbols or displays that amount to "fighting words," the remaining, unmodified terms make clear that the ordinance applies only to "fighting words" that insult, or provoke violence, "on the basis of race, color, creed, religion or gender." Displays containing abusive invective, no matter how vicious or severe, are permissible unless they are addressed to one of the specified disfavored topics. Those who wish to use "fighting words" in connection with other ideas – to express hostility, for example, on the basis of political affiliation, union membership, or homosexuality – are not covered. The First Amendment does not permit St Paul to impose special prohibitions on those speakers who express views on disfavored subjects ...

In its practical operation, moreover, the ordinance goes even beyond mere content discrimination, to actual viewpoint discrimination. Displays containing some words – odious racial epithets, for example – would be prohibited to proponents of all views. But "fighting words" that do not themselves invoke race, color, creed, religion, or gender – aspersions upon a person's mother, for example – would seemingly be usable *ad libitum* in that the placards of those arguing *in favor* of racial, color, etc. tolerance and equality, but could not be used by that speaker's opponents. One could hold up a sign saying, for example, that all "anti-Catholic bigots" are misbegotten; but not that all "papists" are, for that would insult and provoke violence "on the basis of religion." St Paul has no such authority to license one side of a debate to fight freestyle, while requiring the other to follow Marquis of Queensbury Rules ...

St Paul has not singled out an especially offensive mode of expression – it has not, for example, selected for prohibition only those fighting words that communicate ideas in a threatening (as opposed to a merely obnoxious) manner. Rather, it has proscribed fighting words of whatever manner that communicate messages of racial, gender, or religious intolerance. Selectivity of this sort created the possibility that the city is seeking to handicap the expression of particular ideas. That possibility would alone be enough to render the ordinance presumptively invalid, but St Paul's comments and concessions in this case elevate the possibility to a certainty. St Paul argues that the ordinance comes within another of the specific exceptions we mentioned, the one that allows content discrimination aimed only at the "secondary effects" of the speech ...

"The emotive impact of speech on its audience is not a 'secondary effect'" ...

It hardly needs discussion that the ordinance does not fall within some more general exception permitting *all* selectivity that for any reason is beyond the suspicion of official suppression of ideas. The statements of St Paul in this very case afford ample basis for, if not full confirmation of, that suspicion ...

Let there be no mistake about our belief that burning a cross in someone's front yard is reprehensible. But St Paul has sufficient means at its disposal to prevent such behavior without adding the First Amendment to the fire.

The judgment of the Minnesota Supreme Court is reversed, and the case is remanded for proceedings not inconsistent with this opinion.

It is so ordered ...

Stevens, J, concurring ... It is inconsistent to hold that the government may proscribe an entire category of speech is evil ... but that the government may not treat a subset of that category differently without violating the First Amendment; the content of the subset is by definition worthless and undeserving of constitutional protection.

The majority's observation that fighting words are "quite expressive indeed," *ante*, at 2544, is no answer. Fighting words are not a means of exchanging views, rallying supporters, or registering a protest; they are directed against individuals to provoke violence or to inflict injury ...

Therefore, a ban on all fighting words or on a subset of the fighting words category would restrict only the social evil of hate speech, without creating the danger of driving viewpoints from the marketplace. See *ante*, at 2545 ...

By placing fighting words, which the Court has long held to be valueless, on at least equal constitutional footing with political discourse and other forms of speech that we have deemed to have the greatest social value, the majority devalues the latter category ...

[I]f the majority were to give general application to the rule on which it decides this case, today's decision would call into question the constitutionality of the statute making it illegal to threaten the life of the President. 18 USC s. 871. See *Watts v United States*, 394 US 705, 89 SCt 1399, 22 L.Ed.2d 664 (1969) (*per curiam*). Surely, this statute, by singling out certain threats, incorporates a content-based distinction; it indicates that the Government especially disfavors threats against the President as opposed to threats against all others. But because the Government could prohibit all threats and not just those directed against the President, under the Court's theory, the compelling reasons justifying the enactment of special legislation to safeguard the President would be irrelevant, and the statute would fail First Amendment review ...

Contrary to the suggestion of the majority, the St Paul ordinance does *not* regulate expression based on viewpoint. The Court contends that the ordinance requires proponents of racial intolerance to "follow the Marquis of Queensbury Rules" while allowing advocates of racial tolerance to "fight freestyle." The law does no such thing.

The Court writes:

One could hold up a sign saying, for example, that all "all-anti-Catholic bigots" are misbegotten; but not that all "papists" are, for that would insult and provoke violence "on the basis of religion." *Ante*, at 2548.

This may be true, but it hardly proves the Court's point. The Court's reasoning is asymmetrical. The response to a sign saying that "all [religious] bigots are misbegotten" is a way of saying that "all advocates of religious tolerance are misbegotten." Assuming such signs could be fighting words (which seems to me extremely unlikely), neither sign would be banned by the ordinance for the attacks were not "based on ... religion" but rather on one's beliefs about tolerance. Conversely (and again assuming such signs are fighting words), just as the ordinance would prohibit a Muslim from hoisting a sign claiming that all Catholics were misbegotten, so the ordinance would bar a Catholic from hoisting a similar sign attacking Muslims.

The St Paul ordinance is evenhanded. In a battle between advocates of tolerance and advocates of intolerance, the ordinance does not prevent either side from hurling fighting words at the other on the basis of their conflicting ideas, but it does bar *both* sides from hurling such words on the basis of the target's "race, color, creed, religion or gender." To extend the Court's pugilistic metaphor, the St Paul ordinance simply bans punches "below the belt" – *by either party.* It does not, therefore, favor one side of any debate.

Finally, it is noteworthy that the St Paul ordinance is, as construed by the Court today, quite narrow. The St Paul ordinance does not ban all "hate speech," nor does it ban, say, all cross-burnings or all swastika displays. Rather it only bans a subcategory of the already narrow category of fighting words. Such a limited ordinance leaves open and protected a vast range of expression of the subjects of racial, religious, and gender equality. As construed by the Court today, the ordinance certainly does not "'raise the specter that the Government may effectively drive certain ideas or viewpoints from the marketplace.'" *Ante,* at 2545. Petitioner is free to burn a cross to announce a rally or to express his views about racial supremacy, he may do so on private property or public land, at day or at night, so long as the burning is not so threatening and so directed at an individual as to "by its very [execution] inflict injury." Such a limited proscription scarcely offends the First Amendment.

In sum, the St Paul ordinance (as construed by the Court) regulates expressive activity that is wholly proscribable and does so not on the basis of viewpoint, but rather in recognition of the different harms caused by such activity. Taken together, these several considerations persuade me that the St Paul ordinance is not an unconstitutional content-based regulation of speech. Thus, were the ordinance not overbroad, I would vote to uphold it.

NOTES

1 Contrary to Justice White's suggestion, *post,* at 2550–2551, petitioner's claim is "fairly included" within the questions presented in the petition for certiorari, see this Court's Rule 14.1(a). It was clear from the petition and from petitioner's other filings in this Court (and in the courts below) that his assertion that the St Paul ordinance "violat[es] overbreadth ... principles of the First Amendment," Pet. for Cert. i, was *not* just a technical "overbreadth" claim – i.e., a claim that the ordinance violated the rights of too many third parties – but included the contention that the ordinance was "overbroad" in the sense of restricting more speech than the Constitution permits, even in its application to him, because it is content-based. An important component of petitioner's argument is, and has been all along, that narrowly construing the ordinance to cover only "fighting words" cannot cure this fundamental defect. Ibid, at 12, 14, 15–16. In his briefs in this Court, petitioner argued that

a narrowing construction was ineffective because (1) its boundaries were vague, Brief for Petitioner 26, and because (2) denominating particular expression a "fighting word" because of the impact of its ideological content upon the audience is inconsistent with the First Amendment, Reply Brief for Petitioner 5; *ibid.*, at 13 ("[The ordinance] is overbroad, *viewpoint discrimina-tory* and vague as 'narrowly construed'") (emphasis added). At oral argu-ment, counsel for Petitioner reiterated this second point: "It is ... one of my positions, that in [punishing only some fighting words and not others], even though it is a subcategory, technically, of unprotected conduct, [the ordi-nance] still is picking out an opinion, a disfavored message, and making that clear through the State." Tr. of Oral Arg. 8. In resting our judgment upon this contention, we have not departed from our criteria of what is "fairly included" within the petition. See *Arkansas Electric Cooperative Corp. v Arkansas Pub. Serv. Comm'n*, 461 US 375, 382, n. 6, 103 SCt 1905, 1911–1912, n. 6, 76 L.Ed.2d 1 (1983); *Brown v Socialists Workers '74 Campaign Comm.*, 459 US 87, 94, n. 9, 103 SCt 416, 421, n. 9 74 L.Ed.2d 250 (1982); *Eddings v Oklahoma*, 455 US 104, 113, n. 9, 102 SCt 869, 876, n. 9, 71 L.Ed.2d 1 (1982); see generally R. Stern, E. Gressman, & S. Shapiro, Supreme Court Practice 361 (6th ed. 1986).

2 Justice White concedes that a city council cannot prohibit only those legally obscene works that contain criticism of the city government, *post*, at 2555, but asserts that to be the consequence, not of the First Amendment, but of the Equal Protection Clause. Such content-based discrimination would not, he asserts, "be rationally related to a legitimate government interest," ibid. But of course the only *reason* that government interest is not a "legitimate" one is that it violates the First Amendment. This Court itself has occasionally fused the First Amendment into the Equal Protection Clause in this fashion, but at least with the acknowledgment (which Justice White cannot afford to make) that the First Amendment underlies its analysis. See *Police Dept. of Chicago v Mosley*, 408 US 92, 95, 92 SCt 2286, 2289–2290, 33 L.Ed.2d 212 (1972) (ordinance prohibiting only nonlabor picketing violated the Equal Protection Clause because there was no "appropriate governmental interest" supporting the distinction inasmuch as "the First Amendment means that government has no power to restrict expression because of its message, its ideas, its subject matter, or its content"); *Carey v Brown*, 447 US 455, 100 SCt 2286, 65 L.Ed.2d 263 (1980). See generally *Simon & Schuster, Inc v Members of N.Y. State Crime Victims Bd.*, 502 US -, —, — – —, 112 SCt 501, 514, 116 L.Ed.2d 476 (1991) (Kennedy, J, concurring in judgment).

Justice Stevens seeks to avoid the point by dismissing the notion of obscene anti-government speech as "fantastical," *post*, at 2562, apparently believing that any reference to politics prevents a finding of obscenity. Unfortunately for the purveyors of obscenity, that is obviously false. A shockingly hard core pornographic movie that contains a model sporting a political tattoo can be found, "*taken as a whole* [to] lac[k] serious literary, artistic, political, or scientific value," *Miller v California*, 413 US 15, 24, 93 SCt 2607, 2614–2615, 37 L.Ed.2d 419 (1973) (emphasis added). Anyway, it is easy enough to come up with other illustrations of a content-based restriction upon "unprotected speech" that is obviously invalid: the anti-government libel illustration mentioned earlier, for one. See *supra*, at 2543. And of course the concept of racist fighting words is, unfortunately, anything but a "highly speculative hypothetical[l]," *post*, at 2562.

READING QUESTION ON *RAV*

1 How does the court distinguish between expression and action? Is their distinction tenable?

Martha Shaffer
"Criminal Responses to Hate-Motivated Violence: Is Bill C-41 Tough Enough?" (1996)

Shaffer explores the rationale for laws enhancing sentencing for crimes motivated by hate.

Toronto, June 1993. Three Tamil men are violently assaulted by white youths. One of them dies as a result of the attack. Saskatoon, 1991. Aboriginal trapper Leo Lachance is shot to death as he leaves a pawn shop. Pawn shop owner Connie Nerland, a member of the Aryan Nations, pleads guilty to manslaughter and is sentenced to four years in prison. Montreal, November 1992. Two gay men are murdered in separate incidents of gay bashing. Vancouver, September 1992. A gay man requires eight metal plates and thirty-eight screws to reconstruct his face after being attacked by a gang of youths. Toronto, 1993. The Heritage Front, a white supremacist group, sets up a telephone hotline and actively recruits in high schools and on college campuses. Toronto, 1992. The Native Canadian Centre and a book store displaying books opposing fascism are spray painted with swastikas on the same night that a small Jewish cemetery is defaced with anti-Semitic slogans. Within fourteen months of these events, swastikas are painted on four synagogues in Toronto and a Holocaust memorial is defaced with the words "six million isn't enough." In Vancouver, a synagogue is vandalized with blood stains and the Jewish Community Centre receives a bomb threat.

The upsurge in hate-motivated violence Canada appears to be witnessing raises the question whether the criminal justice system is responding adequately to the problem of hate-motivated violence. At present, although the *Criminal Code* contains provisions dealing with hate propaganda,[1] it does not specifically address hate-motivated violence. Hate-motivated violence is prosecuted under the standard criminal provisions governing violent acts, such as assault, manslaughter, or mischief. The bigoted nature of the incident, assuming it enters into the process at all, is considered as a factor in sentencing.

In June 1994, amid a flurry of publicity, Minister of Justice Allan Rock announced his government's intention to take an aggressive stand against hate crime. Rock introduced legislation that would amend the *Criminal Code* to ensure that judges treat an offender's biased motive as a factor increasing the severity of the offence when passing sentence.[2] Although the media greeted Bill C-41 as a significant change and as a potential interference with the independence of the judiciary, in reality the bill does little to alter the current law. Under Rock's bill, hate crimes would continue to be prosecuted under existing provisions sanctioning violent acts. The accused's bigoted motive would, as it is now, only be considered at the point of sentencing. The only difference between existing sentencing principles and the proposed amendments is that under the latter the *Criminal Code* would explicitly provide that an accused's biased motive must be considered.

In contrast to the existing Canadian approach to hate crime (and to Rock's codification of it), many jurisdictions in the United States have enacted specific provisions directed at the problem of hate-motivated violence. These provisions increase the criminal penalties for offences involving violence motivated by hatred above the ordinary penalties which attach to offences where group-based hatred is not an issue. Many also create a civil cause of action for victims of such violence. Despite considerable dispute over the constitutional validity of these statutes, the Supreme Court of the United States recently held that Wisconsin's hate crime law did not violate the Constitution.[3]

In light of the upsurge in hate-motivated violence Canada appears to be witnessing, the time is ripe to consider how the criminal law should respond to this type of violence and specifically whether Bill C-41 is the best approach our criminal law has to offer. ...

My argument in support of U.S.-style hate crime provisions is qualified, however, by a number of concerns. First, although at first glance hate crime legislation may appear to be a progressive measure offering protection and redress to groups who have been victimized by hate-mongers, the reality of such provisions is not so simple. Like many other criminal law reforms, hate crime provisions may be little more than symbolic gestures, incapable of contributing to the solution of deeply entrenched social problems. Second, if hate crime provisions turn out to be ineffective in rendering convictions – as seems to have been the case in the United States – they may do more harm than good. Rather than signalling that hate crime will be treated seriously, they may in fact send the opposite message. Third, once hate crime legislation is in place, we may be tempted to believe that because we have taken measures to combat hate-motivated violence no further action is needed. Notwithstanding these problems, I believe that the creation of strong hate crime legislation is important in a society that prides itself on its ethics of tolerance and multiculturalism and yet is plagued by deep undercurrents of racial and ethnic hate.

Throughout the ensuing discussion, it is important to keep in mind the limited parameters of the debate – namely the response of the criminal justice system to the problem of racist violence. The criminal justice system is only one of many possible mechanisms for addressing hate-motivated violence, and arguably it has only a very small role to play in rooting out the causes of such violence. Hate crime legislation should not be seen as a panacea for eradicating racist violence, as should be clear from the experience of the United State where hate-motivated violence continues to exist at high levels. This paper focuses on the limited question whether the criminal justice system is making the best contribution it can to deterring racist violence and to ensuring that those who commit hate-motivated crime receive appropriate disapprobation ...

Under the current law in Canada, the fact that an accused acted with a racist motive in committing an offence does enter into the criminal process, but only at the point of sentencing. According to accepted sentencing principles, racial motive acts as an aggravating factor which increases the severity of the accused's crime and hence the sentence to be imposed ...

The provisions of Bill C-41 concerned with hate crime would simply codify this practice. Section 718.2 of the Bill provides that a court imposing a sentence shall consider "evidence that the offence was motivated by bias, prejudice or hate based on race, national or ethnic origin, language, colour, religion, sex, age, mental or physical disability, sexual orientation or any other similar factor"[4] as aggravating factors. The fact that an accused was motivated by group hatred would thus lead courts to impose a sentence towards the harsher end of the existing sentencing range, but would *not* permit the courts to *increase* the sentence beyond the maximum currently available.

There are four arguments which suggest that the law's current treatment of hate crime – and, by implication, the proposals contained in Bill C-41 – may be inadequate and which support the enactment of provisions in the *Criminal Code* specifically targeting hate-motivated violence as a distinct criminal offence to which increased penalties attach. First, making hate-motivated violence into a distinct crime is recognition that such violence constitutes a specific form of harm that differs in significant ways from other types of violence. Hate-motivated violence is not simply an attack on the individual who happens to be the immediate target of the assault, but constitutes an affront to minority communities and to the values of equality and multiculturalism that underlie Canadian society. The accused's decision to choose a victim by reason of racial hatred means that the accused's violent conduct is not directed only at the immediate victim, but also against the entire group of which the individual is a member (or is perceived by the perpetrator to be a member). Thus, hate-motivated violence is in effect a form of group intimidation intended to express the loathing its perpetrators feel towards a particular group and to instill fear among that group as a whole. As a result, hate-motivated violence affects entire minority communities, because they know that simply by virtue of who they are they are all potential targets of such violence.[5] Moreover, the harmful effects of hate-motivated violence directed against members of one minority community may not be limited to that community, but may spill over to other minority groups. Bigots seldom limit their hatred to one group and many members of minority groups know that even though they were not targeted this time, they could be next on the list ...

Bill C-41's approach of considering the accused's hateful motive in sentencing implicitly recognizes the harmful effects of hate-motivated violence on minority communities and on Canadian society as a whole as they are what justify treating racist motive as an aggravating factor. However, redressing racial motive through the standard sentencing process may not sufficiently underscore the distinctive nature of hate-motivated crime for two reasons. First, charging the accused with a generic (i.e., non-hate specific) offence may not emphasize the extent to which the accused's action was an expression of hatred of an entire group as effectively as a specific hate crime offence would. Second, the fact that the accused was motivated by group hatred can *at most* increase his or her penalty to the existing maximum for the underlying offence. To take into account fully the extent of the individual and social harms caused by hate crime it is, I would argue, necessary to augment the penalties available where a crime is motivated by hate.

The second argument in favour of enacting provisions specifically directed at hate crime derives from the criminal law's role in demarcating the boundaries between acceptable and unacceptable conduct. By deeming certain activities to be subject to state sanction, the criminal law plays a normative or symbolic role in instructing citizens about the types of conduct that give rise to social disapprobation. The symbolic aspect of the criminal law has featured prominently in feminist scholarship. For example, in advocating law reform to abolish the rule that a man could not rape his wife, to ensure that wife abuse is treated seriously by police and prosecutors, and to criminalize pornography, many feminist scholars have argued that legal rules or their selective implementation have created a cultural climate that condones violence against women. The premise behind feminist arguments for changing the law and for better enforcement is that the messages enshrined in the criminal law can be a powerful force in shaping attitudes and altering behaviour. The symbolic aspect of the criminal law also has a role to play in combatting racism and racially motivated violence. Making hate-motivated violence into a distinct criminal offence sends a strong normative message that such violence is unacceptable and will not be tolerated in a society committed to racial and cultural pluralism. Considering racial motive in the normal sentencing process – as Bill C-41 would have us do – is not as powerful a statement, since it does not constitute an explicit denunciation of racist violence but treats racial motive as one factor among many going to the severity of the accused's conduct.

Third, one can argue that absent an explicit criminal provision condemning hate-motivated violence, the criminal law fails to serve the needs of groups who are most likely to be the victims of hate crime. The argument here is that the criminal law has been formulated primarily by white men and has reflected their views about the kinds of behaviour that ought to be subject to criminal sanction. As white male lawmakers are far less likely to view themselves as potential victims of hate crime than members of minority groups, they may never have contemplated the role of the criminal law in responding to hate crime, nor viewed hate crime as something requiring specifically tailored action. Although racially motivated violence is not new to Canada, the fact that hate crime has not been the subject of significant public disapproval until recently lends credence to this analysis. In light of the fact that minorities are more likely to be targets of hate-motivated violence than members of the majority group, the omission of specially formulated provisions designed specifically to redress such violence raises the question whether the criminal law confers equal protection on all citizens given the different kinds of harm they are likely to face. If one accepts the previous arguments concerning the distinctive nature of hate crime and the importance of the normative messages embodied in the criminal law, the answer even after Bill C-41 is no.

Finally, the creation of a crime of intimidation may make it easier for authorities to compile statistics on the incidence of hate crime. Assuming assiduous charging and prosecution of conduct giving rise to intimidation, the level of hate-motivated violence could be tracked by following the conviction rate for the offence of intimidation, as well as any other hate-specific offence. Determining the frequency of hate-motivated violence under the current system is more complicated since it requires scrutiny of all violence-related offences. In addition, since the hateful nature of the offence will not appear from the charge itself, compilation of hate crime statistics requires devising a recording and retrieval system that takes into account the facts of the case and the factors considered in sentencing, and not simply the disposition. While this argument for creating a specific hate crime is less compelling than the others, it is, nonetheless, worthy of consideration.

The final set of objections to hate crime provisions questions the wisdom of using the criminal law to attempt to eradicate or reduce hate-motivated violence. Commentators in the United States have raised two main concerns in this regard. First, critics speculate that hate crime charges will be laid more often against members of minority groups who lash out against white victims than against white offenders. The prevalence of unconscious bigotry suggests this may indeed be a problem. White police officers, who still constitute the majority in police forces across the country, may be more willing to attribute a hateful motive to a minority offender than to perceive a white offender to be motivated by hate. Officers may, for example, be better able to place themselves in the shoes of white victims, and therefore have a greater ability to perceive the violence as motivated by hate. However, to the extent that unconscious bigotry affects who is charged with hate crimes, it will also be a problem in sentencing. Police officers may be more likely to furnish prosecutors with evidence of hateful motive when the offender is a member of a minority group, with the result that minorities will face stiffer sentences at a disproportionate rate. Thus, regardless of whether Bill C-41 or U.S.-style hate crime legislation is adopted, vigilance will be required to ensure that the law is not being applied in a discriminatory manner.

Second, critics query whether hate crimes legislation will have any significant effect in reducing hate crime or whether it will be largely a symbolic gesture. Although a symbolic denunciation of hate crime may be valuable in itself by performing an educative function, it is clearly not a sufficient response to the problem of hate-motivated violence. Passing a hate crimes provision may, however, end up being the only response because it allows people to believe they have taken effective action and may lessen their inclination to do more ...

A more radical version of this criticism focuses on the reasons the state may find criminal responses to hate crime appealing. Criminal solutions tend to be favourites of government for three reasons. First, enacting criminal legislation is often a relatively easy way for the government to claim it is addressing a social problem. For example, it is much easier to pass a criminal law condemning hate-motivated violence than it is to devise and implement the multiple strategies that a comprehensive response to the problem would demand.

Second, criminal legislation may be comparatively cheap. Although creating additional criminal offences or increasing criminal penalties may increase the costs associated with law enforcement and incarceration, the government will be able to avoid paying for the development and implementation for anti-racist/homophobic education and training programs. At times, the use of the criminal law may in fact be a false economy as the costs to the justice system may end up being greater than the costs of social programs which might avoid engagement with the criminal process. For example, to the extent that improving the economic conditions of lower income Canadians might reduce the rate of addiction to illegal drugs, paying for economic and social programs may be a more cost-effective allocation of resources than paying for all the personnel necessary to fight the drug problem through the criminal justice system. Governments have, however, shown a remarkable degree of resistance to accepting this reality.

Third, the process of enacting criminal provisions in an area such as hate crime is highly visible, attracting considerable media attention. This is also true of trials under hate crime provisions, at least in the law's initial stages. The publicity surrounding these proceedings provides the government with free political mileage in a way that less-visible educational strategies do not. This is particularly significant when, as now, the electorate perceives crime to be a significant problem and accordingly "law and order" responses are politically popular.

A critical perspective provides a final reason to be wary of the criminal law. As numerous critical scholars have noted, the criminal justice system is not usually an instrument of progressive social change. Changes in the criminal law do not tend to bring about fundamental social reform, nor do they normally empower those whom they seek to protect. According to this critique, the criminal law will do little to dismantle the social power structure that gives rise to hate-motivated violence. The symbolic effect claimed of hate crime provisions will be largely illusory.

These concerns with the limitations of the criminal law are important. They are useful reminders that the criminal law is not a sufficient response to social problems and that non-criminal avenues must be explored. However, these criticisms do not offer much guidance on the question of which criminal law remedy to adopt where a number of responses are available. Given that violence, including violence motivated by group hatred, is conduct that should be subject to criminal sanction, the appropriate question is not *whether* criminal remedies should be pursued, but *which* of the criminal remedies can make the best contribution to the problem. These concerns do not tell us whether the fact that violence is motivated by hate should be a factor in sentencing or should be the subject of a specific criminal offence, or even further, should carry no special weight in the criminal process.

CONCLUSION

My assessment of the arguments for and against U.S.-style hate crime provisions leads me to conclude that we should adopt similar legislation in Canada. Hate crime provisions constitute a powerful statement that hate-motivated violence is unacceptable and will not be tolerated in a society committed to equality and multiculturalism. While Bill C-41 also conveys a similar message, it fails to do so as forcefully. Since there seem to be no compelling reasons for adopting the weaker denunciation of hate crime over the stronger, I believe we should embrace the U.S. approach and permit penalty enhancement when violent crime is motivated by group hatred.

I do, however, have some hesitation in making this recommendation. First, I worry that hate crimes provisions, if enacted, might not be appropriately enforced. Such provisions will only make a contribution to reducing hate crime to the extent they are enforced in a non-discriminatory manner and to the extent that they yield convictions where warranted. If they fail on either of these scores, hate crime provisions may in fact be counterproductive, because they will send a message that our opposition to hate crime is purely rhetorical. If hate crime provisions are enacted, they must be carefully monitored to ensure that they are not doing more harm than good.

Second, I fear that the enactment of hate crime legislation may in fact do very little to reduce the level of hate group activity but may let Parliament "off the hook" from taking other potentially more effective measures against hate crime. The enactment of hate crime legislation – whether in the form of Bill C-41 of in the form of U.S.-style intimidation provisions – cannot be the end of the story. The criminal law has only a small role to play in rooting out the underlying causes of group hatred. While it is difficult to know how to combat bigotry, specifically bigotry that culminates in violence, we cannot simply rely on the criminal law to eliminate group hatred. Educational strategies to prevent people from developing bigoted attitudes in the first place have to play a role. Economic measures may also be needed given that economics plays a role in the marginalization and stigmatization of many minority groups and given that hatred of others tends to increase in tough economic times. The passage of hate crimes legislation may provide Parliament with an excuse to avoid undertaking more difficult and more costly measures to combat group hatred, yet may offer the weakest prospect of bringing about significant social change.

Despite these concerns, however, I believe that U.S.-style hate crime provisions are worth enacting. Even if the provisions can make only a modest contribution to the reduction of violence motivated by group hatred, they are at least one part of a broader solution ...

NOTES

1 *Criminal Code*, RSC 1985, c. C-46, ss. 318 and 319. As of July, 1994, only ten charges had been laid under these sections, resulting in seven convictions

and three acquittals for wilful promotion of hatred (*Toronto Star*, July 7, 1994).

2 Bill C-41, *An Act to Amend the Criminal Code (Sentencing) and Other Acts in Consequence Thereof*, 1st Sess., 35th Parl., 1994 [hereinafter *Bill C-41*].

3 *Wisconsin v Mitchell*, 113 SCt 2194 (1993).

4 Bill C-41, *An Act To Amend the Criminal Code (Sentencing) and Other Acts in Consequence Thereof*, 1st Sess., 35 Parl., 1994–1995 (as passed by the House of Commons, June 15, 1995), cl. 178 2(a)(i). Note that this clause was amended after first reading.

5 There are obvious parallels here to male violence against women, particularly to the crime of sexual assault. Like members of minority groups who know they are targets of hate-motivated violence, women know they are potential targets of sexual assault simply because they are women. Many feminists have argued that male violence against women has the effect of curtailing women's activities outside the home because of concerns of personal safety. Of course, a startling degree of violence committed against women actually occurs within the home, or at the hands of persons known to the woman. See "50% of Women Report Assaults: Ground-Breaking Statscan Survey Finds Violence Pervasive," *Globe and Mail* (November 19, 1993), p. A1.

READING QUESTION FOR SHAFFER

1 Shaffer advocates using the criminal law to enforce fundamental moral values. Is this consistent with Mill's "harm principle"?

American Booksellers v Hudnut 771 F.2d 323 (7th Cir. 1985), excerpts

This American case struck down as unconstitutional an ordinance which dealt with pornography as a violation of civil rights.

... Easterbrook, Circuit Judge – Indianapolis enacted an ordinance defining "pornography" as a practice that discriminates against women. "Pornography" is to be redressed through the administrative and judicial methods used for other discrimination. The City's definition of "pornography" is considerably different from "obscenity," which the Supreme Court held is not protected by the First Amendment ...

"Pornography" under the ordinance is "the graphic sexually explicit subordination of women, whether in pictures or in words, that also includes one or more of the following:

(1) Women are presented as sexual objects who enjoy pain or humiliation; or
(2) Women are presented as sexual objects who experience sexual pleasure in being raped; or
(3) Women are presented as sexual objects tied up or cut up or mutilated or bruised or physically hurt, or as dismembered or truncated or fragmented or severed into body parts; or
(4) Women are presented as being penetrated by objects or animals; or
(5) Women are presented in scenarios of degradation, injury, abasement, torture, shown as filthy or inferior, bleeding, bruised, or hurt in a context that makes these conditions sexual; or
(6) Woman are presented as sexual objects for domination, conquest, violation, exploitation, possession, or use, or through postures or positions of servility or submission or display."

Indianapolis Code s. 16–3(q). The statute provides that the "use of men, children, or transsexuals in the place of women in paragraphs (1) through (6) shall also constitute pornography under this section."

The ordinance as passed in April 1984 defined "sexually explicit" to mean actual or simulated intercourse or the uncovered exhibition of the genitals, buttocks or anus. An amendment in June 1984 deleted this provision, leaving the term undefined.

The Indianapolis ordinance does not refer to the prurient interest, to offensiveness, or to the standards of the community. It demands attention to particular depictions, not to the work judged as a whole. It is irrelevant under the ordinance whether the work has literary, artistic, political, or scientific value. The City and many amici point to these omissions as virtues. They maintain that pornography influences attitudes, and the statute is a way to alter the socialization of men and women rather than to vindicate community standards of offensiveness. And as one of the principal drafters of the ordinance has asserted, "if a woman is subjected, why should it matter that the work has other value?" Catharine A. MacKinnon, *Pornography, Civil Rights, and Speech*, 20 Harv.Civ.Rts. – Civ.Lib.L. Rev. 1, 21 (1985).

Civil rights groups and feminists have entered this case as amici on both sides. Those supporting the ordinance say that it will play an important role in reducing the tendency of men to view women as sexual objects, a tendency that leads to both unacceptable attitudes and discrimination in the workplace and violence away from it. Those opposing the ordinance point out that much radical feminist literature is explicit and depicts women in ways forbidden by the ordinance and that the ordinance would reopen old battles. It is unclear how Indianapolis would treat works from James Joyce's *Ulysses* to Homer's *Iliad*; both depict women as submissive objects for conquest and domination.

We do not try to balance the arguments for and against an ordinance such as this. The ordinance discriminates on the ground of the content of the speech. Speech treating women in the approved way – in sexual encounters "premised on equality" (MacKinnon, *supra*, at 22) – is lawful no matter how sexually explicit. Speech treating women in the disapproved way – as submissive in matters sexual or as enjoying humiliation – is unlawful no matter how significant the literary, artistic, or political qualities of the work taken as a whole. The state may not ordain preferred viewpoints in this way. The Constitution forbids the state to declare one perspective right and silence opponents ...

[5] "If there is any fixed star in our constitutional constellation, it is that no official, high or petty, can prescribe what shall be orthodox in politics, nationalism, religion, or other matters of opinion or force citizens to confess by word or act their faith therein." *West Virginia State Board of Education v Barnette*, 319 US 624, 642, 63 SCt 1178, 1187, 87 L.Ed. 1628 (1943). Under the First Amendment the government must leave to the people the evaluation of ideas. Bald or subtle, an idea is as powerful as the audience allows it to be. A belief may be pernicious – the beliefs of Nazis led to the death of millions, those of the Klan to the repression of millions. A pernicious belief may prevail. Totalitarian governments today rule much of the planet, practicing suppression of billions and spreading dogma that may enslave others. One of the things that separates our society from theirs is our absolute right to propagate opinions that the government finds wrong or even hateful ...

Under the ordinance graphic sexually explicit speech is "pornography" or not depending on the perspective the author adopts. Speech that "subordinates" women and also, for example, presents women as enjoying pain, humiliation, or rape, or even simply presents women in "positions of servility or submission or display" is forbidden, no matter how great the literary or political value of the work taken as a whole.

Speech that portrays women in positions of equality is lawful, no matter how graphic the sexual content. This is thought control. It establishes an "approved" view of women, of how they may react to sexual encounters, of how the sexes may relate to each other. Those who espouse the approved view may use sexual images; those who do not, may not.

Indianapolis justifies the ordinance on the ground that pornography affects thoughts. Men who see women depicted as subordinate are more likely to treat them so. Pornography is an aspect of dominance. It does not persuade people so much as change them. It works by socializing, by establishing the expected and the permissible. In this view pornography is not an idea; pornography is the injury.

There is much to this perspective. Beliefs are also facts. People often act in accordance with the images and patterns they find around them. People raised in a religion tend to accept the tenets of that religion, often without independent examination. People taught from birth that black people are fit only for slavery rarely rebelled against that creed; beliefs coupled with the self-interest of the masters established a social structure that inflicted great harm while enduring for centuries. Words and images act at the level of the subconscious before they persuade at the level of the conscious. Even the truth has little chance unless a statement fits within the framework of beliefs that may never have been subjected to rational study.

Therefore we accept the premises of this legislation. Depictions of subordination tend to perpetuate subordination. The subordinate status of women in turn leads to affront and lower pay at work, insult and injury at home, battery and rape on the streets. In the language of the legislature, "[p]ornography is central in creating and maintaining sex as a basis of discrimination. Pornography is a systematic practice of exploitation and subordination based on sex which differentially harms women. The bigotry and contempt it produces, with the acts of aggression it fosters, harm women's opportunities for equality and rights [of all kinds]". Indianapolis Code s. 16–1(a)(2).

Yet this simply demonstrates the power of pornography as speech. All of these unhappy effects depend on mental intermediation. Pornography affects how people see the world, their fellows, and social relations. If pornography is what pornography does, so is other speech. Hitler's orations affected how some Germans saw Jews. Communism is a world view, not simply a *Manifesto* by Marx and Engels or a set of speeches. Efforts to suppress communist speech in the United States were based on the belief that the public acceptability of such ideas would increase the likelihood of totalitarian government. Religions affect socialization in the most pervasive way ...

Many people believe that the existence of television, apart from the content of specific programs, leads to intellectual laziness, to a penchant for violence, to many other ills. The Alien and Sedition Acts passed during the administration of John Adams rested on a sincerely held belief that disrespect for the government leads to social collapse and revolution – a belief with support in the history of many nations. Most governments of the world act on this empirical regularity, suppressing critical speech. In the United States, however, the strength of the support for this belief is irrelevant. Seditious libel is protected speech unless the danger is not only grave but also imminent ...

Sexual responses often are unthinking responses, and the association of sexual arousal with the subordination of women therefore may have a substantial effect. But almost all cultural stimuli provoke unconscious responses ...

Much of Indianapolis's argument rests on the belief that when speech is "unanswerable," and the metaphor that there is a "marketplace of ideas" does not apply, the First Amendment does not apply either. The metaphor is honored; Milton's *Aeropagitica* and John Stuart Mill's *On Liberty* defend freedom of speech on the ground that the truth will prevail, and many of the most important cases under the First Amendment recite this position. The Framers undoubtedly believed it. As a general matter it is true. But the Constitution does not make the dominance of truth a necessary condition of freedom of speech. To say that it does would be to confuse an outcome of free speech with a necessary condition for the application of the amendment.

A power to limit speech on the ground that truth has not yet prevailed and is not likely to prevail implies the power to declare truth. At some point the government must be able to say (as Indianapolis has said): "We know what the truth is, yet a free exchange of speech has not driven out falsity, so that we must now prohibit falsity" ...

At all events, "pornography" is not low value speech within the meaning of these cases. Indianapolis seeks to prohibit certain speech because it believes this speech influences social relations and politics on a grand scale, that it controls attitudes at home and in the legislature. This precludes a characterization of the speech as low value. True, pornography and obscenity have sex in common. But Indianapolis left out of its definition any reference to literary, artistic, political, or scientific value.

The ordinance applies to graphic sexually explicit subordination in words great and small.[1] The Court sometimes balances the value of speech against the costs of its restriction, but it does this by category of speech and not by the content of particular works ...

Any rationale we could imagine in support of this ordinance could not be limited to sex discrimination. Free speech has been on balance an ally of those seeking change. Governments that want stasis start by restricting speech. Culture is a powerful force of continuity; Indianapolis paints pornography as part of the culture of power. Change in any complex system ultimately depends on the ability of outsiders to challenge accepted views and the reigning institutions. Without a strong guarantee of freedom of speech, there is no effective right to challenge what is.

The definition of "pornography" is unconstitutional. No construction or excision of particular terms could save it ...

But the ... Indianapolis ordinance is not neutral with respect to viewpoint. The ban on distribution of works containing coerced performances is limited to pornography; coercion is irrelevant if the work is not "pornography," and we have held the definition of "pornography" to be defective root and branch. A legislature might replace "pornography" in s. 16–3(g)(4) with "any film containing explicit sex" or some similar expression, but even the broadest severability clause does not permit a federal court to rewrite as opposed to excise. Rewriting is work for the legislature of Indianapolis ...

Much speech is dangerous. Chemists whose work might help someone build a bomb, political theorists whose papers might start political movements that lead to riots, speakers whose ideas attract violent protesters, all these and more leave loss in their wake. Unless the remedy is very closely confined, it could be more dangerous to speech than all the libel judgments in history. The constitutional requirements for a valid recovery for assault caused by speech might turn out to be too rigorous for any plaintiff to meet.[2] But the Indianapolis ordinance requires the complainant to show that the attack was "directly caused by specific pornography" (s. 16–3(g)(7)), and it is not beyond the realm of possibility that a state court could construe this limitation in a way that would make the statute constitutional. We are not authorized to prevent the state from trying.

Again, however, the assault statute is tied to "pornography," and we cannot find a sensible way to repair the defect without seizing power that belongs elsewhere. Indianapolis might choose to have no ordinance if it cannot be limited to viewpoint-specific harms, or it might choose to extend the scope to all speech, just as the law of libel applies to all speech. An attempt to repair this ordinance would be nothing but a blind guess.

No amount of struggle with particular words and phrases in this ordinance can leave anything in effect. The district court came to the same conclusion. Its judgment is therefore
Affirmed.

NOTES

1 Indianapolis briefly argues that *Beauharnais v Illinois*, 343 US 250, 72 SCt 725, 96 L.Ed. 919 (1952), which allowed a state to penalize "group libel," supports the ordinance. In *Colin v Smith, supra*, 578 F.2d at 1205, we concluded that cases such as *New York Times v Sullivan* had so washed away the foundations of *Beauharnais* that it could not be considered authoritative. If we are wrong in this, however, the case still does not support the ordinance. It is not clear that depicting women as subordinate in sexually explicit ways, even combined with a depiction of pleasure in rape, would fit within the definition of a group libel. The well received film *Swept Away* used explicit sex, plus taking pleasure in rape, to make a political statement, not to defame. Work must be an insult or slur for its own sake to come within the ambit of *Beauharnais*, and a work need not be scurrilous at all to be "pornography" under the ordinance.

2 See, e.g., *Zamora v CBS*, 480 F.Supp. 199 (S.D.Fla.1979), among the many cases concluding that particular plaintiffs could not show a connection sufficiently direct to permit liability consistent with the First Amendment.

READING QUESTIONS ON HUDNUT

1 Why does Judge Easterbrook put so much weight on the idea that the ordinance is "viewpoint based"? Is it viewpoint based in the sense he suggests?
2 Should speech be protected even when it is harmful? How serious must the harm be to justify censorship?

R v Butler [1992] 1 SCR 452

A decision of the Canadian Supreme Court upholding Canada's obscenity law.

Sopinka, J for the majority: – This appeal calls into question the constitutionality of the obscenity provisions of the *Criminal Code*, RSC, 1985, c. C-46, s. 163. They are attacked on the ground that they contravene s. 2(b) of the *Canadian Charter of Rights and Freedoms*. The case requires the Court to address one of the most difficult and controversial of contemporary issues, that of determining whether, and to what extent, Parliament may legitimately criminalize obscenity. I propose to begin with a review of the facts which gave rise to this appeal, as well of the proceedings in the lower courts.

FACTS AND PROCEEDINGS

In August, 1987, the appellant, Donald Victor Butler, opened the Avenue Video Boutique located in Winnipeg, Manitoba. The shop sells and rents "hard core" videotapes and magazines as well as sexual paraphernalia. Outside the store is a sign which reads:

Avenue Video Boutique; a private members only adult video/visual club.

Notice: if sex oriented material offends you, please do not enter.

No admittance to persons under 18 years.

On August 21, 1987, the City of Winnipeg Police entered the appellant's store with a search warrant and seized all the inventory. The appellant was charged with 173 counts in the first indictment: three counts of selling obscene material contrary to s. 159(2)(a) of the *Criminal Code*, RSC 1970, c. C-34 (now s. 163(2)(a)), 41 counts of possessing obscene material for the purpose of distribution contrary to s. 159(1)(a) (now s. 163(1)(a)) of the *Criminal Code*, 128 counts of possessing obscene material for the purpose of sale contrary to s. 159(2)(a) of the *Criminal Code*, and one count of exposing obscene material to public view contrary to s. 159(2)(a) of the *Criminal Code*.

On October 19, 1987, the appellant re-opened the store at the same location. As a result of a police operation a search warrant was executed on October 29, 1987, resulting in the arrest of an employee, Norma McCord. The appellant was arrested at a later date.

A joint indictment was laid against the appellant doing business as Avenue Video Boutique and Norma McCord. The joint indictment contains 77 counts under s. 159 (now s. 163) of the *Criminal Code*: two counts of selling obscene material contrary to s. 159(2)(a), 73 counts of possessing obscene material for the purpose of distribution contrary to s. 159(1)(a), one count of possessing obscene material for the purpose of sale contrary to s. 159(2)(a), and one count of exposing obscene material to public view contrary to s. 159(2)(a).

The trial judge convicted the appellant on eight counts relating to eight films. Convictions were entered against the co-accused McCord with respect to two counts relating to two of the films. Fines of $1,000 per offence were imposed on the appellant. Acquittals were entered on the remaining charges.

The Crown appealed the 242 acquittals with respect to the appellant, and the appellant cross-appealed the convictions. The majority of the Manitoba Court of Appeal allowed the appeal of the Crown and entered convictions for the appellant with respect to all of the counts ...

RELEVANT LEGISLATION

Criminal Code, RSC, 1985, c. C-46.

163. (1) Everyone commits an offence who,
(a) makes, prints, publishes, distributes, circulates or has in his possession for the purpose of publication, distribution or circulation any obscene written matter, picture, model, phonograph record or other thing whatever; or
(b) makes, prints, publishes, distributes, sells or has in his possession for the purpose of publication, distribution or circulation a crime comic.
(2) Every one commits an offence who knowingly, without lawful justification or excuse,
(a) sells, exposes to public view or has in his possession for such a purpose any obscene written matter, picture, model, phonograph record or other thing whatever;
(b) publicly exhibits a disgusting object or an indecent show;
(c) offers to sell, advertises or publishes an advertisement of, or has for sale or disposal, any means, instructions, medicine, drug or article intended or represented as a method of causing abortion or miscarriage; or
(d) advertises or publishes an advertisement of any means, instructions, medicine, drug or article intended or represented as a method for restoring sexual virility or curing venereal diseases or diseases of the generative organs.
(3) No person shall be convicted of an offence under this section if he establishes that the public good was served by the acts that are alleged to constitute

the offence and that the acts alleged did not extend beyond what served the public good.

(4) For the purposes of this section, it is a question of law whether an act served the public good and whether there is evidence that the act alleged went beyond what served the public good, but it is a question of fact whether the acts did or did not extend beyond what served the public good.

(5) For the purposes of this section, the motives of an accused are irrelevant.

(6) Where an accused is charged with an offence under subsection (1), the fact that the accused was ignorant of the nature or presence of the matter, picture, model, phonograph record, crime comic or other thing by means of or in relation to which the offence was committed is not a defence to the charge.

(7) In this section, "crime comic" means a magazine, periodical or book that exclusively or substantially comprises matter depicting pictorially

(a) the commission of crimes, real or fictitious; or

(b) events connected with the commission of crimes, real or fictitious, whether occurring before of after the commission of the crime.

(8) For the purposes of this Act, any publication a dominant characteristic of which is the undue exploitation of sex, or of sex and any one or more of the following subjects, namely, crime, horror, cruelty and violence, shall be deemed to be obscene.

ISSUES

The following constitutional questions are raised by this appeal:

1. Does s. 163 of the *Criminal Code* of Canada, RSC, 1985, c. C-46, violate s. 2(b) of the *Canadian Charter of Rights and Freedoms*?
2. If s. 163 of the *Criminal Code* of Canada, RSC, 1985, c. C-46, violates s. 2(b) of the *Canadian Charter of Rights and Freedoms,* can s. 163 of the *Criminal Code* of Canada be demonstrably justified under s. 1 of the *Canadian Charter of Rights and Freedoms* as a reasonable limit prescribed by law?

ANALYSIS

... In my view, in the circumstances, this appeal should be confined to the examination of the constitutional validity of s. 163(8) only.

Before proceeding to consider the constitutional questions, it will be helpful to review the legislative history of the provision as well as the

extensive judicial interpretation and analysis which have infused meaning into the bare words of the statute.

Legislative History

The *Criminal Code* did not [in the past] provide a definition of any of the
operative terms, "obscene," "indecent," or "disgusting." The notion of
obscenity embodied in these provisions was based on the test formulated by Cockburn, CJ in *R v Hicklin* (1868), LR 3 QB 360:

> I think the test of obscenity is this, whether the tendency of the matter charged
> as obscenity is to deprave and corrupt those whose minds are open to such
> immoral influences, and into whose hands a publication of this sort may fall.
> (At p. 371)

The focus on the "corruption of morals" in the earlier legislation
grew out of the English obscenity law which made the Court the "guardian of public morals" ...

The current provision, which is the subject of this appeal, entered
into force in 1959 in response to the much criticized former version ...
Unlike the previous statutes, s-s. (8) provided a statutory definition of
"obscene":

> (8) For the purposes of this Act, any publication a dominant characteristic of
> which is the undue exploitation of sex, or of sex and any one or more of the
> following subjects, namely, crime, horror, cruelty and violence, shall be
> deemed to be obscene.

As will be discussed further, the introduction of the statutory definition had the effect of replacing the *Hicklin* test with a series of rules
developed by the courts. The provision must be considered in light of
these tests.

Judicial Interpretation of Section 163(8)

The first case to consider the current provision was *Brodie v The Queen*,
[1962] SCR 681. The majority of this Court found in that case that D.H.
Lawrence's novel, *Lady Chatterley's Lover*, was not obscene within the
meaning of the *Code*. The *Brodie* case lay the groundwork for the interpretation of s. 163(8) by setting out the principal tests which should

govern the determination of what is obscene for the purposes of criminal prosecution. The first step was to discard the *Hicklin* test.

Section 163(8) to be Exclusive Test

In examining the definition provided by s-s. (8), the majority of this Court was of the view that the new provision provided a clean slate and had the effect of bringing in an "objective standard of obscenity" which rendered all the jurisprudence under the *Hicklin* definition obsolete. In the words of Judson, J:

> I think that the new statutory definition does give the Court an opportunity to apply tests which have some certainty of meaning and are capable of objective application and which do not so much depend as before upon the idiosyncrasies and sensitivities of the tribunal of fact, whether judge or jury. We are now concerned with a Canadian statute which is exclusive of all others. [At p. 702]

...

Tests of "Undue Exploitation of Sex"

In order for the work or material to qualify as "obscene," the exploitation of sex must not only be its dominant characteristic, but such exploitation must be "undue." In determining when the exploitation of sex will be considered "undue," the courts have attempted to formulate workable tests. The most important of these is the "community standard of tolerance" test.

"Community Standard of Tolerance" Test
In *Brodie*, Judson, J accepted the view espoused notably by the Australian and New Zealand courts that obscenity is to be measured against "community standards." He cited the following passage in the judgment of Fullager, J in *R v Close*, [1948] VLR 445:

> There does exist in any community at all times – however the standard may vary from time to time – a general instinctive sense of what is decent and what is indecent, of what is clean and what is dirty, and when the distinction has to be drawn, I do not know that today there is any better tribunal than a jury to draw it ... I am very far from attempting to lay down a model direction, but a judge might perhaps, in the case of a novel, say something like this: "It would

not be true to say that any publication dealing with sexual relations is obscene. The relations of the sexes are, of course, legitimate matters for discussion everywhere ... There are certain standards of decency which prevail in the community, and you are really called upon to try this case because you are regarded as representing, and capable of justly applying, those standards. What is obscene is something which offends against those standards."
[At pp. 705–6]

The community standards test has been the subject of extensive judicial analysis. It is the standards of the community as a whole which must be considered and not the standards of a small segment of that community such as the university community where a film was shown ... The standard to be applied is a national one ... With respect to expert evidence, it is not necessary and is not a fact which the Crown is obliged to prove as part of its case ... In *R v Dominion News & Gifts* (1962) Ltd, [1963] 2 CCC 103 (Man. CA), Freedman, JA (dissenting) emphasized that the community standards test must necessarily respond to changing mores:

Community standards must be contemporary. Times change, and ideas change with them. Compared to the Victorian era this is a liberal age in which we live. One manifestation of it is the relative freedom with which the whole question of sex is discussed. In books, magazines, movies, television, and sometimes even in parlour conversation, various aspects of sex are made the subject of comment, with a candour that in an earlier day would have been regarded as indecent and intolerable. We cannot and should not ignore these present-day attitudes when we face the question whether [the subject materials] are obscene according to our criminal law. [At pp. 116–17]

Our Court was called upon to elaborate the community standards test in *Towne Cinema Theatres Ltd v The Queen*, [1985] 1 SCR 494. Dickson, CJ reviewed the case law and found:

The cases all emphasize that it is a standard of *tolerance*, not taste, that is relevant. What matters is not what Canadians think is right for themselves to see. What matters is what Canadians would not abide other Canadians seeing because it would be beyond the contemporary Canadian standard of tolerance to allow them to see it. Since the standard is tolerance, I think the audience to which the allegedly obscene material is targeted must be relevant. The operative standards are those of the Canadian community as a whole, but since what matters is what other people may see, it is quite conceivable that the Canadian community would tolerate varying degrees of explicitness depending upon the audience and the circumstances. [Emphasis in original; at pp. 508–9]

Therefore, the community standards test is concerned not with what Canadians would not tolerate being exposed to themselves, but what they would not tolerate other Canadians being exposed to. The minority view was that the tolerance level will vary depending on the manner, time, and place in which the material is presented as well as the audience to whom it is directed. The majority opinion on this point was expressed by Wilson J in the following passage:

It is not, in my opinion, open to the courts under s. 159(8) of the *Criminal Code* to characterize a movie as obscene if shown to one constituency but not if shown to another ... In my view, a movie is either obscene under the *Code* based on a national community standard of tolerance or it is not. If it is not, it may still be the subject of provincial regulatory control. [At p. 521]

"Degradation or Dehumanization" Test
There has been a growing recognition in recent cases that material which may be said to exploit sex in a "degrading or dehumanizing" manner will necessarily fail the community standards test ...

Among other things, degrading or dehumanizing materials place women (and sometimes men) in positions of subordination, servile submission, or humiliation. They run against the principles of equality and dignity of all human beings. In the appreciation of whether material is degrading or dehumanizing, the appearance of consent is not necessarily determinative. Consent cannot save materials that otherwise contain degrading or dehumanizing scenes. Sometimes the very appearance of consent makes the depicted acts even more degrading or dehumanizing.

This type of material would, apparently, fail the community standards test not because it offends against morals but because it is perceived by public opinion to be harmful to society, particularly to women. While the accuracy of this perception is not susceptible of exact proof, there is a substantial body of opinion that holds that the portrayal of persons being subjected to degrading or dehumanizing sexual treatment results in harm, particularly to women and therefore to society as a whole ... It would be reasonable to conclude that there is an appreciable risk of harm to society in the portrayal of such material. The effect of the evidence on public opinion was summed up by Wilson, J in *Towne Cinema, supra,* as follows:

The most that can be said, I think, is that the public has concluded that exposure to material which degrades the human dimensions of life to a subhuman or merely physical dimension and thereby contributes to a process of moral desensitization must be harmful in some way. [At p. 524]

In *Towne Cinema*, Dickson, CJ considered the "degradation" or "dehumanization" test to be the principal indicator of "undueness" without specifying what role the community tolerance test plays in respect of this issue. He did observe, however, that the community might tolerate some forms of exploitation that caused harm that was nevertheless undue. The relevant passages appear at p. 505:

There are other ways in which exploitation of sex might be "undue." Ours is not a perfect society and it is unfortunate but true that the community may tolerate publications that cause harm to members of society and therefore to society as a whole. Even if, at certain times, there is a coincidence between what is not tolerated and what is harmful to society, there is no necessary connection between these two concepts. Thus, a legal definition of "undue" must also encompass publications harmful to members of society and, therefore, to society as a whole.

Sex related publications which portray persons in a degrading manner as objects of violence, cruelty or other forms of dehumanizing treatment, may be "undue" for the purpose of s. 159(8). No one should be subject to the degradation and humiliation inherent in publications which link sex with violence, cruelty, and other forms of dehumanizing treatment. It is not likely that at a given moment in a society's history, such publications will be tolerated ...

However, as I have noted above, there is no *necessary* coincidence between the undueness of publications which degrade people by linking violence, cruelty or other forms of dehumanizing treatment with sex, and the community standard of tolerance. Even if certain sex related materials were found to be within the standard of tolerance of the community, it would still be necessary to ensure that they were not "undue" in some other sense, for example, in the sense that they portray persons in a degrading manner as objects of violence, cruelty, or other forms of dehumanizing treatment. [Emphasis in original]

In the reasons of Wilson, J concurring in the result, the line between the mere portrayal of sex and the dehumanization of people is drawn by the "undueness" concept. The community is the arbiter as to what is harmful to it. She states:

As I see it, the essential difficulty with the definition of obscenity is that "undueness" must presumably be assessed in relation to consequences. It is implicit in the definition that at some point the exploitation of sex becomes harmful to the public or at least the public believes that to be so. It is therefore necessary for the protection of the public to put limits on the degree of exploitation and, through the application of the community standard test, the public is made the arbiter of what is harmful to it and what is not. The problem is that we know so little of the consequences we are seeking to avoid. Do obscene movies spawn immoral conduct? Do they degrade women? Do they promote violence? The most that can be said, I think, is that the public has concluded that exposure to material which degrades the human dimensions of life to a subhuman or merely physical dimension and thereby contributes to a process of moral desensitization must be harmful in some way. It must therefore be controlled when it gets out of hand, when it becomes "undue." [At p. 524]

"Internal Necessities Test" or "Artistic Defence"
In determining whether the exploitation of sex is "undue," Judson, J set out the test of "internal necessities" in *Brodie, supra*:

What I think is aimed at is excessive emphasis on the theme for a base purpose. But I do not think that there is undue exploitation if there is no more emphasis on the theme than is required in the serious treatment of the theme of a novel with honesty and uprightness. That the work under attack is a serious work of fiction is to me beyond question. It has none of the characteristics that are often described in judgments dealing with obscenity – dirt for dirt's sake, the leer of the sensualist, depravity in the mind of an author with an obsession for dirt, pornography, an appeal to a prurient interest, etc. The section recognizes that the serious-minded author must have freedom in the production of a work of genuine artistic and literary merit and the quality of the work, as the witnesses point out and common sense indicates, must have real relevance in determining not only a dominant characteristic but also whether there is undue exploitation. [At pp. 704–5]

As counsel for the Crown pointed out in his oral submissions, the artistic defence is the last step in the analysis of whether the exploitation of sex is undue. Even material which by itself offends community standards will not be considered "undue," if it is required for the serious treatment of a theme ...

Accordingly, the "internal necessities" test, or what has been referred to as the "artistic defence," has been interpreted to assess whether the exploitation of sex has a justifiable role in advancing the plot or the theme, and in considering the work as a whole, does not merely represent "dirt for dirt's sake" but has a legitimate role when measured by the internal necessities of the work itself.

The Relationship of the Tests to Each Other

This review of jurisprudence shows that it fails to specify the relationship of the tests one to another. Failure to do so with respect to the community standards test and the degrading or dehumanizing test, for example, raises a serious question as to the basis on which the community acts in determining whether the impugned material will be tolerated. With both these tests being applied to the same material and apparently independently, we do not know whether the community found the material to be intolerable because it was degrading or dehumanizing, because it offended against morals or on some other basis. In some circumstances a finding that the material is tolerable can be overruled by the conclusion by the court that it causes harm and is therefore undue. Moreover, is the internal necessities test dominant so that it will redeem material that would otherwise be undue or is it just one factor? Is this test applied by the community or is it determined by the court without regard for the community? This hiatus in the jurisprudence has left the legislation open to attack on the ground of vagueness and uncertainty. That attack is made in this case. This lacuna in the interpretation of the legislation must, if possible, be filled before subjecting the legislation to *Charter* scrutiny. The necessity to do so was foreseen by Wilson, J in *Towne Cinema* when she stated:

The test of the community standard is helpful to the extent that it provides a norm against which impugned material may be assessed but it does little to elucidate the underlying question as to why some exploitation of sex falls on the permitted side of the line under s. 159(8) and some on the prohibited side. No doubt this question will have to be addressed when the validity of the obscenity provisions of the *Code* is subjected to attack as an infringement on freedom of speech and the infringement is sought to be justified as reasonable. [At p. 525]

Pornography can be usefully divided into three categories: (1) explicit sex with violence, (2) explicit sex without violence but which subjects people to treatment that is degrading or dehumanizing, and (3) explicit sex without violence that is neither degrading nor dehumanizing. Violence in this context includes both actual physical violence and threats of physical violence. Relating these three categories to the terms of s. 163(8) of the *Code*, the first, explicit sex coupled with violence, is expressly mentioned. Sex coupled with crime, horror, or cruelty will sometimes involve violence. Cruelty, for instance, will usually do so. But, even in the absence of violence, sex coupled with crime, horror, or cruelty may fall within the second category. As for category (3), subject to the exception referred to below, it is not covered.

Some segments of society would consider that all three categories of pornography cause harm to society because they tend to undermine its moral fibre. Others would contend that none of the categories cause harm. Furthermore, there is a range of opinion as to what is degrading or dehumanizing ... Because this is not a matter that is susceptible of proof in the traditional way and because we do not wish to leave it to the individual tastes of judges, we must have a norm that will serve as an arbiter in determining what amounts to an undue exploitation of sex. That arbiter is the community as a whole.

The courts must determine as best they can what the community would tolerate others being exposed to on the basis of the degree of harm that may flow from such exposure. Harm in this context means that it predisposes persons to act in an anti-social manner as, for example, the physical or mental mistreatment of women by men, or, what is perhaps debatable, the reverse. Anti-social conduct for this purpose is conduct which society formally recognizes as incompatible with its proper functioning. The stronger the inference of a risk of harm the lesser the likelihood of tolerance. The inference may be drawn from the material itself or from the material and other evidence. Similarly evidence as to the community standards is desirable but not essential.

In making this determination with respect to the three categories of pornography referred to above, the portrayal of sex coupled with violence will almost always constitute the undue exploitation of sex. Explicit sex which is degrading or dehumanizing may be undue if the risk of harm is substantial. Finally, explicit sex that is not violent and neither degrading nor dehumanizing is generally tolerated in our society and will not qualify as the undue exploitation of sex unless it employs children in its production.

If material is not obscene under this framework, it does not become so by reason of the person to whom it is or may be shown or exposed nor by reason of the place or manner in which it is shown. The availability of sexually explicit materials in theatres and other public places is subject to regulation by competent provincial legislation. Typically such legislation imposes restrictions on the material available to children ...

The foregoing deals with the inter-relationship of the "community standards test" and "the degrading or dehumanizing" test. How does the "internal necessities" test fit into this scheme? The need to apply this test only arises if a work contains sexually explicit material that by itself would constitute the undue exploitation of sex. The portrayal of sex must then be viewed in context to determine whether that is the dominant theme of the work as a whole. Put another way, is undue exploitation of sex the main object of the work or is this portrayal of sex essential to a wider artistic, literary, or other similar purpose? Since the threshold determination must be made on the basis of community standards, that is, whether the sexually explicit aspect is undue, its impact when considered in context must be determined on the same basis. The court must determine whether the sexually explicit material when viewed in the context of the whole work would be tolerated by the community as a whole. Artistic expression rests at the heart of freedom of expression values and any doubt in this regard must be resolved in favour of freedom of expression.

Does Section 163 Violate Section 2(b) of the Charter?

The majority of the Court of Appeal in this case allowed the appeal of the Crown on the ground that s. 163 does not violate freedom of expression as guaranteed under s. 2(b) of the *Charter* ... [However] [t]he form of activity in this case is the medium through which the meaning sought to be conveyed is expressed, namely, the film, magazine, written matter, or sexual gadget. There is nothing inherently violent in the vehicle of expression, and it accordingly does not fall outside the protected sphere of activity.

In light of our recent decision in *R v Keegstra*, [1990] 3 SCR 697, the respondent, and most of the parties intervening in support of the respondent, do not take issue with the proposition that s. 163 of the *Criminal Code* violates s. 2(b) of the *Charter*. In *Keegstra*, we were unanimous in advocating a generous approach to the protection afforded by s. 2(b) of the *Charter*. Our Court confirmed the view ... that activities cannot be excluded from the scope of the guaranteed freedom on the basis of the content or meaning being conveyed ...

With respect, the majority of the Court of Appeal did not sufficiently distance itself from the content of the materials ...

Meaning sought to be expressed need not be "redeeming" in the eyes of the Court to merit the protection of s. 2(b) whose purpose is to ensure that thoughts and feelings may be conveyed freely in non-violent ways without fear of censure.

In this case, both the purpose and effect of s. 163 is specifically to restrict the communication of certain types of materials based on their content. In my view, there is no doubt that s. 163 seeks to prohibit certain types of expressive activity and thereby infringes s. 2(b) of the *Charter* ...

I would conclude that the first constitutional question should be answered in the affirmative.

Is Section 163 Justified under Section 1 of the Charter?

Is Section 163 a Limit Prescribed by Law?

The appellant argues that the provision is so vague that it is impossible to apply it. Vagueness must be considered in relation to two issues in this appeal: (1) is the law so vague that it does not qualify as "a limit prescribed by law"; and (2) is it so imprecise that it is not a reasonable limit ...

In assessing whether s. 163(8) prescribes an intelligible standard, consideration must be given to the manner in which the provision has been judicially interpreted ...

The fact that a particular legislative term is open to varying interpretations by the courts is not fatal. ... Therefore the question at hand is whether the impugned sections of the *Criminal Code* can be or have been given sensible meanings by the courts ...

Standards which escape precise technical definition, such as "undue," are an inevitable part of the law. The *Criminal Code* contains other such standards. Without commenting on their constitutional validity, I note that the terms "indecent," "immoral," or "scurrilous," found in ss. 167, 168, 173, and 175, are nowhere defined in the *Code*. It is within the role of the judiciary to attempt to interpret these terms. If such interpretation yields an intelligible standard, the threshold test for the application of s. 1 is met. In my opinion, the interpretation of s. 163(8) in prior judgements which I have reviewed, as supplemented by these reasons, provides an intelligible standard.

Objective

The respondent argues that there are several pressing and substantial objectives which justify overriding the freedom to distribute obscene materials. Essentially, these objectives are the avoidance of harm resulting from antisocial attitudinal changes that exposure to obscene material causes and the public interest in maintaining a "decent society." On the other hand, the appellant argues that the objective of s. 163 is to have the state act as "moral custodian" in sexual matters and to impose subjective standards of morality.

The obscenity legislation and jurisprudence prior to the enactment of s. 163 were evidently concerned with prohibiting the "immoral influences" of obscene publications and safeguarding the morals of individuals into whose hands such works could fall. The *Hicklin* philosophy posits that explicit sexual depictions, particularly outside the sanctioned contexts of marriage and procreation, threatened the morals or the fabric of society ... In this sense, its dominant, if not exclusive, purpose was to advance a particular conception of morality. Any deviation from such morality was considered to be inherently undesirable, independently of any harm to society ... [T]his particular objective is no longer defensible in view of the *Charter*. To impose a certain standard of public and sexual morality, solely because it reflects the conventions of a given community, is inimical to the exercise and enjoyment of individual freedoms, which form the basis of our social contract. D. Dyzenhaus, "Obscenity and the Charter: Autonomy and Equality" (1991), 1 CR (4th) 367, at p. 370, refers to this as "legal moralism," of a majority deciding what values should inform individual lives and then coercively imposing those values on minorities. The prevention of "dirt for dirt's sake" is not a legitimate objective which would justify the violation of one of the most fundamental freedoms enshrined in the *Charter*.

On the other hand, I cannot agree with the suggestion of the appellant that Parliament does not have the right to legislate on the basis of some fundamental conception of morality for the purposes of safeguarding the values which are integral to a free and democratic society. As Dyzenhaus, *supra*, writes:

Moral disapprobation is recognized as an appropriate response when it has its basis in *Charter* values. (At p. 376)

As the respondent and many of the interveners have pointed out, much of the criminal law is based on moral conceptions of right and wrong and the mere fact that a law is grounded in morality does not automatically render it illegitimate. In this regard, criminalizing the proliferation of materials which undermine another basic *Charter* right may indeed be a legitimate objective.

In my view, however, the overriding objective of s. 163 is not moral disapprobation but the avoidance of harm to society. In *Towne Cinema*, Dickson, CJ stated:

It is harm to society from undue exploitation that is aimed at by the section, not simply lapses in propriety or good taste. (At p. 507)

The harm was described in the following way in the *Report on Pornography by the Standing Committee on Justice and Legal Affairs* (MacGuigan Report) (1978):

The clear and unquestionable danger of this type of material is that it reinforces some unhealthy tendencies in Canadian society. The effect of this type of material is to reinforce male-female stereotypes to the detriment of both sexes. It attempts to make degradation, humiliation, victimization, and violence in human relationships appear normal and acceptable. A society which holds that egalitarianism, non-violence, consensualism, and mutuality are basic to any human interaction, whether sexual or other, is clearly justified in controlling and prohibiting any medium of depiction, description or advocacy which violates these principles.

The appellant argues that to accept the objective of the provision as being related to the harm associated with obscenity would be to adopt the "shifting purpose" doctrine explicitly rejected in *R v Big M Drug Mart Ltd*, [1985] 1 SCR 295. This Court concluded in that case that a finding that the *Lord's Day Act* has a secular purpose was not possible given that its religious purpose, in compelling sabbatical observance, has been long-established and consistently maintained by the courts. The appellant relies on the words of Dickson, J (as he then was):

... the theory of a shifting purpose stands in stark contrast to fundamental notions developed in our law concerning the nature of "Parliamentary intention." Purpose is a function of the intent of those who drafted and enacted the legislation at the time, and not of any shifting variable.

While the effect of such legislation as the *Lord's Day Act* may be more secular today than it was in 1677 or in 1906, such a finding cannot justify a conclusion that its purpose has similarly changed. In result, therefore, the *Lord's Day Act* must be characterized as it has always been, a law the primary purpose of which is the compulsion of sabbatical observance. [At pp. 335–6]

I do not agree that to identify the objective of the impugned legislation as the prevention of harm to society, one must resort to the "shifting purpose" doctrine. First, the notions of moral corruption and harm to society are not distinct, as the appellant suggests, but are inextricably linked. It is moral corruption of a certain kind which leads to the detrimental effect on society. Second, and more importantly, I am of the view that with the enactment of s. 163, Parliament explicitly sought to address the harms which are linked to certain types of obscene materials. The prohibition of such materials was based on a belief that they had a detrimental impact on individuals exposed to them and consequently on society as a whole. Our understanding of the harms caused by these materials has developed considerably since that time; however, this does not detract from the fact that the purpose of this legislation remains, as it was in 1959, the protection of society from harms caused by the exposure to obscene materials ...

It is the harm to society resulting from the undue exploitation of such matters which is aimed at by the section. The "harm" conceived by Parliament in 1959 may not have been expressed in the same words as one would today. The court is not limited to a 1959 perspective in the determination of this matter ...

A permissible shift in emphasis was built into the legislation when, as interpreted by the courts, it adopted the community standards test. Community standards as to what is harmful have changed since 1959.

This being the objective, is it pressing and substantial? Does the prevention of the harm associated with the dissemination of certain obscene materials constitute a sufficiently pressing and substantial concern to warrant a restriction on the freedom of expression? In this regard, it should be recalled that in *Keegstra, supra*, this Court unanimously accepted that the prevention of the influence of hate propaganda on society at large was a legitimate objective ...

This Court has thus recognized that the harm caused by the proliferation of materials which seriously offend the values fundamental to our society is a substantial concern which justifies restricting the otherwise full exercise of the freedom of expression. In my view, the harm sought to be avoided in the case of the dissemination of obscene materials is similar ... [I]f true equality between male and female persons is to be achieved, we cannot ignore the threat to equality resulting from exposure to audiences of certain types of violent and degrading material. Materials portraying women as a class as objects for sexual exploitation and abuse have a negative impact on "the individual's sense of self-worth and acceptance."

In reaching the conclusion that legislation proscribing obscenity is a valid objective which justifies some encroachment of the right to freedom of expression, I am persuaded in part that such legislation may be found in most free and democratic societies.

The advent of the *Charter* did not have the effect of dramatically depriving Parliament of a power which it has historically enjoyed ...

Finally, it should be noted that the burgeoning pornography industry renders the concern even more pressing and substantial than when the impugned provisions were first enacted. I would therefore conclude that the objective of avoiding the harm associated with the dissemination of pornography in this case is sufficiently pressing and substantial to warrant some restriction on full exercise of the right to freedom of expression. The analysis of whether the measure is proportional to the objective must, in my view, be undertaken in light of the conclusion that the objective of the impugned section is valid only insofar as it relates to the harm to society associated with obscene materials. Indeed, the section as interpreted in previous decisions and in these reasons is fully consistent with that objective. The objective of maintaining conventional standards of propriety, independently of any harm to society, is no longer justified in light of the values of individual liberty which underlie the *Charter*. This, then, being the objective of s. 163, which I have found to be pressing and substantial, I must now determine whether the section is rationally connected and proportional to this objective. As outlined above, s. 163(8) criminalizes the exploitation of sex and sex and violence, when, on the basis of the community test, it is undue. The determination of when such exploitation is undue is directly related to the immediacy of a risk of harm to society which is reasonably perceived as arising from its dissemination.

Proportionality

General
The proportionality requirement has three aspects:

1. the existence of a rational connection between the impugned measures and the objective;
2. minimal impairment of the right or freedom; and

3. a proper balance between the effects of the limiting measures and the legislative objective.

In assessing whether the proportionality test is met, it is important to keep in mind the nature of expression which has been infringed ...

The values which underlie the protection of freedom of expression relate to the search for truth, participation in the political process, and individual self-fulfilment. The Attorney General for Ontario argues that of these, only "individual self-fulfilment," and only in its most base aspect, that of physical arousal, is engaged by pornography. On the other hand, the civil liberties groups argue that pornography forces us to question conventional notions of sexuality and thereby launches us into an inherently political discourse. In their factum, the *BC Civil Liberties Association* adopts a passage from R. West, "The Feminist-Conservative Anti-Pornography Alliance and the 1986 Attorney General's Commission on Pornography Report" (1987), 4 *American Bar Foundation Research Journal* 681, at p. 696:

Good pornography has value because it validates women's will to pleasure. It celebrates female nature. It validates a range of female sexuality that is wider and truer than that legitimated by the non-pornographic culture. Pornography when it is good celebrates both female pleasure and male rationality.

A proper application of the test should not suppress what West refers to as "good pornography." The objective of the impugned provision is not to inhibit the celebration of human sexuality. However, it cannot be ignored that the realities of the pornography industry are far from the picture which the *BC Civil Liberties Association* would have us paint ...

In my view, the kind of expression which is sought to be advanced does not stand on equal footing with other kinds of expression which directly engage the "core" of the freedom of expression values.

This conclusion is further buttressed by the fact that the targeted material is expression which is motivated, in the overwhelming majority of cases, by economic profit ...

I will now turn to an examination of the three basic aspects of the proportionality test.

Rational Connection

The message of obscenity which degrades and dehumanizes is analogous to that of hate propaganda. As the Attorney General of Ontario has argued in its factum, obscenity wields the power to wreak social damage in that a significant portion of the population is humiliated by its gross misrepresentations ...

Accordingly, the rational link between s. 163 and the objective of Parliament relates to the actual causal relationship between obscenity and the risk of harm to society at large. On this point, it is clear that the literature of the social sciences remains subject to controversy ...

While a direct link between obscenity and harm to society may be difficult, if not impossible, to establish, it is reasonable to presume that exposure to images bears a causal relationship to changes in attitudes and beliefs ...

I am in agreement with ... the view that Parliament was entitled to have a "reasoned apprehension of harm" resulting from the desensitization of individuals exposed to materials which depict violence, cruelty, and dehumanization in sexual relations.

Accordingly, I am of the view that there is a sufficiently rational link between the criminal sanction, which demonstrates our community's disapproval of the dissemination of materials which potentially victimize women and which restricts the negative influence which such materials have on changes in attitudes and behaviour, and the objective.

Finally, I wish to distinguish this case from *Keegstra*, in which the minority adopted the view that there was no rational connection between the criminalization of hate propaganda and its suppression. As McLachlin, J noted, prosecutions under the *Criminal Code* for racist expression have attracted extensive media coverage. The criminal process confers on the accused publicity for his or her causes and succeeds even in generating sympathy. The same cannot be said of the kinds of expression sought to be suppressed in the present case. The general availability of the subject materials and the rampant pornography industry are such that, in the words of Dickson, CJ in *Keegstra*, "pornography is not dignified by its suppression." In contrast to the hate-monger who may succeed, by the sudden media attention, in gaining an audience, the prohibition of obscene materials does nothing to promote the pornographer's cause.

Minimal Impairment

In determining whether less intrusive legislation may be imagined ... it is not necessary that the legislative scheme be the "perfect" scheme, but that it be appropriately tailored in the context of the infringed right ...

There are several factors which contribute to the finding that the provision minimally impairs the freedom which is infringed.

First, the impugned provision does not proscribe sexually explicit erotica without violence that is not degrading or dehumanizing. It is designed to catch material that creates a risk of harm to society. It might be suggested that proof of actual harm should be required. It is apparent from what I have said above that it is sufficient in this regard for Parliament to have a reasonable basis for concluding that harm will result and this requirement does not demand actual proof of harm.

Second, materials which have scientific, artistic, or literary merit are not captured by the provision. As discussed above, the court must be generous in its application of the "artistic defence." For example, in certain cases, materials such as photographs, prints, books, and films which may undoubtedly be produced with some motive for economic profit, may nonetheless claim the protection of the *Charter* insofar as their defining characteristic is that of aesthetic expression, and thus represent the artist's attempt at individual fulfilment. The existence of an accompanying economic motive does not, of itself, deprive a work of significance as an example of individual artistic or self-fulfilment.

Third, in considering whether the provision minimally impairs the freedom in question, it is legitimate for the court to take into account Parliament's past abortive attempts to replace the definition with one that is more explicit ... The attempt to provide exhaustive instances of obscenity has been shown to be destined to fail ... It seems that the only practicable alternative is to strive towards a more abstract definition of obscenity which is contextually sensitive and responsive to progress in the knowledge and understanding of the phenomenon to which the legislation is directed. In my view, the standard of "undue exploitation" is therefore appropriate. The intractable nature of the problem and the impossibility of precisely defining a notion which is inherently elusive makes the possibility of a more explicit provision remote. In this light, it is appropriate to question whether, and at what cost, greater legislative precision can be demanded.

Fourth, while the discussion in this appeal has been limited to the definition portion of s. 163, I would note that the impugned section, with the possible exception of s-s. 1 which is not in issue here, has been held by this Court not to extend its reach to the private use or viewing of obscene materials ...

Accordingly, it is only the public distribution and exhibition of obscene materials which is in issue here.

Finally, I wish to address the arguments of the interveners, *Canadian Civil Liberties Association* and *Manitoba Association for Rights and Liberties*, that the objectives of this kind of legislation may be met by alternative, less intrusive measures. First, it is submitted that reasonable time, manner, and place restrictions would be preferable to outright prohibition. I am of the view that this argument should be rejected. Once it has been established that the objective is the avoidance of harm caused by the degradation which many women feel as "victims" of the message of obscenity, and of the negative impact exposure to such material has on perceptions and attitudes towards women, it is untenable to argue that these harms could be avoided by placing restrictions on access to such material. Making the materials more difficult to obtain by increasing their cost and reducing their availability does not achieve the same objective. Once Parliament has reasonably concluded that certain acts are harmful to certain groups in society and to society in general, it would be inconsistent, if not hypocritical, to argue that such acts could be committed in more restrictive conditions. The harm sought to be avoided would remain the same in either case.

It is also submitted that there are more effective techniques to promote the objectives of Parliament. For example, if pornography is seen as encouraging violence against women, there are certain activities which discourage it – counselling rape victims to charge their assailants, provision of shelter and assistance for battered women, campaigns for laws against discrimination on the grounds of sex, education to increase the sensitivity of law enforcement agencies and other governmental authorities. In addition, it is submitted that education is an under-used response.

It is noteworthy that many of the above-suggested alternatives are in the form of responses to the harm engendered by negative attitudes against women. The role of the impugned provision is to control the dissemination of the very images that contribute to such attitudes. Moreover, it is true that there are additional measures which could alleviate the problem of violence against women. However, given the gravity of the harm, and the threat to the values at stake, I do not believe that the measure chosen by Parliament is equalled by the alternatives which have been suggested. Education, too, may offer a means of combating negative attitudes to women, just as it is currently used as a means of addressing other problems dealt with in the *Code*. However, there is no reason to rely on education alone. It should be emphasized that this is in no way intended to deny the value of other educational and counselling measures to deal with the roots and effects of negative attitudes. Rather, it is only to stress the arbitrariness and unacceptability of the claim that such measures represent the sole legitimate means of addressing the phenomenon. Serious social problems such as violence against women require multi-pronged approaches by government. Education and legislation are not alternatives but complements in addressing such problems. There is nothing in the *Charter* which requires Parliament to choose between such complementary measures.

Balance between Effects of Limiting Measures and Legislative Objective

The final question to be answered in the proportionality test is whether the effects of the law so severely trench on a protected right that the legislative objective is outweighed by the infringement. The infringement on freedom of expression is confined to a measure designed to prohibit the distribution of sexually explicit materials accompanied by violence, and those without violence that are degrading or dehumanizing. As I have already concluded, this kind of expression lies far from the core of the guarantee of freedom on expression. It appeals only to the most base aspect of individual fulfilment, and it is primarily economically motivated.

The objective of the legislation, on the other hand, is of fundamental importance in a free and democratic society. It is aimed at avoiding harm, which Parliament has reasonably concluded will be caused directly or indirectly, to individuals, groups such as women and children, and consequently to society as a whole, by the distribution of these materials. It thus seeks to enhance respect for all members of society, and non-violence and equality in their relations with each other. I therefore conclude that the restriction on freedom of expression does not outweigh the importance of the legislative objective.

CONCLUSION

I conclude that while s. 163(8) infringes s. 2(b) of the *Charter*, freedom of expression, it constitutes a reasonable limit and is saved by virtue of the provisions of s. 1. The trial judge convicted the appellant only with respect to materials which contained scenes involving violence or cruelty intermingled with sexual activity or depicted lack of consent to sexual contact or otherwise could be said to dehumanize men or women in a sexual context. The majority of the Court of Appeal, on the other hand, convicted the appellant on all charges.

While the trial judge concluded that the material for which the accused were acquitted was not degrading or dehumanizing, he did so in the context of s. 1 of the *Charter*. In effect, he asked himself whether, if the material was proscribed by s. 163(8), that section would still be supportable under s. 1. In this context, he considered the government objectives of s. 163(8) and measured the material which was the subject of the charges against this objective. The findings at trial were therefore made in a legal framework that is different from that outlined in these reasons. Specifically, in considering whether the materials were degrading or dehumanizing, he did not address the issue of harm. Accordingly, it would be speculation to conclude that the same result would have been obtained if the definition of obscenity contained in these reasons had been applied. The test applied by the majority of the Court of Appeal also differed significantly from these reasons. I therefore cannot accept their conclusion that all of the materials are obscene. Accordingly, I would allow the appeal and direct a new trial on all charges. I note, however, that I am in agreement with Wright, J's conclusion that, in the case of material found to be obscene, there should only be one conviction imposed with respect to a single tape.

I would answer the constitutional questions as follows:

Question 1: Does s. 163 of the *Criminal Code* of Canada, RSC, 1985, c. C-46, violate s. 2(b) of the *Canadian Charter of Rights and Freedoms*?
Answer: Yes.
Question 2: If s. 163 of the *Criminal Code* of Canada, RSC, 1985, c. C-46, violates s. 2(b) of the *Canadian Charter of Rights and Freedoms*, can s. 163 of the *Criminal Code of Canada* be demonstrably justified under s. 1 of the *Canadian Charter of Rights and Freedoms* as a reasonable limit prescribed by law?
Answer: Yes.

READING QUESTION ON BUTLER

1 MacKinnon, as you will see below, approves of this decision. Is there a covert legal moralism of the kind Devlin advocates in Sopinka, J's reasoning?

Catharine MacKinnon
Only Words (1993)

MacKinnon defends the court's approach in *Butler* against the approach taken in *Hudnut*.

The pornography issue, far more than the political speech cases, has provided the setting for the definitive development of the absolutist approach to speech. First Amendment absolutism did not begin in obscenity cases, but it is in explaining why obscenity should be protected speech, and how it cannot be distinguished from art and literature, that much of the work of absolutism has been done, taking as its point of departure and arrival the position that whatever is expressive should be constitutionally protected. In pornography, absolutism found, gained, and consolidated its ground and hit its emotional nerve. It began as a dissenting position of intellectual extremists and ended by reducing the regulation of obscenity to window dressing on violence against women.

Concretely, observe that it was the prospect of losing access to pornography that impelled the social and legal development of absolutism as a bottom line for the First Amendment, as well as occasioned bursts of passionate eloquence on behalf of speech per se; if we can't have this, they seem to say, what can we have? During the same twenty-year period of struggle over obscenity standards, the Court was watching more and more pornography as its mass-marketed forms became more and more intrusive and aggressive. Observing this process from its end point of state protection of pornography, I have come to think that the main principle at work here is that, once pornography becomes pervasive, speech *will* be defined so that men can have their pornography. American obscenity law merely illustrates one adaptation of this principle: some men ineffectually prohibit it while others vaunt it openly as the standard for speech as such.

Consider the picture. The law against pornography was not designed to see harm to women in the first place. It is further weakened as pornography spreads, expanding into new markets (such as video and computers) and more legitimate forums and making abuse of women more and more invisible as abuse, as that abuse becomes more and more visible as sex. So the Court becomes increasingly *unable to tell* what is pornography and what is not, a failing it laments not as a consequence of the saturation of society by pornography, but as a specifically judicial failure, then finally as an impossibility of line-drawing. The stage is thus set for the transformation of pornography into political speech: the excluded and stigmatized "ideas" we love to hate. Obscured is the way this protects what pornography says and ignores what it does, or, alternatively, protects what pornography says as a means of protecting what it does. Thus can a law develop which prohibits restricting a film because it advocates adultery, but does not even notice a film that is made from a rape.

Nothing in the American law of obscenity is designed to perceive the rape, sexual abuse of children, battering, sexual harassment, prostitution, or sexual murder in pornography. This becomes insulting upon encountering obscenity law's search for harm and failure to find any. The law of child pornography, by contrast – based as it is on the assumption that children are harmed by having sex pictures made of them – applies a test developed in areas of speech other than the sexual: if the harm of speech outweighs its value, it can be restricted by properly targeted means. Given the history of the law of pornography of adult women, it is tempting to regard this as a miracle. Child pornography is not considered the speech of a sexually dissident minority, which it is, advocating "ideas" about children and sex, which it does. Perhaps the fact that boys were used in the film in the test case has something to do with it. The ability to see that child pornography is harmful has everything to do with a visceral sense of the inequality in power between children and adults, yet inequality is never mentioned.

Now, in this context of speech and equality concerns, consider again the judicial opinion of the law Andrea Dworkin and I wrote and Indianapolis passed. This law defines the documented harms pornography does as violations of equality rights and makes them actionable as practices of discrimination, of second-class citizenship. This ordinance allows anyone hurt through pornography to prove its role in their abuse, to recover for the deprivation of their civil rights, and to stop it from continuing. Judicially, this was rendered as censorship of ideas.

In *American Booksellers v Hudnut*, the Court of Appeals for the Seventh Circuit found that this law violated the First Amendment. It began by recognizing that the harm pornography does is real, conceding that the legislative finding of a causal link was judicially adequate: "... we accept the premises of this legislation. Depictions of subordination tend to perpetuate subordination. The subordinate status of women in turn leads to affront and lower pay at work, insult and injury at home, battery and rape on the streets. In the language of the legislature, '[p]ornography is central in creating and maintaining sex as a basis of discrimination.'"[1] Writing for the panel, Judge Easterbrook got, off and on, that "subordination" is something pornography does, not something it just says, and that its active role had to be proven in each case brought under the ordinance. But he kept losing his mental bearings and referring to pornography as an "idea,"[2] finally concluding that the harm it does "demonstrates the power of pornography as speech."[3] This is like saying that the more a libel destroys a reputation, the greater is its power as speech. To say that the more harm speech does, the more protected it is, is legally wrong, even in this country.

Implicitly applying the political speech model, Judge Easterbrook said that the law restricted the marketplace of ideas, the speech of outcast dissenters – referring presumably to those poor heads of organized crime families making ten billion dollars a year trafficking women. He said the law discriminated on the basis of point of view, establishing an approved view of what could be said and thought about women and sex. He failed to note at this point that the invalidated causes of action included coercion, force, and assault, rather a far cry from saying and thinking. He reminded us of *Sullivan*, whose most famous dictum is that to flourish, debate must be "uninhibited, robust, and wide-open."[4] Behind his First Amendment facade, women were being transformed into ideas, sexual traffic in whom was protected as if it were a discussion, the men uninhibited and robust, the women wide-open.

Judge Easterbrook did not say this law was not a sex discrimination law, but he gave the state interest it therefore served – opposition to sex inequality – no constitutional weight. He did this by treating it as if it were a group defamation law, holding that no amount of harm of discrimination can outweigh the speech interests of bigots, so long as they say something while doing it. Besides, if we restrict this, who knows where it will end. He is sure it will end with "Leda and the Swan." He did not suggest that bestiality statutes also had to go, along with obscenity's restrictions on depictions of sex between humans and animals. Both restrict a disapproved sexuality that, no doubt, contains an element of "mental intermediation."[5] Nothing in *Hudnut* explains why, if pornography is protected speech based on its mental elements, rape and sexual murder, which have mental elements, are not as well.

A dissent in a recent case invalidating sentence enhancements for crimes of bias could have been a dissent here: "The majority rationalizes their conclusion [that the statute violates the First Amendment] by insisting that this statute punishes bigoted thought. No so. The statute does not impede or punish the right of persons to have bigoted thoughts or to express themselves in a bigoted fashion or otherwise, regarding the race, religion, or other status of a person. It does attempt to limit the effects of bigotry. What the statute does punish is acting upon those thoughts. It punishes the act of [discrimination] not the thought or expression of bigotry."[6]

Perhaps it is the nature of legal inequality that was missed by the Seventh Circuit. Discrimination has always been illegal because it is based on a prohibited motive: "an evil eye and an unequal hand,"[7] what the perpetrator is thinking while doing, what the acts mean. Racial classifications are thought illegal because they "supply a reason to infer antipathy."[8] A showing of discriminatory intent is required under the Fourteenth Amendment. Now we are told that this same motive, this same participation in a context of meaning, this same hatred and bigotry, these same purposes and thoughts, presumably this same intent, *protect* this same activity under the First Amendment. The courts cannot have it both ways, protecting discriminatory activity under the First Amendment on the same ground they make a requirement for its illegality under the Fourteenth. To put it another way, it is the "idea" of discrimination in the perpetrator's mind that courts have required be proven before the acts that effectuate it will be considered discriminatory. Surely, if acts that are otherwise legal, like hiring employees or renting rooms or admitting students, are made illegal under the Constitution by being based on race or sex because of what those who engage in this think about race or sex, acts that are otherwise *illegal*, like coercion, force, and assault, do not become constitutionally protected because they are done with the same thoughts in mind ...

That these tortured consequences result from the lack of an equality context in which to interpret expressive freedoms is clear from the fact that the same issues produced exactly the opposite results in Canada. Canada's new constitution, the *Charter of Rights and Freedoms*, includes an expansive equality guarantee and a serious entrenchment of freedom of expression. The Supreme Court of Canada's first move was to define equality in a meaningful way – one more substantive than formal, directed toward changing unequal social relations rather than monitoring their equal positioning before the law. The United States, by contrast, remains in the grip of what I affectionately call the stupid theory of equality. Inequality here is defined as distinction, as differentiation, indifferent to whether dominant or subordinated groups are hurt or helped. Canada, by contrast, following the argument of the Women's Legal Education and Action Fund (LEAF), repudiated this view in so many words, taking as its touchstone the treatment of historically disadvantaged groups and aiming to alter their status. The positive spin of the Canadian interpretation holds the law to promoting equality, projecting the law into a more equal future, rather than remaining rigidly neutral in ways that either reinforce existing social inequality or prohibit changing it, as the American constitutional perspective has increasingly done in recent years.

The first case to confront expressive guarantees with equality requirements under the new constitution came in the case of James Keegstra, an anti-Semite who taught Holocaust revisionism to schoolchildren in Alberta. Prosecuted and convicted under Canada's hate propaganda provision, Keegstra challenged the statute as a violation of the new freedom of expression guarantee. LEAF intervened to argue that the hate propaganda law promoted equality. We argued that group libel, most of it concededly expression, promotes the disadvantage of unequal groups; that group-based enmity, ill will, intolerance, and prejudice are the attitudinal engines of the exclusion, denigration, and subordination that make up and propel social inequality; that without bigotry, social systems of enforced separation, ghettoization, and apartheid would be unnecessary, impossible, and unthinkable; that stereotyping and stigmatization of historically disadvantaged groups through group hate propaganda shape their social image and reputation, which controls their access to opportunities more powerfully than their individual abilities ever do; and that it is impossible for an individual to receive equality of opportunity when surrounded by an atmosphere of group hate.

We argued that group defamation is a verbal form inequality takes, that just as white supremacy promotes inequality on the basis of race, color, and sometimes ethnic or national origin, anti-Semitism promotes the inequality of Jews on the basis of religion and ethnicity. We argued that group defamation in this sense is not a mere expression of opinion but a practice of discrimination in verbal form, a link in systemic discrimination that keeps target groups in subordinated positions through the promotion of terror, intolerance, degradation, segregation, exclusion, vilification, violence, and genocide. We said that the nature of the practice can be understood and its impact measured from the damage it causes, from immediate psychic wounding to consequent physical aggression. Where advocacy of genocide is included in group defamation, we said an equality approach to such speech would observe that to be liquidated because of the group you belong to is the ultimate inequality.

The Supreme Court of Canada agreed with this approach, a majority upholding the hate propaganda provision, substantially on equality grounds. The Court recognized the provision as a content restriction – content that had to be stopped because of its anti-egalitarian meaning and devastating consequences.[9]

Subsequently, the Winnipeg authorities arrested a whole pornography book store and prosecuted the owner, Donald Victor Butler, for obscenity. Butler was convicted but said the obscenity law was an unconstitutional restriction on his *Charter*-based right of freedom of expression. LEAF argued that if Canada's obscenity statute, substantially different from U.S. obscenity law in prohibiting "undue exploitation of sex, or sex and violence, cruelty, horror, or crime," was interpreted to institutionalize some people's views about women and sex over others, it would be unconstitutional. But if the community standards applied were interpreted to prohibit harm to women as harm to the community, it was constitutional because it promoted sex equality.

The Supreme Court of Canada essentially agreed, upholding the obscenity provision on sex equality grounds.[10] It said that harm to women – which the Court was careful to make "contextually sensitive" and found could include humiliation, degradation, and subordination – *was* harm to society as a whole. The evidence on the harm of pornography was sufficient for a law against it. Violent materials always present this risk of harm, the Court said; explicit sexual materials that are degrading or dehumanizing (but not violent) could also unduly exploit sex under the obscenity provision if the risk of harm was substantial. Harm in this context was defined as "predispos[ing] persons to act in an anti-social manner, as, for example, the physical or mental mistreatment of women by men, or, what is perhaps debatable, the reverse." The unanimous Court noted that "if true equality between male and female persons is to be achieved, we cannot ignore the threat to equality resulting from exposure to audiences of certain types of violent and degrading material." The result rested in part on *Keegstra* but also observed that the harms attendant to the production of pornography situated the problem of pornography differently, such that the appearance of consent by women in such materials could exacerbate its injury. Recognizing that education could be helpful in combating this harm, the court held that that fact did not make the provision unconstitutional.[11]

Although the Canadians considered the U.S. experience on these issues closely in both cases, the striking absence of a U.S.-style political
speech litany suggests that taking equality seriously precludes it, or
makes it look like the excuse for enforcing inequality that it has become.
The decision did not mention the marketplace of ideas. Maybe in Canada,
people talk to each other, rather than buy and sell each other as ideas.
In an equality context, it becomes obvious that those with the most
power buy the most speech, and that the marketplace rewards the powerful, whose views then become established as truth. We were subjected to "Let [Truth] and falsehood grapple; who ever knew Truth put
to the worse, in a free and open encounter." Milton had not been around
for the success of the Big Lie technique, but this Court had.

Nor did the Canadian Court even consider the "slippery slope," a
largely phony scruple impossible to sustain under a contextually sensitive equality rule. With inequality, the problem is not where intervention will end, but when it will ever begin. Equality is the law; if the
slippery slope worked, the ineluctable logic of principle would have
slid us into equality by now. Also, perhaps, because the Canadian law
of equality is moored in the world, and knows the difference between
disadvantaged groups and advantaged ones, it is less worried about the
misfiring of restrictions against the powerless and more concerned about
having nothing to fire against abuses of power by the powerful.

Fundamentally, the Supreme Court of Canada recognized the reality
of inequality in the issues before it: this was not big bad state power
jumping on poor powerless individual citizen, but a law passed to stand
behind a comparatively powerless group in its social fight for equality
against socially powerful and exploitative groups. This positioning of
forces – which makes the hate propaganda prohibition and the obscenity law of Canada (properly interpreted) into equality laws, although
neither was called such by Parliament – made the invocation of a tradition designed to keep government off the backs of people totally inappropriate. The Court also did not say that Parliament had to limit its
efforts to stop the harm of inequality by talking to it. What it did was
make more space for the unequal to find voice.

Nor did the Canadians intone, with Brandeis and nearly every American court that has ruled on a seriously contested speech issue since, that
"[f]ear of serious injury cannot alone justify suppression of free speech
... Men feared witches and burnt women."[12] I have never understood
this argument, other than as a way of saying that zealots misidentify
the causes of their woes and hurt the wrong people. What has to be

added to fear of serious injury to justify doing something about the speech that causes it? *Proof* of serious injury? If we can't restrict it then, when can we? Isn't fear of serious injury the concern behind restricting publication of the dates on which troop ships sail? Is it mere "fear" of injury to children that supports the law against the use of children to make pornography? If that isn't enough, why isn't proof of injury required? "Men feared witches and burnt women." Where is the speech here? Promoting the fear? Nobody tried to suppress tracts against witches. If somebody had, would some women not have been burnt? Or was it the witches' writings? Did they write? So burning their writings is part of the witch-hunt aspect of the fear? The women who are being burned as witches these days are the women in the pornography, and their burning is sex and entertainment and protected as speech. Those who are hunted down, stigmatized, excluded, and unpublished are the women who oppose their burning.

Neither Canadian decision reduces the harm of hate propaganda or pornography to its "offensiveness." When you hear the women next door screaming as she is bounced off the walls by a man she lives with, are you "offended"? Hate speech and pornography do the same thing: enact the abuse. Women's reactions to the presentation of other women being sexually abused in pornography, and the reactions of Jews living in Skokie to having Nazis march through their town, are routinely trivialized in the United States as "being offended." The position of those with less power is equated with the position of those with more power, as if sexual epithets against straight white men were equivalent to sexual epithets against women, as if breaking the window of a Jewish-owned business in the world after Kristallnacht were just so much breaking glass.

In the cases both of pornography and of the Nazi march in Skokie, it is striking how the so-called speech reenacts the original experience of the abuse, and how its defense as speech does as well. It is not only that both groups, through the so-called speech, are forcibly subjected to the spectacle of their abuse, legally legitimized. Both have their response to it trivialized as "being offended," that response then used to support its speech value, hence its legal protection. Both are also told that what they can do about it is avert their eyes, lock their doors, stay home, stay silent, and hope the assault, and the animus it makes tangible, end when the film or the march ends. This is exactly what perpetrators of rape and child sexual abuse tell their victims and what the Jews in Germany were told by the Nazis (and the rest of the world) in the

1930s. Accept the freedom of your abusers. This best protects you in the end. Let it happen. You are not really being hurt. When sexually abused women are told to let the system work and tolerate the pornography, this is what they are being told. The Jews in Germany, and the Jews in Skokie, were told to let the system work. At least this time around, the Jews of Canada were not, nor were sexually abused women.

The final absence in the Canadian decisions, perhaps the most startling, is the failure to mention any equivalent to the notion that, under the First Amendment, there is no such thing as a false idea. Perhaps under equality law, in some sense there is. When equality is recognized as a constitutional value and mandate, the idea that some people are inferior to others on the basis of group membership is authoritatively rejected as the basis for public policy. This does not mean that ideas to the contrary cannot be debated or expressed. It should mean, however, that social inferiority cannot be imposed through any means, including expressive ones.

Because society is made of language, distinguishing talk about inferiority from verbal imposition of inferiority may be complicated at the edges, but it is clear enough at the center with sexual and racial harassment, pornography, and hate propaganda. At the very least, when equality is taken seriously in expressive settings, such practices are not constitutionally insulated from regulation on the ground that the ideas they express cannot be regarded as false. Attempts to address them would not be prohibited – as they were in rejecting the Indianapolis pornography ordinance, for example – on the ground that, in taking a position in favor of equality, such attempts assume that the idea of human equality is true. The legal equality guarantee has already decided that. There is no requirement that the state remain neutral as between equality and inequality – quite the contrary. Equality is a "compelling state interest" that can already outweigh First Amendment rights in certain settings. In other words, expressive means of practicing inequality can be prohibited.

This is not the place to spell out in detail all the policy implications of such a view. Suffice it to say that those who wish to keep materials that promote inequality from being imposed on students – such as academic books purporting to document women's biological inferiority to men, or arguing that slavery of Africans should return, or that Fourteenth Amendment equality should be repealed, or that reports of rape are routinely fabricated – especially without critical commentary, should not be legally precluded from trying on the grounds that the ideas contained in them cannot be assumed false. No teacher should be forced to teach falsehoods as if they must be considered provisionally true, just because bigots who have managed to get published have made their lies part of a debate. Teachers who wish to teach such materials should be prepared to explain what they are doing to avoid creating a hostile learning environment and to provide all students the equal benefit of an education. Wherever equality is mandated, racial and sexual epithets, vilification, and abuse should be able to be prohibited, unprotected by the First Amendment. The current legal distinction between screaming "go kill that nigger" and advocating the view that African-Americans should be eliminated from parts of the United States needs to be seriously reconsidered, if real equality is ever to be achieved. So, too, the current line separating pornography from hate speech and what is done to make pornography from the materials themselves.

Pornography, under current conditions, *is* largely its own context. Many believe that in settings that encourage critical distance, its showing does not damage women as much as it sensitizes viewers to the damage it does to women. My experience, as well as all the information available, makes me think that it is naive to believe that anything other words can do is as powerful as what pornography itself does. At the very least, pornography should never be imposed on a viewer who does not choose – then and there, without pressure of any kind – to be exposed to it. Tom Emerson said a long time ago that imposing what he called "erotic material" on individuals against their will is a form of action that "has all the characteristics of a physical assault."[13] Equality on campuses, in workplaces, everywhere, would be promoted if such assaults were actionable. Why any women should have to attend school in a setting stacked against her equality by the showing of pornography – especially when authoritatively permitted by those who are legally obligated to take her equality seriously – is a question that those who support its showing should have to answer. The answer is not that she should have to wait for the resulting abuse or leave.

Where is all this leading? To a new model for freedom of expression in which the free speech position no longer supports social dominance, as it does now; in which free speech does not most readily protect the activities of Nazis, Klansmen, and pornographers, while doing nothing for their victims, as it does now; in which defending free speech is not speaking on behalf of a large pile of money in the hands of a small group of people, as it is now. In this new model, principle will be defined in terms of specific experiences, the particularity of history, substantively rather than abstractly. It will notice who is being hurt and never forget who they are. The state will have as great a role in providing relief from injury to equality through speech and in giving equal access to speech as it now has in disciplining its power to intervene in that speech that manages to get expressed.

In a society in which equality is a fact, not merely a word, words of racial or sexual assault and humiliation will be nonsense syllables. Sex between people and things, human beings and pieces of paper, real men and unreal women, will be a turn-off. Artifacts of these abuses will reside in a glass case next to the dinosaur skeletons in the Smithsonian. When this day comes, silence will be neither an act of power, as it is now for those who hide behind it, nor an experience of imposed powerlessness, as it is now for those who are submerged in it, but a context of repose into which thought can expand, an invitation that gives speech its shape, an opening to a new conversation.

NOTES

1 Hudnut, 771 F.2d at 328–9.
2 "... above all else, the First Amendment means that government has no power to restrict expression because of its message [or] ideas ..." Ibid. at 328.
3 Hudnut, 771 F.2d at 329.
4 Sullivan, 376 US at 270.
5 Hudnut, 771 F.2d at 329.
6 *State v Mitchell*, 485 NW2d at 820 (Bablitch, J, dissenting).
7 *Yick Wo v Hopkins*, 118 US 356 (1886).
8 *Personnel Administrator v Feeney*, 442 US 256, 272 (1979); *Vance v Bradley*, 440 US 93, 97 (1979).
9 *Regina v Keegstra*, [1991] 2 WWR 1 (1990) (Can.).
10 *Butler v Regina* [1992] 2 WWR 577 (Can.).
11 Ibid. at 594–7, 601, 609.
12 *Whitney v California*, 274 US 357, 376 (1927) (Brandeis, J, concurring).
13 Thomas I. Emerson, *The System of Freedom of Expression* 496 (1970): "A communication of this [erotic] nature, imposed upon a person contrary to his wishes, has all the characteristics of a physical assault" and "can therefore realistically be classified as action." A comparison with his preliminary formulation in *Toward a General Theory of the First Amendment* 91 (1963) suggests that his view on this subject became stronger by his 1970 revisiting of the issue.

READING QUESTION ON MACKINNON

1 What does MacKinnon mean by "silencing"? What view of freedom
   of expression does her argument rest on? What view of equality does
   her argument rest on, and what is the relation between equality and
   freedom of expression on her theory?

Ronald Dworkin,
"Two Concepts of Liberty" (1991)

Dworkin charges that MacKinnon's approach is undemocratic.

When Isaiah Berlin delivered his famous Inaugural Lecture as Chichele
Professor of Social and Political Theory at Oxford, in 1958, he felt it
necessary to acknowledge that politics did not attract the professional
attention of most serious philosophers in Britain and America. They
thought philosophy had no place in politics and *vice versa*; that political
philosophy could be nothing more than a parade of the theorist's own
preferences and allegiances with no supporting argument of any rigour
or respectability. That gloomy picture is unrecognisable now. Political
philosophy thrives as a mature industry; it dominates many distinguished philosophy departments and attracts a large share of the best
graduate students almost everywhere.
    Berlin's lecture, "Two Concepts of Liberty", played an important and
distinctive role in this renaissance. It provoked immediate, continuing,
heated and mainly illuminating controversy. It became, almost at once,
a staple of graduate and undergraduate reading lists, as it still is. Its
scope and erudition, its historical sweep and evident contemporary force,
its sheer interest, made political ideas suddenly seem exciting and fun.
Its main polemical message – that it is fatally dangerous for philosophers to ignore either the complexity or the power of those ideas – was
both compelling and overdue. But chiefly, or so I think, its importance
lay in the force of its central argument. For though Berlin began by
conceding to the disdaining philosophers that political philosophy could
not match logic or the philosophy of language as a theatre for "radical
discoveries" in which "talent for minute analyses is likely to be rewarded",
he continued by analysing subtle distinctions that, as it happens, are

even more important now, in the Western democracies at least, than when he first called our attention to them.

I must try to describe two central features of his argument, though in this short note I shall have to leave out much that is important to them. The first is the celebrated distinction described in the lecture's title: between two (closely allied) senses of liberty. Negative liberty (as Berlin came later to restate it) means not being obstructed by others in doing whatever one might wish to do. We count some negative liberties – like the freedom to speak our mind without censorship – as very important, and others – like driving at very fast speeds – as trivial. But they are both instances of negative freedom, and though a state may be justified in imposing speed limits, for example, on grounds of safety and convenience, that is nevertheless an instance of restricting negative liberty. Positive liberty, on the other hand, is the power to control or participate in public decisions, including the decision how far to curtail negative liberty. In an ideal democracy, whatever that is, the people govern themselves. Each is master to the same degree, and positive liberty is secured for all.

In the Inaugural Lecture Berlin described the historical corruption of the idea of positive liberty, a corruption that began in the idea that someone's true liberty lies in control by his rational self rather than his empirical self, that is, in control that aims at securing goals other than those the person himself recognises. Freedom, on that conception, is possible only when people are governed, ruthlessly if necessary, by rulers who know their true, metaphysical, will. Only then are people truly free, albeit against their will. That deeply confused and dangerous, but nevertheless potent, chain of argument had in many parts of the world tuned positive liberty into the most terrible tyranny. Of course, Berlin did not mean, by calling attention to this corruption of positive liberty, that negative liberty was an unalloyed blessing, and should be protected in all its forms in all circumstances at all costs. He said, later, that on the contrary the vices of excessive and indiscriminate negative liberty were so evident, particularly in the form of savage economic inequality, that he had not thought it necessary much to describe them.

The second feature of Berlin's argument I have in mind is a theme repeated throughout his writing on political topics. He insists on the complexity of political value, and the fallacy of supposing that all the political virtues that are attractive in themselves can be realised in a single political structure. The ancient Platonic ideal, of some master accommodation of all attractive virtues and goals, combined in institutions satisfying each in the right proportion and sacrificing none, is in Berlin's view, for all its imaginative power and historical influence, only a seductive myth.

One freedom may abort another; [he said, summing up later] one freedom may obstruct or fail to create conditions which make other freedoms, or a larger degree of freedom, or freedom for more persons, possible; positive and negative freedom may collide; the freedom of the individual or the group may not be fully compatible with a full degree of participation in a common life, with its demands for cooperation, solidarity, fraternity. But beyond all these there is an acuter issue: the paramount need to satisfy the claims of other, no less ultimate, values: justice, happiness, love, the realisation of capacities to create new things and experiences and ideas, the discovery of the truth. Nothing is gained by identifying freedom proper, in either of its senses, with these values, or with the conditions of freedom, or by confounding types of freedom with one another.[1]

Berlin's warnings about conflating positive and negative liberty, and liberty itself with other values, seemed to students of political philosophy in the great Western democracies in the 1950s to provide important lessons about authoritarian regimes in other times and places. Though cherished liberties were very much under attack in both American and Britain in that decade, the attack was not grounded in or defended through either form of confusion. The enemies of negative liberty were powerful, but they were also crude and undisguised. Joseph McCarthy and his allies did not rely on an Kantian or Hegelian or Marxist concept of metaphysical selves to justify censorship or blacklists. They distinguished liberty not from itself, but from security; they claimed that too much free speech made us vulnerable to spies and intellectual saboteurs and ultimately to conquest. In both Britain and America, in spite of limited reforms, the state still sought to enforce conventional sexual morality about pornography, contraception, prostitution and homosexuality. Conservatives who defended these invasions of negative liberty appealed not to some higher or different sense of freedom, however, but to values that were plainly distinct from and in conflict with freedom: religion, true morality, and traditional and proper family values. The wars over liberty were fought, or so it seemed, by clearly divided armies. Liberals were for liberty, except for the negative liberty of economic entrepreneurs. Conservatives were for that liberty, but against other forms when these collided with security or their view of decency and morality.

But now the political maps have radically changed and some forms of negative liberty have acquired new opponents. Both in America and Britain, though in different ways, racial and gender conflicts have transformed old alliances and divisions. Speech that expresses racial hatred, or a degrading attitude toward women, or that threatens environmental destruction has come to seem intolerable to many people whose convictions are otherwise traditionally liberal. It is hardly surprising that they should try to reduce the conflict between their old liberal ideals and their new acceptance of censorship by some redefinition of what liberty, properly understood, really is. It is hardly surprising, but the result is dangerous confusion, and Berlin's warnings, framed with different problems in minds, are directly in point.

I shall try to illustrate that point with a single example: a lawsuit arising out of the attempt by certain feminist groups in America to outlaw what they consider a particularly objectionable from of pornography. I select this example not because pornography is more important or dangerous or objectionable than racist invective or other highly distasteful kinds of speech, but because the debate over pornography has been the subject of the fullest and most comprehensive scholarly discussion.

Through the efforts of Catherine MacKinnon and other prominent feminists, Indianapolis in Indiana enacted an anti-pornography ordinance. The ordinance defined pornography as "the graphic sexually explicit subordination of women, whether in pictures or words ...", and it specified, as among pornographic materials falling within that definition, those that present women as enjoying pain or humiliation or rape, or as degraded or tortured or filthy, bruised or bleeding, or in postures of servility or submission or display. It included no exception for literary or artistic value, and opponents claimed that applied literally it would outlaw James Joyce's *Ulysses*, John Cleland's *Memoirs*, various works of D.H. Lawrence, and even Yeat's *Leda and the Swan*. But the groups who sponsored the ordinance were anxious to establish that their objection was not to obscenity or indecency, as such, but to the consequences of a particular kind of pornography, and they presumably thought that an exception for artistic value would undermine that claim.

Publishers and members of the public who claimed a desire to read the banned material arranged a prompt constitutional challenge. The federal district court held that the ordinance was unconstitutional because it violated the First Amendment to the United States Constitution, which guarantees the negative liberty of free speech.[2] The Circuit Court for the Seventh Circuit upheld the district court's decision,[3] and the Supreme Court of the United States declined to review that holding. The Circuit Court's decision, in an opinion by Judge Easterbrook, noticed that the ordinance did not outlaw obscene or indecent material generally but only material reflecting the opinion that women are submissive, or enjoy being dominated, or should be treated as if they did. Easterbrook said that the central point of the First Amendment was exactly to protect speech from content-based regulation of that sort. Censorship may on some occasions be permitted if it aims to prohibit directly dangerous speech – crying fire in a crowded theatre or inciting a crowd to violence, for example – or speech particularly and unnecessarily inconvenient – broadcasting from sound trucks patrolling residential streets at night, for instance. But nothing must be censored because the message it seeks to deliver is a bad one, because it expresses ideas that should not be heard at all.

It is by no means universally agreed that censorship should never be based on content. The British Race Relations Act, for example, forbids speech of racial hatred, not only when it is likely to lead to violence, but generally, on the grounds that members of minority races should be protected from racial insults. In America, however, it is a fixed principle of constitutional law that regulation is unconstitutional unless some compelling necessity, not just official or majority disapproval of the message, requires it. Pornography is often grotesquely offensive; it is insulting, not only to women but to men as well. But we cannot consider that a sufficient reason for banning it without destroying the principle that the speech we hate is as much entitled to protection as any other. The essence of negative liberty is freedom to offend, and that applies to the tawdry as well as the heroic.

Lawyers who defend the Indianapolis ordinance argue that society does have a further justification for outlawing pornography: that it causes great harm as well as offence to women. But their arguments mix together claims about different types of kinds of harm, and it is necessary to distinguish these. They argue, first, that some forms of pornography significantly increase the danger that women will be raped or physically assaulted. If that were true, and the danger were clear and present, then it would indeed justify censorship of those forms, unless less stringent methods of control, such as restricting pornographer's audience, would be feasible, appropriate and effective. In fact, however, though there is some evidence that exposure to pornography weakens people's critical attitudes toward sexual violence, there is no persuasive evidence that it causes more actual incidents of assault. The Seventh Circuit cited a variety of studies (including that of the Williams Commission in Britain in 1979) all of which concluded, the Court said, "that it is not possible to demonstrate a direct link between obscenity and rape ..."[4] A recent and guarded report on a year's research in Britain said: "The evidence does not point to pornography as a cause of deviant sexual orientation in offenders. Rather, it seems to be used as part of that deviant sexual orientation."[5]

Some feminist groups argue, however, that pornography causes not just physical violence but a more general and endemic subordination of women. In that way, they say, pornography makes for inequality. But even if it could be shown, as a matter of causal connection, that pornography is in part responsible for the economic structure in which few women attain top jobs or equal pay for the same work, that would not justify censorship under the Constitution. It would plainly be unconstitutional to ban speech directly *advocating* that women occupy inferior roles, or none at all, in commerce and the professions, even if that speech fell on willing male ears and achieved its goals. So it cannot be a reason for banning pornography that it contributes to an unequal economic or social structure, even if we think that it does.

But the most imaginative feminist literature for censorship makes a further and different argument: that negative liberty for pornographers conflicts not just with equality but with positive liberty as well, because pornography leads to women's *political* as well as economic or social subordination. Of course pornography does not take the vote from women, or somehow make their votes count less. But it produces a climate, according to this argument, in which women cannot have genuine political power or authority because they are perceived and understood unauthentically, made over by male fantasy into people very different, and of much less consequence, than the people they really are. Consider, for example, these remarks from the work of the principal sponsor of the Indianapolis ordinance. "[Pornography] institutionalizes the sexuality of male supremacy, fusing the eroticization of dominance and submission with the social construction of male and female

... Men treat women as who they see women as being. Pornography constructs who that is. Men's power over women means that the way men see women defines who women can be."

Pornography, on this view, denies the positive liberty of women; it denies them the right to be their own masters by recreating them, for politics and society, in the shapes of male fantasy. That is a powerful argument, even in constitutional terms, because it asserts a conflict not just between liberty and equality but within liberty itself, that is, a conflict that cannot be resolved simply on the ground that liberty must be sovereign. What shall we make of the argument understood that way? We must notice, first, that it remains a causal argument. It claims not that pornography is a consequence or symbol or symbol of how the identify of women has been reconstructed by men, but an important cause or vehicle of that reconstruction.

That seems strikingly implausible. Sadistic pornography is revolting, but it is not in any general circulation, except for its milder, soft-porn manifestations. It seems unlikely that it has remotely the influence over how women's sexuality or character or talents are conceived by men, and indeed by women, that commercial advertising and soap operas have. Television and other parts of popular culture use sex to sell everything, and they show women as experts in domestic detail and unreasoned intuition and nothing else. The images they create are subtle and ubiquitous, and it would not be surprising to learn, through whatever research might establish this, that they do indeed do great damage to the way women are understood and allowed to be influential in politics. Sadistic pornography, though much more offensive and disturbing, is greatly overshadowed by these dismal cultural influences as a causal force.

Judge Easterbrook's opinion for the Seventh Circuit assumed *arguendo*, however, that pornography did have the consequences the defenders of the ordinance claimed. He said that nevertheless the argument failed because the point of free speech is precisely to allow ideas to have whatever consequences follows from their dissemination, including undesirable consequences for positive liberty. "Under the First Amendment," he said, "the government must leave to the people the evaluation of ideas. Bald or subtle, an idea is as powerful as the audience allows it to be ... [The assumed result] simply demonstrates the power of pornography as speech. All of these unhappy effects depend on mental intermediation."

That is right as a matter of American constitutional law. The Ku Klux Klan and the American Nazi Party are allowed to propagate their ideas in America, and the British Race Relations Act, so far as it forbids abstract speech of racial hatred, would be unconstitutional there. But does the American attitude represent the kind of Platonic absolutism Berlin warned against? No, because there is an important difference between the idea he thinks absurd, that all ideals attractive in themselves can be perfectly reconciled within a single utopian political order, and the different idea he thought essential, that we must, as individuals and nations, choose among possible combinations of ideals a coherent, even though inevitably and regrettably limited, set of these to define our own individual or national way of life. Freedom of speech, conceived and protected as a fundamental negative liberty, is the core of the choice modern democracies have made, a choice we must now honour in finding our own ways to combat the shaming inequalities women still suffer.

This reply depends, however, on seeing the alleged conflict within liberty as a conflict between the negative and positive senses of that virtue. We must consider yet another argument which, if successful, could not be met in the same way, because it claims that pornography presents a conflict within the negative liberty of speech itself. Berlin said that the character, at least, of negative liberty was reasonably clear, that although excessive claims of negative liberty were dangerous, they could at least always be seen for what they were. But the argument I have in mind, which has been offered, among others, by Frank Michelman of the Harvard Law School, expands the idea of the negative liberty in an unanticipated way. He argues that some speech, including pornography, may be itself "silencing", so that its effect is to prevent other people from exercising their negative freedom to speak.

Of course it is fully recognised in First Amendment jurisprudence that some speech is silencing in that way. Government must indeed balance negative liberties when it prevents heckling or other demonstrative speech designed to stop others from speaking or being heard. But Michelman has something different in mind. He says that a woman's speech may be silenced not just by noise intended to drown her out but also by argument and image that change her audience's perceptions of her character, needs, desires and standing, and also, perhaps, change her own sense of who she is and what she wants. Speech with that consequence silences her, Michelman supposes, by making it impossible for her effectively to contribute to the process Judge Easterbrook said the First Amendment protected, the process through which ideas battle for the public's favour. "[I]t is a highly plausible claim", Michelman writes, "... [that] pornography [is] a cause of women's subordination and silencing ... It is a fair and obvious question why our society's openness to challenge does not need protection against repressive private as well as public action."[6]

He argues that if our commitment to negative freedom of speech is consequentialist – if we want free speech in order to have a society in which no idea is barred from entry – then we must censor some ideas in order to make entry possible for other ones. He protests that the distinction American constitutional law makes, between the suppression of ideas by the effect of public criminal law and by the consequences of private speech, is arbitrary, and that a sound concern for openness would be equally concerned about both forms of control. But the distinction the law makes is not between public and private power, as such, but between negative liberty and other virtues, including positive liberty. It would indeed be contradictory for a constitution to prohibit official censorship but also to protect the right of private citizens physically to prevent other citizens from publishing or broadcasting specified ideas. That would allow private citizens to violate the negative liberty of other citizens by preventing them from saying what they wish. But there is no contradiction in insisting that every idea must be allowed to be heard, even those whose consequence is that other ideas will be misunderstood, or given little consideration, or even not be spoken at all because those who might speak them are not in control of their own public identifies and therefore cannot be understood as they wish to be. These are very bad consequences, and they must be resisted by whatever means our constitution permits. But they are not the same thing as depriving others of their negative liberty to speak, and the distinction, as Berlin insisted, is very far from arbitrary or inconsequential.

It is of course understandable why Michelman and others should want to expand the idea of negative liberty in the way they try to do. Only by characterising certain ideas as themselves "silencing" ideas, only by supposing that censoring pornography is the same thing as stopping people from drowning out other speakers, can they hope to justify censorship within the constitutional scheme that assigns a preeminent place to free speech. But the assimilation is nevertheless a confusion, exactly the kind of confusion Berlin warned against in his original lecture, because it obscures the true political choice that must be made. I return to Berlin's lecture, which put the point with that striking combination of clarity and sweep I have been celebrating. "I should be guilt-stricken, and rightly so, if I were not, in some circumstances, ready to make [some] sacrifice [of freedom]. But a sacrifice is not an increase in what is being sacrificed, namely freedom, however great the moral need or the compensation for it. Everything is what it is: liberty is liberty, not equality or fairness or justice or culture, or human happiness or a quiet conscience."

NOTES

1 Berlin, *Four Essays on Liberty*, Oxford Paperbacks, 1969, p. lvi.
2 *American Booksellers Association, Inc et al. v William Hudnut, III, Mayor, City of Indianapolis et al.*, 598 F. Supp. 1316 (S.D. Ind. 1984).
3 771 F2d 323 (US Court Appeals, Seventh Circuit).
4 That court, in a confused passage, said that it nevertheless accepted "the premises of this legislation", which included the claims about a causal connection with sexual violence. But it seemed to mean that it was accepting the rather different causal claim considered in the next paragraph, about subordination. In any case, it said that it accepted those premises only *arguendo*, since it thought it had no authority to reject decisions of Indianapolis based on its interpretation of empirical evidence.
5 See *Daily Telegraph*, December 23, 1990.
6 Frank Michelman, "Conceptions of Democracy in American Constitutional Argument: The Case of Pornography Regulation", 56 *Tennessee Law Review* 291, 1989, pp. 303–4.

READING QUESTIONS ON DWORKIN

1 Should the law in a society marked by pervasive inequalities be the same as it would in a society of equals? Can you think of any exceptions to this claim?
2 Can MacKinnon's argument be restated so that it passes the test for an acceptable moral argument that Dworkin outlines in his response to Devlin?
3 Does the view of politics and law which Dworkin articulates here strengthen the arguments Hutchinson and Monahan make against liberalism and the rule of law?
4 Does Dworkin tacitly rely on a positivistic conception of law in this essay?

Native Women's Association of Canada v Canada
[1992] 3 FC 192

The extracts from this decision of the Federal Court of Appeal deal with the Court's finding that the federal government's failure to fund aboriginal women's organizations while funding male-dominated aboriginal organizations during constitutional deliberations violated freedom of expression.

Mahoney, JA: – This is an appeal from the dismissal, with costs if asked for, of the appellants' application for an order prohibiting the Government of Canada from making any further payments to the Assembly of First Nations, the Native Council of Canada, the Metis National Council, and the Inuit Tapirisat of Canada, hereafter collectively "the designated aboriginal organizations," until (1) it has provided equal funding to the appellant, the Native Women's Association of Canada, hereafter NWAC, and (2) it has provided NWAC an equal right of participation in the constitutional review process as the said organizations, including participation in First Ministers' Conferences to discuss constitutional renewal. As I appreciate their argument, the appellants are primarily concerned with participation in the process; their concern with financing is directed to rendering that participation as informed and effective as that of the designated aboriginal organizations.

THE APPELLANTS

The individual appellants, Gail Stacey-Moore and Sharon McIvor, are respectively a Mohawk of Kahnawake, Quebec, and a member of the Lower Nicola Band of British Columbia. Both are executive members of NWAC. There is ample evidence which need not be reviewed that they individually and native women as a class remain doubly disadvantaged in Canadian society by reason of both race and sex and disadvantaged in at least some aboriginal societies by reason of sex. The uncontradicted evidence is that they are also seriously disadvantaged by reason of sex within the segment of aboriginal society residing on or claiming the right to reside on Indian reservations.

NWAC is a non-profit organization, incorporated in 1974. Its board of directors is comprised of members from all provinces and territories.

The evidence establishes that it is a grass-roots organization founded and led by aboriginal women, at least Metis and both status and non-status Indian women. While I find nothing that would indicate that Inuit women are unwelcome, I find no evidence of their participation. Among its objectives is to be the national voice for native women, to advance their issues and concerns, and to assist and promote common goals towards native self-determination. The record is replete with evidence of NWAC's activities in pursuit of those objectives, including the publication of reports and position papers and appearances before judicial inquiries and Parliamentary committees. NWAC is a bona fide, established, and recognized national voice of and for aboriginal women.

THE CURRENT CONSTITUTIONAL REVIEW PROCESS

In June 1991, the Quebec legislature enacted a law requiring the provincial government to hold a referendum on the sovereignty of Quebec between either June 8 and 22 or October 12 and 26, 1992: *Act Respecting the Process for Determining the Political and Constitutional Future of Quebec,* SQ 1991, c. 34. Shortly before that law came into force, the Canadian government caused the appointment of a *Special Joint Committee of the Senate and House of Commons* "to inquire into and make recommendations to Parliament on ... proposals for a renewed Canada contained in the documents to be referred to it by the Government." Among its 28 proposals was the following:

The Government of Canada proposes an amendment to the Constitution to
entrench a general justiciable right to aboriginal self-government in order
to recognize aboriginal peoples' autonomy over their own affairs within
the Canadian federation ... [Such] a right ... would be exercised within the
Canadian constitutional framework, subject to the Canadian Charter of Rights
and Freedoms. (*Shaping Canada's Future Together – Proposals*, p. 7, A.B. III, at
p. 414)

While the Parliamentary Committee went about its work, the federal government appears to have decided or agreed that a parallel process should take place among the aboriginal peoples. As a result it provided funding to the designated aboriginal organizations. They had been involved in the constitutional conferences convened in 1983, 1984, 1985, and 1987 pursuant to ss. 37 and 37.1 of the *Constitution Act, 1982* ...

which expressly required inclusion of an agenda item "respecting constitutional matters that directly affect the aboriginal peoples of Canada" and that "the Prime Minister of Canada shall invite representatives of those peoples to participate in the discussion on that item."

It is common knowledge that the process has now moved beyond the Parliamentary Committee stage. When this appeal was heard, federal, provincial, and territorial ministers, excluding representation from Quebec but with representation from the designated aboriginal organizations at some, at least, of their meetings, were engaged in designing a constitutional proposal to be put to Quebec. The process has since moved to closed meetings of First Ministers, including the Premier of Quebec, but excluding representatives of the territories and aboriginal peoples.

THE CONTRIBUTION AGREEMENTS

Some $10 million is said to have been allocated among the designated aboriginal organizations. A portion of the funds advanced was specifically earmarked for the study of women's issues. The Assembly of First Nations and the Native Council of Canada each allocated $130,000 of its grant to NWAC and a further grant by the Secretary of State brought the total funding provided to NWAC to about 5 per cent of what had been provided to each of the four organizations under the Contribution Agreements.

The Contribution Agreements are not in evidence. They were entered into under the Aboriginal Constitutional Review Program of the Department of the Secretary of State. Parliamentary authorizations for the expenditures are apparently to be found in items for that department in *Appropriation Acts* Nos. 3 and 4, 1991–92: SC 1991, c. 53, and SC 1992, c. 7. The purpose for which the funds are to be expended has, it seems, not been defined by Act of Parliament or regulation.

THE APPELLANTS' CONCERNS

In the course of the process paralleling the work of the Parliamentary Committee, which included discussions between the designated aboriginal organizations and the federal government as well as among themselves, the appellants became concerned that a constitutional resolution might be agreed upon that did not provide for application of the *Canadian Charter of Rights and Freedoms* to aboriginal self-governments. NWAC asked for equal funding and participation. The federal government's response was that it wished aboriginal women's concerns to be dealt with within the aboriginal community itself and that, to that end, the Contribution Agreements had required the designated aboriginal organizations to spend a portion of the funding on women's issues.

The basis of concerns of NWAC and aboriginal women is eloquently stated in the affidavit of Ms Stacey-Moore.

86. The exclusion of NWAC from direct funding for constitutional matters and from direct participation in constitutional discussions poses a grave threat to the equality of Aboriginal women. The [Assembly of First Nations], in particular is strongly of the view that the *Canadian Charter of Rights and Freedoms* should not apply to Aboriginal self-governments. Without the *Charter*, Aboriginal women will be helpless to resist the discriminatory actions of Band Councils, or any other form of self-government to be developed. This is because the *Canadian Human Rights Act* does not apply to the *Indian Act*, and provincial human rights codes are also inapplicable for jurisdictional reasons. Although the AFN has expressed an interest in establishing an Aboriginal Charter of Rights, Ovide Mercredi, the Grand Chief, has recently advised NWAC that AFN has done nothing towards its development and NWAC should develop a Charter if we are intent on having something soon.

87. Even if a model Aboriginal Charter of Rights were developed, the position of women in the Aboriginal communities would not necessarily be secure. Getting such a Charter accepted by each self-governing entity, and maintaining efficient and well-funded enforcement mechanisms, are major hurdles facing women who seek to rely on such an instrument.

88. As I said in my address to the Chiefs in Assembly, Exhibit "W",
The Assembly of First Nations is proposing an Aboriginal Code of Human Rights which it claims will have more rights assured than the *Charter of Rights and Freedoms*. Will this AFN model code be entrenched in the Canadian Constitution? The answer is likely, no it will not be entrenched. Why? Because First Nation leaders have already expressed concern that no code be imposed on their governments. First Nations do not want any code of human rights, federal or Aboriginal, imposed from outside the community. This means individual women in each community must struggle daily in their own community, isolated from the Aboriginal women's movement, to have a model community code of human rights put in place. Until that community code is in place, human rights of women and children are not guaranteed.

89. If those who advocate that the *Canadian Charter* not apply to Aboriginal self-government are successful, it will mean that Aboriginal women have no protection under any instrument guaranteeing our basic human and equality rights. In those circumstances, we will not be equal partners with Aboriginal males in developing an Aboriginal approach to self-government: their historic dominance will simply be repeated in this new setting.

90. Aboriginal women are at a crisis point. The Government of Canada is funding advocacy for a point of view that will, if successful, see the removal from Aboriginal women of their rights under the *Canadian Charter of Rights and Freedoms*. It has recognized that point of view as the official or "representative" view, while failing to take into account that it is the view of male-dominated organizations, which do not have as much need of the *Charter's* equality guarantees in their own community as do women. As an Aboriginal woman, I face the prospect that the price I will pay for Aboriginal self-government will be the loss of my existing equality rights.

91. Why women are concerned about having no protection of their rights in the Aboriginal community is clear. As I stated in my address to the chiefs, Exhibit "W",

Why are we so worried as women? We have never discussed self governments in our communities. There is much to be learned. We are living in chaos in our communities. We have a disproportionately high rate of child sexual abuse and incest. We have wife battering, gang rapes, drug and alcohol abuse and every kind of perversion imaginable has been imported into our daily lives. The development of programs, services and policies for handling domestic violence has been placed in the hands of men. Has it resulted in a reduction of this kind of violence? Is a woman or a child safe in their own home in an Aboriginal community? The statistics show this is not the case.

92. NWAC wants an equal chance to influence public debate, and to safeguard the destiny of its members, and other Aboriginal women of Canada. It believes that a collectivity cannot be strong if over one-half that collectivity is without rights, and without a voice. It believes that the Government of Canada should not fund advocacy of a position that seeks removal of basic constitutional protection from the Aboriginal women of Canada.

Ms McIvor deposes to having read that affidavit and that she agrees with all Ms Stacey-Moore has deposed.

The Native Council of Canada, hereafter NCC, is a national organization incorporated in 1972 to advance the rights and interests of Metis, non-status Indians, and off-reserve registered Indians throughout Canada. It denies being a male or male-dominated organization. It is composed of provincial and territorial organizations. Each provincial and territorial organization sends delegates to an annual meeting which elects a president and vice-president who, with the president of each constituent organization, constitute the executive. While the president and vice-president are presently both men, the president who negotiated the Contribution Agreement was, in fact, a woman. The presidents of its Alberta, Yukon, and Labrador constituents are presently women, as is a majority of the directors of its BC affiliate. In addition to the $130,000 allocation, it assigned four of its seats at the March 13–15, 1992, Aboriginal Conference on the Constitution to NWAC to permit it to be represented there. (The Government of Canada also allocated four of its seats to NWAC with the result that NWAC had eight of 184 delegates at the table.) It has been active in opposing gender-based discrimination under the *Indian Act*, RSC 1985, c. I-5. As to the *Charter*, NCC's position is that it should apply to "Indian Act governments" but that when aboriginal self-government is achieved, its application should be a matter for each "nation." The record suggests that some "nations" which, notwithstanding the *Charter*, have persisted in exiling Indian women not married to Indian men, but not the reverse, will continue to opt for male domination.

NCC's position is that the learned trial judge [90 DLR (4th) 394, 32 ACWS (3d) 1052] did not err in concluding that the appellants had failed to establish any prima facie breach of their *Charter* rights.

The Metis National Council, hereafter MNC, is a federation of organizations from Ontario, the western provinces, and the Northwest Territories. It denies that NWAC represents Metis women; $130,000 of its grant was earmarked to enable Metis women to address their particular concerns. While Metis women do not by any means comprise half of the executive members of its constituent organizations, the evidence is that they have been a significant proportion over the years. MNC supported proclamation of s. 35(4) of the *Constitution Act*, 1982, and supports application of the *Charter*, specifically including s. 15, to aboriginal self-governments. In addition, it proposes a Metis Charter.

MNC also submits that the learned trial judge did not err in finding no breach of any *Charter* right to have been established and that, in any event, no basis for a remedy affecting it, the deprivation of its funding, had been established.

The Inuit Tapirisat of Canada, hereafter ITC, is a national organization representing Inuit from the Northwest Territories, Quebec, and Labrador. It, too, denies that NWAC represents Inuit women. The specific interests of Inuit women are represented by a national organization known as Pauktuutit, which aims to promote the equality of Inuit women within government institutions and Canadian society. The president of Pauktuutit is a member of the board of directors of ITC and the current president and secretary-treasurer of ITC are women. Inuit concerns on constitutional issues are directed to an ITC committee, whereof three of seven members, including the Pauktuutit president, are presently women. Pauktuutit staff and consultants participate in the technical working groups supporting the committee. Pauktuutit does not seek separate funding from the Government of Canada; it shares ITC's funding. ITC's stated position is that it is willing to consider application of the *Charter* to any Inuit self-government arrangements which may be negotiated between the Inuit and the Government of Canada.

ITC denies that it is a male-dominated organization and that its participation in the constitutional review process and its funding for that purpose infringe any *Charter* right of the appellants.

THE ASSEMBLY OF FIRST NATIONS

The Assembly of First Nations, hereafter AFN, did not intervene in this proceeding. There is no evidence of it but what the appellants have provided. AFN is a national association of Indian chiefs. Its primary, if not only, constituency appears to be status Indians resident on reserves. Sixty of the 633 member chiefs of AFN are women. AFN, and its forerunner the National Indian Brotherhood, has vigorously and consistently resisted the struggle of native women to rid themselves of the gender inequality historically entrenched in the *Indian Act* and has intervened in Parliamentary and legal proceedings to oppose those efforts. It opposed repeal of s. 12(1)(b) of the *Indian Act*

[The following persons are not entitled to be registered [as an Indian], namely, (b) a woman who married a person who is not an Indian, unless that woman is subsequently the wife or widow of a person described in section 11.]

upon the coming into force of s. 15(1) of the *Charter*, and it opposed proclamation of the amendment to the *Constitution Act*, 1982, which added s. 35(4).

As the learned trial judge found and as perusal of the affidavits of Ms Stacey-Moore and Ms McIvor make transparently clear, it is primarily the position of AFN which the appellants fear. The intervenants do not speak for the women of the First Nations whose interests, at least as measured against the norms of Canadian society as a whole, are not only unlikely to be properly represented by AFN but are likely to be injured if AFN's position prevails; NWAC does represent those women. The evidence is clear that AFN is not addressing their concerns. It emphatically rejects imposition of the *Charter* on native self-governments and promises instead an Aboriginal Charter which cannot yet be described as inchoate.

THE ISSUE

The first question is: Has any constitutional right of NWAC, or the individual women it represents, been violated by the Government of Canada funding any or all of the designated aboriginal organizations and permitting their participation in constitutional discussions without providing NWAC equal funding and opportunity to participate? The appellants allege ... the breach of their right to freedom of expression guaranteed by s. 2(b) of the *Charter* which, they stress, must be read together with s. 28 ...

Sections 2(b) and 28 – Freedom of Expression

It is unnecessary that I deal with all of the authorities propounding the central role of freedom of expression in a free and democratic society. They are encapsulated in the following statement by Cory, J, in *Edmonton Journal v (Attorney-General)* (1989), 64 DLR (4th) 577 at p. 607:

It is difficult to imagine a guaranteed right more important to a democratic society than freedom of expression. Indeed a democracy cannot exist without that freedom to express new ideas and to put forward opinions about the functioning of public institutions. The concept of free and uninhibited speech permeates all truly democratic societies and institutions. The vital importance of the concept cannot be over-emphasized.

In the present case, the learned trial judge held [at p. 406]:

On the facts it is evident that the Native Women's Association of Canada has had and will continue to have many opportunities to express its views, both to the appropriate political authorities, to the public and even to the groups which will participate in the conference, some at least of whom share [its] concern respecting the continued application of the *Charter* to aboriginal people. Undoubtedly the more money placed at their disposal the louder their voice could be heard, but it certainly cannot be said that they are being deprived of the right of freedom of speech in contravention of the *Charter*.

With respect to discrimination as to sex, the disproportionate funds provided for [NWAC] results not from the fact that they are women but from the unwillingness of the government to recognize that they should be considered as a separate group within the aboriginal community from the four named groups and treated accordingly. Whether this is fair or contrary to natural justice will be dealt with under another argument respecting the issue of a writ of prohibition, but it does not constitute per se discrimination on the basis of sex in contravention of the *Charter*.

The appellants say he misapprehended their argument as to freedom of expression and erred by taking account only of the purpose or intent of the government's action and not of its effect. They point to the limitations on federal election spending as demonstrating the government's recognition that disparate financing of political points of view enables the ideas of some to command public attention at the expense of others.

In *Irwin Toy Ltd v Quebec (Attorney-General)* (1989), 58 DLR (4th) 577 at pp. 612–13, ... Dickson, CJC, for the majority, said:

Even if the government's purpose was not to control or restrict attempts to convey a meaning, the court must still decide whether the effect of the government action was to restrict the plaintiff's free expression. Here, the burden is on the plaintiff to demonstrate that such an effect occurred. In order to so demonstrate, a plaintiff must state her claim with reference to the principles and values underlying the freedom.

[Those principles and values] can be summarized as follows: (1) seeking and attaining the truth is an inherently good activity; (2) participation in social and political decision-making is to be fostered and encouraged; and (3) the diversity in forms of individual self-fulfilment and human flourishing ought to be cultivated in an essentially tolerant, indeed welcoming, environment not only for the sake of those who convey a meaning, but also for the sake of those to whom it is conveyed. In showing that the effect of the government's action was to restrict her free expression, a plaintiff must demonstrate that her activity promotes at least one of these principles ... [T]he plaintiff must at least identify the meaning being conveyed and how it relates to the pursuit of truth, participation in the community, or individual self-fulfilment and human flourishing.

Communicating one's constitutional views to the public and to governments is unquestionably an expressive activity protected by s. 2(b).

The appellants argue that, by funding and thereby supporting male-dominated aboriginal organizations in that activity, the Canadian government has enhanced their ability to communicate their anti-*Charter* positions to the virtual exclusion of NWAC's pro-*Charter* position. Government action has given the male-dominated organizations an ability to communicate effectively which has been denied aboriginal women, thereby abridging the guarantee of s. 28 that freedom of expression is equally the freedom of male and female persons. They adopt a statement quoted in a recent decision of Nova Scotia Human Rights Tribunal: *Re: A Complaint by Gene Keyes against Pandora Publishing Association*, decision dated March 17, 1992, at p. 40:

[W]omen cannot become powerful or expressive by being spoken to, by being spoken for, or, especially, by being spoken about. It is by being heard that women become empowered.

In my opinion, the question is not whether the designated aboriginal organizations are male dominated but whether they advocate male-dominated aboriginal self-governments. I do not agree that a male-dominated organization is, in fact, necessarily incapable of advocating gender equality on behalf of its female members, nor do I agree that the effect of s. 28 on s. 2(b) dictates that result as a constitutional conclusion.

Measured against the norms of Canadian society as a whole, it is in the interests of aboriginal women that, if, as and when they become the subjects of aboriginal self-governments, they continue to enjoy the protection of the *Canadian Charter of Rights and Freedoms* and, in particular, the rights and freedoms accorded them by ss. 15 and 28, or by equivalent provisions equally entrenched in aboriginal charters, if that be legally possible. It is by no means certain that the latter alternative can or will be realized. The interests of aboriginal women, measured by the only standard this Court can recognize in the absence of contrary evidence, that of Canadian society at large, are not represented in this respect by AFN, which advocates a contrary result, nor by the ambivalence of NCC and ITC.

In my opinion, by inviting and funding the participation of those organizations in the current constitutional review process and excluding the equal participation of NWAC, the Canadian government has accorded the advocates the male-dominated aboriginal self-governments a preferred position in the exercise of an expressive activity, the freedom of which is guaranteed to everyone by s. 2(b) and which is, by s. 28, guaranteed equally to men and women. It has thereby taken action which has had the effect of restricting the freedom of expression of aboriginal women in a manner offensive to ss. 2(b) and 28 of the *Charter*. In my opinion, the learned trial judge erred in concluding otherwise.

That is not to say that equal funding to NWAC would necessarily be required to achieve the equality required by s. 28. The evidence does not permit a concluded opinion as to that. However, the funding actually provided is so disparate as to be prima facie inadequate to accord it the equal freedom of expression mandated by the *Charter*. ...

If I am correct in finding violation of ss. 2(b) and 28, then it is a real, not a speculative, violation. It is clear that, whether or not the impugned funding or the stage of the constitutional review process for which it was made has been exhausted, the process may recur. A remedy, even a declaration, could have a meaningful effect on NWAC's future participation in it ...

The "Floodgates" Argument

The respondent says that a finding of a s. 2(b) violation requiring the equal participation in the constitutional review process and funding of NWAC would require that equal funding and participation be extended to all individuals and interest groups. I do not find this argument persuasive.

Parliament has the right to provide funding or not as it chooses, but, in choosing to fund, it is bound to observe the requirements of the *Charter* ... The government, in exercising a discretion to fund that Parliament has given it, must be equally bound. Generally, I should think a decision to fund will be made on the basis of need to permit effective and informed expression by an otherwise handicapped and particularly concerned interest group. A proper decision to fund one group but not another should be readily justifiable under s. 1 of the *Charter*. The flood-gates argument would be entirely without foundation if the conditions of entitlement to funding were prescribed by law, that is, Act of Parliament or regulation ... The floodgates argument is, in the present circumstances, essentially an argument of administrative convenience which ought not prevail when a constitutionally guaranteed right or freedom has been proved to have been infringed ...

It will be only one who can show a constitutional foundation for a grievance by reason of the favour shown by the government to another who will be able to obtain the assistance of the courts. Not every interest group can complain that, because the designated aboriginal organizations were favoured, its *Charter*-guaranteed freedom of expression was infringed. NWAC can make that complaint and, in my view, with justification. It ought not be denied a remedy by reason of anticipated claims of others not similarly situated with respect to those the government chose to favour, namely, the designated aboriginal organizations.

REMEDY

The remedy sought by the appellants, prohibition of further payments to the designated aboriginal organizations until the federal government has (1) provided equal funding to NWAC and (2) has provided NWAC an equal opportunity to participate in the review process, including participation in relevant First Minister's Conferences, is, in my view, not available in the circumstances.

In the first place, the evidence does not permit a judicial conclusion that funding of NWAC equal to that provided to each of the designated aboriginal organizations is what is necessary to accord aboriginal women the equal measure of freedom of expression guaranteed them by s. 28 of the *Charter*. It may be inadequate or it may be excessive. The appropriate quantum of funding would seem to me very much a matter to be determined by the executive, conscious of the need to accord that equality. Furthermore, equality is not to be achieved by the court interfering with the funding of the designated aboriginal organizations already agreed upon, even if it has not been entirely exhausted. I agree with the submissions of MNC and ITC to the effect that the appellants have established no basis for a remedy depriving the designated aboriginal organizations of their funding.

In the second place, it is notorious that the constitutional review process has now moved beyond consultation. Every such process necessarily will at some point, unless it aborts sooner, pass from a consultative stage to a legislative state in which the courts will not meddle ... I frankly cannot conceive of even *Charter*-based circumstances in which a court could properly interfere, however, indirectly, with the convening of a First Ministers' Conference or any other purely intergovernmental meeting and dictate to them whom they ought to invite to their table.

That said, a court can declare that by including an organization such as AFN proved to be adverse in interest to aboriginal women as measured against the norms of Canadian society generally, while excluding NWAC, an organization that speaks for their interests, in a constitutional review process intended to assist it in deciding, and mustering public and provincial governmental support for, the content of a constitutional resolution affecting aboriginal rights to be put to Parliament, the federal government has restricted the freedom of expression of aboriginal women in a manner offensive to ss. 2(b) and 28 of the *Charter*. That is, in my opinion, to do no more than to declare *Charter*-based rights and duties as between aboriginal women and the Government of Canada.

CONCLUSION

I would allow the appeal ...

READING QUESTIONS ON NATIVE WOMEN'S ASSOCIATION

1 When reading this judgment you should read at the same time Pigeon, J's dissent in *Hofer* and the extracts from *Sovereign Injustice*. Does Mahoney, J, like Pigeon, J, argue that, as a matter of law, all claims of community should be subordinated to fundamental liberal democratic values? Are the Crees committed to the same position in virtue of their argument in *Sovereign Injustice*?
2 What do you make of the fact that the claim made by the native women was one from within the aboriginal community?
3 What are the implications of the fact that the judgment goes beyond a negative liberty conception of the right to free expression, one that merely prevents the government from interfering with individual freedom of expression? Is there a connection here with Catharine MacKinnon's position on law and freedom of expression?

10

Abortion

Political debate about abortion has raged for decades. As such, it probably needs no introduction. The selections included here attempt to articulate views of abortion that treat its regulation as a special case of more general legal principles.

Judith Jarvis Thomson
"A Defence of Abortion" (1971)

Thomson argues that, even if we suppose the foetus to be a person, the limits of moral and legal duties to aid others ensure that abortion cannot be prohibited.

Most opposition to abortion relies on the premise that the foetus is a human being, a person, from the moment of conception. The premise is argued for, but, as I think, not well. Take, for example, the most common argument. We are asked to notice that the development of a human being from conception through birth into childhood is continuous; then it is said that to draw a line, to choose a point in this development and say "before this point the thing is not a person, after this point it is a person" is to make an arbitrary choice, a choice for which in the nature of things no good reason can be given. It is concluded that the foetus is, or anyway that we had better say it is, a person from the moment of conception. But this conclusion does not follow. Similar things might be said about the development of an acorn into an oak tree, and it does not follow that acorns are oak trees, or that we had better say they are. Arguments of this form are sometimes called "slippery slope arguments" – the phrase is perhaps self-explanatory – and it is dismaying that opponents of abortion rely on them so heavily and uncritically.

I am inclined to agree, however, that the prospects for "drawing a line" in the development of the foetus look dim. I am inclined to think also that we shall probably have to agree that the foetus has already become a human person well before birth. Indeed, it comes as a surprise when one first learns how early in its life it begins to acquire human characteristics. By the tenth week, for example, it already has a face, arms and legs, fingers and toes; it has internal organs, and brain activity is detectable.[2] On the other hand, I think that the premise is false, that the foetus is not a person from the moment of conception. A newly fertilized ovum, a newly implanted clump of cells, is no more a person than an acorn is an oak tree. But I shall not discuss any of this. For it seems to me to be of great interest to ask what happens if, for the sake of argument, we allow the premise. How, precisely, are we supposed to get from there to the conclusion that abortion is morally impermissible? Opponents of abortion commonly spend most of their time establishing that the foetus is a person, and hardly any time explaining the step from there to the impermissibility of abortion. Perhaps they think the step too simple and obvious to require much comment. Or perhaps instead they are simply being economical in argument. Many of those who defend abortion rely on the premise that the foetus is not a person, but only a bit of tissue that will become a person at birth; and why pay out more arguments than you have to? Whatever the explanation, I suggest that the step they take is neither easy nor obvious, that it calls for closer examination than it is commonly given, and that when we do give it this closer examination we shall feel inclined to reject it.

I propose, then, that we grant that the foetus is a person from the moment of conception. How does the argument go from here? Something like this, I take it. Every person has a right to life. So the foetus has a right to life. No doubt the mother has a right to decide what happens in and to her body; everyone would grant that. But surely a person's right to life is stronger and more stringent than the mother's right to decide what happens in and to her body, and so outweighs it. So the foetus may not be killed; an abortion may not be performed.

It sounds plausible. But now let me ask you to imagine this. You wake up in the morning and find yourself back to back in bed with an unconscious violinist. A famous unconscious violinist. He has been found to have a fatal kidney ailment, and the Society of Music Lovers has canvassed all the available medical records and found that you alone have the right blood type to help. They have therefore kidnapped you, and last night the violinist's circulatory system was plugged into yours, so that your kidneys can be used to extract poisons from his blood as well as your own. The director of the hospital now tells you, "Look, we're sorry the Society of Music Lovers did this to you – we would never have permitted it if we had known. But still, they did it, and the violinist now is plugged into you. To unplug you would be to kill him. But never mind, it's only for nine months. By then he will have recovered from his ailment, and can safely be unplugged from you." Is it morally incumbent on you to accede to this situation? No doubt it would be very nice of you if you did, a great kindness. But do you *have* to accede to it? What if it were not nine months, but nine years? Or longer still? What if the director of the hospital says, "Tough luck, I agree, but you've now got to stay in bed, with the violinist plugged into you, for the rest of your life. Because remember this. All persons have a right to life, and violinists are persons. Granted you have a right to decide what happens in and to your body, but a person's right to life outweighs your right to decide what happens in and to your body. So you cannot ever be unplugged from him." I imagine you would regard this as outrageous, which suggests that something really is wrong with that plausible-sounding argument I mentioned a moment ago.

In this case, of course, you were kidnapped; you didn't volunteer for the operation that plugged the violinist into your kidneys. Can those who oppose abortion on the ground I mentioned make an exception for a pregnancy due to rape? Certainly. They can say that persons have a right to life only if they didn't come into existence because of rape; or they can say that all persons have a right to life, but that some have less of a right to life than others, in particular, that those who came into existence because of rape have less. But these statements have a rather unpleasant sound. Surely the question of whether you have a right to life at all, or how much of it you have, shouldn't turn on the question of whether or not you are the product of a rape. And in fact the people who oppose abortion on the ground I mentioned do not make this distinction, and hence do not make an exception in case of rape.

Nor do they make an exception for a case in which the mother has to spend the nine months of her pregnancy in bed. They would agree that would be a great pity, and hard on the mother; but all the same, all persons have a right to life, the foetus is a person, and so on. I suspect, in fact, that they would not make an exception for a case in which, miraculously enough, the pregnancy went on for nine years, or even the rest of the mother's life.

Some won't even make an exception for a case in which continuation of the pregnancy is likely to shorten the mother's life; they regard abortion as impermissible even to save the mother's life. Such cases are nowadays very rare, and many opponents of abortion do not accept this extreme view. All the same, it is a good place to begin: a number of points of interest come out in respect to it.

1. Let us call the view that abortion is impermissible even to save the mother's life "the extreme view". I want to suggest that it does not issue from the argument I mentioned earlier without the addition of some fairly powerful premises. Suppose a woman has become pregnant, and now learns that she has a cardiac condition such that she will die if she carries the baby to term. What may be done for her? The foetus, being a person, has a right to life, but as the mother is a person too, so has she a right to life. Presumably they have an equal right to life. How is it supposed to come out that an abortion may not be performed? If mother and child have an equal right to life, shouldn't we perhaps flip a coin? Or should we add to the mother's right to life her right to decide what happens in and to her body, which everybody seems to be ready to grant – the sum of her rights now outweighing the foetus's right to life?

The most familiar argument here is the following. We are told that performing the abortion would be directly killing[3] the child, whereas doing nothing would not be killing the mother, but only letting her die. Moreover, in killing the child, one would be killing an innocent person, for the child has committed no crime, and is not aiming at his mother's death. And then there are a variety of ways in which this might be continued. (1) But as directly killing an innocent person is always and absolutely impermissible, an abortion may not be performed. Or, (2) as directly killing an innocent person is murder, and murder is always and absolutely impermissible, an abortion may not be performed.[4] Or, (3) as one's duty to refrain from directly killing an innocent person is more stringent than one's duty to keep a person from dying, an abortion may not be performed. Or, (4) if one's only options are directly killing an innocent person or letting a person die, one must prefer letting the person die, and thus an abortion may not be performed.[5]

Some people seem to have thought that these are not further premises which must be added if the conclusion is to be reached, but that they follow from the very fact that an innocent person has a right to life.[6] But this seems to me to be a mistake, and perhaps the simplest way to show this is to bring out that while we must certainly grant that innocent persons have a right to life, the theses in (1) through (4) are all false. Take (2), for example. If directly killing an innocent person is murder, and thus is impermissible, then the mother's directly killing the innocent person inside her is murder, and thus is impermissible. But it cannot seriously be thought to be murder if the mother performs an abortion on herself to save her life. It cannot seriously be said that she *must* refrain, that she *must* sit passively by and wait for her death. Let us look again at the case of you and the violinist. There you are, in bed with the violinist, and the director of the hospital says to you, "It's all most distressing, and I deeply sympathize, but you see this is putting an additional strain on your kidneys, and you'll be dead within the month. But you *have* to stay where you are all the same. Because unplugging you would be directly killing an innocent violinist, and that's murder, and that's impermissible." If anything in the world is true, it is that you do not commit murder, you do not do what is impermissible, if you reach around to your back and unplug yourself from that violinist to save your life.

The main focus of attention in writing on abortion has been on what a third party may or may not do in answer to a request from a woman for an abortion. This is in a way understandable. Things being as they are, there isn't much a woman can safely do to abort herself. So the question asked is what a third party may do, and what the mother may do, if it is mentioned at all, is deduced, almost as an afterthought, from what it is concluded that third parties may do. But it seems to me that to treat the matter in this way is to refuse to grant to the mother that very status of person which is so firmly insisted on for the foetus. For we cannot simply read off what a person may do from what a third party may do. Suppose you find yourself trapped in a tiny house with a growing child. I mean a very tiny house, and a rapidly growing child – you are already up against the wall of the house and in a few minutes you'll be crushed to death. The child on the other hand won't be crushed to death; if nothing is done to stop him from growing he'll be hurt, but in the end he'll simply burst open the house and walk out a free man. Now I could well understand it if a bystander were to say, "There's nothing we can do for you. We cannot choose between your life and his, we cannot be the ones to decide who is to live, we cannot intervene." But it cannot be concluded that you too can do nothing, that you cannot attack it to save your life. However innocent the child may be, you do not have to wait passively while it crushes you to death. Perhaps a pregnant woman is vaguely felt to have the status of house, to which we don't allow the right of self-defence. But if the woman houses the child, it should be remembered that she is a person who houses it.

I should perhaps stop to say explicitly that I am not claiming that people have a right to do anything whatever to save their lives. I think, rather, that there are drastic limits to the right of self-defence. If someone threatens you with death unless you torture someone else to death, I think you have not the right, even to save your life, to do so. But the case under consideration here is very different. In our case there are only two people involved, one whose life is threatened, and one who threatens it. Both are innocent: the one who is threatened is not threatened because of any fault, the one who threatens does not threaten because of any fault. For this reason we may feel that we bystanders cannot intervene. But the person threatened can.

In sum, a woman surely can defend her life against the threat to it posed by the unborn child, even if doing so involves its death. And this shows not merely that the theses in (1) through (4) are false; it shows also that the extreme view of abortion is false, and so we need not canvass any other possible ways of arriving at it from the argument I mentioned at the outset.

2. The extreme view could of course be weakened to say that while abortion is permissible to save the mother's life, it may not be performed by a third party, but only by the mother itself. But this cannot be right either. For what we have to keep in mind is that the mother and the unborn child are not like two tenants in a small house which has, by an unfortunate mistake, been rented to both: the mother *owns* the house. The fact that she does adds to the offensiveness of deducing that the mother can do nothing from the supposition that third parties can do nothing. But it does more than this: it casts a bright light on the supposition that third parties can do nothing. Certainly it lets us see that a third party who says "I cannot choose between you" is fooling himself if he thinks this is impartiality. If Jones has found and fastened on a certain coat, which he needs to keep him from freezing, but which Smith also needs to keep him from freezing, then it is not impartiality that says "I cannot choose between you" when Smith owns the coat. Women have said again and again "This body is *my* body!" and they have reason to feel angry, reason to feel that it has been like shouting

into the wind. Smith, after all, is hardly likely to bless us if we say to him, "Of course it's your coat, anybody would grant that it is. But no one may choose between you and Jones who is to have it."

We should really ask what it is that says "no one may choose" in the face of the fact that the body that houses the child is the mother's body. It may be simply a failure to appreciate this fact. But it may be something more interesting, namely the sense that one has a right to refuse to lay hands on people, even where it would be just and fair to do so, even where justice seems to require that somebody do so. Thus justice might call for somebody to get Smith's coat back from Jones, and yet you have a right to refuse to be the one to lay hands on Jones, a right to refuse to do physical violence to him. This, I think, must be granted. But then what should be said is not "no one may choose", but only, "*I* cannot choose", and indeed not even this, but "*I* will not *act*", leaving it open that somebody else can or should, and in particular that anyone in a position of authority, with the job of securing people's rights, both can and should. So this is no difficulty. I have not been arguing that any given third party must accede to the mother's request that he perform an abortion to save her life, but only that he may.

I suppose that in some views of human life the mother's body is only on loan to her, the loan not being one which gives her any prior claim to it. One who held this view might well think it impartiality to say "I cannot choose". But I shall simply ignore this possibility. My own view is that if a human being has any just, prior claim to anything at all, he has a just, prior claim to his own body. And perhaps this needn't be argued for here anyway, since, as I mentioned, the arguments against abortion we are looking at do grant that the woman has a right to decide what happens in and to her body.

But although they do grant it, I have tried to show that they do not take seriously what is done in granting it. I suggest the same thing will reappear even more clearly when we turn away from cases in which the mother's life is at stake, and attend, as I propose we now do, to the vastly more common cases in which a woman wants an abortion for some less weighty reason than preserving her own life.

3. Where the mother's life is not at stake, the argument I mentioned at the outset seems to have a much stronger pull. "Everyone has a right to life, so the unborn person has a right to life." And isn't the child's right to life weightier than anything other than the mother's own right to life, which she might put forward as ground for an abortion?

This argument treats the right to life as it if were unproblemantic. It is not, and this seems to me to be precisely the source of the mistake.

For we should now, at long last, ask what it comes to, to have a right to life. In some views having a right to life includes having a right to be given at least the bare minimum one needs for continued life. But suppose that what in fact *is* the bare minimum a man needs for continued life is something he has no right at all to be given? If I am sick unto death, and the only thing that will save my life is the touch of Henry Fonda's cool hand on my fevered brow, then all the same, I have no right to be given the touch of Henry Fonda's cool hand on my fevered brow. It would be frightfully nice of him to fly in from the West Coast to provide it. It would be less nice, though no doubt well meant, if my friends flew out to the West Coast and carried Henry Fonda back with them. But I have no right at all against anybody that he should do this for me. Or again, to return to the story I told earlier, the fact that for continued life that violinist needs the continued use of your kidneys does not establish that he has a right to be given the continued use of your kidneys. He certainly has no right against you that *you* should give him continued use of your kidneys. For nobody has any right to use your kidneys unless you give him such a right; and nobody has the right against you that you shall give him this right – if you do allow him to go on using your kidneys, this is a kindness on your part, and not something he can claim from you as his due. Nor has he any right against anybody else that *they* should give him continued use of your kidneys. Certainly he had no right against the Society of Music Lovers that they should plug him into you in the first place. And if you now start to unplug yourself, having learned that you will otherwise have to spend nine years in bed with him, there is nobody in the world who must try to prevent you, in order to see to it that he is given something he has a right to be given.

Some people are rather stricter about the right to life. In their view, it does not include the right to be given anything, but amounts to, and only to, the right not to be killed by anybody. But here a related difficulty arises. If everybody is to refrain from killing that violinist, then everybody must refrain from doing a great many different sorts of things. Everybody must refrain from slitting his throat, everybody must refrain from shooting him – and everybody must refrain from unplugging you from him. But does he have a right against everybody that they shall refrain from unplugging you from him? To refrain from doing this is to allow him to continue to use your kidneys. It could be argued that he has a right against us that *we* should allow him to continue to use your kidneys. That is, while he had no right against us that we should give him the use of your kidneys, it might be argued that he anyway has a right against us that we shall not now intervene and deprive him of the use of your kidneys. I shall come back to third-party interventions later. But certainly the violinist has no right against you that *you* shall allow him to continue to use your kidneys. As I said, if you do allow him to use them, it is a kindness on your part, and not something you owe him.

The difficulty I point to here is not peculiar to the right to life. It reappears in connection with all the other natural rights; and it is something which an adequate account of rights must deal with. For present purposes it is enough just to draw attention to it. But I would stress that I am not arguing that people do not have a right to life – quite to the contrary, it seems to me that the primary control we must place on the acceptability of an account of rights is that it should turn out in that account to be a truth that all persons have a right to life. I am arguing only that having a right to life does not guarantee having either a right to be given the use of or a right to be allowed continued use of another person's body – even if one needs it for life itself. So the right to life will not serve the opponents of abortion in the very simple and clear way in which they seem to have thought it would.

4. There is another way to bring out the difficulty. In the most ordinary sort of case, to deprive someone of what he has a right to is to treat him unjustly. Suppose a boy and his small brother are jointly given a box of chocolates for Christmas. If the older boy takes the box and refuses to give his brother any of the chocolates, he is unjust to him, for the brother has been given a right to half of them. But suppose that, having learned that otherwise it means nine years in bed with that violinist, you unplug yourself from him. You surely are not being unjust to him, for you gave him no right to use your kidneys, and no one else can have given him any such right. But we have to notice that in unplugging yourself, you are killing him; and violinists, like everybody else, have a right to life, and thus in the view we were considering just now, the right not to be killed. So here you do what he supposedly has a right you shall not do, but you do not act unjustly to him in doing it.

The emendation which may be made at this point is this: the right to life consists not in the right not to be killed, but rather in the right not to be killed unjustly. This runs a risk of circularity, but never mind: it would enable us to square the fact that the violinist has a right to life with the fact that you do not act unjustly toward him in unplugging yourself, thereby killing him. For if you do not kill him unjustly, you do not violate his right of life, and so it is no wonder you do him no injustice.

But if this emendation is accepted, the gap in the argument against abortion stares us plainly in the face: it is by no means enough to show that the foetus is a person, and to remind us that all persons have a right to life – we need to be shown also that killing the foetus violates its right to life, i.e., that abortion is unjust killing. And is it?

I suppose we may take it as a datum that in a case of pregnancy due to rape the mother has not given the unborn person a right to the use of her body for food and shelter. Indeed, in what pregnancy could it be supposed that the mother has given the unborn person such a right? It is not as if there were unborn persons drifting about the world, to whom a woman who wants a child says "I invite you in."

But it might be argued that there are other ways one can have acquired a right to the use of another person's body than by having been invited to use it by that person. Suppose a woman voluntarily indulges in intercourse, knowing of the chance it will issue in pregnancy, and then she does become pregnant; is she not in part responsible for the presence, in fact the very existence, of the unborn person inside here? No doubt she did not invite it in. But doesn't her partial responsibility for its being there itself give it a right to the use of her body?[7] If so, then her aborting it would be more like the boy's taking away the chocolates, and less like your unplugging yourself from the violinist – doing so would be depriving it of what it does have a right to, and thus would be doing it an injustice.

And then, too, it might be asked whether or not she can kill it even to save her own life: If she voluntarily called it into existence, how can she now kill it, even in self-defence?

The first thing to be said about this is that it is something new. Opponents of abortion have been so concerned to make out the independence of the foetus, in order to establish that it has a right to life, just as its mother does, that they have tended to overlook the possible support they might gain from making out that the foetus is *dependent* on the mother, in order to establish that she has a special kind of responsibility for it, a responsibility that gives it rights against her which are not possessed by any independent person – such as an ailing violinist who is a stranger to her.

On the other hand, this argument would give the unborn person a right to its mother's body only if her pregnancy resulted from a voluntary act, undertaken in full knowledge of the chance a pregnancy might result from it. It would leave out entirely the unborn person whose existence is due to rape. Pending the availability of some further argument, then, we would be left with the conclusion that unborn persons whose existence is due to rape have no right to the use of their mothers' bodies, and thus that aborting them is not depriving them of anything they have a right to and hence is not unjust killing.

And we should also notice that it is not at all plain that this argument really does go even as far as it purports to. For there are cases and cases, and the details make a difference. If the room is stuffy, and I therefore open a window to air it, and a burglar climbs in, it would be absurd to say, "Ah, now he can stay, she's given him a right to the use of her house – for she is partially responsible for his presence there, having voluntarily done what enabled him to get in, in full knowledge that there are such things as burglars, and that burglars burgle." It would be still more absurd to say this if I had had bars installed outside my windows, precisely to prevent burglars from getting in, and a burglar got in only because of a defect in the bars. It remains equally absurd if we imagine it is not a burglar who climbs in, but an innocent person who blunders or falls in. Again, suppose it were like this: people-seeds drift about in the air like pollen, and if you open your windows, one may drift in and take root in your carpets or upholstery. You don't want children, so you fix up your windows with fine mesh screens, the very best you can buy. As can happen, however, and on very, very rare occasions does happen, one of the screens is defective; and a seed drifts in and takes root. Does the person-plant who now develops have a right to the use of your house? Surely not – despite the fact that you voluntarily opened your windows, you knowingly kept carpets and upholstered furniture, and you knew that screens were sometimes defective. Someone may argue that you are responsible for its rooting, that it does have a right to your house, because after all you *could* have lived your life with bare floors and furniture, or with sealed windows and doors. But this won't do – for by the same token anyone can avoid a pregnancy due to rape by having a hysterectomy, or anyway by never leaving home without a (reliable!) army.

It seems to me that the argument we are looking at can establish at most that there are *some* cases in which the unborn person has a right to the use of its mother's body, and therefore *some* cases in which abortion is unjust killing. There is room for much discussion and argument as to precisely which, if any. But I think we should side-step this issue and leave it open, for at any rate the argument certainly does not establish that all abortion is unjust killing.

5. There is room for yet another argument here, however. We surely must all grant that there may be cases in which it would be morally indecent to detach a person from your body at the cost of his life. Suppose you learn that what the violinist needs is not nine years of your life, but only one hour: all you need do to save his life is to spend one hour in that bed with him. Suppose also that letting him use your kidneys for that one hour would not affect your health in the slightest. Admittedly you were kidnapped. Admittedly you did not give anyone permission to plug him into you. Nevertheless it seems to me plain you *ought* to allow him to use your kidneys for that hour – it would be indecent to refuse.

Again, suppose pregnancy lasted only an hour, and constituted no threat to life or health. And suppose that a woman becomes pregnant as a result of rape. Admittedly she did not voluntarily do anything to bring about the existence of a child. Admittedly she did nothing at all which would give the unborn person a right to the use of her body. All the same it might well be said, as in the newly emended violinist story, that she *ought* to allow it to remain for that hour – that it would be indecent in her to refuse.

Now some people are inclined to use the term "right" in such a way that it follows from the fact that you ought to allow a person to use your body for the hour he needs, that he has a right to use your body for the hour he needs, even though he has not been given that right by any person or act. They may say that it follows also that if you refuse, you act unjustly toward him. This use of the term is perhaps so common that it cannot be called wrong; nevertheless it seems to me to be an unfortunate loosening of what we would do better to keep a tight rein on. Suppose that box of chocolates I mentioned earlier had not been given to both boys jointly, but was given only to the older boy. There he sits, stolidly eating his way through the box, his small brother watching enviously. Here we are likely to say "You ought not to be so mean. You ought to give your brother some of those chocolates." My own view is that it just does not follow from the truth of this that the brother has any right to any of the chocolates. If the boy refuses to give his brother any, he is greedy, stingy, callous – but not unjust. I suppose that the people I have in mind will say it does follow that the brother has a right to some of the chocolates, and thus that the boy does act unjustly if he refuses to give his brother any. But the effect of saying this is to obscure what we should keep distinct, namely the difference between the boy's refusal in this case and the boy's refusal in the earlier case, in which the box was given to both boys jointly, and in which the small brother thus had what was from any point of view clear title to half.

A further objection to so using the term "right" that from the fact that A ought to do a thing for B, it follows that B has a right against A that A do it for him, is that it is going to make the question of whether or not a man has a right to a thing turn on how easy it is to provide him with it; and this seems not merely unfortunate, but morally unacceptable. Take the case of Henry Fonda again. I said earlier that I had no right to the touch of his cool hand on my fevered brow, even though I needed it to save my life. I said it would be frightfully nice of him to fly in from the West Coast to provide me with it, but that I had no right against him that he should do so. But suppose he isn't on the West Coast. Suppose he has only to walk across the room, place a hand briefly on my brow – and lo, my life is saved. Then surely he ought to do it, it would be indecent to refuse. Is it to be said "Ah, well, it follows that in this case she has a right to the touch of his hand on her brow, and so it would be an injustice in him to refuse"? So that I have a right to it when it is easy for him to provide it, though no right when it's hard? It's rather a shocking idea that anyone's rights should fade away and disappear as it gets harder and harder to accord them to him.

So my own view is that even though you ought to let the violinist use your kidneys for the one hour he needs, we should not conclude that he has a right to do so – we should say that if you refuse, you are, like the boy who owns all the chocolates and will give none away, self-centred and callous, indecent in fact, but not unjust. And similarly, that even supposing a case in which a women pregnant due to rape ought to allow the unborn person use her body for the hour he needs, we should not conclude that he has a right to do so; we should conclude that she is self-centred, callous, indecent, but not unjust, if she refuses. The complaints are no less grave; they are just different. However, there is no need to insist on this point. If anyone does wish to deduce "he has a right" from "you ought", then all the same he must surely grant that there are cases in which it is not morally required of you that you allow that violinist to use your kidneys, and in which he does not have a right to use them, and in which you do not do him an injustice if you refuse. And so also for mother and unborn child. Except in such cases as the unborn person has a right to demand it – and we were leaving open the possibility that there may be such cases – nobody is morally *required* to make large sacrifices, of health, of all other interests and concerns, of all other duties and commitments, for nine years, or even for nine months, in order to keep another person alive.

6. We have in fact to distinguish between two kinds of Samaritan: the Good Samaritan and what we might call the Minimally Decent Samaritan. The story of the Good Samaritan, you will remember, goes like this:

A certain man went down from Jerusalem to Jericho, and fell among thieves, which stripped him of his raiment, and wounded him, and departed, leaving him half dead.

And by chance there came down a certain priest that way; and when he saw him, he passed by on the other side.

And likewise a Levite, when he was at the place, came and looked on him, and passed by on the other side.

But a certain Samaritan, as he journeyed, came where he was; and when he saw him he had compassion on him.

And went to him, and bound up his wounds, pouring in oil and wine, and set him on his own beast, and brought him to an inn, and took care of him.

And on the morrow, when he departed, he took out two pence, and gave them to the host, and said unto him, "Take care of him; and whatsoever thou spendest more, when I come again, I will repay thee."

(Luke 10:30–5)

The Good Samaritan went out of his way, at some cost to himself, to help one in need of it. We are not told what the options were, that is, whether or not the priest and the Levite could have helped by doing less than the Good Samaritan did, but assuming they could have, then the fact they did nothing at all shows they were not even Minimally Decent Samaritans, not because they were not Samaritans, but because they were not even minimally decent.

These things are a matter of degree, of course, but there is a difference, and it comes out perhaps most clearly in the story of Kitty Genovese, who, as you will remember, was murdered while thirty-eight people watched or listened, and did nothing at all to help her. A Good Samaritan would have rushed out to give direct assistance against the murderer. Or perhaps we had better allow that it would have been a Splendid Samaritan who did this, on the ground that it would have involved a risk of death for himself. But the thirty-eight not only did not do this, they did not even trouble to pick up a phone to call the police. Minimally Decent Samaritanism would call for doing at least that, and their not having done it was monstrous.

After telling the story of the Good Samaritan, Jesus said "Go, and do thou likewise." Perhaps he meant that we are morally required to act as the Good Samaritan did. Perhaps he was urging people to do more than is morally required of them. At all events it seems plain that it was not morally required of any of the thirty-eight that he rush out to give direct assistance at the risk of his own life, and that it is not morally required of anyone that he give long stretches of his life – nine years or nine months – to sustaining the life of a person who has no special right (we were leaving open the possibility of this) to demand it.

Indeed, with one rather striking class of exceptions, no one in any country in the world is *legally* required to do anywhere near as much as this for anyone else. The class of exceptions is obvious. My main concern here is not the state of the law in respect to abortion, but it is worth drawing attention to the fact that in none of the United States is any man compelled by law to be even a Minimally Decent Samaritan to any person; there is no law under which charges could be brought against the thirty-eight who stood by while Kitty Genovese died. By contrast, in most states in this country women are compelled by law to be not merely Minimally Decent Samaritans, but Good Samaritans to unborn persons inside them. This doesn't by itself settle anything one way or the other, because it may well be argued that there should be laws in this country – as there are in many European countries – compelling at least Minimally Decent Samaritanism.[8] But it does show that there is a gross injustice in the existing state of the law. And it shows also that the groups currently working against liberalization of abortion laws, in fact working toward having it declared unconstitutional for a state to permit abortion, had better start working for the adoption of Good Samaritan laws generally, or earn the charge that they are acting in bad faith.

I should think, myself, that Minimally Decent Samaritan laws would be one thing, Good Samaritan laws quite another, and in fact highly improper. But we are not here concerned with the law. What we should ask is not whether anybody should be compelled by law to be a Good Samaritan, but whether we must accede to a situation in which somebody is being compelled – by nature, perhaps – to be a Good Samaritan. We have, in other words, to look now at third-party interventions. I have been arguing that no person is morally required to make large sacrifices to sustain the life of another who has no right to demand them, and this even where the sacrifices do not include life itself; we are not morally required to be Good Samaritans or anyway Very Good Samaritans to one another. But what if a man cannot extricate himself from such a situation? What if he appeals to us to extricate him? It seems to me plain that there are cases in which we can, cases in which a Good Samaritan would extricate him. There you are, you were kidnapped, and nine years in bed with that violinist lie ahead of you. You have your own life to lead. You are sorry, but you simply cannot see giving up so much of your life to the sustaining of his. You cannot extricate yourself, and ask us to do so. I should have thought that – in light of his having no right to the use of your body – it was obvious that we do not have to accede to your being forced to give up so much. We can do what you ask. There is no injustice to the violinist in our doing so.

7. Following the lead of the opponents of abortion, I have throughout been speaking of the foetus merely as a person, and what I have been asking is whether or not the argument we began with, which proceeds only from the foetus's being a person, really does establish its conclusion. I have argued that it does not.

But of course there are arguments and arguments, and it may be said that I have simply fastened on the wrong one. It may be said that what is important is not merely the fact that the foetus is a person, but that it is a person for whom the woman has a special kind of responsibility issuing from the fact that she is its mother. And it might be argued that all my analogies are therefore irrelevant – for you do not have that special kind of responsibility for that violinist, Henry Fonda does not have that special kind of responsibility for me. And our attention might be drawn to the fact that men and women both *are* compelled by law to provide support for their children.

I have in effect dealt (briefly) with this argument in section 4 above; but a (still briefer) recapitulation now may be in order. Surely we do not have any such "such responsibility" for a person unless we have assumed it, explicitly or implicitly. If a set of parents do not try to prevent pregnancy, do not obtain an abortion, and then at the time of birth of the child do not put it out for adoption, but rather take it home with them, then they have assumed responsibility for it, they have given it rights, and they cannot *now* withdraw support from it at the cost of its life because they now find it difficult to go on providing for it. But if they have taken all reasonable precautions against having a child, they do not simply by virtue of their biological relationship to the child who comes into existence have a special responsibility for it. They may wish to assume responsibility for it, or they may not wish to. And I am suggesting that if assuming responsibility for it would require large sacrifices, then they may refuse. A Good Samaritan would not refuse – or anyway, a Splendid Samaritan, if the sacrifices that had to be made were enormous. But then so would a Good Samaritan assume responsibility for that violinist; so would Henry Fonda, if he is a Good Samaritan, fly in from the West Coast and assume responsibility for me.

8. My argument will be found unsatisfactory on two counts by many of those who want to regard abortion as morally permissible. First, while I do argue that abortion is not impermissible, I do not argue that it is always permissible. There may well be cases in which carrying the child to term requires only Minimally Decent Samaritanism of the mother, and this is a standard we must not fall below. I am inclined to think it a merit of my account precisely that it does *not* give a general yes or a general no. It allows for and supports our sense that, for example, a sick and desperately frightened fourteen-year-old schoolgirl, pregnant due to rape, may *of course* choose abortion, and that any law which rules this out is an insane law. And it also allows for and supports our sense that in other cases resort to abortion is even positively indecent. It would be indecent in the woman to request an abortion, and indecent in a doctor to perform it, if she is in her seventh month, and wants the abortion just to avoid the nuisance of postponing a trip abroad. The very fact that the arguments I have been drawing attention to treat all cases of abortion, or even all cases of abortion in which the mother's life is not at stake, as morally on a par ought to have made them suspect at the outset.

Secondly, while I am arguing for the permissibility of abortion in some cases, I am not arguing for the right to secure the death of the unborn child. It is easy to confuse these two things in that up to a certain point in the life of the foetus it is not able to survive outside the mother's body; hence removing it from her body guarantees its death. But they are importantly different. I have argued that you are not morally required to spend nine months in bed, sustaining the life of that violinist; but to say this is by no means to say that if, when you unplug yourself, there is a miracle and he survives, you then have a right to turn round and slit his throat. You may detach yourself even if this costs him his life; you have no right to be guaranteed his death, by some other means, if unplugging yourself does not kill him. There are some people who will feel dissatisfied by this feature of my argument. A woman my be utterly devastated by the thought of a child, a bit of herself, put out for adoption and never seen or heard of again. She may therefore want not merely that the child be detached from her, but more, that it die. Some opponents of abortion are inclined to regard this as beneath contempt – thereby showing insensitivity to what is surely a powerful source of despair. All the same, I agree that the desire for the child's death is not one which anybody may gratify, should it turn out to be possible to detach the child alive.

At this place, however, it should be remembered that we have only been pretending throughout that the foetus is a human being from the moment of conception. A very early abortion is surely not the killing of a person, and so is not dealt with by anything I have said here.

NOTES

1 I am much indebted to James Thomson for discussion, criticism, and many helpful suggestions.
2 Daniel Callahan, *Abortion: Law, Choice and Morality* (New York, 1970), p. 373. This book gives a fascinating survey of the available information on abortion. The Jewish tradition is surveyed in David M. Feldman, *Birth Control in Jewish Law* (New York, 1968). Part 5, the Catholic tradition in John T. Noonan, Jr., "An Almost Absolute Value in History", in *The Morality of Abortion*, ed. John T. Noonan, Jr. (Cambridge, Mass., 1970).
3 The term "direct" in the arguments I refer to is a technical one. Roughly, what is meant by "direct killing" is either killing as an end in itself, or killing as a means to some end, for example, the end of saving someone's life. See n. 6, below, for an example of its use.
4 Cf. *Encyclical Letter of Pope Pius XI on Christian Marriage*, St Paul Editions (Boston, n.d.), p. 32: "however much we may pity the mother whose health and even life is gravely imperiled in the performance of the duty allotted to her by nature, nevertheless what could ever be a sufficient reason for excusing in any way the direct murder of the innocent? This is precisely what we are dealing with here". Noonan (*The Morality of Abortion*, p. 43) reads this as follows: "What cause can ever avail to excuse in any way the direct killing of the innocent? For it is a question of that."
5 The thesis in (4) is in an interesting way weaker than those in (1), (2), and (3): they rule out abortion even in cases in which both mother *and* child will

die if the abortion is not performed. By contrast, one who held the view expressed in (4) could consistently say that one needn't prefer letting two persons die to killing one.

6 Cf. the following passage from Pius XII, *Address to the Italian Catholic Society of Midwives:* "The baby in the maternal breast has the right to life immediately from God. – Hence there is no man, no human authority, no science, no medical, eugenic, social, economic or moral 'indication' which can establish or grant a valid juridical ground for a direct deliberate disposition of an innocent human life, that is a disposition which looks to its destruction either as an end or as a means to another end perhaps in itself not illicit. – The baby, still not born, is a man in the same degree and for the same reason as the mother" (quoted in Noonan, *The Morality of Abortion,* p. 45).

7 The need for a discussion of this argument was brought home to me by members of the Society for Ethical and Legal Philosophy, to whom this paper was originally presented.

8 For a discussion of the difficulties involved, and a survey of the European experience with such laws, see *The Good Samaritan and the Law,* ed. James M. Ratcliffe (New York, 1966).

READING QUESTIONS ON THOMSON

1 Is it appropriate to think of the relation between a pregnant woman and a foetus in the terms Thomson suggests?

2 Why does Thomson talk so much about avoidability? How does it change the rights of the parties involved?

3 Thomson maintains that the law should not place larger burdens on women than on men. How is this claim related to the rest of her argument?

John Finnis
"The Rights and Wrongs of Abortion: A Reply to Judith Jarvis Thomson" (1973)

Finnis appeals to traditional moral understandings to argue that abortion is indistinguishable from murder because it requires the intentional taking of life.

Fortunately, none of the arguments for and against abortion *need* be expressed in terms of "rights". As we shall see, Judith Thomson virtually admits as much in her "A Defence of Abortion".[1] But since she has chosen to conduct her case by playing off a "right to life" against a "right to decide what happens in and to one's body", I shall begin by showing how this way of arguing about the rights and wrongs of abortion needlessly complicates and confuses the issue. It is convenient and appropriate to speak of "rights" for purposes and in contexts which I shall try to identify; it is most inconvenient and inappropriate when one is debating the moral permissibility of types of action – types such as "abortions performed without the desire to kill", which is the type of action Thomson wishes to defend as morally permissible under most circumstances. So in section I of this essay I shall show how her specification and moral characterization of this type of action are logically independent of her discussion of "rights". Then in section II I shall outline some principles of moral characterization and of moral permissibility, principles capable of explaining some of the moral condemnations which Thomson expresses but which remain all too vulnerable and obscure in her paper. In section III I shall show how the elaboration of those principles warrants those condemnations of abortion which Thomson thinks mistaken as well as many of those attributions of human rights which she so much takes for granted. In section IV I briefly state the reason (misstated by Thomson and also by Wertheimer[2]) why the foetus from conception has human rights, i.e. should be given the same consideration as other human beings.

I

Thomson's reflections on rights develop in three states. (A) She indicates a knot of problems about what rights are rights to; she dwells particularly on the problem "what it comes to, to have a right to life" (p. 687). (B) She indicates, rather less clearly, a knot of problems about the source of rights; in particular she suggests that, over a wide range (left unspecified by her) of types of right, a person has a right only to what he has "title" to by reason of some gift, concession, grant or undertaking to him by another person. (C) She cuts both these knots by admitting (but all too quietly) that her whole argument about abortion concerns simply what is "morally required" or "morally permissible"; that what is in question is really the scope and source of the mother's responsibility (and only derivatively, by entailment, the scope and source of the unborn child's rights). I shall now examine these three stages a little more closely, and (D) indicate why I think it useful to have done so.

(A) How do we specify the content of a right? What is a right a right to? Thomson mentions at least nine different rights which a person might rightly or wrongly be said to have.[3] Of these nine, seven have the same logical structure;[4] viz., in each instance, the alleged right is a right with respect to P's action (performance, omission) as an action which may affect Q. In some of these seven instances,[5] the right with respect to P's action is P's right (which Hohfeld[6] called a privilege and Hohfeldians call a liberty). In the other instances,[7] the right with respect to P's action is Q's right (which Hohfeldians call a "claim-right"). But in all these seven instances there is what I shall call a "Hohfeldian right": to assert a Hohfeldian right is to assert a three-term relation between two persons and the action of one of those persons in so far as that action concerns the other person.

The other two rights mentioned by Thomson have a different logical structure.[8] In both these instances, the alleged right is a right with respect to a thing (one's "own body", or the state of affairs referred to as one's "life"). Here the relation is two-term: between one person and some thing or state of affairs. Rights in this sense cannot be completely analysed in terms of some unique combination of Hohfeldian rights.[9] P's right to a thing (land, body, life) can and normally should be secured by granting or attributing Hohfeldian rights to him or to others; but just which combination of such Hohfeldian rights will properly or best secure his single right to the thing in question will vary according to time, place, person, and circumstance. And since moral judgments centrally concern *actions*, it is this specification of Hohfeldian rights that we need for moral purposes, rather than invocations of rights to things.

Since Thomson concentrates on the problematic character of the "right to life", I shall illustrate what I have just said by reference to the "right to one's own body", which she should (but seems, in practice, not to) regard as equally problematic. Now her two explicit versions of this right are: one's "just, prior claim to his own body", and one's "right to decide what happens in and to one's body". But both versions need much specification[10] before they can warrant moral judgments about particular sorts of action. For example, the "right to decide" may be *either* (i) a right (Hohfeldian liberty) to do things to or with one's own body (e.g. to remove those kidney plugs, or that baby, from it – but what else? anything? do I have the moral liberty to decide not to raise my hand to the telephone to save Kitty Genovese from her murderers?); *or* (ii) a right (Hohfeldian claim-right) that other people shall not (at least without one's permission) do things to or with one's own body (e.g. draw sustenance from, or inhabit, it – but what else? anything?); *or* (iii) some combination of these forms of right with each other or with other forms of right such as (a) the right (Hohfeldian power) to change another person's right (liberty) to use one's body by making a grant of or permitting such use (*any* such use?), or (b) the right (Hohfeldian immunity) not to have one's right (claim-right) to be free from others' use of one's body diminished or affected by purported grants or permissions by third parties. And as soon as we thus identify these possible sorts of right, available to give concrete moral content to the "right to one's body", it becomes obvious that the actions which the right entitles, disentitles, or requires one to perform (or entitles, disentitles, or requires others to perform) *vary* according to the identity and circumstances of the two parties to each available and relevant Hohfeldian right. And this, though she didn't recognize it, is the reason why Thomson found the "right to life" problematic, too.

(B) I suspect it was her concentration on non-Hohfeldian rights ("title" to things like chocolates or bodies) that led Thomson to make the curious suggestion which appears and reappears, though with a very uncertain role, in her paper. I mean, her suggestion that we should speak of "rights" only in respect of what a man has "title" to (usually, if not necessarily, by reason of gift, concession, or grant to him).

This suggestion,[11] quite apart from the dubious centrality it accords to ownership and property in the spectrum of rights, causes needless confusion in the presentation of Thomson's defence of abortion. For if the term "right" were to be kept on the "tight rein" which she suggests (p. 691), then (a) the Popes and others whose appeal to the "right to life" she is questioning would deprive her paper of its starting-point and indeed its pivot by simply rephrasing their appeal so as to eliminate all reference to rights (for, as I show in the next section, they are not alleging that the impropriety of abortion follows from any grant, gift, or concession of "rights" to the unborn child); and (b) Thomson would likewise have to rephrase claims she herself makes, such as that innocent persons certainly have a right to life, that mothers have the right to abort themselves to save their lives, that P has a right not to be tortured to death by Q even if R is threatening to kill Q unless Q does so, and so on. But if such rephrasing is possible (as indeed it is), then it is obvious that suggestions about the proper or best way to use the term "a right" are irrelevant to the substantive moral defence or critique of abortion.

But this terminological suggestion is linked closely with Thomson's substantive thesis that we do not have any "special [sc. Good Samaritan or Splendid Samaritan] responsibility" for the life or well-being of others "unless we have assumed it, explicitly or implicitly" (p. 695). It is this (or some such) thesis about *responsibility* on which Thomson's whole argument, in the end, rests.

(C) Thomson's explicit recognition that her defence of abortion *need* not have turned on the assertion or denial of rights comes rather late in her paper, when she says that there is "no need to insist on" her suggested reined-in use of the term "right":

If anyone does wish to deduce "he has a right" from "you ought", then all the same he must surely grant that there are cases in which it is not morally required of you that you allow that violinist to use your kidneys ... [12] And so also for mother and unborn child. Except in such cases as the unborn person has a right to demand it ... nobody is morally *required* to make large sacrifices ... in order to keep another person alive (pp. 692–3).

In short, the dispute is about what is "morally required" (i.e. about what one "must" and, for that matter, "may" or "can" [not] do: see p. 687; that is to say, about the rights and wrongs of abortion. True, on page 695 there is still that "right to demand large sacrifices" cluttering up the margins of the picture. But when we come to the last pages of her paper (pp. 696–7) even that has been set aside, and the real question is identified as not whether the child has a "right to demand large sacrifices" of its mother, but whether the other has a "special responsibility" to or for the child (since, if she has, then she may be morally required to make large sacrifices for it and *therefore* we will be able to assert, by a convenient locution, the child's "right to [demand] those sacrifices").

(D) So in the end most of the argument about rights was a red herring. I have bothered to track down this false trail, not merely to identify some very common sorts and sources of equivocation (more will come to light in the next two sections), but also to show how Thomson's decision to conduct her defence in terms of "rights" makes it peculiarly easy to miss a most important weak point in her defence. This weak point is the connection or relation between one's "special responsibilities" and one's ordinary (not special) responsibilities; and one is enabled to miss it easily if one thinks (a) that the whole problem is essentially one of rights, (b) that rights typically or even essentially depend on grant, concession, assumption, etc., (c) that special responsibilities likewise depend on grants, concessions, assumptions, etc., and (d) that therefore the whole moral problem here concerns one's *special* responsibilities. Such a train of thought is indeed an enthymeme, if not a downright fallacy; but that is not surprising, since I am commenting here not on an argument offered by Thomson but on a likely effect of her "rhetoric".

What Thomson, then, fails to attend to adequately is the claim (one of the claims implicit, I think, in the papal and conservative rhetoric of rights) that the mother's duty not to abort herself is *not* an incident of any special responsibility which she assumed or undertook for the child, but is a straight-forward incident of an ordinary duty everyone owes to his neighbour. Thomson indeed acknowledges that such ordinary nonassumed duties exist and are as morally weighty as duties of justice in her reined-in sense of "justice"; but I cannot discern the principles on which she bases, and (confidently) delimits the range of, these duties.[13]

She speaks, for instance, about "the drastic limits to the right of self-defence": "If someone threatens you with death unless you torture someone else to death, I think you have not the right, even to save your life, to do so" (p. 685). Yet she also says: "If anything in the world is true, it is that you do not ... do what is impermissible, if you reach around to your back and unplug yourself from that violinist to save your life" (p. 685). So why, in the first case, has one the strict responsibility not to bring about the death demanded? Surely she is not suggesting that the pain ("torture") makes the difference, or that it *is* morally permissible to kill *painlessly* another person on the orders of a third party who threatens you with death for noncompliance? And, since she thinks that "nobody is morally *required* to make large sacrifices, of health, of all other interests and concerns, of all other duties and commitments, for nine years, or even for nine months, in order to keep another person alive" (p. 693), will she go on to say that it is permissible, when a third party threatens you with such "large sacrifices" (though well short of your life), to *kill* (painlessly) another person, or two or ten other persons?

If Thomson balks at such suggestions, I think it must be because she does in the end rely on some version of the distinction, forced underground in her paper, between "direct killing" and "not keeping another person alive".

The more one reflects on Thomson's argument, the more it seems to turn and trade on some version of this distinction. Of course she starts by rejecting the view that it is always wrong to directly kill, because that view would (she thinks) condemn one to a lifetime plugged into the violinist. But she proceeds, as we have noted, to reject at least one form of killing to save one's life, on grounds that seem to have nothing to do with consequences and everything to do with the formal context and thus structure of one's action (the sort of formal considerations that usually are wrapped up, as we shall see, in the word "direct"). And indeed the whole movement of her argument in defence of abortion is to assimilate abortion to the range of Samaritan problems, on the basis that having an abortion is, or can be, justified as *merely* a way of *not rendering special assistance*. Again, the argument turns, not on a calculus of consequences, but on the formal characteristics of one's choice itself.

Well, why should this apparently *formal* aspect of one's choice determine one's precise responsibilities in a certain situation whatever the other circumstances and expected consequences or upshots? When we know *why*, on both sides of the debate about abortion, we draw and rely on these distinctions, then we will be better placed to consider (i) whether or not unplugging from the violinist is, after all, direct killing in the sense alleged to be relevant by Popes and others, and (ii) whether or not abortion is, after all, just like unplugging the captive philosopher from the moribund musician.

II

Like Thomson's moral language (setting off the "permissible" against the "impermissible"), the traditional rule about killing doubtless gets its peremptory sharpness primarily (historically speaking) from the injunction, respected as divine and revealed: "Do not kill the innocent and just."[14] But the handful of peremptory negative moral principles correspond to the handful of really basic aspects of human flourishing, which in turn correspond to the handful of really basic and controlling human needs and human inclinations. To be fully reasonable, one must remain *open* to every basic aspect of human flourishing, to every basic form of human good. For is not each irreducibly basic, and none merely means to end? Are not the basic goods incommensurable? Of course it is reasonable to concentrate on realizing those forms of good, in or for those particular communities and persons (first of all oneself), which one's situation, talents, and opportunities most fit one for. But concentration, specialization, particularization is one thing; it is quite another thing, rationally and thus morally speaking, to make a choice which cannot but be characterized as a choice *against* life (to kill), *against* communicable knowledge of truth (to lie, where truth is at stake in communication), *against* procreation, *against* friendship and the justice that is bound up with friendship. Hence the strict negative percepts.[15]

The general sense of "responsibility", "duty", "obligation", "permissibility" is not my concern here, but rather the *content* of our responsibilities, duties, obligations, of the demands which human good makes on each of us. The general demand is that we remain adequately open to, attentive to, respectful of, and willing to pursue human good in so far as it can be realized and respected in our choices and dispositions. Now most moral failings are not by way of violation of strict negative precepts – i.e. are not straightforward choices against basic values. Rather, they are forms of negligence, of *insufficient* regard for these basic goods, or for the derivative structures reasonably created to support the basic goods. And when someone is accused of violating directly a basic good, he will usually plead that he was acting out of a proper care and concern for the realization of that or another basic value in the *consequences* of his chosen act though not in the act itself. For example, an experimenter accused of killing children in order to conduct medical tests will point out that these deaths are necessary to these tests, and these tests to medical discoveries, and the discoveries to the saving of many more lives – so that, in view of the foreseeable consequences of his deed, he displays (he will argue) a fully adequate (indeed, the only adequate) and reasonable regard for the value of human life.

But to appeal to consequences in this fashion is to set aside one criterion of practical reasonableness and hence of morality – namely, that one remain open to each basic value, and attentive to some basic value, in each of one's chosen acts – in favour of quite another criterion – namely, that one choose so to act as to bring about consequences involving a greater balance of good over bad than could be expected to be brought about by doing any alternative action open to one. Hare has observed that *"for practical purposes* there is no important difference" between most of the currently advocated theories in ethics; they all are "utilitarian", a term he uses to embrace Brandt's ideal observer theory, Richards's (Rawls's?) rational contractor theory, specific rule-utilitarianism, universalistic act-utilitarianism and his own universal prescriptivism.[16] All justify and require, he argues, the adoption of "the principles whose general inculcation will have, all in all, the best consequences."[17] I offer no critique of this utilitarianism here; Thomson's paper is not, on its face, consequentialist. Suffice it to inquire how Hare and his fellow consequentialists know the future that to most of us is hidden. How do they know what unit of computation to select from among the incommensurable and irreducible basic aspects of human flourishing; what principle of distribution of goods to commend to an individual considering his own interests, those of his friends, his family, his enemies, his *patria* and those of all men present and future? How do they know how to define the "situation" whose universal specification will appear in the principle whose adoption (singly? in conjunction with other principles?) "will" have best consequences;[18] whether and how to weigh future and uncertain consequences against present and certain consequences? And how do they know that net good consequences would in fact be maximized (even if *per impossible* they were calculable) by general adoption of consequentialist principles of action along with consequentialist "principles" to justify nonobservance of consequentialist "principles" in hard cases?[19] One cannot understand the Western moral tradition, with its peremptory negative (forbearance-requiring) principles (the positive principles being relevant in all, but peremptory in few, particular situations), unless one sees why that tradition rejected consequentialism as mere self-delusion – for Hare and his fellow consequentialists can provide no satisfactory answer to any of the foregoing lines of inquiry, and have no coherent rational account to give of any level of moral thought above that of the man who thinks how good it would be to act "for the best."[20] Expected total consequences of one's action do not provide a sufficient ground for making a choice that cannot but be regarded as *itself* a choice directly against a basic value (even that basic value which it is hoped will be realized in the *consequences*) — for expected total consequences cannot be given an evaluation sufficiently reasonable and definitive to be the decisive measure of our response to the call of human values, while a choice directly against a basic good provides, one might say, its own definitive evaluation of itself.

I do not expect these isolated and fragmentary remarks to be in themselves persuasive. I do not deny that the traditional Western willingness (in theory) to discount expected consequences wherever the action itself could not but be characterized as against a basic value, is or was supported by the belief that Providence would inevitably provide that "all manner of things shall be well" (i.e. that the whole course of history would turn out to have been a fine thing, indisputably evil deeds and their consequences turning out to have been "all to the good" like indisputably saintly deeds and their consequences). Indeed, the consequent-ialist moralist, who nourishes his moral imagination on scenarios in which by killing an innocent or two he saves scores, thousands, mil-lions, or even the race itself, rather obviously is a post-Christian phe-nomenon – such an assumption of the role of Providence would have seemed absurd to the pre-Christian philosophers[21] known to Cicero and Augustine. I am content to suggest the theoretical and moral context in which the casuistry of "direct" and "indirect" develops, within the wider context of *types* of action to be considered "impermissible" (I leave the term incompletely accounted for) because *inescapably* (i.e. whatever the hoped-for consequences) choices *against* a basic value of human living and doing. In short, one's responsibility for the realization of human good, one's fostering of or respect for human flourishing in future states of affairs at some greater or lesser remove from one's present action, does not override one's responsibility to respect each basic form of human good which comes directly in question in one's present action itself.

But how does one choose "directly against" a basic form of good? When is it the case, for example, that one's choice, one's intentional act, "cannot but be" characterized as "inescapably" anti-life? Is abortion always (or ever) such a case? A way to tackle these questions can be illustrated by reference to three hard cases whose traditional "solutions" contributed decisively to the traditional judgment about abortion. The relevance of these "hard cases" and "solutions" to the discussion with Thomson should be apparent in each case, but will become even more apparent in the next section.

(i) Suicide

Considered as a fully deliberate choice (which it doubtless only rather rarely is), suicide is a paradigm case of an action that is always wrong because it cannot but be characterized as a choice directly against a fundamental value, life. The characterization is significant, for what makes the killing of oneself attractive is usually, no doubt, the prospect of peace, relief, even a kind of freedom or personal integration, and sometimes is an admirable concern for others; but no amount of con-centration on the allure of these positive values can disguise from a clear-headed practical reasoner that it is *by* and *in* killing himself that he intends or hopes to realize those goods. And the characterization is given sharpness and definition by the contrast with heroic self-sacrifices in battle or with willing martyrdom.[22] Where Durkheim treated martyrdom as a case of suicide,[23] anybody concerned with the intentional structure of actions (rather than with a simplistic analysis of movements with foreseen upshots) will grant that the martyr is not directly choosing death, either as end or as means. For, however certainly death may be expected to ensue from the martyr's choice not to accede to the tyrant's threats, still it will ensue through, and as the point of, *someone else's* deliberate act (the tyrant's or the executioner's), and thus the martyr's chosen act of defiance need not be interpreted as itself a choice against the good of life.

The case of suicide has a further significance. The judgments, the characterizations, and the distinctions made in respect of someone's choices involving his *own* death will be used in respect of choices involving the death of *others*. In other words, *rights* (such as the "right to life") are not the fundamental rationale for the judgment that the killing of other (innocent) persons is impermissible. What is impermissible is an intention set against the value of human life where that value is directly at stake in any action by virtue of the intentional and causal structure of that action; and such an impermissible intention may concern my life or yours – and no one speaks of his "right to life" as against himself, as something that would explain why *his* act of self-killing would be wrongful.

Indeed, I think the real justification for speaking of "rights" is to make the point that, when it comes to characterizing intentional actions in terms of their openness to basic human values, those human values are, and are to be, realized in the lives and well-being of others as well as in the life and well-being of the actor. That is, the point of speaking of "rights" is to stake out the relevant claims to equality and nondiscrimination (claims that are not to absolute equality, since *my* life and my well-being have some reasonable priority in the direction of *my* practical effort, if only because I am better placed to secure them). But the claims are to equality of *treatment*; so, rather than speak emptily of (say) a "right to life", it would be better to speak of (say, *inter alia*) a "right not to be killed intentionally" – where the meaning and significance of "intentional killing" can be illuminated by consideration of the right and wrong of killing oneself (i.e. of a situation where no "rights" are in question and one is alone with the bare problem of the right relation between one's acts and the basic values that can be realized or spurned in human actions).

Finally, the case of suicide and its traditional solution remind us forcefully that traditional Western ethics simply does not accept that a person has "a right to decide what shall happen in and to his body", a right which Thomson thinks, astonishingly (since she is talking of Pius XI and Pius XII), that "everybody seems to be ready to grant". Indeed, one might go so far as to say that traditional Western ethics holds that, because and to the extent that one does *not* have the "right" to decide what shall happen in and to one's body, one *therefore* and to that extent does not have the right to decide what shall, by way of one's own acts, happen in and to anyone else's body. As I have already hinted, and shall elaborate later, this would be something of an oversimplification, since one's responsibility for one's own life, health, etc. is reasonably regarded as prior to one's concern for the life, health, etc. of others. But the oversimplification is worth risking in order to make the point that the traditional condemnation of abortion (as something one makes happen in and to a baby's body) *starts* by rejecting what Thomson thinks everyone will admit.

(ii) D's Killing an Innocent V in Order to Escape Death at the Hands of P, Who Has Ordered D to Kill V

This case has been traditionally treated on the same footing as cases such as D's killing V in order to save Q (or Q_1, Q_2 ... Q_n) from death (perhaps at the hands of P) or from disease (where D is a medical researcher); for all such cases cannot but be characterized as choices to act directly against human life. Of course, in each case, the reason for making the choice is to save life; but such saving of life will be effected, if at all, through the choices of other actors (e.g. P's choice not to kill D where D has killed V; or P's choice not to kill Q) or through quite distinct sequences of events (e.g. Q's being given life-saving drugs discovered by D).

Hence the traditional ethics affirms that "there are drastic limits to the right of self-defence" in much the same terms as Thomson. "If someone threatens you with death unless you torture someone else to death ... you have not the right, even to save your own life, to do so" (p. 685). And it was this very problem that occasioned the first ecclesiastical pronouncement on abortion in the modern era, denying that "it is licit to procure abortion before animation of the foetus in order to prevent a girl, caught pregnant, being killed or dishonoured".[24] The choice to abort here cannot but be characterized as a choice against life, since its intended good life- or reputation-saving effects are merely expected consequences, occurring if at all through the further acts of other persons, and thus are not what is being *done* in and by the act of abortion itself. But I do not know how one could arrive at any view of this second sort of hard case by juggling, as Thomson seems to be willing to, with a "right to life", a "right to determine what happens in and to your own body", a "right to self-defence" and a "right to refuse to lay hands on other people" – all rights shared equally by D, V, P, and Q, $Q_1, Q_2 \dots$!

(iii) Killing the Mother to Save the Child

This was the only aspect of abortion that Thomas Aquinas touched on, but he discussed it thrice.[25] For if it is accepted that eternal death is worse than mere bodily death, shouldn't one choose the lesser evil? So if the unborn child is likely to die unbaptized, shouldn't one open up the mother, rip out the child and save-it-from-eternal-death-by-baptizing-it? (If you find Aquinas's problems unreal, amend it – consider instead the cases where the child's life seems so much more valuable, whether to itself or to others, than the life of its sick or old or low-born mother.) No, says Aquinas. He evidently considers (for reasons I consider in section III) that the project involves a direct choice against life and is straightforwardly wrong, notwithstanding the good consequences.

So the traditional condemnation of therapeutic abortion flows not from a prejudice against women or in favour of children but from a straightforward application of the solution in the one case to the other case, on the basis that mother and child are *equally* persons in whom the value of human life is to be realized (or the "right to life" respected) and not directly attacked.[26]

III

But now at last let us look at this "traditional condemnation of abortion" a little more closely that Thomson does. It is not a condemnation of the administration of medications to a pregnant mother whose life is threatened by, say, a high fever (whether brought on by pregnancy or not), in an effort to reduce the fever, even if it is known that such medications have the side effect of inducing miscarriage. It is not a condemnation of the removal of the malignantly cancerous womb of a pregnant woman, even if it is known that the foetus within is not of viable age and so will die. It is quite doubtful whether it is a condemnation of an operation to put back in its place the displaced womb of a pregnant woman whose life is threatened by the displacement, even though the operation necessitates the draining off of the amniotic fluids necessary to the survival of the foetus.[27]

But why are these operations not condemned? As Foot has remarked, the distinction drawn between these and other death-dealing operations "has evoked particularly bitter reactions on the part of non-Catholics. If you are permitted to bring about the death of the child, what does it matter how it is done?"[28] Still, she goes some way to answering her own question; she is not content to let the matter rest where Hart had left it, when he said:

Perhaps the most perplexing feature of these cases is that the overriding aim in all of them is the same good result, namely ... to save the mother's life. The differences between the cases are differences of causal structure leading up to the applicability of different verbal distinctions. There seems to be no relevant moral difference between them on any theory of morality ... [to attribute moral relevance to distinctions drawn in this way] in cases where the ultimate purpose is the same can only be explained as the result of a legalistic conception of morality as if it were conceived in the form of a law in rigid form prohibiting all intentional killing as distinct from knowingly causing death.[29]

Foot recognizes that attention to "overriding aim" and "ultimate purpose" is not enough if we are to keep clear of moral horrors such as saving life by killing innocent hostages, etc. As a general though not exclusive and not (it seems) at-all-costs principle, she proposes that one has a duty to refrain from doing injury to innocent people and that this duty is stricter than one's duty to aid others; this enables her to see that "we might find" the traditional conclusion correct, that we must not crush the unborn child's skull in order to save the mother (in a case where the child could be saved if one let the mother die): "for in general we do not think that we can kill one innocent person to rescue another".[30] But what is it to "do injury to" innocent people? She does not think it an injury to blow a man to pieces, or kill and eat him, in order to save others trapped with him in a cave, *if he is certain to die soon anyway*.[31] So I suppose that, after all, she *would* be willing (however reluctantly) to justify the killing by D of hostages V, V_1, V_2, whenever the blackmailer P threatened to kill *them too*, along with Q, Q_1, Q_2, unless D killed them himself. One wonders whether this is not an unwarranted though plausible concession to consequentialism.

In any event, Foot was aware, not only that the "doctrine of the double effect" "should be taken seriously in spite of the fact that it sounds rather odd",[32] but also of what Thomson has not recorded in her brief footnote (p. 697, n. 3) on the technical meaning given to the term "direct" by moralists using the "doctrine" to analyse the relation between choices and basic values, namely that the "doctrine" requires more than that a certain bad effect or aspect (say, someone's being killed) of one's deed be not intended either as end or as means. If one is to establish that one's death-dealing deed need not be characterized as directly or intentionally against the good of human life, the "doctrine" requires further that the good effect or aspect, which *is* intended, should be proportionate (say, saving someone's life), i.e. sufficiently good and important relative to the bad effect or aspect: otherwise (we may add, in our own words) one's choice, although not directly and intentionally to kill, will reasonably be counted as a choice inadequately open to the value of life.[33] And this consideration alone might well suffice to rule out abortions performed in order simply to remove the unwanted foetus from the body of women who conceived as a result of forcible rape, even if one were to explicate the phrase "intended directly as end or as means" in such a way that the abortion did not amount to a directly intended killing (e.g. because the mother desired only the removal, not the death of the foetus, and would have been willing to have the foetus reared in an artificial womb had one been available).[34]

Well, how *should* one explicate these central requirements of the "doctrine" of double effect? When *should* one say that the expected bad effect or aspect of an action is not intended either as end or as means and hence does not determine the moral character of the act as a choice not to respect one of the basic human values? Since it is in any case impossible to undertake a full discussion of this question here, let me narrow the issue down to the more difficult and controverted problem of "means". Clearly enough, D intends the death of V *as a means* when he kills him in order to conform to the orders of the blackmailer P (with the object of thereby saving the lives of Q *et al.*), since the good effect of D's act will follow only by virtue of *another* human act (here P's). But Grisez (no consequentialist!) argues that the bad effects or aspects of some *natural* process or chain of causation need not be regarded as intended as means to the good effects or aspects of that process even if the good effects or aspects *depend* on them in the causal sense (and provided that those good effects could not have been attained in some other way by that agent in those circumstances).[35] So he would, I think, say that Thomson could rightly unplug herself from the violinist (at least where the hook-up endangered her life) even if "unplugging" could only be effected by chopping the violinist in pieces. He treats the life-saving abortion operation in the same way, holding that there is no direct choice against life involved in chopping up the foetus if what is intended as end is to save the life of the mother and what is intended as means is no more than the removal of the foetus and the consequential relief to the mother's body.[36] As a suasive, he points again to the fact that *if* an artificial womb or restorative operation were available for the aborted foetus, a right-thinking mother and doctor in such a case would wish to make these available to the foetus; this shows, he says, that a right-thinking mother and doctor, even where such facilities are *not* in fact available, need not be regarded as intending the death of the foetus they kill.[37] For my part, I think Grisez's reliance on such counter-factual hypotheses to specify the morally relevant meaning or intention of human acts is excessive, for it removes morally relevant "intention" too far from common-sense intention, tends to unravel the traditional and common-sense moral judgments on suicide (someone would say: "It's not death I'm choosing, only a long space of peace and quiet, after which I'd willingly be revived, if that were possible"!), and likewise disturbs our judgments on murder and in particular on the difference between administering (death-hastening) drugs to relieve pain and administering drugs to relieve-pain-by-killing.

In any event, the version of traditional nonconsequentialist ethics which has gained explicit ecclesiastical approval in the Roman church these last ninety years treats the matter differently; it treats a bad or unwanted aspect or effect of act A_1 as an *intended* aspect of A_1, not only when the good effect (unlike the bad) follows only by virtue of another human act A_2, but also *sometimes* when both the good effect and the bad effect are parts of one natural causal process requiring no further human act to achieve its effect. *Sometimes*, but not always; so when?

A variety of factors are appealed to explicitly or relied on implicitly in making a judgment that the bad effect is to count as intended-as-a-means; Bennett would call the set of factors a "jumble",[38] but they are even more various than he has noted. It will be convenient to set them out while at the same time observing their bearing on the two cases centrally in dispute, the craniotomy to save a mother's life and that notable scenario in which "you reach around to your back and unplug yourself from that violinist to save your life".

(1) Would the chosen action have been chosen if the victim had not been present? If it would, this is ground for saying that the bad aspects of the action, viz. its death-dealing effects on the victim (child or violinist), are not being intended or chosen either as end or means, but are genuinely incidental side effects that do not necessarily determine the character of one's action as (not) respectful of human life. This was the principal reason the ecclesiastical moralists had for regarding as permissible the operation to remove the cancerous womb of the pregnant woman.[39] And the "bitter" reaction which Foot cites and endorses – "If you are permitted to bring about the death of the child, what does it matter how it is done?" – seems, here, to miss the point. For what is in question, here, is not a mere matter of technique, or different ways of doing something. Rather it is a matter of the very reason one has for acting in the way one does, and such reasons can be constitutive of the act as an intentional performance. One has no reason even to want to be rid of the foetus within the womb, let alone to want to kill it; and so one's act, though certain, causally, to kill, is not, intentionally, a choice against life.

But of course, *this* factor does not serve to distinguish a craniotomy from unplugging that violinist; in both situations, the oppressive presence of the victim is what makes one minded to do the act in question.

(2) Is the person making the choice the one whose life is threatened by the presence of the victim? Thomson rightly sees that this is a relevant question, and Thomas Aquinas makes it the pivot of his discussion of self-defensive killing (the discussion from which the "doctrine" of double effect, as a theoretically elaborated way of analysing intention, can be said to have arisen). He says:

Although it is not permissible to intend to kill someone else in order to defend oneself (since it is not right to do the act "killing a human being", except [in some cases of unjust aggression] by public authority and for the general welfare), still it is not morally necessary to omit to do what is strictly appropriate to securing one's own life simply in order to avoid killing another, for to make provision for one's own life is more strictly one's moral concern than to make provision for the life of another person.[40]

As Thomson has suggested, a bystander, confronted with a situation in which one innocent person's presence is endangering the life of another innocent person, is in a different position; to choose to intervene, in order to kill one person to save the other, involves a choice to make himself a master of life and death, a judge of who lives and who dies; and (we may say) this context of his choice prevents him from saying, reasonably, what the man defending himself can say: "I am not choosing to kill; I am just doing what – as a single act and not simply by virtue of remote consequences or of someone else's subsequent act – is strictly needful to protect my own life, by forcefully removing what is threatening it." Now the traditional condemnation of abortion[41] concerns the bystander's situation: a bystander cannot but be choosing to kill if (a) he rips open the mother, in a way foreseeably fatal to her, in order to save the child from the threatening enveloping presence of the mother (say, because the placenta has come adrift and the viable child is trapped and doomed unless it can be rescued, or because the mother's blood is poisoning the child, in a situation in which the bystander would prefer to save the child, either because he wants to save it from eternal damnation, or because the child is of royal blood and the mother low born, or because the mother is in any case sick, or old, or useless, or "has had her turn", while the child has a whole rich life before it); or if (b) he cuts up or drowns the child in order to save the mother from the child's threatening presence. "Things being as they are, there isn't much a woman can safely do to abort herself", as Thomson says (p. 684) – at least, not without the help of bystanders, who by helping (directly) would be making the same choice as if they did it themselves. But the unplugging of the violinist is done by the very person defending herself. Thomson admits that this gives quite a different flavour to the situation, but she thinks that the difference is not decisive, since bystanders have a decisive reason to intervene in favour of the *mother* threatened by her child's presence. And she finds this reason in the fact that the mother *owns* her body, just as the person plugged in to the violinist owns his own kidneys and is entitled to their unencumbered use. Well, this too has always been accounted a factor in these problems, as we can see by turning to the following question.

(3) Does the chosen action involve not merely a denial of aid and succour to someone but an actual intervention that amounts to an assault on the body of that person? Bennett wanted to deny all relevance to any such question,[42] but Foot[43] and Thomson have rightly seen that in the ticklish

matter of respecting human life in the persons of others, and of characterising choices with a view to assessing their respect for life, it *can* matter that one is directly injuring and not merely failing to maintain a life-preserving level of assistance to another. Sometimes, as here, it is the causal structure of one's activity that involves one willy-nilly in a choice for or against a basic value. The connection between one's activity and the destruction of life may be so close and direct that intentions and considerations which would give a different dominant character to mere nonpreservation of life are incapable of affecting the dominant character of a straightforward taking of life. This surely is the reason why Thomson goes about and about to represent a choice to have an abortion as a choice *not* to provide assistance or facilities, *not* to be a Good or at any rate a Splendid Samaritan; and why too, she carefully describes the violinist affair so as to minimize the degree of intervention against the violinist's body, and to maximize the analogy with simply refusing an invitation to volunteer one's kidneys for this welfare (like Henry Fonda's declining to cross America to save Judith Thomson's life). "If anything in the world is true, it is that you do not commit murder, you do not do what is impermissible, if you reach around to your back and unplug yourself from that violinist to say your life." Quite so. It might nevertheless be useful to test one's moral reactions a little further: suppose, not simply that "unplugging" required a *bystander's* intervention, but also that (for medical reasons, poison in the bloodstream, shock, etc.) unplugging could not safely be performed unless and until the violinist had first been dead for six hours and had moreover been killed outright, say by drowning or decapitation (though not necessarily while conscious). Could one then be *so* confident, as a bystander, that it was right to kill the violinist in order to save the philosopher? But I put forward this revised version principally to illustrate *another* reason for thinking that, within the traditional casuistry, the violinist-unplugging in Thomson's version is *not* the "direct killing" which she claims it is, and which she *must* claim it is if she is to make out her case for rejecting the traditional principle about direct killing.

Let us now look back to the traditional rule about abortion. If the mother needs medical treatment to save her life, she gets it, subject to one proviso, even if the treatment is certain to kill the unborn child – for after all, her body is *her* body, as "women have said again and again" (and they have been heard by the traditional casuists!). And the proviso? That the medical treatment not be *via* a straightforward assault on or intervention against the child's body. For after all *the child's body is the child's body, not the woman's.* The traditional casuists have admitted the claims made on behalf of one "body" up to the very limit where those claims became *mere (understandable) bias, mere (understandable) self-interested* refusal to listen to the *very same* claim ("This body is *my* body") when it is made by or on behalf of another person.[44] Of course, a traditional casuist would display an utter want of feeling if he didn't most profoundly sympathise with women in the desperate circumstances under discussion. But it is vexing to find a philosophical Judith Thomson, in a cool hour, unable to see when an argument cuts both ways, and unaware that the casuists have seen the point before her and have, unlike her, allowed the argument to cut both ways impartially. The child, like his mother, has a "just prior claim to his own body", and abortion involves laying hands on, manipulating, that body. And here we have perhaps the decisive reason why abortion cannot be assimilated to the range of Samaritan problems and why Thomson's location of it within that range is a mere (ingenious) novelty.

(4) But is the action against someone who had a duty not to be doing what he is doing, or not to be present where he is present? There seems no doubt that the "innocence" of the victim whose life is taken makes a difference to the characterizing of an action as open to and respectful of the good of human life, and as an intentional killing. Just how and why it makes a difference is difficult to unravel; I shall not attempt an unravelling here. We all, for whatever reasons, recognize the difference and Thomson has expressly allowed its relevance.

But her way of speaking of "rights" has a final unfortunate effect at this point. We can grant, and have granted, that the unborn child has no Hohfeldian *claim-right* to be allowed to stay within the mother's body under all circumstances; the mother is not under a strict duty to allow it to stay under all circumstances. In *that* sense, the child "has no right to be there". But Thomson discusses also the case of the burglar in the house; and he, too, has "no right to be there", even when she opens the window! But beware of the equivocation! The burglar not merely has no claim-right to be allowed to enter or stay; he also has a strict duty *not* to enter or stay; i.e., he has no Hohfeldian *liberty* – and it is *this* that is uppermost in our minds when we think that he "has no right to be there": it is actually unjust for him to be there. Similarly with Jones who takes Smith's coat, leaving Smith freezing. And similarly with the violinist. He and his agents had a strict duty not to make the hook-up to Judith Thomson or her gentle reader. Of course, the violinist himself may have been unconscious and so not himself at fault; but the whole affair is a gross injustice to the person whose kidneys are made free with, and the injustice to that person is not measured simply by the degree of moral fault of one of the parties to the injustice. Our whole view of the violinist's situation is coloured by this burglarious and persisting wrongfulness of his presence plugged into his victim.

But can any of this reasonably be said or thought of the unborn child? True, the child had no *claim-right* to be allowed to come into being within the mother. But it was not in breach of any *duty* in coming into being nor in remaining present within the mother; Thomson gives no arguments at all in favour of the view that the child is in breach of duty in being present (though her counter examples show that she is often tacitly assuming this). (Indeed, if we are going to use the wretched analogy of owning houses, I fail to see why the unborn child should not with justice say of the body around it: "That is my house. No one *granted* me property rights in it, but equally no one *granted* my mother any property rights in it." The fact is that both persons *share* in the use of this body, both by the same sort of title, viz, that this is the way they happened to come into being. But it would be better to drop this ill-fitting talk of "ownership" and "property rights" altogether). So though the unborn child "had no right to be there" (in the sense that it never had a claim-right to be allowed to *begin* to be there), in another straight-forward and more important sense it *did* "have a right to be there" (in the sense that it was not in breach of duty in being or continuing to be there). All this is, I think, clear and clearly different from the violinist's case. Perhaps forcible rape is a special case; but even then it seems fanciful to say that the child is or could be in any way at fault, as the violinist is at fault or would be but for the adventitious circumstance that he was unconscious at the time.

Still, I don't want to be dogmatic about the justice or injustice, innocence or fault, involved in a rape conception. (I have already remarked that the impermissibility of abortion in any such case where the mother's life is not in danger, does not depend necessarily on showing that the act is a choice directly to kill.) It is enough that I have shown how in three admittedly important respects the violinist case differs from the therapeutic abortion performed to save the life of the mother. As presented by Thomson, the violinist's case involves (i) no bystander, (ii) no intervention against or assault upon the body of the violinist, and (iii) an indisputable injustice to the agent in question. Each of these three factors is absent from the abortion cases in dispute. Each has been treated as relevant by the traditional casuists whose condemnations Thomson was seeking to contest when she plugged us into the violinist.

When all is said and done, however, I haven't rigorously answered my own question. When should one say that the expected bad effect or aspect of an act is not intended even as a means and hence does not determine the moral character of the act as a choice not to respect one of the basic human values? I have done no more than list some factors. I have not discussed how one decides which combinations of these factors suffice to answer the question one way rather than the other. I have not discussed the man on the plank, or the man off the plank; or the woman who leaves her baby behind as she flees from the lion, or the other women who feeds *her* baby to the lion in order to make good her own escape; or the "innocent" child who threatens to shoot a man dead, or the man who shoots that child to save himself;[45] or the starving explorer who kills himself to provide food for his fellows, or the other explorer who wanders away from the party so as not to hold them up or diminish their rations. The cases are many, various, instructive. Too generalized or rule-governed an application of the notion of "double effect" would offend against the Aristotelian, common-law, Wittgensteinian wisdom that here "we do not know how to draw the boundaries of the concept" – of intention, or respect for the good of life, and of action as distinct from consequences – "except for a special purpose".[46] But I think that those whom Aristotle bluntly calls wise can come to clear judgments on most of the abortion problems, judgments that will not coincide with Thomson's.

IV

I have been assuming that the unborn child is, from conception, a person and hence is not to be discriminated against on account of age, appearance, or other such factors in so far as such factors are reasonably considered irrelevant where respect for basic human values is in question. Thomson argues against this assumption, but not, as I think, well. She thinks (like Wertheimer,[47] mutatis mutandis) that the argument in favour of treating a newly conceived child as a person is merely a "slippery slope" argument (p. 681), rather like (I suppose) saying that one should call all men bearded because there is no line one can confidently draw between beard and clean shavenness. More precisely, she thinks that a newly conceived child is like an acorn, which after all is not an oak! It is discouraging to see her relying so heavily and uncritically on this hoary muddle. An acorn can remain for years in a stable state, simply but completely an acorn. Plant it and from it will sprout an oak sapling, a new, dynamic biological system that has nothing much in common with an acorn save that it came from an acorn and is capable of generating new acorns. Suppose an acorn is formed in September 1971, picked up on 1 February 1972, and stored under good conditions for three years, then planted in January 1975; it sprouts on 1 March 1975 and fifty years later is a fully mature oak tree. Now suppose I ask: When did that oak begin to grow? Will anyone say September 1971 or February 1972? Will anyone look for the date on which it was first noticed in the garden? Surely not. If we know it sprouted from the acorn on 1 March 1975, that is enough (though a biologist could be a trifle more exact about "sprouting"); that is when *the oak* began. A *fortiori* with the conception of a child, which is no *mere* germination of a seed. Two cells, each with only twenty-three chromosomes, unite and more or less immediately fuse to become a new cell with forty-six chromosomes providing a unique genetic constitution (not the father's, not the mother's, and not a mere juxtaposition of the parents') which thenceforth throughout its life, however long, will substantially determine the new individual's makeup.[48] This new cell is the first stage in a dynamic integrated system that has nothing much in common with the individual male and female sex cells, save that it sprang from a pair of them and will in time produce new sets of them. To say that *this* is when a person's life began is not to work backwards from maturity, sophistically asking at each point "How can one draw the line *here*?" Rather it is to point to a perfectly clear-cut beginning to which each one of us can look back and in looking back see how, in a vividly intelligible sense, "in my beginning is my end". Judith Thomson thinks she began to "acquire human characteristics" "by the tenth week" (when fingers, toes, etc. became visible). I cannot think why she overlooks the most radically and distinctively human characteristic of all – the fact that she was conceived of human parents. And then there is Henry Fonda. From the time of his conception, though not before, one could say, looking at his unique personal genetic constitution, not only that "by the tenth week" Henry Fonda would have fingers, but also that in his fortieth year he would have a cool hand. That is why there seems no rhyme or reason in waiting "ten weeks" until his fingers and so on actually become visible before declaring that he *now* has the human rights which Judith Thomson rightly but incompletely recognizes.

NOTES

1 *Philosophy and Public Affairs*, vol. 1, no. 1 (Fall 1971), 47–66. Otherwise unidentified page references in the text are to this article.

2 Roger Wertheimer, "Understanding the Abortion Argument", *Philosophy and Public Affairs*, vol. 1, no. 1 (Fall 1971), pp. 67–95.

3 Rights which Thomson is willing to allow that a person has:

R1. a right to life (p. 682);

R2. a right to decide what happens in and to one's body (p. 682) (to be equated, apparently, with a just prior claim to one's own body, p. 686);

R3. a right to defend oneself (i.e. to self-defence, p. 685);

R4. a right to refuse to lay hands on other people (even when it would be just and fair to do so, p. 686) – more precisely, a right not to lay hands on other people.

Rights which she thinks it would be coherent but mistaken to claim that a person has or in any event always has:

R5. a right to demand that someone else give one assistance (p. 692) – more precisely, a right to be given assistance by ...;

R6. a right to be given whatever one needs for continued life (p. 687);

R7. a right to the use of (or to be given, or to be allowed to continue, the use of) someone else's body (or house) (p. 686);

R8. a right not to be killed by anybody (p. 687);

R9. a right to slit another's throat (an instance, apparently, of a "right to be guaranteed his death") (pp. 696–97);

4 Namely, R3 through R9 in the list of note 3 above.

5 Namely, R3, R4, and, in one of their senses, R7 and R9.

6 W.H. Hohfeld, *Fundamental Legal Conceptions* (New Haven, 1923).

7 Namely, R5, R6, R8, and, in another of their senses, R7 and R9.

8 Namely, R1 and R2.

9 This proposition is elaborated in a juridicial context by A.M. Honore, "Rights of Exclusion and Immunities against Divesting", *University of Tulane Law Review*, vol. 34 (1960), p. 453.

10 Insufficient specification causes needless problems, besides those mentioned in the text. For example, against "so using the term 'right' that from the fact that A ought to do a thing for B, it follows that B has a right against A that A do it for him", Thomson objects that any such use of the term "right" is "going to make the question of whether or not a man has a right to a thing turn on how easy it is to provide him with it" (p. 692); and she adds that it's "rather a shocking idea that anybody's rights should fade

away and disappear as it gets harder and harder to accord them to him" (p. 692). So she says she has no "right" to the touch of Henry Fonda's cool hand, *because*, although he ought to cross the room to touch her brow (and thus save her life), he is not morally obliged to cross America to do so. But this objection rests merely on inadequate specification of the right as against Henry Fonda. For if we say that she has a right that Henry Fonda should cross-the-room-to-touch-her-fevered-brow, and that she has no right that he should cross-America-to-touch-her-fevered-brow, then we can (if we like!) continue to deduce rights from duties.

11 It is perhaps worth pointing out that, even if we restrict our attention to the rights involved in gifts, concessions, grants, trusts, and the like, Thomson's proposed reining-in of the term "right" will be rather inconvenient. Does only the donee have the "rights"? Suppose that uncle U gives a box of chocolates to nephew N1, with instructions to share it with nephew N2, and asks father F to see that this sharing is done. Then we want to be able to say that U has a right that N1 and N2 shall each get their share, that N1 shall give N2 that share, that F shall see to it that this is done, and so on; and that N1 has the right to his share, the right not to be interfered with by F or N2 or anyone else in eating his share, and so on; and that N2 has a similar set of rights; and that F has the right to take steps to enforce a fair distribution, the right not to be interfered with in taking those steps, and so on. Since disputes may arise about any one of these relations between the various persons and their actions and the chocolates thereby affected, it is convenient to have the term "right" on a loose rein, to let it ride round the circle of relations, picking up the action in dispute and fitting the competing claims about the "right thing to do" into intelligible and typical three-term relationships. Yet some of the rights involved in the gift of the chocolates, for example U's rights, are not acquired by any grant to the right-holder.

12 The sentence continues: "and in which he does not have a right to use them, and in which you do not do him an injustice if you refuse". But these are merely remnants of the "rhetoric" in which she has cast her argument. Notice, incidentally, that her suggestion that "justice" and "injustice" should be restricted to respect for and violation of rights in her reined-in sense is of no importance since she grants that actions not in her sense unjust may be self-centred, callous, and indecent, and that these vices are "no less grave".

13 Perhaps this is the point at which to note how dubious is Thomson's assertion that "in no state in this country is any man compelled by law to be even a Minimally Decent Samaritan to any person", and her insinuation that this is a manifestation of a discrimination against women. This sounds

so odd coming from a country in which a young man, not a young woman, is compelled by law to "give up long stretches of his life" to defending his country at considerable "risk of death for himself". True, he is not doing this for "a person who has no special right to demand it"; indeed, what makes active military service tough is that one is not risking one's life to save *anybody* in particular from any *particular* risk. And are we to say that young men have *assumed* a "special responsibility" for defending other people? Wouldn't that be a gross fiction which only a lame moral theory could tempt us to indulge in? But it is just this sort of social contract-arianism that Thomson is tempting us with.

14 Exodus 23:7; cf. Exodus 20:13, Deuteronomy 5:17, Genesis 9:6, Jeremiah 7:6 and 22:3.

15 These remarks are filled out somewhat in my "Natural Law and Unnatural Acts", *Heythrop Journal* 11 (1970): 365. See also Germain Grisez, *Abortion: the Myths, the Realities and the Arguments* (New York 1970), Ch. 6. My argument owes much to this and other works by Grisez.

16 R.M. Hare, "Rules of War and Moral Reasoning", *Philosophy and Public Affairs*, vol. 1, no. 2 (winter 1972), pp. 167, 168.

17 Ibid., p. 174.

18 Cf. H.-N. Castaneda, "On the Problem of Formulating a Coherent Act-Utilitarianism", *Analysis* 32 (1972), p. 118; Harold M. Zellner, "Utilitarian-ism and Derived Obligation", *Analysis* 32 (1972), p. 124.

19 See D.H. Hodgson, *Consequences of Utilitarianism* (Oxford, 1967).

20 Cf. Hare, op. cit, p. 174: "The defect in most deontological theories ... is that they have no coherent rational account to give of any level of moral thought above that of the man who knows some good simple moral principles and sticks to them ... [The] simple principles of the deontologist ... are what we should be trying to inculcate into ourselves and our children if we want to stand the best chance ... of doing what is for the best."

21 Not to mention the Jewish moralists: see D. Daube, *Collaboration with Tyranny in Rabbinic Law* (Oxford, 1965).

22 Note that I am not asserting (or denying) that self-sacrificial heroism and martyrdom are moral duties; I am explaining why they need not be regarded as moral faults.

23 *Le Suicide* (Paris, 1897), p. 5. Cf. also Daube's remarks on Donne in "The Linguistics of Suicide", *Philosophy and Public Affairs*, vol. 1, no. 4 (summer 1972), pp. 418ff.

24 Decree of the Holy Office. 2 March 1679, error no 34; see Denzinger and Schönmetzer, *Enchiridion symbolorum definitionum et declaratjonum de rebus fidei er morum* (Barcelona, 1967), par. 2134; Grisez, *Abortion: the Myths, the*

Realities and the Arguments, p. 174; John T. Noonan, Jr., "An Almost Absolute Value in History", in *The Morality of Abortion*, ed. John T. Noonan, Jr. (Cambridge, Mass., 1970), p. 34.

25 See *Summa Theologiae III*, q. 68, art. II; in 4 *Sententiarum* d. 6, q. 1, a. 1, q. 1, ad. 4; d. 23, q. 2. a. 2, 1. q. 1, ad 1 & 2; Grisez, op. cit., p. 154; Noonan, op. cit., p. 24.

26 Pius XII's remark, quoted by Thomson, that 'the baby in the maternal breast has the right to life immediately from God' has its principal point, not (*pace* Thomson, p. 683) in the assertion of a premise from which one could deduce the wrongfulness of direct killing, but in the assertion that *if* anybody – e.g. the mother – has the right not to be directly killed, *then* the baby has the same right, since as Pius XII goes on immediately "the baby, still not born, is a man in the same degree and for the same reason as the mother".

27 The three cases mentioned in this paragraph are discussed in a standard and conservative Roman Catholic textbook: Marcellino Zalba, *Theologiae Moralis Compendium* (Madrid, 1958), i. 885.

28 Philippa Foot, "The Problem of Abortion and the Doctrine of Double Effect", *The Oxford Reveiw*, vol. 5 (1967), p. 6.

29 H.L.A. Hart, "Intention and Punishment", *The Oxford Review*, vol. 4 (1967), p. 13; reprinted in Hart, *Punishment and Responsibility* (Oxford, 1968), pp. 124–5.

30 Foot, op. cit., p. 15.

31 Ibid., p. 14.

32 Ibid., p. 8.

33 Ibid., p. 7. This is the fourth of the four usual conditions for the application of the "Doctrine of Double Effect"; see e.g. Grisez, op. cit., p. 329. G.E.M. Anscombe, "War and Murder", in *Nuclear Weapons and Christian Conscience*, ed. W. Stein, (London, 1961), p. 57, formulates the "principle of double effect", in relation to the situation where "someone innocent will die unless I do a wicked thing", thus: "you are no murderer if a man's death was neither your aim nor your chosen means, *and if you had to act in the way that led to it or else do something absolutely forbidden*" (emphasis added).

34 Grisez argues thus, op. cit., p. 343; also in "Toward a Consistent Natural-Law Ethics of Killing", *American Journal of Jurisprudence*, vol. 15 (1970), p. 95.

35 Ibid., p. 333 and pp. 89–90 respectively.

36 Ibid., p. 341 and p. 94 respectively.

37 Ibid., p. 341 and p. 95 respectively. I agree with Grisez that the fact that, if an artificial womb were available, many women would *not* transfer their aborted offspring to it shows that those women are directly and wrongfully

intending the *death* of their offspring. I suspect Judith Thomson would agree.

38 Jonathan Bennett, "'Whatever the Consequences'," *Analysis*, vol. 26 (1966), p. 92 n. 1.

39 See the debate between A. Gemelli and P Vermeersch, summarized in *Ephemerides Theologicae Lovaniensis*, ii (1934), 525–61; see also Noonan, op. cit., p. 49; Zalba, *Theologiae Moralis Compendium*, i. 885.

40 *Summa Theologiae* II-II, q. 64, art. 7: "Nec est nesessarium ad salutem ut homo actum moderatae tuterae practermittat ad evitandum occisionem alterius; quia plus tenetur homo vitae suae providere quam vitae alienae. Sed quia occidere hominem non licet nisi publica auctoritate propter bonum commune, ut ex supra dictis patet [art. 3], illicitum est quod homo intendat occidere hominem ut seipsum defendat."

41 Ibid., arts. 2 and 3.

42 Bennett, op. cit.

43 Foot, op. cit, pp. 11–13.

44 Not, of course, that they have used Thomson's curious talk of "owning" one's own body with its distracting and legalistic connotations and its dualistic reduction of subjects of justice to objects.

45 This case is (too casually) used in Brody, "Thomson on Abortion", *Philosophy and Public Affairs*, vol. 1, no. 3 (spring 1972), p. 335.

46 Cf. Wittgenstein, *Philosophical Investigations* (Oxford, 1953), sec. 69.

47 "Understanding the Abortion Argument."

48 See Grisez, op. cit., Ch. 1 and pp. 273–87, with literature there cited.

READING QUESTIONS ON FINNIS

1 Finnis distinguishes between takings of life that are intended and those that are merely foreseen. Explain the distinction.

2 How does Finnis know that it is right to classify abortion as an intentional taking of life rather than a foreseeable loss of life? How might Thomson reply?

3 Suppose that Finnis is right about the moral significance of the distinction he draws. Does he need to show anything further to conclude that it ought to be the basis for legal enforcement?

Morgentaler, Smolling and Scott v The Queen [1988] 1 SCR 30

The Supreme Court of Canada case overturning the *Criminal Code* provision outlawing abortion. The court held that the law violated women's equality rights.

Dickson, CJC: – The principal issue raised by this appeal is whether the abortion provisions of the *Criminal Code* infringe the "right to life, liberty and security of the person and the right not to be deprived thereof except in accordance with the principles of fundamental justice" as formulated in s. 7 of the Canadian *Charter* of Rights and Freedoms. The appellants, Dr Henry Morgentaler, Dr Leslie Frank Smoling, and Dr Robert Scott, have raised 13 distinct grounds of appeal. During oral submissions, however, it became apparent that the primary focus of the case was upon the s. 7 argument. It is submitted by the appellants that s. 251 of the *Criminal Code*, RSC 1970, c. C-34, contravenes s. 7 of the Canadian *Charter* of Rights and Freedoms and that s. 251 should be struck down. Counsel for the Crown admitted during the course of her submissions that s. 7 of the *Charter* was indeed "the key" to the entire appeal. As for the remaining grounds of appeal, only a few brief comments are necessary. First of all, I agree with the disposition made by the Court of Appeal of the non-*Charter* issues, many of which have already been adequately dealt with in earlier cases by this court. I am also of the view that the arguments concerning the alleged invalidity of s. 605 under ss. 7 and 11 of the *Charter* are unfounded. In view of my resolution of the s. 7 issue, it will not be necessary for me to address the appellants' other *Charter* arguments and I expressly refrain from commenting upon their merits ...

SECTION 7 OF THE *CHARTER*

In his submissions, counsel for the appellants argued that the court should recognize a very wide ambit for the rights protected under s. 7 of the *Charter*. Basing his argument largely on American constitutional theories and authorities, Mr Manning submitted that the right to "life, liberty and security of the person" is a wide-ranging right to control one's own life and to promote one's individual autonomy. The right would therefore include a right to privacy and a right to make unfettered decisions about one's own life.

In my opinion, it is neither necessary nor wise in this appeal to explore the broadest implications of s. 7 as counsel would wish us to do. I prefer to rest my conclusions on a narrower analysis than that put forward on behalf of the appellants. I do not think it would be appropriate to attempt an all-encompassing explication of so important a provision as s. 7 so early in the history of *Charter* interpretation. The court should be presented with a wide variety of claims and factual situations before articulating the full range of s. 7 rights. I will therefore limit my comments to some interpretive principles already set down by the court and to an analysis of only two aspects of s. 7, the right to "security of the person" and "the principles of fundamental justice."

Interpreting Section 7

The goal of *Charter* interpretation is to secure for all people "the full benefit of the *Charter's* protection": To attain that goal, this court has held consistently that the proper technique for the interpretation of *Charter* provisions is to pursue a "purposive" analysis of the right guaranteed.

In *Re Singh and Minister of Employment and Immigration* (1985), 17 DLR (4th) 422 at p. 458, Justice Wilson emphasized that there are three distinct elements to the s. 7 right, that "life, liberty, and security of the person" are independent interests, each of which must be given independent significance by the court (pp. 458-9 DLR, p. 205 SCR). It is therefore possible to treat only one aspect of the first part of s. 7 before determining whether any infringement of that interest accords with the principles of fundamental justice ...

I have no doubt that s. 7 does impose upon courts the duty to review the substance of legislation once it has been determined that the legislation infringes an individual's right to "life, liberty and security of the person." The section states clearly that those interests may only be impaired if the principles of fundamental justice are respected. Lamer J emphasized, however, that the courts should avoid "adjudication of the merits of public policy" (p. 299 CCC, p. 546 DLR, p. 499 SCR). In the present case, I do not believe that it is necessary for the court to tread the fine line between substantive review and the adjudication of public policy. As in the *Singh* case, it will be sufficient to investigate whether or not the impugned legislative provisions meet the procedural standards of fundamental justice. First it is necessary to determine whether s. 251 of the *Criminal Code* impairs the security of the person.

Security of the Person

The law has long recognized that the human body ought to be protected from interference by others. At common law, for example, any medical procedure carried out on a person without that person's consent is an assault. Only in emergency circumstances does the law allow others to make decisions of this nature. Similarly, art. 19 of the *Civil Code of Lower Canada* provides that "[t]he human person is inviolable" and that "[n]o person may cause harm to the person of another without his consent or without being authorized by law to do so." "Security of the person," in other words, is not a value alien to our legal landscape. With the advent of the *Charter*, security of the person has been elevated to the status of a constitutional norm. This is not to say that the various forms of protection accorded to the human body by the common and civil law occupy a similar status. "Security of the person" must be given content in a manner sensitive to its constitutional position. The above examples are simply illustrative of our respect for individual physical integrity:

The appellants submitted that the "security of the person" protected by the *Charter* is an explicit right to control one's body and to make fundamental decisions about one's life. The Crown contended that "security of the person" is a more circumscribed interest and that, like all of the elements of s. 7, it at most relates to the concept of physical control, simply protecting the individual's interest in his or her bodily integrity.

The case law leads me to the conclusion that state interference with bodily integrity and serious state-imposed psychological stress, at least in the criminal law context, constitute a breach of security of the person. It is not necessary in this case to determine whether the right extends further, to protect either interests central to personal autonomy, such as a right to privacy, or interests unrelated to criminal justice.

I wish to reiterate that finding a violation of security of the person does not end the s. 7 inquiry. Parliament could choose to infringe security of the person if it did so in a manner consistent with the principles of fundamental justice. The present discussion should therefore be seen as a threshold inquiry and the conclusions do not dispose definitively of all the issues relevant to s. 7. With that caution, I have no difficulty in concluding that the encyclopedic factual submissions addressed to us by counsel in the present appeal establish beyond any doubt that s. 251 of the *Criminal Code* is prima facie a violation of the security of the person of thousands of Canadian women who have made the difficult decision that they do not wish to continue with a pregnancy ...

At the most basic, physical and emotional level, every pregnant woman is told by the section that she cannot submit to a generally safe medical procedure that might be of clear benefit to her unless she meets criteria entirely unrelated to her own priorities and aspirations. Not only does the removal of decision-making power threaten women in a physical sense; the indecision of knowing whether an abortion will be granted inflicts emotional stress. Section 251 clearly interferes with a woman's bodily integrity in both a physical and emotional sense. Forcing a woman, by threat of criminal sanction, to carry a foetus to term unless she meets certain criteria unrelated to her own priorities and aspirations, is a profound interference with a woman's body and thus a violation of security of the person. Section 251, therefore, is required by the *Charter* to comport with the principles of fundamental justice.

Although this interference with physical and emotional integrity is sufficient in itself to trigger a review of s. 251 against the principles of fundamental justice, the operation of the decision-making mechanism set out in s. 251 creates additional glaring breaches of security of the person. The evidence indicates that s. 251 causes a certain amount of delay for women who are successful in meeting its criteria. In the context of abortion any unnecessary delay can have profound consequences on the woman's physical and emotional well-being.

If forced to apply to several different therapeutic abortion committees, there can be no doubt that a woman will experience serious delay in obtaining a therapeutic abortion ... [T]he implications of any delay, according to the evidence, are potentially devastating. The first factor to consider is that different medical techniques are employed to perform abortions at different stages of pregnancy. The testimony of expert doctors at trial indicated that in the first 12 weeks of pregnancy, the relatively safe and simple suction dilation and curettage method of abortion is typically used in North America. From the 13th to the 16th week, the more dangerous dilation and evacuation procedure is performed, although much less often in Canada than in the United States. From the 16th week of pregnancy, the instillation method is commonly employed in Canada. This method requires the intra-amniotic introduction of prostaglandin, urea, or a saline solution, which causes a woman to go into labour, giving birth to a foetus which is usually dead, but not invariably so. The uncontroverted evidence showed that each method of abortion progressively increases risks to the woman.

The second consideration is that even within the periods appropriate to each method of abortion the evidence indicated that the earlier the abortion was performed, the fewer the complications and the lower the risk of mortality.

It is no doubt true that the over-all complication and mortality rates for women who undergo abortions are very low, but the increasing risks caused by delay are so clearly established that I have no difficulty in concluding that the delay in obtaining therapeutic abortions caused by the mandatory procedures of s. 251 is an infringement of the purely physical aspect of the individual's right to security of the person.

Secondly, were it nevertheless possible in this case to dissociate purpose and administration, this court has already held as a matter of law that purpose is not the only appropriate criterion in evaluating the constitutionality of legislation under the *Charter*. Even if the purpose of legislation is unobjectionable, the administrative procedures created by law to bring that purpose into operation may produce unconstitutional effects, and the legislation should then be struck down.

In summary, s. 251 is a law which forces women to carry a foetus to term contrary to their own priorities and aspirations and which imposes serious delay causing increased physical and psychological trauma to those women who meet its criteria. It must, therefore, be determined whether that infringement is accomplished in accordance with the principles of fundamental justice, thereby saving s. 251 under the second part of s. 7.

The Principles of Fundamental Justice

Although the "principles of fundamental justice" referred to in s. 7 have both a substantive and a procedural component, I have already indicated that it is not necessary in this appeal to evaluate the substantive content of s. 251 of the *Criminal Code*. My discussion will therefore be limited to various aspects of the administrative structure and procedure set down in s. 251 for access to therapeutic abortions.

In outline, s. 251 operates in the following manner. Subsection (1) creates an indictable offence for any person to use any means with the intent "to procure the miscarriage of a female person." Subsection (2) establishes a parallel indictable offence for any pregnant woman to use or to permit any means to be used with the intent "to procure her own miscarriage." The "means" referred to in s-ss. (1) and (2) are defined in s-s. (3) as the administration of a drug or "other noxious thing," the use of an instrument, and "manipulation of any kind." The crucial provision for the purposes of the present appeal is s-s. (4) which states that the offences created in s-ss. (1) and (2) "do not apply" in certain circumstances.

The procedure surrounding the defence is rather complex. A pregnant woman who desires to have an abortion must apply to the "therapeutic abortion committee" of an "accredited or approved hospital." Such a committee is empowered to issue a certificate in writing stating that in the opinion of a majority of the committee, the continuation of the pregnancy would be likely to endanger the pregnant woman's life or health. Once a copy of the certificate is given to a qualified medical practitioner who is not a member of the therapeutic abortion committee, he or she is permitted to perform an abortion on the pregnant woman and both the doctor and the woman are freed from any criminal liability ...

As is so often the case in matters of interpretation, however, the straightforward reading of this statutory scheme is not fully revealing. In order to understand the true nature and scope of s. 251, it is necessary to investigate the practical operation of the provisions. The court has been provided with a myriad of factual submissions in this area ... In other words, the seemingly neutral requirement of s. 251(4) that at least four physicians be available to authorize and to perform an abortion meant in practice that abortions would be absolutely unavailable in almost one-quarter of all hospitals in Canada.

Other administrative and procedural requirements of s. 251(4) reduce the availability of therapeutic abortions even further. For the purposes of s. 251, therapeutic abortions can only be performed in "accredited" or "approved" hospitals. As noted above, an "approved" hospital is one which a provincial minister of health has designated as such for the purpose of performing therapeutic abortions. The minister is under no obligation to grant any such approval. Furthermore, an "accredited" hospital must not only be accredited by the Canadian Council on Hospital Accreditation, it must also provide specified services. Many Canadian hospitals do not provide all of the required services, thereby being automatically disqualified from undertaking therapeutic abortions. Moreover, even if a hospital is eligible to create a therapeutic abortion committee, there is no requirement in s. 251 that the hospital need do so.

A further flaw with the administrative system established in s. 251(4) is the failure to provide an adequate standard for therapeutic abortion committees which must determine when a therapeutic abortion should, as a matter of law, be granted. Subsection (4) states simply that a therapeutic abortion committee may grant a certificate when it determines that a continuation of a pregnancy would be likely to endanger the "life or health" of the pregnant woman. It was noted above that "health" is not defined for the purposes of the section. The Crown admitted in its supplementary factum that the medical witnesses at trial testified uniformly that the "health" standard was ambiguous, but the Crown derives comfort from the fact that "the medical witnesses were unanimous in their approval of the broad World Health Organization definition of health." The World Health Organization defines "health" not merely as the absence of disease or infirmity, but as a state of physical, mental, and social well-being.

I do not understand how the mere existence of a workable definition of "health" can make the use of the word in s. 251(4) any less ambiguous when that definition is nowhere referred to in the section. There is no evidence that therapeutic abortion committees are commonly applying the World Health Organization definition.

Various expert doctors testified at trial that therapeutic abortion committees apply widely differing definitions of health. For some committees, psychological health is a justification for therapeutic abortion; for others it is not. Some committees routinely refuse abortions to married women unless they are in physical danger, while for other committees it is possible for a married woman to show that she would suffer psychological harm if she continued with a pregnancy, thereby justifying an abortion. It is not typically possible for women to know in advance what standard of health will be applied by any given committee.

When the decision of the therapeutic abortion committee is so directly laden with legal consequences, the absence of any clear legal standard to be applied by the committee in reaching its decision is a serious procedural flaw ... The combined effect of all of these problems with the procedure stipulated in s. 251 for access to therapeutic abortions is a failure to comply with the principles of fundamental justice. One of the basic tenets of our system of criminal justice is that when Parliament creates a defence to a criminal charge, the defence should not be illusory or so difficult to attain as to be practically illusory. The criminal law is a very special form of governmental regulation, for it seeks to express our society's collective disapprobation of certain acts and omissions. When a defence is provided, especially a specifically tailored defence to a particular charge, it is because the legislator has determined that the disapprobation of society is not warranted when the conditions of the defence are met.

The Crown argues in its supplementary factum that women who face difficulties in obtaining abortions at home can simply travel elsewhere in Canada to procure a therapeutic abortion. That submission would not be especially troubling if the difficulties facing women were not in large measure created by the procedural requirements of s. 251 itself. If women were seeking anonymity outside their home town or were simply confronting the reality that it is often difficult to obtain medical services in rural areas, it might be appropriate to say "let them travel." But the evidence establishes convincingly that it is the law itself which in many ways prevents access to local therapeutic abortion facilities. The enormous emotional and financial burden placed upon women who must travel long distances from home to obtain an abortion is a burden created in many instances by Parliament.

SECTION 1 ANALYSIS

Section 1 of the *Charter* can potentially be used to "salvage" a legislative provision which breaches s. 7.

The appellants contended that the sole purpose of s. 251 of the *Criminal Code* is to protect the life and health of pregnant women. The respondent Crown submitted that s. 251 seeks to protect not only the life and health of pregnant women, but also the interests of the foetus. On the other hand, the Crown conceded that the court is not called upon in this appeal to evaluate any claim to "foetal rights" or to assess the meaning of "the right to life." I expressly refrain from so doing. In my view, it is unnecessary for the purpose of deciding this appeal to evaluate or assess "foetal rights" as an independent constitutional value. Nor are we required to measure the full extent of the state's interest in establishing criteria unrelated to the pregnant woman's own priorities and aspirations. What we must do is evaluate the particular balance struck by Parliament in s. 251, as it relates to the priorities and aspirations of pregnant women and the government's interests in the protection of the foetus.

Section 251 provides that foetal interests are not to be protected where the "life or health" of the woman is threatened. Thus, Parliament itself has expressly stated in s. 251 that the "life or health" of pregnant women is paramount. The procedures of s. 251(4) are clearly related to the pregnant woman's "life or health" for that is the very phrase used by the subsection. As McIntyre, J states in his reasons, the aim of s. 251(4) is "to restrict abortion to cases where the continuation of the pregnancy would, or would likely, be injurious to the life or health of the woman concerned, not to provide unrestricted access to abortion." I have no difficulty in concluding that the objective of s. 251 as a whole, namely, to balance the competing interests identified by Parliament, is sufficiently important to meet the requirements of the first step in the Oakes inquiry under s. 1. I think the protection of the interests of pregnant women is a valid governmental objective, where life and health can be jeopardized by criminal sanctions. Like Beetz and Wilson, JJ, I agree that protection of foetal interests by Parliament is also a valid governmental objective. It follows that balancing these interests, with the lives and health of women a major factor, is clearly an important governmental objective.

I am equally convinced, however, that the means chosen to advance the legislative objectives of s. 251 do not satisfy any of the three elements of the proportionality component of *R v Oakes*. The evidence has led me to conclude that the infringement of the security of the person of pregnant women caused by s. 251 is not accomplished in accordance with the principles of fundamental justice. It has been demonstrated that the procedures and administrative structures created by s. 251 are often arbitrary and unfair. The procedures established to implement the policy of s. 251 impair s. 7 rights far more than is necessary because they hold out an illusory defence to many women who would prima facie qualify under the exculpatory provisions of s. 251(4). In other words, many women whom Parliament professes not to wish to subject to criminal liability will nevertheless be forced by the practical unavailability of the supposed defence to risk liability or to suffer other harm such as a traumatic late abortion caused by the delay inherent in the s. 251 system. Finally, the effects of the limitation upon the s. 7 rights of many pregnant women are out of proportion to the objective sought to be achieved. Indeed, to the extent that s. 251(4) is designed to protect the life and health of women, the procedures it establishes may actually defeat that objective. The administrative structures of s. 251(4) are so cumbersome that women whose health is endangered by pregnancy may not be able to gain a therapeutic abortion, at least without great trauma, expense and inconvenience.

Section 251 of the *Criminal Code* cannot be saved, therefore, under s. 1 of the *Charter*.

Beetz, J: – I have had the advantage of reading the reasons for judgment written by the Chief Justice, as well as the reasons written by Mr Justice McIntyre and Madam Justice Wilson.

Like the Chief Justice and Wilson, J, I would allow the appeal and answer the first constitutional question in the affirmative and the second constitutional question in the negative. This, however, is a result which I reach for reasons which differ from those of the Chief Justice and those of Wilson, J.

I find it convenient to outline at the outset the steps which lead me to this result:

Before the advent of the *Charter*, Parliament recognized, in adopting s. 251(4) of the *Criminal Code*, that the interest in the life or health of the pregnant woman takes precedence over the interest in prohibiting abortions, including the interest of the state in the protection of the foetus, when "the continuation of the pregnancy of such female person would or would be likely to endanger her life or health." In my view, this standard in s. 251(4) became entrenched at least as a minimum when the "right to life, liberty and security of the person" was enshrined in the *Canadian Charter of Rights and Freedoms* at s. 7.

"Security of the person" within the meaning of s. 7 of the *Charter* must include a right of access to medical treatment for a condition representing a danger to life or health without fear of criminal sanction. If an Act of Parliament forces a pregnant woman whose life or health is in danger to choose between, on the one hand, the commission of a crime to obtain effective and timely medical treatment and, on the other hand, inadequate treatment or no treatment at all, her right to security of the person has been violated.

According to the evidence, the procedural requirements of s. 251 of the *Criminal Code* significantly delay pregnant women's access to medical treatment resulting in an additional danger to their health, thereby depriving them of their right to security of the person.

The deprivation referred to in the preceding proposition does not accord with the principles of fundamental justice. While Parliament is justified in requiring a reliable, independent, and medically sound opinion as to the "life or health" of the pregnant woman in order to protect the state interest in the foetus, and while any such statutory mechanism will inevitably result in some delay, certain of the procedural requirements of s. 251 of the *Criminal Code* are nevertheless manifestly unfair. These requirements are manifestly unfair in that they are unnecessary in respect of Parliament's objectives in establishing the administrative structure and that they result in additional risks to the health of pregnant women.

The primary objective of s. 251 of the *Criminal Code* is the protection of the foetus. The protection of the life and health of the pregnant woman is an ancillary objective. The primary objective does relate to concerns which are pressing and substantial in a free and democratic society and which, pursuant to s. 1 of the *Charter*, justify reasonable limits to be put on a woman's right. However, rules unnecessary in respect of the primary and ancillary objectives which they are designed to serve, such as some of the rules contained in s. 251, cannot be said to be rationally connected to these objectives under s. 1 of the *Charter*. Consequently, s. 251 does not constitute a reasonable limit to the security of the person.

It is not necessary to decide whether there is a proportionality between the effects of s. 251 and the objective of protecting the foetus, nor is it necessary to answer the question concerning the circumstances in which there is a proportionality between the effects of s. 251 which limit the right of pregnant women to security of the person and the objective of the protection of the foetus. But I feel bound to observe that the objective of protecting the foetus would not justify the severity of the breach of pregnant women's right to security of the person which would result if the exculpatory provision of s. 251 was completely removed from the *Criminal Code*. However, a rule that would require a higher degree of danger to health in the latter months of pregnancy, as opposed to the early months, for an abortion to be lawful, could possibly achieve a proportionality which would be acceptable under s. 1 of the *Charter* ...

If a rule of criminal law precludes a person from obtaining appropriate medical treatment when his or her life or health is in danger, then the state has intervened and this intervention constitutes a violation of that man's or that woman's security of the person. "Security of the person" must include a right of access to medical treatment for a condition representing a danger to life or health without fear of criminal sanction. If an Act of Parliament forces a person whose life or health is in danger to choose between, on the one hand, the commission of a crime to obtain effective and timely medical treatment and, on the other hand, inadequate treatment or no treatment at all, the right to security of the person has been violated.

This interpretation of s. 7 of the *Charter* is sufficient to measure the content of s. 251 of the *Criminal Code* against that of the *Charter* in order to dispose of this appeal. While I agree with McIntyre, J that a breach of a right to security must be "based upon an infringement of some interest which would be of such nature and such importance as to warrant constitutional protection," I am of the view that the protection of life or health is an interest of sufficient importance in this regard.

McIntyre, J (dissenting): – I have read the reasons for judgment prepared by my colleagues, the Chief Justice and Beetz and Wilson, JJ. I agree that the principal issue which arises is whether s. 251 of the *Criminal Code*, RSC 1970, c. C-34, contravenes s. 7 of the *Canadian Charter of Rights and Freedoms*. I will make some comments later on other issues put forward by the appellants. The Chief Justice has set out the constitutional questions and the relevant statutory provisions, as well as the facts and procedural history. He has considered the scope of s. 7 of the *Charter* and, having found that it has been offended, he would allow the appeal. I am unable to agree with his reasons or his disposition of the appeal. I find myself in broad general agreement with the reasons of the Court of Appeal, and I would dismiss the appeal on that basis and for reasons that I will endeavour to set forth.

PROCEDURAL FAIRNESS

I now turn to the appellant's argument regarding the procedural fairness of s. 251 of the *Criminal Code*. The basis of the argument is that the exemption provisions of s-s. (4) are such as to render illusory or practically illusory any defence arising from the subsection for many women who seek abortions. It is pointed out that therapeutic abortions are available only in accredited or approved hospitals, that hospitals so accredited or approved may or may not appoint abortion committees, and that "health" is defined in vague terms which afford no clear guide to its meaning. Statistically, it was said that abortions could be lawfully performed in only 20 per cent of all hospitals in Canada. Because abortions are not generally available to all women who seek them, the argument goes, the defence is illusory, or practically so, and the section therefore fails to comport with the principles of fundamental justice ...

It would seem to me that a defence created by Parliament could only be said to be illusory or practically so when the defence is not available in the circumstances in which it is held out as being available. The very nature of the test assumes, of course, that it is for Parliament to define the defence and, in so doing, to designate the terms and conditions upon which it may be available.

[I]t is apparent that the court's role is not to second-guess Parliament's policy choice as to how broad or how narrow the defence should be. The determination of when "the disapprobation of society is not warranted" is in Parliament's hands. The Court's role when the enactment is attacked on the basis that the defence is illusory is to determine whether the defence is available in the circumstances in which it was intended to apply. Parliament has set out the conditions, in s. 251(4), under which a therapeutic abortion may be obtained, free from criminal sanction. It is patent on the face of the legislation that the defence is circumscribed and narrow. It is clear that this was the Parliamentary intent and it was expressed with precision. I am not able to accept the contention that the defence has been held out to be generally available. It is, on the contrary, carefully tailored and limited to special circumstances. Therapeutic abortions may be performed only in certain hospitals and in accordance with certain specified provisions. It could only be classed as illusory or practically so if it could be found that it does not provide lawful access to abortions in circumstances described in the section. No such finding should be made upon the material before this court. The evidence will not support the proposition that significant numbers of those who meet the conditions imposed in s. 251 of the *Criminal Code* are denied abortions.

It is evident that what the appellants advocate is not the therapeutic abortion referred to in s. 251 of the *Code*. Their clinic was called into being because of the perceived inadequacies of s. 251. They propose and seek to justify "abortion on demand." The defence in s. 251(4) was not intended to meet the views of the appellants and provide a defence at large which would effectively repeal the operative subsections of s. 251. Some feel strongly that s. 251 is not adequate in today's society. Be that as it may, it does not follow that the defence provisions of s. 251(4) are illusory. They represent the legislative choice on this question and, as noted, it has not been shown that therapeutic abortions have not been available in cases contemplated by the provision.

Wilson, J: – At the heart of this appeal is the question whether a pregnant woman can, as a constitutional matter, be compelled by law to carry the foetus to term. The legislature has proceeded on the basis that she can be so compelled and, indeed, has made it a criminal offence punishable by imprisonment under s. 251 of the *Criminal Code*, RSC 1970, c. C-34, for her or her physician to terminate the pregnancy unless the procedural requirements of the section are complied with.

My colleagues, the Chief Justice and Beetz, J, have attacked those requirements in reasons which I have had the privilege of reading. They have found that the requirements do not comport with the principles of fundamental justice in the procedural sense and have concluded that, since they cannot be severed from the provisions creating the substantive offence, the whole of s. 251 must fall.

With all due respect, I think that the court must tackle the primary issue first. A consideration as to whether or not the procedural requirements for obtaining or performing an abortion comport with fundamental justice is purely academic if such requirements cannot as a constitutional matter be imposed at all. If a pregnant woman cannot, as a constitutional matter, be compelled by law to carry the foetus to term against her will, a review of the procedural requirements by which she may be compelled to do so seems pointless. Moreover, it would, in my opinion, be an exercise in futility for the legislature to expend its time and energy in attempting to remedy the defects in the procedural requirements unless it has some assurance that this process will, at the end of the day, result in the creation of a valid criminal offence. I turn, therefore, to what I believe is the central issue that must be addressed.

THE RIGHT OF ACCESS TO ABORTION

Section 7 of the Canadian *Charter* of Rights and Freedoms provides:

7. Everyone has the right to life, liberty and security of the person and the right not to be deprived thereof except in accordance with the principles of fundamental justice.

I agree with the Chief Justice that we are not called upon in this case to delineate the full content of the right to life, liberty, and security of the person. This would be an impossible task because we cannot envisage all the contexts in which such a right might be asserted. What we are asked to do, I believe, is define the content of the right in the context of the legislation under attack. Does s. 251 of the *Criminal Code* which limits the pregnant woman's access to abortion violate her right to life, liberty, and security of the person within the meaning of s. 7?

Leaving aside for the moment the implications of the section for the foetus and addressing only the s. 7 right of the pregnant woman, it seems to me that we can say with a fair degree of confidence that a legislative scheme for the obtaining of an abortion which exposes the pregnant woman to a threat to her security of the person would violate her right under s. 7 ... But this, of course, does not answer the question whether even the ideal legislative scheme, assuming that it is one which poses no threat to the physical and psychological security of the person of the pregnant woman, would be valid under s. 7. I say this for two reasons: (1) because s. 7 encompasses more than the right to security of the person; it speaks also of the right to liberty, and (2) because security of the person may encompass more than physical and psychological security; this we have yet to decide.

It seems to me, therefore, that to commence the analysis with the premise that the s. 7 right encompasses only a right to physical and psychological security and to fail to deal with the right to liberty in the context of "life, liberty and security of the person" begs the central issue in the case. If either the right to liberty or the right to security of the person or a combination of both confers on the pregnant woman the right to decide for herself (with the guidance of her physician) whether or not to have an abortion then we have to examine the legislative scheme not only from the point of view of fundamental justice in the procedural sense but in the substantive sense as well. I think, therefore, that we must answer the question: what is meant by the right to liberty in the context of the abortion issue? Does it give the pregnant woman control over decisions affecting her own body? If not, does her right to security of the person give her such control? I turn first to the right to liberty.

The Right to Liberty

In order to ascertain the content of the right to liberty, we must commence with an analysis of the purpose of the right. We are invited, therefore, to consider the purpose of the *Charter* in general and of the right to liberty in particular.

The *Charter* is predicated on a particular conception of the place of the individual in society. An individual is not a totally independent entity disconnected from the society in which he or she lives. Neither, however, is the individual a mere cog in an impersonal machine in which his or her values, goals, and aspirations are subordinated to those of the collectivity. The individual is a bit of both. The *Charter* reflects this reality by leaving a wide range of activities and decisions open to legitimate government control while at the same time placing limits on the proper scope of that control. Thus, the rights guaranteed in the *Charter* erect around each individual, metaphorically speaking, an invisible fence over which the state will not be allowed to trespass. The role of the courts is to map out, piece by piece, the parameters of the fence ...

The idea of human dignity finds expression in almost every right and freedom guaranteed in the *Charter*. Individuals are afforded the right to choose their own religion and their own philosophy of life, the right to choose with whom they will associate and how they will express themselves, the right to choose where they will live and what occupation they will pursue. These are all examples of the basic theory underlying the *Charter*, namely, that the state will respect choices made by individuals and, to the greatest extent possible, will avoid subordinating these choices to any one conception of the good life.

Thus, an aspect of the respect for human dignity on which the *Charter* is founded is the right to make fundamental personal decisions without interference from the state ... In my view, this right, properly construed, grants the individual a degree of autonomy in making decisions of fundamental personal importance ... Liberty in a free and democratic society does not require the state to approve the personal decisions made by its citizens; it does, however, require the state to respect them.

In my opinion, the respect for individual decision making in matters of fundamental personal importance reflected in the American jurisprudence also informs the Canadian *Charter*. Indeed, as Chief Justice pointed out in *R v Big M Drug Mart Ltd*, beliefs about human worth and dignity "are the *sine qua non* of the political tradition underlying the *Charter*." I would conclude, therefore, that the right to liberty contained in s. 7 guarantees to every individual a degree of personal autonomy over important decisions intimately affecting their private lives.

The question then becomes whether the decision of a woman to terminate her pregnancy falls within this class of protected decisions. I have no doubt that it does. This decision is one that will have profound psychological, economic, and social consequences for the pregnant woman. The circumstances giving rise to it can be complex and varied and there may be, and usually are, powerful considerations militating in opposite directions. It is a decision that deeply reflects the way the woman thinks about herself and her relationship to others and to society at large. It is not just a medical decision; it is a profound social and ethical one as well. Her response to it will be the response of the whole person.

It is probably impossible for a man to respond, even imaginatively, to such a dilemma not just because it is outside the realm of his personal experience (although this is, of course, the case) but because he can relate to it only by objectifying it, thereby eliminating the subjective elements of the female psyche which are at the heart of the dilemma ...

[T]he history of the struggle for human rights from the eighteenth century on has been the history of men struggling to assert their dignity and common humanity against an overbearing state apparatus. The more recent struggle for women's rights has been a struggle to eliminate discrimination, to achieve a place for women in a man's world, to develop a set of legislative reforms in order to place women in the same position as men. It has not been a struggle to define the rights of women in relation to their special place in the societal structure and in relation to the biological distinction between the two sexes. Thus, women's needs and aspirations are only now being translated into protected rights. The right to reproduce or not to reproduce which is in issue in this case is one such right and is properly perceived as an integral part of modern woman's struggle to assert her dignity and worth as a human being ...

Given then that the right to liberty guaranteed by s. 7 of the *Charter* gives a woman the right to decide for herself whether or not to terminate her pregnancy, does s. 251 of the *Criminal Code* violate this right? Clearly it does. The purpose of the section is to take the decision away from the woman and give it to a committee. Furthermore, as the Chief Justice correctly points out, the committee bases its decision on "criteria entirely unrelated to [the pregnant woman's] priorities and aspirations." The fact that the decision whether a woman will be allowed to terminate her pregnancy is in the hands of a committee is just as great a violation of the woman's right to personal autonomy in decisions of an intimate and private nature as it would be if a committee were established to decide whether a woman should be allowed to continue her pregnancy. Both these arrangements violate the woman's right to liberty by deciding for her something that she has the right to decide for herself.

The Right to Security of the Person

Section 7 of the *Charter* also guarantees everyone the right to security of the person. Does this, as Mr Manning suggests, extend to the right of control over their own bodies?

I agree with the Chief Justice and with Beetz, J that the right to "security of the person" under s. 7 of the *Charter* protects both the physical and psychological integrity of the individual. State-enforced medical or surgical treatment comes readily to mind as an obvious invasion of physical integrity. [T]he present legislative scheme for the obtaining of an abortion clearly subjects pregnant women to considerable emotional stress as well as to unnecessary physical risk. I believe, however, that the flaw in the present legislative scheme goes much deeper than that. In essence, what it does is assert that the woman's capacity to reproduce is not to be subject to her own control. It is to be subject to the control of the state. She may not choose whether to exercise her existing capacity or not to exercise it. This is not, in my view, just a matter of interfering with her right to liberty in the sense (already discussed) of her right to personal autonomy in decision-making, it is a direct interference with her physical "person" as well. She is truly being treated as a means — a means to an end which she does not desire but over which she has no control. She is the passive recipient of a decision made by others as to whether her body is to be used to nurture a new life. Can there be anything that comports less with human dignity and self-respect? How can a woman in this position have any sense of security with respect to her person? I believe that s. 251 of the *Criminal Code* deprives the pregnant woman of her right to security of the person as well as her right to liberty.

THE SCOPE OF THE RIGHT UNDER SECTION 7

I turn now to a consideration of the degree of personal autonomy the pregnant woman has under s. 7 of the *Charter* when faced with a decision whether or not to have an abortion or, to put it into the legislative context, the degree to which the legislature can deny the pregnant woman access to abortion without violating her s. 7 right. This involves a consideration of the extent to which the legislature can "deprive" her of it under the second part of s. 7 and the extent to which it can put "limits" on it under s. 1.

The Principles of Fundamental Justice

Does s. 251 deprive women of their right to liberty and to security of the person "in accordance with the principles of fundamental justice"? I agree with Lamer, J who stated in *Reference re s. 94(2) of Motor Vehicle Act* (1985), 23 CCC (3d) 289 at p. 311, that the principles of fundamental justice "cannot be given any exhaustive content or simple enumerative definition, but will take on concrete meaning as the courts address alleged violations of s. 7". In the same judgment Lamer, J also stated at p. 302 CCC, p. 550:

In other words, the principles of fundamental justice are to be found in the basic tenets of our legal system. They do not lie in the realm of general public policy but in the inherent domain of the judiciary as guardian of the justice system ...

While Lamer, J draws mainly upon ss. 8 to 14 of the *Charter* to give substantive content to the principles of fundamental justice, he does not preclude, but seems rather to encourage, the idea that recourse may be had to other rights guaranteed by the *Charter* for the same purpose. The question, therefore, is whether the deprivation of the s. 7 right is in accordance not only with procedural fairness (and I agree with the Chief Justice and Beetz, J for the reasons they give that it is not) but also with the fundamental rights and freedoms laid down elsewhere in the *Charter*.

In my view, the deprivation of the s. 7 right with which we are concerned in this case offends s. 2(a) of the *Charter*. I say this because I believe that the decision whether or not to terminate a pregnancy is essentially a moral decision, a matter of conscience. I do not think there is or can be any dispute about that. The question is: whose conscience? Is the conscience of the woman to be paramount or the conscience of the state? I believe, for the reasons I gave in discussing the right to liberty, that in a free and democratic society it must be the conscience of the individual. Indeed, s. 2(a) makes it clear that this freedom belongs to "everyone", i.e., to each of us individually. I quote the section for convenience:

2. Everyone has the following fundamental freedoms:
(a) freedom of conscience and religion;

It seems to me, therefore, that in a free and democratic society "freedom of conscience and religion" should be broadly construed to extend to conscientiously held beliefs, whether grounded in religion or in a secular morality. Indeed, as a matter of statutory interpretation, "conscience" and "religion" should not be treated as tautologous if capable of independent, although related, meaning. Accordingly, for the state to take sides on the issue of abortion as it does in the impugned legislation by making it a criminal offence for the pregnant woman to exercise one of her options, is not only to endorse but also to enforce, on pain of a further loss of liberty through actual imprisonment, one conscientiously held view at the expense of another. Legislation which violates freedom of conscience in this manner cannot, in my view, be in accordance with the principles of fundamental justice within the meaning of s. 7.

READING QUESTIONS ON MORGENTALER

1 Can you think of a statute regulating abortion that would pass the tests the court outlines?
2 Wilson, J uses the metaphor of a "fence" protecting individual rights. How is this type of argument related to the debate about negative liberty, above?

Lorraine Weinrib,
"The Morgentaler Judgment: Constitutional Rights, Legislative Intention, and Institutional Design" (1992)

Weinrib examines the consequences of the court's decision in Morgentaler. She criticizes the judgment, although she argues that it is the beginning of the realization that women are rights-holders first, breeders second.

IV THE FUTURE OF CANADIAN ABORTION LAW

The *Morgentaler* judgment does not incapacitate our legislatures from regulating abortion or even prohibiting abortion in some circumstances. Nor is there, in the absence of legislation, a legal vacuum, as repeatedly declared by the press in the aftermath of the decision. On the contrary, we have abundant law on the subject of abortion – constitutional law that circumscribes the permissible exercise of state power. Any state action must honour the *Charter* guarantee of expeditious access to therapeutic health care for women throughout pregnancy, without prejudice attaching to gender and without moral overtones.

The diversity of analysis in the three majority judgments is often cited as proof that *Charter* analysis lies in the subjective leanings of the individual judge rather than in the realm of legal discourse. But diversity is not disparity. Each opinion is a study in legal, rather than political or moral, analysis; each presents a distinctively judicial approach to elaboration of guaranteed rights; each expresses disdain for the subordination of the substantive rights of women to therapeutic health care to the lesser ranked interests of doctors, hospitals, and politicians. The taint of subjectivism lies, if anywhere, in the dissent.

Proof of a majority consensus as to the substantive dictates of the supreme law of Canada lies in the remedy afforded. If Justice Beetz's concern applied only to the procedural delivery of the therapeutic standard, he would have left that standard in place, leaving those charged with the offence of procuring miscarriages with the defence of therapeutic need. Similarly, if Chief Justice Dickson's interest was limited to securing a fair procedure unrelated to the "priorities and aspirations" of the pregnant woman, he too would have left women and doctors with the defence of therapeutic cause. The working of the criminal law system would have been an orderly reprieve from the lottery established by section 251. In sum, if the Court's concerns had really been restricted to procedure, four members of the Court's panel of seven should have been satisfied with a more minimal remedy than invalidation of section 251 in toto.

The remedy accords best with the reasoning of Justice Wilson, the view that a pregnant woman's liberty includes the right to access in early abortion, period. This result may appear startling, until one comes to appreciate that the positions of the other judges in the majority are closer to her view than generally understood. The logic of the Chief Justice's approach as well as the remedy he affirms take him to autonomy over procreation, because "priorities and aspirations" are subjective values and thus inappropriate to substitute decision-making, especially by doctors. Justice Beetz is not far from this camp. His acceptance of a non-stringent therapeutic standard for early pregnancy, which appears to include reactive stress, as an exercise of medical judgment unsupervised by the institutions of public hospital administration or the politics of the medical profession, his rejection of any conditions unrelated to therapeutic concerns, his refusal to rule out liberty as a ground for access to abortion, and his insistence upon a therapeutic exemption as a *Charter* right, all suggest how he agreed to invalidate section 251 in its entirety. The majority opinions also share another important element. They accord a woman's claim to therapeutic health care the highest constitutional stature, above the claims of the foetus and above the conscientious, political and economic claims of the public, the medical profession, and politicians.[1]

The majority position therefore precludes, on *Charter* grounds, the blanket criminalization of abortion. It also precludes restriction without a therapeutic exemption in early pregnancy, at least on the common law standard. In later pregnancy, the state may impose a more stringent therapeutic standard. There need be no legislated abortion policy, least of all in exercise of the federal jurisdiction over criminal law.

It was in this mesh of constitutional strictures that the federal government proposed Bill C-43 as an exercise of its criminal law jurisdiction. Its conformity to the principles established by the majority in *Morgentaler* is not clear. In my view, features of Bill C-43, the proposed amendment to the *Criminal Code* that failed to pass the Senate in January of 1991, ran contrary to the Supreme Court of Canada's reasons for judgment.

The Infirmities of Bill C-43

General Conditions

Bill C-43 contained no conditions unrelated to the delivery of therapeutic health care.[2] The absence of such requirements reflected the denunciation by Beetz, J and Dickson, CJC of general conditions that restricted access to abortion in the name of health and professional standards, financial constraints, and ease of enforcement.

Personal Standards

The proposed bill would have extended the personal therapeutic standard in section 251.[3] In addition to retaining the terms included in section 251, Bill C-43 specified that physical, mental, and psychological health were included. Interpretive material provided by the minister of justice incorporated a wider range of circumstances than accepted by the Court as coming within the therapeutic standard.[4] Some may use this extended usage of the word "health" to argue that the statutory standard moves beyond therapeutic health care (by including stress reaction to the pregnancy due to socio-economic circumstances, for example) into the realm connoted by the terms "priorities and aspirations" or even "abortion on demand." If so, one may question, on *Charter* grounds, whether the state can require women to seek permission from doctors for abortions that are based on subjective considerations rather than grounds recognizable by medical expertise.

One can also question whether this kind of prohibition-exception undermines the jurisdiction of Parliament to enact the law in exercise of its criminal law power. At issue is the elastic quality of the category of "therapy" in the current societal context, reflected in the federal government's interpretation of the proposed legislation and medical practice. While the Parliament of Canada can say that a cow is a pig, it cannot alter its legislative jurisdiction by so doing.

When doctors and the health-care system deal not only with disease and its prevention, but also with well-being on a broader socio-economic basis, including consideration of an individual's relationships and life circumstances, then the concept of therapy loses its hard edges. Consequently, one cannot continue to differentiate between expert medical assessments of the presence of illness or likely deleterious impact on health, on the one hand, and findings that a pregnant woman is suffering stress because she sincerely believes that she should not continue a pregnancy, on the other.

The wide understanding of therapy impinges on the criminal quality of the prohibition-exemption in the following way. *Morgentaler* establishes that any prohibition against abortion must include a therapeutic exemption. But if therapy is as expansive a category as indicated, then the *criminal* prohibition admits an exemption based on expert determination that the individual is experiencing reactive stress. This condition combines a reaction to the situation of unwanted pregnancy as well as to the prohibition itself. One satisfies the exemption by reacting negatively to the prohibition, and its attendant interruption of one's control over intimate decision-making. In result, the most basic understanding of the nature of criminal law, that it condemns certain conduct as unacceptable to the fabric of society, is abandoned. The norm established by the prohibition is self-contradictory to the extent it admits of an exception that is merely an objection to the norm.[5]

This feature of the proposed legislation also undercuts the argument for foetal protection under section 1 of the *Charter*. The majority opinions in *Morgentaler* accept the claims on behalf of the foetus as grounds for justifying restrictions in later pregnancy on the pregnant woman's access to therapeutic health care. To the extent that the grounds for permitted abortion are relaxed to include what is in effect elective abortion, the credibility of the state's argument that it acts to protect the foetus in any meaningful way is weakened.

This same difficulty follows from another feature of the proposed legislation, the inapplicability of the prohibition before implantation.[6] While this window of opportunity may lessen the impact of criminalization by increasing the frequency of very early pregnancy termination, it may also weaken the state's claim to act to protect the foetus.

The majority judges each justified encroachment upon women's rights in terms of foetal interests. While formulated differently by each judge, the common ground appears to be that the state can provide increasing protection to the foetus as the pregnancy progresses against the pregnant women's constitutional rights to security of the person and/or to liberty.[7] None of the judgments, however, adequately addresses the principled basis for this position.

The task of articulating the principled grounds of justification for increasing recognition of foetal claims, however, is made all the more difficult by the proposed open-ended "therapeutic" standard and the early dispensation period, generally accepted as part of pregnancy, in which no protection is afforded whatsoever. The pre-implantation dispensation suggests that the state's interest is not in the fertilized ovum that develops into the foetus, but in the pregnancy. The argument for increasing foetal rights was beyond the majority's grasp in *Morgentaler*. Bridging the gap between no protection and protection is a greater challenge.[8]

Decision-Making

If *Morgentaler* makes anything clear, it is the requirement of an accessible, expeditious, and medically expert decision-making instrumentality where a therapeutic standard is imposed as a precondition for access to legal abortion. Justice Beetz gives the clearest direction in suggesting that the attending doctor solicit a second opinion from another doctor and that permission be transferable. The proposed legislation, however, would have required even less: the opinion of the doctor performing or overseeing the abortion, on generally accepted professional standards.

This arrangement might appear to provide the ready access that *Morgentaler* demands. However, appearances are often deceptive. It is true that the proposed legislation would not have imposed the infamous general conditions that formerly impeded and restricted decision-making. But it contained another feature of the invalidated legislative arrangements, one that might impede decision-making in an equally impermissible way although not to the same extent. The reasons for judgment in *Morgentaler* did not dwell on this deficiency because the gross deficiencies of section 251 rendered more subtle analysis unnecessary. The offensive feature in the new legislation is once again the unconstrained discretion given to doctors.

One of the primary desiderata in the formulation of the provision invalidated in *Morgentaler* was the delegation of complete authority over abortions to the medical profession in large public hospitals. That discretion included freedom to establish therapeutic committees, or not, as well as the authority to set the acceptable attitudes for members of those committees, the basis for permitting abortions, the conditions attached to permission, the eligible population of applicants, the mode of application, the number of abortions, and the abortion methods. The 1969 amendment, it must be emphasized, created *no entitlement* to abortion for women who could satisfy the therapeutic standard. There was only "permission," as the minister of justice had made clear in 1969, for doctors to operate within the statutory arrangements prescribed.

In formulating the therapeutic exemption, legislators took care that doctors retained discretion on grounds of conscience. No doctor was to be forced against conscience to participate in the decision-making process or in the provision of abortion services. Amendments to make this protection explicit were abandoned only on the assurance of the minister of justice that they were unnecessary.[9]

The infirmity of the proposed legislation was not that it failed to honour the conscience of doctors in regard to abortion, but that it maintained the doctors' option on access to the exemption beyond the exercise of conscience. Even though the Supreme Court of Canada made it clear that the exemption must be easily and widely available, because otherwise the securing of therapeutic health care is constitutionally fettered by criminal sanction, Parliament in Bill C-43 made no arrangements to provide a functioning and accessible decision-making process. Nor did it ensure that, once permission was given, abortion would be available.

Much of the discussion about Bill C-43 focused on the possible criminal and civil liability of doctors who perform abortions. In addition to exposure to criminal liability[10] for failing to apply the therapeutic standard properly, or at all, the spectre of civil proceedings[11] put doctors on guard. The only response of the federal government was to stress that the provincial attorneys general would exercise discretion as to criminal proceedings.

This response was unsatisfactory for two reasons. First, in practical terms, it did not diminish the anxiety of doctors who did not want exposure to criminal liability to cast a pall over their practices. Second, on a more legal plane, it manifested an odd reluctance by the federal government to make clear that it would exercise *its* prosecutorial responsibility to stop frivolous or vexatious prosecutions.[12] This reluctance to give some direct and meaningful assurance to doctors in order to guarantee that the new system would accommodate all applicants demonstrated, at least, a failure to appreciate the constitutional obligation that follows from the creation of an exemption from criminalization.

To no one's surprise, many doctors and groups of doctors indicated that they would no longer provide abortions and thereby reduce and delay the availability of abortion beyond the well-known problem areas, for example, in the Atlantic provinces and non-urban centres generally. In the light of this development it was highly unrealistic for the federal government to assume that the day-to-day functioning of the medical system would accommodate the constituency with constitutional claim to its services.

Without legislated assurance that such accommodation was in place, Bill C-43 would put pregnant women in the same situation in which they found themselves under section 251, namely, hostage to the monopoly of a medical profession under no statutory or constitutional obligation to provide abortion.

The Parliament of Canada, however, enjoys no such option. Once it embarks on criminalization, it must provide a therapeutic exemption, the administration of which dictates exercise of medical expertise. It is not enough to refrain from imposing impediments. No considerations in conflict with the right of access to therapeutic health care – expense constraint, the exclusive legislative jurisdiction of the provinces over the health-care system, garden-variety paternalism, or reluctance to conscript the medical profession – dissolve that obligation. *Morgentaler* makes that abundantly clear.

It is unreasonable, unfair, and unconstitutional to leave the administration of an exemption from criminal liability to the unconstrained discretion of the medical profession. It is unreasonable because members of the profession, licensed and professionally bound to offer health-care services, also stand liable to prosecution for every asserted or manipulated misstep. Moreover, doctors' behaviour under section 251 signals that they are not better able than anyone else to put personal prejudices, stereotypes, and self-interest before constitutional rights. It is unfair because giving doctors the authority, but not the duty, to consider applications for exemption renders the proposed system potentially as arbitrary, unpredictable, and mysterious as that rejected by the Supreme Court. And, one must remember, women seeking abortion approach the medical profession in the physical and emotional throes of early and unwanted pregnancy. Finally, it is unconstitutional because the federal government assumes constitutional responsibility to provide access to therapeutic health care if it chooses to criminalize abortions that do not pass this standard.[13]

Beyond Bill C-43

If the federal government chose not to act under the *Criminal Code*, each province would regulate abortion, either specifically or within the larger organization of the health-care system. Could a province establish criteria for abortion, such as a therapeutic standard? That would depend on the grounds for the standard. The province cannot legislate criminal law, although it can enforce its own regulatory schemes.[14] Accordingly, it could not impose criteria for abortion reflecting the disapprobation of society, for example, in respect to the "proper" role for procreation in the lives of women or the morality of abortion. The *Morgentaler* judgment also precludes giving priority to foetal interests at the expense of therapeutic health care for pregnant women.

The provinces are also subject to the *Charter's* equality guarantees. The stipulation of equality before and under the law, without discrimination on the ground of sex, in section 15, precludes any fetter upon access to abortion as a matter of therapeutic health care that is not generally applicable to other therapeutic and elective services.

Similarly, payment for the procedure under provincial health-care plans would also have to be consistent with payment for any comparable therapeutic or elective treatment. To the extent that treatment for birth control, sterilization, infertility, and birth are funded, therapeutic abortion should be as well. Also, since early abortion is less expensive than late abortion and much less expensive than medical supervision of a pregnancy, birth, and infant care, expeditious access is required, without restrictions or rationing for the sake of reducing health-care expenditures.

V CONCLUSION: WOMEN AND THE CONSTITUTION

No one should regret the demise of section 251, an ill-conceived and manifestly unfair legislation provision. The ability of the Court to decide *Morgentaler* as it did, given the political volatility of the issue, stands to its credit. In the future it may be obvious that women are

Charter rights-holders first, breeders second. As we look back on *Morgentaler*, we will see the preliminary attempts to give shape to that idea as constitutional law.

NOTES

1 For the view that the anti-abortion argument, that the foetus's right to life trumps all other claims, is "on very weak ground" because the right of a mature moral agent must prevail over the right of an unborn, potential person, see R. Whitaker "Rights in a 'Free and Democratic Society': Abortion" in *Federalism and Political Community* 331. Once one looks at the abortion issue from the point of view of women as gestators, birth-givers, and primary caretakers of children, especially in a society that devalues and disadvantages women because of the procreative role, this conclusion seems to follow. The weakness of the position in terms of legal argument is also demonstrated by written argument submitted to the Supreme Court of Canada in *R v Borowski* [1989] 1 SCR 342, 57 DLR (4th) 231 by Borowski and by REAL Women.

2 An Act Respecting Abortion
1. S. 287 & 288 of the *Criminal Code* are repealed and the following substituted therefore:

s. 287(1) Every person who induced an abortion on a female person is guilty of an indictable offence and liable to imprisonment for a term not exceeding 2 years, unless the abortion is induced by or under the direction of a medical practitioner who is of the opinion that, if the abortion were not induced, the health or life of the female person would be likely to be threatened.

(2) For the purposes of this section, "health" includes, for general certainty, physical, mental and psychological health; "medical practitioner," in respect of an abortion induced in a province, means a person who is entitled to practice medicine under the laws of that province; "opinion" means an opinion formed using generally accepted standards of the medical profession;

(3) For the purposes of this section and s. 288, inducing an abortion does not include using a drug, device or other means on a female person that is likely to prevent implantation of a fertilized ovum.

s. 288 Everyone who unlawfully supplies or procures a drug or other noxious thing or an instrument or thing, knowing that it is intended to be used or employed to induce an abortion on a female person, is guilty of an indictable offence and liable to imprisonment for a term not exceeding two years.

2. This Act shall come into force on a day to be fixed by order of the Governor in Council.

3 Four judges approved this standard: Justices Beetz, Estey, McIntyre, and La Forest. The Chief Justice and Justice Lamer would form part of this group if one reads their judgment as dispensing with wider grounds for the exemption, that is, accepting therapeutic grounds rather than the applicant's "priorities and aspirations," positing fair access to the exemption. While this is a possible reading of the Dickson judgment, his unswerving commitment to the status of women and free and equal members of the polity militates against it. I would argue that the Dickson opinion should be read as mandating the therapeutic exemption.

4 In correspondence to the medical profession Justice Minister Kim Campbell expressed the view that Bill C-43 would permit doctors to consider "such factors as rape, incest, genetic defects and socio-economic factors" with their opinion on "health." This view was also contained in explanatory material released with Bill C-43 on 3 November 1989. Both documents are on file with the author.

5 An analogy might clarify this argument. The insanity defence to a criminal charge denotes some sort of mental or emotional disability relating to the essential features of the offence. Such a condition is understood to be beyond the individual's control and to vitiate responsibility for the commission of the offence. If the range of the defence were expanded to include stress reaction to the urge to commit the offence or to the prohibition against commission of the act, then the defence itself would swallow up the prohibition.

6 Bill C-43, supra note 2, new section 287(3). The dispensation from criminalization is significant. Most abortions are now performed in early pregnancy at the time when the procedure is simple, inexpensive, and minimally traumatic. Most women prefer very early abortion. Later abortions under the regime of section 251, as the Beetz and Dickson judgments make clear, were a function of statute-induced and other delay. Relatively recent developments, such as the morning-after pill (routinely administered to rape victims in many centres) and the abortion pill, facilitate early, non-surgical intervention. Later abortions are usually precipitated by acquisition of information as to the health of the pregnant woman or of the foetus, which was unavailable earlier. Foetal abnormality, although per se not a therapeutic indication for the gestator, was widely understood in medical practice to satisfy the therapeutic standard under section 251, because of its traumatic effect upon the pregnant woman. Breakthroughs in medical science that advance the detection of foetal

abnormality at earlier stages of pregnancy will lead to earlier abortions. (One unresolved issue is the use of abortion for gender selection, a practice that might slip into the therapeutic stress reaction category. This possibility could be eliminated by provincial regulations prohibiting reporting of the gender of the foetus unless the information is related to the likelihood of transmission of genetic defects or disease. Such a prohibition might also be promulgated by medical associations and regulatory bodies as a matter of professional ethics. Any resistance to such a regulation could be met by section 15(2) of the *Charter*, which provides a basis for state action that works against discrimination based, inter alia, on sex.)

7 For Justice Beetz this justification applies, on a rising scale of therapeutic cause; for the Chief Justice this justification is a balance between the interests of pregnant women and the unborn. For Justice Wilson the justification arises in the latter half of pregnancy, on therapeutic grounds.

8 Principled argumentation in favour of an autonomy approach is not diminished but that is of no assistance because Bill C-43, *supra* note 2, as a criminal formulation, does not and cannot accommodate an autonomy-based right.

9 Justice Beetz confirmed this right to conscience under the *Charter*; see text, *supra*.

10 One can imagine, in the intense atmosphere infusing this issue, that anti-abortion activists might attempt to "trap" doctors into decisions that could be the basis for laying private informations.

11 Civil proceedings might arise at the initiative of third parties to stop abortions or by successful but regretful applicants, after the fact, for negligent exercise of the decision-making function. While it is exceedingly unlikely that any would succeed, the nuisance value of instituting proceedings might prove very effective in inducing doctors to withdraw their services.

12 See *A.G. Can. v C.N. Transportation* [1983] 2 SCR 206, 3 DLR (4th) 16 and *R v Wetmore* [1983] 2 SCR 284, 2 DLR (4th) 577.

13 Analogies may clarify the argument. If the government criminalized the possession, sale, and use of proscribed drugs, with an exemption based on a determination of eligibility by qualified medical practitioners, it would be constitutionally obligated to ensure that persons who wanted to qualify for the exemption could have their eligibility determined. If the determination process was time consuming, tedious, and involved the doctor in long-term supervision, and also provided inadequate remuneration, doctors might decide not to provide the service. Persons for whom an exemption to criminal liability had been provided by Parliament would thus find

themselves exposed to criminal liability. Here, where there is a much weaker case for constitutional claim to the exemption than in the context of abortion, one can see the contours of a credible section 7 argument. Another analogy, perhaps closer to the abortion issue, would involve claims of insanity at the time of commission of an offence. Imagine a requirement that an individual, who committed an offence involving serious bodily harm and wanted to make an insanity defence, consult a psychiatrist within two months of the commission of the offence. (This time frame is close to the time frame for securing a first-trimester abortion.) And let us say that psychiatrists did not want to be burdened with the public outcry that medical practitioners would be harbouring the incriminating secrets of persons who had committed criminal acts, but had not yet been charged. If many psychiatrists refused to do this work and persons were for that reason denied access to defences to criminal charges, a credible section 7 argument could be made.

14 This power is provided in section 92(15) of the *Constitution Act, 1867.*

READING QUESTION ON WEINRIB

1 Why does Weinrib insist that any abortion law must contain a therapeutic exemption? Do you agree?

The Canada Act and the Charter of Rights

CANADA ACT 1982
U.K., 1982, c.11
An Act to give effect to a request by the Senate and House of
Commons of Canada

Whereas Canada has requested and consented to the enactment of an Act of the Parliament of the United Kingdom to give effect to the provisions hereinafter set forth and the Senate and the House of Commons of Canada in Parliament assembled have submitted an address to Her Majesty requesting that Her Majesty may graciously be pleased to cause a Bill to be laid before the Parliament of the United Kingdom for that purpose.

Be it therefore enacted by the Queen's Most Excellent Majesty, by and with the advice and consent of the Lords Spiritual and Temporal, and Commons, in this present Parliament assembled, and by the authority of the same as follows:

1. The *Constitution Act, 1982* set out in Schedule B to this Act is hereby enacted for and enacted shall have the force of law in Canada and shall come into force as provided in that Act.

2. No Act of the Parliament of the United Kingdom passed after the *Constitution Act, 1982* comes into force shall extend to Canada as part of its law.

3. So far as it is not contained in Schedule B, the French version of this Act is set out in Schedule A to this Act and has the same authority in Canada as the English version thereof.

4. This Act may be cited as the *Canada Act 1982*.

CONSTITUTION ACT, 1982
Schedule B to Canada Act 1982 (U.K.)

PART I
CANADIAN CHARTER OF RIGHTS AND FREEDOMS

Whereas Canada is founded upon principles that recognize the supremacy of God and the rule of law:

Guarantee of Rights and Freedoms

1. *The Canadian Charter of Rights and Freedoms* guarantees the rights and freedoms set out in it subject only to such reasonable limits prescribed by law as can be demonstrably justified in a free and democratic society.

Fundamental Freedoms

2. Everyone has the following freedoms:
- (a) freedom of conscience and religion;
- (b) freedom of thought, belief, opinion and expression, including freedom of the press and other media of communication;
- (c) freedom of peaceful assembly; and
- (d) freedom of association.

Democratic Rights

3. Every citizen of Canada has the right to vote in an election of members of the House of Commons or of a legislative assembly and to be qualified for membership therein.

4. (1) No House of Commons and no legislative assembly shall continue for longer than five years from the date fixed for the return of the writs at a general election of its members.

(2) In time of real or apprehended war, invasion or insurrection, a House of Commons may be continued by Parliament and a legislative assembly may be continued by the legislature beyond five years if such continuation is not opposed by the votes of more than one-third of the members of the House of Commons or the legislative assembly, as the case may be.

5. There shall be a sitting of Parliament and of each legislature at least once every twelve months.

Mobility Rights

6. (1) Every citizen of Canada has the right to enter, remain in and leave Canada.

(2) Every citizen of Canada and every person who has the status of a permanent resident of Canada has the right
(a) to move and to take up residence in any province; and
(b) to pursue the gaining of a livelihood in any province.

(3) The rights specified in subsection (2) are subject to
(a) any laws or practices of general application in force in a province other than those that discriminate among persons primarily on the basis of province of present or previous residence; and
(b) any laws providing for reasonable residency requirements as a qualification for the receipt of publicly provided social services.

(4) Subsections (2) and (3) do not preclude any law, program or activity that has as its object the amelioration in a province of conditions of individuals in that province who are socially or economically disadvantaged if the rate of employment in that province is below the rate of employment in Canada.

Legal Rights

7. Everyone has the right to life, liberty and security of the person and the right not to be deprived thereof except in accordance with the principles of fundamental justice.

8. Everyone has the right to be secure against unreasonable search or seizure.

9. Everyone has the right not to be arbitrarily detained or imprisoned.

10. Everyone has the right on arrest or detention
(a) to be informed promptly of the reasons therefor;
(b) to retain and instruct counsel without delay and to be informed of that right; and
(c) to have the validity of the detention determined by way of *habeas corpus* and to be released if the detention is not lawful.

11. Any person charged with an offence has the right
(a) to be informed without unreasonable delay of the specific offence;
(b) to be tried within a reasonable time;

(c) not to be compelled to be a witness in proceedings against that person in respect of the offence;

(d) to be presumed innocent until proven guilty according to law in a fair and public hearing by an independent and impartial tribunal;

(e) not to be denied reasonable bail without just cause;

(f) except in the case of an offence under military law tried before a military tribunal, to the benefit of trial by jury where the maximum punishment for the offence is imprisonment for five years or a more severe punishment;

(g) not to be found guilty on account of any act or omission unless, at the time of the act or omission, it constituted an offence under Canadian or international law or was criminal according to the general principles of law recognized by the community of nations;

(h) if finally acquitted of the offence, not to be tried for it again and, if finally found guilty and punished for the offence, not to be tried or punished for it again; and

(i) if found guilty of the offence and if the punishment for the offence has been varied between the time of commission and the time of sentencing, to the benefit of the lesser punishment.

12. Everyone has the right not to be subjected to any cruel and unusual treatment or punishment.

13. A witness who testifies in any proceedings has the right not to have any incriminating evidence so given used to incriminate that witness in any other proceedings, except in a prosecution for perjury or for the giving of contradictory evidence.

14. A party or witness in any proceedings who does not understand or speak the language in which the proceedings are conducted or who is deaf has the right to the assistance of an interpreter.

Equality Rights

15. (1) Every individual is equal before and under the law and has the right to the equal protection and equal benefit of the law without discrimination and, in particular, without discrimination based on race, national or ethnic origin, colour, religion, sex, age or mental or physical disability.

(2) Subsection (1) does not preclude any law, program or activity that has as its object the amelioration of conditions of disadvantaged individuals or groups including those that are disadvantaged because of race, national or ethnic origin, colour, religion, sex, age or mental or physical disability.

Official Languages of Canada

16. (1) English and French are the official languages of Canada and have equality of status and equal rights and privileges as to their use in all institutions of the Parliament and government of Canada.

(2) English and French are the official languages of New Brunswick and have equality of status and equal rights and privileges as to their use in all institutions of the legislature and government of New Brunswick.

(3) Nothing in this Charter limits the authority of Parliament or a legislature to advance the equality of status or use of English and French.

17. (1) Everyone has the right to use English or French in any debates and other proceedings of Parliament.

(2) Everyone has the right to use English or French in any debates and other proceedings of the legislature of New Brunswick.

18. (1) The statutes, records and journals of Parliament shall be printed and published in English and French and both language versions are equally authoritative.

(2) The statutes, records and journals of the legislature of New Brunswick shall be printed and published in English and French and both language versions are equally authoritative.

19. (1) Either English or French may be used by any person in, or in any pleading in or process issuing from, any court established by Parliament.

(2) Either English or French may be used by any person in, or in any pleading in or process issuing from, any court of New Brunswick.

20. (1) Any member of the public in Canada has the right to communicate with, and to receive available services from, any head or central office of an institution of the Parliament or government of Canada in English or French, and has the same right with respect to any other office of any such institution where
    (a) there is a significant demand for communications with and services from that office in such language; or
    (b) due to the nature of the office, it is reasonable that communications with and services from that office be available in both English and French.

(2) Any member of the public in New Brunswick has the right to communicate with, and to receive available services from, any office of an institution of the legislature or government of New Brunswick in English or French.

21. Nothing in sections 16 to 20 abrogates or derogates from any right, privilege or obligation with respect to the English and French languages, or either of them, that exists or is continued by virtue of any other provision of the Constitution of Canada.

22. Nothing in sections 16 to 20 abrogates or derogates from any legal or customary right or privilege acquired or enjoyed either before or after the coming into force of this Charter with respect to any language that is not English or French.

Minority Language Educational Rights

23. (1) Citizens of Canada

(a) whose first language learned and still understood is that of the English or French linguistic minority population of the province in which they reside, or

(b) who have received their primary school instruction in Canada in English or French and reside in a province where the language in which they received that instruction is the language of the English or French linguistic minority population of the province,

have the right to have their children receive primary and secondary school instruction in that language in that province.

(2) Citizens of Canada of whom any child has received or is receiving primary or secondary school instruction in English or French in Canada, have the right to have all their children receive primary and secondary school instruction in the same language.

(3) The right of citizens of Canada under subsections (1) and (2) to have their children receive primary and secondary school instruction in the language of the English or French linguistic minority population of a province

(a) applies wherever in the province the number of children of citizens who have such a right is sufficient to warrant the provision to them out of public funds of minority language instruction; and

(b) includes, where the number of those children so warrants, the right to have them receive that instruction in minority language educational facilities provided out of public funds.

24. (1) Anyone whose rights or freedoms, as guaranteed by this Charter, have been infringed or denied may apply to a court of competent jurisdiction to obtain such remedy as the court considers appropriate and just in the circumstances.

(2) Where, in proceedings under subsection (1), a court concludes that evidence was obtained in a manner that infringed or denied any rights or freedoms guaranteed by this Charter, the evidence shall be excluded if it is established that, having regard to all the circumstances, the admission of it in the proceedings would bring the administration of justice into disrepute.

General

25. The guarantee in this Charter of certain rights and freedoms shall not be construed so as to abrogate or derogate from any aboriginal, treaty or other rights or freedoms that pertain to the aboriginal peoples of Canada including

(a) any rights or freedoms that have been recognized by the Royal Proclamation of October 7, 1763; and

(b) any rights or freedoms that now exist by way of land claims agreements or may be so acquired.[1]

26. The guarantee in this Charter of certain rights and freedoms shall not be construed as denying the existence of any other rights or freedoms that exist in Canada.

27. This Charter shall be interpreted in a manner consistent with the preservation and enhancement of the multicultural heritage of Canadians.

28. Notwithstanding anything in this Charter, the rights and freedoms referred to in it are guaranteed equally to male and female persons.

29. Nothing in this Charter abrogates or derogates from any rights or privileges guaranteed by or under the Constitution of Canada in respect of denominational, separate or dissentient schools.

30. A reference in this Charter to a province or to the legislative assembly or legislature of a province shall be deemed to include a reference to the Yukon Territory and the Northwest Territories, or to the appropriate legislative authority thereof, as the case may be.

31. Nothing in this Charter extends the legislative powers of any body or authority.

Application of Charter

32. (1) This Charter applies

(a) to the Parliament and government of Canada in respect of all matters within the authority of parliament including all matters relating to the Yukon Territory and Northwest Territories; and

(b) to the legislature and government of each province in respect of all matters within the authority of the legislature of each province.

(2) Notwithstanding subsection (1), section 15 shall not have effect until three years after this section comes into force.

33. (1) Parliament or the legislature of a province may expressly declare in an Act of Parliament or of the legislature, as the case may be, that the Act or a provision thereof shall operate notwithstanding a provision included in section 2 or sections 7 to 15 of this Charter.

(2) An Act or a provision of an Act in respect of which a declaration made under this section is in effect shall have such operation as it would have but for the provision of this Charter referred to in the declaration.

(3) A declaration made under subsection (1) shall cease to have effect five years after it comes into force or on such earlier date as may be specified in the declaration.

(4) Parliament or the legislature of a province may re-enact a declaration made under subsection (1).

(5) Subsection (3) applies in respect of a re-enactment made under subsection (4).

Citation

34. This Part may be cited as the *Canadian Charter of Rights and Freedoms.*

NOTE

1   Paragraph 25 (b) was amended by the *Constitution Amendment Proclamation, 1983.* It originally read "(b) any rights or freedoms that may be acquired by the aboriginal peoples of Canada by way of land claims settlement."

An Overview of the Canadian Legal System: Divisions of Powers and Essentials of Procedure

While the focus of most of the readings in this book is the role of moral reasoning in the law, understanding of those issues is enhanced by an understanding of the ways in which particular issues arise and are resolved within a legal order. Not every dispute involves legal rights, and not every dispute involving legal rights makes it to trial. Canada's legal order shares important features with many of the world's legal systems, though it differs from other systems in various ways. This appendix is meant as a quick tour through the structure of legal order in general and in particular the structure of the Canadian legal order.

The Canadian legal system exhibits the classic liberal division of powers between three branches of government – the legislature, the executive, and the judiciary. According to the doctrine of the division of powers, the legislature – the democratically elected representatives of the people – make law, while the executive – a body of professional government employees – implement and enforce the law. The judiciary, who in Canada are unelected officials appointed by the government, interpret the law when a question arises about what it requires in a particular case.

The rationale for dividing power in this way is doing so secures the rule of law. Law is legitimate when it is made by the legislature for it then reflects the will of the people. Executive action to implement and enforce the law is legitimate as long as the officials stay within the limits set by the law. Thus, civil servants are charged with carrying out broadly defined government policies. Judicial interpretation of the law is legitimate as long as it is confined to seeing to it that the executive officials stay within the limits set by the law rather than whatever they would themselves consider appropriate.

In this scheme, judges are given the role of ultimately determining what the law is, but are subject to the duty to confine their determinations to what the law requires. If they confine their interpretative role in this way, society is governed by laws rather than by the personal whims of people holding power. Citizens can be secure in the knowledge that government officials may not act except when the law gives them the warrant to do so.

In Canada, the role of determining the law is the task of the superior courts of general jurisdiction of each province. These have different names according to the province, for example, Ontario Court (General Division), or in Alberta and other provinces, the Court of Queen's Bench. These courts have general jurisdiction in that they have the power to hear and decide any question of law. Appeals against their decisions are to the provincial courts of appeal. In addition, federal courts hear some cases in specialized areas of the law. Appeals against the decisions of both provincial and federal courts can be made to the Supreme Court of Canada. The Supreme Court agrees to hear only a small proportion of the cases appealed to it, and normally decides which cases to hear based on the legal significance of the issues they raise. Judges are appointed to all of these courts by the federal government, and enjoy lifetime tenure so as to protect their independence.

In order to bring a case before a court, the person bringing it must have *standing*. In private disputes, private citizens who claim to have been wronged by others have standing to sue. In general private citizens only have standing to challenge government action if they can claim that some right of theirs is jeopardized by it. However, in certain circumstances, parties before a court can argue on the basis of the constitutional rights of third parties. Also, courts have discretion to grant intervenor status to interested parties in appellate cases in which they have an indirect interest. Intervenors can raise broader constitutional issues that the parties to the dispute may not have raised themselves.

Public law governs the relationship between government and citizen as well as between the different branches of government. But judges also decide cases arising in private law, the law which regulates the interactions between individuals. The courts may have to decide whether an agreement between two people is a valid contract, or who is liable in the case of an unintended injury. They may have to determine who owns a piece of land, or whether someone can recover from someone else who was unjustly enriched at their expense. In Canada (unlike the United States) questions of private law are always tried by judges rather than juries. In answering questions in a private law case, judges often need to sort out difficult questions of fact – who did what, and when – as well as questions of law concerning the legal rights and duties of the parties. In considering facts in matters of private law, judges decide in favor of the party whose claim is supported by the balance of the evidence. Since one of the two parties will lose in a private dispute, fairness requires that the one with the stronger case should prevail. In order to limit frivolous litigation, the losing party in a private suit must pay the legal expenses of the winner. In private law cases, both parties enjoy the right of appeal. However, only issues of law can be raised on appeal. Facts must be taken to be as the trial court found them.

Canada has two distinctive systems of private law. In Quebec, private law is codified in the *Code Civile*. In the rest of Canada, private law is largely a matter of common law. The difference is important, because at the core of common-law reasoning is the appeal to precedent – the way cases have been decided before. Precedents can be drawn from other common-law jurisdictions, including foreign ones. By contrast, decisions in civil law systems are presented as the consequences of the explicit provisions of the civil code. As a result, decisions sometimes look as though they are the result of a straightforward deductive process. However, the generality with which such provisions must be framed still leaves space for judicial creativity, and judges are aware of prior judicial understandings of how the law should be interpreted.

In private law, judges are upholding the rule of law because individuals know that any private dispute which the law regulates will be settled by an impartial application of the law. Just as it is essential that citizens know that judges will keep government officials within the law, so it is essential that individuals know that their fellows will have to deal with them in the manner prescribed by law.

Criminal law falls into public rather than private law, because the state investigates and prosecutes criminal offences. Because of the grave consequences which attend criminal conviction, the standard of proof is higher in criminal law – facts must be proven beyond a reasonable doubt. For the same reasons, people accused of crimes are presumed innocent until proven guilty. Those accused of crimes with sentences of less than two years are subject to summary trial without a jury. Those accused of more serious crimes are entitled to trial by jury, though they may elect to be tried by a judge. In a jury trial, the jury's role is limited to determining facts. In Canada (unlike the United States) both the Crown and the accused are allowed to appeal a criminal decision, but only on the basis of questions of law. Often the grounds for appeal turn on the judge's instruction to the jury, or on the trial judge's decisions about the admissibility of evidence. The criminal law in Canada is codified in a single federal *Criminal Code*.

In common-law systems, it is sometimes difficult to determine what principle or principles a judicial decision stands for, since principles must be inferred from the judge's reasoning or argument justifying the decision. If several judges hear the matter, some might dissent from the majority on some issues but not others, while others concur with the result, but offer different reasons for it. Finally, even when all the judges support the judgment given by one judge, the opinion might include arguments which are in tension with each other. The common law is found in the judgments of the superior courts and changes over time at the hands of judges. When a judge decides an issue in a common-law legal order, that judgment becomes a precedent – it has authority for judges deciding similar issues. The weight of the authority it has will vary on a number of dimensions, the extent to which it has been followed, the place of the judge in the judicial hierarchy, and, indeed, the merits of the judgment. In some parts of the law, especially private law, the law in a common-law legal order might be made almost entirely by judges. In other parts, such as the criminal law, the common law will be a complex overlay of judicial interpretation of statutory codification. But it will also serve as an underlay, or a background for interpretation, since the principles that were codified were in the first instance principles developed by judges. The role of precedent in common-law systems means that the subsequent development of the law will often depend on the particular cases that make it to trial, which in turn depends in part on the resources available to the parties.

Public law includes the rules of public international law, the law which governs relations between states. Public international law also governs the interpretation of treaties. For example, if Canada and the United States have an extradition treaty, and some American states have the death penalty while Canada does not, does Canada need to send an American fugitive convicted of a capital crime in one of those states to certain death? (In private matters, the rules governing the choice of laws are no less complex, and govern such questions as which law applies to the property of a couple married in France, but residing in Canada at the time of their divorce.)

Public law also includes constitutional law and administrative law. Some issues in constitutional law seem to have little to do with particular individuals, as in the questions relating to the division of political power in the Canadian federal system between the central federal government and the provincial governments. But the division of powers is important to the ability of various bodies to make law. If a lawmaking body overreaches its mandate, individuals may be illegally deprived of advantages to which they are entitled. Since the enactment of the *Charter* in 1982, Canada has had a written constitution. Even in jurisdictions without a written constitution (such as Britain), courts sometimes engage in constitutional review.

Issues of public law reveal the complexities of the division of powers. Governments often enact statutes which delegate broad powers to officials to elaborate and implement policies, rather than attempting to anticipate details in advance. In order to protect their agencies from the intrusion of the superior courts into this kind of policy making, governments have often at the same time set up tribunals to decide the legal questions which arise in the course of elaborating and implementing the statute. For example, questions of labour law are decided by provincially appointed labor relations boards, and human rights codes by specially appointed tribunals. To what extent can the decisions of such bodies be immunized from the supervision by the superior courts? Courts have generally recognized the authority of tribunals to decide such issues, subject to their own "review power." Courts will intervene if the tribunal either overreaches what the court deems to be its statutory authority, or offends against any of the procedural values – the values of fair process – which the courts deem it their constitutional duty to protect. Courts always retain a residual power of review because of their role as final arbiters of the boundaries between the branches of government.

Since the enactment of the *Charter of Rights and Freedoms* in 1982, a new range of constitutional issues has preoccupied the courts. These of course pertain to whether statutes or official action under statutes offend against *Charter*-protected rights and values. The Canadian *Charter* has an unusual structure in two respects. First, Section 1 requires a court to ask a further question after a finding that a *Charter*-protected right or value has been violated. This is the question whether that violation can itself be justified by the values of a "free and democratic society," and whether the violation is proportional to the problem it is supposed to address. Second, Section 33 permits a legislature or parliament to "override" a judicial determination of constitutionality subject to the conditions set out in the section. Thus, while judges have the final say over what the law is, legislatures retain the power to temporarily override those decisions.

The *Charter* may seem to undermine the division of powers. It clearly gives judges the power to decide on whether the laws made by democratically elected parliaments are valid in accordance with their interpretation of very broadly defined values, for example, the right to free speech. That is, judges may not merely be keeping officials within the limits of the law as it is, but deciding what the law ought to be. In this the *Charter* only makes more visible and dramatic a pervasive feature of legal orders. Virtually all legal systems include such concepts as "good faith," "reasonableness," and "fair play," all of which are open to moral interpretation. That judicial interpretation is partly creative and not merely deductive is explicitly recognized in the Canadian legal system.

Glossary of Legal and Philosophical Terms

Terms and Definitions

This section contains some technical terms that will be found in the readings. The definitions and discussions are intended to give a bare handle on the terms, and thus are an aid to the readings rather than a replacement for them.

Atomism.   The view that the social world is made up of isolated individuals each making perfectly independent choices about how to live. The label "atomism" is more often offered as a criticism of others' view than as a view put forward by anyone.

Autonomy.   The individual's right to decide for herself how to live her life.

Comity.   The recognition by one legal system of another legal system's laws. Extradition treaties are one example of comity; the acceptance of marriages or divorces made abroad is another.

Common law.   Systems of law descended from the British common-law system. (The common law was originally the law common to the King's courts, and thus contrasted with manorial and cannon law.) The distinctive feature of common-law systems is the way in which judges appeal to previously decided cases in deciding novel ones. The law is to be found in cases, rather than statutes. Most modern common-law systems include statutes as well, but these are standardly interpreted in light of settled cases.

Commensurability.   Two things are said to be commensurable if there is some basis for comparing them. Things are said to be incommensurable if no such basis exists. For example, love and money are usually thought to be incommensurable, because no amount of money can replace a lost love.

Communitarianism.   The view that an individual is the product of a particular social and cultural environment. The meaningful choices as to how to live for an individual are the choices informed by this environment. Thus, communitarians suppose that choices to reject the ways of one's culture are often not worthy of protection.

Consequentialism.   The moral position which evaluates actions based on the balance of good over bad consequences which they bring or might bring about. An argument in favor of something that claims its implementation would reduce violent crime is consequentialist. Consequentialist arguments always require factual support because they depend on claims about what would happen if various policies were adopted.

Constitutionalism.   The view that the basic essentials of a political regime should lie outside the reach of ordinary processes of majority rule. Not all advocates of constitutional democracy suppose a written constitution is necessary. In Britain, for example, there is no written constitution, but the powers of government are limited.

Deontological.   The moral position that supposes that acts should be evaluated on the basis of some intrinsic quality. For example, claims about rights, and appeals to fairness and desert are deontological. Both deontological and consequentialist arguments can be found on both sides of almost every political debate. Many complex positions will appeal to both kinds of arguments.

Egalitarianism.   The view that the allocation of resources and opportunities has to be substantially equal.

Habeas corpus.   The right against unlawful imprisonment. For example, prisoners who have not been promptly charged with any crime can be freed under *habeas corpus.*

Legal moralism.   The position that the state can legitimately coerce people into ways that do not accord with their own views of the best way to live. *Pure* legal moralists suppose that there is a correct answer about how best to live; *impure* legal moralists suppose it is up to each society to answer questions about the appropriate moral content of law for itself. Opponents of legal moralism often appeal to the "harm principle," which holds that the only legitimate basis for restrictions on liberty is the prevention of harm to others.

Legal positivism.   The view that the law that exists on any matter exists as a matter of publicly ascertainable fact. That is, finding out what the law is does not require any sort of controversial moral argument.

Liberalism.   The view that the fundamental role of the state is to enable people to freely decide how best to live their own lives. Different liberals have very different views about how best to protect individual liberty, as well as different views about which individual choices are most important. Some suppose that liberty requires an unregulated capitalist market; others that the state must make sure that individuals have a fair share of resources and opportunities in order to be able to freely decide what life is best for them. All liberals share an abstract commitment to rejecting paternalism, though they disagree about the implications of this commitment.

Libertarianism.   The view that the only legitimate role of the state is in protecting negative liberty. Libertarians standardly reject economic redistribution as an illicit interference with property rights.

Majoritarianism.   The view that the law should implement the preferences of the majority whatever these happen to be. Majoritarianism can be understood as a democratic position, but is at odds with the view that democracy requires certain constitutional safeguards.

Natural law.   Defenders of natural law insist that whether or not anything counts as law will depend on its specific content. For the natural lawyer, wicked legal systems are not legal systems at all; they need to be understood as exercises of naked power. Natural lawyers disagree among themselves about just what moral content a legal system must have, but they agree that the proper role of positive law is to articulate and implement natural law.

Negative liberty.   Defenders of negative liberty understand liberty as the absence of external impediments to individual preferences. One has this kind of liberty when the state limits its coercive interference in the lives of individual to the minimum necessary to prevent individuals from harming each other.

Neutrality.   The refusal by the state to take a stand on contested views about the good life. A neutral state will not treat opera any differently than it does football. A difficult question for theories of liberal neutrality is whether traditional practices that discriminate against women are best thought of as contested conceptions of the good which the state has no business correcting, or as injustices which are within the scope of its proper concern.

Normative claim.   A claim about how things should be. Normative claims aim to guide action. Thus, they contrast with descriptions of how things are. There are a wide variety of types of normative claims. Moral claims are normative, as are aesthetic claims and claims of etiquette, though few suppose that any of these is simply a special case of the others. Legal claims are also action-guiding. One of the central questions of jurisprudence concerns the nature of legal normativity. The dispute between positivists and anti-positivists turns on whether the normative element in legal claims is a special case of the normativity of moral claims.

Paternalism.   Actions by the state that are done to protect people from themselves. For example, a law outlawing bungee-jumping is paternalistic because it seeks to protect people from the consequences of their own choices. By contrast, drunk-driving laws are not paternalistic because one of their aims is to protect people from the choices of others.

Perfectionism.   The position which requires the state to aid or even coerce people into living out their lives in accordance with some ideal of what makes life valuable. For example, state support of the arts is sometimes defended on perfectionist grounds.

Positive liberty.   The view that individuals have to have certain things before the idea of negative liberty and autonomy makes any sense. Defenders of positive liberty differ in their views about what it requires. Some emphasize the role of various social conditions that are said to enable individual choice. Others stress the importance of such things as political participation or community to any life that is truly free.

Reasonable person.   Anglo-American legal systems use the construct of a reasonable person to articulate standards of care and judgment. The reasonable person is neither the rational person who acts effectively to realize his or her ends, nor the typical or average person. Instead, the reasonable person is the person who shows appropriate regard for the interests of others, and takes appropriate care in avoiding injury to them. Reasonableness standards reflect views both about what is important to the security of those who might be harmed, and about the importance of people being able to go about their own affairs. The reasonable person also appears in the law of self-defence, as the measure of the care one must take in assessing whether one's life is in peril. The reasonable person standard is sometimes called an *objective* standard because it abstracts away from the personal features of the person being judged.

Utilitarianism.   The most prominent kind of consequentialist position. Utilitarians say that policies and institutions should be assessed on the basis of their ability to bring about the best overall balance of good over bad consequences. The most popular candidate for good consequences is the satisfaction of people's preferences – that is, the aggregate sum of what various people in fact want and desire.

Sources and Credits

Anthony J. Sebok, "Judging the Fugitive Slave Acts," 100 *Yale Law Journal* 1835 (1991) (notes omitted), reprinted by permission of the Yale Law Journal Company and Fred B. Rothman & Company.

W.J. Waluchow, "Charter Challenges: A Test Case for Theories of Law?" (1991) 29 *Osgoode Hall Law Journal* 183–214 (some notes omitted; remaining notes renumbered), reprinted by permission of the author and of the editors of the *Osgoode Hall Law Journal*.

John Finnis, "Natural Law and Legal Reasoning," in Robert P. George, ed., *Natural Law Theory: Contemporary Essays* (1994) (some notes omitted; remaining notes renumbered), reprinted by permission of Oxford University Press.

Catharine A. MacKinnon, "The Liberal State," in *Towards a Feminist Theory of the State* (1989) 223–33 (notes omitted), reprinted by permission of Harvard university Press and the author; copyright by Harvard University Press; this extract may not be reproduced in whole or in part, in any form without written permission from the publishers.

Martha Minow, "Foreword: Justice Engendered," 101 *Harvard Law Review* 10 (1987) (some notes omitted; remaining notes renumbered), reprinted by permission of the author and of the editors of the *Harvard Law Review*.

Patricia Williams, *The Alchemy of Race and Rights* (1991) 146–8, reprinted by permission of Harvard University Press; copyright by Harvard University Press; this extract may not be reproduced in whole or in part, in any form without written permission from the publishers.

John Stuart Mill, *On Liberty* (1859), reprinted by permission of University of Toronto Press.

F.A. von Hayek, "Planning and the Rule of Law," in *The Road to Serfdom* (1994) 80–96, reprinted by permission of the executors of the estate of F.A. von Hayek and of University of Chicago Press; copyright by University of Chicago Press; this extract may not be reproduced in whole or in part, in any form without written permission from the publishers.

Charles Taylor, "What's Wrong with Negative Liberty," in *Philosophy and the Human Sciences* (1985) 213–29 (some notes omitted; remaining notes renumbered), reprinted by permission of the author and of Cambridge University Press.

Patrick Devlin, "Morals and the Criminal Law," in *The Enforcement of Morals* (1965) 1–25 (some notes omitted; remaining notes renumbered), reprinted by permission of Oxford University Press.

Ronald Dworkin, "Civil Disobedience" and "Liberty and Moralism," in *Taking Rights Seriously* (1977) 206–22; 248–55, reprinted by permission of Duckworth and Company.

Allan C. Hutchinson and Patrick Monahan, "Democracy and the Rule of Law," in Hutchinson and Monahan, eds., *The Rule of Law: Ideal or Ideology* (1987) 97–123, reprinted by permission of the authors and of Carswell.

Jody Freeman, "Defining Family in *Mossop v DSS*: The Challenge of Anti-Essentialism and Interactive Discrimination for Human Rights Litigation" (1994) 44 *University of Toronto Law Journal* 42–92 (some notes omitted; remaining notes renumbered), reprinted by permission of the author and of University of Toronto Press.

John Rawls, "Civil Disobedience," in *A Theory of Justice* (1971) 36–91 (notes omitted), reprinted by permission of Harvard University Press; copyright by Harvard University Press; this extract may not be reproduced in whole or in part, in any form without written permission from the publishers.

Martin Luther King, Jr, "Letter from Birmingham City Jail," reprinted by arrangement with The Heirs to the Estate of Martin Luther King, Jr, c/o Writers house, Inc., as agent for the proprietor. Copyright 1968 by Martin Luther King, Jr, copyright renewed 1991 by Coretta Scott King.

Queen's University Letter, reprinted by permission of the authors.

Sovereign Injustice: Forcible Inclusion of James Bay Crees and Cree Territory into a Sovereign Québec (October 1995), reprinted by permission of the Grand Council of the Crees (of Quebec).

Joel Feinberg, "Pornography and the Criminal Law" (1979) 40 *University of Pittsburgh Law Review* 567–73, reprinted by permission of the author and of the editors of the *University of Pittsburgh Law Review*.

T.M. Scanlon, "A Theory of Freedom of Expression," *Philosophy and Public Affairs* vol. 1, no. 2 (winter 1972) 204–26 (some notes omitted; remaining notes renumbered), reprinted by permission of Princeton University Press.

Mayo Moran, "Talking about Hate Speech: A Rhetorical Analysis of American and Canadian Approaches to the Regulation of Hate Speech" (1994) 6 *Wisconsin Law Review* 1497–1514 (some notes omitted; remaining notes renumbered), reprinted by permission of the author and of the editors of the *Wisconsin Law Review*.

Martha Shaffer, "Criminal Responses to Hate Motivated Violence: Is Bill C-41 Tough Enough?" (1995) 41 *McGill Law Journal* 199 (some notes omitted; remaining notes renumbered), reprinted by permission of the author and of the editors of the *McGill Law Journal*.

Catharine A. MacKinnon, *Only Words* (1993) 89–110 (some notes omitted; remaining notes renumbered), reprinted by permission of Harvard University Press and the author; copyright by Harvard University Press; this extract may not be reproduced in whole or in part, in any form without written permission from the publishers.

Ronald Dworkin, "Two Concepts of Liberty," in Edna Ulman-Margalit and Avishai Margalit, eds., *Isaiah Berlin: A Celebration* (Hogarth Press, Chatto and Windus, 1991), 100–9, reprinted by permission of the author.

Judith Jarvis Thomson, "A Defence of Abortion," *Philosophy and Public Affairs* vol. 1, no. 1 (Fall 1971) 47–66, reprinted by permission of Princeton University Press.

John Finnis, "The Rights and Wrongs of Abortion: A Reply to Judith Jarvis Thomson," *Philosophy and Public Affairs* vol. 2. no. 2 (Winter 1973) 117–45, reprinted by permission of Princeton University Press.